RUSSIA UNDER KHRUSHCHEV

RUSSIA UNDER KHRUSHCHEV

An Anthology from
Problems of Communism

Edited by

ABRAHAM BRUMBERG

FREDERICK A. PRAEGER, *Publisher*

New York

BOOKS THAT MATTER

Published in the United States of America in 1962 by
Frederick A. Praeger, Inc., Publisher
64 University Place, New York 3, N.Y.

© 1962 by Frederick A. Praeger, Inc.

Library of Congress Catalog Card Number: 62-13165

RUSSIA UNDER KHRUSHCHEV is published in two editions:
A paperback edition (PPS-19)
A clothbound edition

This book is Number 105 in the series of
Praeger Publications in Russian History and World Communism

Manufactured in the United States of America

Preface

THE ARTICLES IN this anthology are taken from the bimonthly journal *Problems of Communism*, published by the United States Information Agency. They provide a chronological and thematic commentary on internal developments in the U.S.S.R., ranging from the changes in the official ideology to the latest developments in Soviet agriculture. They constitute, essentially, a report on what might be called "the Khrushchev era." At the same time, it is hoped that they will broaden the reader's comprehension not only of what is new in the Soviet Union, but also of what is old; not only of what is changing, but of what has remained the same—reforms, upheavals, purges, and sputniks notwithstanding.

In compiling this volume, the editor must confess to having struggled against numerous odds, not the least of which was the wealth of material from which a relatively modest selection had to be made. *Problems of Communism* has been in existence since 1952. It has thus spanned some of the most exciting and momentous chapters in the history of the U.S.S.R.: the last year of Stalin's reign, with its "vigilance campaigns," xenophobia, and deadening intellectual climate; Stalin's death, the struggle for succession, and the eventual emergence of Khrushchev as the undisputed (though perhaps not all-powerful) leader of the Soviet Party and state; the "de-Stalinization" drive, which started haltingly in 1953 and burst forth with dramatic swiftness in 1956, following Khrushchev's "secret speech" in February of that year; the cultural "thaw" and the subsequent reimposition of stringent controls on writers and intellectuals; economic, administrative, and social reforms, changes in foreign policy, eruptions in the Soviet bloc and the international Communist movement as a whole—all these events were recorded and analyzed in the journal by noted observers of Soviet affairs. Which of these numerous articles—some, no doubt, of lasting significance—were to be chosen, and which left out? Even the decision to begin (approximately) with the year 1956 did not fully resolve the dilemma, for a truly comprehensive survey of Soviet policies over the past five years alone would take up more space than a single volume can offer.

It was inevitable, therefore, that what would finally emerge would not be exhaustive in any sense. Aside from the conspicuous omission of material on Soviet foreign policy, relations with Eastern Europe, and—to be sure—Sino-Soviet relations, a number of articles dealing with such diverse topics as educational and agricultural reforms, achievements (and failures) of Soviet science, and the history and current status of the Komsomol (Communist Youth League) also had to be deleted. What *has* been placed within the covers of this volume are those studies that provide the broadest picture of the political, economic, and cultural trends of Khrushchev's Russia. Although not perfect, perhaps the result nevertheless will provide both the student of Soviet affairs and the interested layman with material whose scope and variety compensate for the occasional gap or lack of detail.

Another difficulty faced in the compilation of this anthology was that of timeliness. While some of the articles reprinted here had appeared as late as in May, 1961, others were published three, four, and even seven years ago. The reader might therefore be tempted to question the applicability of some of the remarks and observations to current-day problems and circumstances. In reply, it should be pointed out that articles of little or no contemporary relevance have not been included in this volume; that others, of clearly historic importance, have been brought up to date by the authors either by means of additional documentation or postscripts; that some of the articles have been revised, and thus do not appear in their original form; that all have been carefully scrutinized and minor changes, deletions, or corrections have been made. Finally, some of the articles have been listed in chronological order (e.g., the chapters *"Kto Kavo?"* and "The Economy: Problems, Prospects"), so as to give the reader a greater sense of the drama and turbulence of recent Soviet history.*

In conclusion, I should like to express my gratitude to my three colleagues on the magazine without whose help this volume would have never come to fruition: the Managing Editor, Miss Marie Thompson, who has been with *Problems of Communism* since its inception and has been responsible for editing most of the original articles; to Mr. Clarke Kawakami, Associate Editor since 1955; and to the other Associate Editor, Mr. Cary O. Fisher, whose special assistance in the preparation of the economic section I gratefully acknowledge.

Abraham Brumberg

Washington, D.C.
July, 1961

---

* The Twenty-second Congress of the Soviet Communist Party took place at the end of October, 1961. In view of the singular importance of this event, an article describing and analyzing its highlights has been included in this volume just as it was about to go to press. (See "The Twenty-second Party Congress," by Merle Fainsod, pp. 127–49.)

To the Memory of Z.

Contents

THE IDEOLOGICAL
SETTING

Introduction

PERHAPS NO SUBJECT related to Communism has engendered so much punditry as that of ideology—the role, significance, and precise textual interpretation of what is known as Marxism-Leninism. Why this is so is not difficult to fathom. To read Lenin, for example, is to participate in an exercise of medieval scholasticism: The authority of the "scriptures" (i.e., the writings of Marx and Engels) having been established beyond any doubt, Lenin essentially saw his task as that of elaborating, commenting, and applying the doctrinal formulas to the very concrete problems of revolutionary strategy that his party was facing. In Stalin's writings, this kind of exegesis was carried one (or two) steps further, for not only did Stalin, in his zeal to justify the construction of a totalitarian order, subject Marx's and Engels' works to additional reinterpretation and reaffirmation, but he did so with Lenin's and—not infrequently—his own works as well. ("The pamphlet *The Foundations of Leninism* [by J. V. S.]," reads the first sentence of Stalin's *On the Problems of Leninism*, "contains the well-known definition of Leninism which seems [note the coyness] to have received general recognition. It runs as follows: 'Leninism is Marxism of the era of imperialism and of the proletarian revolution. To be more exact, Leninism is the theory and tactics of the proletarian revolution in general, the theory and tactics of the dictatorship of the proletariat in particular.' Is this definition correct? I think it is correct.")

3

Stalin, of course, made sure that *his* ideological pronouncements would in turn be quoted and nurtured by countless Soviet "theoreticians." (Curiously—or perhaps not so curiously—"Talmudism" is a pejorative term in the Communist lexicon.) And matters have hardly changed since Stalin's death. True, the new Soviet leadership has tried to dissociate itself not only from some of Stalin's deeds but also from some of his words, but it has done so in a manner that is singularly reminiscent of the way in which Stalin carried on his ideological discourses: In order to refute some of Stalin's doctrines, for instance, Khrushchev has found it necessary to invoke the authority of Lenin—thus perpetuating, of course, the very spirit and method of Stalinist (that is, Soviet) scholasticism.

Faced, then, with the sheer bulk of Soviet writings on ideology, it is small wonder that the printed reaction of non-Communist scholars has been equally bulky. Yet it would seem that in all these voluminous writings one question, perhaps the central one, has not been posed, or answered, with sufficient clarity—namely, what role does ideology play in the shaping of Soviet policy, both domestic and foreign? Or put another way, how seriously do Soviet leaders take their ideological doctrines—do they use them merely as spectacles through which to view the world, or as actual tools with which to remake it? The symposium "Ideology and Power Politics" addresses itself to this very problem. The differences in the views of the authors, while clearly expressed in the original articles in the March–April, 1958, issue of *Problems of Communism*, were further contested and debated in the May–June, 1958, issue. Leopold Labedz's article also deals, in part, with the general role of Soviet ideology, but is primarily concerned with the change of the role—and the substance—of Soviet ideology since Stalin's death.

Ideology and Power: A Symposium

The Importance of Doctrine

——R. N. CAREW HUNT

THE TERM IDEOLOGY is one that is more often used than defined. As the present study will be concerned with what the Russian Communists, and Communists in general, mean by it, a definition taken from a Soviet source is in order. The *Filosoficheskii slovar* (*Philosophical Dictionary*, 1954 ed.), calls ideology "a system of definite views, ideas, conceptions, and notions adhered to by some class or political party," and goes on to say that it is always "a reflection of the economic system predominant at any given time." In a class-divided society, the ideology will be that of one or another of the struggling classes, but under socialism, when there is no longer any class division, it will be that of society as a whole. A quotation from Lenin is added to the effect that there can be no "middle way" between the ideology of the bourgeoisie and that of the proletariat—the one is false and the other true.

Such a summation, albeit neat, is not altogether satisfactory. Broadly speaking, Marx was right in contending that the ideology of a society—the complex of ideas that determines its "way of life"—will be that of its dominant class, that is, of those whose abilities (whether used rightly or wrongly is irrelevant in this context) have raised them above the common herd. But this sociological fact applies equally to the Soviet Union, where the Party certainly constitutes such a class and indeed is assigned the duty of fertilizing the masses with its ideas. Undoubtedly the current Soviet ideology is intended to strengthen the Party and reinforce its claim to rule. But one must probe further to explain why the Party should have adopted the particular body of doctrine that it has. The fact is that the ideology has been largely determined by the type of collective society that has been established in the Soviet Union.

The authors of the October Revolution were Marxists and thus were committed to abolishing the capitalist system and replacing it by a nationwide planned economy. For a brief period, the experiment of allowing the workers to take charge was tried out, but, when this led to chaos, the Party assumed control and has retained it ever since.

If a Communist regime is to be set up in a backward country, the first prerequisite, as Lenin realized, is industrialization; this is likely to be carried out as rapidly as possible since the quicker the country is developed—particularly its war potential—the stronger will be the position of its rulers. The execution of such a program of necessity demands the centralization of power in the hands of a small group of leaders, along with the adoption of such unpopular measures as the fixing of wages, the direction of labor, and the prohibition of strikes. And since large-scale planning geared to an expanding economy is impracticable if the plan is liable to be upset at any moment by a vote in a popular assembly, it is not to be expected that the planners will long tolerate any opposition. Furthermore, they will be tempted to interfere in one branch of human activity after another, seeing that all can be so manipulated as to assist the execution of their grand design.

All this has happened in the Soviet Union, and the outcome has been an ideology that derives from the logic of collectivism. Its basic principles are to be found in Marx's revolutionary doctrine, the implications of which were spelled out by Lenin and Stalin when confronted with the practical problem of setting up the type of social order Marx had advocated. Communist literature and propaganda have made us familiar with the doctrine, and there is no need to analyze it here, even if space permitted such an analysis. The issue to be decided is what role ideology plays today, and how far it influences Soviet policy.

Myths and the Masses

Virtually all analysts would agree that in the years of struggle before the October Revolution, the Bolsheviks took the theory upon which their movement was based in deadly earnest; there is also general agreement that in the 1920's the doctrine acted as a stimulus to the workers, who took pride in building up their country. In the 1930's, however, the situation changed. Stalin assumed absolute power. The machinery of the state and of the secret police was greatly strengthened, and all prospects of establishing a genuine classless society disappeared. With the Stalin-Hitler Pact, if not before, the Soviet Union entered an era that can plausibly be represented as one of naked power politics, perpetuated after World War II in the aggressive and obstructive policies pursued by the regime. Hence it is sometimes argued that Communist ideology has now ceased to possess any importance; that it is simply a top-dressing of sophistries designed to rationalize measures inspired solely by Soviet interests; and that apart from a few fanatics, such as may be found in any society, no one believes in the doctrine any longer, least of all the leaders themselves.

Yet such unqualified assertions are erroneous. Consider, first, the outlook of the ordinary Soviet citizen vis-à-vis the ideology. Day in, day out, he is subjected to intensive and skillfully devised propaganda through every known medium, designed to demonstrate that the ideology on which the Soviet Union is based makes it the best of all possible worlds, and that on this account it is encircled with jealous enemies bent on its destruction. The Soviet leadership has always considered it essential that every citizen possess as deep an understanding of Communist principles as his mind is capable of assimilating, and those holding positions of consequence are obliged recurrently to pass through carefully graded schools of political instruction.

It is significant that whenever the leaders feel themselves in a tight corner—as in the recent aftermath of de-Stalinization and the intervention in Hungary—their invariable reaction is to intensify indoctrination in an attempt to refocus public attention on "first principles." As hard-headed men, they would certainly not attach such importance to indoctrination if they did not know that it paid dividends—and experience has proved that the persistent repetition of a body of ideas that are never challenged is bound to influence the minds of their recipients. Of course, the present generation does not react to the formal ideology with the same fervor as did its forebears who made the Revolution, and there are doubtless those who view official apologetics with a large degree of cynicism. But between total commitment and total disillusionment there are many intermediate positions. It is quite possible for a man to regard much of what he is told as nonsense while still believing that there is something of value behind it, especially if he identifies that "something" with the greatness of his country as "the first socialist state" and believes in its historic mission.

Leadership Credence—A Hope or a Habit?

More significant, in the present context, than the attitude of the ordinary citizen is that of the ruling elite responsible for policy. What its top-ranking members believe is a question no one, of course, can answer positively. But before surmising, as do some analysts, that the Soviet leadership cannot possibly believe in the myths it propounds, we should remind ourselves that no class or party ever finds it difficult to persuade itself of the soundness of the principles on which it bases its claim to rule.

The Soviet leaders are fortified in this conviction by the very nature of their creed. They have been nurtured in it from birth, and it would be strange indeed if they had remained unaffected. It has become second nature to these men to regard history as a dialectical process—one of incessant conflict between progressive and reactionary forces, which can only be resolved by the victory of the former. The division of the world into antagonistic camps, which is an article of faith, is simply the projection onto the international stage of the struggle within capitalistic society between the bourgeoisie, which history has condemned, and the proletariat, whose ultimate triumph it has decreed. The leaders seem to be confident that history is on their side, that all roads lead to Communism, and that the contradictions of capitalism must create the type of situation they can turn to their advantage.

Inefficiency—An Index of Ideology

Indeed, if the analysis presented earlier in this article of the genesis of the Communist ideology is correct, the attitude of the Soviet leaders *must* be attributed, at least in part, to the theoretical principles that distinguish Communist regimes from other forms of dictatorship. Certainly the leaders shape and phrase their domestic and foreign policies to fit the general framework established by these principles, and the latter often do not allow much room for maneuver. In fact, their application may sometimes weaken rather than strengthen the country.

To take a simple example, much waste would be avoided if small traders were permitted to operate on a profit basis; the fishmonger, for instance, would have an incentive to put his fish on ice, which he frequently fails to do, to the discomfort of the public. Allowance of profits, however, would constitute a return to private enterprise, which cannot be tolerated.

Similarly, in the Communist view it has long been regarded as indefensible to subordinate a higher form of socialized enterprise to a lower one. Thus, while it has been apparent for years that Soviet agriculture would be more efficient if the Machine Tractor Stations were handed over to the collective farms, the issue has been consistently dodged, because the MTS are fully state-owned organs and therefore "higher" than the farms, which still belong in part to the peasants. When the economist Venzher advocated this measure, he was slapped down at once by Stalin, and the fact that it had already been adopted in Yugoslavia only made his suggestion the more objectionable. In 1956, Khrushchev launched an extensive program to strengthen the organization and power of the MTS. Very recently, however, he indicated that the regime was—at long last—prepared to yield to practical necessity on this point; in a speech on farm policy, he advocated the transfer of farm machinery to the collectives, and although his proposals are not yet legalized, it would appear that a number of MTS have already been dissolved. (The MTS were abolished in 1958.—*Ed.*)

The principle of hierarchy has not been repudiated, however, and still governs other aspects of agricultural organization—for example, the relative status of the two forms of agricultural enterprises. From the standpoint of productive efficiency, the collective farms are bad, but the state farms are worse. Nonetheless, the latter represents a "higher type" of organization, and thus the virgin-lands campaign has been based upon them.

Dogmatism in Foreign Policy

The same point can be scored by examining the Soviet Union's treatment of its satellites. Poland affords a good example. With the country at its mercy after World War II, the Soviet regime decided, among other measures, to integrate the Polish economy with its own. Had Poland been regarded merely as a colony to be exploited, the operation would have been viewed primarily as a business proposition, and due attention would have been paid to such questions as the nature of the country's resources and the aptitudes of its people. The need to proceed with caution was very evident. The traditional hostility of the Poles to everything Russian should have been taken into account, as well as the fact that the Polish Communist Party had no public support (due in part to the liquidation of its established leaders during the Great Purges). Yet it was decided that the country must pass through, in shorter time intervals, precisely those stages of development that the Soviet Union had traversed. The result was a serious disruption of the economy through the erection of a top-heavy industrial structure on the base of a depressed agriculture. This policy cannot be attributed to Stalin alone, since it was continued after his death. It proved disastrous and is intelligible only on the assumption that it was primarily motivated by ideological considerations.

The argument can be carried further. By its behavior throughout its history, the Soviet Union has incurred the hostility, or at least the suspicion, of the entire free world. Yet there was no practical reason why it should have done so. After the October Revolution, the Bolshevik regime was faced with appalling domestic problems, and it had nothing to gain by courting the animosity of the West. The Soviet leaders might well have built up their country in accordance with the principles to which they were committed without exciting such widespread hostility. What governments do at home is commonly regarded as their own affair. Fundamentally, the regime in Yugoslavia is as Communist as that of the Soviet Union and was established with equal ruthlessness. But, Tito, having asserted his independence from Moscow, has muffled his attacks on the West, and the Western governments in turn have demonstrated their desire—albeit tempered with caution—to believe in his good faith.

What no country will tolerate is the attempt, deliberately engineered by a foreign power, to overthrow its form of government; yet this has been the persistent aim and effort of the Soviet regime in defiance of its diplomatic guarantees of noninterference. It is hard to see how this strategy has assisted the development of Soviet Russia, and that it has never been abandoned cannot be dissociated from those messianic and catastrophic elements in the Communist creed that influence, perhaps even impel, the Soviet drive for world power.

In conclusion, it is frequently stated that Communism has created an ideological cleavage between the West and the Soviet bloc. Yet this statement would be meaningless if the issue today were, as some believe, simply one of power politics. An ideology is significant only if it makes those who profess it act in a way they would not otherwise do. The fact that large numbers of persons accept Communism would not constitute a danger if it did not lead them to support policies that threaten the existence of those who do not accept it. It is true that many people, especially in underdeveloped countries, call themselves Communists without having any clear idea of what it means. Yet the movement would not be the force it has become were there not in every country men and women who sincerely believe in the ideas that collectively form what we call its ideology.

To represent this ideology as a species of opium with which the Soviet leaders contrive to lull the people, while taking care never to indulge in it themselves, is to attribute to them an ability to dissociate themselves from the logic of their system— an ability they probably do not possess. For the concepts that make up that system, fantastic as many of them appear to be, will be found on examination to be interrelated and to be logical extensions of the basic principles to which all Communists subscribe.

To turn it the other way around, Communists claim a theoretical justification for the basic principles in which they believe. But these principles must be translated into appropriate action; and action, if directed by the rulers of a powerful country like the Soviet Union, will take the form of *Realpolitik*. There is no yardstick that permits a measure of the exact relation between power politics and ideology in the policies that result; but surely neither factor can be ignored.

National Interest: Key to Soviet Politics

——SAMUEL L. SHARP

AN ENORMOUS BODY of Western research and analysis focuses on Marxist-Leninist ideology as a clue to an understanding of Kremlin policy. This extensive and intensive preoccupation with matters doctrinal is, at least in part, the result of a rather widely circulated belief that the democratic world was guilty of neglect when it refused to take seriously the "theoretical" writings and pronouncements of Adolf Hitler. It has been alleged that these writings later guided Hitler's actions and that a ready key to his conduct was thus overlooked.

When, at the end of World War II, the Soviet Union appeared on the international scene as a power—and a menace—of the first order, led by a group consistently claiming its adherence to a body of doctrine as a guide to action, legions of experts began to dissect that body in a search for a key to Soviet behavior, current and future. The material at hand was certainly more promising than the intellectually scrawny homunculus of Nazi or Fascist "ideology." After all, Marxism has its not entirely disreputable roots in legitimate Western thought. Even in terms of sheer bulk, there was more to operate on, what with Lenin's and Stalin's additions and modifications of the original scriptures and the voluminous exegetic output of a generation of Soviet propagandists.

The massive study of Communist ideology has had one happy result: Some serious scholarly output has been provided to counterbalance Party-line apologias, thereby destroying a number of primitive notions concerning the Soviet system and what makes

15

it tick. At the same time, in this writer's view, preoccupation with the search for a formula of interpretive and predictive value had produced its own distortions. These distortions seem to be the composite result of Cold War anxieties, faulty logic, and disregard of some of the elementary principles and practices of international relations. To these causes must be added the human tendency to look beyond the simple and obvious for the complicated and mysterious in attempting to explain any condition that is exasperating and is therefore perceived as strange and unique. Baffled by the Soviet phenomenon, millions in the Western world have found a negative consolation of sorts in the famous statement made by Winston Churchill in a broadcast on October, 1939, that Russian policy is "a riddle wrapped in a mystery inside an enigma." But how many have bothered to read the qualifying words that followed? Having disclaimed ability to forecast Soviet actions, Churchill added: *"But perhaps there is a key. That key is Russian national interest."* (Italics added.)

Clearly implied in this observation was the logical supposition that the policy-makers of the Soviet Union act in what they believe to be the best interest of the state over whose destinies they are presiding. In this sense, the Soviet Union is to be looked upon as an actor, a protagonist, on the stage of international politics; and in this writer's view, its actions can be interpreted most fruitfully in terms of behavior *germane* to the practice of international politics. Without denying the possible pitfalls of this approach, the writer proposes to argue its usefulness as a key to understanding a phenomenon that the non-Communist world can ill afford to envelop in a fog of self-generated misinterpretation.

The Doubtful Art of Quotation

Whenever the suggestion is made that the concept of national interest be applied as an explanation of Soviet behavior on the international scene, objections are raised in many quarters. The most vigorous protests come, of course, from Soviet sources. It is a standard claim of Soviet spokesmen that their state is by definition something "different" (or "higher"), and that the foreign policy of this entity is different in principle (*printsipialno otlichna*) from that of other states, because the latter are capitalist and the former is socialist. It would seem that only uncritical adherents of Communism could take such statements seriously. Yet non-Communists very often cite them as a convenient *ipse dixit* in support of their own claim that the Soviet Union is indeed "different," though not in the way Soviet propaganda wants one to believe. The claim is that the Soviet Union is, at best, "a conspiracy disguised as a state" and cannot be viewed as a "normal" member of the world community of nations. There is no attempt to explain on what basis some Soviet statements are to be taken as reliable indexes of regime motivations, while other statements, no less abundantly scattered throughout the Marxist-Leninist scriptures, are rejected as lie and deception.

It is surely dubious scholarship to collect quotations (sometimes reduced to half a sentence) from Lenin and Stalin without regard to the time, place, circumstances, composition of the audience, and, whenever ascertainable, immediate purposes of such utterances. What results from such compilations, no matter how laboriously and ingeniously put together, is, as Marshall Knappen has pointed out in his *Introduction to American Foreign Policy,* "a collection of such loose generalizations and so many exceptions and contradictions that few readers can find much guidance in it." Stalin, for example, can be quoted as once having said that "with a diplomat, words must diverge from facts," and that "a sincere diplomat would be like dry water or wooden iron"; yet this not too astute observation was made in 1913, in an article dealing with bourgeois diplomacy written by an obscure Georgian revolutionary who probably had never met a diplomat. His view in this instance is identifiable as a variant of the classic image of the diplomat as "an honorable gentleman sent abroad to lie for his country." This image may very well have stayed with the congenitally suspicious and pessimistic Stalin in later life and thus might indeed afford us a clue to his "real" nature. However, sound scholarship would seek to reconstruct the attitudes of the Kremlin ruler out of words and deeds of a more relevant period of his life rather than from this loose piece of Djugashvili prose torn out of context.

The Vital Factor of Feasibility

Some objections to the interpretation of Soviet policies in terms of national interest are rooted in the aforementioned line of analysis, which conjures up the ghost of Adolf Hitler. The democracies erred, did they not, in initially looking upon Hitler's aims as an expression of "legitimate" (we will return to this phrase in a moment), however distasteful, national aspirations, only to discover later that they were dealing with a maniac whose appetites were unlimited. Since it is generally agreed that Soviet policy, like Hitler's, belongs to the totalitarian species, would it not be unpardonable to repeat the same mistake by looking upon the aims of the Soviet leaders as the expression of the aspirations of a "normal" nation–state?

Two points should be made here. First, Hitler bears comparison with no one; there is no other leader in history who has combined his precise mental make-up with his enormous concentration of power. He was, as his biographer Allan Bullock pointed out, a man "without aims," i. e., without *limited* and therefore tractable aims. At one point in his career, Hitler began to disregard the cardinal rule of politics—the necessity of aligning ambition with capacity to translate them into reality. He broke the barrier of the *feasible,* motivated by what could most likely be diagnosed as the death wish. Whatever else may be said about the Soviet leaders, no one, including people who suspect them of ideological self-deception, has denied them the quality of caution. Far from seeking self-destruction, they are lustily bent on survival. This in itself, even in the complete absence of scruples, makes their aims *limited.*

Mr. Carew Hunt argues elsewhere in these pages that there are "messianic and catastrophic elements in the Communist creed that influence . . . the Soviet drive for world power." While there may indeed be a degree of messianism in the Soviet leadership's view of its mission, the "catastrophic" tendency seems to be held carefully in check. Hitler was propelled by the absurd notion that he had to accomplish certain aims before he reached the age of sixty—an arrogant and, from the point of view of German national interest, totally irrelevant assumption. Granted that the

Soviet leaders aim at "world power" (a concept that in itself should be defined more explicitly than it usually is), they have long since decided not to fix any specific time limit for the achievement of this ultimate aim. Certainly the present generation of leaders has acted to modify (perhaps "refine" is a better word) the aggressive drive for power abroad, at least to an extent that will allow some enjoyment at home of the tangible fruits of the Revolution this side of the Communist heaven. Even back in the early days of Bolshevik rule, Lenin, though at times carried away by expectations of spreading revolution, never sacrificed practical caution to missionary zeal; repeatedly, he warned his followers to look after the "bouncing baby" (the Soviet state), since Europe was only "pregnant with revolution" (which it was not).

An Applicable Concept of Interest

The second point to be made is a crucial one. Reluctance to analyze Soviet aims in terms of national interest is due, in part, to the aura of legitimacy that surrounds the "normal" run of claims of nation–states, giving rise to the notion that the term itself infers something legitimate. However, suggesting that Kremlin moves can best be understood in terms of what the leaders consider advantageous to the Soviet state by no means implies subscribing to their aims or sympathizing with them. In international relations, the maxim *tout comprendre c'est tout pardonner* does not apply. The concept of national interest, by focusing attention on the *objective sources of conflict*—i.e., those that *can* be explained rationally as issues between nations— permits us to view the international scene in terms of a global problem of power relations rather than a cops-and-robbers melodrama. We can then perceive which are the *tractable* elements in the total equation of conflict and devote our energies to reducing or altering these factors.

This approach seems to the writer to be indispensable both to the scholar and to the statesman. The scholar who accepts the "natural" (in terms of the nature of international politics) explanation for Kremlin behavior is not likely to violate the "law of

parsimony" by unnecessarily piling up hypotheses that are un-
provable and, in any case, simply confuse the issue, insofar as
dealing practically with the Soviet Union is concerned. The
statesman finds that he is coping with a phenomenon he knows
how to approach both in accommodation and in opposition,
rather than with some occult and other-worldly force.

Those who object to the framework of analysis here proposed
would say, as does Mr. Hunt, that there are many cases on record
when the Soviet leaders have acted in a manner clearly inconsistent with the Russian national interest, and intelligible only
in terms of ideological dogmatism. The answer to this argument
is simple: It does not matter what Mr. Hunt—or anybody else—
considers to be the Russian national interest; as the term is defined here, the only view that matters is that held by the Soviet
leaders. By the same token, it is a rather fruitless thing to speak
of "legitimate" versus "illegitimate" Soviet interests. One of the
essential attributes of sovereignty (and the Soviet leaders are
certainly jealous where their own is involved!) is that it is up to
the sovereign to determine what serves him best.

Yet does not this reasoning render pointless the entire conceptual approach proposed? If Soviet national interest is what
the Soviet leaders take it to be, and if one agrees—as one must—
that their view of the world is derived largely from their adherence to Marxism-Leninism, is this not another way of saying
that Soviet behavior is the result of ideological conditioning? Not
quite. The point at issue is whether the "pure" Soviet view of
the world is important *as a guide to action,* whether the *ultimate*
aims of the Communist creed are operative in policy determinations. In the present writer's view they are not. The fault of the
opposing line of analysis is that in dwelling on the supposed
impact of ideology on the leadership, it tends to ignore the degree to which the pursuit of ultimate goals has been circumscribed in time and scope by considerations of *the feasible.* In
simple arithmetic, doctrine minus those aspects that are not
empirically operative equals empirically determined policy. If a
policy action is called "revolutionary expediency," it is still expediency. Why then introduce into the equation an element that
does not affect the result?

A supporting view in this respect is W. W. Rostow's character-ization of Soviet foreign policy as a series of responses to the outside world that, especially before 1939, "took the form of such actions as were judged most likely, *on a short-range basis,* to maintain or expand the national power of the Soviet regime." Despite the Soviet Union's vastly greater ability to influence the world environment in the postwar era, says Rostow, "there is no evidence that the foreign-policy criteria of the regime have changed." If some instances of Soviet behavior appear to have produced results actually detrimental to the Soviet interest, we must not only refrain from applying to our view of Soviet in-terest, but also—as Rostow's viewpoint suggests—judge the policy decisions involved in terms of their validity at the time they were made and not in the light of what happened later (remembering, too, that mistakes and miscalculations are common to all policy-makers, not just those who wear "ideological blinders").

The words "on a short-range basis" have been underscored above to stress that the term policy, if properly applied, excludes aims, ambitions, or dreams not visibly accompanied by action, and within a reasonable time, capable of producing the results aimed at or dreamed of. In the case of the Soviet leaders, con-centration on short-range objectives and adjustment to political realities has, in the brilliant phrase suggested by Barrington Moore, Jr., *caused the means to eat up the ends.*

The objection will still be raised that the Soviet leaders mouth every policy decision in terms of ideological aims. Enough should have been said on this score to obviate a discussion here; as able students of the problem have pointed out, the Soviet leaders' claim to rule rests on their perpetuation of the ideology and their insistence on orthodoxy; they have no choice but to continue pay-ing lip service to the doctrine, even if it is no longer operative. The liberal mind somehow balks at this image of total manipula-tion of an exoteric doctrine for public consumption that has no connection with its esoteric counterpart—that is, the principles or considerations that really govern Kremlin behavior. Yet allow-ance must be made for this possibility.

Moscow and International Communism

One serious argument of those who reject the image of the Soviet Union as a "legitimate" participant in the balance-of-power game played in the arena of international politics is that the Soviet leaders consistently violate the rules of the game by enlisting out-of-bounds help from foreign Communist parties. This point invites the following brief observations:

1) Early in its history, the Communist International was transformed into a tool of Soviet foreign policy, at a time when few other tools were available to Moscow.

2) As soon as the Soviet state felt at all sure of its survival (after the period of civil war, foreign intervention, and economic chaos), it reactivated the apparatus of foreign policy along more traditional lines.

3) Under Stalin, the Third International was reduced to a minor auxiliary operation. An index of Stalin's attitude toward it is the fact that he never once addressed a Comintern congress. Probably the International was kept up in the interwar period because it seemed to produce marginal dividends in terms of nuisance value. Moreover, Stalin could hardly have divorced himself from it officially at a time when he was jockeying for total power inside Russia, since this would have helped to confirm his opponents' accusations that he was "betraying the Revolution." But he certainly did everything to show his disdain for the ineffectiveness of the organization and its foreign components, in comparison with the growing power of the Soviet state.

4) When the entire record of Soviet success and failure is summed up, the achievements are clearly attributable to Soviet power and diplomacy, with no credit due to the international Communist movement. Furthermore, the ties between the Soviet Union and foreign Communist parties have never deterred Moscow from useful alliances or cooperation with other governments —including, from one time to another, the astutely anti-Communist Turkish government of Ataturk; the more brutally anti-Communist regime of Adolf Hitler; and, during World War II, the Western powers. That the Soviet leaders, by virtue of their doctrine, entertained mental reservations about the durability of

friendly relations with these governments can hardly be doubted. But it is equally clear that the cessation of cooperation was due in each case to the workings of power politics rather than Soviet ideological dictate—that is, to the historical tendency of alliances to disintegrate when that which binds them (usually a common enemy) disappears.

5) Finally, it might be argued that the Soviet appeal to foreign Communist parties is not dissimilar to the practice of various governments of different periods and persuasions to appeal for support abroad on the basis of some sort of affinity—be it *Hispanidad,* Slav solidarity, *Deutschtum,* or Pan-Arabism. The Soviet appeal is admittedly broader and the "organizational weapon" seems formidable, but their importance should not be exaggerated. Actually, there is no way at all to measure the effectiveness of the appeal per se, since Communist "success" or "failure" in any situation always involves a host of other variables—including military, geographical, social, political, or economic factors. In the last analysis, virtually every instance where Moscow has claimed a victory for Communism has depended on Soviet manipulation of traditional levers of national influence.

An Exception to Prove the Rule

There remains one area of Soviet "foreign policy" where the Soviet leaders have supplemented power politics—or more accurately, in this instance, naked force—with an attempt to derive special advantage, a sort of "surplus value," from claiming ideological obeisance to the Soviet Union as the seat of the secular church of Communism. This area is the so-called Soviet orbit in Eastern Europe.

The term foreign policy is enclosed in quotation marks here because Stalin obviously did not consider areas under the physical control of Soviet power as nations or governments to be dealt with in their own right. He was clearly impatient with the claim of at least some Communist parties that their advent to power had changed the nature of their relationship to Moscow, and that the party-to-party level of relations must be separated from the government-to-government level (as Gomulka argued in 1948).

In Stalin's thinking, especially after 1947, the East European regimes were not eligible for more real sovereignty than the "sovereign" republics of the Soviet Union. He attempted to extend the principle of "democratic centralism" (a euphemism for Kremlin control) to these countries, allowing them only as much of a façade of sovereignty as was useful for show toward the outside world.

One need not necessarily dig into doctrine to explain this attitude; in fact, doctrine until recently said nothing at all about relations between sovereign Communist states. The explanation lies to a large extent in Stalin's personal predilection for total control, plus the need to tighten Moscow's bonds to the limit, by whatever means or arguments possible, in the face of the bipolarization of global power after World War II.

Stalin's successors began by pressing the same claims of ideological obeisance from the satellites. But rather strikingly—in the same period that their foreign policy has scored substantial success in other areas in traditional terms of diplomatic advances and manipulation of the economic weapon—they have failed in the one area where they attempted to substitute the ties of ideology for the give and take of politics. Communist parties in power, it turned out (first in the case of Yugoslavia, while Stalin still reigned, and later in Poland, not to mention the very special case of China), claimed the right to be sovereign—or at least semisovereign—actors on the international scene. Whether or not this makes sense ideologically to the Soviet leaders is unimportant; they have recognized the claim.

It is not necessary to review here the post-Stalin history of fluctuating Soviet relations with Eastern Europe that began with the B. & K. pilgrimage to Belgrade. Let us take only the most recent attempt to reformulate the nature of relations between the U.S.S.R. and other Communist countries—the inter-Party declaration issued on the occasion of the fortieth anniversary of the Bolshevik Revolution. On the surface, the declaration—adopted at a meeting held on November 14–16, 1957, and published in *Pravda* on November 22—in the name of twelve ruling Communist parties, seems to reimpose a pattern of ideological uniformity as well as to recognize the special leadership position of the Soviet Union. However, the circumstances of the gathering and the internal evidence of the declaration together with the reports of some of the participants, show a far more complex situation.

The following aspects of the conference deserve attention: First, the very fact that the parties representing governments of sovereign countries were singled out for a special meeting and declaration, instead of being lumped together with the mass of parties (many of them illegal, some leading no more than a paper existence) is a significant departure from past practice. Second, the Yugoslav Party, though represented at the festivities, refused to sign the declaration, apparently after long negotiations. Third, attempts to revive in any form an international, Moscow-based organization resembling the Comintern were unsuccessful. Gomulka's report on the meeting, which appeared in *Trybuna Ludu* on November 29, 1957, made it clear that the Polish Party opposed both a new Comintern (for which it nevertheless had a few good words) and a new Cominform (for which it had nothing but scorn).

A point of particular significance was the revelation that future international gatherings of Communist parties, especially those in power, are to be based on previous agreements concerning the agenda. According to Gomulka, problems that each Party thinks it can best solve *"for itself and its country"* will not be decided by inter-Party conferences.

Perhaps most significant for the purposes of the present discussion was a statement by Mao Tse-tung, who, next to Khrushchev and Suslov, was the main speaker at the meeting of the "ruling" parties and was billed as co-sponsor of the declaration. Mao bolstered his argument for the recognition of the leading position of the Soviet Union in the "socialist camp" with the remark that "China does not even have one fourth of a Sputnik, while the Soviet Union has two." Now, the possession of a Sputnik is a symbol of achievement and a source of prestige for the Soviet Union, but certainly not in terms of ideology. It was Soviet national power to which Mao paid deference.

In sum, the entire circumstances of the gathering indicate a disposition on the part of the Soviet Union to substitute—

wherever it has to—the give and take of politics for its former relationship with the orbit countries, which relied on naked power to enforce demands of ideological subservience.

From all the foregoing, it should be clear that the task of the non-Communist world is not to worry itself sick over the ultimate goals of the Soviet leadership or the degree of its sincerity, but to concentrate on multiplying situations in which the Soviet Union either will be forced or will choose to play the game of international politics in an essentially traditional setting. How the Kremlin leaders will square this with their Marxist conscience is not really our problem.

The Logic of One-Party Rule

——RICHARD LOWENTHAL

To WHAT EXTENT are the political decisions of the Soviet leadership influenced by its belief in an official ideology—and to what extent are they empirical responses to specific conflicts of interest, expressed in ideological terms merely for purposes of justification? The phrasing of the question at issue suggests the two extreme answers that are prima facie conceivable—on the one hand, that ideology provides the Kremlin with a ready-made book of rules to be looked up in any situation; on the other, that its response to reality takes place without any reference to ideology. Yet any clear formulation of this vital issue will show that both extremes are meaningless nonsense.

A ready-made book of rules for any and every situation—an unvarying road map to the goal of Communism, which the Soviet leaders must predictably follow—cannot possibly exist, both because the situations to be met by them are not sufficiently predictable, and because no government behaving in so calculable a manner could conceivably retain power. On the other hand, empirical *Realpolitik* without ideological preconceptions can exist as little as can "empirical science" without categories and hypotheses based on theoretical speculation. Confronted with the same constellation of interests and pressures, the liberal statesman will in many cases choose a different course of action from the conservative—and the totalitarian Communist's choice will often be different from that of either.

It seems surprising, therefore, that at this late stage of discussion, Professor Sharp is apparently in earnest in defending the

27

extreme of the *Realpolitik* interpretation and in denying completely the relevance of the Communist ideology for the formation, and hence the understanding, of Soviet foreign policy. The latter, he assures us, can be adequately understood in terms of national interest, just as it can in any other state. When reminded by Mr. Carew Hunt of certain irrational features of Soviet foreign policy, he replies that what matters is not any outsider's concept of Soviet interests, but the Soviet leaders' own. Yet this reduces his thesis to a tautology: He "proves" that national interest motivates Soviet foreign policy by the simple device of labeling whatever motivates it "national interest."

Surely Professor Sharp cannot have it both ways. Either there are objective criteria of national interest, recognizable by the scholar—and then the view that these interests explain Soviet actions is capable of proof or refutation; or else it is admitted that different statesmen may interpret national interest in different but equally "legitimate" ways—and then a consideration of the internal structures of different national communities and of the "ideologies" reflecting them becomes indispensable for an understanding of their foreign policies.

The latter observation does not, of course, apply to Communist states alone, although it is only reasonable to expect the influence of the monopolistic ideology of a single-party state to be specially pervasive. George Kennan, in his 1950 lectures on American diplomacy, has convincingly shown the relevance of ideological factors to an understanding of modern United States foreign policy as well. To deny this influence a priori and to admit, as Professor Sharp apparently would, only the *Ding an sich* of national interest on the one side, and the accidental element of human error or pathology (such as Hitler's "death wish") on the other, seems to this writer to be an unjustifiable renunciation of one of the limited roads to understanding that are available to present-day political science.

The Function of Doctrine

Assuming, then, that the Soviet leaders' ideology is relevant to their conduct, the real problem remaining is to discover which are the actual operative elements in it and in what way they affect policy decisions. Clearly, it would be folly to expect that Soviet policy could be predicted solely from an exegetic study of the Marxist-Leninist canon. Not only is it impossible for any group of practical politicians to base their decisions on an unvarying book of rules; there is any amount of historical evidence to show that the rules have been altered again and again to fit the practical decisions ex post facto. Moreover, there are vast parts of the Communist ideological structure, such as the scholastic refinements of "dialectical materialism" or the labor theory of value, that in their nature are so remote from the practical matters to be decided that their interpretation cannot possibly affect policy decisions. They may be used in inner-Party arguments to *justify* what has been decided on other grounds, but that is all.

How, then, are we to distinguish those elements of Soviet ideology that are truly operative politically from those that are merely traditional scholastic ballast, linked to the operative elements by the historical accident of the founding fathers' authorship? The answer is to be found by going back to the original Marxian meaning of the term "ideology"—conceived as a distorted reflection of social reality in the consciousness of men, used as an instrument of struggle. The fundamental, distinctive social reality in the Soviet Union is the rule of the bureaucracy of a single, centralized, and disciplined party that wields a monopoly of political, economic, and spiritual power and permits no independent groupings of any kind. The writer proposes as a hypothesis that the operative parts of the ideology are those that are indispensable for maintaining and justifying this state of affairs. "Marxism-Leninism" matters inasmuch as it expresses, in an ideologically distorted form, the logic of one-party rule.*

* While this comes close to the position outlined in Mr. Carew Hunt's paper, I cannot follow him in his assumption that the totalitarian party monopoly is a by-product of the attempt to establish collectivist economic planning or to achieve the speedy industrialization of a backward country. This neo-Marxist view, held by such otherwise divergent authors as Professor Hayek and Milovan Djilas, is contradicted by the fact that the Bolshevik Party monopoly, including the ban on inner-Party factions, was fully established by Lenin at the time of the transition to the New Economic

Totalitarian Parallels

There are a few interconnected ideological features common to all the totalitarian regimes of our century—whether of the nationalist-fascist or of the Communist variety. We may designate them as the elements of chiliasm, of collective paranoia, and of the representative fiction. Each totalitarian regime justifies its power and its crimes by the avowed conviction, first, that its final victory will bring about the millennium—whether defined as the final triumph of Communism or of the master race—and second, that this state of grace can only be achieved by an irreconcilable struggle against a single, omnipresent, and multiform enemy—whether Monopoly Capitalism or World Jewry—whose forms include every particular opponent of the totalitarian power. Each also claims to represent the true will of the people—the *volonté générale*—independent of whether the people actually support it, and argues that any sacrifice may be demanded from the individual and the group for the good of the people and the defeat of its devilish enemies.

The Communist version of these basic beliefs is superior to the Nazi version in one vital respect. Because the appeal of racialism is in its nature restricted to a small minority of mankind, the Nazis' goal of world domination could not possibly have been attained without a series of wars, preferably surprise attacks launched against isolated opponents. Because the appeal of Communism is directed to all mankind, it can be linked with the further doctrine of the inevitable victory of the rising forces of socialism over the imperialist enemy that is disintegrating under

---

Policy (1921), when economic planning was reduced to a minimum and forced industrialization not yet envisaged. Independent of the concrete economic program, totalitarianism was implicit in the centralized, undemocratic structure of a party consciously created as an instrument for the conquest of power, and in the ideological characteristics resulting (to be discussed further in this article). Of course, totalitarian power, once established, favors total economic planning and the undertaking of revolutionary economic tasks by the state; but this is a consequence, not a cause. Marx never developed a concept of total planning, and even Lenin never imagined anything of the kind before 1918. But Marx, in his youth at least, equated the "dictatorship of the proletariat" with the Jacobin model, and Lenin followed this model throughout.

the impact of its own internal contradictions. This central ideological difference, and not merely the psychological difference
between Hitler and the Soviet leaders, explains why the latter
are convinced that history is on their side and that they need not
risk the survival of their own regime in any attempt to hasten its
final triumph: They believe in violence, revolutionary and military, as one of the weapons of policy, but they do not believe
in the inevitability of world war.

Awkward Aims and Claims

Yet the Communist version of totalitarian ideology also suffers
from some weaknesses and contradictions from which the Nazi
and fascist versions are free. In the first place, its vision of the
millennium has more markedly utopian features—the classless
society, the end of exploitation of man by man, the withering
away of the state—which made awkward yardsticks for the real
achievements of Communist states. Second, in a world where
nationalism remains a force of tremendous strength, an internationalist doctrine is bound to come into conflict with the interests of any major Communist power or with the desire of smaller
Communist states for autonomy.

Third, by rejecting the "Führer principle" and claiming to be
"democratic," Communist ideology makes the realities of Party
dictatorship and centralistic discipline more difficult to justify;
yet because appeal to blind faith is not officially permitted,
justification is needed in "rational" terms. It is precisely this
continuous need for the pretense of rational argument—the awkward heritage of Communism's origin from revolutionary Western
democracy—that has led to the far greater elaboration of its
ideology, compared to that of "irrationalist" right-wing totalitarianism, and that gives its constant interpretation so much
greater importance in preserving the cohesion of the Party
regime. Due to the fictions of democracy and rationality, the
morale of Party cadres has been made dependent on the appearance of ideological consistency.

The result of these inherent weaknesses of Communist ideology
is that the doctrines dealing with the "dictatorship of the prole-

tariat," the Party's role as a "vanguard" embodying the "true" class consciousness, "democratic centralism," "proletarian internationalism," and the "leading role of the Soviet Union" become focal points of ideological crises and targets of "revisionist" attacks whenever events reveal the underlying contradictions in a particularly striking way. Yet these are the very doctrines the regime cannot renounce, because they are the basic rationalizations of its own desire for self-preservation.

We can expect, then, that Communist ideology will have an effective influence on the policy decisions of Soviet leaders when, and only when, it expresses the needs of self-preservation of the Party regime. We can further expect that ideological changes and disputes within the Communist "camp" will offer clues to the conflicts and crises—the "contradictions"—that are inseparable from the evolution of this, as of any other, type of society. The fruitful approach, in this writer's view, consists neither in ignoring Communist ideology as an irrelevant disguise, nor in accepting it at its face value and treating it as a subject for exegesis, but in using it as an indicator of those specific drives and problems that spring from the specific structure of Soviet society—in regarding it as an enciphered, continuous self-disclosure whose cipher can be broken by sociological analysis.

Two Camps—One Enemy

Let us now apply this approach to the doctrine of the "two camps" in world affairs. The two-camp concept was not, of course, a Stalinist invention, although this is sometimes believed. The postwar situation with its alignment of the Communist and Western powers in two openly hostile politico-military blocs merely gave plausibility to a world image that was inherent in Leninism from the beginning, but that attracted little attention in the period when the Communist "camp" was just an isolated fortress with several outposts. Nor has the doctrine disappeared with the post-Stalin recognition of the importance of the uncommitted, ex-colonial nations and of the tactical value of incorporating them in a "peace zone"; it remains one of the basic ideas of the Moscow twelve-party declaration of November, 1957, and one of the fundamental subjects of ideological disagreement between the Soviets and the Yugoslav Communists.

The Yugoslavs can reject the two-camp doctrine because they admit the possibility of "roads to socialism" rather than Communist Party dictatorship—"reformist" roads for advanced industrial countries with parliamentary traditions, "national revolutionary" roads for ex-colonial countries. It follows from this view that Communist states have no monopoly on progress, and that alliances have no ultimate ideological meaning.

The Soviets still assert that while there can be different roads to Communist power, and minor differences in the use of power once gained, there is no way of achieving socialism except by the "dictatorship of the proletariat exercised by its vanguard." It follows that tactical agreements with semisocialist neutrals are not different in kind from the wartime alliance with the Western "imperialists," or the prewar pact with Hitler—maneuvers that are useful in dividing the forces of the "class enemy" but that remain subordinate to the fundamental division of the world into the Communists versus the Rest.

In other words, the two-camp doctrine is the Communist version of what we have called the element of "collective paranoia" in totalitarian ideology—its need for a single, all-embracing enemy who is assumed to pull the wires of every resistance to the Party's power. The term "paranoia" is used here not to infer that the phenomenon in question is due to psychotic processes in either the leaders or the mass following of totalitarian parties, but merely to describe, through a convenient psychological analogy, the ideological mechanism of projection that ascribes the regime's drive for unlimited power to an imagined all-enemy. The essential point is that in the nature of totalitarianism, any independent force—either inside or outside the state—is regarded as ultimately hostile; the concept of "two camps" and that of "unlimited aims" are two sides of the same phenomenon.

Moscow's Double-Indemnity Tactics

Now Professor Sharp is, of course, entirely right in asking where this doctrine impinges on actual Soviet foreign policy—

given the undoubted facts that actual Soviet aims, and the risks incurred in their pursuit, are limited at any given moment; that the Soviets are perfectly capable of concluding "temporary" alliances with "bourgeois," "imperialist," or even "fascist" states; and that most other alliances in this impermanent world are proving to be "temporary" as well, for quite nonideological reasons. This writer would suggest to him that the difference has manifested itself in the peculiar suspicion with which the Soviets treated their "imperialist" allies even at the height of the war, seeking in particular to isolate their own population from contact; in the manner in which they sought to create additional "guarantees" for the reliability of those allies by the use of local Communist parties wherever this was possible; and, above all, in the difference between the traditional and the Communist concepts of "spheres of influence," as illuminated by the different interpretations of the Yalta agreements.

The peculiar forms taken by Moscow's suspicion of its wartime allies are too well known to need elaboration here; but it is less generally realized that such behavior was merely the reverse side of Soviet efforts to "strengthen" such temporary alliances, where possible, by the use of Party ties. Existence of the Party channel has not, of course, been a *sine qua non* for Moscow's intragovernmental deals, as is shown by the examples of Russo-Turkish cooperation after World War I, the Stalin-Hitler Pact, and to some extent recent Soviet support for Nasser's Egypt. But wherever Communist parties were tolerated by the partner, Soviet foreign policy has assigned to them a vital role.

In the 1920's, Stalin's Chinese policy was openly run in double harness; diplomatic support for the Nationalist advance to the North was supplemented by an agreement of affiliation between the Chinese Communist Party and the Kuomintang, enabling the Communists to occupy influential political and military positions —an attempt no less serious for its ultimate total failure in 1927. In the 1930's, a variant of the same "dual policy" was evident when Moscow supported the League of Nations and "collective security," while Communist parties in France and Spain pursued "popular-front" policies that soft-pedaled economic and social demands for the sake of influencing governmental foreign policy.

In the case of Spain, the Communists, aided by the Republicans' dependence on Soviet supplies, ended up in virtual control of the Republic on the eve of its final collapse.

Again during World War II, Communists in the resistance movements and in the free Western countries were ordered to pursue the same tactics of social moderation and occupation of key positions as were practiced in China in the 1920's and in Spain in the 1930's. Wartime military and political cooperation between "Soviet China" and Chiang Kai-shek was urged in the same spirit, with considerable success. All these are the foreign-policy methods of a state *sui generis*—a one-party state enabled by its ideology to make use of a disciplined international movement organized for the struggle for power. To compare them—and the secondary opportunities for infiltration and espionage that they offer in addition to their main political objectives—to the use of vague cultural influences like *Hispanidad* is to show a notable degree of innocence.

Yalta—A Historic "Misunderstanding"

The crucial example to illustrate the role of ideology in Soviet foreign policy, however, remains the history of the postwar division of Europe. The writer is not concerned here with the political controversy over whether this division, as first laid down in the wartime agreements at Teheran and Yalta, was inevitable in the light of the military situation as seen at the time or whether the Western statesmen committed an avoidable mistake of disastrous dimensions. What matters in the present context is the different meaning attached by the Western and Communist leaders, in concluding these agreements, to the concept of "spheres of influence," and the consequences of this "misunderstanding."

That great powers are in a position to exert a measure of influence over their smaller neighbors, and that they use this influence in one way or another to increase as far as possible their security against attack by other great powers, is a general experience in the politics of sovereign states and unlikely to be superseded by any amount of declamation about "equality of rights"; hence, the

fact that the wartime allies, in drawing a military line of demarcation from north to south across the center of Europe, should
have tried to agree about their postwar spheres of influence is,
by itself, proof of realistic foresight rather than morally repre-
hensible cynicism.

To Roosevelt and Churchill, however, these spheres of influence meant what they had traditionally meant in the relations
of sovereign states—a gradual shading over from the influence of
one power or group of powers to that of the other, which might
even be loosely described in terms of "percentages of influence,"
ranging from 50-50 to 90-10. To the Soviets, "spheres of influence" meant something completely different in the framework of
their ideology—the ideology of the single-party state. To them
there could be no securely "friendly" government except a government run by a Communist party under their discipline; no
sphere of influence but a sphere of Communist rule; no satisfactory percentage short of 100. Hence the consistent Soviet efforts,
which began even before the end of the European war, to impose
total control by Communist parties in every country on their side
of the demarcation line—an effort that was finally successful
everywhere but in Finland and Eastern Austria; hence also the
indignant protests of the Western powers that the Soviets had
broken the agreements on free elections and democratic development, and the equally indignant Soviet retort that they were
only installing "friendly governments" as agreed, that theirs was
the truly "democratic" system, and that they had kept scrupulously to the essential agreement on the military demarcation
line.

A large section of Western opinion has concluded from this
experience that agreements with the Soviets are useless in principle, because "you cannot trust them"; and Professor Sharp's
insistence on national interest as the sole key to Soviet policy is
probably at least in part a reaction against this emotional and
moralizing approach. In fact, any interpretation of the postwar
experience overlooking the fact that the Soviets have, for reasons
of national self-interest, kept to the "self-enforcing" agreement
on the demarcation line, would be as seriously one-sided as one
overlooking the fact that they have, for reasons of ideology or

party interest, broken every agreement on "percentages" and free elections.

There is no need, however, to base future policy on either of two one-sided views equally refuted by experience. Nobody in the Western world has argued more powerfully against the "moralizing" approach to foreign policy, and for a return to the give and take of diplomacy based on real interests, than George Kennan; yet in his 1958 Reith lectures, as before, he has insisted that the specific ideological distortion in the Soviet leaders' image of the world, far from being magically cured by such a return to diplomacy, has to be taken into account continuously in judging which kind of agreements are possible and which are not. After all, the peoples of Eastern Europe are still paying for the illusion of the West that the Soviet Union was a state like any other, pursuing its power interests without regard to ideology.

The Soviet Dilemma in Eastern Europe

If we now turn to interstate and interparty relations within the Communist camp, we seem at first sight to have entered an area where ideology is adapted quite unceremoniously to the changing requirements of practical politics. Lenin, having barely seized power in Russia and looking forward to an early spreading of Communist revolution, could talk airily enough about the sovereign "socialist" states. Stalin, having determined after the failure of short-term revolutionary hope to concentrate on "socialism in a single country," came to regard international Communism as a mere tool of Soviet power and to believe that revolutionary victories without the backing of Soviet arms were neither possible nor desirable; he wanted no sovereign Communist allies, only satellites, and he got them in postwar Eastern Europe.

The independent victories of the Yugoslav Communists at the end of the war and of the Chinese Communists in 1949, nevertheless posed the problem he had sought to avoid, and thus required a revision of policy and ideology. But, so one argument goes, the stubborn old man had lost the flexibility to accept the situation; he precipitated a needless quarrel with the Yugoslavs and generally prevented the necessary adjustment while he lived. His heirs, however, hastened to correct his mistakes and put inter-Communist relations back on a basis of sovereign equality and diplomatic give and take, not only with China and Yugoslavia, but, after some trial and error, with all Communist states. Or did they?

In the above "common-sense" account, not only the facts of the final phase are wrong; by deliberately neglecting the ideological aspect, it loses sight of all the real difficulties and contradictions that remain inherent in the situation. Because the Soviet Union is both a great power and a single-party state tied to an international ideology, it cannot be content either to oppress and exploit other Communist states or to come to terms with them on a basis of expediency; it must act in a way that will ensure the ideological unity of the Communist "camp" and its own authority at the center.

Stalin's insistence on making the "leading role of the Soviet Union" an article of the international creed expressed not just the idiosyncrasies of a power-mad tyrant, but his perception of one side of the dilemma—the risk that a recognition of the sovereign equality of other Communist states might loosen the solidarity of the "camp" in its dealings with the non-Communist world and weaken the ideological authority of the Soviet Party leaders, with ultimate repercussions on their position in the Soviet Union itself. His successors disavowed him because his Yugoslav policy had failed and because they perceived the other side of the dilemma—that rigid insistence on Soviet hegemony might break up the unity of the "camp" even more quickly and might, in particular, lead to open conflict with China. But by going to Peking and Belgrade and admitting the "mistakes" of Stalin's "Great Russian chauvinism" (as well as the "mistakes" of his internal terrorist regime), they precipitated the very crisis of authority he had feared.

The Reassertion of Soviet Primacy

Even Khrushchev and his associates, however, never intended to grant effective sovereign equality to the other Communist

satellite regimes of Eastern Europe, which, in contrast to Yugoslavia and China, had come into being exclusively through the
pressure of Soviet power; they merely had planned to make the
satellite regimes more viable by reducing Soviet economic exploitation and administrative interference, while maintaining
full policy control. In the one case in which effective internal
autonomy, although not full sovereignty, was in fact granted—the
case of Poland—the Soviet leaders were forced to act against
their will as a result of open local defiance in a critical international situation. To say that the other East European participants
in the Moscow twelve-party meeting of November, 1957, or for
that matter the participants from Outer Mongolia and North
Korea, represented "governments of sovereign countries" is to
mistake the fancies of Communist propaganda for political facts.
Nor do the facts bear out Professor Sharp's interpretation that
the outcome of the conference showed the Soviet leaders' willingness to rely, in their future relations with these "sovereign
governments," on the give and take of diplomacy. Rather, they
confirm Mr. Carew Hunt's view that the need for a single center
of international authority is inherent in the Soviet Communist
Party's conception of its own role and in its ideology.

The real purpose of that conference was to exploit the recent
successes of the Soviet Union as a military and economic power
in order to restore the indispensable, but lately damaged, ideological authority of its leaders in the international Communist
movement. The principle of "proletarian internationalism"—i.e.,
unity in foreign policy—had been recognized by all participants,
including for the first time in many years the Yugoslavs, before
the conference started. Now Moscow was aiming at the further
recognition both of its own leadership role and of the need for
doctrinal unity; a joint struggle against "revisionism" on the
basis of common principles was to abolish once and for all the
heresy of "polycentrism" (i.e., the concept of a plurality of truly
autonomous Communist movements).

As it turned out, the Yugoslavs refused both propositions,
while the Polish Communists and the nonruling but important
Italian Communist Party accepted them only with mental reservations, insisting in practice on their right to decide for them-

selves how the "common principles" would be applied in their own countries. As opposed to this partial failure, however, Moscow was successful in winning full acceptance of the new dispensations by the Chinese Communists and the satellites, as well as in getting agreement on a new, elaborate international liaison machinery within the Secretariat of the Soviet Communist Central Committee, in the implementation of its renewed claim to international authority.

Moscow's partial failure, therefore, did not indicate that the Soviets would be content with less than they had demanded; on the contrary, it proved the prelude to an all-out offensive against "revisionism" in Eastern Europe. After preparatory articles in the Soviet theoretical journals during the winter, the campaign was unleashed in the spring of 1958, when the draft of the new Yugoslav Party program showed the determination of its authors not to join the "camp" in a military alliance under Soviet discipline. After last-minute mediation attempts by the Polish and Hungarian Communists had proved futile, the instruction issued to all "loyal" Communist parties early in April to refrain from sending fraternal delegates to the Yugoslav Party Congress renewed in effect the ideological excommunication of the "neutralist" deviators. The lesson was hammered home when Imre Nagy was executed in June as a "traitor," because he had tried to take Hungary out of the Soviet bloc, and when all the spokesmen of orthodox Communism explained that Nagy's treason had been the logical consequence of his ideological revisionism. With Gomulka's condemnation of the Yugoslav heresy and his defense of Nagy's execution as an "internal Hungarian affair," the full submission of the Polish Communists in matters of ideology as well as of foreign policy had been secured, even though Moscow continued to tolerate, in return, their continued autonomy in the domestic application of the "general line." Khrushchev had achieved the objective required by the logic of his one-party regime—the restoration of Soviet authority in international Communism as a precondition for unity in both foreign policy and ideological principles, based on some of the very doctrines he had rashly thrown overboard in 1955–56.

Ideology on the Home Front

Ultimately, the need to fight "revisionism" in Eastern Europe, even at the price of renewed difficulties with both Yugoslavia and Poland, arises from the need to strengthen the ideological defenses of the Party regime in Russia itself. To admit that in Hungary the workers rose against a Communist government would call into question the basic identification of the ruling party with the working class—the fiction of the "dictatorship of the proletariat." To let Yugoslav propaganda for "workers' management" pass unchallenged would confirm the implication that Soviet factories, having no workers' councils with similar rights, are managed in the interest not of the workers but of the privileged bureaucracy. To keep silent when the Poles proudly report the improvement of their agricultural yields since the dissolution of most of their collective farms would encourage Soviet peasants to dream of similar reforms. To condone the increased, if still limited, freedom of artistic, literary, and philosophical discussion now permitted in Poland and Yugoslavia would strengthen the demands of Soviet writers and scholars for similar freedom.

The obvious and intended implication here is that Soviet reconciliation with Yugoslavia and the near-revolutionary changes in Poland merely aggravated pressures for change that *already* existed in Russia itself. Thus the present account would be incomplete without some attempt to indicate, however sketchily, how ideological changes can be used as aids in interpreting the Soviet domestic scene as well as Kremlin foreign policy and bloc relations.

Earlier in this article, reference was made to some of the basic tenets that seem inseparably bound up with the preservation and justification of a Communist one-party regime. But within this unchanging framework, considerable variations in detail have taken place in the history of the Soviet Union. The appearance or disappearance of one of these "ideological variables" may be a valuable indicator of the kind of pressures that are exerted on the regime by the growing society and of the manner in which the leaders try to maintain control, sometimes by partly ceding to such pressures and seeking to canalize them, other times by a sharp frontal counterattack.

The "Permanent" Revolution

Among the most revealing of these variables are Soviet doctrines dealing with the economic role of the state and with the "class struggle" within Soviet society. The underlying reality is that a revolutionary party dictatorship, once it has carried out its original program and thus has contributed to the emergence of a new privileged class, is bound to disappear sooner or later—to fall victim to a "Thermidor"—unless it prevents the new upper class from consolidating its position by periodically shaking up the social structure in a "permanent revolution from above." The ideological expression of this problem is the classical doctrine that the dictatorship of the proletariat should gradually "wither away" after it has succeeded in destroying the old ruling classes; thus, if continued dictatorship is to be justified, new goals of social transformation must be set and new "enemies" discovered.

In the early period of Stalin's rule, the new "goal" was the forced collectivization of the Russian countryside; the prosperous peasants—the kulaks—took the place of the former landowners and capitalists as the "enemy class" that had to be liquidated. Summing up the achievement in 1937, Stalin wrote in his *Short Course* on Party history that collectivization had been a second revolution, but a revolution carried out from above, by state power "with the help of the masses," not just by the masses from below. The ideological groundwork was thus laid for assigning the state a function of continuous economic transformation from above, not just a once-for-all revolutionary function.

The second step, also taken by Stalin in 1937, at the height of the Great Blood Purge, consisted in proclaiming the doctrine that the "class struggle" in the Soviet Union was getting more acute as the "construction of socialism" advanced, because the "enemies" were getting more desperate. This was the ideological justification of the Purge itself; at the same time, it was a veiled indication that another revolution from above was in effect taking place, although this time Stalin refrained from trying to define the "enemies" in social terms. In fact, what Stalin accomplished was a mass liquidation of both the bearers of the Party's older revolutionary tradition—considered unsuited to the tasks of a bureaucratic state party—and of the most confident and independent-minded elements of the new privileged bureaucracy; the end result was a transformation of the Party's social and ideological composition through the mass incorporation of the surviving frightened bureaucrats.

Stalin's final ideological pronouncement was contained in his political testament, *Economic Problems of Socialism*, published in 1952. In this work he mapped out a program for the further revolutionary transformation of Soviet society, with the taking over of kolkhoz property by the state as its central element.

Khrushchev's Formula for Perpetual Rule

The first major renunciation of these Stalinist ideological innovations was made by Khrushchev in his "secret speech" at the Twentieth Congress. Apart from his factual disclosures concerning Stalin's crimes, he denounced Stalin's doctrine of the sharpening class struggle with the advance of socialist construction as dangerous nonsense, calculated to lead to the mutual slaughter of loyal Communists after the real class enemy had long been liquidated. This statement affords the master clue to the puzzle of why Khrushchev made the speech: It was a "peace offering" to the leading strata of the regime in the Party machine, army, and managerial bureaucracy alike—a response to their pressure for greater personal security. But by his concession, Khrushchev reopened the problem that Stalin's doctrine and practice had been intended to solve—that of preserving and justifying the Party dictatorship by periodic major shake-ups of society.

By the spring and summer of 1957, Khrushchev showed his awareness of the practical side of the problem: His dismantling of the economic ministries, breaking up the central economic bureaucracy, and strengthening the power of the regional Party secretaries, was another such revolutionary shake-up. By November, he responded to the ideological state of the problem. First he repeated, in his solemn speech on the fortieth anniversary of the Bolshevik seizure of power, his rejection of Stalin's doctrine of ever-sharpening class struggle and ever-present enemies, thus indicating his wish to avoid a return to Stalin's terroristic methods even while following his social recipe of permanent revolution. Then he proceeded to develop his own alternative justification for maintaining the Party dictatorship—a unique argument that equated the strengthening of Party control with the "withering away of the state" predicted by Lenin.

Reviving this formula for the first time since it was buried by Stalin, Khrushchev explained that the military and police apparatus of the state would have to be maintained as long as a hostile capitalist world existed outside; but he added that the economic and administrative functions of the state bureaucracy would henceforth be steadily reduced by decentralization and devolution, thus strengthening the organs of regional self-government and of national autonomy within the various republics. At the same time, he quietly took steps to strengthen the control of the central Party Secretariat—his own seat of power—over the republican and regional Party organs, thus following the old Leninist principle that the fiction of national autonomy must be balanced by the fact of centralized discipline within the ruling party.

In short, the same aim of maintaining the social dynamism of the Party dictatorship and justifying its necessity, which Stalin achieved by exalting the economic role of the state, is pursued by Khrushchev by means of the reverse device of claiming that the state's economic functions have begun to "wither away." On the face of it, this doctrinal manipulation seems to reduce the role of ideology to that of ingenious trickery, obscuring rather than reflecting the underlying social realities. Yet in fact, the very need for a change in the ideological argument, and its further elaboration by Khrushchev in his report to the Twenty-first Party Congress, reflects the change that is taking place in the underlying social situation—the resistance against a return to naked terrorism, the growing desire for a lessening of state pressure, and a greater scope for local activity. Whether in industry or agriculture, in the control of literature or in relations with the satellite states, the basic conditions that the regime needs for its self-perpetuation have remained the same—but they can no longer be assured in the same way. That, too, is reflected in the variables of the official ideology.

Ideology: The Fourth Stage

——LEOPOLD LABEDZ

MARXISM IN RUSSIA has gone through three stages and now seems to be entering its fourth. The first stage was that of transplantation. Marxism was a doctrine born in the West, and the members of the Russian intelligentsia who adopted it had for decades been subject to Western cultural and political influences. The doctrine emerged in the wake of the German romantic movement, of the disenchantment of the intelligentsia with the results of the French revolution, of the abortive revolutions of 1848, and of the revulsion from the social effects of early industrialization. It contained two essential ingredients that strengthened its appeal to the intelligentsia of a backward country: revolutionary fervor and a chiliastic hope. It called for modernization, and not, like *Narodnichestvo* (populism), for a revival of moribund peasant institutions. But although its millenarianism suited the Russian messianic tradition, the premises of its class analysis were not in line with Russian revolutionary attitudes, which had little patience with an evolutionary process, even a Marxist one.

Intellectually, however, the early Marxists under Plekhanov emerged victorious from the debate with the *Narodniks* about what would now be called the "Russian road to socialism." They demonstrated "conclusively" that the hopes of Russian socialism were naïve, that the stage of capitalism could not be skipped, that the peasant commune (*obshchina*) was in process of disintegration under the impact of market relationships, that the Russian peasant was not "a Communist by nature," and that capitalism had already established itself in Russia and was rapidly developing.

46

This, the Plekhanov phase of the Marxist movement, came to an end soon; with Lenin's *What is to be Done?*, Bolshevism—or Leninism—was born. It created the premises for the triumph of the very heresy that Russian Marxism had begun by opposing— the concept of jumping the economic stages Marx himself had postulated. The organizational principle of the party "of the new type"—closely knit, revolutionary, and highly centralized—was, of course, the most important among these premises, but not the only one.

Marxism in Practice

The second stage in the destinies of Marxism in Russia was that of adaptation. Bolshevism has often been described as a blend of Marxism and populism. This is true but incomplete. Other Marxist trends were also affected by the historical background and environmental pressures in Russia: Mensheviks were often no less "impatient," and it was Trotsky's idea of permanent revolution—the notion that the two classic Marxist revolutions, the "bourgeois" and the "proletarian," could be "telescoped" into one—that was implemented by Lenin in October, 1917, after his abandonment (in the April Theses) of his previous views on the character and perspectives of the Revolution. But there is little doubt that it was in Bolshevism that some of the most characteristic ideas of the Populist theoreticians of the nineteenth century found their safest anchor: Pisarev's utilitarian ethics, Tkachev's attribution of a special role to the revolutionary elite, Nechaev's acceptance of the use of force and fraud as "normal," Lavrov's emphasis on the role of the Party, and the general fascination with the idea of the dictatorship of the revolutionary minority. Despite the obvious continuity between Bolshevism and its predecessors, however, there is also an element of genuine novelty in Leninism: In the principle of "democratic centralism" it contained the nucleus of a totalitarian chain reaction.

The third stage, that of implementation, came with the victory of the Revolution. The Marxists had "solved" the problem of how to win power in the un-Marxist conditions presented by a proletarian island in a peasant sea; now they were confronted with the problem of exercising that power in a backward country lacking, according to their own Marxist premises, the industrial prerequisites of socialism. The hope, based on these premises, of a "proletarian revolution" in the more advanced countries soon vanished, and the next step beyond the original orthodoxy became inevitable: Stalinism replaced Leninism. Lenin had replaced the Marxist theory of revolution with his own, more practicable theory in the given circumstances. Stalin abandoned other tenets of the original Marxist creed as well.

The process has been referred to as a transition from theory to ideology. But it was both more and less than that. Having suffered a theoretical defeat through its own victory after the Revolution in Russia, Marxism was caught up in a vicious circle of theoretical contradictions. It was not the unity but the disunity of theory and practice that began to be embodied in Soviet institutions. The theory therefore could not simply be thrown overboard while the ideology was retained; both had to undergo a complex transformation. The theory was elevated to the status of a state doctrine; orthodoxy crystallized into a ritual, and policies were justified by invoking first principles that had no relation to the circumstances. It was not that the theory was "betrayed"; it simply became more irrelevant. The facts that did not fit it had to be explained away.

The reason why the theory could not be abandoned and replaced by another was, of course, because the legitimacy of the system itself was based upon it. Therefore, subordinate propositions had to be introduced with each new twist of policy; such propositions often logically nullified the original theory, but they helped to preserve it by shifting the emphasis from its heuristic aspect (purporting to explain past and current experience) to the future it envisaged. The theory thus acquired an autonomous sphere of existence largely impervious to the facts of the present and therefore invulnerable to logical argument.

Even earlier, Marxism, in becoming an ideology of mass movements and acquiring the characteristic features of systems of mass belief, had come to assume the inadmissibility of doubts lest the faith of the believers be endangered. Despite the fact that *de omnibus dubitandum* was one of Marx's favorite maxims, his followers soon became accustomed to settling their arguments by an appeal to the "scriptures," and quotation-mongering became an obligatory game. When the doctrine became the basis of a state, the believers could no longer appeal to the scriptures on their own; interpretations were prescribed by those who controlled the state.

An Ideology, Not a Theory

As a total *Weltanschauung*, Marxism was a theory that aspired both to explain the facts of nature and society and at the same time to evaluate those facts. The statements of fact and value were thus intrinsically mixed, and despite its protestations to the contrary, Marxism was from the first an "ideology" in its own sense of the term—that is, a "false consciousness" and not, as it claimed to be, a "scientific theory of socialism." Unlike a scientific theory, it was not ready to revise its assumptions in the light of experience, so that revisionism always presented a mortal danger. Previously, Marxism had merely been "an illusion of an epoch"; after becoming a ruling ideology, it was transformed into a falsified consciousness, with all the instruments of the state devoted to this falsification. Indoctrination was geared to fill the gap between experience and theory, not merely to expound a certain system of values. The new scholastic species, the ideological functionaries, performed the task of doctrinal exposition according to the requirements of the moment. Like other casuists before them, they could always find a suitable quotation.

It is this last aspect that led many Western commentators to conclude that under Stalin, ideology had become a mere appendage of Machiavellian *Realpolitik*—a cynical camouflage playing no role whatever in political decisions, which were dictated by hard-headed considerations of the interests of the Party or the state.

The reality was more complex. It is true that when the "Stalinist school of falsification" replaced the Leninist school of rationalization, ideology seemed to be reduced to a secondary role. But this was partly a matter of degree and partly an optical illusion. Lenin had a strong element of *Realpolitik* in him, without ceasing to be an *ideologue;* Stalin, the "realist politician," aspired all his life to be the supreme ideologist. The question here is not one of personalities. The Party could not exist without the ideology providing its doctrinal legitimacy. Ideology may be manipulated to suit policy, but it is still there, not merely reflecting the needs of the rulers, but shaping their mentalities as well. Doctrinal rationalization has not ended with Lenin, nor has falsification ended with Stalin.

The Stalinist Legacy

The vicissitudes of "de-Stalinization" and "re-Stalinization" tended to obscure the simple fact that the post-Stalin regime emerged as a continuation of the one he left; all the leaders struggling for the succession were members of the victorious Stalinist faction in the 1920's and 1930's, and the repudiation of its role would have amounted to a repudiation of themselves. Khrushchev went furthest in his "secret speech" of 1956, but limited his denunciation to Stalin personally. This stand has since been modified, or at least clarified, in the newly published version of Party history, which explicitly approves Stalin's actions in the 1920's and 1930's—with the exception of the Great Purge. Thus the need to legitimize the post-Stalinist regime set the limit to doctrinal change.

Such changes as have been made are presented only as a continuation of Leninist orthodoxy, straightening the path where Stalin strayed from it. This is, of course, quite deceptive. "Khrushchevism," despite historical continuity, is no more a return to Leninism than Stalinism was a straight continuation of it. The new adaptation takes those elements from Lenin's ambiguous legacy that suit its present purposes, as Stalin did in his time, and as Lenin himself did with Marx.

The history of Soviet thought can be regarded as a struggle of doctrine with reality, or as a process of adjustment to intractable reality. When the latter is finally accepted, the doctrinal formula of acceptance is referred to as "the creative development of Marxism." Before such a formula emerges, a period of groping precedes it, in which various formulations are thrashed out in esoteric discussions until finally one of them is consecrated in the official orthodoxy. The evolution of such formulas can be traced as precisely as that of a species in a museum of natural history. The Stalinist contributions to the "creative development of Marxism"—"socialism in one country," the theory of the reinforced state, class structure in the socialist society, the new twists given to the problems of egalitarianism, "the law of value," and the relation between the economic base and the ideological superstructure—all of these had a long history of gradual reformulation until they acquired their ultimate shape in the Stalinist dogma. It is possible to trace their emergence to political or economic needs, and to see how in their final form they were related to such needs—with the least apparent damage done to the doctrine.

Yet ideological inconsistencies became routine in the Soviet system and they continue under Khrushchev. There have been obvious signs in recent years of groping for new theoretical adjustments, and now that Khrushchev's writ is law, it is probable that some of the new experimental formulas that have been put forward will be proclaimed as his contributions to the "creative development of Marxism." Indeed, the expression is already being used in respect to some such formulations, and if they serve the ideological requirements of the new situation they may become a part of the new theodicy.

The Fourth Stage of Marxism

The Stalinist phase in Soviet ideology was doctrinally characterized as "the building of socialism." Khrushchev has announced that the process is completed and has promised the achievement of Communism in the near future. Indeed, according to his pronouncements, the Soviet Union has already entered the "higher stage" and is engaged in attaining the final doctrinal aim, the Communist society.

This may well be the most difficult period for the doctrine. In the past, its dynamic appeal was preserved as a result of its teleological view of history and its retention of certain ideas derived from nineteenth-century utopian socialism. However, these elements could not stand up to a confrontation with reality, and therefore the doctrine had to operate "beyond the reality principle" by projecting ultimate aims into the future. Obviously the moment of reckoning would come once the aims could be considered to have been achieved, the historical mission of the proletariat fulfilled, and the *terminus ad quem* of prehistory attained.

The achievement of Communism can, of course, be repeatedly postponed, but ultimately there are only limited ways out of the doctrinal dilemma. One is for the ideology to become a set of dead formulas, not only to the population at large but to the Party as well. It is perfectly obvious, however, that the *apparatchiki* have a vital vested interest in the perpetuation of the ideology. It is this feature that makes Soviet Communism historically *sui generis*. In the case of the French Revolution, the revolutionary dynamic had been exhausted long before forty years had passed, the Jacobin formulas and even Thermidor were forgotten, and *"liberté, égalité, fraternité"* was becoming a motto for the façades of public buildings (including prisons). Should ideology cease to be an operative factor in the Soviet Union, the Party could not hold out for long against divisive social forces and sectional interests. It would be the end of the unity of the political elite and of the permanent revolution from above.

But nothing at the moment warrants such a forecast. The chiliastic element in the ideology cannot be reconciled with "the achievement of Communism," but it can be projected beyond the geographic frontiers of the Communist bloc to perpetuate the "ideological" dynamic. Herein lies one alternative to abandonment of the doctrine. Needless to say, it is incomparably more dangerous to free societies and to the prospects of "peaceful coexistence."

Effects of Ritualization

The outcome is, of course, not predetermined and will depend not only on internal Soviet developments but on outside factors —the courses pursued in the non-Communist world, the direction taken by Chinese revolutionary fervor, etc. Internally, the ideological future will depend on the rate of *embourgeoisement* and the degree to which this affects the Party. Both the content and the role of ideology are bound to be affected by general social change as the Soviet Union acquires a more mature industrial economy. The Party, which is not the ruling social class but the ruling political elite, is aware of these antithetical elements and tries to perpetuate its position at the top of society by new injections of social mobility. Khrushchev's educational reform and the recent wage and salary changes are two instances of the Bonapartist technique of playing lower strata of the population against the higher to preserve the Party's equilibrating position. But such attempts cannot be effective indefinitely. The Soviet social structure is crystallizing, and no amount of permanent revolution from above (especially without terror) can arrest the process in the long run.

With *embourgeoisement*, the doctrinate fanaticism of the *apparatchiki* may subside, or they may be corrupted by cynicism. It is clear that as the doctrine to which they adhere has become more ritualistic it has lost its positive content. But if ritual diminishes the meaning of a religion to the believer, it helps on the other hand to preserve the church. Since there are different degrees of initiation according to rank, the ritual sterilization of ideology has varying impacts at different levels of the hierarchy. Eventually the "historical purpose" of Marxist eschatology may cease to be convincing at any level. Even those initiated into the tactical motivation of changes in the Party line may cease to regard them as simple teleological detours, necessary to reach the ultimate goal. It has happened before that those charged with the administration of the faith end by losing it.

Yet the sophistication of the Soviet *apparatchiki* of today does not really match that of the Renaissance cardinals. And at their apex is a ruler for whom simplified Marxism is a part of folklore, a vital element that shaped his mentality in the *rabfak* (workers' school), as the popular wisdom of Russian proverbs did before he received his formal education. Here is a very different figure from those of the past.

The Leninist generation of Bolshevik leaders, recruited from the intelligentsia, consisted of ideologues. Stalin, a member of the semi-intelligentsia, resented their intellectual superiority, yet aspired to provide ideological guidance, entering personally into doctrinal disputes. While it is true that his main venture into philosophy (the celebrated section on dialectical and historical materialism in the fourth chapter of the *Short Course* of the Party history) was written with the help of Yudin, until recently Soviet Ambassador in Peking, Stalin never left his doctrinal pronouncements entirely to ghost writers.

Khrushchev, on the other hand, relies on his *vydvizhentsy* (those promoted from the bench or the plough) who are even cruder intellectually than their Stalinist predecessors. He leaves doctrinal formulations to these ideological functionaries, and it is only when a formula is ready for *oformleniie* (final formulation) that he puts his stamp on it. While the appearance is maintained that ideology has acquired a new Supreme Interpreter without whom the system could not properly function, the new interpretation is no longer made by him personally, but rather by the Party ideologists. The era of philosopher-kings in the Soviet Union is ended. It is therefore more likely that social factors and forces will become a greater influence in shaping doctrinal change.

Doctrinal Innovations

What specific changes can already be discerned in the content and the role of ideology in this early period of the post-Stalin era, and what is likely to be the physiognomy of the fourth stage of Marxism in Russia?

First—and perhaps inevitably—with the announcement that the ultimate goal of Communism was in sight, the ambivalence so characteristic of Marxism and Leninism seems to have become even more marked.

The economic and administrative reforms of Khrushchev have again raised the perennial problems of the theory of state and the law of value. In general, Stalin's doctrinal legacy in this area is approved, but with certain important exceptions and modifications. Those of his ideas that have been repudiated are neatly summarized in *Politicheskii slovar* (*Political Dictionary*):

The Economic Problems of Socialism in the U.S.S.R. [Stalin's last opus, written in 1952] had a great influence on the elaboration of some theses of the political economy of social-ism. At the same time, the work contains a series of erroneous and questionable theses, such as for instance the statement that commodity circulation begins to hinder the development of the productive forces of the country and that a gradual transition to natural exchange is necessary; the underestimation of the role of the law of value in the sphere of productivity, in particular in relation to the means of production; the assertion about the inevitability of the contraction of capitalist production after World War II and about the inevitability in contemporary conditions of wars between the capitalist countries.*

In simple language this means that under Khrushchev, monetary economy is taken for granted, at least for the time being, and that direct distribution through rationing is not yet contemplated; that the problem of pricing capital goods has been recognized as a problem; that the prospects for capitalism set out in the postwar "Varga controversy" have finally been recognized as fallacious,† and that Stalin's hope of wars between the Western countries is taken for what it was, a nonsensical fantasy of a paranoidal dictator.

With the greater importance attached to "the law of value," Soviet economic theory has begun to show signs of stirring out of the long slumber into which it had fallen during Stalin's lifetime. Although the Polish and Yugoslav economic revisionists are attacked, and the more heretical Soviet economists (like Kronrod) scorned, there are indications that the pragmatic needs of the Soviet economy in its more mature phase force the acceptance of the economic facts of life, including the problem of the price mechanism and market relationships.

* B. N. Ponomarev, *Politicheskii slovar* (2nd ed.; Moscow, 1958), p. 556. One concept mentioned perhaps requires elucidation. According to the "law of value," the commodity exchange is correlated with the amount of abstract, socially necessary labor used in the production of commodities. In Soviet usage, the "law of value" refers euphemistically also to the market relationships permitted in the Soviet economy.

† Cf. M. E. Varga, "The Problems of the Postwar Cycles and the New Crisis of Overproduction," *Kommunist*, No. 8 (June, 1948).

The Case for a Strong State

In contrast to the critical assessment of Stalin's doctrinal positions in the economic sphere, his contributions to the "creative development of Marxism" in the political sphere are now accepted almost in toto.

After initial waverings in 1956, the Soviet theoreticians reached a new doctrinal equilibrium on the theory of state.

Khrushchev in his secret speech condemned as erroneous the doctrinal premise of Stalin's terrorism, his thesis that class struggle grows more intense with the advance of socialism. This thesis had served as a basis for the Stalinist theory of state under socialism; since the internal class struggle was becoming more acute, the state—far from "withering away"—had to grow stronger. (His other ingenious justification of the strong state was, of course, the concept of "capitalist encirclement.")

During 1956–57, the condemned thesis was referred to in Soviet publications as one of Stalin's mistaken notions, although it was not linked with its logical Marxist corollary concerning the diminishing role of the state. On the contrary, Soviet dialecticians indulged in an involved argument that pointed to the old conclusion that the state must remain strong even under Communism.

Though Stalin was "rehabilitated" in 1957, his thesis on the intensification of the class struggle under socialism has not returned to favor. But neither is it treated any more as one of his doctrinal sins. It has been quietly forgotten, as witnessed by the fact that it got no critical mention at all in the two most recent authoritative publications on theory, *Politicheskii slovar* (1958) and the new Party history (1959).

On the other hand, Stalin's theory of state is now accepted in principle, and full credit is given to him by M. V. Kharlamov (*The Activity of the CPSU for Further Strengthening of the Soviet Socialist State*, Moscow, 1958):

Generalizing the historical experience accumulated by the Party after the death of V. I. Lenin, a new contribution to the Marxist-Leninist teaching on the state was made by J.

V. Stalin. In particular, he showed the necessity of strengthening the Soviet state in every respect in conditions of capitalist encirclement, boldly posed the question of the insufficiency of the well-known formula of F. Engels about the withering away of the state, and gave a new formulation to the question of the possibility of preserving the state even under Communism, if the danger of an attack from outside still exists.

The sanctioned view of the state's role—at least for the present—seemed clear enough, as expressed by Khrushchev himself, in an interview with a United Press correspondent in *Pravda*, November 19, 1957: "It would be a serious error, a Leftist deviation, if we were now to weaken our state organs of rule, to abolish the organs of coercion." This line has been elaborated by the ideologists, e.g., by Kharlamov in the above-cited work:

> The Communist Party takes constant care at the present time to strengthen the Soviet state and to make it more efficient in every respect. The theses "On the Fortieth Anniversary of the Great Socialist October Revolution" proclaim: "In present conditions, Soviet society still needs a strong popular state for the defense of its socialist achievements and for taking charge of the building of Communism."

Changing State Functions

In rather startling contradiction to such statements, however, certain modifications have been made concerning the role of the state in the future. The theory inherited by today's ideological functionaries from the Stalin epoch divided the basic phases of societal development into two: first, the revolutionary transition from capitalism to socialism; and second, the gradual transition to Communism. In each of these phases the state has certain functions to fulfill. Among the functions listed in the first phase were: suppression of the overthrown exploiting classes, defense of the country, and performance of administrative-organizational and cultural-educational work by state organs. In the second phase, the first of these functions is abolished, but the other two are retained and another is added: the task of safeguarding socialist property from thieves and embezzlers of the national wealth.

While the basic stages of development have remained the same in present theory, there has been a subtle twist in scholastic argumentation to emphasize the Khrushchevian shift from methods of direct coercion to those of persuasive pressure. The argument centers on a semantic nuance. V. V. Nikolaev (*Voprosy filosofi*, No. 4, 1957, p. 10) declared Stalin wrong in regarding "the administrative-organizational and cultural-educational work of the state organs as one function of the Soviet state." His view was incorrect because, "as a result of joining these two functions, an impression is involuntarily created of the subordinate significance of cultural-educational work in relation to administrative-organizational activity." It is expedient to delimit the two, because "the methods and forms of performing these two functions, [as well as] the organization and activity of the administrative organs of the economy and [those of] culture have their own peculiarities."* The Soviet intelligentsia supposedly can now rest assured that the peculiarities of the administrative function will not be applied in the intellectual sphere.

The functions of the Soviet state in the period of transition to Communism remain the same as those enumerated in the Stalinist theory of state, but their content and relationship to the society are now presented differently. By a new dialectical turn, Soviet scholastic experts have again tried to deal with that thorn in their flesh, the "withering away of the state." The abatement of terror and Khrushchev's administrative and judicial reforms have been hailed as steps in the direction of a diminution of state power. K. V. Ostrovitianov, for example, has stated:

The socialist state remains during the whole period of the construction of Communism, but the content of its functions and the forms of its activity change. Gradually, the role of

---

* P. S. Romashkin, "The Development of the Functions of the Soviet State in the Process of Transition to Communism," in *Voprosy stroitelstva kommunizma v SSSR* (Moscow: Soviet Academy of Science, 1959), p. 113. This book and the new Party history are the two basic texts on Soviet ideology under Khrushchev.

the administrative functions, connected with state coercion, is diminished. Thus the premises are being created for the withering away of the state, which will take place at the higher stage of Communism provided there is no danger of attack by the imperialist powers. At the higher stage of Communism, the importance of the planned direction of production and distribution . . . and [of] cultural values will increase even more. The state organs performing these functions under socialism will be replaced at the higher phase of Communism by social organs of economic-cultural self-government.*

At the Twenty-first Congress, Khrushchev gave as an example of such "self-government" the action of the extrajudicial bodies set up under the so-called antiparasite laws. On November 23, 1958, *Trud* also hailed the formation of the workers' militia (which existed previously as *Brigadmils*—Brigades for Cooperation with the Militia) as "a step in the handing over of state functions to social organizations," and therefore as part of the process of the withering away of the state. Various ossified institutions, including trade unions and soviets, are now claimed to contribute to the same end.

A skeptical observer may have some difficulty in visualizing how much more "withered away" the Soviet state under Communism will be in comparison to the capitalist states, with whom it will presumably "coexist." The Soviet theoreticians have shown no such doubts, boldly proclaiming that "the Twenty-first Congress of the CPSU has elaborated the problem of the concrete forms of the withering away of the state." They do confirm, however, that progress toward the goal will be a "protracted process." According to the theoretical organ of the Party, *Kommunist* (No. 11, July, 1959, pp. 9–20):

[The organs of state coercion] are still necessary in present conditions, but the social content of their activity has already changed essentially. At the Twenty-first Congress it was

* K. V. Ostrovitianov, "Some Problems of the Construction of Communism in the U.S.S.R. and the Tasks of the Social Sciences," *ibid.*, p. 21.

noted that drastic coercion is at present directed against thieves, crooks, embezzlers of socialist property, parasites, malicious hooligans, murderers, and other criminal elements. Together with the creation of the conditions of the transition to Communism, with the increase of the consciousness of the masses, coercion inside the country will diminish more and more. . . . In the Soviet Union the sprouts of Communist social self-government have already appeared, and they represent the forms that will secure the further development of socialist democracy.

One may wonder what "further development" these "sprouts" can accomplish—if, as is claimed in the new Party history, socialist democracy already "secures to all Soviet citizens genuine freedom of speech, of the press, of assembly, meetings, and demonstrations. . . ." But then, the dialectical process is unending.

In elaborating his aforementioned theories of class struggle and state power during the building of socialism, Stalin argued "dialectically" that "any dialectical thinker understands that, in order to wither away, the state must first grow stronger." (Speech before the Sixteenth Party Congress.) According to Khrushchev, the new phase of building Communism has initiated the process of the withering away of the state. But he has made use of Stalin's argument for other purposes—and primarily for the defense of the strong Party.

Although at the higher stage of Communism both the Party and the state are destined to disappear, only the state seems to be involved in the process for the indefinite future according to G. Shitarev (*Kommunist*, No. 12, August, 1958, pp. 12–13):

To be sure, the Party will not exist forever. Marxism-Leninism teaches that when the Party has accomplished the construction of the higher stages of Communism, which then ceases to be an object of struggle, only then will there be no more necessity for the Party as a political organization. This means that class differences will then finally disappear, as well as the essential differences between physical and mental labor, between town and country, and that the consciousness of all the toilers will be raised to the level of their Communist vanguard. But this is a question of the distant future. All the present practice of the construction of Communism points to one necessity: the steadfast strengthening of the guiding role of the Party in all spheres of life in Soviet society.

In short, as with the state, in order to wither away, the Party must first grow stronger. Although Engels' third dialectical law, the negation of negation, which fell into disfavor in Stalin's time, is now readmitted, it is still the second dialectical law, the interpenetration of opposites, that reigns supreme.

Commodity Circulation

When Stalin proclaimed the achievement of socialism, he justified it theoretically on the ground that with collectivization and the liquidation of the NEP, private ownership of the means of production had ceased to exist in the U.S.S.R. Henceforth, there existed two sectors in the Soviet socialist economy: the state sector, consisting of nationalized industry and sovkhozes (state farms), and the cooperative sector, consisting of kolkhozes (collective farms) and artels (cooperatives). The transition to Communism was said to involve "the raising of the private, cooperative sector to the level of the public, state sector"—in other words, total nationalization, not only of industry but also of agriculture.

Khrushchev's dissolution of the MTS (Machine Tractor Stations), and his pronouncements on the withering away of the state have introduced new difficulties in doctrinal formulations and explanations touching upon the above concept.

Previously, the MTS were regarded as the nuclei of Communism in the countryside. Stalin wrote in his *Economic Problems of Socialism* that selling the MTS to the collective farms would extend commodity circulation and would thereby hinder the transition to Communism, which was incompatible with commodity circulation. But as this "retrograde step, turning back the wheel of history" (Stalin's words) has in fact been taken by his successor, Soviet theories have had to be revamped.

The theoretician Ostrovitianov produced the new rationale by applying the familiar dialectical argument, this time not to the withering away of the state or of the Party, but to commodity circulation:

> The dialectics of the development of socialist economy consists in the fact that we will reach the withering away of commodity production and money circulation at the highest phase of Communism, as a result of the all-round development of commodity and money relationships at the socialist stage of development.

The innovations on the withering away of the state create an even greater doctrinal quandary. How can the higher phase of Communism be defined as a transition to the stage when the state takes over all productive property, if at the same time this transition is characterized by the gradual withering away of the state itself?

But as Stalin himself has said, "there are no fortresses that the Bolsheviks cannot conquer"—especially semantic fortresses besieged by theoreticians. P. Fedoseev, the head of the Institute of Philosophy—who ranks with Pospelov, Ponomarev, and Ostrovitianov as a leading ideologist of the Khrushchev regime—provided a somewhat involved answer:

> As long as the state exists, the public (*obshchenarodnaia*) form of property remains the nationalized means of production, i.e., state property. When the state withers away, the public means of production will cease to be state property. However, until then, the state socialist sector of production, based on public property, will play a leading role in the advancement of society to Communism. There is no basic, qualitative difference between state socialist property and the future Communist nonstate form of property; the difference here is only in the degree of development at different stages of one and the same social-economic formation.*

Stalin might well admire this display of dialectical dexterity.

* *Loc. cit.*, pp. 71–72.

The social effect of the transition to Communism should be the classless society—the economic effect, the change to the distribution principle, "to each according to his needs."

Today, as in Stalin's time, it is asserted that class distinctions in the U.S.S.R. are being obliterated: But now the additional claim is made that the difference between mental and physical labor has already begun to disappear. The reduction in the number of unskilled workers and Khrushchev's educational reform are mentioned in substantiation of this thesis.

The distribution of products "according to needs," which in the orthodox theory was incompatible with commodity circulation and monetary exchange, now gets another doctrinal twist. At the Twenty-first Congress, Khrushchev declared that "an individual's needs are not unlimited," but cautiously added: "Of course, when we speak about satisfying the needs of the people, we do not mean capricious demands and pretentions to luxury, but the healthy needs of a civilized man."

Who decides what these "healthy needs" are is not made explicit. Presumably not the individual, but the state—in the time it has to spare from withering away. Nor are the criteria of distribution "according to needs" under Communism made explicit, though Ostrovitianov has explained that they will not be too egalitarian:

> The tendency to decrease differentiation in the remuneration of labor during the period of the transition to Communism by no means signifies a tendency toward a leveling off in consumption. . . . The Communist principle of distribution does not signify equalitarianism and leveling of consumption, but a full satisfaction of the variegated and rising needs and tastes of the members of society.

The Evolution of Khrushchevism

The evolution of Khrushchevism has not, of course, depended on domestic developments alone, nor will it in the future. More attention is being paid to the international aspect of Communism. According to the present doctrine, socialism has become a world system. One of the new functions of the Soviet state, according to Romashkin, is "the strengthening of the inviolable friendship, brotherly cooperation, and mutual help of the countries of the world system of socialism." The new Party history, unlike the old *Short Course*, offers tribute to foreign Communist leaders. The chasm between the "socialist" and "capitalist" systems is stressed in Soviet publications as much as ever, although the present emphasis is on proving the superiority of the Communist system through "peaceful competition."

The basic ambivalence of Russian Marxism remains. Communism in one bloc is an even greater anomaly in doctrinal terms than socialism in one country. The two "souls" of Bolshevism, the Marxist and the Jacobin, have as their historical roots orthodox universality on the one hand and the populist nationalist appeal on the other. These two aspects of Bolshevism have so far been reinforcing each other, thus increasing the danger of expansionism against the outside world. While there has always been a potential conflict between nationalist and universalist messianism in the motivation of Soviet policy, the contradiction is still not antinomical, although conceivably it might become so.

More important at present as a cause of ambivalence is the growing discrepancy between the maturing Soviet social structure and fundamentalist ideological prescriptions. The gap is steadily widening, and the legitimacy of the system is therefore under constant threat. Industrial development has introduced the necessity of rationalism in the organization of the economy, an element the Soviet rulers can neglect only at their own peril and at the risk of undermining the international position of the U.S.S.R. The formal rationality of organization, the rationality of means, can of course co-exist with the substantive irrationality of ideological ends. But the divorce between the two in Soviet society contributes further to the atrophy of faith. The *apparatchiki* have long ceased to believe that the average man will rise to the stature of Aristotle or Goethe, an idea expressed by Trotsky and shared by others in the romantic period of the Revolution. The Soviet "organization man" is probably disinclined to believe that the "new Soviet man" will ever rise "above these heights to the new peaks," and must find it increasingly difficult to swallow the rest of the ideological nonsense with which he is bombarded

—on the state withering away, on the disappearance of the differences between mental and manual occupations, on the imminence of distribution "according to needs," etc. Whereas Lenin suggested that the establishment of a Communist society might require a century or two, Khrushchev is promising it here and now, or in the not-too-distant future—thereby bringing nearer the day of reckoning, the confrontation of utopia with reality. Surely he must realize the utter incongruity of reducing the problem of achieving the Realm of Freedom to a question of per-capita production of meat and milk.

The alternative possibilities of the evolution of Khrushchevism remain open. The tension between ideology and rationality is becoming more—not less—acute. As suggested earlier, one way out of this dilemma is a withering away not of the state, or the Party, or commodity circulation, but of the Marxist faith itself. The other is a renewed cycle of ideological "restructuring of reality," either through new attempts to make Soviet reality conform to Marxist blueprints or through the application of fundamentalism to the global community of nonbelievers, resulting in increased pressure on the "bourgeois world."

The history of Bolshevism offers many examples of such alternating cyclical phases. The NEP was hailed as a return to normalcy, the end of revolutionary romanticism, and the beginning of a new stability. Khrushchev's reforms, the easing of the position of the masses, the great degree of security for the Soviet elite, and the higher role given to rationality in the productive process, do not eliminate the basic cause of tension created by the issue of the legitimacy of the system. The flying pyramids, the Sputniks and Luniks, may perhaps divert attention from the chasm between theory and practice, but they hardly can bridge it. The present reformist phase of internal adjustment may well give way to another attempt to change this world before conquering other worlds.

Those who hope that Khrushchevism will evolve harmlessly in and by itself, who ignore the expansionist element within it, do not understand the nature of the Communist system. Doctrines have a way of resisting social change, and doctrinaires change their views with utmost reluctance. Only when repeated attempts to violate reality are to no avail do they adjust themselves to it and proceed to produce another "creative contribution to Marxism." Resistance to Communist expansion is the best way to direct Soviet ideology toward internal euthanasia. Only in this way can the process of *embourgeoisement* come to fruition and ideology and utopia be replaced by a domesticated ideological ritual and semiutopia. When and if this happens, it will be legitimate for Soviet citizens to say along with Oscar Wilde: "The map of the world which does not contain an island of utopia is not even worth looking at."

KTO KAVO?
THE POLITICS
OF THE
STRUGGLE FOR POWER

Introduction

Some time ago, this writer participated in a conversation with a young man who was visiting the United States as a member of a delegation of Soviet youth leaders. As the conversation, which at first was concerned with rather innocuous matters, became more openly polemical, the young man was asked: "Can you explain to us why the mightiest Communist country in the world, the Soviet Union, has put so many more Communists in jails and concentration camps, and has in fact *murdered* so many more Communists, than the capitalist and anti-Communist United States?" Nonplussed, and with little time to cast about for a suitable reply, the young man said: "Well, it is because we have so many more Communists than you do!"

The Soviet youth leader was no doubt unaware of the chilling implications of his reply, but if he was at a loss to provide a better explanation, it may well be because he was aware of the implications of the question. In his *A Study of Bolshevism*, Nathan Leites observes that "the essential question" for the Communist Party in its relations with the rest of the world is best described by the phrase *kto kavo*—who (will destroy) whom? The truth of the matter, however, is that this phrase summarizes not only the attitude of the Party toward its external enemies, but toward its perennial internal enemies as well. Indeed, the entire history of the Soviet Union, certainly since the time of Lenin's death in 1924, could be written from the standpoint of the struggle for power—Stalin versus Trotsky (assassinated), Stalin versus Zinoviev and Kamenev (executed), Stalin versus Bukharin and Rykov (executed)—the list is long and impressive and includes thousands of Party and government functionaries, diplomats, military figures, and foreign Communist leaders—men who had been prominent before and after the Revolution, but who somehow became "enemies of the people" as Stalin consolidated his personal dictatorship, finally making himself *vozhd* (leader) and undisputed authority in all matters, from running a war to "planting eucalyptus trees on the coast of the Black Sea."

After Stalin's death, however, it seemed for a while as if the Soviet method of replacing government officials by rigged trial and execution had finally come to an end. And indeed, with the exception of Beria—and, lest it be forgotten, Nagy—no prominent Soviet official has lost his life (unnaturally) within the past eight years. But have the essentials of the system *really* changed? A mere glance at the history of the post-Stalin era will provide the answer: the rise and ignominious fall of Malenkov; the abortive revival of "collective leadership"; the virtual disappearance from the political arena of all prominent Soviet leaders—Bulganin, Molotov, Kaganovich, Perukhin, Saburov, Zhukov, Kirichenko—all, that is, with the exception (not counting Mikoyan, who remains conveniently in the background) of Nikita Khrushchev. To be sure, none of them has suffered the ultimate penalty that Stalin had meted out to his adversaries; still, they all had to go—their reputations defiled and their erstwhile services to the Soviet state relegated to the "memory hole"—to make way for the man who had risen from relative obscurity to become the ruler of the U.S.S.R.

The articles comprising the following section deal with this process—the *kto-kavo* process of the Khrushchev era. Arranged chronologically, they depict and analyze the events surrounding the struggle for power from the time of Khrushchev's attack on Stalin in 1956 to the present. With all the allowances (and they *must* be made) for the differences between the current and past practices, the articles make it clear that the "who" part of the process has been fairly well established; the list of "whom" is long—and yet to be exhausted.

Iconoclasm in Moscow—A Commentary

THE FULL IMPLICATIONS of the Twentieth Congress of the Communist Party of the Soviet Union, which convened in Moscow (February 14–25, 1956), will not be apparent for some weeks—perhaps months—to come. Yet there is little doubt that the Congress will go down in history as an event of signal importance.

The most spectacular development at the CPSU Congress was the virtual dethronement of the once-omnipotent dictator of the U.S.S.R., Joseph Vissarionovich Stalin. The foundation for it was provided by the address of the First Secretary of the Party, Nikita Khrushchev. Speaking with the confidence that comes from a consciousness of power, Khrushchev startled his audience and the world by asserting that Communists—Leninist and Stalinist teachings notwithstanding—do not necessarily stand for the violent overthrow of the capitalist order; that parliaments (which, according to Lenin, were to be utilized for the express purpose of their eventual *destruction*) may serve as organs of "genuine democracy for the working people"; that "cooperation with social democrats" is "possible and essential"; and that the concept of "separate paths to socialism" was completely acceptable from the Marxist-Leninist point of view (thus in effect giving sanction to an erstwhile deviation for which many a dedicated Communist paid with his life).

The most significant statement, however, came toward the end of the speech. Said Khrushchev:

> The Central Committee adopted measures for wide-scale enlightenment on the Marxist-Leninist position of the role

of personality in history. The Central Committee resolutely opposes the cult of personality alien to the spirit of Marxism-Leninism, which turns one or another leader into a miracle-performing hero and, at the same time, minimizes the role of the Party and the popular masses.

Though Khrushchev refrained from mentioning names, there was little doubt to whom he was referring: The "miracle-performing hero" was none other than the late dictator of the U.S.S.R., Joseph Stalin.

This theme was soon reiterated and expanded by other speakers. M. A. Suslov, Secretary of the CPSU Central Committee, bluntly condemned the "cult of personality . . . which was spread prior to the Nineteenth Congress" (in 1952), and which "inflicted considerable damage both to organizational and ideological work of the Party." And the veteran Bolshevik leader Anastas Mikoyan sharpened the edge of the attack by admitting that "in the course of about twenty years [!] we in fact had no collective leadership" and by denouncing "certain ossified forms of Soviet diplomacy," which had flourished until three years ago (a theme later developed by Molotov). He sharply attacked that holy of holies, the *Short Course on the History of the CPSU*, as well as other Party histories (particularly those dealing with regions where Stalin had ostensibly played a prominent role in the early years of this century) for distortion of historical truth, especially for their mendacious treatment of "certain" personalities. Finally, he criticized Stalin's *Economic Problems of Socialism in the U.S.S.R.* for its mistaken notions about the nature of contemporary capitalism.

The extent of this repudiation of the Stalin cult can only be fathomed by recalling the incredible lengths to which it was driven while the dictator was still alive. The greatest "genius on earth"; "great architect of Communism"; "wise teacher and leader"; "inspirer of our glorious victories"; foremost authority on science, literature, linguistics, music—these are but a handful of the panegyrics showered upon him. What has caused this process to come to such an ignominious end?

At the outset, it must be realized that the Soviet leadership is more than aware of the salutory effect that the liquidation of the Stalin cult will have on its subjects. The average man and woman, to whom Stalin meant—*inter alia*—privation, terror, purges, fear, and suspicion, cannot fail to welcome the repudiation as proof of good will on the part of the present regime, as an expression of its desire to break away from the bleak legacy it inherited in 1953. Viewed in this light, the latest step, marking the logical culmination point of a process that was initiated in 1953, can surely be considered one of the most astute tactics instituted by Stalin's successors.

But it is more than a tactic. The dethronement is indicative of a deep malaise with which all layers of Soviet society had been afflicted and which the present leadership has found it imperative to terminate. Yet it would be probably incorrect to assume—as some commentators do—that the leadership has been faced with a crisis of major proportions. Indeed, despite the minor upheavals that have rocked the country since Stalin's death, the policies of his heirs have given every evidence of goal-consciousness, flexibility, and stability. The dethronement of Stalin may very well be taken as proof (though not conclusive, of course) that the Soviet regime does not find it necessary to *legitimize* its rule by relying on the myth of invincibility that the name of Stalin represented.

Before the world accepts the *new* myth concocted in Moscow, a few words of caution seem to be in order.

First, the dethronement of Stalin by no means and in no way can be equated with the restoration of democracy within the Party or the country at large—if, indeed, one can at all speak of a democratic *restoration* in Soviet Russia. This is clearly demonstrated by the way in which the cult of personality is now being decried, as well as by the tenor of the Congress *in toto*. The new line is being handed down *from above*—this time, in particular, by Khrushchev—and the assembled delegates dutifully accept it, and dutifully go through the customary rites of officially sponsored enthusiasm ("animation in the hall"; "stormy and long applause, turning into ovation; all rise"; etc.). There is no disagreement from any quarter, no debate, nothing that even remotely resembles an honest exchange of opinion. On the contrary, the entire Congress bears the earmarks of the spurious spontaneity that Communist leaders love so well. As *Pravda* (February 16, 1956) phrased it:

> The working people of the Soviet Union have been and are declaring their unanimous support for the domestic and foreign policy of the Communist Party and for its general line. . . . Everywhere, in towns and villages of our country, at factories and works, in pits and power stations . . . on collective farms, MTS's, in scientific research establishments, and in army units, talks devoted to the Twentieth Party Congress are taking place. . . . Everywhere the working people are expressing fervent approval. . . .

There is hardly a line here that does not resemble the hosannas sung at the Nineteenth Congress, or at any other important event in the history of the Soviet state.

Secondly, in deference to historical truth, which Mikoyan has now rediscovered, it seems only fair to be reminded that the very people who are now attacking Stalin are the same ones who in the past vied with each other in their extravagant tributes to him. It was only in October, 1952, at the Nineteenth Congress, that Mikoyan stated:

> At the present stage in world history and the history of our Motherland, it is unthinkable to live, build, fight without thorough mastery of all the new concepts Comrade Stalin has contributed to the Marxist-Leninist science. . . . After the Nineteenth Party Congress, our Party will go forward still more calmly and confidently to the victory of Communism under the guidance of our leader and teacher, the brilliant architect of Communism, our own beloved Comrade Stalin. Glory to the great Stalin!" (Stormy, prolonged applause. All rise.)—*Pravda*, October 12, 1952.

Those who are now burying Stalin are those who brought him to power, who—though exposed to Stalin's paranoiac wrath—

were also the beneficiaries of his exalted status—in short, those who had, in the course of the past quarter of a century, taken the place of the men who made the Revolution and then fell victim to it. Their present protestations, therefore, inevitably have a hollow ring of insincerity.

In his speech, Mikoyan resurrected two Bolshevik figures who had disappeared during the Great Purge in the 1930's: Antonov-Ovseenko and Kossior. Yet are we to expect any further and more fundamental rehabilitations of erstwhile idols turned into "nonpersons"? It is sufficient to read Khrushchev's denunciation of "Trotskyites, Bukharinites, bourgeois nationalists, and other enemies of the people" (that is, people who were actually brought to trial and did not merely vanish, as those mentioned by Mikoyan) to realize how far the Party is from renouncing its favorite bogeymen and from cleansing its historical record. Furthermore, the Party can hardly be expected to give up the instrument of the purge—even though its form may be radically altered. It is a truism worth repeating that a society that knows of no orderly procedure of governmental change must resort to the purge in its effort to keep the machinery of the state from stagnating. And a party that claims to be infallible in its *essential* ideological premises—and *at any given time*—must perforce resort to scapegoats to explain its past failings, mistakes, and shortcomings.

By using the term "scapegoats" we may, perhaps, arrive at the crux of the matter, not only insofar as the Stalin myth is concerned, but also as regards the Communist system at large. The country is suffering from famine? It is the fault of the kulaks. The economy of the state is on the verge of collapse? It is the sabotage of the Mensheviks, the Trotskyites, the Bukharinites, the Zinovievites. Bureaucratic inefficiency? It is not the system that is at fault—it is the slovenly, corrupt, and incorrigible small-fry functionaries and officials. And so on and on, *ad infinitum.*

Since Stalin's death, Beria has been the chief culprit—the man responsible for all and sundry calamities—for fomenting hatred between nationalities, for depriving the Soviet citizen of his legal rights, for rupturing relations with Yugoslavia and for the deterioration of relations with Turkey, for unjustly dissolving the Polish CP in 1938, for despoiling Marxism-Leninism. Now, perhaps, we see the beginning of the most horrendous, the most ironic jest ever perpetrated in the annals of the Soviet State: Stalin, until recently the "glorious sun" of the U.S.S.R., is becoming its *bête noire*. The Soviet people may indeed breathe more easily now that the leadership is telling them that an oppressive chapter is over, and that a new era is dawning. But can they be sure? Can they have confidence in the promises of their leaders? Strange things have happened at the Twentieth Congress of the CPSU, but who knows what stranger things will happen during the next few years, before a new Congress is convened? Today, Khrushchev is burying Stalin. Who, one is tempted to wonder, will bury Khrushchev?

A. B.

Anatomy of Tyranny: Khrushchev's Attack on Stalin

—JANE DEGRAS

RARELY HAS A document aroused more interest and speculation than the paper issued by the U.S. State Department, purporting to be the text of the speech delivered on February 25, 1956, by Nikita Khrushchev, First Secretary of the Communist Party of the Soviet Union, to the Twentieth Congress. The United States Government does not vouch for its authenticity; nevertheless, it has been received everywhere as plausible. It is in keeping with the tenor of statements made by responsible officials of non-Soviet Communist Parties, and Communist newspapers in the West have made no attempt to denounce it as a forgery. On the contrary, they have treated it as genuine.

To read this paper is to recall a dozen highlights of Soviet history between the assassination of Kirov in 1934 and Stalin's death in 1953. Of these two events, the first is presented in a highly equivocal light, suggesting a plot by the secret police in collusion with Stalin, the second as a release from unparalleled tyranny. Overshadowing all the rest is the somber horror of the Great Purge of the later 1930's.

The ostensible purpose of the speech was to destroy Stalin's reputation, or, in its own terms, to destroy the "cult of the individual." Khrushchev's picture of the Soviet Union between 1934 and 1953, as given here, bears a startling resemblance to the more lurid efforts of the extreme anti-Communist school. They, too, spoke of Stalin's dictatorship by terror, of mass injustice, of the execution of thousands of innocents, of cringing judges and confessions, extorted by torture, to crimes that were never committed, of the distortion of history, of the paralyzing rule of fear —all of it smothered under choking clouds of servile adulation.

In contrast to Lenin, Khrushchev is alleged to have said, Stalin "abandoned the method of ideological struggle for that of administrative violence, mass repressions, and terror." Whoever opposed him was "doomed to moral and physical annihilation." But not only those who opposed him. Stalin used terror against "many honest Communists, against those Party cadres who had borne the heavy load of the Civil War and the first and most difficult years of industrialization and collectivization." It was enough to be "suspected of hostile intent." Mass arrests and executions without trial "created conditions of insecurity, fear, and even desperation"; in his "intolerance and brutality" Stalin condemned to summary death many thousands who had committed no crimes at all, but who were forced to confess to the most "unlikely crimes" by the use of "cruel and inhuman tortures." The military collegium of the Soviet Supreme Court is now reviewing these cases. Since 1954, it has "rehabilitated 7,679 persons, many of whom were rehabilitated posthumously."

Stalin is also declared to have been responsible for "the mass deportation from their native places of whole nations." These actions were "not dictated by any military considerations"; others, by implication, were, and it is therefore not surprising that Khrushchev did not include in his list of the uprooted the Volga Germans, the Poles, and the Balts. For these, apparently, the Stalin regime is not yet at an end.

To attribute to Stalin alone the responsibility for these and innumerable other acts is to carry the cult of the individual far indeed. It imposes too great a strain on credulity to believe that for twenty years one man could terrorize 200 million, while his colleagues in the Party, the government, and the army remained utterly helpless. Khrushchev deplored the tendency to "elevate one person, transform him into a superman possessing supernatural characteristics akin to those of a god"; yet in his own fashion this is precisely what he himself has done.

Khrushchev's contention was a curious one for a Marxist. No revolutionary of Czarist days would have accepted as a reason for inactivity the plea that the tyrant "treated all others in such a way that they could only listen and praise him"; or that "a situation was created where one could not express one's own will." It is tantamount to an admission that the revolutionary terror had succeeded—where Czarist persecution had failed—in destroying the spirit and traditions of the Party that elevates revolution against oppressors to the highest level of social obligation.

The alternative plea of ignorance due to Stalin's failure to convene the Central Committee or inform his colleagues of action about to be taken cannot even have been intended seriously; it might have some validity for a few months, but not for twenty years. The present rulers of the U.S.S.R. saw their colleagues, their superiors, and their subordinates fall by the thousands. It is difficult to believe that they had to wait for Stalin's death to learn that the victims were innocent. In any case, the plea of ignorance cannot be advanced to excuse inactivity when, on Khrushchev's own showing, Stalin's policies threatened the country, in the opinion of the army chiefs, with immense losses and dangers during the war. (Neither ignorance nor obedience to orders was accepted as a valid plea at Nuremberg; in his final speech there, the chief Soviet prosecutor, General Rudenko, said that the Nazi leaders "were necessary to Hitler just as much as he was necessary to them. Göring, Frick, Rosenberg . . . are inconceivable without Hitler, just as Hitler is inconceivable without them.")

In fact, neither plea was meant to be taken at face value. Khrushchev was not talking to a gathering of schoolchildren, but to his country's outstanding political figures. What he was saying in effect was that they were *all* equally responsible. As witnesses and accomplices, none had the right to claim a pre-eminence on moral or historical grounds. If there was collective leadership, there was also collective guilt.

There were two interesting exceptions. Khrushchev appeared to go out of his way to suggest that Malenkov's guilt was greater than average by recalling two occasions during the war when he acted as Stalin's spokesman, and to display in a favorable light Marshal Zhukov, whom Stalin denigrated. (Malenkov, it may be remembered, was highly critical of Khrushchev's agricultural policies at the Nineteenth Congress in 1952.)

Why was the risk taken of bringing the details of this nightmare of tyranny out into the open? Why not have continued the policy of silence that was pursued up to the Twentieth Congress, while eradicating the worst abuses of the earlier years? For three years, the Party leaders had been cautiously refashioning many facets of Soviet society, executing or getting rid of leading officials of the secret police, encouraging local initiative, loosening the stranglehold that had virtually killed the arts, and generally reducing the extreme tensions and fears of the Stalin era. It might have been thought that this was a settled policy, which would be followed until the present itself denied the past and the dead tyrant's name sank unremarked into oblivion without explicit disavowal.

There is no convincing answer to be found in the "objective situation," for reasons that were valid in the spring of 1956 were equally valid three years earlier. The answer can lie only in the situation *within* the Communist Party, and here there are only slender indications to support speculation.

In the published records of the Twentieth Congress there is only one speech that departed from the practice of silent repudiation. That is the speech of Mikoyan, which contained the first explicit attack on Stalin. It seems reasonable to assume either that this section of Mikoyan's speech came as a surprise to his colleagues or that it had been inserted by agreement "to test audience reaction"—the first being the more likely. It was presumably a step in the maneuvering for position within the leadership. The popularity of the measures taken after Stalin's death to mitigate the harshness of the regime suggested that support could be won by the open denunciation of its chief architect, and if prestige was to be enhanced by these means, Khrushchev was unlikely to allow it to be won by a colleague. The response to Mikoyan's attack probably convinced the Party Presidium that the risks were smaller than they had supposed. (There is, in fact, a strong suggestion, implicit in the parentheses found in the written report of the speech indicating the mood of the audience, that the Party cadres welcomed this opportunity to purge themselves of feelings of guilt, to find a more telling and significant scapegoat than Beria.)

There was no suggestion in Khrushchev's opening speech at the Congress of any crisis of authority. The forces making for change, embodied in the technical and administrative personnel of the country, received full recognition. But it must be assumed, *post facto*, that the air of confidence was in part fictitious, that the Communist leaders still felt the need to create fresh bonds between themselves and the members generally, to build relations of confidence and understanding between the rulers and the mass of the ruled. No better way could have been found—given the political narrowness of the regime—than to denounce the man who had destroyed all earlier bonds and made a virtue of mistrust.

In any case, once the conspiracy of silence was broken, it would have been difficult to stop at the point to which Mikoyan ventured. Whether a landslide has been set in motion by this drastic action it is too early to say. But the subterranean forces were already there, imprisoned within the petrified Stalinist mold. They would in any case have sought an outlet, and it is more likely that they can be kept under control and guided if the initiative in their release comes from above.

What cannot be in doubt is that the dual process of establishing a hierarchy within the leadership and of reaching a new social equilibrium will take time to work itself out. The Soviet rulers must hope that the revelations—or rather admissions—will prove no more than a nine-day wonder, that their own part in twenty years of tyranny and misrule will be overlooked in thankfulness that it has ended, and that they will be able to go ahead untrammeled by the discarded garments of their past.

It is difficult, unless one has lived in a totalitarian country, to understand the pressures to which its inhabitants are subjected. But what of the Communist leaders in the decadent democracies, over whom no secret police kept watch? They found no difficulty in approving the Purge and apparently as little in approving the rehabilitation of its victims. They were prepared to subscribe to the belief in Stalin's infallibility and now appear equally prepared to tread his reputation into the mud. Was none of them capable of distinguishing between theory and dogma, between dissent and treason? What of their historians, for whom the records were available, their scientists, technicians, writers, and artists, who were in a position to compare the Soviet output with that in other countries? It is not Stalin's writings, or genetics, or the quality of Madame Pankratova's history, or the technical standing of Western industry that have changed, but the Party line.

This is not to suggest that the leaders of Communist parties in the West will have as little freedom in the future as they have had hitherto. On the contrary, it seems probable that they will have a far wider scope for initiative thrust on them. The Soviet leaders have emancipated themselves from the cramping obsession that there is only one pattern of revolution; it will now be up to the leaders of other parties to seek, under license, their own road.

Khrushchev dated Stalin's degeneration from the Seventeenth Congress of the CPSU, that is, from 1934. The choice of date is significant, not because more than half the delegates who attended the Congress—and 70 per cent of the members of the Central Committee it elected—fell victim to the Purge, but because it implies endorsement of the policy with which Stalin's name will always be associated, the policy of "revolution from above," of forced collectivization and industrialization—whose victims were probably no fewer than those of the Great Purge. To have denounced him wholly, as Beria is denounced, would have destroyed too much. To deny him altogether would be to deny the present leaders' own legitimacy and the very essence of the system they are operating. For if it would be foolish not to admit that Stalin's insanely suspicious and envious character, his megalomania, ignorance, and vanity account for some of the worst abuses of his rule, it is equally incontestable that a policy that imposed such burdens, pains, and punishments could not have been applied except in a society where there are no alternative parties, alternative policies, and alternative rulers. How, indeed, except in a totalitarian system, could Stalin have concentrated such power in his own hands?

This is the cardinal feature of the Soviet system, which

Khrushchev could not attack. And it is to preserve this that Stalin's crimes were said to have been committed from a mistaken view of the interests of the Party and the masses. "In this lies the whole tragedy."

The more striking excrescences of the dictatorship, the paralyzing rigidity and conformity of Stalin's last years, can be condemned and abandoned now that the painful and costly stage of "primitive accumulation" is past. There is no risk that relaxation will start the whole system sliding backwards. (In the same way, the forced labor camps have largely fulfilled their economic function and can be in part dissolved: The roads and railways and houses have been built, the mines have been mechanized. Inducements can now be combined with pressure in varying degrees to get labor to the uninviting wastes of the Arctic region.) Industry now has a broad enough basis and sufficient momentum to expand without subjecting the population to conditions that only brutal terrorism could persuade them to endure in silence. The endorsement of Stalin's earlier policies implies that criticism of the Communist Party, of its position in the country, and of its monopoly of power, will still not be tolerated.

The resignation of Molotov and Kaganovich from their ministerial posts (while remaining deputy premiers) continues the program of disavowing the past, leaving, of Stalin's old guard, only Mikoyan and the figurehead President, Marshal Voroshilov. The balance of power within the Presidium has shifted, and Malenkov now seems to hold a fairly isolated position. While the newly released forces find channels of expression and eventually settle down into a pattern that reflects the Soviet Union's changed position, internally and externally, the machinery of political power remains unchanged, and the new elite appear to have full control of its operations. They are aware of the need for experiment and adoption and are prepared to initiate these themselves. Stalin is said not to have visited the rural areas after 1928, whereas Khrushchev spends a good deal of his time traveling around his own as well as other countries.

The men who now rule were the beneficiaries of the policy they have discarded. They are operating a new policy. For the inhabitants of the Soviet Union and its East European bloc, the change is most welcome. The extent to which "controlled relaxation" may be permitted can perhaps be gauged from the way in which this policy has operated in Yugoslavia; there, nothing has been allowed to encroach on the unique position of the Communist Party, and the reduction in the size of maximum landholdings testifies to the belief that an independent peasantry is potentially an enemy of the Communist regime.

Externally, the change in policy antedates the Twentieth Congress. The rapprochement with Yugoslavia (the quarrel was singled out by Khrushchev as a particularly glaring example of "Stalin's shameful role" for which the Soviet Union "paid dearly") and the rapid development of friendly relations with the countries of Asia were all set in motion before the Congress. Broadly, Soviet foreign policy continues to aim at the neutralization of Europe, the isolation of America, and advance through the underdeveloped countries. But these aims are pursued with far greater flexibility and in more conventional terms than before; "during Stalin's leadership, our peaceful relations with other nations were often threatened." There is basically no difference between competitive coexistence and Cold War, but the current term emphasizes that the struggle will be waged by other than military means. For its part, the U.S.S.R. cannot begin to compete successfully until it approximates the level of productivity achieved in the United States, and this requires not the sullen acquiescence of an intimidated working class, but voluntary cooperation and the belief that initiative and independence will not have fatal consequences. The largest obstacle of all—the stagnation of agriculture—remains, and there is no sign that in this respect the essentials of Stalin's policy have been abandoned. Twenty-five years of collectivized agriculture have failed to attract the peasants, who, after all, represent nearly half the working population.

The Permanent Revolution Is On Again

——RICHARD LOWENTHAL

ON THE EVE of the fortieth anniversary of the Bolshevik seizure of power in November, 1917, the Soviet Union was launched on yet another social revolution—on yet another turn of the wheel, that is, of the permanent revolution from above by which the rule of the Communist Party is maintained. This and nothing less is the meaning of the recent dramatic victory scored by Khrushchev over his opponents in the Presidium of the Party. (The author's reference here is to the June, 1957, Plenum of the Central Committee, which saw the purge of Molotov, Malenkov, Kaganovich, and Shepilov.—*Ed.*)

It is obvious to all that by eliminating his chief rivals, Khrushchev has ended the fiction of "collective leadership" and restored the primacy of the head of the Party machine, familiar to us from Stalin's time. It is equally obvious that he has done so in the name of new policies—policies which he claims represent neither a return to Stalin's system, nor a repudiation of the main line of the Stalinist tradition, but a bold advance forward from Stalinism. What is not yet generally understood is just what these new policies are.

Yet it seems to this observer that the signs are plain enough for all to read. Khrushchev's primary objective is neither "de-Stalinization," nor "decentralization," least of all "democratization." It is nothing less than the ending of the dualism of Party and state machine by which the Soviet Union has been governed for the past four decades—the institution of direct rule over the country, including direct management of its economy, by Party

85

secretaries. The Soviet state is to "wither away" at last, as Lenin promised—but only in the technical sense of having its bureaucracy no longer controlled but replaced by that of the Party.

It is a tremendous undertaking, without precedent in the annals of modern totalitarianism, and it may fail. But let us first examine the evidence for saying that it has started.

During recent months, the Soviet Union has been without a "government" in the traditional sense of the term. Not only have twenty-five industrial ministries been dissolved; not only have the prime ministers of the sixteen constituent republics been granted membership in the all-Union government, thus making it a representative rather than an executive body; but the life and soul of the government, the "inner cabinet" of deputy prime ministers, has disappeared, and nothing has taken its place— nothing, that is, on the governmental plane. Some of the former deputy premiers have become sectional heads in the reorganized Gosplan (State Planning Commission); five of them, who were leading figures and also members of the Party Presidium, have been demoted as a result of Khrushchev's purge (Malenkov, Molotov, Kaganovich, Pervukhin, and Saburov). Only the ever-lasting Mikoyan and the new head of Gosplan, Y. Y. Kuzmin, are left, with the title of "first deputy premier."

It may be objected that the real policy-making body was the Party Presidium all the time. Consider, then, the changes in the composition of the Presidium. It has now been inflated to comprise fifteen voting members and nine candidates—including all the eight members of the Party's Central Secretariat. Only once before has the Presidium been larger—after Stalin's last Party Congress, in November, 1952, when twenty-five full members and eleven candidates were elected. But in that body of thirty-six, the ten members of the Secretariat and three provincial Party secretaries were balanced by twelve deputy premiers and four other ministers of the Union government, with Premier Stalin and Deputy Premier Malenkov combining functions in the government and the Party Secretariat. In the new Presidium of twenty-four, the eight members of the Central Secretariat, together with the first secretaries of Leningrad, Gorki, and Sverdlovsk, of the Ukraine, Belorussia, Latvia, Georgia, and Uzbekistan, add up to sixteen representatives of the Party machine, while the Union government is represented only by Premier Bulganin, Deputy Premier Mikoyan, Marshal Zhukov, and Ministers Pervukhin and Kosygin. The balance is gone; the men formally charged with carrying on the government are not in a position decisively to influence policy.

This disorganization and demotion of the government is, of course, the direct consequence of Khrushchev's scheme for the reorganization of economic planning. The need for such a reorganization was recognized on all sides; its direction was bitterly contested—indeed, it formed one of the two central issues in the struggle between Khrushchev and his opponents. It was the critics of Khrushchev who first raised the demand for an overhaul of the planning machinery (as well as a revision of current plans) in December, 1956, when Khrushchev's authority stood lowest on the morrow of the Polish and Hungarian events. They called for more realistic targets, better coordination, and less disturbance of the plan by sudden "campaigns"—in fact, for more rationality and less propaganda; and they won, besides some investment cuts, the creation of a greatly strengthened State Economic Commission of high-powered economic administrators, which was to submit its reform proposals in February, 1957. Yet by February, Khrushchev was politically on top again; he, not Pervukhin, the Chairman of the Commission, proposed the reforms and got approval for an outline suggesting the creation of regional planning organs under control of the Party. Between then and March 30, when Khrushchev published his theses, that idea had hardened into the proposal to make the regional Councils for National Economy the "basic link" in the new planning machinery under the Gosplan, and to abolish the industrial ministries of the Union and of the national republics altogether.

At its first appearance, this proposal was widely interpreted outside the U.S.S.R. as a step toward "decentralization" of the economy in the Yugoslav sense, however strongly Khrushchev himself denied this intention; nor was it recognized that the sudden switch from having recently strengthened the State

Economic Commission to replacing it by a Gosplan with increased powers was due to the objections raised against Khrushchev's scheme by the experienced economic administrators attached to the Commission. But when the scheme was presented to the Supreme Soviet in May (with minor amendments preserving, for the time being and with reduced powers, a few industrial ministers in the Union and republican governments) and when the economic councils came to be appointed subsequently, two things became clear—that none of Khrushchev's Presidium colleagues concerned with economic administration had supported him in the discussion, and that the presidents of the new economic councils were generally Party secretaries— usually the second secretaries of the regions concerned. What had started as a drive for more economic rationality had turned into a drive for more direct Party rule in the economic field.

This was not at all inconsistent with Khrushchev's record. After he took over as First Secretary of the Party, he became noteworthy for the attention he paid to technical economic detail—to methods of sowing potatoes, to the value of planting corn for fodder, and to the advantages of building with concrete. Some Western observers hailed him on that account as a practical man who had no time for ideological nonsense and was turning the Communist Party into a kind of glorified polytechnic. Yet against this there was the evidence of his passion for foreign travel and speech making—the evidence, in fact, that he is a primitive but perfectly genuine believer in the Leninist concept of world revolution. The ideal he put before the young generation of *apparatchiki* was that of a man who would combine a universal competence in the technical problems of production with a perfect Marxist-Leninist understanding of the international scene. It may be a difficult ideal to fulfill, but there is no reason to doubt that Khrushchev believes in it sincerely. In one and the same speech at the Twentieth CPSU Congress, he developed the advantages of taking power by such "legal" and "parliamentary" methods as were employed in Czechoslovakia in 1948, and suggested that Party regional secretaries ought to be paid salaries in proportion to the production successes of their region! The latter proposal seemed strange enough at a time when a formal separation of Party and administration was still the official doctrine; it makes perfect sense in the framework of Khrushchev's revolution.

But does the revolution itself make sense? Khrushchev is turning the top-heavy administrative machinery of a gigantic command economy upside down. He is breaking overnight the customary links, thus clogging the well-worn channels of command; he is driving all the most competent higher administrators into frantic opposition, without arousing enthusiasm from the managers in the field—who still will be under strict orders—but from new and usually less competent, though somewhat nearer people. He is, in short, running the risk of destroying the over-complicated mechanism of detailed planning from the center, without daring to replace it by bold reliance on market forces and managerial initiative within a broadly planned framework. And he is taking sole responsibility for the consequences—even to the point of appointing one of his assistants from the Party Secretariat, a man without high-level experience of decision-making, as head of Gosplan and first deputy premier!

What, then, impelled him along this course? The old planning system was certainly creaking, but its crisis was not desperate. It is true that following the immediate postwar reconstruction period, the rates of Soviet industrial growth had gradually slowed down; this was inevitable, since the phase of "primitive accumulation" had ended, since industry could no longer rely on a steady influx of new millions of workers from the countryside, and since even natural population growth had slowed down. It had been the common conviction of the post-Stalin leaders that such a situation required increased attention to the raising of output per man-shift, and hence increased reliance on incentives rather than coercion; the gradual transformation of the labor camps into forced settlements of "free" workers and the material concessions to both workers and peasants had their origin in this conviction. For the same reasons, there was certainly growing pressure to eliminate the shocking bureaucratic waste of the command economy, to improve cost accounting, and to decentralize the power of decision. There was pressure, in other words, to move toward greater economic rationality by adopting a broadly planned market economy, as the Yugoslavs had done as early as 1953. But that is not what Khrushchev is doing.

Must we explain his scheme, then, purely in terms of the struggle for personal power? The "rational" solution, with its greater scope for the managers, might have appealed to Malenkov and some of the "technocrats" in the Economic Commission; the old "Stalinists," like Molotov and Kaganovich, would have tended to defend the old forms of centralized departmental control. Did Khrushchev devise his scheme—with its reliance on his own appointees and natural supporters, the regional Party secretaries—as the best means to defeat both groups of opponents and secure full control? That, I believe, is at least part of the truth; for even though the urgency of the economic situation was not desperate, that of Khrushchev's personal situation in the winter of 1956 probably was.

At the December, 1956, Plenum, Malenkov and the Stalinist "conservatives" seem to have united in blaming Khrushchev's rash advances to Tito and his "de-Stalinization" speech at the Twentieth CPSU Congress for having lowered Russia's international authority and produced the upheaval in Eastern Europe. Khrushchev had his back to the wall; he may have been saved only by Chinese support for his views that the unity of the Soviet bloc could not be restored by a simple return to Stalin's "great power chauvinism," and that a precarious compromise with Gomulka, one which maintained unity in foreign policy, was preferable to another Hungary nearer home. He saw that unless he got rid of his opponents, his opponents would sooner or later get rid of him; and just as Stalin took the great foreign-policy defeat of his early years—the break-up of the alliance between the Chinese Communists and the Kuomintang in 1927— as a signal to force the surrender or expulsion of his critics in the same year, so Khrushchev may have resolved to force an issue of his own choice as soon as he got a chance.

It was, then, the crucial decisions demanded by the East European revolution of 1956 that led to irreconcilable conflict within the "collective leadership" and that made the present crisis inevitable. The planning reform was the issue chosen by

Khrushchev himself for fighting it out. But the reform plainly raised even more resistance than Khrushchev had expected; and the question remains how so risky, so patently irrational a scheme could win at all against such strongly entrenched opposition.

The answer, in this writer's view, is that a "rational" solution of the problem of economic planning was—and is—in conflict with the interests of single-party rule. Khrushchev chose this issue for the decisive intra-Party struggle, and won on it because his policy coincides with the Party's interest in preserving its power in the new industrial society it has helped to create.

A genuine economic "decentralization"—the granting of freedom for managerial initiative and the forces of supply and demand—would deprive the Party of a tremendous lever of power over the new managerial class. It would strengthen the feeling—which inevitably has grown with the development of a modern industry, army, and administration—that the Party is a kind of parasitic appendix to this modern society, no longer needed for its proper functioning. If accompanied—as it must be in order to create a genuine market economy—by the abolition of forced agricultural deliveries, it would reduce the Party's power over the peasants to the same extent. (When both steps were taken in Yugoslavia, the managerial class was still very weak, but the growth in peasant self-confidence and independence proved very marked and led fairly soon to a dissolution of most collective farms. The difference was, of course, that the pressure toward economic rationality in the Yugoslav situation was much more severe than in the U.S.S.R. today.)

The Soviet Communist Party has been concerned with this problem of the new industrial upper class ever since it emerged from the First Five Year Plan. At that time, in 1934, the Party still contained many of the old revolutionaries from the working class and prewar intelligentsia, while the new upper class had developed largely outside the Party. It was the basic function of Stalin's Blood Purge of the 1930's to overcome this discrepancy; by eliminating the traditional revolutionary element from the Party and driving the new bureaucracy into its fold, he created a personal union between the organ of power and the class of

privilege. Once the profiteers of the Revolution had joined the
Jacobin Club, there could be no more Thermidor!

Twenty years later, history has shown that despite the personal
union between the ruling Party and the governing bureaucracy,
the division of function remains a source of conflict. The manager or economic administrator, even though a Party member,
tends to think in terms of personal security, social stability, and
economic rationality: Confident in his own competence, he feels
sure he could hold an equal job even if there were no Party—
and perhaps with less troublesome interference. The Party secretary or editor, even though a privileged bureaucrat, tends
to think in terms of power and its ideological justification: he sees
industry and the army, the whole modern Soviet society, as the
creation of the Party, and the end of Party control to him would
be the end of everything. But with the passage of time since the
Revolution, and with the discredit into which the Party has fallen
as a result of its purges, vacillations, abuses, and, lately, the
shock of the East European revolution, his outlook has become
less typical and more isolated.

Now Khrushchev is trying once again to bridge the gap: If
a union of persons was not enough, a union of functions must
be created. No doubt he hopes to get along without a blood
purge of comparable scale; though Malenkov and Molotov have
been attacked for forming an "anti-Party group" and, more
ominously, for their share in the frame-ups of the past, the
recalcitrant economic bureaucrats are not yet being pilloried as
"enemies of the people." But what will Khrushchev do if his
scheme breaks down?

Before proceeding further, it may be useful to try to relate the
present analysis to the discussion of over-all trends in Soviet
society now going on among Western students of Communist
affairs. Leaving aside the optimists who foresee "democratization," and the professional exhorters who look at every change
in the Soviet orbit as mere "trickery" designed to deceive the
unwary, there remain two principal approaches. On one side are
those who argue that the growth of a modern industrial society
with universal literacy and widespread technical competence,

and of a self-confident new upper and middle class, will exert pressure toward more rational methods of rule, which is ultimately bound to prove irresistible—that as society matures and revolutionary fervor subsides, the regime itself is bound to "mellow." On the other side are those who stress the unique character of the totalitarian party regime, which reacts to social pressures neither by giving in nor by resisting change, but by manipulating the inevitable changes in such a way as to preserve its own power and dynamism—that is, in a manner that remains revolutionary and "irrational" from a purely economic point of view.

What has been said so far constitutes an implicit criticism of the first-named approach: it is the "irrational" Khrushchev with his Party bosses, not the "rational" Malenkov with his managers and economic administrators, who has won the latest round; and the reason is to be found precisely in the logic of self-preservation of the Party regime, which, after forty years, still remains a revolutionary regime in its origin and justification. Revolutionary regimes do not mellow; they continue until they are overthrown and their social and economic results are incorporated into a different kind of regime. The people may long since have lost their faith in the revolutionary shibboleths; but the Party cannot abandon its ideology without abandoning power. The Party leadership maintains this power by using it to twist society into an artificial preconceived pattern, by allowing none of the basic classes to settle down in stability and security, by reacting to every pressure from growing social forces with another turn of the screw of permanent revolution from above. After the recovery of peasant agriculture in the 1920's came the forced collectivization; after the rise of the new managerial class in the 1930's, the Blood Purge; after the new consolidation of this class in the 1950's, following Stalin's death, Khrushchev's move toward direct Party rule. . . .

Yet there is something dangerously one-sided in this picture. The Party, after all, is not God; if it does make history, it cannot do so arbitrarily. Not all the changes to which it reacts were foreseen in its theory; not all the measures it takes were part of its original program. If it seeks to respond to every pressure in such a way as to preserve its power, there is no preordained guarantee that it will always succeed in doing so. The true history of the Soviet system is certainly not that of the automatic modification of the regime by outside social and economic forces, but neither is it that of the pure unfolding of the grand design of the totalitarian regime: it is the history of dynamic interaction between the logic of economic and social growth and the logic of totalitarianism—an interaction that frequently takes the form of conflict, and in which measures taken in order to preserve the regime may well have the unforeseen effect of undermining it. The Party, we said, cannot mellow; but it may fail.

Let us now apply this "dialectical" approach to the history of the past four years. On the morrow of Stalin's death, the Party was at its lowest point in vitality and prestige; Malenkov, when faced by the "collective" with the choice between leadership of the government or of the Party machine, seems voluntarily to have preferred the premiership; and the initiative passed for a time to state organs. (Among the ten members and four candidates of the Party Presidium as then reconstructed, there was only one representative of the Central Party Secretariat—Khrushchev—and two provincial Party secretaries, whereas there were, besides Premier Malenkov himself, four "first deputy premiers," three deputy premiers, and one minister—an imbalance as strong as the present one, but in the opposite direction.) But while Malenkov busied himself to restore confidence and keep the economy going by material concessions, Khrushchev set to work to revive the Party. The most urgent condition for this was the downgrading of the secret police, which, by being used as the instrument of Stalin's personal rule, had come to exert power over the constituted Party organs. The execution of Beria and Abakumov and the accompanying campaign enabled Khrushchev gradually to reassert the primacy of the Party machine, to oust Malenkov from the premiership, and finally, at the Twentieth Congress, to pack the Central Committee with his own nominees.

Yet at this very same congress, Khrushchev was made aware of the extent of the accumulated social pressure for greater security and stability—a pressure that had had a chance to make itself felt after the downgrading of the secret police, and one that was now turned on the Party itself—largely from inside. Behind the pressure was the obvious fear that the revival of the Party, and of the control of the First Secretary over the Central Committee, would lead eventually to the rise of another Stalin, with all the well-remembered horrors of his rule. So strong was this fear that Khrushchev had to appease it with a triple moral guarantee. First, by his "secret" speech he "disclosed" Stalin's methods and explicitly disowned the doctrine on which the purges were based—the theory avowing the "sharpening of the class struggle" with every step forward in the construction of "socialism," which could conveniently be used to discover new "class enemies" for every new phase in the permanent revolution. Second, he allowed opponents whom he had already defeated politically—Malenkov on the question of economic policy, Molotov on the concessions to Yugoslavia and the satellites and on the partial disavowal of Stalin—to be re-elected to the Party Presidium, although in his new, hand-picked Central Committee he could have prevented their election even then. Third, he had the head of the army, Marshal Zhukov (who had become Deputy War Minister when Stalin died and War Minister when Malenkov fell), elected to the Presidium as a candidate—an unprecedented concession to the political weight of the army.

The essential point is that all these concessions were *not* made for strictly intra-Party reasons: They amounted to a peace offering to the nation's leading strata and to the other pillars of the administration by the Party machine. These elements were, in fact, assured that if they put up with the restored primacy of the Party machine, there would be no more insecurity, no more hunt for "enemies," no return to paranoia as a system of government; there would, on the contrary, be a respectful hearing for the spokesmen of the economic bureaucracy and the army within the highest Party councils. The "compromise," such as it was, was reflected in the balance within the new Party Presidium: among eleven members and six candidates, there were eight government members (Bulganin, six deputy premiers, and Zhukov), five members of the Central Secretariat, and two provincial Party secretaries.

It is this compromise that Khrushchev has now torn up, this balance that he has shattered. The truce between the Party machine and Soviet society is broken: The permanent revolution is on again. Rather than submit to the gradual erosion of the Party's primacy by the economic bureaucracy, which a rational solution of the planning problems would have implied, Khrushchev has preferred to declare war on the economic bureaucracy and to attempt direct Party rule in economic life.

Now, as at the Twentieth Congress, it was the Party machine that decided the outcome. But the two opposite decisions—then for a compromise in order to restore confidence, now for the repudiation of that compromise in order to prevent the gradual undermining of Party rule—are not just the result of Khrushchev's Machiavellian trickery: They express a genuine dilemma. The social pressures have become stronger, after all, with the growth of a modern industrial society. The road of concessions leads ultimately to the Thermidor. The road of open defiance of the new social forces leads to the Party's growing isolation.

Traditionally, Soviet administration has rested on four main hierarchical pillars—the Party machine, the secret police, the economic bureaucracy, and the army. Throughout the history of the Soviet Union, they have all been represented in varying proportions in the highest policy-making organ, the Politburo or Party Presidium, though most of the time the army was represented only by a political minister. After Beria's fall, the downgraded secret police ceased to have top-level representation; now the spokesmen of the economic bureaucracy have disappeared. Khrushchev and his Party bosses are left alone with the representative of the last pillar—the army.

What Happened to "Collective Leadership"?

——MERLE FAINSOD

ON APRIL 19, 1959, two days after Khrushchev's sixty-fifth birthday, the Soviet press erupted in a rash of congratulatory tributes, the tenor of which evoked vivid memories of the Stalinist cult of personality condemned only a few years ago. Of the many messages that were printed, the most important came from Khrushchev's fellow members of the Party Presidium, who saluted his career as a "model" and "example" of "devoted service" and referred to him deferentially as "senior comrade and friend, true disciple of Lenin, and outstanding leader of the Communist Party, the Soviet state, and the entire international Communist and workers' movement." While the reasons for the press delay in celebrating Khrushchev's birthday remain somewhat mysterious, the contents of the congratulatory messages came as no surprise. They had been foreshadowed by an outpouring of lavish tributes at the Twenty-first Party Congress in the course of which delegate after delegate joined in praising Khrushchev's "Leninist firmness," "profound practical knowledge," "fatherly solicitude," and "tireless energy," as well as his "brilliant, comprehensive, and profound report."

At the Twentieth Party Congress, Khrushchev had denounced Stalin's craving for flattery and his insistence on presenting himself as a superman who "knows everything, sees everything . . . can do anything"; at the subsequent Party gathering, Khrushchev interposed no objections as one speaker after another offered effusive thanks for the personal guidance and initiative Khrushchev had supplied in every sector of Soviet life from foreign policy and the development of guided missiles to cotton growing in Tadjikistan. If these genuflections still represented a far cry from the heights of glorification witnessed during the Stalin cult, they left little doubt that Khrushchev had reached the summit of the Soviet power structure and that his position of undisputed leadership was universally acknowledged.

The image of Khrushchev's personal leadership that emerged from the Twenty-first Congress was obviously modeled on that of Lenin. As Khrushchev himself put it in his secret speech to the previous Congress:

> Lenin resolutely stood against every attempt aimed at belittling or weakening the directing role of the Party in the structure of the Soviet state. . . . He tried to convince; he patiently explained his opinion to others. Lenin always diligently insisted that . . . the Party statute be enforced, that the Party congresses and the plenary sessions of the Central Committee take place at the proper intervals. . . .

Taking his cue from these precepts, Khrushchev sought to project himself as the true custodian of the Leninist tradition—a leader who maintains his contact with the masses, who embodies his authority in the Party and its Central Committee, and who insists on rigorous observance of the Leninist norms of Party life. It is in this sense, and perhaps in this sense only, that it was still possible for delegates to the Twenty-first Congress to refer to collective leadership at all.

If by collective leadership is meant an equal sharing of authority by all members of the Party Presidium, then collective leadership must clearly be regarded as a thing of the past. The proceedings of the last Congress provide unmistakable evidence that Khrushchev now towers high above all his associates. While future events may demonstrate that his position is not impregnable, the possibility that he will soon be dislodged by another cabal in the Party Presidium seems remote indeed. The levers of power in the Soviet system appear to be firmly in his hands, and the charismatic qualities of popular leadership he has displayed contribute to give his authority a secure base. At the present time it is difficult to discern the direction from which a challenge to his supremacy might arise.

Disorder and Forgotten Sorrow

What happened to collective leadership? A retrospective analysis of the struggle for the succession may help to shed light on the problems of collective rule. When Stalin died, no single member of the Presidium loomed as the clearly anointed heir with an unquestioned title to supreme power. In the first few days after Stalin's entombment, there were some signs that Malenkov aspired to Stalin's role. But the *Pravda* announcement on March 21, 1953, that Malenkov had been "released" from his duties as Party Secretary "at his own request" seemed to indicate that his colleagues in the Presidium were making a determined and successful effort to dilute his power. At the same time, the delicate problems attendant on the transition and the need to consolidate the authority of the new regime compelled the new rulers to submerge their differences in the interest of presenting a united front to the nation and to the world. In these circumstances, collective leadership emerged as the natural formula to describe the divided and uncertain distribution of power.

Its long-term stability was in question from the start. Collective rule may attain a degree of solidity when those who share power are bound together by common dangers, interests, and purposes that outweigh their individual interests, where no one of the group possesses the ability, ambition, or will to stake out a claim to supremacy, and where power is so dispersed within the group as to make it dangerous for any member to try to dominate the rest. On the other hand, the stability of collective leadership is obviously endangered when deep policy differences begin to divide the group and one or more members strike out for the additional increments of power that make them a real threat to their colleagues.

The legacy Stalin bequeathed to his successors did not easily adapt itself to collective rule. In the absence of the Supreme Despot, power was precariously apportioned and distributed, with no point of coordination short of the Presidium itself. Malenkov, as Chairman of the Council of Ministers, rested his authority on command of the administrative apparatus and on such informal connections as he retained in the Party organization itself. Beria, as head of the MVD, had a formidable weapon in his hands. Molotov, as Foreign Minister and Old Bolshevik, enjoyed the prestige of an elder statesman but lacked an organizational power base. Khrushchev, who succeeded Malenkov as senior Party Secretary, identified his authority with that of the Party functionaries, but in the first months of the new regime he remained largely in the background. Bulganin, as Defense Minister, supervised the armed forces, but the degree of personal control he exercised over them was unclear. With Stalin gone, the interrelation of these plural power centers was, to say the least, ambiguous. Since Party, police, and administrative controls overlapped and penetrated each other, it was difficult to envisage how a clash of wills and interests could be avoided.

Moves and Countermoves

The possibility of conflict was magnified by the issues that confronted the collective leadership. Should the Soviet ship of state continue to be steered on a Stalinist course, or should new departures in policy be ventured? Should the new regime strive for a *détente* in its relations with the outside world, and if so, on what terms and conditions? Should large-scale concessions be made to the desire of the populace for more consumer goods, or should heavy industry and armaments continue to enjoy top priority in planning future economic developments? With power dispersed in the ruling groups and ambitions unleashed, a complete harmony of outlook on questions such as these could hardly be anticipated. In a political system where opposition is outlawed, policy conflicts ordinarily lead to the suppression or elimination of one or another of the antagonistic forces. This deeply rooted Party practice augured ill for the stability of collective leadership.

The first challenge came from Beria. The very existence of a powerful secret police controlled by one member of the oligarchy posed a constant threat to his colleagues, and their fears were doubtless reinforced by the uses to which the secret police had been put in past Party struggles. Even though the charge that Beria endeavored to use his subordinates in the police hierarchy to gain control of the Party and administrative apparatus cannot be fully documented, the remark attributed to Khrushchev (by the French Socialist Senator Pierre Commin) that Beria "was clearly preparing a conspiracy against the Presidium" has a ring of authenticity. It expressed the underlying concern that ultimately resulted in Beria's liquidation.

While the arrest of Beria in July, 1953, eliminated one of the chief contenders for supremacy, it left the problem of control of the police still to be resolved. The appointment of Kruglov, a professional police officer, as head of the MVD and the strengthening of Party controls over the police at all levels served both to downgrade the police and to neutralize its role in the power struggle. The decision in the spring of 1954, to transfer the political police from MVD jurisdiction to a newly organized Committee on State Security (KGB) under Colonel-General Serov marked another phase in the dilution of police power. By the same token, these actions also served to underline the residual importance of control of the armed forces.

The designation of Khrushchev as First Secretary in September, 1953, set the stage for his bid for supreme power. After Lenin's death, Stalin had used his position as General Secretary to consolidate his control of the Party apparatus and to extend his authority into other spheres. Khrushchev's associates in the Presidium undoubtedly were aware of the precedent, and one must conclude that they either underestimated Khrushchev or displayed excessive confidence in their capacity to contain such ambitions as he cherished. The series of moves he initiated, beginning in the fall of 1953, to install his henchmen in leading Party posts in Moscow, Leningrad, and other key areas could hardly fail to arouse concern among his colleagues in the Presidium; one can only surmise that at this juncture some of them, at least, saw an even greater danger in the ambitions and programs of Malenkov.

Malenkov Versus Khrushchev

The search for an explanation of the alignments of the early post-Stalinist period cannot be limited to moves on the chessboard of power. Important policy differences divided the ruling group, and while they are only faintly illumined by Soviet press comment, they are visible enough so that patterns can be discerned. During this period, Malenkov and Khrushchev emerged as the major antagonists. In the area of foreign affairs, Malenkov saw nuclear war as spelling "the destruction of world civilization," developed a thesis of peace, based on mutual deterrence, that minimized the danger of war, and called for improvement in relations with the United States through a process of patient negotiations. Khrushchev took a harder line. Speaking before the Tenth Congress of the Czech Communist Party on June 12, 1954, he hailed a nuclear war as inevitably leading to a collapse of capitalism rather than of "world civilization." He accused reactionary capitalist circles of seeking a way out of their difficulties "by the preparation of a new war" and stressed the aggressive intentions of the imperialist camp. Similar views were expressed in a series of speeches delivered by Molotov, Kaganovich, Voroshilov, and Bulganin.

Malenkov's optimistic outlook on the prospects for peace found its reflection on the domestic scene in his identification with the consumer-goods program. Here again it was Khrushchev who took the "hard" line. In calling for a reassertion of the priority of heavy industry and armaments, he drew on the support of the armed forces as well as on those members of the Presidium who shared his world outlook. The alignment on such new agricultural programs as the opening of the virgin lands was somewhat different. Here it was Khrushchev who was the innovator, while, if later testimony is to be credited, Malenkov was joined by Molotov and Kaganovich in conservative opposition.

These crosscurrents suggest the danger of viewing the struggle for the succession as merely a series of maneuvers for power and place. Coalitions were cemented by principle as well as by calculations of advantage and fear. The opposition to the Malenkov program provided a powerful rallying point, which reinforced the position of Khrushchev. The erosion of Malenkov's strength can be traced at least from the spring of 1954. In a speech on April 26, 1954, which represented a complete concession to the views of his opponents, he declared that a third world war "would inevitably lead to the collapse of the capitalist social system." It was not without significance that this speech of the Chairman of the Council of Ministers was addressed to the Council of Nationalities of the Supreme Soviet, while the greater honor of addressing the Council of the Union was reserved for Khrushchev.

Meanwhile, the battle over the priority of heavy industry versus consumer goods continued to be fought. The conflict came into sharp focus with the appearance of a curious pair of editorials on December 21, 1954. *Izvestia*, presumably the organ of Malenkov, called for the increased production of consumer goods; *Pravda*, the organ of Khrushchev, summoned "the Soviet people to direct their main attention to fulfillng plans for the further growth of heavy industry." The issue between Khrushchev and Malenkov came to a head at the meeting of the Central Committee in late January, 1955. The published version of Khrushchev's speech (*Pravda*, February 3, 1955) to a plenary session on January 25, 1955, named no names, but its intent was unmistakable. Said Khrushchev:

> In connection with the measures lately taken for increasing output of consumer goods, some comrades have confused the question of the pace of development of heavy and light industry in our country. . . . These pseudo theoreticians try to claim that at some state of socialist construction the development of heavy industry ceases to be the main task, and that light industry can and should overtake all other branches of industry. This is profoundly incorrect reasoning, alien to the spirit of Marxism-Leninism—nothing but slander of our Party. This is a belching of the Rightist deviation, a regurgitation of views hostile to Leninism, views that Rykov, Bukharin, and their ilk once preached.

The denouncement was not long in coming. On February 8, 1955, Malenkov "resigned" his chairmanship of the Council of

Ministers, after signing a letter acknowledging his administrative "inexperience" and his past "guilt and responsibility for the unsatisfactory state of affairs in agriculture" (*Pravda*, February 9, 1955).

By previous standards, his punishment was mild indeed. Although demoted to the positions of Minister of Power Stations and Deputy Chairman of the Council of Ministers, he remained on the Party Presidium.

The Shrinking Collective

The demotion of Malenkov opened the way to a reconstruction of the top leadership. Bulganin replaced Malenkov as Chairman of the Council of Ministers and at the same time yielded his post as Minister of Defense to Marshal Zhukov. Khrushchev remained First Secretary. Five Presidium members—Molotov, Kaganovich, Mikoyan, Saburov, and Pervukhin—served as First Deputy Chairmen of the Council of Ministers. Voroshilov, the senior member of the Presidium group, continued to discharge the protocol functions of head of state. At the July, 1955, session of the Central Committee, two new Presidium members were elected—A. I. Kirichenko, First Secretary of the Ukrainian Party, and M. A. Suslov, the senior Central Committee Secretary after Khrushchev.

At this same session of the Central Committee, Molotov was marked out as the next candidate for demotion and disgrace. As was subsequently revealed, the chief subject of discussion at this meeting—which came soon after the B. & K. state visit to Belgrade—was the question of policy toward Tito. Khrushchev favored reconciliation and an attempt to recapture Tito for the Soviet cause; Molotov opposed concessions to Tito as unnecessary and dangerous. But Molotov's views found little support in the Central Committee, and from that point on, his influence sharply declined. The Party theoretical journal, *Kommunist*, in its issue of September, 1955, administered an added blow to his prestige as an Old Bolshevik when it published a strange letter of recantation signed by Molotov. In it he acknowledged that in a speech delivered some seven months earlier, he had committed a major ideological error by describing the Soviet Union as only having constructed "the foundations of a socialist society" instead of adhering to the orthodox formula that the Soviet Union had achieved socialism and was now building Communism. A further sharp rebuff followed in June, 1956, when Molotov was replaced as Foreign Minister by D. T. Shepilov.

Meanwhile, Kaganovich was undergoing a similar process of downgrading. In March, 1955, his authority in the industrial sphere was reduced when Mikoyan, Pervukhin, and Saburov joined him as First Deputy Chairmen of the Council of Ministers. His appointment as Chairman of the State Committee on Labor and Wage Problems in May, 1955, was terminated in June of the next year, and in September, 1956, he was transferred to the still lower post of U.S.S.R. Minister of the Construction Materials Industry. Despite these humiliations, which were shared with Molotov and Malenkov, all three remained members of the Party Presidium, where, it can reasonably be assumed, they continued to harbor their grievances and thoughts of revenge.

The Hard Climb to the Summit

The maneuverings that attended the Twentieth Party Congress marked a further stage in the development of the intra-Presidium struggle. The attack on Stalin and on the cult of personality, which was first launched by Mikoyan and then documented in detail in Khrushchev's secret speech, was interpreted at the time as an effort to bar the way to the emergence of another Stalin. Yet if we assume, as in the light of later events we must, that Khrushchev was determined to consolidate his authority, his secret speech can also be read as an effort to discredit his major opponents in the Presidium. In the process of attacking Stalin, he made a studied effort to dissociate himself from responsibility for Stalin's excesses, and to single out others—particularly Malenkov, Molotov, and Kaganovich—as having been tarred with the brush of their master's misdeeds. Conversely, he attempted to demonstrate—though somewhat lamely—that he and Bulganin had opposed Stalin's methods and policies. Despite the fact that Khrushchev had served as one of Stalin's proconsuls during the Great Purge, first in the Moscow Party organization and after January, 1938, in the Ukraine, he insisted that he had nothing to do with the Purge, that it was engineered by Stalin and Yezhov, and that they alone were responsible for the liquidation of Postyshev, Kossior, and other prominent Party figures in the Ukraine whom Khrushchev both succeeded and, at the time, denounced. Even though the explanations were labored, their intent was unmistakable. Khrushchev was seeking to demonstrate that the Party had nothing to fear from him, while it had a great deal indeed to fear from those who had been more intimately involved in Stalin's crimes.

Meanwhile, Khrushchev also moved to use his powers as First Secretary to extend his influence in the leading organs of the Party. More than a third of the Central Committee members— 53 out of 133—and more than half of the candidate members of the Central Committee—76 out of 122—were newly elected at the Twentieth Congress, and in numerous instances their elevation in the Party apparatus was directly traceable to earlier associations with Khrushchev. Five additions were made to the alternate membership list of the Presidium—Marshal Zhukov; Brezhnev, First Secretary of the Kazakhstan Party organization; Mukhitdinov, the Uzbek First Secretary; Furtseva, head of the Moscow Party organization; and Shepilov, editor of *Pravda*. All of them appeared to owe their appointments to Khrushchev, although both Marshal Zhukov and Shepilov were later to break with him. Khrushchev strengthened his hold over the Central Committee Secretariat through the appointments of Brezhnev, Furtseva, and Shepilov as Party secretaries. In addition, a special Russian Republic Bureau of the Central Committee was established with Khrushchev as Chairman; of its ten members, at least nine could plausibly be identified as part of Khrushchev's entourage.

The Twentieth Congress was followed by a series of blows directed at the Stalinist Old Guard. On June 2, 1956, Shepilov replaced Molotov as Minister of Foreign Affairs, and Molotov was moved to the lesser post of Minister of State Control. Soon thereafter, Kaganovich was demoted. By mid-1956, Khrushchev appeared to be riding high, with no competitor on the horizon to offer a serious challenge.

But appearances were deceptive. The shock of Khrushchev's revelations at the Twentieth Congress opened up a Pandora's box of wholly unintended consequences. The Hungarian uprising in October and the political overturn in Poland threatened the Soviet satellite system with disintegration. All this gave powerful ammunition to Khrushchev's Presidium opponents, who could now argue that Khrushchev's policies at the Twentieth Congress had placed the entire Soviet bloc in jeopardy.

During this period, evidence accumulated that Khrushchev was in trouble. The delegation that was hastily dispatched to Warsaw on October 19, to discuss "topical problems" with the Polish Politburo included Molotov and Kaganovich, as well as Khrushchev and Mikoyan—a juxtaposition that seemed to point to a new correlation of forces in the Presidium. The break with Tito, which followed the Hungarian events, served to discredit Khrushchev's policy of reconciliation. Increasing difficulties on the industrial front, which were complicated by the need to buttress the shaky satellite economies, contributed to undermine Khrushchev's leadership. Significantly, at the Central Committee session in December, 1956, which revised the industrial targets downward and sought to tighten the planning machinery, Khrushchev did not even deliver an address. The main speeches were made by Bulganin, Saburov, and Baibakov. At this session, the Central Committee greatly broadened the powers of the State Economic Commission, which was charged with current planning. Pervukhin was designated Chairman of the Commission and became something of an "overlord of overlords," exercising primary responsibility for the operation of the national economy. The effect of this move was to strengthen the authority of elements in the Presidium identified with the state, rather than the Party machine. The scheme was approved by the Supreme Soviet on February 12, 1957.

The very next day, Khrushchev launched a counterattack. Appearing before a specially summoned session of the Central Committee, he offered a plan that was designed to emasculate the Economic Commission, to strengthen the role of Gosplan as the supreme planning authority, to abolish a number of central ministries, and to devolve many of their operational responsibilities on new regional economic councils, or *sovnarkhozy*. The plan that Khrushchev espoused was clearly calculated to weaken the power of his ministerial competitors, to enlist support from local and regional managerial personnel, and to leave the field free for the Party apparatus to become the primary integrating and centralizing force. This bold move by Khrushchev to consolidate his authority served to bring matters to a head.

Open Conflict

The question may well be raised why Khrushchev was prepared to throw down the gage to his opponents in February when he was not willing to do so in December. While the answer must be speculative, certain considerations appear to be relevant. By February, far more than in December, the unrest in the satellite empire appeared to be under firm restraint and less of a threatening factor. The bountiful harvest in the virgin lands provided a vindication of Khrushchev's agricultural program and strengthened his position. And perhaps most important of all, Khrushchev's readiness to act indicated that he counted on the program he had devised to rally the Party apparatus to his banner.

From this point on, Khrushchev moved swiftly to consolidate his position. A law approved by the Supreme Soviet on May 10, 1957, established the regional economic councils, abolished the State Economic Commission, and made Gosplan the dominant economic planning agency. By a decree of the Presidium of the Supreme Soviet a week earlier, I. I. Kuzmin, one of Khrushchev's subordinates in the Central Committee apparatus, had already been installed as Chairman of Gosplan and First Vice Chairman of the Council of Ministers.

Meanwhile, Khrushchev's opponents in the Presidium were also gathering their forces. By June, Khrushchev found himself in a minority in the Presidium. Malenkov, Molotov, and Kaganovich were joined by Bulganin, Voroshilov, Pervukhin, and Saburov, a total of seven out of eleven full members of the Presidium;

they also enlisted the support of Shepilov, an alternate member of the Presidium. The details of the cabal remain obscure, but judging by the special violence of the attack on Malenkov at the Twenty-first Party Congress in January, 1959, it is probable that he was the moving and organizing spirit. Despite previous disagreements with both Molotov and Kaganovich, he was able to find common ground with them in the effort to curb Khrushchev's bid for supremacy. Bulganin, Pervukhin, and Saburov were late-comers to the conspiracy. Bulganin, in his speech at the December, 1958, Plenum of the Central Committee, abjectly confessed to having been not only an "accomplice" of the anti-Party group, but, as Chairman of the Council of Ministers, its "nominal leader as well."

Pervukhin's participation was directly traceable to the dispute over industrial reorganization. As he put it in his speech to the Twenty-first Congress:

> In the Central Committee discussion on the problem of reorganizing the management of industry and construction, I cast doubts on and objected to certain propositions in the suggested reorganization. My incorrect position in this most important matter and the discontent connected with it caused me to commit a gross political mistake; namely that I upheld the attacks of the anti-Party group on Comrade Khrushchev at the sessions of the Central Committee Presidium that preceded the Plenum in June, and consequently, as I later became aware, also attacks on his stand with regard to several problems of internal and foreign policy.

But he also added that "once the anti-Party group openly put forth the question of a change of leadership in the Central Committee, I disagreed and did not support this request." Saburov similarly confessed at the Twenty-first Congress to having manifested "political instability" prior to the June Central Committee meeting. Nevertheless, in a subsequent speech at the Congress, Kuzmin took both Pervukhin and Saburov sharply to task for seeking to minimize their parts in the conspiracy, and Pervukhin was singled out as having played a particularly active role, together with Molotov and Shepilov, in resisting Khrushchev's plans for industrial reorganization.

The opposition group's attempt to unseat Khrushchev by confronting him with a hostile majority in the Presidium misfired. Khrushchev refused to resign and took his appeal to a hastily assembled special session of the Central Committee where, according to the official report, he received unanimous support, with only Molotov abstaining. The resolution of the Central Committee, which was published on July 4, centered its fire on Malenkov, Kaganovich, and Molotov, as well as on Shepilov, "who joined them." That the conspiracy had wider ramifications could be inferred from the fact that Saburov was dropped from the Presidium and that Pervukhin was demoted to alternate membership. In the resolution, the "anti-Party group" was accused of having used "factional methods in an attempt to change the composition of the Party's leading bodies" and of having disagreed with and fought the Party line on a number of issues, including industrial reorganization, agricultural policy, and foreign policy. Malenkov, Kaganovich, and Molotov were expelled from the Presidium and the Central Committee; Shepilov lost his posts as a Central Committee Secretary, Presidium alternate, and Central Committee member.

From Rout to Triumph

The reconstruction of the membership of the Presidium, which followed the June Plenum, represented a striking triumph for Khrushchev. The Presidium was enlarged to fifteen members. Marshal Zhukov was promoted from alternate to full membership, an action which seemed to imply that the Marshal had given full support to Khrushchev in the struggle against the "anti-Party" group. The other new members of the Presidium—Furtseva, Aristov, Belyayev, Brezhnev, Ignatov, Kozlov, Kuusinen, and Shvernik—had all been closely associated with Khrushchev in his rise to power and were appropriately rewarded.

The treatment of the conspirators was far less harsh than might have been anticipated. All of them retained their Party membership. Molotov was honorably exiled to Outer Mongolia as an

Ambassador; Malenkov was dispatched to manage an electric-power station in Kazakhstan; Kaganovich was sent to the Urals to run a cement plant; and Shepilov was reported as occupying a teaching position somewhere away from Moscow. The other major participants in the conspiracy, who were not publicly identified at the time of the June Plenum, suffered a series of retaliatory demotions. Pervukhin, after stepping down to an alternate membership in the Presidium, lost his position as a First Deputy Chairman of the Council of Ministers, became Chairman of the State Committee for Foreign Relations, and was then shifted to East Germany as Ambassador. Saburov's disgrace was more complete. After losing his Presidium membership, he became a Deputy Chairman of the State Committee for Foreign Economic Relations under Pervukhin, was subsequently moved from that post, and at the Twenty-first Congress was identified merely as a "factory manager in Syzran."

The treatment of Bulganin followed a particularly curious course. After the June Plenum, he retained both his seat in the Presidium and his position as Chairman of the Council of Ministers. Although his public role as government spokesman declined greatly, he was not replaced as Chairman of the Council of Ministers by Khrushchev until March 27, 1958, remained on the Presidium until September 5, 1958, and was not formally linked with the anti-Party group until Khrushchev's speech of November 14, 1958. His consignment to the relatively obscure post of Chairman of the Stavropol Economic Council completed his humiliation.

Voroshilov was dropped from the Presidium in July, 1960. Meanwhile, Khrushchev also found it necessary to settle accounts with Marshal Zhukov. While it is at least possible that the Marshal had Bonapartist pretentions, it is more likely that the purge of the popular World War II hero was a prophylactic action taken to eliminate a potential rallying point of military discontent. The issue was precipitated by friction between the Party's political apparatus in the armed forces and the more professionally oriented officers who followed Marshal Zhukov in seeking to subordinate political indoctrination to combat training and military control. Even before the Twentieth Congress, the

Army newspaper *Krasnaia zvezda* reported in its issue of January 25, 1956, that Marshal Zhukov—speaking at a Party conference of the Moscow military district—had complained: "Certain efforts have been made to subject the official activity of commanders to criticism at Party meetings. Such efforts are blameworthy. Our task is the comprehensive strengthening of the authority of the commanders, giving support to exacting officers and generals." This doctrine proved unpalatable to Khrushchev. The Central Committee resolution of October, 1957, approving the ouster of Zhukov from his positions as Minister of Defense and member of the Presidium and Central Committee, charged that he had "pursued a policy" of underestimating and curtailing Party leadership of the army and navy. It reminded the armed forces of the paramount role of the Party and called for an intensification of political work in the armed forces. The reorganization of the military high command in the wake of the Zhukov purge also involved the elevation of such Khrushchev protégés as Marshal Konev to top command responsibilities.

The consolidation of Khrushchev's authority was manifest in every sphere of Soviet society. His assumption of the chairmanship of the Council of Ministers in late March, 1958, represented merely a formal recognition of the leadership he already exercised in the area of governmental administration. His own Party henchmen were increasingly moved into key control positions. The so-called Ukrainian contingent, which had formed part of Khrushchev's entourage during his long period of service in the Ukraine, forged rapidly ahead under Khrushchev's tutelage. This was also true of assorted functionaries in the Central Committee Secretariat who worked closely with Khrushchev as First Secretary. As early as February 1, 1956, the professional police officer S. N. Kruglov was replaced as MVD chief by N. P. Dudorov, a former Khrushchev associate in the Ukraine and a section chief in the Central Committee Secretariat. On December 26, 1958, *Pravda* announced that A. N. Shelepin, former head of the Komsomol, would succeed General Serov as KGB chairman, and it was not without interest that Shelepin's successor as Komsomol chief for a period was one V. E. Semichatnyi, who had earlier occupied a corresponding post in the Ukraine.

The published proceedings of the December, 1958, Plenum of the Central Committee provide particularly dramatic evidence of Khrushchev's supremacy. Almost every important speaker at the meeting was interrupted by Khrushchev with questions or comments, and the kowtowing to Khrushchev that took place left no doubt that homage was being paid to the leader. The speeches at the Twenty-first Congress represented variations on the same theme and were sufficiently fulsome in their praise to suggest that Khrushchev was being lifted to a new pedestal.

What then has happened to collective leadership? In an interview with Henry Shapiro, chief Moscow correspondent of the United Press, on November 14, 1957, and published in *Pravda* on November 19, Khrushchev was asked: "When you speak of the collective leadership, do you mean the Central Committee, or its Presidium?" Khrushchev replied: "I mean the Central Committee of our Party. The Presidium is an executive body of the Central Committee. . . . The collective leadership consists not only of the members of the Central Committee. Collective leadership is exercised in our Party from top to bottom. . . ."

Those who accept Khrushchev's assurance that collective leadership still prevails in the Soviet Union may point to the undoubted fact that the Party Central Committee assembles with considerable frequency and that local Party organizations function with greater regularity than was true during the latter part of Stalin's reign. But it may be worth remembering that Stalin at one time was also lavish in his praise of collective leadership and that he, too, made effective use of the Central Committee in his march to supreme power. Khrushchev's style of governance has its own distinctive characteristics, but the swiftness with which he has moved to consolidate his authority leaves little doubt that he is now not merely *primus inter pares,* but the new master of the Soviet state.

The Nature of Khrushchev's Power

——RICHARD LOWENTHAL

WHEN KHRUSHCHEV BROKE UP the summit conference for which he had been working hard for more than two years, the question was raised as to how much of a free agent he had been in doing so. Basing their conjectures on a combination of explicit facts about Peking's opposition to Khrushchev's foreign policy and indications (or mere rumors) of dissatisfaction in the top echelons of the Soviet hierarchy itself, a number of observers concluded that Khrushchev was either on his way out or at least had been forced to yield control over policy to a hostile majority in the Presidium of the Central Committee. Accordingly, those who had come to hold this view proceeded to search all the records of recent domestic developments in the U.S.S.R. for clues to this presumed shift of power and to the composition of the new majority.

In following these speculations, this author must confess that he had not found them particularly persuasive on the subject of the scope and nature of foreign-policy disagreements in the Kremlin; if anything, they have served to underscore the wide divergencies of opinion among Western commentators on the present nature of the Soviet regime. The following remarks, therefore, are concerned with the latter rather than with the former. In other words, the purpose of this article is not to re-open the controversy on the motives of Khrushchev's volte-face and its likely sequel, but to examine—in the light of what we know about the structure and evolution of the Soviet Communist regime—the contradictory assumptions about the nature and the limits to Khrushchev's power. Such an examination may help us in establishing some standards for drawing distinctions between legitimate hypotheses about internal Soviet developments (based, as they inevitably must be, on insufficient data) and what is properly called "demonology"—i.e., the attempt to establish *unproved* policy shifts by reference to *unproved* conspiracies.

Historical Parallels

In what sense does a single-party dictatorship require a personal dictator? Official Communist (as distinct from fascist) doctrine has never admitted that need; according to the official formula, Party dictatorship rests upon "democratic centralism"— the determination of Party policy by elected congresses and central organs after democratic discussion, followed by their disciplined and unanimous execution under central control. In practice, Stalin in the late years of his rule largely dispensed with this fictitious formula and ruled fairly openly as a despot; but Khrushchev, in denouncing Stalin's "abuses," pledged a return to Leninist observance of Party rules—i.e., to "democratic centralism." He has in fact called regular meetings of the full Central Committee, and has asserted that in the intervals decisions of the Presidium are taken by majority vote.

But while this clearly suggests that the possibility of frank discussion and temporary disagreement without serious risk has been restored in the leading Party organs, it does not affect the ban on organized "factions," introduced by Lenin at the Tenth CPSU Congress in 1921. Under this ban, the minority of a leading Party organ is not entitled to carry any dispute to the next broader organ and, ultimately, to the Party congress; if it tries to do so, it automatically becomes guilty of "factionalism"—that is, of "anti-Party" activity. By the same token, Party members who disagree with the Central Committee's policy between congresses do not have the right to draw up a counterplatform for discussion at the next congress and to collect support for it. It follows, therefore, that all policy initiative is concentrated at the top, that the Central Committee is presented with prepared decisions by its Presidium, and the Party congress by the Central Committee.

Any other practice would indeed spell deadly danger for a one-party regime: For once a monopolistic party permits the growth of a plurality of organized groups or wings in its own ranks, it becomes, in fact, a democratic multiparty regime under another name, and the advantages of its monopoly are gone. But any regime that wishes to mold society in a predetermined pattern into which it would not grow of its own accord—and that is the essence of both Leninism and Stalinism—must insist on the totalitarian principle of concentrating all power and initiative at a single point.

Soviet practice has consistently corresponded to this principle —in the last years of Lenin, during most of Stalin's reign, and also under Khrushchev—except in the two crises of succession. For it turned out that the kind of collective discipline that enables disagreements to remain confined within a small leading group depends on the concentrating of power and authority in a single, undisputed leader. But when no such leader exists, every policy disagreement becomes linked with a struggle for his position among rival aspirants; and rivals in a struggle for dictatorial power do not keep to the rules of the party statutes. Hence the ban on factions was in fact wholly or partly ignored between 1923, when the struggle for Lenin's succession came into the open while he was still alive, and 1928–29, when Stalin defeated the last openly organized group opposed to his policies and his leadership—the so-called Right Opposition led by Bukharin and Rykov. Only after each oppositional faction had been defeated was it condemned for its "factionalism."

Similarly, the death of Stalin was followed by several years of half-open factional maneuverings among the rival members of the collective leadership, culminating in the First Secretary's successful appeal—from a "factional" Presidium majority hostile to his policies—to a plenary session of the Central Committee in June–July, 1957. Until Khrushchev emerged as undisputed leader with the defeat of the anti-Party group and the subsequent removal of Zhukov, the fundamental question of the Party machine's supremacy over the police, the government and economic bureaucracies, and the army had itself been in doubt. The domination of a single political will over the potential pluralism of these power machines could not be ensured without its embodiment in a single leader, any more than could the Party's own freedom from factionalism.

In both succession crises, the head of the Party Secretariat—that is, the head of the executive machinery of the organization that embodies legitimate authority in the single-party state—emerged victorious. The reason for both victories is simple: As head of the Secretariat, Khrushchev is favored not only by the prestige of his office, but more importantly by the fact that the Secretariat is charged with preparing the meetings of the Presidium and presenting the facts to its members, with executing its decisions, and above all with the powers of appointment and publicity. Within the Secretariat—an executive organ—no voting takes place; there is only subordination and division of labor; he who dominates it is in a position—by virtue of his control of the press and radio—to influence the outcome of any factional struggle, to appoint regional and republican secretaries who will pack the next Party congress with his supporters, and to arrange the composition of the next Central Committee according to his wishes. But once he has won the succession struggle and, by the aid of these organizational techniques, has emerged publicly as the new and acclaimed political leader, his power becomes both more vast and more secure.

Khrushchev's Climb to Power

It is worth recalling the most important stages of this process in the case of Khrushchev. On March 14, 1953, when the collective of Stalin's heirs forced Malenkov to yield his position as Secretary of the Central Committee, Khrushchev became the only representative of the Secretariat in the Presidium. During that year, Khrushchev emerged as the policy-maker in the field of agriculture, as well as the power behind several key appointments in the Party organization, and by the summer of 1954, he became strong enough to cause the Party to be listed first in all pronouncements issued jointly with the government. In the autumn of 1954, Khrushchev went to Peking, taking along with him Bulganin and Mikoyan—but not Malenkov; and in February,

1955, Malenkov was ousted from the premiership, following open attacks on his policies in the Soviet press.

At the Twentieth Congress of the CPSU (February, 1956), Khrushchev felt strong enough to attack the dogma of Stalin's infallibility and to influence decisively the composition of the new Central Committee. Nevertheless, the position of his rivals in the other segments of the bureaucracy—notably in the economic administration—was substantial enough to force the inclusion of their representatives in the Party Presidium, thus confronting Khrushchev with a continuous opposition to his policies as well as to his drive for supreme power. It was only in the wake of the serious setback suffered by Khrushchev as a result of the Polish and Hungarian events that he managed (with the support of the Party machine) to break the resistance of the economic bureaucracy, to win the decisive showdown against the majority in the Presidium, and—after defeating Marshal Zhukov's bid for greater army autonomy—to emerge finally as the supreme and unchallenged leader.

Until that time—i.e., until the second half of 1957—Khrushchev's rise to one-man leadership had been closely linked with the restoration of the pre-eminence of the Party machine in all areas of Soviet life. Now, however, matters took a new turn as Khrushchev began to expand his direct influence in other power machines, and as his personal appointees increasingly took over top positions in the army, police, and the government apparatus. After the defeat of the anti-Party group in the summer of 1957, the government, under the untrustworthy Bulganin, had almost ceased to function, with the inner cabinet of deputy prime ministers reduced to rudimentary proportions; by December, the supremacy of the Party machine was visibly expressed in the numerical domination of the Party Presidium by members of the Secretariat. In the spring of 1958, however, Khrushchev took over as premier and began rebuilding the "inner cabinet" to a point where it was no longer necessary to have all economic life controlled by the Secretariat. Accordingly, the Secretariat's numerical domination of the Party Presidium was also reduced; moreover, the frequently absent leader has decided not to entrust all his varied powers to any single deputy, and has increasingly divorced his own creation, the Party Bureau for the R.S.F.S.R., from the Central Committee Secretariat.

The result of all these changes is that, following the latest reshuffle announced on May 4, 1960, the majority of the seats on the Party Presidium are no longer held by the CC Secretariat alone, but by Khrushchev and three completely separate groups of his subordinates: four members from the Secretariat—Suslov, Kozlov, Mukhitdinov, Kuusinen—(or five, if Brezhnev, the new chief of state, is still counted); two members and two candidates from the R.S.F.S.R. Party Bureau—Aristov, Polyansky, Pospelov, Kirilenko; and four members from the Government—Mikoyan, Kosygin, Ignato, Furtseva—a total (with Khrushchev) of eleven out of fifteen full Presidium members, not counting Brezhnev. This singular concentration of personal power in Khrushchev's hands—foreshadowed by the steady chorus of public eulogies for the "leader and teacher," the "continuator of Lenin," the "foremost shock worker of the Soviet Union," and culminating in Kuusinen's recent (and quite unconstitutional) reference to Khrushchev as "head of the Soviet State"—would indicate that the simultaneous changes in the high command of the Soviet armed forces were part of the same process, outwardly symbolized by Khrushchev's affixing of his personal signature to the decree promoting 300 officers to the rank of general.

This record of Khrushchev's unremitting consolidation of power seems quite incompatible with the assumption that his leadership could still be seriously challenged at the present stage by any "neo-Stalinist" or "pro-Chinese" faction. Such a faction would have to start with an incomparably weaker base than the anti-Party group Khrushchev defeated in 1957—without control of any one of the great power machines, without the nationwide prestige of any of the old leaders, and with the whole accumulated force of the "Khrushchev cult" against it. In fact, assumptions about the formation of such a faction and its success in gaining a majority simply reflect a failure to distinguish between the conditions of an unresolved succession crisis, in which such developments may occur—indeed have occurred—and the conditions of firmly re-established one-man leadership, which is the normal rule of life in the one-party state.

Pressures—Direct and Indirect

Yet if we make the opposite assumption—namely, that Khrushchev is the unchallenged successor of Lenin and Stalin as head of the Party and the state—it does not follow that his power is subject to no limitations whatsoever. If he is not in danger of being overthrown or put under tutelage by a majority of the Presidium, he still has to take account of the weight of social forces and the movement of opinion in the leading strata of society upon which his power is based.

It is by now a commonplace that any attempt to run the Soviet Union at its present stage of economic development by mass terrorism, with an army of labor slaves, and so on, would be vastly more irrational than it was when Stalin first introduced these methods, and that Khrushchev is fully aware of this. But any regime that does not wish, or is unable, to achieve its aims by methods of mass terrorism has to take some account of the needs and desires of all the forces whose cooperation it requires. This is not necessarily—and in the Soviet Union not normally— a matter of conscious political pressure. The Soviet government grants wage increases not chiefly because it has reason to fear that the workers might go on strike, but because it wants to give them an incentive to work harder; it grants better prices to the kolkhoz peasants not because they have either made representations through Party channels or formed secret organizations for sabotaging the harvest, but because it recognizes that this is a precondition for raising agricultural productivity after a quarter century of Stalinist stagnation. In just the same way, it must take into account the discontent in the officer corps, not because the high command sends ultimatums to Khrushchev or concludes an alliance with the alleged "neo-Stalinists" in the Presidium, but simply because the existence of high morale in the armed forces is of utmost concern to the regime.

The above distinction between the organized pressures that may be exercised on policy in a pluralistic society, or during a temporary crisis in a totalitarian society, and the social facts of life that the government of any modern society, however totalitarian and secure, must take into account, is not a mere conceptual nuance; the effects in each case are likely to be of a different order. Other things being equal, a working class organized in independent trade unions will be able to extract higher wages than those granted—as an incentive—by an all-powerful state to its state-controlled workers. Similarly, an army not subject to effective civilian control, either of a constitutional or of a totalitarian kind, may be able to dictate policy by threats; an army subordinated to the all-pervading control of a totalitarian party, if seriously discontented, may obtain an extra round of promotions and welfare measures combined with a liberal dose of rhetoric on matters affecting military prestige, but hardly more.

Recent developments in the U.S.S.R. suggest the latter pattern rather than the former. There is no sign that the cuts in the armed forces, announced in January, 1960, will be abandoned, despite the uneasiness they may well have caused in the officer corps. In addition, an increased stress on consumer goods was announced at the same session of the Supreme Soviet at which the U-2 incident was disclosed. Marshal Malinovsky, far from trying to exert pressure to reverse these policies by turning against their originator, has publicly praised both the policies and the man. All of this still would not exclude the possibility that the latest round of promotions, as well as Khrushchev's repeated threats *after* the U-2 flights had been stopped, may have been prompted by due concern about military morale.

But there may indeed be more direct limitations on Khrushchev's power. It is worth recalling that in the early days of the Soviet regime, even Lenin occasionally found himself in the minority in his Central Committee—sometimes on vital questions such as the peace treaty with Germany in 1918—and chose temporarily to bow to the majority, even when he foresaw how heavy the cost would be, rather than risk forcing through policies before he could carry an overwhelmingly united leadership with him. Stalin, too, met effective delaying resistance to the expansion of his Blood Purge in the Central Committee as late as the autumn of 1936, after all opponents of his major policies had long disappeared from its ranks; only in the following spring did he feel ready to drive ahead ruthlessly and kill the resisters along with those they had tried to protect. Such temporary concessions to majorities, which express not a systematic opposition to the leader but a temporary climate of opinion in the leading Party organs, are the inevitable price for maintaining the fiction of democratic centralism, or in more realistic terms, for wishing to maintain a genuine exchange of opinions within the leading circle: When Stalin decided to do away with such concessions in principle, he also ended both the possibility of such discussion and the "democratic" fiction—and he became an undisguised despot, except in the eyes of some naïve outsiders.

Power and Authority

Khrushchev, having restored the climate of top-level discussion among his supporters, must thus be prepared to be put into a minority occasionally—at least in matters of detail. For though he has prompted a personality cult at once vaster and more servile than Lenin would have tolerated, his real authority—as distinct from his power—is nevertheless still far inferior to that of the founder of the Soviet state, or, for that matter, to that of the man who led Russia through the bitter years of forced collectivization and World War II. In short, Khrushchev disposes of all the levers of command, but he is not yet regarded as infallible within the inner circle.

This distinction between what may be termed mechanical power and moral authority is, in this author's opinion, as crucial to an understanding of the present stage in the evolution of the Soviet regime as the previous distinction drawn between the direct political pressures of social forces and their indirectly felt weight. One aspect of the present situation is Khrushchev's lack of historical achievement; ergo, his hunt for spectacular prestige successes abroad, or his proneness to a quick sequence of extravagant promises at home. If he fails to make good on any particular promise, whether in regard to overtaking the U.S.A. in meat consumption per head or to running the Western powers out of Berlin, he is not yet strong enough simply to drop the subject "down the memory hole," or to silence criticism by liquidating the critics. He is compelled instead to initiate a new and equally exciting venture, thus diverting attention from his previous failures.

Khrushchev *is* strong enough, however, to be beyond a serious challenge to his position. There is all the difference in the world between the hypothesis of an angry, disappointed mood in the Soviet leadership following the decline of prospects for a summit victory on Berlin, the U-2 incident, and President Eisenhower's assumption of responsibility for it—a mood to which Khrushchev would have had to pay attention in handling the situation—and the hypothesis of a hostile faction using that mood to send the leader, who for years has acted as exclusive and plenipotentiary Soviet spokesman on world affairs, to a crucial negotiation with detailed "instructions" removing his freedom of action, or having the power to reverse such instructions, or to withdraw his negotiating powers after his back was turned. The first hypothesis assumes a common embarrassment of Khrushchev and his team at having been made to look foolish in their dispute with the Chinese Communists; the second assumes a majority of his team turning on him to tell him that the Chinese had been right and he had better admit it and adopt their policy. Both hypotheses might explain some aspects of Khrushchev's behavior during the critical days, but the first is compatible with what we know of the power situation in Russia and the second is not. The latter amounts to assuming a head-on, deliberate challenge to Khrushchev's leadership, which could only end either with his downfall or with the purging of his critics; and for the reasons indicated above, such a reopening of the power struggle would be extremely difficult to conceive at the present stage.

Moreover, there is not a shred of real evidence to indicate a challenge on this scale. The record of recent events, and indeed of recent years, shows many examples of Khrushchev's eagerness to solidify his domestic authority and popularity by quick adjustments to changing situations; it shows none of uncertainty in his position. The two should not be confused.

Some Methodological Questions

A final word on the canons for judging evidence about conflicts within the Soviet leadership. If we wish to interpret events as they are unfolding, it is clearly impossible to confine ourselves to documentation that is both official and explicit: None such will be forthcoming until a particular conflict is decided, and even then it most likely will be one-sided as well as fragmentary. This is particularly true insofar as the struggles among the aspirants for the next succession are concerned: There is no doubt that in Stalin's lifetime keen rivalry existed first between Zhdanov and Malenkov, and later between Malenkov and Khrushchev, but even today our knowledge of the issues and turning points is tenuous at best. Today, we may guess that the fall of Kirichenko, once Khrushchev's favorite within the Party Secretariat, has been connected with similar rivalries—perhaps with a defeated attempt to extend his and his Ukrainian "clan's" influence to the R.F.S.F.R. Party Bureau; but there is no direct documentation for that.

But while there is an extreme dearth of official and explicit documentation, one must be on guard against supplementing it liberally with information based on the private statements made by Soviet officials to Westerners, or even to Poles and Yugoslavs. Most, though of course not all, of these private statements are made for an immediate tactical purpose; while the official documents are studied inside the Soviet Communist Party and government apparatus, the private statements can be made deliberately for their effect on Western opinion and policy. It follows, therefore, as an elementary rule of thumb, that official Soviet Party documents, if read with due regard to the known element of ideological and propagandist distortion, are more trustworthy than almost all of the so-called inside information available to the West.

This means that if analysts wish to learn more than they are told, they must concentrate their attention above all on official documents, including public speeches, debates, resolutions, appointments, etc., and study them for their hidden implications— as would, indeed, a trained Soviet Communist. There are, of course, risks in such a method, but they are smaller than the risks of believing in "confidential information" that may have been planted for outside consumption; also, they can be diminished by using the "decoding" method, not in isolation, but by relating it to known facts and general criteria of plausibility.

There is, however, one more rule: No serious struggle, however secret, can take place for any length of time without leaving identifiable traces in *some* public statement or political act of the protagonists. Thus, the prediction of a possible clash between Malenkov and Khrushchev was based on Malenkov's slighting remarks about Khrushchev's "agro-cities" project at the Nineteenth Party Congress in October, 1952, and on Khrushchev's personal participation in the removal of Malenkov's Leningrad appointee, Andrianov, in the autumn of 1953. Similarly, the final clash between Khrushchev and his opponents in the Party Presidium in the summer of 1957, was foreshadowed by the puzzling fact that in all the prior public discussions of Khrushchev's proposals for the reorganization of industrial planning, the Presidium and government members hitherto in charge of these matters had maintained a solid front of silence.

Where such positive or negative evidence of conflict is wholly lacking, one is entitled to regard speculation as "demonology" in the proper sense of the term—namely, the construction of theories about invisible agents, theories that, by their nature, are not open to verification. This seems to apply to an extraordinary extent to the cycle of legends that in the past few years has grown around the person of Mikhail Suslov, who is widely described as the last identifiable "Stalinist" in the Presidium and Secretariat of the Central Committee, and the presumed rallying point of the "neo-Stalinist"—or "pro-Chinese"—opposition to Khrushchev. Now there is some evidence that Suslov, who performed the same functions of ideological coordination under Zhdanov and Malenkov in Stalin's lifetime that he is performing now, has been less in a hurry than some younger Presidium members to join in public eulogies for Khrushchev. But it is also a documented fact that he was among the first of the leaders to voice public criticism of Stalin at the Twentieth Congress, and that he belonged to the minority of Presidium members who stood by Khrushchev against the "Old Stalinists" in the crisis of June, 1957, in fact presiding over the Central Committee meeting that expelled them. His reputation as a neo-Stalinist appears to have stemmed from Yugoslav accounts of the international conference of Communist Parties in Moscow in November, 1957, at which gathering Suslov was responsible for pushing through the new doctrinaire theses that the Poles found difficult and the Yugoslavs impossible to accept. Yet there has never been any evidence at all that this was not also Khrushchev's policy; and, there is to this day not a single policy speech or article by Suslov that shows disagreement with Khrushchev. That he is a man of very different character and temper from the First Secretary and has a very different way of doing things may readily be granted; but surely, in the absence of any proof of policy differences, this is hardly enough reason for imagining him to be the center of an opposing group.

It is not the purpose of these remarks to discourage speculation on Soviet internal politics, which is inevitable owing to the insufficiency of direct documentation, and in many cases highly legitimate. Rather, the author would like to see some of this speculation directed into more fruitful and promising channels. If Khrushchev's position is reasonably secure, then a struggle for influence over him and for his eventual succession must be in process. The fall of Kirichenko and the signs of a general decline of Ukrainian influence at Moscow headquarters may be part of this struggle; so may be the stricter separation of the Central Committee Secretariat and the R.S.F.S.R. Party Bureau, as well as the simultaneous rise of a number of men with shorter or longer histories in the Leningrad Party organization, including Kozlov, Kosygin, and Ignatov. These moves do not lend themselves easily to dramatic assumptions about implications for foreign policy, but they are facts; and they may well be the sort of facts that will determine the lineup for the next *real* power struggle in Russia—the struggle for Khrushchev's eventual succession.

The Twenty-second Party Congress

——MERLE FAINSOD

THE TWENTY-SECOND CPSU CONGRESS will surely go down in history as one of the more dramatic events in the life of a party from which drama has rarely been absent. The highlights of the Congress were the open airing of Sino-Soviet differences over the treatment of the Albanian Workers Party and the full-scale attack on Stalin and the anti-Party group. Neither was foreshadowed in the agenda announced for the Congress. All the advance preparations pointed to the new Party program and the revision of the Party rules as the sun and the moon around which the convocation would revolve. This was to be the Congress that would illumine the future, outline the road to Communism, and celebrate the triumphal march of Soviet power to a dominant position in the world.

Whether planned or unplanned, this was not quite the direction that the Congress took. Khrushchev did devote a long speech to the new Party program, and Kozlov made the expected report on the new Party rules, but as the Congress unfolded, both program and rules disappeared into the wings, and a host of absent figures—Stalin and Mao, Hoxha and Shehu, Molotov, Kaganovich, and Malenkov—moved into the center of the stage. The past and the present invaded and displaced the future, and the delegates found themselves being escorted on a journey into Hades instead of concentrating on the vision of the Promised Land. As the crimes of Stalin and the anti-Party group were unfolded, one sensed in the performance almost a ritual act of sacrifice, as if the

Party could not be readied for the future until the horrors of the past had been exorcised.

The Background

To see the Congress in perspective, one must view it in the context of developing events. On the domestic front, Khrushchev could point with justified pride to continued rapid industrial progress and striking military and scientific-technical achievements in the space realm. As he openly acknowledged at the Congress, too much capital was tied up in too many unfinished plants, and investment plans were consequently overextended, but despite these evidences of inefficient planning, the industrial-growth rate remained high. In agriculture, the picture was less rosy. The banner harvest of 1958 was followed by two mediocre crops, and the 1961 harvest, although improved, also fell short of that of 1958. Shortages of meat and dairy products were admitted, though Khrushchev placed the blame on a great increase in effective consumer demand.

On the eve of the Party Congress, Khrushchev gave every evidence of being solidly in command of his Party machine. The so-called anti-Party group had been humiliated and demoted, and they seemed to offer no threat to his power. Yet, in one sense their status was anomalous. Labeled anti-Party, they still retained their Party membership, and, in some cases, even occupied positions of dignity and prominence. For reasons that are still obscure, the cries heard at the Twenty-first Party Congress demanding that Molotov, Kaganovich, and Malenkov be expelled from the Party were not carried through. In this respect, at least, the anti-Party group represented unfinished business; the Twenty-second Party Congress offered Khrushchev an opportunity for a final settlement.

Within the international Communist movement, trouble was brewing, with ideological and policy differences between the Chinese and Soviet Communist leadership still unresolved. The compromise declaration patched together at the Moscow meeting of the eighty-one Communist parties in November–December,

1960, provided a surface show of unity, but the subsequent exac-
erbation of relations between Moscow and Albania, and the
Chinese adoption of the Albanians as a client Party, gave protestations of amity an increasingly hollow ring. Thus Khrushchev
was confronted by a challenge that presented him with unpalatable alternatives. If Chinese and Albanian defiance were allowed
to go unanswered, there was the risk of spreading ideological
infection and the danger that Soviet leadership of the bloc and
of the world Communist movement would be further undermined. If the issue were brought into the open and the demand
for capitulation too sharply posed, there was the possibility of a
split in the ranks of the international Communist movement that
would deal it a serious blow. It is against this background that
one must understand Khrushchev's decision to make the Twenty-
second Party Congress the occasion for a show of strength and
to concentrate his fire on the Albanian Party leaders rather than
on the Chinese. Whether he hoped, through this maneuver, to
avoid a direct confrontation with the Chinese while still asserting
Soviet leadership we do not know; if that was his design, the
Congress was soon to reveal that it miscarried.

Problems of foreign policy also engaged the attention of the
Congress planners. In this area, the Soviet leadership professed
satisfaction with the state of its relations with the so-called un-
aligned nations of Asia and Africa, and the presence of delegations from the ruling parties of Guinea, Ghana, and Mali was
hailed as a harbinger of the magnetic attraction of Communism
for all ex-colonial peoples. Cuba occupied a special niche at the
Congress, the symbol of Latin American liberation from the imperial oppression of the United States and the supposed forerunner of a series of revolts that would carry the anticolonial struggle
into the inner preserve of the leader of the imperialist camp.
There were indications, both before and during the Congress, that
Soviet policy in the underdeveloped parts of the world was undergoing re-examination and that its distribution of future largesse
would provide special encouragement for "friendly" neutrals that
followed the Soviet foreign-policy line, cut their economic ties
with the West, organized their economies on a "socialist" basis,

and made room for local Communists in their governing arrangements.

Relations with the West cast a darker shadow over the Congress. Here the most disturbing developments from the Soviet point of view were the rearmament of West Germany, its growing economic strength, the prosperity of the Common Market countries, and the prospect that an integrated Western Europe including Britain would present a formidable barrier to Soviet expansion in Europe. The immediate tasks of Soviet foreign policy as seen from Moscow were to arrest these tendencies toward unity, to bring disintegrative forces into play, and to force the West to make concessions to rising Soviet power without igniting a nuclear holocaust.

The Berlin crisis and such far-flung Soviet operations as Laos and the Congo take on meaning in this context. In their different ways, they represented probing operations designed to test the stamina of the Western community and to take advantage of such opportunities as opened up to extend Soviet influence or power. Pressure continued to be exerted, both before and during the Congress, in the form of the Soviet resumption of testing, the demonstrative terror of the 50-plus megaton bomb, the firing of ballistic missiles into the mid-Pacific, and the demand that the Finns join in "defensive" actions against West Germany. Since the cumulative effect of these measures was to precipitate a war scare, Khrushchev also used the platform of the Congress to temper his brinkmanship by postponing his December 31 deadline for the conclusion of the treaty with East Germany and by indicating through Gromyko that the road to a resolution of the Berlin crisis was still open, though the terms of a possible settlement were left vague.

The Issues

The problem Khrushchev faced at the Congress was to demonstrate that the cause of Communism could be effectively advanced on a world scale without risking the destruction of a thermonuclear war. The perspective he set forth emphasized the rising military and economic power of the Soviet bloc, the declining position of the West, and the expectation that the West would adjust to this changing correlation of forces by peacefully surrendering positions it was no longer capable of defending by force. While Khrushchev did not exclude the possibility that the West, in an act of madness, might embark on a thermonuclear war, he tended to minimize the danger on the assumption that superior Soviet military power and counsels of peace and reason within the Western camp would operate as restraints. In the Khrushchevian vision, the West might have to be prodded along into yielding its positions by pressure and threat and by coaxing and guile, but on the inevitability of surrender he permitted himself no doubts.

For most people in the Soviet Union who remember the casualties of the last war, Khrushchev's promise of victory without H-bombs holds out great appeal. The fact that the Soviet government found it necessary to withhold from its own citizens news of the resumption of nuclear testing and that the test series, when finally reported, was presented as a necessary defensive measure to ward off the threat of Western aggression, testifies to a widespread yearning for peace among the Soviet people—a sentiment the leadership can manipulate but not wholly disregard. The ambiguous formula of peaceful coexistence that Khrushchev has chosen as his springboard to world power has its semantic attractions inside the Soviet Union as well as outside.

But there are also those in the Communist camp who see the Khrushchevian vision as a rationalization for inaction and as a betrayal of the revolutionary cause. It was to these views that Khrushchev referred in his October 27 speech (*Pravda*, October 29) to the Party Congress when he said:

> Some attack us, accusing us of allegedly simplifying or softening our assessment of the international atmosphere when we emphasize the need for peaceful coexistence under present conditions. We are told that he who insists on peaceful coexistence allegedly displays some kind of underestimation of the essence of imperialism and even sinks into contradiction with the Leninist assessment of imperialism.

Reaffirming his own faith in victory as a result of the emerging conjuncture of forces, he went on to condemn those "hopeless dogmatists who, having learned by rote the general formulas about imperialism, stubbornly turn away from life. . . . It is such a position that the diehard Molotov still upholds. He and his like do not understand the changes in the world atmosphere and the new phenomena in life. They follow in the wake of events and have long since become a brake and a ballast."

Khrushchev chose to point the finger at Molotov, but it was the Chinese whom he really had in mind. From the beginning, the Chinese Communist leaders displayed the deepest skepticism toward Khrushchev's thesis that the imperialists could be defeated without war. In Chinese eyes, the Khrushchev strategy with its long-drawn-out prospect of competitive coexistence and eventual peaceful capitalist surrender was founded on illusions, and they did not hesitate to propagate their views in the international Communist movement, where they found some open and more covert support among impatient Party leaders seeking a quick road to power.

Among those who rallied to the Chinese banner were the leaders of the Albanian Party, Enver Hoxha and Mehmet Shehu. Disaffected in the first instance by Khrushchev's efforts to woo their enemy, Tito, back into the bloc, critical of the consequences of the 1956 de-Stalinization campaign, resenting Soviet intervention on behalf of their intra-Party enemies, they came increasingly to share the Chinese evaluation of Khrushchev as a revisionist lacking in revolutionary ardor. After breaking with Khrushchev, they adopted the Chinese as their protectors and patrons.

Attack and Counterattack

It is against this background that the Soviet-Chinese confrontation at the Twenty-second Party Congress assumes its special drama. The first sign of impending trouble was the failure of a delegation from the Albanian Workers Party to appear at the Congress. Then came Khrushchev's attack on the Albanian Party leaders in his Central Committee report (*Pravda*, October 18), in which he charged them with departing from "the generally agreed line of the whole Communist movement on the most important questions of modern times," reviving Stalinist methods in Albania, and "coming out against the course of the Twentieth Party Congress." While the meaning of the indictment was clear, and perhaps as much aimed at the unmentioned Chinese as at the Albanians, it was still phrased in general terms, more in sorrow than in anger, and it appeared to leave the door open to the Albanians to "abandon their mistaken views" and to return "to the path of unity" and "friendship with the CPSU."

Two days later, Chou En-lai rose to bring the greetings of the Chinese Communist Party to the Congress. After some polite words praising Soviet achievements, he launched into a diatribe strikingly different in tone from Khrushchev's report. Where Khrushchev had expressed the hope for a "normalization" of relations with the United States, Chou En-lai denounced the Americans as "the most vicious enemy of peace," and the Kennedy administration as "more deceptive and adventurous" than its predecessor. He insisted that "all the activities of American imperialism show that we are still confronted with the danger of war and that the people of all countries must heighten their vigilance." Where Khrushchev condemned Yugoslav revisionism in rather cursory fashion, Chou coupled "the Yugoslav revisionist clique" and American imperialism as the main enemies. Chou's most biting remarks were reserved for Khrushchev's attack on the Albanian Party. Said Chou (*Pravda*, October 20):

We hold that if a dispute or difference unfortunately arises between fraternal parties or fraternal countries, it should be resolved patiently in the spirit of proletarian internationalism and on the principles of equality and unanimity through consultations. Any public, one-sided censure of any fraternal party does not help unity and is not helpful in resolving problems. To lay bare a dispute between fraternal parties or fraternal countries openly in the face of the enemy cannot be regarded as a serious Marxist-Leninist attitude. Such an attitude will only grieve those near and dear to us and gladden our enemies. The CCP sincerely hopes that fraternal parties that have disputes or differences will unite afresh on the basis of Marxism-Leninism and on the basis of mutual respect, independence, and equality. This, in my opinion, is the position we Communists ought to take on this question.

Perhaps to emphasize his displeasure, Chou En-lai shortly afterwards departed for Peking, where he was given a full-dress welcome by leading Communist dignitaries, including Mao. Meanwhile, speaker after speaker at the Congress joined in the denunciation of the absent Albanians. But there were also a few conspicuous abstentions: the North Koreans and the Vietnamese remained silent.

In the course of the whole debate, there was no direct reference to the Chinese, until Khrushchev in his concluding remarks replied to the absent Chou as follows:

The leader of the delegation of the Communist Party of China, Comrade Chou En-lai, in his speech expressed anxiety over the matter of openly raising the question of Albanian-Soviet relations at our Congress. As far as we understand it, the main thing in his speech was alarm that the present state of our relations with the Albanian Workers Party might influence the cohesion of the socialist camp. We share the anxiety of our Chinese friends and appreciate their concern for the strengthening of unity. If the Chinese Comrades desire to apply their efforts to a normalization of relations between the Albanian Workers Party and the fraternal parties, then hardly any one can make a better contribution to the solution of this problem than the Communist Party of China. This would really benefit the Albanian Workers Party and would correspond to the interest of the whole commonwealth of Socialist countries (*Pravda*, October 29).

Then Khrushchev launched into a violent attack on Hoxha and Shehu, charged them with having imposed a reign of terror on their Party, accused them of having taken the initiative in openly ventilating their differences with the Soviet Union, and left little doubt that the break with the Albanian Party leaders was irrep-

arable. Peking, meanwhile, went out of its way to identify itself
with the Albanians, and there was not even the hint of a reply
to Khrushchev's suggestion that Chou En-lai might use his good
offices to heal the breach.

As a result, the Twenty-second Party Congress can hardly be
considered a success in asserting Khrushchev's leadership of the
Communist camp. The effect of the Chou En-lai–Khrushchev
confrontation was to dramatize disunity. While Khrushchev's denunciations were directed at tiny Albania, and Chou En-lai's
most bitter barbs were reserved for the Kennedy administration
and Tito, no special ingenuity was required to recognize the two
main antagonists and the sharpness of their differences on underlying Communist strategy.

What Khrushchev hoped to accomplish by airing his grievances
against the Albanians at the Party Congress must remain a matter
of conjecture. Did he suppose that Chinese economic difficulties,
their dependence on Soviet aid, and their interest in not further
embittering Sino-Soviet relations would prompt them to keep
silent while their Albanian ally was being humiliated and isolated? If so, the miscalculation was a serious one. Or did he take
the possibility of a Chinese reaction into account and decide
nevertheless to bring the issue into the open as a way of showing
his strength and demonstrating the overwhelming character of
his support in the Soviet Party and in the world Communist
movement? If that was his purpose, there can be no question that
he was able to mobilize what, in another connection, he described
as an "arithmetical majority," but the victory was won by flouting
Chinese sensitivities, and the cost has yet to be measured in the
deterioration of Sino-Soviet relations.

Purge of the Purgers

In the grand design of the Congress, the attack on the Stalinism of the Albanian leaders was coupled with a much broader
and more far-reaching indictment of the repressions of the Stalinist era and its alleged exemplars, the leaders of the anti-Party
group. The assault on Stalin followed a curious course. Although
Khrushchev's opening report on behalf of the Central Committee

quoted Lenin's demand that Stalin be removed from his position as Secretary-General of the Party and offered general criticism of the "mistakes" and "distortions" associated with the "personality cult," there was no bill of specifications, and indeed there were even a few words of praise for the *vozhd*. ("Of course, Stalin had great merits in the Party and the Communist movement, and we give him his due.") But as the Congress gathered momentum, the indictment of Stalin and the wealth of detail cited to illustrate his crimes and to involve Molotov, Kaganovich, Malenkov, and Voroshilov in them went far beyond anything contained in Khrushchev's secret speech to the Twentieth Congress.

Drawing on police archives, A. N. Shelepin, the Chairman of the KGB, charged Stalin, Molotov, and Kaganovich with personal responsibility for sanctioning the executions of Postyshev, Kossior, Eiche, Rudzutak, Chubar, Krylenko, Unshlicht, Bubnov, and many other Party and government leaders during the Great Purge (*Pravda*, October 27). He told the story of General Yakir, who, condemned to death, sent a last plea to Stalin proclaiming his innocence and ending, "I die with words of love for you, the Party, and the country, with limitless faith in the triumph of Communism." On the letter, Stalin had written, "A rascal and a prostitute," and Voroshilov, Molotov, and Kaganovich had added similar notations. Shelepin also described how in June, 1937, the Old Bolshevik Lomov, a member of the Bureau of the Soviet Control Commission, was arrested and executed at the order of Molotov and Stalin on the grounds that he had had "friendly relations" with Rykov and Bukharin. Shelepin charged Malenkov with personal responsibility for the "Leningrad Affair," for the execution of Voznesensky, Kuznetsov, and many other prominent workers.

Khrushchev's concluding speech (*Pravda*, October 29) was in some respects even more sensational. "You have heard Comrade Shelepin's speech," he declared. "He disclosed a great deal at the Congress, but, of course, he did not by any means tell all that has now been revealed. Thousands of absolutely innocent people perished, and each person is a whole story. Many Party leaders, statesmen, and military leaders lost their lives." He described in great detail the suspicious circumstances surrounding Kirov's assassination and the subsequent investigation, and left the inference that the whole affair was organized by Stalin and by Kirov's jealous rivals. He confirmed the fact that Ordzhonikidze committed suicide after his brother had been arrested and shot, and that Svanidze, the brother of Stalin's first wife, was also executed as a spy for Germany after he refused to ask Stalin's pardon. He also verified the story that had long circulated in the West that Marshal Tukhachevsky, General Yakir, and the other distinguished military leaders who were sent to their death on the charge of being agents of the German General Staff were executed on the basis of false documents planted by Nazi intelligence. And perhaps Khrushchev revealed more than he intended when he told how within the year, while attending a conference in Alma Ata, he was approached by General Yakir's son, who asked him to explain the death of his father. "What could I tell him?" he asked the Congress. More than most rhetorical questions, it left a great deal unsaid.

The climax of the attack on Stalin came with Khrushchev's suggestion that a monument be erected in Moscow "to perpetuate the memory of comrades who fell victim to arbitrary rule" and with the decision of the Congress to remove Stalin's body from the mausoleum in Red Square. One of the high points of the Congress was the speech of Mme. D. A. Lazurkina, Party member since 1902, who rose to support the proposal that Stalin be ejected from the mausoleum. Mme. Lazurkina, an old lady who worked with Lenin in her youth, described how, together with many other Old Bolsheviks, she had been arrested without cause in 1937, had suffered through two and a half years in prison, a sentence to a forced labor camp, and seventeen years in exile, during all of which time she had defended Stalin and argued with her fellow prisoners that it was impossible that he could have sanctioned their arrests. Rehabilitated at the time of the Twentieth Party Congress, she at last had her eyes opened to Stalin's evil deeds by Khrushchev's secret speech. "I consider," Mme. Lazurkina stated, "that our marvelous Vladimir Ilyich, that most human man, must not lie side by side with that person, who, even though he rendered services in the past, before 1934, should not be next to Lenin." At which point Khrushchev interrupted her recital by calling out "Correct." And Lazurkina continued, "I always carry Ilyich in my heart, always, Comrades, in the most difficult moments . . . and yesterday evening I counseled with Ilyich; it was as if he stood alive before me, and he said: It is unpleasant for me to lie side by side with Stalin, who brought so much harm to the Party." The next day Stalin was moved.

Observers of the Soviet scene will probably long debate the reasons that impelled Khrushchev to use the forum of the Twenty-second Party Congress to reopen the subject of Stalin's crimes and to crown his attack with that last act of total repudiation, symbolized by the removal of Stalin's body from the mausoleum. Khrushchev's own official version in his concluding speech suggests that he would have gone much further in exposing Stalin's abuses of power at the Twentieth Party Congress had he not been hampered by the leaders of what later was to become known as the anti-Party group. According to him, they continued after the Twentieth Congress to sabotage his efforts, "fearing lest their part as accessories to mass repressions be brought to light." With the rout of the anti-Party group, the obstacle presumably was removed. "Our Party is doing this," Khrushchev proclaimed, "so that similar phenomena will never be repeated."

In saying this, Khrushchev may well have articulated the heartfelt hopes of the bulk of the Party membership, but the circumstances of the Congress suggest that Khrushchev's own motives were probably more complex. In assailing Stalin, Khrushchev was also attacking and seeking to denigrate the remnants of the anti-Party opposition within his own Party as well as the opposition outside. The elaborate documentation of the involvement of Molotov, Malenkov, Kaganovich, and Voroshilov in Stalinist repressions and the assault on the Stalinism of the Albanian Party leaders (and by implication also the Chinese) represented an effort to tar all these opposition elements with the same brush, to discredit and cauterize any past, present, or future opposition that might seek to rally under the Stalinist flag, which his most formidable rivals, the Chinese, still held high.

In launching this massive exposure of Stalinist repressions, Khrushchev appeared to be playing a somewhat dangerous game. It could hardly escape the notice of thoughtful people in the Soviet Union or outside that the Party leaders of Khrushchev's generation—personalities such as Mikoyan, Kuusinen, Shvernik, and the First Secretary himself—were themselves deeply involved in Stalin's crimes, and the question might well be raised as to why they still sit in the seats of the mighty, while Molotov and Company have been cast out. It may or may not be significant that Mikoyan, in the course of a long speech to the Congress (*Pravda*, October 29), made no reference to Stalinist repressions or to the involvement of the anti-Party group in them, but largely confined himself to setting forth his ideological differences with its members. Whether this much more cautious and gingerly approach to the problem points to differences with Khrushchev on how Stalin and the anti-Party group should have been handled must, in the present state of our knowledge, remain a matter for speculation. Perhaps more immediately meaningful is Khrushchev's obvious confidence that, as the winner in the intra-Party struggle, he can separate himself from all responsibility for the repressions of the Stalinist era. Since it is the victor who writes Soviet history, Khrushchev's confidence may not be misplaced.

The Plot That Failed

The role assigned to the anti-Party group at the Congress forms a fascinating story in itself. For the first time the Soviet public has been given a detailed, if still official, version of what happened in June, 1957, when the anti-Party group organized its so-called "arithmetical majority" in the Presidium to unseat Khrushchev. While much of the material now released on the June events became known outside the Soviet Union at the time through the unusually revealing dispatches of Giovanni Boffa in the Italian Communist paper *Unità* and of Michael Lucki in *Trybuna Ludu* (Warsaw), within the Soviet Union itself information was much more tightly restricted, and the wide-reaching ramifications of the conspiracy were only gradually divulged with the fall of Bulganin in 1958, and with the confessions of Pervukhin and Saburov at the Twenty-first Congress in early 1959. Now the Soviet populace has been officially informed that Voroshilov also joined in the plot, thus making clear that the so-called anti-Party group in the Presidium mobilized seven votes to Khrushchev's four, and that it was only the appeal to a hastily summoned special meeting of the Central Committee that saved Khrushchev.

The assault on the anti-Party group at the Congress had its antecedents in previous actions. At the Twenty-first Party Congress, I. V. Spiridonov, the Leningrad Party Secretary, N. V. Podgorny, the Ukrainian Party Secretary, and others close to Khrushchev launched a bitter attack on the anti-Party group and demanded that stern measures be taken against it. Despite their call for retribution, no further disciplinary action was invoked, and the members of the group were permitted to retain their Party cards. It was reasonably inferred at the time that there was a powerful segment of Party opinion that was not then prepared to support any form of drastic retaliation. While Khrushchev's decision to renew the attack at the Twenty-second Congress did not necessarily mean that such qualms had entirely evaporated, it did reflect his determination to crush his opponents and his confidence that the existing constellation of forces in the Party would support him.

The treatment of the anti-Party group at the Congress varied with its members. Saburov and Pervukhin were virtually ignored; both had previously confessed their sins and both were duly punished—Saburov by losing his seat on the Central Committee and by demotion to an obscure post as a factory manager, and Pervukhin by being deprived of his alternate status in the Party Presidium and his membership in the Central Committee. Bulganin, whose confession of "nominal" leadership of the anti-Party group had been made at the December, 1958, Central Committee Plenum, was also largely disregarded, except for a rather ominous passage in Shelepin's speech, in which he accused Bulganin of having stationed his bodyguards around the government building where the Party Presidium met in June, 1957, and charged that there was "evidence that the plotters were ready to resort to the most extreme measures to achieve their dirty aims." Shepilov, as an old *Pravda* editor, was reserved as a special target for Pavel Satyukov, the present occupant of that post. Denouncing Shepilov as a "careerist, political schemer, and double-dealer," who thought he saw how the wind was blowing and moved over to what he expected would be the winning side, Satyukov called for his expulsion from the Party along with the leaders of the anti-Party group (*Pravda*, October 27).

The role assigned to Voroshilov was uniquely piquant. Chosen as a member of the Congress Presidium, he was condemned to sit in silence while his reputation was besmirched. Rumor has it that he tried to gain the floor to reply when Polyansky taunted him with "the repression of innocent people, especially the cadres of military leaders" (*Pravda*, October 24), but that the chairman gaveled him down. His statement of recantation, which, "for health reasons," was read for him by someone else, was a pathetic tale of an old man who "had been led astray" (*Pravda*, October 29), but it provided an opening for Khrushchev to show clemency and forgiveness, and Khrushchev reveled in the part. Said Khrushchev (*Pravda*, October 29):

> Comrade Voroshilov has been sharply criticized. This criticism has been correct because he has made great mistakes, and Communists cannot forget them. But I feel that our approach to Comrade Voroshilov should be considerate and magnanimous. I believe he is sincere in condemning his actions and in his repentances. [He] has lived a long life, has done much good for our Party and the people. . . . I think that Klementi Yefremovich will actively fight together with us for the cause of our Party. (Stormy applause.)

If there was mercy for Voroshilov, there was none at all for Malenkov, Kaganovich, and Molotov, the leaders of the anti-Party group. Malenkov was denounced as a close associate of Yezhov and, later, Beria; he was accused of having been responsible with Yezhov for the decimation of the Belorussian Party in 1937, of having played equal havoc in Armenia and many other areas, and of bearing primary responsibility with Beria for the Leningrad purges in 1949 and 1952. Kaganovich was described as a sadist who had been responsible for mass arrests of leading transport workers and for similar purges in the Russian Republic and the Ukraine.

Molotov, too, was accused of direct responsibility for mass repressions, of cold inhumanity and stony indifference to the sufferings of the innocent, but the attack on him assumed broader dimensions. As an Old Bolshevik with a record of Party service that antedated Khrushchev's by far, and as an ideological spokesman of orthodox Leninism in its most revolutionary form, he posed a threat that the others did not. His most serious crime, it would appear, was that he remained unregenerate in his beliefs and that his ideological position largely coincided with that of the Chinese. As Satyukov described it (*Pravda,* October 27):

The delegates to the Congress must know that in October of this year, prior to the very opening of the Congress, Molotov sent a letter to the Central Committee. In this letter, without once mentioning his undermining factional activities against the Leninist Party, against the decisions of its Twentieth Congress, he again tried to appear in the role of an interpreter of Leninism and again attacked the Central Committee and the CPSU Draft Program.

... Molotov asserts that the new program is allegedly antirevolutionary in spirit. . . . Molotov declares that the Draft Program, if you please, does not tie up Communist construction in the U.S.S.R. with the prospects of revolutionary struggle of the working class in the capitalist countries, with the prospects for the world-wide Socialist revolution. . . .

Molotov goes so far as to make the monstrous statement that the Draft Program circumvents the difficulties of the struggle and orients the Party and people [toward the view] that the further advance toward Communism . . . will take place without revolutionary struggle. . . . Molotov asserts that the Draft Program contains pacifism and even revisionism. . . .

Without access to Molotov's letter, it is, of course, impossible to know how accurately Satyukov summed up its contents, but if its general direction is as represented, its resemblance to the Chinese position is striking. Indeed, it is not too farfetched to suggest that when Khrushchev's ideological spokesmen were directing their heaviest fire against Molotov, they were at the same time polemicizing with their Chinese adversaries. Khrushchev sought to make sure that the Chinese platform would have no resonance or response within the Soviet Party, on whose monolithic support he counted in his struggle for leadership of the world Communist camp.

The renewal of the attack on the anti-Party group inevitably raised the question of the strength it commanded in the Party. Did it still pose a threat to Khrushchev's hegemony in any way? Perhaps anticipating this question, Shelepin in his speech to the Congress declared: "We are speaking at our Congress about the anti-Party group not because it represents some kind of danger for the Party. Oh, no! The members of the anti-Party group are political corpses who do not represent any danger now, not even the shadow of a danger. We speak about these reactionaries to lay bare once more their true face, to underline once more their utter insignificance. . . ." On the basis of such information as is available, it is impossible to challenge Shelepin's description of the state of internal Party affairs. This much perhaps can be said. Even if the anti-Party group retained some secret sympathizers in the Party after the events of 1957, it is highly unlikely that they would have come out into the open in organized form once Khrushchev's strengthened position became so powerfully manifest. If this interpretation is correct, the resumption of the attack on the anti-Party group must be seen not as a testimonial to the immediate threat its members posed, but rather as a prophylactic action designed to destroy them forever as possible rallying points for any future opposition, to warn against the danger of factionalism in general, and to emphasize that those who are tempted to take such a path will have to pay a heavy price.*

* At this writing (November 11, 1961), no official announcements have been forthcoming on the fate of the anti-Party group. At the Congress, many delegates loudly demanded that Molotov, Malenkov, and Kaganovich

Insurance for the Future

The new Party rules adopted by the Congress (see *Pravda*, November 3) make clear that factional activity of any kind will not be tolerated. In a rather extraordinary paragraph (No. 27), which appears on its face to endorse the principle of inner-Party democracy, there is a warning that "broad discussion, especially discussions on an all-Union scale, of questions of Party policy must be carried out in such a way as to . . . prevent the possibility of attempts to form fractional groupings destructive to Party unity or of attempts to split the Party." To underline the point, F. R. Kozlov, in his report on the new Party rules (*Pravda*, October 29), stated:

> Naturally one must not allow a situation to come about in which the Party can be drawn into a sterile discussion at the whim of some small group of muddleheaded or immature people, in which individual anti-Party elements can undertake actions leading to the subversion of Party unity. . . . That is why the rules provide guarantees against attempts by an insignificant minority to force its will on the majority, as well as against attempts to form factional cliques and to split the Party.

The most important novelty in the Party rules is the adoption, in modified form, of the principle of rotation in office. Under the

---

be expelled from the Party, but it perhaps deserves notice that Mikoyan conspicuously refrained from joining in this demand, and that Khrushchev, while violently denouncing the group and never referring to any of its members except Voroshilov as "comrades," did not specifically call for their ejection from the Party. The Congress resolution on Khrushchev's Central Committee report also omitted any such demand, although it approved the measures taken by the Central Committee in exposing and "ideologically" routing the anti-Party group, and it also "indignantly" condemned their "subversive factional activity" (*Pravda*, October 31). According to *The New York Times* (November 8), when reporters asked Khrushchev at the preceding day's Kremlin reception if it had been decided what was to be done with Molotov, Khrushchev replied, "We have not decided. It is a matter of no practical importance."

new system, not less than one quarter of the members of the Presidium and of the Central Committee will be "renewed" at all regular elections, and Presidium members will "as a rule" not be elected for more than three successive terms. Outstanding individuals of proved usefulness, however, may serve in these bodies for longer terms, provided that they are re-elected by not less than three quarters of the votes cast in secret ballot. Central Committees of the Union-republic, territorial, and regional committees are to have at least one third of their membership "renewed" at each regular election, while lower Party committees will be similarly required to "renew" at least half their membership. Members of executive Party bodies at these levels "may be elected for not more than three terms," while secretaries of primary Party bodies "may be elected for not more than two successive terms." Again, special exceptions are to be made for highly qualified individuals, provided that they are re-elected by the necessary three-quarters majority.

In explaining these changes to the Congress, Khrushchev pointed out (*Pravda,* October 19) that they were designed to accomplish three purposes: (1) "to provide a guarantee against any recurrence of the cult of personality," (2) to open the way to the promotion of talented young people to leading Party posts, and (3) to enable the Party to root out leaders who organize "family circles" around them and engage in "mutual concealment of shortcomings and mistakes in work." While the rules on their face provide a formal mechanism by which even Khrushchev could be voted out of office, it is highly unlikely that this prospect occasions him any loss of sleep. More important than statutory niceties is the actual structure of power within the Party, and as long as Khrushchev retains a tight grip on the Party apparatus, it can safely be predicted that he will emerge as one of those Party workers who, in the language of the Party rules, "by virtue of their recognized authority and high political, organizational, or other abilities" are eligible to re-election to executive bodies "for a longer period." As Kozlov put it, "It is essential to say that the principle of a systematic renewal of the Party organs is closely linked with the principle of continuity of leadership. . . .

Without a more or less steady group of leaders, the continuity of leadership or the transfer of accumulated experience cannot be insured.

On the other hand, the Party rules sanction and legitimize what can only be described as a new form of permanent purge. In the hands of a strong Party leader like Khrushchev they can be manipulated not only to rid the Party apparatus of the inefficient and to make way for the able, but also to eliminate those who prove troublesome, to reward the faithful, and to maintain sufficient uncertainty about future prospects to evoke sustained effort as well as loyalty to the leader's cause.

Turnover in the Echelons

Data released at the Congress indicate that these processes of "renewal" are well under way (see Titov's Credential Commission Report, *Pravda*, October 22). At the present time, the Party includes 8,872,516 members and 843,489 candidates—9,716,005 in all—of whom more than one third have been added since the Twentieth Congress. According to Kozlov, "the composition of the central committees of Communist parties of Union republics and [of] *kraikoms* and *obkoms* at the last elections was renewed by 45 per cent, and the composition of *gorkoms* and *raikoms* by 40 per cent. The new Central Committee chosen by the Twenty-second Party Congress is substantially larger than its Twentieth Congress predecessor: 175 members and 155 candidates, compared with the respective 1956 totals of 133 and 122. Of the 1956 contingent of full members, less than one half were re-elected, and among the new alternate members, the overwhelming majority are new names.

Turnover at the Presidium level, although less drastic, was still substantial. Four members of the old Presidium—Mme. E. A. Furtseva, A. V. Aristov, N. A. Mukhitdinov, and N. G. Ignatov—were dropped from that body, and one new member—G. I. Voronov—added. Voronov, one-time First Secretary of the Orenburg *obkom*, where his leadership in producing a series of consistently good harvests attracted attention, was elevated to an alternate membership in the Presidium group in January, 1961, at which time he also became the First Deputy Chairman of the Russian Bureau of the Party. His promotion to membership in the Presidium recognizes his important role in leading a successful drive to lift agricultural output in the Russian Republic in 1961. As a result of these changes, the size of the Presidium has been reduced from fourteen to the following eleven full members: Khrushchev, Kozlov, Mikoyan, Suslov, Brezhnev, Kosygin, Podgorny, Polyansky, Kuusinen, Shvernik, and Voronov. Casualties among the alternate members were more extensive: A. E. Kalnberzin, A. P. Kirilenko, D. S. Korotchenko, P. N. Pospelov, and N. G. Pervukhin lost their places, while only two new alternates—S. R. Rashidov, the Uzbek First Secretary, and V. V. Scherbitsky, Chairman of the Ukrainian Council of Ministers—were added. The effect of these changes was to reduce the alternate list from nine to five, with only three alternates—Grishin, Mazurov, and Mahavanadze—re-elected.

At the same time, the number of the Central Committee secretaries was expanded from five to nine. Khrushchev, Kozlov, Suslov, and Kuusinen carried over from the old Secretariat, while the following five newcomers were added: A. N. Shelepin, head of the Soviet security police; P. N. Demichev, Moscow First Secretary; I. V. Spiridonov, Leningrad First Secretary; L. F. Ilyichev, in charge of Agitprop activities for the Union republics in the Central Committee Secretariat; and B. N. Ponomarev, a department chief in the Secretariat responsible for relations with the international Communist movement.

In announcing the composition of the new Secretariat, the Soviet press departed from the usual practice of listing members in alphabetical order and put Kozlov in second place, immediately after Khrushchev. Since Kozlov had already been singled out as the only official, aside from Khrushchev, to present a major report to the Congress, these moves were widely interpreted as implying that Kozlov was the designated heir apparent. Whether he will succeed over the years in validating his claims remains to be demonstrated.

The Congress on Balance

For the moment at least, Khrushchev's status as leader of the Soviet Communist Party appears to be beyond challenge. The paeans that were heaped on him at the Congress provided an almost embarrassing reminder of the Stalinist cult of personality that the Party was ostensibly repudiating. Indeed, so apparent was the parallel that Khrushchev himself was impelled to take note of it (*Pravda*, October 29):

> In many speeches at the Congress, and not infrequently in our press, special emphasis is laid on my person in discussing the activities of the Central Committee. My role is stressed in carrying out the most important measures of the Party and the government. Now I appreciate the kind sentiments guiding these comrades. May I, however, emphasize most emphatically that everything said about me should be addressed to the Central Committee of our Leninist Party, to the Presidium of the Central Committee. Not a single major measure, not a single responsible speech has been made on anyone's personal instructions; rather, these are the result of collective discussion and collective decisions. . . .

Even though historians with long memories will recall that Stalin, too, in his early days sang the virtues of collective leadership, there is danger in pushing the parallel too far. Unlike Stalin, Khrushchev seeks where he can to rest his power on persuasion rather than terror, and his style of leadership makes a place for consultative procedures both within and outside the ruling group. In contrast to Stalin, he has sought to incorporate his authority in the Party and to make it the paramount instrument of his rule. But, as the Twenty-second Congress demonstrated, Khrushchev remains a Stalinist in one important respect. There is no room in his formula of governance for oppositional factions, and any effort to derogate his personal authority is likely to receive short shrift.

If the result of the Congress was to confirm Khrushchev's place at the pinnacle of the Soviet power pyramid, the same cannot be said of his position in the international Communist movement. Despite his show of strength at the Congress, the Albanian Party leaders continued to defy him from Tirana, and the Chinese Party leadership openly identified itself with the Albanian cause. The effect of the Congress was to dramatize the rift in the world Communist movement and to set the stage for a continuing struggle for ascendancy between Khrushchev and Mao. While the reverberations of the struggle will probably be contained within the Soviet Union itself, the severity of the attack on Molotov's criticism of the Party program may well have been intended not merely as a rebuke to the Chinese, but as a warning to those elements in the Soviet Party who might be tempted to echo his heretical views. The perspective that Khrushchev unveiled at the Congress—its promise that Communism will eventually triumph on a world scale without a nuclear *Götterdämmerung*—is likely to find a much more powerful sounding board of support within the Soviet Union and the other more industrially advanced nations in the Soviet bloc than it will with Communist leaders in the less advanced nations who seek a quick road to power and find themselves held back by Soviet counsels of restraint. The Chinese demand for a more aggressive strategy undoubtedly appeals to the latter group. The fissures that have already revealed themselves in such important outposts of Asian Communism as the Indian and Indonesian parties, as well as elsewhere, are symptomatic of the strain.

The Twenty-second Party Congress did not relieve these tensions. If anything, it exacerbated them. The Chinese leaders were not overawed by the loyal legions Khrushchev succeeded in mobilizing. The vision of the Communist future unveiled at the Congress left a most important question unanswered: Whose vision, Khrushchev's or Mao's?

THE ECONOMY:
PROBLEMS, PROSPECTS

Introduction

The Soviet economy under Stalin was unique in a number of ways, including in its extreme, thorough centralization and in its neglect of the consumer in favor of the industrial and military might of the state. These features gave rise to various phenomena: There was (and still is) the widespread practice of corruption and pilfering (described in Joseph Berliner's article); to hypocrisy, stemming from the need to reconcile a glaringly inequitable system with an ideology that claims to be concerned with the welfare and happiness of the individual (see the article by Leon Herman); there was the allegiance to Marxist economic theories that clashed with the rational imperatives of an increasingly intricate industrial system (a contradiction that became more and more conspicuous toward the end of the Stalin era—see the articles by Alec Nove and Gregory Grossman). Above all, there was the growing realization that the Stalinist system, while fulfilling the immediate function of converting a backward agricultural society—quickly, brutally, and regardless of the human cost—into a powerful industrial state, in many respects proved to be an obstacle rather than an asset to the further expansion of the Soviet economy: Agriculture was in a state of near-collapse; Soviet living standards were abysmally low; and the population at large was apathetic, exhausted after years of continuous sacrifices, and lacking in any incentives for further exertions.

It was inevitable, therefore, that the economy, just as any other

area of Soviet life, would have to undergo some changes once a
new leadership, more rationally oriented and somewhat more
responsive to the needs of the population, came into power. The
way in which the new leaders set about to correct the unhappy
state of affairs, their successes and failures—the latter stemming,
above all, from the unwillingness to change any essential aspect
of the Soviet economic system—form the substance of the following articles. The first two (by Berliner and Herman) are mainly
concerned with certain basic features of the Soviet economy;
the others examine some of the most important policies of the
Khrushchev regime. For other analyses of the Soviet economic
system, the reader is referred to the articles by Arcadius Kahan
in the fourth section of the book ("The Society") and to the
symposium "Toward a 'Communist Welfare State'?"

Blat *Is Higher Than Stalin*

——JOSEPH S. BERLINER

THAT ANYTHING AT ALL was "higher" than the late almighty lord of the Communist world may come as a surprise. Yet the proverb "*blat* is higher than Stalin" falls easily from the lips of any former Soviet citizen when talking about life in the U.S.S.R. An investigation of the meaning and function of this phenomenon opens the door to some interesting observations on the role of illegality in Soviet industrial organization.

The word *blat* is an old one in the Russian language, but it has taken on a new meaning in Soviet society. In the pre-Revolutionary period, the jargon of underworld thieves and hoodlums was known as the *blat* language. Modern Soviet dictionaries define the expression "by *blat*" as "by protection or patronage," or "in an illegal manner." In common Soviet usage, *blat* refers to the use of personal influence to secure some favor to which a person is not lawfully entitled. Thus the proverb "*blat* is higher than Stalin" means that any law or regulation can be circumvented if one has the right connections. Other common folk sayings that refer to the same theme are: "*Blat* is higher than the Council of Peoples' Commissars," and "You've got to have ZIS." (In this proverb, ZIS is a play on words. It refers both to the famous Soviet-make automobile known as the ZIS and to the initial letters of the expression "acquaintanceship and connections" [*znakomstvo i sviazy*].

In the sphere of industrial management, the use of *blat* is most important as a means of expediting the supply of materials. The Soviet manager faces the perpetual threat that promised materials will neither be delivered on time nor in the right quantity and quality; in trying to make good these deficiencies, he is hampered by a maze of regulations and restrictions imposed by the state. Unable to obtain the materials through legal channels, he turns to the use of *blat*. If he or the members of his staff have the right connections in the right places, it is usually possible to obtain needed materials by unlawful means. A typical illustration of the technique is the following verbatim statement of a former citizen who had been a supply agent in a Soviet plant:

Say the factory needs some writing paper. The chief of the purchasing department does not worry about this. He will simply tell his agent to go out and get it. We did receive an allocation of paper, but it was not sufficient. We needed 150 kilograms more than we were allowed by allocation. We got this by *blat*. Say I had an allocation for 250 kilograms. I always used to get my paper from a particular store in Leningrad. Since I always got it there, I soon developed an acquaintanceship there. I need 500 kilograms, but my allocation is only for 250. The accountant gives me only enough money for 250 kilograms, but the director gives me enough money out of the director's fund to get the extra paper.* Then I go out to the warehouse, or perhaps to the store itself. The store is not allowed to give me so much paper at retail, but I know the manager personally, and he can give me 1,000 sheets instead of only 10. In the warehouse I also get another 100 sheets by *blat*.

That the practice of obtaining supplies illegally is widespread is indicated by frequent denunciations of individual managers in the Soviet press. But a full understanding of the technique of *blat* can only be gained from people who no longer live in the Soviet Union. The nature of the personal influence needed to arrange such *blat* negotiations varies from case to case. Most

* The director's fund is a fund into which a certain proportion of the enterprise's profits are paid. The money is supposed to be spent on such things as workers' housing and bonuses, but apparently the director sometimes uses it for helping the enterprise out of financial difficulties.

deals are based upon some sort of reciprocation—the person who receives the favor today repays with a like favor in the future. If a paint-manufacturing enterprise illegally supplies paint to a furniture manufacturer, the furniture manufacturer reciprocates by declaring one of its tables "damaged" and selling it to the paint manufacturer at a nominal price. Since such deals are illegal, a certain degree of mutual trust must exist between the persons involved. This trust is based upon family kinship or upon friendship developed in the course of a long business or social intercourse. Since every manager or official realizes his own fate may some day depend upon being able to obtain a favor by *blat*, most are willing to risk rendering favors. The use of friendship to arrange an illegal deal is illustrated by a case exposed in the Soviet industrial newspaper *Chernaia metallurgia* (November 30, 1940). A certain Iakov Lukich Karnarukov, an official in the Commissariat of Agriculture, had been ordered to obtain 150 tons of coke, for which he did not have an allocation and which, therefore, he had no legal right to purchase. He forthwith wrote to his "former colleague but now just good friend" Konstantin Mikhailovich Zolotarevskii, who was Deputy Commercial Director of the Nikitovsk Dolomite Combine. Unfortunately, he did not take the precaution of stamping the letter "personal." Zolotarevskii was out of town on business when it arrived, and someone in the office opened it. The contents eventually found their way into the newspaper of the Commissariat. The relevant part of the letter, after the usual friendly greeting and news, is as follows:

I am approaching you as a magician and wizard in commercial matters. This is the problem. We have to obtain 150 tons of coke for the use of the Commissariat of Agriculture. Since we have no way of getting it, I have arranged with my boss to pay out a certain sum of wages, the amount of which you yourself are to name. And I am approaching you with the request that you figure out and name the sum that will satisfy you if you can arrange to ship 100 tons of coke to Leningrad and 50 tons to Moscow. You there in Khanzhenkov have a hand that has always come to the rescue in

time of need. Payment will be made immediately upon presentation of the bill. Do not fail to state the price of the coke.

I am sure that you, Konstantin Mikhailovich, will not
refuse to satisfy my request and earn a little milk for the
kiddies.

So important to the success of an enterprise is a widely cultivated *blat* that it could not be left to the haphazard personal
acquaintanceship of the individual members of the staff of the
enterprise. As often happens in a social system when a certain
essential function has to be performed, the process of the division
of labor operated to create a special occupational category. In
the Soviet economy this occupation is performed by the "pusher,"
or *tolkach*. The pusher is a man who specializes in *blat*, who
makes a profession of cultivating a large number of acquaintances
upon whom he can rely to obtain certain materials illegally.
Soviet citizens have some very definite ideas about the stereotype
of the pusher. He is a lively, energetic man who knows how to
"drink with people," how to talk his way into the inner offices of
a factory, how to establish a working friendship with the proper
officials. He usually resides in a city in which he has a large
number of connections, and he has as his "accounts" a number
of out-of-town enterprises that carry him on their staff lists as
"representative," although on paper he works for just one of
them. Sometimes his influence is limited to a particular range of
products—he may be a specialist in "leather *blat*" or "coal *blat*."
Other pushers are able to obtain anything at all, for a price. The
boldness of the approach of a pusher is indicated in the following
report by a correspondent of the newspaper *Industriia* (April 5,
1940):

Recently N. S. Kovezo arrived at the Dnepropetrovsk Office
of the Chief Purchasing Administration of Nonferrous
Metals* and introduced himself:
   "Let's get acquainted!"

---

* This organization purchases many of the materials needed by enterprises
of the Commissariat of Nonferrous Metallurgy, and resells them to the
enterprises.

"I beg your pardon? What has brought you here?"

"Here is the telegram. I have to get something from you. . . ."

The arrangement, of course, did not come off.

We asked Comrade Dudnitskii to describe the "activity" [of Kovezo] more fully. It seems that this man comes as the representative of various organizations, receiving from each of them huge salaries. There are many such people, if you please, in Dnepropetrovsk. Very often they are spawned by the purchasing organizations themselves. It is usually done in this way. Suppose that an office has to obtain a quantity of decentralized materials in Zaporozh'e.* In order to get around the law, which forbids them to have special representatives for this, inhabitants of Zaporozh'e are taken into employment as "consultants" and are listed as "residing" in Dnepropetrovsk. They even keep a list of them. Such "business" is engaged in by many of the purchasing organizations of the Commissariats of Nonferrous Metallurgy, Construction, Petroleum, etc.

Since the work of the pusher is illegal, it is potentially dangerous, and he is therefore recompensed with extremely high earnings. Part of his earnings is direct salary, but much is in the form of special gifts from grateful plant managers, liberal expense accounts, and profitable transactions he is able to negotiate because of his wide knowledge of sources of supply and demand. In this respect he is the Soviet prototype of the capitalist "middleman," although he might be said to be "socialist in form, capitalist in content." From time to time the authorities have made efforts to eliminate the abuses involved in this illegal method of getting things done. Limits have been established on the amount of time officials may spend away from their enterprises on travel missions. Imprisonment of from two to five years has been prescribed for people guilty of selling or exchanging materials or equipment illegally. But the importance of the

---

* Decentralized materials are nonpriority goods that may be purchased freely by the user without an allocation. The implication here is that pushers deal only in decentralized materials and would not dare to negotiate illegal deals in centrally allocated materials.

pusher's function in helping the enterprise to fulfill its plan is so great that mere legislation has not been able to stamp it out. There are indications that state officials whose prime concern is production tend to "close one eye" to the activities of these helpful persons who are willing to stick their necks out for high remuneration. Even officials of the secret police are not above accepting little gifts, such as a bottle of vodka or a few pairs of shoes, to "look the other way." As noted before, the best hint of the continued and vigorous activity of the pushers is provided by condemnation of the practice in the Soviet press. In the humor magazine *Krokodil* (March 30, 1952), for example, there appears a delightful line drawing of a typical pusher and a poem describing his activity. The poem is so revealing that it merits quotation in part:

Anton Fomich is irreplaceable,
One feels safe with him, comfortable with him.
However much the official estimates interfere,
He always finds a roundabout way
Of arranging this, of fixing that,
Of working out any business problem,
Of getting from the warehouse, without an allocation,
Everything that is needed and even what is not needed,
And having received a wagonload of this,
Of exchanging this for that,
Of making the plan easier, of writing something off,
Of concealing reserves, of passing off rejects . . .
Iron, nails, lumber, bricks,
Who will get it? Anton Fomich.
How will he get it? Right out of the ground.
All hush-hush, under cover,
So that no one can ever trip him up . . .
Without him management often
Cannot move a step.
Management is always so comfortable with him.
Always, in every kind of weather,
He dives into the coldest water for management,
And always emerges dry . . .

The use of *blat* is only one of several illegal methods to which management is forced to resort in order to carry out the production tasks imposed by the state. A study of official Soviet sources reveals a number of other interesting practices, among which *strakhovka* is one of the most prominent. Literally, the word means "insurance" or "security." The concept covers a wide variety of specific actions, all of which have in common the desire for a bit of slack, for a safety factor unknown to the state authorities, upon which management can draw when it is unable to fulfill its plan. One incidence of *strakhovka* concerns the attempts by management to have the planned production target of their enterprises set at a level well below what they know can be produced. For example, if the managers know they can produce a million yards of cloth, they falsely report their maximum capacity at 900,000 yards, hoping thereby to allow a margin for error and mishap. Proof of the widespread practice of this unlawful "reduced planning" comes from the frequent condemnations of enterprises, and indeed of ministries too, that indulge in it. "In the Ministry of the Coal Industry," writes a Soviet commentator, "production capacities that were below the output which had actually been achieved were used for a number of mines. . . . In the Ministry of the Lumber and Paper Industry, the production capacities used were below the output actually achieved." Despite repeated exhortations from the state authorities, managerial officials at all levels apparently indulge in this practice.

Errors and inefficiency occur most frequently in the supply and delivery of materials, and the desire for a "safety valve" is most keenly felt in this area. A common device to which management resorts is the deliberate overstatement of the quantity of materials the enterprise needs to fulfill the production plan. As a former accountant in a Soviet enterprise put it: "We always submitted estimates for materials with a little bit of fat." If, for example, an enterprise knows that 100,000 pounds of cotton are sufficient to produce the planned output of textiles, it reports its requirements as 110,000 pounds. Sometimes the Ministry will cut the "fat" off, but often it does not, in part because it cannot check on the needs of every enterprise, and more likely because it also has a stake in seeing the plan fulfilled. This "padding of estimates" of materials has been roundly condemned again and again in words that clearly emphasize its unlawful character. Yet the practice persists:

> Thus in 1950, some consumers presented to the planning organs statements of material requirements for metal, equipment, automatic machines, lumber products, and other kinds of products that exceeded their actual consumption by 20 to 30 per cent. . . . The striving by some managers and purchasing officials to receive excess materials and to "preserve" them is a manifestation of enterprise-centered, narrow-minded bureaucratic and essentially antistate tendencies; it is a manifestation of the remnants of capitalism in the consciousness of the people.*

A companion device to overordering is the practice of hoarding stocks of materials in case the materials ordered do not arrive. To restrain the hoarding tendencies of managers, the state requires that an upper limit be placed upon the quantity of materials an enterprise may hold in inventory at any time. The unlawful hoarding of materials in excess of the official upper limits is one of the most persistent problems with which the Soviet state has to deal. Again and again, managers are severely criticized for keeping in stock millions of rubles worth of excess materials and equipment for which they have no need but which they hold in store "just in case." In the Engine of the Revolution Plant, "538,000 rubles worth of metal products have not been touched for about a year and a half." In 1950, the Kirov Plant had fifty machines, some of which had lain idle since 1939, and some since 1945. To the manager, always seeking to protect himself against the failure of deliveries or against the breakdown of worn-out equipment, every extra ton of coal in the bins and every idle machine kept on hand constitutes another inch of safety margin.

* E. Lokshin, "Problems of the Planning of Material-Technical Supply in the National Economy of the U.S.S.R.," *Planovoe khoziaistvo*, No. 2 (1950), p. 54.

Stocking against future shortages is not the only motive behind the hoarding of materials: There is also benefit to be derived from the unlawful exchange or outright sale of excess materials or equipment. Officially, materials and equipment are put at the disposal of a manager to be used for production targeted in advance by the state. To redirect these resources to other enterprises is to devote them to uses that have not been planned, and the plan, as the manager is repeatedly warned, is law. Nevertheless, in the prewar period, the practice of trading, exchanging, and reselling materials and equipment was commonplace. This was especially true of industrial commodities having alternative uses as consumer goods, such as linoleum, leather, work clothes, and so forth. An official of a purchasing organization complained in the *Chernaia metallurgia* (April 26, 1941): "Everybody took work clothes to excess. Right here, around my desk, stood the supply agents, and they asked for everything which fell into their hands. And once they left the office and entered the street they exchanged gloves for iron, bedding for paints...."

Managers and their supply agents and pushers spent a good deal of time rummaging about other enterprises and supply depots seeking to purchase or exchange anything that might some day be of conceivable use to the enterprise. Malenkov related the following incident in his report to the Eighteenth Conference of the Communist Party in early 1941:

In 1940, the Central Urals Copper Refining Plant in Sverdlovsk region sold an armature to the Office of the Chief Purchasing Administration of Nonferrous Metals for 100,000 rubles. And then a curious thing happened. At the same time the director sold this armature, the so-called agent of this plant was out looking for all kinds of materials and equipment for the enterprise. In the course of his searching he came to the warehouse of the Chief Purchasing Administration of Nonferrous Metals and saw there an armature that seemed good to him. Not knowing that this armature had just been sold by his own plant, the agent bought it and brought it home to the plant, having paid 111,000 rubles. Can you imagine, Comrades, what sort of order exists in this enterprise?

In reality, in the case of such "operations," if you will excuse the expression, the director should have been thrown out of business, but since it is generally taken for granted that all such stupidities are carried out at the state's expense, the director feels perfectly at ease. I suppose the director even received a bonus for a shrewd sale and the agent received a bonus for a shrewd purchase.

One more group of illegal activities merits reporting because of its wide prevalence and its intimate relation to the normal problems of management. This is referred to by the Soviets as "simulation," or "pulling the wool over someone's eyes." The price of failure is high in the Soviet Union, and the expedient manager will spare no effort to fulfill his production plan in any way he can. If the target simply cannot be met, then plan fulfillment must be simulated by one of a number of devices. The most obvious one is the falsification of production records, that is, reporting a higher output than has actually been achieved. That indulgence in this practice is widespread is again attested to by former Soviet citizens and by indirect references in Soviet literature and the press. In 1940, the state bank harshly criticized enterprises that resorted to such falsification, citing as an example the Dynamo Plant, whose plan fulfillment, reported as being 110 per cent, was later found to be only 77 per cent. Similar complaints have continued in the postwar period. In a case reported in *Izvestia* (November 21, 1952), a plant director "entered into the shipping department's invoices footwear that, in fact, had not been received," thus simulating his December plan fulfillment at 100.8 per cent, when actually it was 73.9 per cent. A loom manager, fearing that his August plan would not be fulfilled, "made up some kind of statistics" and then gave "strict orders to include the output of the first days of September in the August plan, and, of course, to draw up appropriate 'records' for this purpose" (*Vecherniaia Moskva*, November 22, 1952). These are not isolated instances.

Falsifying production records is the most obvious, and perhaps

declared to be his "holy obligation" in the "burning, passionate defense of the state's interest." To inspire the "proper" managerial attitude, the state has established a number of incentives. First, because of the socialist ideology in which Bolshevism was nurtured, official literature stresses such social incentives as service to the people and to socialism. Great esteem is accorded the successful manager, his picture is published in papers, and he is awarded medals and decorations. But the regime also knows the value of material self-interest, and since the inception of the Five Year Plans, it has not allowed old socialist ideas of equality to stand in the way of material incentives. Thus the manager's social position is bolstered by certain material privileges: He enjoys a high salary, is often furnished a good apartment and perhaps a summer cottage in the country, and has access to an automobile and chauffeur provided by the enterprise. The important role officially ascribed to the self-interest principle is illustrated in the following excerpt from the special volume on the U.S.S.R. of the *Great Soviet Encyclopedia*, in words strikingly reminiscent of the "invisible hand" of Adam Smith:

> Socialism not only does not deny the material self-interest of working people in the results of their labor, but in fact raises this self-interest to a higher plane than any previous production method. The material self-interest of socialist working people in raising the productivity of their labor is directed toward the good of all the people, toward the strengthening and growth of the social wealth.

Material incentives for the managers also take the form of special bonuses for successful performance. Most of these bonuses are awarded for overfulfillment of the production plan, and they are large. For example, the director of a machine-building plant may earn up to 37 per cent of his basic salary simply for fulfilling his plan, and up to 4 per cent for every overfulfillment of his plan. In 1947, of the total earnings of engineering and technical personnel in the Ministry of Ferrous Metallurgy, 51.4 per cent were bonuses. All evidence points to the fact that these bonuses constitute a major motivating factor among managerial officials at all levels, from director down to shop chief. The state has further enhanced the importance placed upon bonuses by identifying them with successful performance; bonuses are now desired not only for their own sake but as a symbol of good work. The manager who does not earn large bonuses is considered a manager of dubious ability; if he is less motivated by material advantage than by love of creation or patriotism, he must nevertheless engage in the same action as those who are interested mainly in their own incomes and their careers.

Assuming, then, that the manager desires above all to fulfill and overfulfill the plan, whether for the sake of bonuses or for other reasons, there are two conditions of the economic milieu under which he must operate that lead to the widespread use of the illegal practices described above. The first is the effort of the state to obtain the maximum possible output from the enterprise. Toward this end the state requires that the production plan of the enterprise be as high as possible. The target is always set at least as high as the output actually produced in the past period, and if possible higher. Thus, every time the manager succeeds in overfulfilling his plan, he knows that in the next period his plan will be higher; and the more he overfulfills his plan the harder it will be to overfulfill next time. The consequence is a perpetual drive for more and more production, which keeps the manager in a constant state of tension.

The second condition is the general scarcity of commodities and the system of controls over the supply of materials. Since the total output of the economy can be increased to the extent that a smaller quantity of materials are used per unit of output, the state seeks to set the allocation of materials for each enterprise at an absolute minimum. At the same time, control over the distribution of important commodities is shared by a number of organizations, which results in a maze of bureaucratic inefficiency. With output plans set maximally high and materials minimally low, enterprises frequently fail to fulfill their plans or just as frequently indulge in some sort of simulation, such as producing an unplanned combination of products or reducing the quality of output. As a result, other enterprises are unable to obtain needed materials and they, too, fail to fulfill their plans.

Underfulfillment in one enterprise leads to a chain of underfulfillments in other enterprises that fail to receive even the minimum of material they were promised by plan. In the reality of
Soviet plant management, then, the manager is never sure that
the materials ordered will be delivered on time or in the right
quantity and quality; and if the ordered commodities are not
delivered, the enterprise is legally barred from buying them elsewhere. The problems associated with the supply of materials are
perhaps the greatest bane in the work of the manager. "An
especially large number of complaints by plant officials," wrote
the editors of the industrial newspaper *Mashinostroenie* on January 11, 1940, "deal with the completely unsatisfactory system
of planning the supply of materials to factories and with the
allocation and sale of centrally controlled materials." The reasons
for the serious deficiencies of the system of supply cannot be
explored here, but they are closely related both to the high rate
of investment the state has imposed upon the economy and to the
bureaucratic inefficiencies of a highly centralized system of industrial allocation. To the manager it means that the operation of
his plant is constantly threatened by a shortage of one or another
material.

This, then, is the situation in which the manager finds himself.
His own material interests in fulfilling the plan for the sake of
bonuses and the advancement of his career are encouraged by
the social honors accorded to the manager who regularly fulfills
his plan. Fulfillment of the plan is the gateway to managerial
success. Yet all the force of the state, mobilized in the Party,
trade unions, and other social organizations, is directed at the
periodic raising of the level of the plan and the reduction of the
planned use of labor and materials. If the production plan is
overfulfilled in one year, the plan for the following year must be
raised and thereby becomes more difficult to achieve; and if the
manager succeeds in raising labor productivity in one year, he
will be allowed less labor for fulfilling a higher plan the next
year. At the same time, there hovers over his head the constant
danger that his machines will not stand the pace and will break
down; that spare parts will not be readily available to repair
defective machines, that the crucial materials needed for ful-

filling the plan will not arrive, or that they will be of poor quality. Nor are there any reasons that are accepted as valid for
failure to fulfill the plan. To plead "objective conditions" is to
admit defeat—there are no "objective conditions" the Bolshevik
manager cannot overcome. The order, indeed the law, is to fulfill
the plan: If you cannot do it, someone else will be found who can.

This depiction of the managerial role, based on numerous
interviews with former Soviet economic officials, on Soviet economic writings, and on Soviet novels, explains the widspread
evasion of laws and regulations. Rather than suffer the consequences of failure to fulfill the plan, the manager will seek some
way of simulating plan fulfillment. He will report as completed
in the present month output on which work has not even begun.
He will greatly overproduce those products that count for most
in the computation of plan fulfillment and neglect products that
are in short supply. He will produce tractors without headlights
and toothbrushes with vanishing bristles, if only the value of
output is fulfilled. To secure a low target level and thereby gain
a margin of safety, he will conceal some of his machines. He will
insist that he needs not 1,000 tons of coal but 2,000, hoping that
if he is allowed 2,000 tons, perhaps 1,000 will be delivered. And
if the 1,000 tons do not arrive, he will send his agents out to
other enterprises, armed with scarce commodities to give as gifts,
with orders to buy or exchange some of his hoarded materials for
the material that threatens to hold up his production.

The widespread evasion of laws is encouraged not only by the
system of incentives and the conditions of operation, but, finally,
by forces at work in the system that lead the manager to expect
to get away with his illegal action. For many of these illegal
actions actually help rather than hinder the functioning of the
economy. For example, management's manipulations to secure a
safety margin help assure that plans will not be set unrealistically
high; hence, since underfulfillment in one plant leads to a chain
of successive underfulfillments in other enterprises, the safety
factor helps keep down the extent of underfulfillment in the
system as a whole. And *blat* undoubtedly succeeds in moving
into production machines and materials that otherwise might
have lain idle in enterprises for an indefinite period. Take, for

example, the following typical situation described by Mikoyan, which illustrates the inefficiencies that frequently arise because of the bureaucratic red tape in which Soviet industry is snarled:

There are cases in which a large amount of cement is lying around on one construction project because there is not enough iron. On another construction project in the same city, iron is lying around idle because there is no cement, and therefore work is held up in both places. All that is required is that the cement and iron be transferred between the two construction projects, and both would continue working. But since they are different construction projects, different commissariats, the materials are frozen. This leads to the idleness of keenly needed materials, instead of using them up as rapidly as possible.

It is precisely in such a situation that the pusher makes his usefulness felt. It is he who learns that one project has some extra cement and another has some extra iron, and it is through his *blat* connections that he arranges a mutually satisfactory exchange. Without him, both projects might fail to meet their plans while waiting months for permission from the "proper" officials of both ministries to exchange the materials legally. Not only the construction enterprises but the ministries, too, benefit, since it is to their advantage to have their enterprises fulfill their plans. The Party secretary in the enterprise and the local Party organization benefit as well, since plan fulfillment by their enterprises reflects well upon their own records. In short, plan fulfillment is so important in the Soviet economy that—all the way up the line of the hierarchy, perhaps to the Politburo itself—the major measure by which a senior judges the performance of a junior is the successful plan fulfillment of the enterprises within his jurisdiction. Realizing this measure of performance, and aware that some evasion of the law is necessary if the plan is to be fulfilled, persons at all levels of authority are motivated to "look the other way" at the successful transgressions of their successful managers. Because all are dependent upon plan fulfillment, the honest man who refuses to break a law or who impedes the execution of an illegal action will soon be forced out. Malenkov hinted at this situation in his speech to the Nineteenth Congress of the Soviet CP in October, 1952:

> Not infrequently, officials who are honest and competent, but alert to and intolerant of defects and therefore disturbing to the peace of mind of the administration, are ousted under various pretexts and replaced with individuals of dubious merits or even wholly unfit for the job but compliant and pleasing to certain administrators. . . . As a consequence of such distortions of the Party line in the selection and advancement of personnel, there emerge in some organizations close coteries of people who are bound together by mutual protection and who place the interests of the group above the interests of the Party and state. It is no wonder that such situations ordinarily lead to corruption and degeneration.

The pressure upon the manager to fulfill the plan and the conditions in which he has to operate explain why he has to resort to illegal action. But it is the "mutual protection" referred to by Malenkov that explains the *extent* of illegality. For the manager knows that many of the officials responsible for enforcement of the laws are, for the sake of their own careers, too dependent upon his ability to fulfill his plans to report him when he evades the laws. Even the minister himself wants to be able to report that the plan has been fulfilled, and can therefore be expected to "look the other way" if the quality of output has been reduced or *blat* has been used. Of course, certain state organizations, such as the Ministry of State Control or the Ministry of Finance, are not as dependent for their own records upon the successful performance of the enterprise, and it is these organizations that have to be feared. Because of these controlling agencies, the manager does not commit his illegal acts without trepidation, for he knows that from time to time some managers are caught and end up in jail. But if he lets fear stand in his way, the conditions of the economic system will soon make it impossible for him to fulfill his plan. Undoubtedly many persons succumb to their fears, but these are the unsuccessful managers, those who are replaced by others more willing to take chances. The successful manager, the one who climbs swiftly to the top and makes a brilliant career, is the one who is willing to hazard arrest and imprisonment. There is a selective process at work that raises the risktaker to the top and causes the timid to fall by the wayside. It is in this sense that breach of law is an integral part of the operation of the Soviet economy.

Postscript

In the more than half-dozen years since this article was written, a number of dramatic reforms have been introduced in the Soviet industrial organization. The published sources are not very helpful in providing information on the impact of the reforms on managerial practice, but they do afford some indication of the areas in which change may have occurred.

One series of reforms has eliminated the criminal sanctions that used to bedevil the lives of managers. Unauthorized exchange or resale of supplies is no longer a criminal offense, and the procedures for obtaining authorization have reportedly been simplified. Thus the volume of illegal activity must, by definition, have been reduced, even if there has been no actual reduction in the volume of unauthorized activity. Moreover, the abolition of criminal sanctions may well have encouraged the practice of hoarding, for there is now less danger in exchanging hoarded surpluses for other materials.

The volume of unauthorized exchange of supplies depends on the manager's confidence in the efficiency of the supply system. We have evidence that managers are not yet prepared to trust the planning system to provide them with a smooth flow of the supplies they need to meet their targets. Sharp denunciations of the army of *tolkachi* and of the abuse of expense accounts continue to appear in the Soviet press.

A second group of reforms granted enterprise directors more authority by widening the scope of their discretionary powers and making them somewhat less dependent on higher agencies. The merits of such changes are clear enough, but the dangers are not as readily apparent. According to *Izvestia* (April 4, 1959), an official of the State Control Commission has recently given us a fascinating illustration of the unintended consequence of administrative change. A decree of 1956 relieved managers of the duty to provide detailed accounts of all their plant expenditures, with the meritorious objective of increasing their scope of independent action. The consequence, according to the official, is a sharp increase in the employment of *tolkachi*. Indeed, the patchwork pattern of the post-Stalin reforms is reflected in the numerous instances in which a new measure designed to remedy a problem in one area led to an unintended resurgence of an old problem in another area.

Something of the sort has happened as a result of the most celebrated of the reforms, the replacement of the central ministries by regional councils of the national economy (sovnarkhozes). The reform did eliminate the old problem of *vedomstvennost*—that is, of collusion between directors and their ministries—at the expense of enterprises subordinated to other ministries. But any old hand could have predicted that the measure would, as it did, lead to a distressing surge of *mestnichestvo*—that is, of collusion between directors and their new local chiefs—at the expense of enterprises in other geographical jurisdictions.

There is one recent development that, more than any of the administrative reforms, may lead to a radical change in the practices of management. There seems to be a hesitant move toward more realistic production targets. In 1957, the unprecedentedly low figure of 7.1 per cent was announced for the annual planned increase in industrial production. To be sure, the persons responsible for that low target were subsequently fired from their jobs,[*] but the pressure for more realistic targets later reasserted itself in the repudiation of the Sixth Five Year Plan and the substitution of the Seven Year Plan with its much less ambitious targets. Should the new, more realistic approach to planning assert itself

---

[*] At the time the 1957 plan was formulated, there were two all-Union planning agencies, the State Economic Commission and the State Planning Commission. M. G. Pervukhin was chairman of the former, and N. K. Baibakov of the latter. Three months after the presentation of the unfortunate 7.1 per cent target, both men were reassigned to other jobs. See *Pravda*, February 6, 1957; May 3, 1957; and May 5, 1957.

permanently—if, in other words, production goals should become more capable of fulfillment rather than being inordinately high figures designed to mobilize extraordinary effort—then the atmosphere within which managerial activity is conducted will be fundamentally altered. The *tolkach* thrives in an economic soil watered by shortages and fertilized by unrealistic targets.

Taxes and the Soviet Citizen

——LEON M. HERMAN

THE ECONOMY OF THE Soviet Union, like that of most other nations, is based on money. Goods and services are regularly paid for in currency, at conventional prices, regardless of whether they are exchanged between the government and the population or among the economic agencies of the state. In the course of discharging its functions, the Soviet government, too, annually incurs the standard "overhead" expenses for defense, administration, education, and other public services. Like its counterparts everywhere, the regime solves its budgetary problems with the time-honored device of taxation.

At this point, however, the similarity ceases. For in collecting revenues, just as in other matters of public policy, the Soviet government is unhampered by the constraints of political consent. The Soviet citizen has no voice in deciding how large his tax burden will be nor in the methods of collection. In fact, he does not even know how much tax money he is paying at any given time, because, unlike all modern states, the Soviet Union chooses to collect the bulk of its tax moneys through a system of indirect, hidden taxation. Today, nearly 50 per cent of all budget revenue and 85 per cent of all taxes on the population are raised through excise taxes on goods sold to consumers in the stores. The Soviet tax system is thus something of an iceberg: Only about 15 per cent rides above the surface, while most of the tax-collecting operation takes place out of sight, in the form of a special mark-up over and above profits and distribution costs, on all goods sold to the population.

In token form, an income tax still exists in the U.S.S.R. In 1958, it provided less than 8 per cent of the total revenue in the state budget, and its fiscal role is thus quite negligible. But by displaying prominently the very low sums levied on income, and reporting them officially as the only tax moneys collected "from the population"—as opposed to the huge excise taxes collected "from the economy"—the Soviet regime has made the best of the income tax in the field of political propaganda. And so, satisfied no doubt with the ingenious use to which the tax was put, the Soviet leaders have long watched the downward drift in the relative fiscal importance of direct taxation without any visible signs of interest.

It was left to an old political practitioner like Nikita Khrushchev to discover still another way of pressing the moribund income tax into political service. His plan, revealed in his seven-hour speech to the Twenty-first Party Congress, is quite simple. Some time in the near future, he intends to announce that the Soviet Union has found a way to dispense with this trivial item of budget revenue; and the action will be billed as "the end of tax collection" in the U.S.S.R. Khrushchev's formal pronouncement on the subject reads as follows (*Pravda*, January 28, 1959):

> Under present conditions, the existence of taxes levied upon the population is unnecessary either from the point of view of its class significance . . . or from the point of view of securing revenue for the state budget of the U.S.S.R.; the more so, as the share of taxes raised amounts to only 7.8 per cent of budget revenue. All this will make it possible to do away with the collection of taxes from the population in the next few years.

In the light of this startling treatment of the subject of taxes, two questions are likely to arise in the mind of the reader interested in Soviet developments: (1) What is the actual tax burden of the Soviet citizen? and (2) How much does he stand to gain by the reform so solemnly adumbrated by Khrushchev?

The Size of the Turnover Tax

Ever since the basic reform of the Soviet fiscal structure in September, 1930, the principal source of tax money in the

U.S.S.R. has been the so-called "turnover tax." This tax began its life as a modest special levy on all transactions involving the sale of consumer goods (there was an exception to the rule in that petroleum was also made subject to the tax). The innovation proved a huge success, and it was soon extended to other areas, such as movie-house admissions, repairs, laundry, and other consumer services. In short, it gradually evolved into a universal excise tax and into "a means of withdrawing from circulation part of the wages and other payments made to the population."* This withdrawal, as will be seen later, has been carried out at a rather heavy rate.

With the aid of this new, rich source of taxation, the government's tax receipts doubled in one year, rising from 6 billion to 12 billion rubles by the end of 1931. In due course, the government began to experiment with the tax rates, raising the levy on one commodity after another as much as the traffic would bear. The tax on bread, for example, went up in several successive steps from the original rate of 8 per cent of the sales price, in 1931, to 76 per cent, in 1934. While the price paid to the peasant for grain remained unchanged, the government raised the price of bread to the consumer from 12 to 50 kopeks per kilogram during this three-year period.

As could be expected, yields from the turnover tax rose briskly during the first decade of its life. By 1940, they were nearly ten times as large as in 1931, namely 106 billion rubles, while average wages during the same period increased only fourfold (from 84 to 338 rubles a month). Inevitably, too, the share of this tax in total government revenue increased conspicuously, so that by 1940 it accounted for 58.8 per cent of all treasury receipts. In 1959, the turnover tax is expected to yield 332.4 billion rubles, or 47 per cent of total budget revenue.†

---

* R. W. Davies, *The Development of the Soviet Budgetary System* (Cambridge, Mass.: Cambridge University Press, 1958), p. 216.

† The revenue resources of the Soviet Government, as planned for 1959, may be summarized as follows: 1) The turnover (excise) tax: 332.4 billion rubles, or 47 per cent of total revenue. 2) Direct taxes, chiefly the income tax: 56 billion rubles, or somewhat under 8 per cent of total revenue. 3) Deductions from profits of state economic enterprises: 155 billion rubles, or about 21 per cent of total revenue. 4) The remainder, some 24 per cent

Economic Functions

From the standpoint of size alone, then, the turnover tax is important enough a phenomenon to merit a position of honor in the Soviet financial system. Its economic significance, however, is even more far-reaching. What gives the turnover tax its unique influence over the economic process in the U.S.S.R. is the fact that it is employed as a device for subsidizing the state sector at the expense of the consumer sector.

More specifically, the turnover tax is deployed strategically to accomplish two basic objectives of Soviet economic policy. First, because it is levied almost entirely on consumer articles, the tax raises the price of all goods bought by the population by roughly 100 per cent on the average over and above the full economic price. By sopping up purchasing power at this greedy rate, the turnover tax acts as a powerful brake on consumption and enables the government to pursue its policy of heavy investment in the capital-goods and armament industries with diminished inflationary pressures in the consumer market.

Secondly, this tax, though collected from the consumer sector, does its most "creative" work in the state sector. Just how this is accomplished may be briefly described as follows: Since the Soviet government exercises a virtually exclusive monopoly of both the economic and the political authority in the country—producing, taxing, pricing, and distributing all goods, with very minor exceptions—it is under no obligation to show a profit on each individual product. Neither does it have to seek an economic return in full from any large group of products. All that is required for the purpose of general economic viability is that the sum of the prices of all goods sold by the state recapture the cost of production of all goods, plus a given margin of profit. The latter is needed, of course, for the replacement of outworn equipment and for further capital expansion. Within this broad

---

of the total expected revenue of 723.4 billion rubles, will be drawn from a group of minor revenue sources, such as the social insurance tax, the timber tax, the tax on collective farms, and others. See the annual budget report of Finance Minister A. Zverev in *Pravda*, December 23, 1958.

framework of economic constraint, however, there is ample room for maneuver.

Having the power to do so, the Soviet government proceeds to overprice the goods sold to the consumer by approximately the amount by which it wishes to underprice the goods it sells to itself, namely capital goods and military matériel. This Herculean task of "compensation," as some Soviet economists prefer to call it, is carried out by the turnover tax. Its use has made it possible over the years to depress the share of consumer goods in total industrial output from 60 per cent in the late 1920's, to less than 30 per cent at present.

The Tax Bite

In its own way, the Soviet government pays a special tribute to the "strategic" character of the turnover tax by taking the utmost precaution to keep all details on specific rates out of the public view. The tax is therefore built into the sales price of each article before it enters retail channels. Only the total amount to be collected through this tax in the course of a year is made public. Beyond that, however, discussion of the subject is usually couched in broad, theoretical terms.

For information on actual tax rates we have to go to a few fragmentary figures released during the prewar years. According to this information, the turnover tax takes a specific "bite" out of every consumer ruble spent in the state stores. But the rates are extremely varied. Thus, when the Soviet citizen buys such articles as beef, butter, or laundry soap, the final retail price he pays consists of 60 to 70 per cent tax. (In practice, a tax component of 60 per cent of the selling price means that the basic economic price of the good is increased 2.5 times before it enters retail channels.) Other goods, such as sugar, salt, cigarettes, or vodka, are covered by a still heavier tax layer, amounting as much as 70 to 88 per cent of the retail price.

Some articles sold to the consumer, like yardgoods, shoes, and apparel, appear to escape with a tax bite of "only" 40 to 55 per cent of the retail price. In fact, however, these articles are taxed twice, the first time upon emerging from the factory as intermediate products in the form of yarn, cloth, leather, etc., and the second time as finished goods.

The taxing of admission taxes to the movies provides another illustration of indirect taxation in the U.S.S.R. The Russian movie-goer pays 3.3 rubles for attending an average urban movie house, which in terms of earning power represents almost one hour's wages of the average worker. In the U.S., this cost would be the equivalent of about $1.75 for an average wage earner. What makes the price so high is the fact that it is compounded of two charges. There is, first, the basic charge of 1.6 rubles, which represents the economic price of admission. As such, it already includes a profit for the government in its capacity as owner of the movie house. The second, and larger, charge consists of 1.9 rubles of turnover tax, going directly into the coffers of the treasury for the strategic budget expenditures.

Methods of Collection

For the Soviet government, the turnover tax has two prime virtues. It is relatively painless, and it is easy to collect. Because it enters into the price of all goods behind the scenes, the taxpayer is spared the agony of counting out his tax money. At the same time, the government does not have to employ tax collectors. The retail stores throughout the country serve as the tax-gathering agencies. And so long as all citizens, urban and rural alike, must buy their food, clothing, and other essentials at stores, the tax will be collected in the process, approximately as planned in the fiscal offices of the government.

For his part, the Soviet citizen enters the state stores with currency that has already been pretaxed. In the course of making his purchases and paying the tax-laden official prices, he automatically helps to implement the government plan for recapturing a fixed proportion of the money placed in circulation. By the end of the year, when the balance sheet is drawn, it is easy to see what an impressive job of tax collecting is accomplished by the stores. In 1957, for instance, the retail-trade network sold a volume of goods valued at 625 billion rubles. The tax component of these sales was equally imposing. Receipts from the turnover tax came to 276 billion rubles. In other words, some 45 per cent of all money paid out by the consumer at the stores went for the payment of excise taxes, and because of the surreptitious nature of this levy, no tax receipts were issued in the process. That, too, was all to the good; the morale of the consumer was spared possible injury, while the government saved on the cost of printing receipts.

With its heavy incidence on the necessities of life, the Soviet turnover tax is of course heavily regressive. The rates are, by and large, determined by two basic considerations: the revenue requirements of the government and the volume of consumer goods available for distribution. Whatever the budgeted expenditures, the turnover tax must supply the bulk of the revenue. If the volume of available goods in a particular year is expected to be relatively small, the rate of the turnover tax on each commodity is raised accordingly. This is in fact what happened in the years immediately following World War II. For four consecutive years, from 1947 through 1950, the state collected through the stores about 240 billion rubles of turnover tax annually, in spite of the scarcity of goods available for sale. The claims of capital investment and armament were served to the hilt; the consumer got along as best he could.

That was austerity of a high order indeed. Since 1950, however, the tax share in retail trade has been drifting downward, dropping from 78 per cent in 1948 to 45 per cent in 1957.

The Elastic Ruble

The practice of injecting varying doses of excise tax into every article the consumer buys has the effect of distorting the ruble as a yardstick of value. As a result, there is no way of finding a general purchasing-power equivalent of the ruble in relation to any other currency. What the ruble buys in each commodity class will depend on the amount of tax the article is supposed to raise.

Measured against dollar prices, the Soviet worker's expenses for food and clothing abound with incongruity. Thus when he buys a pound of meat or fish, tea or milk, the ruble buys as

TURNOVER TAXATION IN THE U.S.S.R.

	Retail Value of Trade (in billion rubles)	Turnover Tax (in billion rubles)	Average Rate of Tax (in per cent)
1940	175.1	105.9	60.5
1945	160.1	123.1	76.9
1946	247.2	190.9	77.2
1947	308.0	239.9	77.8
1948	332.0	247.3	74.5
1949	348.0	245.5	70.5
1950	359.6	236.1	65.7
1951	379.8	247.8	65.2
1952	393.6	246.9	62.7
1953	430.7	243.6	56.6
1954	481.9	224.3	46.5
1955	501.5	242.4	48.3
1956	547.0	258.6	47.2
1957	617.3	275.6	44.6
1958	668.5	301.5	45.1

Source: F. D. Holzman, "Taxes in the U.S.S.R.," National Tax Journal, June, 1957, p. 144. Data for last two years drawn from the Annual Report of the U.S.S.R. Central Statistical Administration for the respective years.

much as 6 cents would in the United States. In the case of items like butter, sugar, and fruits, the purchasing power of the ruble is about 3 cents. In the nonfood categories, there is also extreme variation. When buying a shirt or nylon stockings, the Soviet citizen's ruble will command the value of only 2 cents. In the case of a suit, about 3 cents. The purchasing power of a ruble for shoes comes to 4 cents.

The following two examples may illustrate just how tax-packed ordinary articles of wear are in the Soviet Union. A delegation of the British weavers' trade union visiting the Moscow Oblast in September, 1956, was questioned in private by a group of earnest Russian workers as to how many days they had to work to earn the suits they were wearing. The Russians' findings were startling indeed. As it turned out, the British weaver had to work seven and a half days, the Russian forty-three.* To cite another example, a shoe salesman in the U.S.S.R. earns one tenth of the price of a pair of shoes (250 rubles) in a day. His American counterpart earns the full price of a pair in one day.

Of all consumer goods, durable goods are treated most favorably by the Soviet tax writers. But in this category, too, we find the usual range of diversity. Measured against dollar prices, musical instruments, for example, are lower-priced than cooking utensils; prices of television sets are more favorable to the consumer than the price of bicycles. Within the category as a whole, however, the ruble buys approximately as much as 11 cents would buy in the United States.

On the average, counting all the purchases he makes during the year, the retail purchasing power of a ruble is equivalent to 7.5 cents in the United States. At this rate, the average wage earner who receives 4 rubles per hour and spends 90 per cent of his money through the stores earns the equivalent of $15 weekly.

So far, only the consumer's ruble has been considered. The story is quite different in the state sector. There, the ruble comes close to commanding as much value as the official rate of exchange claims for it. We know from recent public Soviet statements that it takes only 3.5 times as many rubles as dollars to buy a tank. Similarly, as shown by the official price books, the price the government pays for a ton of steel, coal, cement, or machinery also comes close to the official rate of exchange. Within the category of investment goods, the purchasing-power equivalent of the ruble lies between 20 and 30 cents.

Embarrassment for Official Theorists

The problem of explaining the turnover tax has plagued official Soviet ideologists for a long time. The tax is much too unpleasant a device to extol as a great "socialist" innovation, and too impor-

* Report on *Visit to the U.S.S.R.* (September 16–30, 1956), Amalgamated Weavers' Association, Lewis Wright, General Secretary, Manchester, 1956, p. 8.

tant to ignore. It should be remembered that indirect taxes of this kind have long been recognized by Marxist and liberal writers alike as "regressive" and socially iniquitous, for a tax system that taxes all individuals at the same rate without regard to their earnings imposes a relatively heavier burden on low-income recipients by exacting a larger share of their income.* Most modern governments have therefore adopted the more equitable "progressive" tax structures—usually the income tax—under which tax rates rise progressively with increasing rates of income.

It is not surprising, therefore, that most of the "explanations" of the turnover tax found in official Soviet textbooks are tortured and far-fetched. One can read, for example, that the turnover tax cannot be compared to any other known levy because it is a unique form of "self-taxation," imposed by the workers, as the true owners of the wealth of society, upon themselves.† Another typical explanation will argue that the practice of singling out the consumer industries for such heavy-handed taxation is merely a matter of economy in collection, since plants in the capital-goods sector are growing too rapidly.

Writing on the same subject, the Soviet economist A. K. Suchkov argues that the government is justified in applying the heaviest tax rates to the food and light industries because of the shorter production cycle in these branches. Hence, profit-taking can proceed at a more rapid pace. Still another explanation falls back on the old Marxian argument that only goods reaching the consumer through the market are depositories of exchange value, and thus "commodities." By definition, then, all

* The same policy of nominal equality, incidentally, is followed by the Soviet government in regard to rent. All occupants pay at the rate of 1.32 rubles per square meter, a charge that is admittedly below the cost of re-placing any kind of housing today. The average citizen who now occupies 5.5 meters of space is thus not heavily burdened by rent, although he has to pay as much again for his utilities. Nor is he amply provided with living space. The real beneficiary is the high-paid functionary of the state. He gets ample space as well as the benefit of the low cost per unit of housing. See T. Sosnovy, "Rent in the USSR," *The American Slavic and East European Review*, XVII, No. 2 (April, 1959), pp. 174–81.

† For a detailed treatment of the whole subject of official explanations of the turnover tax, see F. D. Holzman, *Soviet Taxation* (Cambridge, Mass.: Harvard University Press), Chapter 6.

capital goods produced by and for the state fall outside the sphere of "commodity" production and therefore beyond the reach of the taxing authority.

Within the past few years, however, Soviet economists have been encouraged to discuss the problems of price formation in the U.S.S.R. in more realistic terms. A few writers, for instance, have expressed themselves in favor of a more equal distribution of the turnover tax, and quite recently *Finansy SSR* (No. 2, 1959, p. 37), an official economic journal, even admitted that some "practical workers" treat the turnover tax as a "universal excise tax." But those who now attempt to treat seriously the economic function of the turnover tax tread very carefully and generally carry on their discussion in rather obscure language. Nevertheless, such meaning as does escape leaves no doubt that the turnover tax is essentially a scheme for depressing the cost of capital goods to the state. Here is a sample of the language in which D. D. Kondrashev, a Soviet economist, has recently tackled the effect of the turnover tax on prices in his book on industrial price formation in the U.S.S.R.:

> The essence of the matter is as follows: Prices of producer goods include only part (the lesser part at that) of the money accumulation in the form of profits. The other part of the accumulation, designated in practice as a tax on turnover, does not as a rule enter into that price. At the same time, prices on consumer goods contain a higher level of monetary accumulation, taking the form of profits as well as tax on turnover.

While the meaning is unmistakable, the language is painfully abstract. We need, therefore, some concrete figures to illustrate this most important point. In 1955, the state extracted from industry a total amount of "surplus product" (savings) of 321.7 billion rubles, made up of 88.7 billions in the form of "profits" and 233 billions in "turnover tax." To this amount heavy industry, which accounted for 70.5 per cent of all industrial goods produced in that year, contributed 53.4 billion rubles, or only 17 per cent of the total amount skimmed off into the treasury.

This high degree of favoritism toward heavy industry has

evoked the following reaction from another prominent Soviet economist, Y. Kronorod, writing in *Voprosy ekonomiki* (No. 25, 1957, p. 87):

> If prices in the capital-goods sector were correlated with the value of goods, heavy industry should also have yielded about 70 per cent of the value of the "surplus product" (savings) obtained through the prices of all industrial goods produced.

In other words, here we have a tax that works wonders. By its magic, every unit of currency used by the government in payment for goods becomes a "privileged" currency, exempt from paying the full economic price. By the same token, every ruble paid out by the government to the citizen is "debased," in that the price of the goods it will buy is inflated by an extra amount of profit in the form of a turnover tax.

By any test of performance, the present system of extracting tax money from the economy has worked well for the Moscow rulers. So much so, that even the reform-bent Soviet Premier seems disposed to leave the basic scheme intact. All that Mr. Khrushchev proposes to do, in effect, is to add a further refinement. Instead of relying upon indirect taxes to the extent of 85 per cent, as is the case now, he proposes to make it 100 per cent— and call it "abolition of all taxes."*

* On May 7, 1960, the Supreme Soviet issued a decree providing for the gradual abolition of the personal income tax, to be carried out over a period of six years. On October 1, persons earning up to 500 rubles were relieved of their income-tax payments. During the next four years, workers and employees earning between 500 and 900 rubles per month are to be gradually relieved of their payments. Finally, on October 1, 1965, all wage earners will cease paying income taxes. In an attempt to narrow the very wide wage gap (see the article by Robert A. Feldmesser on pp. 223–39.—Ed.), those wage earners with an income up to 1,000 rubles will be compensated by having the sum formerly paid in income tax added to their wages; those earning between 1,000 and 2,000 rubles will only receive part of it in wages; whereas those earning more than 2,000 rubles a month will receive nothing at all.

As a result of this gradual abandonment of the income tax, the state budget will sustain an annual loss of about 1 per cent of its total revenue— a sum that will be easily compensated for by the increased revenues from the tax on profits and from the turnover tax resulting from the steadily rising level of economic activities in the country.

In substance, nothing will be abolished, nothing sacrificed. The 50 billion rubles a year now raised through direct taxes will be collected in some other way. It is clearly not a formidable figure. To collect it, the global volume of the turnover tax would have to be increased only modestly, by some 17 per cent. As it is, the turnover tax collections have been inching upward recently at the rate of 30 billion rubles a year. Surely from the standpoint of the ruling new class, the prospect of governing a "taxless society" is worth the price of a modest boost in the present turnover-tax rates. The Soviet public will simply have to learn to view this change in the same "correct" light.

The Soviet Industrial Reorganization

——ALEC NOVE

On July 1, 1957, THE Khrushchev regime launched a major reform of the Soviet economy under which the bulk of industrial and building enterprises passed from the control of various central ministries to newly created regional economic councils, or sovnarkhozes. The reform was accompanied by a drastic political shake-up in the top echelons of the CPSU, leading many commentators to interpret Khrushchev's new program as primarily an outgrowth of the political struggle for power. Khrushchev, so it has been argued, sought to smash the ministerial machines in which his enemies were entrenched while strengthening the grip of the Party machine on economic life. It is clear that the power struggle played an important role in the processes of elaborating and promulgating the reform; its measures were controversial, affecting numerous vested interests, and they probably were of key significance in the struggle between Khrushchev and the so-called "anti-Party group" within the leadership. On the other hand, it would be misleading to regard the reorganization as solely a power maneuver, for such a view ignores its intrinsic importance as an attempt to deal with real problems that beset the Soviet economy. The present instance would not be the first time that a major reform rooted in social or economic conditions has been carried through by an ambitious politician intent on strengthening his personal power position. Stalin, in launching his collectivization campaign in 1928–29, was no doubt plotting to isolate and defeat the Bukharin-Rykov group, but this aspect of

189

his policy hardly merits priority in assessing its historic significance.

There were, then, economic considerations of great importance behind the recent reorganization. The background situation against which the reform must be viewed was discussed at some length in articles by Gregory Grossman and this writer in *Problems of Communism* for March-April, 1957, both of which were written prior to the announcement of Khrushchev's proposals. The Soviet economy, it was pointed out there, has long been laboring under strain. Many factors have contributed to this condition; essentially, however, the problem of the regime is one of reconciling its quest for maximum growth ("overtaking the most advanced capitalist countries at the earliest date") with other insistent demands on Soviet resources (arising out of necessary concessions to the population in the form of consumer goods, the need to increase agricultural production, the economic requirements of foreign policy, etc.)—and this in a period in which labor was no longer abundant.

"Departmentalism"—A Fundamental Defect

These various pressures on the economy obviously called for the most efficient possible use of available resources, and the top-heavy structure of planning and control inherited from Stalin simply was not doing the job. At least as early as July, 1955, at a Party plenum called to discuss problems of industry, the Soviet leadership began to hint publicly that difficulties were due to shortcomings in the economic system itself. When the strains became so great as to compel—in December, 1956—a downward revision of the tempo of growth envisaged in the Sixth Five Year Plan, the issue of economic organization became manifestly urgent. It is very likely that the need for radical changes of some kind was appreciated by all leaders, though they were to come to blows over what action should be taken.

One of the more serious obstacles to efficiency arose out of the centralization of planning and operational control in Moscow, with responsibility divided among some forty economic ministries. Under heavy pressure to fulfill ambitious plans, each ministry understandably tended to look after its own enterprises, and rational cooperation between enterprises belonging to different ministries was rendered difficult. While the sins of "departmentalism" were possibly overstressed by the Soviet press in its efforts to prepare public opinion for the reform, there is little doubt that a great deal of waste was incurred as a result of the lack of coordination in the operations of ministries. Among examples cited in the press (*Pravda*, April 15, 1957) was the case of a large quarry worked by eight small quarrying enterprises, each representing a different user ministry seeking to ensure its own supplies. Another instance involved two steamer fleets operated under different ministries on the same river; one sailed empty in one direction, the other in the opposite direction. There also have been numerous cases cited of waste in transporting materials to and from factories within one ministerial system, and repeated complaints concerning delays due to the need to refer decisions to distant Moscow.

Obviously these defects were real, and there was need for corrective action. In determining what course to take, the Soviet leaders had a choice between two alternative approaches: They could delegate much wider powers at the actual production level, i.e., to the managers of enterprises, or they could create more effective operational and planning units in the localities. The first of these implied a radical departure from established methods of bureaucratic control through the government and Party apparatuses, and would necessarily leave instead a much wider use of the price and market mechanism. Considering both Khrushchev's character and the Party's traditional view of its functions, it is hardly surprising that the second alternative was chosen. However, a scheme along the latter lines could have many variants, and clearly the political struggle had a direct effect on the version finally adopted.

Plans and Politics

The essentials of the new forms of organization are doubtless familiar to most readers. In 1957, the Soviet Union was divided into 105 regions, of which 70 were in the Russian Republic

(R.S.F.S.R.) and 11 in the Ukraine. In each, a regional economic council was established to act as the planning and operational authority for nearly all industrial and construction enterprises situated within its borders. In almost all cases, industrial ministries have been abolished in Moscow as well as in the republic capitals. Within a few months, only the Ministry of Electric Power Stations was left, and this because of the necessity to control a nationally interconnected electric-power system. State committees were created for the principal defense industries, and also for chemicals, automation, and machine building; their purpose is to give general guidance in matters of design and planning, but, formally at least, they have no direct operational control.

The typical Soviet enterprise, both in heavy and light industry, now takes its orders from its sovnarkhoz.* The latter is subordinated to the council of ministers of its republic (subject in turn to the usual Party controls). The all-Union government, particularly Gosplan, and the Party apparatus are supposed to ensure the necessary degree of central leadership.

These proposals were adopted after a hard struggle within the leadership; but while the existence of dissension over this and other aspects of Soviet policy became increasingly obvious, the interplay of political forces in the course of the struggle presented a confused picture. It is virtually impossible to analyze the complex motivations that governed Khrushchev or his opponents at different phases of the "debate" over economic organization, the conflicting viewpoints that determined the alignment of forces, or the extent to which differences over other policies were involved. The indications are, however, that if Khrushchev's position was ever shaky, it was in the aftermath of the Hungarian revolution in the fall of 1956. Insofar as economic policy was concerned, the decisions of a Party Plenum in December, 1956, indicated that the prevailing opinion within the leadership favored tackling the disease of departmentalism through the subordination of almost all of the economic ministries to the State

---

* Small industrial units of purely local significance, which are under the control of municipal Soviets, are also beyond the purview of the reform and of this article.

Economic Commission, with M. Pervukhin at its head. This agency had been created in May, 1955, to take over responsibility for current economic affairs from Gosplan, whose functions were reduced at the time to long-term planning and research. Even the two ministries dealing with agricultural affairs, Khrushchev's special interest, were placed under Pervukhin, leading some observers to interpret the plan as an attempt to limit Khrushchev's interference in economic affairs.

At any rate, Khrushchev's first proposals, put forward in his "theses" of April, 1957, preserved the idea adopted in December of combining planning and administrative power in one central body, though he referred to the latter by the old designation of Gosplan. He suggested that the old ministries be abolished (significantly, however, agriculture was now excluded from the reform) and that an undetermined number of sovnarkhozes be created. The latter were to be under "dual subordination"—i.e., controlled directly from Moscow as well as by the respective republic authorities.

During the following month, there was an unusually open debate of the theses in the Soviet press, indicative of the intensive discussion and maneuvering that must have been going on behind the closed doors of the leadership councils. The result was a number of significant changes in Khrushchev's plan, as finally adopted by the Supreme Soviet in May. First, Gosplan was reassigned responsibility for both long-term and current planning, but was stripped of all executive power, while the State Economic Commission was abolished altogether. An unknown Party bureaucrat, Kuzmin, was appointed to head the new Gosplan, to the surprise of all observers. The republics were given undivided control over their sovnarkhozes (as opposed to "dual" control, first proposed by Khrushchev; the republic governments and Party organs remain subject, of course, to control from the center). It was also left to the republics to decide the number of regions into which they would be divided.

As noted, it is by no means clear how these various changes were related to the political struggle going on in the Party Presidium. Thus, for example, while Khrushchev first proposed a strong Gosplan, he may have come to favor a limitation of its powers as a means to prevent the rise of Pervukhin as an economic "rival," if he thought the latter would be appointed its head (this might have seemed a strong likelihood in view of the December actions of the Party Plenum). On the other hand, Khrushchev may have decided that a weak Gosplan would tend to throw more responsibility for economic administration on the Party apparatus; this might have seemed attractive to him quite apart from any immediate desire to down an opponent.

Political rather than economic considerations clearly influenced certain other aspects of the scheme that was finally adopted. For instance, why were as many as 105 economic regions created? A number of voices were raised in public discussion favoring far fewer regions—one for the Urals, one for East Siberia, and so on. It was pointed out that the split-up of these and other natural economic regions under the jurisdiction of three of four sovnarkhozes would create awkward problems. An official of the Gosplan research institute by the name of Omarovski argued in print in favor of ten to twelve sovnarkhozes for the R.S.F.S.R., rather than the seventy that were created. Why, then, were there so many?

Intra-Party Pressures from Below

The only possible explanation is that the leadership wanted to avoid interfering with existing administrative boundaries, or, in political-personal terms, with the areas of influence of local Party secretaries, who have always been the key personalities at the oblast (district) level. An oblast Party secretary's status would inevitably be threatened if his territory were linked to a neighbor's. Suppose, for example, that the adjoining oblasts of Belgorod, Bryansk, and Kursk were made into one economic region. Who would be the Party man in charge? Either a new boss would be sent out from headquarters, or one of the three secretaries would have to be placed in authority over the others. In either case, some Party officials would be aggrieved, which might result in strengthening any group of malcontents in a factional struggle. It is therefore probable that, in the R.S.F.S.R. at any rate, the line of least resistance was followed: With very few exceptions, the boundaries of the new regions have coincided with those of existing oblasts.

Politics probably also accounted for the granting of additional powers to the republics. As was noted above, Khrushchev's original proposals gave Moscow direct access to the regions, over the heads of the republics. Such a bypassing arrangement would have tended to curtail the political-economic role of the republics' governmental and Party leaderships. When the proposals became known, these authorities doubtless exerted pressure to obtain full jurisdiction within the line of command, making the regions subordinate in the first instance to the republic capitals. A significant illustration of their attitude is afforded by the behavior of the then Uzbek Party leader, Mukhitdinov. At first he pressed for only one region for Uzbekistan. However, when the scheme in its final form ensured that Moscow could not bypass Tashkent, he changed his mind, and in May, 1957, four sovnarkhozes were set up in Uzbekistan.

These examples suggest that Khrushchev, relying as he did on the support of provincial Party secretaries, adapted the reforms to their ambitions and tried to avoid treading on their political sore spots. In this respect, as in some others, politics seems to have played a primary role. Yet the problems being tackled are real enough; they were not simply conjured up by Khrushchev in order to smash his opponents. Some action was necessary; the fact that the actual measures taken were adapted to, and influenced by, the political struggle should not be surprising. Few politicians in any country act in a wholly disinterested manner, and they seldom overlook the effects of their policies on their personal position. There is no reason why Khrushchev should be an exception.

Achievements of the Reform

Has the system worked well? Has it, at least, worked better than the ministerial system it replaced? Experience shows that certain improvements have been achieved, principally the following:

a) The sovnarkhozes are able to study local productive resources and to initiate plans that, however much they may be altered at higher levels, do at least initially represent an attempt to utilize these resources in the best possible manner. This was made impossible in the past by the vertical bureaucratic structure of the ministerial system. The local plans are particularly valuable in new areas in process of development, notably in Siberia.

b) Once an output plan for a sovnarkhoz is confirmed, there is a possibility of concentrating production in the most efficient local plants and of transferring underutilized capital assets. Unnecessary "inputs" from remote sources of supply can be eliminated if the sovnarkhoz is able to produce the necessary items in its own factories, thereby reducing the strain on transport.

c) It was an inherent weakness of the ministerial system that by-products of factories "belonging" to one ministry could not be utilized by other industries without great bureaucratic complications. The chemical industry in particular suffered from this. Much of this type of inflexibility has now undoubtedly been eliminated.

d) Various minor matters that had to be referred to Moscow can now be settled on the spot, and directors of enterprises find this a considerable convenience, since it reduces bureaucratic delays, and they often can exercise their local influence to useful effect.

While it would certainly be wrong to neglect the advantages of the sovnarkhoz system, the disadvantages are also considerable. The most important of them is *mestnichestvo*, i.e., so-called localist or regionalist tendencies, a disease inherent in regional control. Any territorial authority must inevitably feel primary responsibility for enterprises under its wing. Therefore, in any choice between alternatives, it will be guided by the economic interests of its own region. These, under Soviet conditions, consist of fulfilling and, if possible, overfulfilling the plan. It is by this criterion that enterprises and sovnarkhozes are judged by the superior authorities. Consequently, the sovnarkhozes, just like the defunct ministries, must tend to insure themselves against uncertain delivery of supplies from outside the area under their control by producing as much as possible within their own borders, and they naturally give priority to deliveries to "their" enterprises. This is not due to ill will or lack of "socialist consciousness." In an economy based on planning and hierarchical authority, the fulfillment of plans and instructions is the essential criterion of behavior. The central and republican authorities, to be sure, issue many detailed orders to sovnarkhozes, and failure to obey these orders—notably in respect of planned deliveries to other regions—can lead to trouble. Nevertheless, as one object of the reform was to encourage local initiative—and in any event all contingencies cannot be covered by central orders—the sovnarkhozes, within the sphere of their authority, are driven toward *mestnichestvo* by the planning system itself.

To make the point clearer, we must note that in a planned economy not based on the market-and-price mechanism, only a central office can possibly know what the requirements of the economy are. Industries inevitably require supplies from many different regions. For example, the Minsk tractor works relies on about a hundred enterprises situated outside the Belorussian sovnarkhoz. This complex pattern of production and supply can be seen from the center only, and in the past, the ministries underwrote important contracts and interfered to impose priorities on a national scale when things went wrong. All this cannot be done in or by any one of the supplying sovnarkhozes. In a market economy, the necessary signals would be transmitted through the price mechanism, but in the U.S.S.R. they can be communicated only by administrative instructions—a process that cannot be effectively decentralized and that in itself severely limits any possibilities of thoroughgoing economic decentralization.

Evidence that *mestnichestvo* would cause serious difficulties began accumulating almost immediately after the reform was instituted. Thus on September 2, 1957, the chairman of the Belorussian sovnarkhoz wrote in *Pravda:*

> There are instances when officials bother only about enterprises subordinate to them and do not think of the difficulties their irregularities cause for enterprises in other regions. It is necessary to speak about this frankly, so that these defects do not grow worse. . . . *We have met clear instances of*

tendencies towards autarchy. [Author's italics.] The Dzerzhinski factory of the Dnepropetrovsk region supplies rolled
wire to the Rezhitsa nail-making works. In July, the Dzerzhinski factory underfulfilled its plan by 15 per cent, but
sent to Rezhitsa only 300 instead of 1,020 tons of rolled wire.
When this outrageous fact was investigated, the managers
of the Dzerzhinski factory declared that they had orders
from the Dnepropetrovsk sovnarkhoz to give priority to
enterprises in their own region and to supply them in full.

In a similar case cited by the chairman, suppliers from Nikopol
arbitrarily cut deliveries of pipes to Minsk by 41 per cent, while
similar deliveries to Kharkov (which is in the same republic as
the supplying factory) were cut by only 7 per cent. Another
example came from Central Asia, where *Pravda Vostoka* of
March 29, 1957, reported that components from Stalingrad had
stopped arriving at the Tashkent farm-machinery plant. On July
25, 1957, *Pravda* devoted an editorial to the subject of such
defaults in deliveries from one region to another, and the central
Party organ has repeatedly voiced similar complaints in subsequent years. Another strong editorial appeared on February 26,
1958, and as recently as June 23, 1960, the Leningrad Party
Secretary, Spiridonov, wrote in the same paper about the difficulties encountered by the Leningrad shipbuilding industry in
connection with delivery of components from other sovnarkhozes.
It is true that the national interest is supposed to be defended
by Party secretaries in the localities. In practice, however, they
frequently connive at, or even encourage, *mestnichestvo*, because
ultimately they are judged by plan fulfillment in their area of
responsibility. Indeed, Khrushchev himself has argued in favor
of a direct connection between the salaries of Party officials and
the fulfillment of economic plans. Party officials even encourage
the use of centrally allocated investment funds for local purposes, as may be seen from an attack on several such officials
published in *Partiinaia zhizn* (No. 15, 1958). On another occasion, the same Party journal (No. 7, 1957) reported that the
Party office at Omsk forbade local government officials to obey
an order from Moscow to send trucks to the neighboring Kus-

tanai oblast; Omsk was to have 100 per cent priority, regardless of what any one said. Yet, local Party officials, like the sovnarkhoz officials, have no compass to guide them—except clear orders from above—and can only strive to fulfill their own plans. Since the plans are themselves prescribed from above, the Party secretary may well give his own area priority in the honest belief that what is good for Omsk is good for Russia.

Matters are not helped by the small size of most of the sovnarkhozes. They are not in any sense self-contained geographical-economic areas, and most decisions taken within them affect other areas in ways the local officials usually have no means of knowing. True, sovnarkhoz officials who obstruct interregional deliveries were threatened with punishment by a decree announced early in 1958 by Kozlov (*Pravda*, January 31, 1958), but such punishment presupposes the existence of clear orders that have been disobeyed, rather than referring to the use made by sovnarkhozes of such powers of decision as they themselves possess.

Under the circumstances, an enormous weight of responsibility was necessarily thrown upon the coordinating agencies, i.e., primarily on Gosplan, which took over at the all-Union level many of the planning, supply, and allocation functions of the former ministries. The problems of planners on the republic level have varied. In the smaller republics, only moderate difficulties have been encountered, but in the giant Russian Republic (R.S.F.S.R. with its sixty-eight sovnarkhozes),* it has been quite another matter. Numerous complaints about the R.S.F.S.R.'s ineffectiveness in planning and administration have been published in the press, emphasizing not only muddle but also lack of executive authority. The latter accusation is hardly surprising, as the republic Gosplans cannot issue binding orders and must frequently refer matters to the appropriate council of ministers. These difficulties, and perhaps also some political reason, led to the dismissal of Baibakov from the chairmanship of the R.S.F.S.R. Gosplan in 1958. The persistent appearance of similar criticisms,

*Originally, there were seventy. The Balashov and Kamensk oblasts and sovnarkhozes were liquidated in 1957–58.

however, and the continuous reorganizations of the R.S.F.S.R. administrative structure indicate that the problems remain unresolved.

Old Problems in New Forms

It is essential to appreciate that neither this nor any other reorganization can solve certain problems inherent in the Soviet system of centralized economic planning based on instructions from above. A modern industrial economy is exceedingly complex, and any investment or production decision involves a very large number of consequential decisions in many regions and many branches of industry. Thus a change of an output plan for a given commodity in a large factory affects not only the allocation of materials and components to this factory—and therefore the output and delivery plans of the industries providing them— but also those branches of the economy throughout the U.S.S.R. that use the products of the factory concerned.

The cumulative complications are enormous. Theoretically, of course, an all-seeing brain at planning headquarters could foresee everything and take fully coordinated decisions, but in practice it cannot be so. The job is divided between many offices, some concerned with the common problems of an industry, some with the common problems of an area in which there are several industries, and still others with problems common to many industries and many areas (e.g., new techniques, labor, etc.). Naturally, different organizational forms enable certain questions to be dealt with more expeditiously, but usually at the cost of creating new difficulties in other areas. The ministerial system, superseded in 1957, neglected regional problems. The sovnarkhoz system registers a gain in this sector, at the cost of throwing heavier burdens on the functions of coordination. In fact, the history of the reform since 1957 is one of a steady increase in the powers of the central coordinators and a decline in the effective importance of the sovnarkhozes, since the government and Party strive to implement the central plan and to combat such regionalist tendencies as obstruct the uninterrupted functioning of at least the priority sectors of the economy. Thus sovnarkhozes were forbidden to reallocate investment funds between branches, and their powers to allocate materials and components to "their" enterprises were severely restricted. Continuous gravitation of authority and control toward the central bodies, which command a bird's-eye view, has been the natural result.

Newest Administrative Changes

Meanwhile, efforts have been made to mitigate the disadvantages inherent in the small size of the regions. The press referred several times to *ad-hoc* committees of neighboring sovnarkhozes, which meet to coordinate their activities. The regions involved are: the three Baltic states, the three Transcaucasian republics, the East Siberian sovnarkhozes, and the eight sovnarkhozes in and around the Urals. It must be remembered, however, that these committees could hardly possess any powers of decision. A more important event was the setting up within the R.S.F.S.R. Gosplan of divisions corresponding to main geographic regions, grouping together many sovnarkhozes. Eminent Soviet academicians have criticized this arrangement as quite inadequate (*Promyshlenno-ekonomicheskaia gazeta*, September 19, 1958), and the existence within Gosplan of regional as well as functional departments caused considerable administrative confusion, which was eloquently described by Kulyov in the Party journal *Kommunist* (No. 9, 1959). The substitution of big regions for the existing sovnarkhozes, or the grouping of them into superregions, has consequently been widely advocated. If the small size of the original regions was a by-product of Khrushchev's desire to retain the support of the oblast Party secretaries at a time when his political future was at stake, then at present we may well expect him to advocate bigger regions, since he is surely strong enough now to opt for the more rational solution. As these lines are being written, Uzbekistan has liquidated its regions, or rather the entire republic has become a sovnarkhoz (Decree of the Council of Ministers of the Uzbek Republic, reported in the London *Times*, July 4, 1960), while the Ukraine chose to increase the number of its sovnarkhozes from eleven to fourteen.[*] This

___

[*] This was accomplished by the creation of new sovnarkhozes for Poltava, Cherkassy, and the Crimea, as reported in *Pravda*, July 14, 1960.

makes an all-Union total of 102 at the present time. More reductions are likely, affecting above all the R.S.F.S.R. with its unwieldy sixty-eight regions.

At the all-Union level, quiet, little-publicized changes, which must surely have altered the balance of economic power to a marked degree, have continued. Gosplan, in its material allocation and its industrial branches, now has a tight grip on what the sovnarkhozes actually do, and its relationship to enterprises is such that I. V. Spiridonov described the machinery output of the Kirov (former Putilov) Works in Leningrad (*Pravda*, June 23, 1960) as "subordinated . . . to the Department of Heavy Machine Building of Gosplan U.S.S.R." and then complained that the metal production of the same factory is "an orphan," because no one at the center is responsible for it. In this context, he does not mention the sovnarkhoz at all, though it is the nominal master of the factory. Thus it does seem as if the current planning functions of Gosplan had grown vast in scope and detail.

On the other hand, the political weight and area of responsibility of Gosplan seem, paradoxically, to have been reduced by the proliferation of other state committees and an increase in their importance. Thus in 1960, A. N. Kosygin, who had taken over Gosplan from I. I. Kuzmin, was promoted to what appears to be a general economic overlordship, and a little-known official, V. N. Novikov, was promoted from the R.S.F.S.R. Gosplan to be the head of the all-Union Gosplan. A more senior functionary, A. F. Zasyadko, became head of a greatly expanded State Scientific and Economic Council (*Nauchno-Ekonomicheskii Sovet*) of the U.S.S.R. Council of Ministers, and it is unofficially reported that this council is now charged with long-term planning. The division made between long- and short-term planning in 1955–56 is thus reappearing once again (except that, confusingly enough, Gosplan was the name given in the earlier period to the body charged with *long-term* planning).

Still another body with increased, though undefined, powers is the Scientific and Technical Committee (*Nauchno-Tekhnicheskii Komitet*), and several other state committees of various grades and designations have also come into being. With the proliferation of these new committees, a new problem in coordination arises—this time between central bodies. It may be that Kosygin has been charged with this responsibility, or perhaps it is done within the machinery of the Party's Central Committee. The details are still unknown. In the R.S.F.S.R., where presumably these various committees also exist, a dramatic change came about in June, 1960, when the creation of an all-Russian super-sovnarkhoz, using the old designation VSNKh (or *Vesenkha*), was announced and charged with operational control over the sovnarkhozes of this vast republic in all matters concerned with plan fulfillment. The Ukraine and Kazakhstan have followed suit. It is too early to say how these new bodies will fit into the administrative and planning pattern, or whether similar changes will occur in other republics or at the all-Union level. It may or may not presage a sharp cut in the number of sovnarkhozes. One thing, however, is certain: These newest changes add to the effective power of supervision exercised over the sovnarkhozes of the R.S.F.S.R. from Moscow, and those of the Ukraine from Kiev, and thus continue the trend toward restricting the area of sovnarkhoz autonomy.

Some Conclusions

What, then, are the conclusions we can draw from the working of the reforms of 1957?

In this author's original article on this topic (*Problems of Communism*, November–December, 1957), written a few months after the promulgation of the reform, the following passage appeared:

What seems most likely, therefore, is that as difficulties become apparent, there will be a gradual return to centralization. Venturing a guess at the pattern of development, there probably will be a continuing stream of complaints reaching Moscow from enterprises and various authorities protesting the delays in production due to irregular arrival of supplies from other regions, asking for help in obtaining this or that item, and so on. The occasional interference of the center will be found insufficient. It will be necessary to set up or strengthen day-to-day organs of supervision to ensure the uninterrupted functioning of at least the priority sectors of the economy. . . . In other words, the center is likely to be compelled to limit greatly the range of choice open to the sovnarkhozes in order to ensure that they conform to a national plan.

This, indeed, is very largely what has occurred. Yet it would be wrong to regard the reform as purely negative in effect, or the sovnarkhozes as mere helpless puppets. The existence of regional authorities facilitates the initiation of local plans, and, within the national plan, all kinds of minor adjustments can still be made at the local level, various small expenditures by enterprises authorized, unused productive capacity redistributed, useful technical innovations encouraged and financed. However, we can now see how right Khrushchev was in refusing to use the word "decentralization" to describe the industrial reorganization of 1957. The sovnarkhoz reform was and remains a matter of reorganizing central planning.

Meanwhile, the imperfections and stresses inherent in the Soviet system of central planning are still there. In order to permit wider scope for free contract based on rational prices, reduce the area of administrative decision, and increase the importance of "automatic" forces in economic life, many Soviet economists are urging a major recasting of the system. The voices of Kantorovich and Novozhilov are advocating the use of linear programming methods, which would necessitate theoretical and practical changes of the first magnitude. So far, none of this has been realized by the actual reforms. The Party leadership is, by tradition and self-interest, averse to automatic economic forces and will probably resist reforms on these lines. Yet this same Party leadership is actively searching for new ways of achieving efficiency in its self-imposed task of "overtaking America." Thus there will be more hesitation, more experiments, and perhaps conflict as the search for a more rational basis of economic organization continues.

Communism in a Hurry:
The "Time Factor" in Soviet Economics

——GREGORY GROSSMAN

THE COMMUNIST ATTITUDE toward time is not without paradoxes. In a sense, by virtue of its historical determinism, Marxism is a philosophy of the relation of man to time, of the logical and orderly succession of historical stages, and of the necessity and imminence of events. Yet the Leninist does not leave the inevitable to its own progress; he must be ever watchful for opportunities. The right moment for action must be seized lest it slip by forever. Time to the Communist is a faithful but recalcitrant ally.

Take Marxian economics. One of its most important axioms is that labor time is the basis of exchange value. On this crucial assumption (largely rejected by the major economists even in Marx's own day) rest elaborate theorems of class relations, of exploitation, of capitalist crises, and of the eventual breakdown of the capitalist system. Applied by Marx only to unplanned market economies, the "labor theory of value" was in the early 1940's, declared to hold as an "economic law" in the Soviet Union. This position is still officially maintained, although its exact meaning and practical consequences have never been specified. But—and this is a major difficulty with which Soviet economics and planning have had to contend—if value is determined by labor time, how does one compare values over a period of time? For example, is an hour's labor today equivalent to an hour's work five years hence? The labor theory of value, at least in the naïve form adopted by Soviet economists, would seem to say "yes." But this is patently absurd to any economist, planner, or statesman. Thus in a country that has proclaimed a race against time, the formal relation between economic value and time has been a bothersome theoretical problem and a drag on the efficiency of planning for several decades.

Three events in mid-1958 underscore the pressing problem of time in Soviet planning. One was the apparent decision to step up the pace in the economic contest with the United States. Another was the resolution—more accurately, perhaps, near-resolution—of the long-smoldering debate regarding the formal handling of time in economic calculations, where there is a choice among different time patterns of outlays that result in identical benefits to the economy. And third, resting on both of these developments came Khrushchev's pronouncement—in the course of the ceremonies marking the commissioning of the hydroelectric station at Kuibyshev on the Volga—that henceforth such grandiose hydroelectric projects would be reappraised from the standpoint of the "time factor." According to Khrushchev, they take too much capital and too much time to build. Granted that the electrical energy generated by water power is cheaper than that generated by steam, still, according to *Pravda* of August 11, 1958:

The element of time is worth more in this matter than any immediate material outlays, for time lost cannot be compensated by any amount of money. We have to gain 10 to 15 years in the peaceful competition with capitalist countries. And when we have gained them and have developed our industry even further, then we shall be able to allot the funds necessary for constructing hydroelectric stations.

Momentum and Timing

The problem of formal incorporation of time into the economic calculus should not, of course, be confused with the art of timing tactical and strategic moves. In the latter respect, Khrushchev has shown himself to be very skillful. A good example is his agricultural program, in which, by an appropriate sequence and timing of steps, he has been able to create a definite upward momentum and to exploit it for further advances.

There can be little doubt that the predictions surrounding the launching of the Seven Year Plan (1959–65) are also primarily designed to produce a new momentum, and in this case on more fronts than one. The world is being told over and over again with an air of utmost confidence that by 1970, or even sooner, the U.S.S.R. will have caught up with the United States in per-capita production, and that consequently the Soviet "material standard of living" will then have caught up with the American living standard. (This does not follow logically at all, because consumption accounts for a considerably smaller portion of the total national product in the U.S.S.R. than it does in the U.S.; conversely, investment and military uses take considerably larger portions.) The road of catching up with the U.S. will also take the Soviet society to "Communism" in the sense of the ultimate society of abundance and perfect harmony. The Seven Year Plan, we are told, is to take a long stride in this direction.

Setting the goal of catching up on a per-capita basis with the most opulent country in the world—and specifying a target date (ten to twelve years hence) for the attainment of that goal—is a very clever move. It attracts the world's attention in the most vivid fashion possible to the dynamic nature of the Soviet economy and, by implication, to the lagging pace of capitalism. It focuses on "peaceful competition" (though nothing in the Seven Year Plan indicates any reduction in the volume of resources devoted to military use). It raises spirits and mobilizes energies at home by means of a vision of the American standard of living at the end of another big push for a decade or so. In short, it is intended to create a momentum on which the U.S.S.R. and Khrushchev himself, can capitalize internally and externally.

It seems to have escaped general notice, in part because of the studied silence on this point by the Soviet press itself, that the present "catch-up-and-overtake" campaign is a repetition of a very similar campaign launched by Stalin twenty years earlier.

The time has come to take practical measures to solve the basic economic task of the U.S.S.R.: to catch up with and overtake . . . economically the most developed capitalist countries of Europe and the United States of America. . . . Then and then only will the significance of the new era in the development of the U.S.S.R. unfold itself, the era of transition from a socialist to a Communist society.

And:

Only in the event that we overtake economically the main capitalist countries shall we be able to regard our country as fully saturated with consumer goods, and we shall [then] be able to go from the first to the second phase of Communism. What do we need in order to overtake the economically most powerful capitalist countries? . . . A determined and unremitting desire to move ahead and a readiness to bear sacrifices . . . and, lastly, time . . . ten to fifteen years.

These are not Khrushchev's words at the Twenty-first Party Congress in 1959. They are the words of Molotov and Stalin speaking at the Eighteenth Congress in March, 1939, and their clear purpose then, as their successor's is now, was to instill an impression of strength and invincibility abroad, and to spur production efforts at home.

Obviously, this is not 1939. While clouds of war again loom on the international horizon, the economy is not now, as it was temporarily then, in a stagnant condition, and the outlook for the average man is not as bleak. Why then impose a deadline, ten to twelve years hence, to "catch up" with the United States?

The answer seems to lie, at least in part, in the fact that Soviet economic growth, though still rapid, has been slowing down and is bound to continue to slow down in comparison with the first five years after Stalin's death. The great post-Stalin advance in agriculture has already taken place, thanks chiefly to the "new lands" and to favorable weather conditions. Any future gains in agricultural production will have to be wrested with greater effort. Nor can the rest of the economy, including industry, count on continuing at the old rates of growth, mainly due to the limited opportunity (for demographic and economic reasons) to expand the nonagricultural labor force.*

But the population is still growing at over 1.5 per cent per year. If the U.S.S.R. is not to slow down seriously in its self-proclaimed economic race with the United States, or if improvements in consumer welfare are not to be sacrificed drastically for the sake of this race, the mobilization of popular energies and efforts by means of an inspiring and not-too-distant goal is in order. American productivity and the American standard of living provide this goal, and the Soviet population is therefore exhorted to put its shoulders to the wheel so as to attain this goal in a decade.†

As a rousing slogan and a rallying cry, "catching up with America" has much in its favor. Not only is the idea superficially comprehensible to the simplest mind—surely more so than the notion of "passing over to the higher phase of Communism"—but also few save the statistically sophisticated appreciate the practical and conceptual difficulties and the quantitative indeterminacy of comparing the over-all outputs of two complex modern economies. The American and the Soviet economies each produce many thousands, perhaps hundreds of thousands, of commodities and services, only few of which are completely identical. They differ in numberless ways: in size, quality, appearance, functional and aesthetic characteristics, durability, serviceableness, and so forth, ad infinitum. It is a most difficult, perhaps impossible task to match a substantial proportion of the products of the two countries.

* These and other retarding factors in Soviet economic growth have been discussed by the author in "Thirty Years of Soviet Industrialization," *Soviet Survey* (London), October–December, 1958. The control figures for the Seven Year Plan, which appeared since, indicate that nearly 12 million persons—a large number—are to be added to the category of "workers and employees" over the septennium (this category essentially comprises non-peasant employment). However, this figure must be interpreted with considerable caution. It undoubtedly includes the young people who, under the latest educational reform, are now to go to work at the ages of fourteen and fifteen, instead of continuing in school as in the past. It may also include a substantial number of peasants who are to be reclassified as workers by virtue of the transformation of their collective farms into state farms.

† In even starker fashion, the slogan of catching up with the British level of production is used in Chinese propaganda.

But matching the products of the two countries is only the beginning of the problem. Comparing the *totality* of the goods produced in one country with the *totality* of the goods produced in the other—and this is what "catching up" means in statistical terms—implies that all the goods in *both* countries must be brought to a common denominator. Apples and oranges, shoes and ships and sealing wax, must be added to yield a synthetic total for each country, and then the totals must be compared to determine how large the total (or per-capita) output of one country is in relation to the total (or per-capita) output of the other. The common denominator is usually some monetary unit —dollar, ruble, pound sterling—and each commodity or service must be assigned its relative importance—the statistician calls it the commodity's "weight"—in terms of that unit. Alas, even the competent and conscientious statistician has many systems of weights to choose from, each with a perfectly valid logic of its own, but each resulting in a different ratio between the total (or per-capita) outputs of the two countries.

Consider then the problem of comparing the total outputs of two economies, one of which is characterized by a boundless variety of products, by emphasis on quality and finish, by catering to the needs and conveniences of the customer—the other, by an austere assortment of products, by frequent sacrifice of quality for quantity, and by taking the customer for granted. Add to this the complexities of statistical weighting. The result is a fertile field for questionable comparisons and for impressing an uninitiated audience to whom the notion of "catching up" is a very simple one.

Another great advantage of the catching-up campaign is that partial successes can be periodically proclaimed. Today one catches up in butter production, tomorrow in coal output or in wooden fabrics. Each instance provides cause for rejoicing and serves as a reminder of the ground still to be won. Of course, not everything is suitable for this purpose. The particular product must not evoke preindustrial images (horse carts will not do). A prestige item, like butter is to be preferred.*

* Implementation of the campaign to catch up with the U.S. in the production of milk, butter, and meat has provided numerous interesting hints

The Turning Point in Mid-1958

The year from mid-1957 to mid-1958 was marked by a relatively high degree of attention to the consumer on the part of the regime. Khrushchev's campaign to catch up with the United States in the per-capita production of milk, butter, and meat was proclaimed during the latter part of May, 1957. At the end of July, the Party and the government announced a bold program "to liquidate the housing shortage in the course of ten to twelve years" (Pravda, August 2, 1957). When Khrushchev, speaking at the ceremonies marking the fortieth anniversary of the Revolution on November 7, revealed some of the targets of the fifteen-year plan for 1972, those for consumer goods did not appear to be much more modest than those for producer goods. Early in 1958, the cotton-growing republics of the Soviet Union pledged themselves to ambitious targets for raw-cotton output in 1965, and two and one-half months later, Khrushchev published his far-reaching program for chemicals and synthetics—two steps that promised a substantial improvement in the supply of fabrics and other goods.

Yet much as the signs pointed in that direction, it would have been an error at the time to expect a "soft" (i.e., relatively consumer-oriented) Seven Year Plan. When the control figures for the Plan were published in mid-November, 1958, they showed a stepping-up in the annual rate of industrial growth compared with Khrushchev's fifteen-year targets of a year earlier, and a "hardening" of targets as if to reflect heightened impatience to catch up with the U.S. Thus the spread between the over-all

---

as to how similar campaigns may be handled in the future. To mention just a few points: (a) The statistical definitions of "milk" and of "meat" were expanded a year before the campaign was launched, thereby making these categories noncomparable with earlier Soviet series; (b) Usually campaign slogans refer to catching up with the per-capita levels "in the United States of America, the foremost capitalist country," thereby giving the impression that these per-capita levels are also the highest in the world. In point of fact, however, per-capita milk, butter, and even meat production in the U.S. are not the highest in the world by substantial margins; (c) No mention is made of margarine, the consumption of which now exceeds that of butter in America, nor of cheese, the U.S. production of which approximates that of butter, in comparison to the U.S.S.R.'s relatively small output.

targets for producer goods and consumer goods widened in favor of the former.* Especially notable in relation to other targets is the large investment program. If the agricultural equipment to be purchased by collective farms is to be included with state investment (as it previously was), the volume of state investment over the whole seven years, as planned, will be 90 or more per cent larger than over the preceding septennium. In addition, sizable increases in the investment by and in collective farms on their own account, and in private homes by the population, are anticipated. Compare this with the expected increase in the "consumption fund" of 60–63 per cent,† and of 62 per cent in the volume of retail sales by state and cooperative stores,‡ between 1958 and 1965.

In this connection, it may be interesting to trace the evolution of the long-range targets for steel. Speaking at the Supreme Soviet session in May, 1957, I. P. Bardin, the most authoritative figure in Soviet steel planning, called for an output of 125–50 million metric tons of steel in 1980, which implies an average annual increase of 4–5 per cent. In November, 1957, Khrushchev set a target of 100–120 million tons by 1972, implying an average

* The original (and since discarded) control figures for the Sixth FYP (1956–60) called for the following increases (over five years): gross output of all industry, 65 per cent; gross output of producer goods, 70 per cent; of consumer goods, 60 per cent. The control figures for the Seven Year Plan call for the following increases: all industry, 78 per cent; producer goods, 85–88 per cent; consumer goods, 62–65 per cent. Cf. Leon M. Herman, "The Seven Year Haul," *Problems of Communism*, March–April, 1959.

† The "consumption fund" is presumably the portion of the national product going into consumption, but its composition and derivation are not clear. It probably includes consumption of material goods for military and other government use.

‡ The retail-sales figure must be interpreted with considerable caution, for it almost certainly exaggerates the prospective increase in consumption. Consider: (a) Sales in the so-called collective-farm markets, not included in this figure, have been declining and will undoubtedly continue to decline relative to other retail sales; (b) The shift from collective farms to state farms, from grain to technical crops, and from remuneration in kind to payment in cash, as well as the pressure against peasants' private plots, are likely to make peasants more dependent on "official" retail sales and less on self-supply; (c) It is not clear whether sales of parts and supplies for agricultural equipment to collective farms, or even of the equipment itself, will henceforth be counted as retail sales.

annual increase of 5–6 per cent. In April, 1958, (according to a *Tass* release broadcast by Radio Moscow on April 23, 1958), Bardin revealed the Seven Year Plan's target for 1965 as 80 million tons—representing a 6 per cent average annual rate of increase. Finally, the control figures for the SYP posit a target of 86–91 million tons by 1965, calling for an average annual rate of increase of 6.5–7.5 per cent from 1958. These figures suggest that the Seven Year Plan was substantially "hardened" sometime in mid-1958. The reader may wish to speculate as to what domestic or international developments may have prompted this redirection of Soviet long-range planning.

Toward Greater Rationality?

A country bent on winning an economic race in a short period of time against a formidable adversary would, if it proceeded rationally, choose a favorable yardstick for measuring its progress against that of the opponent, would mobilize popular support and enthusiasm for the race, would plow back into the expansion of its productive capacity as high a fraction of its current resources as possible, and would distribute its resources among the various alternative uses so as to obtain the most out of them for the task at hand. The first three of these the Soviet leaders are more or less doing, as we have already seen. The yardstick with which to measure their progress in the race is in their own hands and of their own choosing. An intense effort is being made to elicit popular support for the race through the use of the "catch-up-with-America " slogan. And, following the setback resulting from the poorly constructed and overly optimistic control figures for the Sixth Five Year Plan, investment is once again being stepped up in relation to other end uses, although the imperatives of military defense and the need to satisfy the popular desire for substantial improvement in the standard of living are keeping the volume of investment within bounds.

The fourth consideration—efficient allocation of available resources to meet the posited goals—has also been receiving much more careful attention than ever before. Concomitantly, a radical reorientation of Soviet economics has come into effect, one not without serious implications for the governing ideology on the one hand and the evolving society and polity on the other.

The great industrial advance under Stalin was accomplished largely by drawing on four well-nigh limitless reservoirs (or so they seemed to be at the time): the large surplus of manpower of the villages, the rich natural resources of the country, the bountiful technology of the industrial world, and the capacity of the Soviet consumer to endure—to be sure, under political repression and police control—prolonged and heavy privation. Vast resources were mobilized for "socialist construction" in this manner, but no one who has looked into the record can say that these resources were efficiently used. In fact, they were wasted at an appalling rate due to the lack of a clear conception of what efficient resource allocation entails, to confusion and stupidity in planning, to various institutional factors, and to the unpreparedness of the population for rapid industrial advance. By the time Stalin's successors took over, the reservoirs were no longer full; indeed some of them, especially the pool of surplus manpower, were nearly empty. Thus the question of better husbanding of resources, of economic rationality, was crucial.

A number of steps in the direction of greater economic rationality either have been taken in the past few years or are now being intensely debated. Among them, the problem of price formation in the state sector should be particularly noted. It has been under discussion for two years now, and an official resolution of the issues is probably not far away. Whether the price reform to come will lean more in the direction of rationality, producing a price structure reasonably expressive of opportunity costs within the Soviet economy and thus facilitating the efficient allocation of resources, or will bow to Marxian doctrine and enthrone the labor theory of value even more firmly, remains to be seen.

Victory for the "Rationalists"

Of very great interest in this regard, and of direct relevance to the problem of the "time factor," is the resolution in mid-1958 of the long-smoldering issue of choice among alternative technologies, an issue that revolved around the validity of applying, under Soviet conditions, an interest rate (or some surrogate thereof) in order to decide how much capital should be invested to produce a given amount of a certain product.

The matter has had a long and sinuous history in the U.S.S.R. Briefly, the use of the interest rate in economic calculation was abolished in the early 1930's as a "bourgeois category." The effect was to make capital (investible resources) a free good when in fact it was extremely scarce during the five-year-plan era, and to lead to a preference for unnecessarily capital-intensive variants of investment projects. In fact, of course, the full demand for capital could not be satisfied, and it was allocated "administratively" according to a scale of priorities and certain rule-of-thumb criteria. To meet this problem, some of the planners, mostly at intermediate levels, were led to set up for their own guidance "minimum admissible recoupment periods." That is to say, they would use additional capital on investment projects only if the consequent savings in current cost paid for the extra capital in no more than a given number of years. Thus, in a backhanded way, by means of the minimum recoupment periods* (additional capital/annual savings in operating cost resulting therefrom), these planners were introducing the concept of a minimum rate of return on capital (annual savings in operating cost/additional capital)—that is, in effect, an interest rate.

For about a decade these methods remained relatively unnoticed. In 1948–49, they were discovered by some Soviet economists and condemned on Marxian theoretical and ideological grounds. However, the condemnation did not bring about the complete abandonment of the "recoupment-period" device, and indeed, only a year after Stalin's death, a partial and cautious authoritative approval of the device was published in *Voprosy ekonomiki* (No. 3 [1954], pp. 99–113), which seems to have led to its widespread adoption in Soviet economic planning. This was not entirely surprising, since the device, primitive as it is, is a very convenient—indeed almost an unavoidable—aid to plan-

---

* In American business practice, the recoupment period is usually called the "pay-off period" or the "pay-out period."

ning. In August, 1956—this time not only in response to the needs of planning but also in response to an urgent need to develop a system of rewards for innovators—the State Commission for New Technology (*Gostekhnika*) issued a "temporary model methodology" for computing the efficiency of capital investment, which once again permitted the use of the recoupment period as a criterion of selection among alternative technologies.

In mid-1958, the issue was finally resolved. The solution took the form of "recommendations" by a special conference on the subject convened by the Institute of Economics of the Academy of Sciences of the U.S.S.R. Significantly, the recommendations went almost full length in the "rationalist" direction, calling for the extensive use of recoupment periods and interest rates (though not so called) in economic calculation in connection with investment planning. However, the determination of appropriate interest rates and maximum admissible recoupment periods was left to the individual industries, and little theoretical guidance was given on this score by the recommendations (as indeed may have been expected because of the peculiar inability of the Marxian theory of value to cope with this problem).

The immediate practical significance of this event should perhaps not be overrated. Chances are that in itself the formal incorporation of the "time factor" into the economic calculus is going to add only moderately to the effectiveness of resource utilization in Soviet investment planning—and to that modest extent, only after the more fundamental problem of rationalizing the whole price structure is resolved. Its import lies, rather, in the clear-cut major victory for the "rationalists" as against the "dogmatists," and in the sign of the times that it represents.

Present Versus Future

As for the third development in 1958, mentioned earlier in the article—the change of policy with regard to hydroelectric stations —very little sophisticated economic calculus was needed to arrive at it. For various reasons, among which prestige considerations must have ranked high, the Soviet leadership until recently showed a preference for hydroelectric power stations, particularly the grandiose ones, as against thermal stations. This preference was buttressed by certain bases in economic calculation, such as the failure to charge interest on capital invested (which is, of course, much larger in hydroelectric stations) and the failure to ascribe any value to the land flooded behind the dams.

However, hydroelectric construction was taking a long time (at least from the standpoint of the race with the U.S.) and was using a considerable fraction of investible resources. With the emphasis on quick returns and postponement of outlays that the economic race logically calls for (Khrushchev's "time factor"), a shift from hydroelectric power to thermal power, based especially on the cheap and plentiful but hitherto neglected resource of natural gas, makes sense. From the standpoint of actual planning, of course, it is not so much a matter of emphasizing the one against the other as finding the optimal balance between the two. Whether Soviet thinking is sufficiently clear-headed on this subject at the moment—and it appears from remarks at the Twenty-first Congress of the CPSU that political interests and personal passions are heavily involved in the matter—and whether the Soviet economic calculus is sufficiently precise to bring about the proper balance remains to be seen.

In a sense, the latest educational reform also represents a deference to the time factor. To the extent that it emphasizes the immediate absorption of young people into the labor force, it necessarily de-emphasizes the accumulation of technical and scientific skills through advanced study, or, if one will, the accumulation of "human capital" for the future; in other words, the educational reform in effect sacrifices some of the nation's future productive capacity for production in the near term.

The Soviet economy is in a hurry; it is pressing hard against its means. This more than anything else is pushing its leaders toward more prudent (i.e., rational) techniques of husbanding and utilizing resources. Thus the time factor in economic calculation is now receiving formal attention and official obeisance. Whether greater economic rationality in this sense must eventually remold the spirit of the society and thereby affect benignly the very ends the Soviet regime seeks and the values it professes

—whether, in effect, the servant will humanize the master—remains to be seen. Those who so believe cannot overlook the fact that more rational paths are also more direct and speedier paths to the posited goals. In the meantime, the commitment of Soviet society to an all-out economic contest under dictatorial direction, the thoroughgoing enlistment of the population's energies and minds to this end, and the staking of so much by the regime on the race, do not seem to be especially favorable conditions for accelerating the transformations in the body politic for which economic rationality is reputedly a catalyst.

THE SOCIETY

Introduction

Among the changes that have taken place in the Soviet Union since Stalin's death, and particularly since Khrushchev's assumption of power, two trends—seemingly contradictory, yet essentially complementary in character—emerge in sharp relief. One is the trend toward a partial lowering of the rigid social and economic barriers that have separated the distinctly privileged from the distinctly unprivileged in Stalin's "socialist" society; the other is the gradual enhancement of the position of the Communist Party in all spheres of public life.

These two trends form the subject matter of the first four articles in this section. In the first of these, Mr. Feldmesser traces the progress as well as the limitations of "social undifferentiation" and offers a provocative explanation of its causes. In the second, Mr. Bialer provides a somewhat different interpretation of recent Soviet developments in this area; the bulk of his article, however, is concerned with the intricate relation between the seemingly increased emphasis on egalitarianism on the one hand, and the strengthening of the actual ruling stratum in Soviet society—the officialdom of the Communist Party of the U.S.S.R.—on the other. The articles by Paul Barton and Arcadius Kahan continue the survey of equality and inequality by examining the status of what, in Communist terminology, is referred to as the two "non-antagonistic classes" in Soviet society—workers and peasants. Mr. Barton's article deals specifically with recent developments in

labor legislation, while Mr. Kahan presents a historical sketch
of the relation between the peasantry and the regime, as well as
an analysis of current agricultural policies.

The Soviet claim of having eliminated the gross inequalities of
capitalism does not pertain only to class distinctions but, of
course, to national injustices as well. Indeed, the establishment
of "harmonious" and "friendly" relations between the more than
100 national minorities inhabiting the U.S.S.R. has always been
one of the major claim of Soviet propaganda. How valid that
assertion is may be gathered from the two other articles by Alex
Inkeles and Erich Goldhagen. Mr. Inkeles, in his article, sets up
a number of criteria that would have to be met by any successful policy toward national minorities and then examines the
actual Soviet record in relation to each of these criteria. Mr.
Goldhagen discusses the position of the Jews in the U.S.S.R.—a
unique case in the annals of Soviet nationality policy, but one
that may indeed be the exception that proves the rule.

Equality and Inequality Under Khrushchev

——ROBERT A. FELDMESSER

A GREAT DEAL HAS BEEN written on the emergence of gross inequalities of wealth, privilege, and official honor in Soviet society. The process, fully described and documented, may be said to have begun with a famous speech by Stalin in 1931, in which he denounced "equality mongering" in the wage structure and called for a new attitude of "solicitude" toward the intelligentsia; it manifested itself in highly differentiated incomes, in a change in the composition of the Communist Party, in the establishment of tuition fees and other more subtle obstacles to higher education, in elegant uniforms and elaborate titles, and in a host of other ways. By the end of World War II, and particularly during the last years of Stalin's life, the trend was clear: The Soviet Union was well advanced along a seemingly irreversible course toward a rigid system of social stratification, in which the upper classes would remain upper, the lower classes lower, and the twain would rarely meet.

Yet the irreversible has now been reversed. With that breathtaking facility that so often startles us, the Soviet leadership has launched a series of measures calculated to reduce the degree and rigidity of differentiation in Soviet society to a very considerable extent. Many observers have not yet fully apprehended this turn of events, if only because all its component parts had not been assembled in one place: To do so is one objective of the present study. But partly, too, the lack of comprehension is due to a reluctance to credit Soviet leaders with the desire or ability to achieve so "virtuous" an aim as social equality—or rather, it is due to a failure to appreciate the *meaning* of equality in the Soviet system. A second objective here is to define that meaning.

The "Revival of Democracy"

[He] began to trample crudely on the methods of collectivity in leadership . . . to order people around and push aside the personnel of Soviet and economic organizations. . . . [He] decided questions great and small by himself, completely ignoring the opinions of others.

[He] flattered himself with the belief that all [improvements] were due only to his own merits. The more successfully things went, the more conceited he became, the more airs he gave himself.

You get the impression that everything other people do is bad, and only the things [he] does are good.

These scathing remarks could well have been taken from Khrushchev's secret speech to the Twentieth Congress exposing the incredible extremes to which Stalin's method of one-man rule had gone. A common reaction to this speech abroad was to see in it a confirmation of the trend toward inequality. The intelligentsia, or the "state bourgeoisie" (a term coined by Hugh Seton-Watson) despite their privileges vis-à-vis other elements of the population, had long resented the Stalinist tyranny. Now, as a result of their increasing power in an industrialized and militarized state, they had reached the point where they could force Khrushchev to confess that they had been unjustly treated, to promise them the freedom of decision-making, and to guarantee the security of their status.

Subsequent comments in the Soviet press have belied this interpretation. The quotations do not come from the secret speech; they are attacks on, respectively, a *raion* Party secretary, the chairman of a city soviet executive committee, and a factory director. For, as it now appears, the secret speech was directed not only at the one big Stalin, but also at all the other little Stalins who had grown up in his image. It has been followed up not with praise for Soviet administrators, but with denunciations of *administrirovanie*—the high-handed, arrogant ways of officials who have exercised "petty tutelage" over their subordinates; who have glossed over shortcomings, suppressed criticism, and persecuted their critics; who have been "inattentive to the workers and their needs"; who have, in short, violated the letter of Soviet law and the spirit of "Communist morality."

Denunciations of this sort are not, of course, new; but what is interesting today is not only the frequency and vehemence of such attacks, but the implicit admission that the inspiration for bad administrative habits came from very high up. Accordingly, Khrushchev's own behavior, so sharply at variance with Stalin's, has been held up as an example for others to follow: Soviet officials have been urged to get closer to the people, to pay more attention to them, and not to rely exclusively on existing channels of authority. Sessions of local soviets are being held more frequently; there have been occasional reports of ministers and department heads being subjected to questioning by deputies; in some instances, agendas of meetings have been posted and public hearings held on the items under discussion. The number of deputies in local soviets has been increased by 1.8 million, and unpaid activists have been taking on tasks formerly performed by the executive staff—as if housewives were indeed to run the state. Along the same lines, there has been a large-scale effort to reinvigorate the system of worker and peasant correspondents, to protect them from reprisals by the targets of their criticism, and to have them do more of the newspapers' work in place of the professional journalistic staff. *Partiinaia zhizn* (No. 14, July, 1959, p. 55) has told *raion* newspapers that they were not limited to criticizing "only rank-and-file workers and 'second-rank' officials of *raion* organizations."

The appeal for "popular participation" to reform the deeply ingrained bureaucratic habits of Soviet officialdom has even been extended to the Party-controlled trade unions, which have been urged to shake off their submissiveness to factory executives and to offer vigorous opposition when necessary. Instances of rambunctious local trade-union committees have been held up for emulation, and workers enjoined to criticize "without being afraid that it will upset some director or other," and without having their remarks "prepared" or "cleared" by higher authorities.

Another indication of the new spirit, antedating the Twentieth Congress, has been the abolishment of the uniforms, insignia of rank, and titles that had been authorized for many civilian occupations during and after the war. There has been an appeal for more informal relations and less social distance between those of high rank and those of low, and for an end to such practices in the armed forces as separate dining rooms for the several ranks.

In general, the Party seems to have been going out of its way to assert its respect for "ordinary" workers and peasants, a development reminiscent, as are many aspects of this campaign, of the attitude prevailing during the first decade after the October Revolution. Reversing a trend of more than twenty years' duration, the Party has made a deliberate attempt to recruit more workers and peasants into its ranks: so much so, that Khrushchev was able to report at the Twenty-first Congress that two thirds of current admissions were in those categories, a figure which he accurately called a "considerable increase." In addition, the Soviet press has published numerous editorials, articles, and letters passionately proclaiming the honor and worth of manual labor in a socialist society, filled with glowing words about citizens who are not afraid of soiling their hands, who are "creating material values for the people" rather than "sitting in offices and filing papers." While this line of propaganda is not new, it has never been pursued so intensely. In recent speeches and articles, the third member has often been missing from the traditional trinity of "workers, collective-farm peasants, and intelligentsia."

The rights and privileges mentioned thus far may seem to be only honorific. To be sure, they do not signify any real diffusion of the locus of power in Soviet society. Nevertheless, their importance should not be underrated: They do, after all, attempt to raise the ordinary worker's self-respect, and to imbue him with the consciousness—denied to him under Stalin—of his own contribution to the country's industrial progress. Having for years been exposed to harassment, incessant exhortations, and an attitude on the part of the authorities bordering on contempt, he is not likely to scorn even this—however mild—token of recognition and respect.

Adjustments in the Income Structure

In any event, more tangible rewards have also resulted from the new policy. Although we need not take too literally all of the promises made by Khrushchev—and by Malenkov before him—to increase the output of consumer goods, there is every indication that the lowest-paid Soviet workers and peasants have been placed in a better competitive position to buy whatever is available.

On the one hand, minimum wages were raised in 1956, and two more increases scheduled in the current plan will bring the wage floor up to 500–600 rubles a month by 1965—hardly a level of luxury, but approximately twice what it is now; raises have also been promised to "medium-paid workers and employees." Old-age and disability pensions have been increased, too. Income taxes have been revised in favor of the lowest income brackets.

On the other hand, there has been a good deal of talk, and some action, aimed at reducing the incomes of managerial and scientific personnel. In particular, the awarding of lavish bonuses to administrative, Party, and other officials has been repeatedly attacked, and it is almost certain that the worst abuses are being corrected, "voluntarily" if not otherwise. A decree of the Council of Ministers has warned against excessive expense accounts on *komandirovki* (business trips)—another common source of added income for economic staffs. Sputniks notwithstanding, the scientists have come in for their share of criticism, too, for holding multiple jobs and for receiving high incomes "merely" because they have higher degrees.

The range of differentiation is being contracted not only between manual and nonmanual workers, but within the manual group as well. Wages in a number of industries have been sporadically revised over the past five years, the guiding principle being "a rise in the proportion of basic wage rates in workers' earnings." Although the primary motives seemed to be economic and bookkeeping concerns—to restrain inflationary forces and restore simplicity to the wage structure—it was implied that many of the premiums and increments that had permitted the rise of an inner aristocracy among the workers would be curtailed or eliminated. It has now been authoritatively stated that greater equality of wages is a deliberate intention. A. Volkov, who succeeded Kaganovich as head of the Committee on Labor and Wages, has declared that, "with the aim of decreasing the gap between maximum and minimum wage rates," such measures as these are to be undertaken: a reduction in the number of skill categories and in the ratio between the highest and lowest rates to "no more than" two to one; a "sharp" decrease in the use of progressive piecework rates; and a replacement of individual bonuses by collective bonuses, spreading the benefits of a single worker's accomplishment to his whole work team.*

Rural Remedies

Even more striking have been the changes in the agricultural sector. Adjustments in crop-purchase prices and agricultural taxes and other steps taken since 1953 have raised the income of collective farmers in general while diminishing the range of earnings among and within the collectives. On several occasions, Khrushchev has referred to the "excessively high incomes" of some collective farms (as he has to the "unjustifiably high incomes" of some workers). One remedy, analogous to the industrial wage reform, has been the establishment of a uniform pricing system for agricultural purchases, without bonuses for exceeding the purchase plan, with the result, according to Khrushchev, that "many collective farms will undoubtedly get more, while the leading collective farms will receive . . . somewhat less than now. And this," he added, "will be entirely fair" (*Pravda*, June 21, 1958). Especially interesting is his implicit denial of the principle laid down by Stalin in 1931: that wide income differentials were needed as incentives to raise produc-

---

* *Pravda*, November 25, 1958. At the Twenty-first Congress, Khrushchev remarked that it was also time to eliminate the differential paid for work in remote places (*Pravda*, February 1, 1959). Premiums evidently will be preserved for hot or underground jobs and hard physical labor.

tion. Khrushchev, on the contrary, has asserted that the farms
with low income due to poor production are discouraged from
increasing their output:

> Collective farms that did not achieve the planned harvest
> . . . were penalized, as it were. . . . This, of course, did not
> spur them on. . . . The goal here must be a more correct
> determination of pay . . . in order to provide incentive not
> only to the leading, but to all collective farms.

In connection with the shift, now apparently underway, from
payment by workdays to guaranteed cash payments, the whole
problem of income differentiation in agriculture has been discussed in three articles in *Voprosy ekonomiki* (No. 2, February,
1959), the Soviet Union's leading economic journal. Among situations they cited as "unjustifiable" are: income differentials among
collective farms due to varying locations, soil fertility, or crops;
differentiations between peasants and farm executives due to the
closer linking of peasant earnings to the volume of output; and
differentiations among the peasants themselves due to too many
pay-rate categories with too steep increases and to inequitable
discrepancies in output norms. The remedies are fairly obvious,
and cases are cited in which they are already being applied.

Reform in Education

The school system initiated in the 1930's was one of the major
props of social differentiation. Its salient features, for present
purposes, were these: Seven years of education were nominally
compulsory, although it has been revealed that as late as 1958,
only 80 per cent of the young people were completing the course.
After the seven-year school, a youngster might (a) go to work
in a job requiring little or no skill; (b) be drafted into a labor-
reserves school, providing training of up to two years for occupations of moderate skill; (c) enter a *tekhnikum*, a three- or four-
year school for highly skilled manual and some nonmanual
occupations; or (d) proceed to the upper grades of a ten-year
school for essentially "academic" training, preparatory in almost
all cases to matriculation at a *vuz* (higher educational institution). Tuition fees were charged in the *vuzes*, ten-year schools,

and *tekhnikums*. Scholarships were available at *tekhnikums*, while room, board, and uniforms were free in the labor-reserves schools; but no such aids were offered to pupils of the ten-year school. For both material and "cultural" reasons, therefore, the tendency was for children from lower-status families to attend the vocational schools and enter the same sort of occupations already held by their parents, while children of the "elite" were more likely to take the academic sequence preparing them for professional and administrative positions. The greater informal influence which highly placed parents could exercise on those responsible for *vuz* admission strengthened this tendency. The schools thus contributed to the cleavage between manual and nonmanual groups.

The decision, adopted at the Nineteenth Congress and re-affirmed at the Twentieth, to implement universal ten-year education wreaked havoc with this arrangement. Since ten-year schooling was to be compulsory, tuition fees made little sense, and they were accordingly abolished. On the other hand, *vuz* enrollments were not expanded; most of the ten-year graduates were expected to go directly to work, or into *tekhnikums* or other vocational schools. This meant, in turn, a revision of the ten-year-school curriculum: physical education, music, art, mechanical drawing, and other "practical studies" were increased at the expense of academic courses, and the latter were simplified in content, with fewer examinations and less homework. The effect of these changes—again in part intended—was to make school more accessible and more comfortable for the children of workers and peasants, improving their chances for scholastic success, and to blur the distinction between education for the manual worker and education for his occupational and social superior.

New Problems and a New Program

But the reform proved unsatisfactory in important respects. In particular, graduates of the ten-year schools clung to the idea that they were entitled to a higher education. Many of them resented going either to work or to a vocational school, preferring to wait until they could gain admission to a *vuz*—and this in the face of an imminent labor shortage caused by the birth deficiencies of the war years. One attempt at solving this problem was the campaign, referred to above, stressing anew the dignity of manual labor; but it proved futile. Khrushchev then struck boldly: rejecting the ten-year principle, he declared that eight years of education were all that was necessary, and that such training should be "close to life"—i.e., primarily vocational. He proclaimed a "sacred slogan": "All students must prepare for useful work" and take a full-time job upon completion of the eighth grade. "This . . . will be democratic, since more equal conditions will be created for all citizens: neither the position nor the pleas of parents will exempt anyone, whoever he may be, from productive labor. . . ."

This program met two related goals: a labor force would be trained, in a minimum amount of time, for the kind of work that would be the lot of most;* and the notion of an automatic transition from secondary school to higher education would be dispelled. The purpose and atmosphere of the new type of school are suggested by the fact that pupils will combine their studies with productive work and with such chores as cleaning classrooms, tending shrubbery, and preparing and serving lunches. After the educational overhaul is completed, in three to five years, all students who wish to receive full secondary schooling (now to be of eleven years' duration)† will do so by correspondence or in evening or off-season schools, without taking time away from their jobs. Although there was much discussion of schools for the "gifted," in which students would not be required to work while studying, it is significant that no provision was made for them (except in the areas of music and dance) in the reform as it was finally enacted. The labor-reserves system as such now seems to be a dead letter, though it might be more accurate to say that in effect it has been extended to embrace all schools and all young people.

---

* Khrushchev estimated an annual increment of 2 to 3.5 million youths in the labor force two years sooner than under the old program; this gain is exclusive of the part-time work to be performed by pupils in most grades.

† It should be pointed out that the eight-year school is not a condensation of the ten-year curriculum, but an expansion of the seven-year school—again indicative of the relaxation of academic rigor.

Regulation of Vuz Admissions

At the same time, changes have been effected to improve the chances of workers' and peasants' children competing for entrance to higher educational institutions. Khrushchev and others had repeatedly deplored the handicaps faced by children of lower-status families, scoring in particular the fact that the "competition of parents" with influence was as important in determining *vuz* admissions as was the competition in entrance examinations. In Moscow's higher schools, said Khrushchev, children of workers and collective farmers made up only 30 to 40 per cent of the enrollment. The abolition of tuition fees in the *vuzes*, along with those in the secondary schools, was one move calculated to alter this situation. It is particularly revealing that this step was taken at a time when pressure for admission to higher education from the growing ranks of ten-year graduates was reaching its peak—that is, when selectivity in admissions was becoming most necessary. If there were truth in the hypothesis of growing class stratification under pressure from a powerful "state bourgeoisie," just the opposite might have been expected—i.e., a rise in the tuition fees as a convenient way of shutting out low-income applicants.

Very different rules of competition were instead set up. A rising proportion (currently, 80 per cent) of *vuz* admissions was reserved for applicants with at least two years of work experience or military service; presumably, this will become a universal requirement when the secondary-school reform is complete. Meanwhile, honor graduates of the ten-year schools and the *tekhnikums* are now obliged to compete in entrance examinations along with everybody else—and, for the sake of "objectivity," the written part of the examinations is turned in under a pseudonym.* In most fields, the first two or three years of higher education are to be combined with full-time work, in order both

* *Pravda*, June 4 and November 12, 1958; *Izvestia*, April 4, 1959. Since honor graduates formerly were admitted without entrance examinations, high-status parents (according to Khrushchev) often put pressure on secondary-school teachers to give their children good grades (*Pravda*, September 21, 1958).

to weed out the less serious students and to impress the future *vuz* graduates with the "glorious traditions of our working class and collective-farm peasantry"—i.e., to blunt the forces making for social separateness. The method of awarding scholarships has been revised to take more account of the material needs of the student, and somewhat less of his grades; special courses are being organized to help *vuz* applicants who have not completed secondary education or who have been out of school for a while; and all applicants must present recommendations from places of work and also from Party, Komsomol, or trade-union organizations, whose representatives also will sit on admissions boards—all of which recalls the days when the official aim was to "proletarianize" the higher schools. Given the recent Soviet willingness to publish more figures (so long as they "look good"), it may be predicted that we shall soon have, for the first time since 1938, comprehensive data on the social origins of students in higher education.*

The subject of educational reform cannot be passed over without taking notice of the boarding schools. When Khrushchev first broached the topic at the Twentieth Congress, observers assumed (as in the case of the secret speech) that his proposal demonstrated the influence of the elite and that the new schools—despite his protestations to the contrary—would be exclusive institutions for the privileged.

The reality of the boarding school has been a far cry from these suppositions. Priority in admission has gone—as, after all, Khrushchev said it should—to children from large or low-income families, and to others from disadvantaged environments. Fees are charged, but they have been waived for those who could not

* Another prediction that might be ventured is the resurrection of intelligence and aptitude tests, abolished in the 1930's on the grounds that they emphasized inherited rather than acquired traits and discriminated against children of workers and peasants. In effect, the criteria of "ability" became instead school examinations, grades, and *vuz* entrance examinations, which actually discriminate more heavily against low-status students in terms of the motivational or "cultural" influences in their lives. Intelligence-test scores are now considered less immutable than was once thought to be the case, and Khrushchev may "discover" that IQ tests are a more "objective" (i.e., less class-biased) measure of ability than achievement tests.

afford them—again in accord with Khrushchev's original suggestion. Moreover, the curriculum has been strictly polytechnical,
providing training for such occupations as lathe operators, elec-
tricians, farm-machine operators, stenographers, typists, etc.—
hardly pursuits becoming to an aristocratic caste.

Is the Classless Society Coming?

The scope and force of the trend away from extreme differentiation are unmistakable. There are many clues other than those
which have already been cited: criticism of the practice of
assigning chauffered cars to officials; a pervasive, if still partial,
change in the method of awarding medals and orders; a demand
that the Soviet fashion journal concern itself less with evening
gowns and furs and more with "everyday" clothes. To dismiss
all this evidence as mere window dressing, as ritual obeisance
to an ideology, explains nothing; for why is it happening *now?*
Why should Khrushchev feel compelled to renew rituals that
Stalin had long neglected, rituals that offend the sensibilities of
the "elite"? What, then, does account for the change? Is the end
of class distinctions to be one facet of the "transition to Communism"?

Stalin, it seems clear, had felt that a high degree of differentiation was necessary to achieve his overriding goal—a very rapid
process of industrialization subject to his absolute control. This
meant, in the first place, that a group of loyal and competent
administrators and other brainworkers had to be created, and
quickly. It also meant that large segments of the population
would have to be deprived, at least "temporarily," of material
returns from their labor, in order that greater proportions of
production could be applied to the expansion of industrial capacity. Stalin sought to turn the consequently depressed condition of the workers and peasants to good purpose by offering
them great rewards for joining the administrative and technical
corps—hence the wealth, privilege, and prestige that came to
define the upper end of the occupational hierarchy. The need
for upward mobility to escape a life of privation would induce
people to strive for educational training and vocational achieve-

ment and would encourage obedience to Stalin's dictates, while the chance for upward mobility would serve as a substitute for the more prosaic benefits of a slow and moderate rise in the general standard of living.

The gap thus generated between the higher statuses and the lower ably served Stalin's purposes in some respects. Those in high position came to live a different kind of life, free from the material anxieties of those over whom they stood. They became, in short, "insulated" from the less fortunate—blind or indifferent to the needs and wishes of the masses. For they learned that success was to be had by winning the favor not of those below them but of those above them, which was exactly what Stalin wanted them to learn. Now that the policy has come under fire, the attitude it engendered has been amply described in the Soviet press, for example in *Izvestia* of January 18, 1958, in this criticism of the "self-willed" official as a type: "Tell such an official that he has disturbed his subordinate's state of mind, and he will probably be amazed: 'His state of mind? Brother, we're having trouble meeting our plan here, and I have no time to look into all sorts of cases of melancholia.'"

The Problems of Stalinist Policy

Nevertheless, extreme social differentiation had its less desirable aspects, too. For one thing, it "overmotivated" the population: anything less than a higher education, and the higher occupation it brought, was regarded as a disgrace for an upper-status child and as a sad fate for a lower-status child—hence, the intense pressure exerted on the educational institutions, the reluctance of youths to commit themselves to factory jobs. For another and more important thing, it interfered with the operation of the impersonal selection system necessary to an efficient economy and to the reward function of upward mobility. Those in higher and better-paid positions were able to use their influence and their money to assure similar places for their children, at the expense of potentially more capable or more loyal children from less-favored families. Perhaps even worse, some children from well-to-do families neither studied nor worked, but lived off their parents' income—an idle existence that not only meant a loss to the labor force but also, if the Soviet press is to be believed, led in many cases to alcoholism, crime, or even to the acceptance of "bourgeois ideology."

This excessive measure of status security perverted adults as well as children. Once a man was granted local power, he was able to suppress or punish, if not ignore, criticism from his inferiors, and he cooperated with his colleagues to evade the regime's cross-checks on him. This had been intermittently acknowledged in the Soviet Union under the label of *semeistvennost* ("familyness"), but the full dimensions of the problem are only now being revealed. One of the many instances that may be cited concerns the chairman of a city soviet executive committee who "forbade his assistants and the heads of the city executive committee departments to appeal to Party organs without his consent" (*Izvestia*, January 16, 1958). Thus, higher authorities were precluded from receiving the information they needed to keep tabs on their own subordinates. Or, if the Party did manage to find out about and remove some incompetent or dishonest official, he often reappeared in another responsible position— partly, at least, as the result of friendships formed and mutual obligations exacted. Indeed, an integral part of the pattern has been the concern of officials to find places in the *apparat* for friends and relatives who could reciprocally provide a haven if necessary.

All of this was simply the obverse side of the arbitrary power delegated to local officials for the sake of allowing them to carry out their instructions from above without interference from below. But it was ironically self-defeating: By being freed of criticism from below, administrators were able to free themselves of supervision from above. This threatened to contravene the cardinal dogma of the Soviet system, which has come to be known as Stalinism, though it could as well be called Leninism or Khrushchevism: that ultimate power belongs exclusively to the Party—or more accurately, to the head of the Party. Whenever any group jeopardizes that principle, it must be struck down, and that is what Khrushchev is doing. Stalin, in other words, forgot his Stalinism; and Khrushchev is not repudiating Stalinism; he is, if anything, reinstating it.

Khrushchev's Two-Sided Task

No doubt, the Soviet press, in characteristic fashion, has exaggerated the threat. Stalin was not a complete fool, and when all is said and done, he does seem to have kept things pretty well under control. If the group whose growth he fostered was an "elite," then surely no elite has ever proved so utterly helpless in preventing actions that, like those at present, affect it so adversely. The danger was a distant cloud—but a good Bolshevik tries not to wait until the storm has swept away his fortifications. Khrushchev's task, then, is to rid the "state bourgeoisie" of its cockiness, to disabuse it of the notion that it is safe regardless of its actions, to infuse fresh blood—personnel more responsive to orders—into it. Yet because of the positions these people occupy, the task will not be easy, and the plan may be "under-fulfilled." But given the Soviet political structure, the odds are on Khrushchev's side.

The nature of the targets at which Khrushchev has taken aim makes his crusade sound like an echo of earlier revolutionary periods; but in actuality, the development does not connote a return to the situation that prevailed in the early 1920's, for Khrushchev has learned something from Soviet history. The extremes of high and low incomes are to be moderated—but "equality-mongering" is still wrong. Mass participation and criticism from below are to be permitted—but not "violations of state discipline" or "slander of the Party and its leaders." Executives should be more humble, more attentive to their subordinates—but the principle of "one-man management" is to be preserved. "The struggle against the cult of the individual does not at all mean a belittling of the significance of leadership and leaders. . . . The Party does not advocate the denial of authorities" (*Partiinaia zhizn,* No. 7, April, 1956, p. 5). Moreover, Khrushchev has expressly defended the nonmanual pursuits—"those who work in offices are not at all bureaucrats, they are the creative people who originate that which is new"—and he has strongly implied that, even under Communism, there will still be the bosses and the bossed: Communist society will be "highly organized." Complete equality is not just around the corner, nor is it even being contemplated.

"Classlessness" Defined

Nevertheless, Khrushchev *is* seeking a classless society, in the proper sense of the term. If an "upper class," for example, means anything, it means a group of people who share fairly distinctive values and advantages that they are able to hold on to for some length of time even against the resistance of others. Yet in the totalitarian scheme of things, it is essential to the preservation of party supremacy that no group become so entrenched in positions of strength as to become insulated against further demands from the party. An "upper class," or any other "class," is no more admissible than an autonomous trade union or ethnic group. Hence the party must insist—in the long run—that every man be individually and continuously on trial, that status and rewards remain contingent and ephemeral. The greatest threat to the party is the development of a sense of identification or solidarity within a group—or class—and this is precisely what was happening to the Soviet elite. Khrushchev's war against the bourgeoisie is, in fact, only an extension of the battle with the bureaucrats that has long been a part of Soviet policy, even if it was sometimes muted. In short, "classlessness" is essentially a corollary of Stalinism.

Khrushchev, however, believes himself to be in a better position to attain it than Stalin ever was. The creation of a substantial industrial base has relieved him of the urgency that Stalin felt so acutely. Automation, as he has frequently pointed out, really has diminished the differences between mental workers and manual. The spread of education has freed him from dependence on a relatively small group as the only source of administrative and intellectual personnel; workers and peasants can now be brought into the *vuzes* with less risk of lowering the quality of education (as happened in the 1920's). Finally, he evidently presumes that a long period of enforced political homogeneity has led to the withering away of deviant values among Soviet citizens. Criticism from below would thus be less dangerous, since it is more likely to accord with what the Party wants. The only social unit that still enables Soviet man to maintain and transmit both "hostile" values and favored positions, with even a small degree of success, is the family—hence the significance of the boarding schools (and other attempts to loosen family bonds). For the boarding schools are not destined to be elite institutions, but universal ones: the instrument by which the regime hopes finally to achieve control over the last remaining semi-autonomous activity, the rearing of children.* This, too, is an objective that will be familiar to students of Soviet history, but unlike the earlier situation, Soviet leaders may well feel that they now have, or can produce, the material facilities with which to realize it.

Yet it is unlikely that the regime has solved, once and for all, the problem of inequality. Power corrupts—even delegated power. Workers and peasants, no less than the intelligentsia, will sooner or later try to put their privileges to uses that, so far as the Party is concerned, are "selfish." They may, for example, try to develop a monopoly of their own on higher education, or act "prematurely" to increase the production of consumer goods or raise wages, in a kind of latter-day "workers' opposition." Or, once terror is removed, they may turn out not to have lost all their hostile values, after all. When that happens, they will once more be put back in the inferior position they knew up to Stalin's death. No end is in sight to this ancient practice of playing one off against the other, this alternate granting of status privilege within a basically classless framework, as the Soviet system struggles with its perennial and fundamental problem: the need to control the controllers.

---

* "The sooner we provide nurseries, kindergartens, and boarding schools for all children, the sooner and the more successfully will the task of the Communist upbringing of the growing generation be accomplished": Khrushchev's theses on the Seven Year Plan, *Pravda*, November 14, 1958. See also the decree on the boarding schools in *Pravda*, May 26, 1959.

"...But Some Are More Equal Than Others"

———SEWERYN BIALER

IT WILL STILL take us a long time, but whatever the circumstances, we must see to it that our specialists—who constitute and will continue to constitute a distinct social stratum until we attain the highest degree of development of Communist society—live better under socialism than under capitalism.[*]

In these words of Lenin we find the origin of the privileged caste of technical intelligentsia and executive officialdom that has long been a distinctive feature of Soviet society. Stalin extended Lenin's principle of privilege to political and administrative "specialists" as well as to experts in the art of coercion; at the same time he created a system of social stratification that, in the degree of its rigidity and class differentiation, has had no equal in contemporary industrial societies.

Among the evolutionary shifts that have taken place since Stalin's death, changes affecting this aspect of Soviet society have attracted special attention—not wholly by chance or without reason. On the one hand, the new leadership has spared no effort to publicize the favorable features of such changes both at home and abroad; along with sputniks, they have increasingly become the trump cards of official propaganda. On the other hand, the policy moves and measures involved here have been a natural focus of outside interest, since they have important effects both on the Soviet economy and on the relations of the Party to the

[*] V. I. Lenin, *Collected Works* (Russian ed., 1952), XXXIII, 169.

rest of the society. There is a tendency in the non-Communist world—more conscious in some quarters, of course, than in others—to search for signs of a democratic evolution in the Soviet system, as the most comfortable and simplest escape from the problems and dangers of perpetuated East-West competition. The policy shifts under discussion offer rich food for such hopes, because they constitute, without question, significant departures from the past; it therefore becomes a crucial matter to assess them in broad perspective, to see—in short—whether they have affected the essential totalitarian features of the Soviet system.

Types of Change

These shifts can be divided into two groups. In the first group are those that have brought about a distinct improvement in the general living standard and working conditions of the Soviet population. Borrowing from the Marxist-Leninist lexicon, one could justifiably say that the "law of absolute pauperization"—the concept of the inevitable growing poverty of the laboring masses under capitalism—well describes the conditions that prevailed for the great majority of the Soviet populace during Stalin's rule. If there were occasional intervals that saw some amelioration of these conditions, still the over-all living standard, by any yardstick, hovered continuously on the verge of destitution. By contrast, there is not the slightest doubt that a constant rise in living standards has taken place during the last seven years among a broad segment of the population. A great deal of evidence has been compiled to substantiate this trend (see, e.g., the comprehensive article by Alec Nove in the January–February, 1960, issue of *Problems of Communism*); and while there are still discrepancies between Soviet propaganda claims and actual achievements, it seems pointless to waste debate on them, since—assuming a continuation of present policies—the gap will narrow with time.

In the second group are shifts that actually or seemingly affect the class structure of the Soviet Union—that is, the relative status of the different social strata. Again applying Marxist-Leninist concepts, if under Stalinism the "law of absolute pauperization" of the worker and peasant masses occasionally "let up" a little, the "law of [their] relative pauperization" operated without interruption from the late 1920's until very recently. In plainer terms, paralleling the retreat from early "revolutionary romanticism" and the growth of the bureaucracy, there was increasing isolation of the various social strata and increasing disparity between the living conditions and social privileges of the higher and lower classes (or, as Flora Lewis has aptly described them, the "upper classless" and the "lower classless"). As will be shown, the changes that would bring about a genuine reversal of this trend are of quite a different caliber than those in the first group.

The issue has been raised whether Stalin—had he lived and faced the same opportunities as Khrushchev—would have acted to raise the living standard of the Soviet people. In this writer's view, there are no grounds for maintaining that Stalin opposed a rise in the living standard per se: To suppose that he kept it in a depressed state as an absolute goal rather than as a relative necessity (from his viewpoint) is to demonize his medieval personality and to regard his policy as completely detached from the economic and political facts of life as he saw them. A policy of raising the living standard could be characterized as "anti-Stalinist" if the price of its pursuit were a renunciation of the priority of heavy industry, a slowing down of Soviet military growth, and a decrease in the accumulation-consumption ratio of the economy. Such a policy was pursued by Imre Nagy in Hungary during 1953–54, to a certain extent by Malenkov in the U.S.S.R. during the same period, and by Gomulka in Poland after 1956.*

Khrushchev's program to raise the living standard is no such anti-Stalinist policy. It does not reject the basic system of priorities of the Stalinist era. In point of fact, the terms "anti-" or "pro-Stalinist," or "anti-" or "pro-totalitarian," have no more rele-

---

* The Polish example raises the question whether such an "anti-Stalinist" policy can in fact be successfully pursued in a Communist state: While Nagy's and Malenkov's aborted policies are inconclusive in this respect, Gomulka's longer experiment led to deepening economic crisis and, ultimately, to major revisions in his policy.

vancy to his efforts in this area than they have to Soviet successes in the exploration of space. In raising the living standard, Khrushchev has simply actualized *existing potentials* in the economic situation; he has not initiated social changes or ideological revisions.

The situation is different when it comes to changes in the second category. A lessening of class differentiation in Soviet society—if it should prove to be a genuine trend and not a short-term tactical maneuver—would constitute a basic social reform and a political phenomenon of import. The question is whether the present regime has in fact adopted such a policy—and if so, whether it constitutes a long-range trend comparable to the effort to raise the living standard. There is no doubt that a number of developments attest to some leveling off of class differentiation, but in the author's view this tendency is limited in important respects. The economic effects are the most easily measured, and it is to these that we will first turn attention.

The Status of Peasants vis-à-vis Workers

Regarding the industrial workers as the basic layer of Soviet society, the economic stratification initiated under Stalin took place in two directions, both downward and upward.

The peasant became the main victim of the differentiation downward. It is something of a paradox that for long years the only "economic" privilege extended to the peasant—that is, the only hope he had of raising his standard of living—was the right to escape from the countryside to the city. Some recently released statistics give an inkling of the desperate situation that prevailed among the peasantry at the end of the Stalin era: During 1953, 13 per cent of the kolkhozes in Tadzhikistan were unable to pay their farmers any cash for collective labor, while 28 per cent paid only one ruble per labor day—this in a republic strongly favored by the existing agricultural price structure (in 1950, it might be noted, Tadzhikistan and two other cotton-growing republics received 30 per cent of all kolkhoz money income in the U.S.S.R., though containing only 4 per cent of the collective farms).

The disproportion between peasant and worker incomes, in Soviet writings euphemistically called "the differences between town and country," has decreased dramatically in the later years of the post-Stalin era. Between 1952–58, the average payment per labor day on the collectives has about tripled, and the total sum of the collectives' payment for labor has almost quadrupled. Nothing close to such an increase has affected industrial wages or the urban standard of living.

The present regime's policy on peasant income may be explained, in the main, as follows: In the era of "primary socialist accumulation"—and then during the postwar reconstruction and development of industry—agriculture was designated as the basic source of accumulation, the payer of what Stalin called the "tribute" necessary to achieve industrialization. But as Soviet industrial power grew, a more equitable distribution of the burden of accumulation between the city and the country, between industry and agriculture, became not only possible, but absolutely necessary if further progress was to be achieved. Lags in agricultural production had become a stumbling block, hindering the expansion of industry, the raising of urban living standards, and not least of all the Kremlin's expansionist plans. Forcible methods of collectivization had been sufficient to ensure the siphoning off of produce from the country to the town, but not to stimulate agricultural development. The introduction of genuine incentives into agriculture—that is, incentives that would raise the standard of living—became imperative.

A New Retreat?

The Soviet leaders have vigorously pursued this objective over a period of years. Recent evidence suggests, however, that they are now more concerned with the reverse of the problem: namely, how to slow down the pace of the process that they set in motion—in fact, how to prevent the peasants' income from reaching the level of the workers' income. Some indications of this concern were manifested at the December, 1959, Plenum of the Central Committee of the CPSU, where a concerted attack was launched against the present index of purchasing prices for agricultural commodities. One after another, high functionaries of the Party took the stand against the current price scale. The First Secretary of the Tadzhik S.S.R., T. Uldzhabayev, declared that at meetings of activists and on higher Party levels, "a unanimous opinion concerning the need to lower prices for cotton, fruit, and other products had been expressed."[*] Georgia's First Secretary, V. Mzhavanadze, asserted that it was "necessary to work out new proposals for lowering the purchase prices of tea, citrus fruits, bay leaves, and industrial crops."[†] The speeches of C. Polyansky of the R.S.F.S.R., N. Podgorny of the Ukraine, V. Akhundov of Azerbaijan, and many others were keyed to the same theme.

Two future courses were suggested at the Plenum. On the one hand, it was proposed that kolkhoz commodity prices be adjusted, on a step-by-step basis, to approximate more closely the prices "paid" to sovkhozes (the state farms). "It is necessary," said Polyansky, "to work toward a closer approach between kolkhoz and sovkhoz costs of production . . ." and "toward a closer approach between kolkhoz purchase prices and the contractual prices of the sovkhozes."[‡] An indication of the differences between kolkhoz and sovkhoz delivery prices was provided by N. Belyaev, in data on Kazakhstan for 1958:[§]

	Kolkhoz Price	Sovkhoz Price
	(in rubles per centner)	
Wool	4,213.00	1,821.00
Mutton	578.92	320.92
Beef	773.50	416.72
Sunflower Seed	138.72	60.30

If these figures are representative of the whole country, it would seem necessary to lower kolkhoz prices by some 40 to 60 per cent to meet sovkhoz levels.

[*] *Pravda*, December 24, 1959.
[†] *Ibid.*, December 25, 1959.
[‡] *Ibid.*, December 23, 1959.
[§] *Ibid.*

The second proposal advanced at the Plenum—by N. Podgorny, N. Belyaev, and others—was to introduce a maximum wage for the collective farmers. While no exact figure was set, there have been various indications that the *maximum* collective wage under consideration would approximate the *average* industrial wage. It is worth noting that the proposal was put forward following complaints by several speakers that kolkhoz workers in some regions were earning more than the average workers in the area. That such cases must be few and far between, however, seems indicated by data revealing that during 1958, the average monthly earning of kolkhoz workers—combining payments in money and in kind—was below the minimum wage of 270 rubles established for rural areas.* It seems clear from these figures that no more than a small percentage of kolkhoz workers could, in the near future, reach the proposed maximum wage, whether it is adopted or not.

The complaints and proposals aired at the December Plenum bring into focus the problem confronting the leadership. The current price level for the purchase of collective commodities has been one of the mainsprings responsible for the improvement of agricultural production. Its importance is underscored by the fact that in 1958, for the first time in the history of collectivization, cash payments for collective labor overtook the gross income earned by the kolkhoz workers from the sale of produce raised on their private plots.† Any downgrading of the price index is bound to lead to a drop in peasant incomes—or at very least to hold them in check—and the adverse psychological effects of such a move could be serious in the extreme.

The dilemma that confronts the regime is how to continue encouraging the development of agriculture—necessary if it is to fulfill its projected goal of overtaking the United States in per-capita agricultural production—while at the same time guarding against the increase of peasant income at a greater pace than that of the rest of society, specifically the workers. The leadership

---

* Based on the author's extrapolation of data in *Comparisons of the United States and Soviet Economies*, Report of the Joint Committee of the U.S. Congress (Washington, D.C., 1960), p. 274–76.

† *Ibid.*, p. 275.

wants only to narrow, not to close, the gap between the peasants'
and the workers' living standard—at least until such time as it
feels able to transform the collectives into a completely state-
owned system of agriculture. In view of the complexities of this
situation, it is pointless for the moment to speak of a dominant
trend toward the leveling of the economic inequities that have
separated these two groups.

Shifts in "Upward" Differentiation

Whether the process of stratification that took place upward
from the working class, separating it from the "higher" levels of
the society, has now been set in reverse is a much more complicated question. There is a great deal of statistical evidence available concerning the improved circumstances of the workers. But
there is very little hard data to show the effects of recent policies
on the upper strata; and the higher a particular group stands in
the hierarchy, the less is said about it in official sources. Moreover, the higher the group, the more its status must be measured
in terms not just of money income, but in terms of a broad range
of privileges—both economic and noneconomic—which indirectly
favor its welfare.

Starting, then, with the clearest evidences of change, there is
no doubt that steps have been taken to lessen the fantastic ranges
in earning power, and hence in living conditions, within the
industrial working class. There is also not much doubt that the
chasm between the workers on the one hand, and the lower-level
"organizational" men and technical intelligentsia on the other,
has been closed to some extent. The differences of economic
position both within and between these groups are indicated
fairly accurately by the simple dimension of nominal earnings.
The basic intent of the regime in this respect is clear from the
wage and salary provisions of the Seven Year Plan: The minimum wage is to increase by some 60 to 70 per cent between 1959
and 1965, compared to an average increase in all money wages
of 26 per cent. Since, by some estimates, 20 per cent or more of
all workers in the main sectors of the state economy are in the
minimum wage bracket, it seems safe to assume that the most

glaring wage disparities—in the broad range from unskilled workers at one end to technical specialists and middle-ranking professionals or officials at the other—will be lessened considerably.

Moving on up the scale, we come to the question of economic differentiation between the above-mentioned groups and the Party and governmental managerial strata. It is at this level that information concerning direct monetary remuneration is most difficult to come by. There have been rumors that the salaries of some very high-ranking bureaucrats—for example, government ministers—have recently been reduced.* But how wide or how deep the scythe has cut nobody knows; there are not even solid grounds for speculation.

This, however, is the least of the problem. For at the higher levels, excessive inequalities in nominal wages cease to be the only yardstick for measuring differences in economic status. From the medium strata of officialdom on upward, economic privileges of a nonmonetary character increasingly affect and determine the living standard of their recipients. These privileges are hard to measure, not only because they are rarely discussed in detail in Soviet publications, but also because they are largely qualitative rather than quantitative in nature.

Economic Immeasurables

Some examples will be useful. In the catastrophic housing situation that exists in the Soviet Union today, the allotment of dwelling space depends much less on a person's ability to pay than on his official status. His position in the power set-up determines the size and the quality of the housing he can procure. In urban areas, a great portion of the Party apparatus, for example, lives in specially built blocks of apartments—well above average in their appointments—that are the property of the Party and are excluded from the supervision of the local authorities.

* E.g., the Moscow correspondent of the French newspaper *Le Monde*, Michel Tatu, reported on January 5, 1960, that he received "indications" from M. Volkov, the Chairman of the Soviet Governmental Commission for Labor and Wages, that many top ministerial, military, and administrative officials have had their salaries cut.

Since, moreover, these units cannot accommodate all Party personnel, a certain number of units in newly built apartment houses are systematically assigned to the Party from the general housing pool administered by the local government. Once these units are assigned, control passes entirely to the Party, which can choose or change tenants at will. Cases have even been reported where unoccupied apartments have been held in reserve by local Party committees. In this situation, housing has inevitably become a political instrument with which to reward the worthy or to punish the recalcitrant.

Other nonmonetary economic privileges can again be exemplified by Party practice, though also available through separate channels to all groups of the elite. First of all, the Party owns and operates a whole chain of so-called rest homes—in effect, vacation resorts—offering free and relatively high-class accommodations to all Party personnel and their families.* In addition, Party workers have access to a Party-run network of medical facilities, complete with highly trained personnel, modern methods of treatment, and scarce domestic or imported medicines not generally available to the public. A ruble in the hands of a Party *apparatchik* has a "usable value" no less important than its nominal purchasing power: It may be spent at any of a number of stores, service shops, cafeterias, and canteens run by the Party outside the public retail-trade network and offering a line of "deficit" or luxury goods and services rarely obtainable elsewhere. Among other economic sidelines, the Party even maintains a so-called "loan-assistance fund," from which Party workers can borrow money without interest, paying it back in small installments. These are only a few of the operations through which the Party disperses its favors.

* Rest homes are, of course, supposed to be available to all deserving Soviet workers, but some simple arithmetic raises questions about this claim. According to an official Soviet source, as of 1958, there were 836 rest homes in the U.S.S.R., accommodating 160,000 people for two-week vacation periods. According to the same source, the total working force in the nationalized economy and state administration in the same year totaled 54.4 million people. Extrapolating these figures, it is seen that the rest homes can accommodate only about 7 to 8 per cent of the working population. The opportunities for "privilege-mongering" become clear. Source: *Narodnoe khoziaistvo SSSR v 1958 godu* (Moscow, 1959), pp. 101, 666, 895.

The privileges spoken of here do not just pertain to the few hundred officials in Khrushchev's inner circle—they are already living in a "Communist" society where everybody receives according to his needs. These privileges are enjoyed—to a greater or lesser degree, of course—by the entire political bureaucracy and a considerable part of the state bureaucracy. When the sum of such peripheral benefits is considered, it is clear that economic differentiation between the political or administrative official and the average citizen is much more than a matter of difference in pay.

Are these privileges now being eliminated—or even modified? It is impossible to answer definitively. More than likely, they have simply assumed a more "sophisticated"—that is, less obvious —character as a result of the general improvement on the "open" market and the decrease in consumer-goods shortages. The Soviet system, at present and for the foreseeable future, will remain a system where the conveyance of goods from the producer to the consumer is primarily determined not by simple laws of supply and demand—i.e., by a free circulation of commodities in exchange for money—but by planned distribution, allowing regime authorities to decide to a large degree what will be sold where, when, and to whom. The wealth of published testimony bearing witness to the differences in the quantity and quality of goods available in Moscow compared to the provincial cities, or again in industrial towns compared to rural areas, indicates the broad pattern established by distribution controls up to the present. Within this framework, it is clear that planning decisions have been based on both economic and political priorities—and the shorter the supply of particular goods, the greater the influence of political considerations in their distribution.

In the absence of any indications to the contrary, it is fair to assume that these priorities continue to operate.* The indirect

---

* The parallel situation in Poland is interesting in this respect. During the Polish "October," a great number of the nonmonetary economic privileges of the ruling bureaucracy were abruptly liquidated. Yet in the subsequent period of "stabilization," Gomulka has found it necessary to restore the system of privilege to some extent—this despite his own notably ascetic tastes (which would seem to militate against such a retreat) and despite the inevitable negative impact on public opinion.

economic privileges described above may be "survivals from the past," but they have an incentive value among the upper strata that the regime would be loathe to sacrifice. It would be neither possible, given the inadequate level of consumer goods and services, nor politic, given the professed policy of wage equalization, for the regime to compensate for any abandonment of these privileges with some form of direct monetary return. Taking all of the above into consideration, any talk of a trend aimed at undercutting the privileged economic position of Soviet officialdom is—to say the least—premature.

The War on Permanent Privilege

There is, however, a category of policies adopted by the Soviet leadership that in a special and distinct sense has been directed against these upper strata; such policies have had as their common target the perpetuation of privileged status without regard to performance, the "bequest" of such status from one generation to another, and the companion tendency in Soviet society toward class immobility.

Thus, in the case of Khrushchev's educational reforms, for example, steps have been taken to equalize the opportunities and competition for higher education among youths from all social classes of the population, and to curb the abuses of social privilege and power whereby upper-class families have often secured the enrollment of their children in the universities. These measures should help to increase upward mobility and, in time, to make class standing more dependent on ability and less on heredity.

Another step in the same direction has been the prolonged and vigorous press campaign attacking the laws of inheritance and other privileges of the so-called "golden youth"—the sons of "good" family who for all practical purposes do not work, but instead live off their parents' incomes or inheritances left to them.

The regime's attack is directed not only against the sons, but against the fathers—that is, against the assumed privilege of "life membership" in the hierarchy. While this privilege has never, of course, been set forth as a positive right, its foundations were laid during Stalin's time. In the development of the "new class" under Stalin, upward mobility was restricted—though for the ablest the road led to ever-higher honors. On the other hand, downward mobility was even more restricted: The road of descent was limited almost exclusively to political "liquidation" and/or the grave. Assuming that a careerist steered clear of political deviations, did not antagonize superiors, and had some talent for flattery, he could attain a permanent berth among the privileged, once he was "in" with those who counted. The hero of a collection of stories by N. Troyepolski published in Moscow in 1955 (*Prokhor semnadsatii i drugie*) (*Prokhor the Seventeenth and Others*)—a Party functionary named Prokhor—exemplifies and perhaps immortalizes the "staying power" of the privileged group. When questioned about his professional speciality, Prokhor characterizes himself as "Party activist" or "leader" (*rukovoditel*). He not only fails to discharge duties, but disrupts operations in one after another of the positions he holds—yet another place is always offered to him. Why? Because in the files of the Party committee he is a Party activist, a member of the privileged group; he is not guilty of political deviations, and is generally a "nice fellow"; therefore he must be given a responsible post.

The current leadership is clearly at war against this concept of permanent privilege. One of the weapons it has used has been to cut back the size of the Party and state elite.* In this process it has relegated officials who have not shown administrative or leadership ability to jobs in direct production.

The Motivations

These several policies certainly do damage to the position of the bureaucratic and managerial strata, and they have not been undertaken merely for the sake of propaganda—though they are

---

* Very little information is available on the size of these cuts, though there is no doubt that some have taken place, particularly in the state bureaucracy. With regard to the Party apparatus, a delegation of the Italian Communist Party, in a report on talks with Soviet Party officials, quoted a high-level deputy's statement that cuts have been made and are still being made *Problemi e realita dell'URSS* (Rome: Riunitti, 1958), p. 52.

widely exploited as such. Do they, on the other hand, constitute an attack on the *existence* of the new class, or on its basic right to a privileged position in Soviet society? It would seem not. Khrushchev's new-found taste for greater equipotentiality among social groups is not an attempt to destroy the "new class," but rather, in a sense, to "rescue" it from itself—and in the process, to make sure that it remains dependent on the Party leadership.

If the slogan "Back to Leninism," so frequently employed by Khrushchev, means anything at all, it means an attempt to return to a more aggressive, ambitious, and imaginative policy in all spheres of Soviet activity. But the shape in which he found the new class when he acceded to power was inadequate to the tasks and goals he had in mind; its muscles, so to speak, had lost their flexibility and had grown fat. Inflexibility among cadres is desirable in the sphere of ideological adherence, but not at the level of practical performance. Accordingly, Khrushchev has set about making the new class not only more flexible but more dynamic. From his point of view, this class should have a right to enjoy special economic privileges, but not as an end in itself. It should be a hard-working elite, not a leisure class. It should have the drive of the "empire builders" of the nineteenth century, not the comfort-seeking self-complacency of an aristocracy.

At the same time, Khrushchev's reforms have had another—and perhaps even more important—end in view. The new class cannot be allowed to grow strong enough to achieve even partial independence from the central authority, the Party leadership. If the control of the leaders is to be maintained, there should be no people of "independent means," and no groups with a "guaranteed" permanent place in the bureaucratic hierarchy. When such guarantees exist or are taken for granted, a caste loses its zest and becomes preoccupied with its own private affairs—and the ties making it dependent on the leadership begin to weaken. Hence all blessings must come from on high; it must remain within the province of the leadership to grant or withhold them, and to demand that they constantly be earned anew.

In Stalin's time any tendency toward the weakening of ties between the upper strata and the regime was kept in check by the constant threat and frequent use of terror, in wholesale violation of so-called "socialist legality." With the abolishment of organized terror, the regime has been faced with the task of curbing this tendency by "lawful" measures—i.e., by strong and continuous economic and organizational checks. This factor is important in considering how Khrushchev has been able to carry through his "reforms" without greater and more effective opposition on the part of the upper strata. It should be kept in mind that freedom from fear and terror is a very fresh sensation for these people. Khrushchev has demonstrated on more than one occasion that he can be ruthless in the face of resistance, and the choice between accepting his reforms and inviting even a partial retreat toward coercive methods of "persuasion" had probably not been difficult to make. To use an old adage, the elite probably recognizes that it cannot eat its cake and have it, too.

Evolutionary Trends

Adjusting our focus once again to the whole society, it can be shown that a very curious and seemingly contradictory process is taking place in the Soviet Union. On the one hand, the structure and functions of the primary productive and administrative units of the economy have been influenced, to an increasing degree, by factors of rationality; both the managers and the workers, at their respective levels of responsibility, have been allowed to exercise far more initiative than was the case under Stalin. On the other hand, the control of the central authority—its ability to render and to enforce basic policies—has not been diminished, but in fact has increased in certain important respects. In short, *the monistic character of the Soviet system of governance*—which is the heart of the meaning of totalitarianism—has become even more pronounced.

This phenomenon merits close examination. In analyses of the recent evolution of Soviet totalitarianism, the main stress has been laid on the absence of one-man dictatorship in the first years after Stalin's death and on the relative weakness of the recent dictatorship of Khrushchev. Totalitarianism is not, of course, identical with one-man dictatorship. Today, there are dictatorships in a number of countries (e.g., the U.A.R., Iraq,

Portugal, and Spain), but these regimes cannot be labeled totalitarian. But does the opposite hold true? Can a totalitarian system endure for long without some form of dictatorship, of domination by an individual, at the top? The Soviet experience would indicate that it cannot. The inner logic of totalitarianism creates a tendency toward the concentration of power in the hands of a single leader.

What explains this tendency? The *sine qua non* of a totalitarian system is the existence of central authority to make and to enforce basic decisions affecting all spheres of life. When there is a fluctuating balance of power at the center, in turn causing fluctuation or frequent change in basic policies, then the efficiency and discipline of the society are dangerously weakened. Such periods of instability may occur in any totalitarian system, but almost immediately the search for a new condition or form of stability begins.

The process that is set in motion can best be demonstrated by drawing a contrast. In a parliamentary democracy, basic policies are determined by the opinion of the majority. In the parliamentary body itself, there must be a so-called working majority if the business of state is to be accomplished; in the absence of such a majority over any period of time, policy determinations remain in a state of suspension and the parliamentary system itself is threatened. (The crisis in the Fourth French Republic before De Gaulle's accession is a good example of this situation.)

It has been supposed by some that the top policy-making bodies in the Soviet system—the Presidium and the Central Committee of the Party—similarly operated on the basis of a working majority during the period of so-called collective leadership. In point of fact, the concept of collective leadership, invoked after Stalin's death and finally dropped in the summer of 1957, was adopted precisely because of the lack of such a majority. It is sufficient to recall the countless shifting alliances and conflicts among the Soviet leaders to realize the ridiculousness of supposing that any real working majority could have existed (e.g., Khrushchev, Malenkov, and others vs. Beria in 1953; Khrushchev, Molotov, Bulganin, and others vs. Malenkov in 1954; Khrushchev, Bulganin, Kaganovich, Shepilov, and others vs. Molotov in 1955;

Malenkov, Molotov, Kaganovich, Shepilov, and Bulganin vs. Khrushchev, Mikoyan, and Zhukov in 1956–57; Khrushchev and others vs. Zhukov in 1957—enough instances, one would hope, to prove the point). The concept of collective leadership endured as long as there was a relative equilibrium of power within the Soviet leadership, *preventing* the formation of a working majority. The process of elimination necessary before such a working majority could be formed left—in the end—a "majority of one."

Khrushchev's rise demonstrates that the present Soviet system is not much different from its predecessor in so far as the inexorable tendency toward a concentration of power is concerned. The power he now commands does not, of course, approach the degree or scope of the power wielded by Stalin in the prime of his dictatorship, and possibly it never will attain that level. In this sense it might be claimed that the Soviet system is "less totalitarian" than in the past. There are, however, other factors to be considered that preclude such a judgment.

Shifts in the Power Pattern

Let us turn, then, to a consideration of the means and channels by which regime policies are put into effect. For it is in this area the writer finds basis for claiming that the monistic character of Soviet totalitarianism—far from "fading away"—has been intensified.

It falls, of course, to the Soviet bureaucratic hierarchy to communicate the policies and decisions of the leadership down to the operational level, to organize their implementation, and to oversee and ensure their fulfillment. This broad hierarchy can be divided, in terms of function, into four main groups: the political bureaucracy (the Party apparatus); the bureaucracy of coercion (the police and the legal system); the military bureaucracy (the permanent professional army); and the administrative and managerial bureaucracy (the state apparatus).

It can be shown that the boundaries between these groups, in terms of their functions and power, have never before been so sharply drawn—or differentiated—as they are now. In Stalin's

time there was a kind of dualism—or quadruplism, if one will—
apparent in the respective jurisdictions and relative power of
these groups. It was manifested above all in the peculiar, fluctuating equilibrium of power that existed between the political
bureaucracy and the coercive apparatus. Neither of these groups
established clear superiority or control over the other;* on the
other hand, both were more powerful than the remaining two
bureaucracies. Yet the latter groups, though in a subordinate
position, were able to create their own highly centralized organizations, with certain internal features that restricted or counter-
acted outside interference.

In the seven years since Stalin's death, the position of the
political apparatus has been enhanced to a point where it is
both absolutely and relatively the most powerful element in the
bureaucratic hierarchy. This has been accomplished both by
curtailing the power of the other groups and by increasing the
prerogatives and functions of the Party *apparatchiki.*

It would not take much persuasion to convince anyone that
the role and the power of the coercive bureaucracy has been
radically decreased, eliminating it as a challenge to the Party.
It would also seem that since the purge of Zhukov, the relative
power and independence of the military bureaucracy has declined vis-à-vis the political apparatus. The area in which the
author's assertions may be questioned concerns the present influence of the administrative and managerial bureaucracy as compared to the Party. The fact that administrators and managers

---

* In the Stalin era, the ubiquitous police apparatus had rights of inspection and control in all spheres of the society. It interfered with the work of
the other apparatuses in a number of ways—not only in security matters
but in the implementation of the political line, cadre, policy, etc. It was only
in relation to the Party apparatus (and to some extent the military apparatus) that certain limitations were in force.

The Party apparatus, for its part, had no reciprocal power to control or
inspect the operations of the police apparatus. Only in matters of political
indoctrination and propaganda did the Party have a right to impose its
decisions upon the police. And even this right was more formal than real,
since Party committees in the police apparatus were under the jurisdiction
of the Ministry of Public Security itself—unlike their counterparts in, say,
the military apparatus, which were responsible in the last instance to the
Party's Central Committee.

have been allowed a great deal more initiative in conducting their work has led some to assume that their specific gravity in the Soviet power mechanism has increased as well. A comparison of the changing structure and functions of the state and political bureaucracies shows that this assumption is unwarranted.

Emergence of the "Supreme" Party

In the first place, the Party apparatus has remained highly centralized. To the extent that personnel cuts have taken place, they have mainly affected the lowest levels of the Party. By contrast, the state apparatus has been substantially decentralized, especially in the economic field, and many of its central ministries and agencies have been abolished.

With the dissolution of a large part of the central state apparatus, the Party bureaucracy has assumed much greater responsibility at higher levels for the functions of communicating regime decisions downward and overseeing their execution. At the same time, its role in the direct organization of production has greatly increased at the intermediate level of operations, as a result of the creation of the sovnarkhozes (the regions constituting the basic economic and administrative units in Khrushchev's decentralization scheme). Perhaps most dramatic has been the increase of its power at the oblast (district) level, where the long-standing problem of dual authority between the local Party and government organs has generally been resolved in favor of the former. The one real blow to local Party strength in the rural areas, the liquidation of the machine-tractor stations, is being compensated in part by granting the Party organizations in the kolkhozes more power to influence production decisions.

In another and quite different area—the conduct of Soviet relations with the international Communist movement and with other regimes in the Soviet empire—the Party apparatus has again assumed a much larger role than it played in the past, frequently acting as the direct channel for contacts that in Stalin's time were handled by state officials and diplomatic representatives.

It would seem that the record speaks for itself. The Party bureaucracy is at present the only remaining apparatus that is centralized in its organization, that operates at all levels of the society, and that "specializes" in every sphere of societal activity. In its functions of communicating, controlling, and, to an ever greater degree, directly organizing the tasks set forth by the leadership, it influences the operations of the other bureaucratic apparatuses, but is not in turn subject to any outside interference. It is subordinate only to the top leadership and to its own hierarchical line of authority. The individual member of the apparatus has, of course, a clearly defined and limited area of operation, but the apparatus as a whole is under no such limitations. In short, it has assumed an exclusive, ubiquitous, and all-pervasive role in the society.

It is *this* narrow group, then—narrow in relation both to the size of the entire Party and to the size of other groups within the Communist bureaucracy—that has come to constitute the new ruling stratum in the Soviet Union.* While its ranks include a number of "experts" with specialized functions and authority, the role of the apparatus as a whole is perhaps best expressed in the functions and powers of the hierarchy of Party "first" secretaries. The activity of the Party secretary is restricted only by the territorial limits of his jurisdiction and by the decisions of the next secretary up the line; he may exercise his authority in any sphere, imposing his will on the economic administration, the educational system, the local governmental apparatus, etc. He is, in effect, the one representative of the Communist bureaucracy within "his" area whose scope of professional interests and right of interference are virtually absolute and all-embracing. In this sense, he personifies the omnipotence of the Party apparatus within the society at large.

It may be argued that the role of the managerial bureaucracy is to an extent parasitical compared to its counterpart in a free economic system; yet once the means of production are nationalized, once a state economy is established, the managerial

---

* According to the author's calculations (based on various factors that cannot be presented here for lack of space), the Party apparatus in the Soviet Union is composed of about 200,000 officials—that is, some 3 per cent of the Party membership and only a fraction of a per cent of the total population.

apparatus can at least be defended as economically necessary and socially justifiable. This justification is lacking in the case of the political bureaucracy; its *raison d'être* is solely to perpetuate the supremacy of the Party.

The Nature of the New "Democracy"

Perhaps no one has better defined the character of "democracy" in the Soviet Union than the American economist David Granick in his book *The Red Executive:*

> The essence of Soviet "democracy" is the activity of large numbers of people in interpreting to their local scene the decisions made higher in the organization . . . taking part in carrying out these decisions . . . supervising their execution by others, and finally . . . trying to mobilize support for these decisions among the general Soviet public. In short, *democracy consists of participation in everything except basic decision-making.*

This, in simplest terms, expresses the barrier that continues to divide and distinguish the *rulers* from the *ruled* in Soviet society. The Party leadership has been willing—as industrial development made it possible—to share the ruling group's position of *economic* privilege with other strata of the population, to extend the "fruits of the revolution" on an ever greater scale to an ever greater number of people. But more closely and jealously than ever, it guards the ruling group's position of *political* privilege—that is, its monopoly of power and final authority over the basic decisions that determine the direction and character of the society. A number of non-Party specialists and even some outstanding workers in certain occupations (e.g., mining), may enjoy a living standard close to that of the ruling group; in fact, the highest-paid managerial personnel and specialists may be "better off" than the preponderant majority of the political apparatus. But here any equality of status ends. The economic privileges granted at any level represent payment for services rendered on order of the political rulers; and at any level they are incentives aimed at binding the recipients to the Party regime. In the last analysis, even the highest-ranking specialists—as long as they are *only* specialists and not members of the political bureaucracy—have no more right than the lowliest citizens to affect or participate in the basic policy-making function.

The same barrier applies to the so-called freedom of initiative in Soviet life. Any initiative to make decisions has remained tightly within the grasp of the Party apparatus; what has been granted—and in fact widely encouraged in the regime's own interest—is the initiative to implement decisions. One could not wish for a more succinct definition of this difference than that offered in a Soviet pedagogical textbook: "Initiative is an independent search for the best way to fulfill a command."

Progress—Toward What?

The fierce struggle for power within the Kremlin, and the final victorious emergence of Khrushchev, was the inevitable product —the other side of the coin, so to speak—of the myth of collective leadership. Similarly, the concentration and "universalization" of the power of the political bureaucracy is the other side of the coin of Khrushchev's decentralization and democratization reforms. If, as a result of these reforms, the political regime is less preoccupied with petty interference in the lives of its citizens and in the day-to-day determinations necessary in their work, then it is more preoccupied than ever with the basic decisions by which its policies are implemented, with the control of fundamental managerial activities. The lessening of terror—the most fearful and brutal characteristic of Soviet totalitarianism in Stalin's era—and the downgrading of the role of the apparatus that stood behind it has gone hand in hand with the extension of political control and the elevation of the Party apparatus to a unique position of authority. To interpret this process as a diminution of totalitarianism is an utter fallacy.

A Polish writer, back in the days of the October upheaval of 1956, posed the pointed question: "If a cannibal eats with a fork and knife, does it mean progress?" By dictionary definition, progress means "moving forward, developing to a higher stage, gradual betterment." Does the Kremlin's adoption of more civilized means to accomplish its ends mean "gradual betterment"? From the point of view of the average Soviet citizen, it probably does. Perhaps it does from the leadership's point of view, too: The notion of "progress," after all, is highly subjective in character. In addition, any concept of progress, as applied to a whole society, embraces various fields of human and social activity—some complementary, some bearing no relation to each other.

It is important to keep in mind that "progress"—or, for that matter, "regress"—is not the same as "change." In the Soviet Union, changes are taking place in all spheres of the national life; if these constitute progress in some respects, they do not necessarily mean progress in others. There is no doubt that certain changes have initiated a progressive betterment in the living conditions and standards of Soviet society at every level. But changes that would diminish—rather than merely reorganize—the totalitarian features of the Soviet system are yet to come.

While the future is never entirely predictable, it seems improbable that a genuine retreat from totalitarianism will come about through reform from above, so long as those in control—men who took part in building Stalin's empire and who are well schooled in the ways of the "old master"—remain at the helm of Soviet society. To quote another Polish writer's remark at the time of the revolution: "Woe to us, so long as the principle remains in force that only the people who damaged the machine are entitled to repair it."

The Current Status of the Soviet Worker

——PAUL BARTON

THE CLASS STRUCTURE of Soviet society and its development can, and indeed should, be studied from different vantage points. Thus, for example, one may concentrate on the privileges and burdens of the different social groups, or the relationship between the groups in terms of power as well as of material conditions, the links of the various groups with the ruling apparatus, the degree of social mobility, and so on. Social science now offers complex and often subtle techniques to deal with the various aspects of the problem. But if these studies are to be based on firm ground, it still is essential to proceed in the classical fashion and begin by analyzing the status of each of the important classes. This article is an inquiry into the present position of the Soviet worker, as it emerges after the many reforms—some more, some less important—it has been undergoing.

Diffusion of Coercion

On April 25, 1956, with a minimum of publicity, a decree was promulgated in Moscow that produced the most significant changes in the Soviet worker's status since the death of Stalin: Prosecution of workers absenting themselves from work without valid reason was discontinued, the prohibition of unauthorized changes of employment was repealed, and the authority to effect compulsory transfers of workers from plant to plant was withdrawn.

Soon after it had appeared in print, the new law was exhaustively analyzed in *Problems of Communism* (July–August, 1956, p. 2) by the late Jerzy Gliksman, an authority on Soviet labor, whose article also succeeded in reconstructing certain unpublished amendments that, as early as 1951, had already modified Stalin's oppressive labor decrees of 1940. Gliksman convincingly identified the rising concern of the Soviet rulers with the problem of increasing labor productivity as the underlying motivation for the new trend in Soviet labor policy: With the advance of technological development in the Soviet Union and the emergence of an urban proletariat, the brutally coercive measure of the old labor legislation had become antiquated, and they impeded rather than promoted efficiency. Before that, the element of compulsion in Soviet labor policy had been increasing gradually since 1928, and the periodic disruption of industrial relations caused thereby had more than once forced the Soviet government to relax pressure on the wage earners. It is now clear that toward the end of Stalin's rule, labor relations in Soviet Russia had degenerated to the point of complete chaos.

Gliksman also showed that the 1956 decree had by no means put an end to the use of coercion in maintaining labor discipline. He stressed in particular the coercive effect of Soviet seniority rules, of the penalties for unexcused absence from work, of the "labor book," and of the manipulation of social-insurance benefits. Subsequent development has fully confirmed this diagnosis: Indeed, the network of constraint entangling the Soviet worker today remains, if anything, even tighter than Mr. Gliksman supposed. While the recent changes generally tend to soften the harshest provisions of earlier legislation, they also introduce additional severities.

What, then, is the present position of the Soviet worker who desires to leave his job? According to the 1956 decree, he need only inform the plant management a fortnight in advance, except where he may have been employed for a specified period of time or until completion of a specific work assignment. Nevertheless, there remain various effective means of influencing his decision. First of all, economic pressure. For example, if the worker is cultivating a plot of land, he will lose it upon leaving his job, since it is the plant management that assign plots to its employees; furthermore, current legislation provides that the wage earner may use his plot only as long as he is employed by the enterprise that assigned it to him. Thus, the worker who leaves his job automatically loses a substantial portion of his food supply. Furthermore, most social-security benefits, particularly paid leave, sick pay, pregnancy and maternity benefits, are scaled according to the length of uninterrupted employment in the same enterprise. With every change in jobs, moreover, the wage earner loses his right to sick pay for a period of six months.

In addition to these economic pressures, a number of administrative measures remain in force. Specifically, these are connected with the labor book, the interior passport, and the recruitment of labor for industries in which working conditions are particularly hard and the pay is low. Every wage earner must possess a labor book containing information about himself, his successive jobs, the medals and prizes he has been awarded, and the reasons for any separation from his work. The plant management keeps the book for every worker in its employ until he is paid off. In view of the official attitude, which condemns labor turnover as a symptom of demoralization, the wage earner whose book shows several job changes will encounter serious difficulties when he tries to find better-paid work.

All Soviet citizens must also have a passport issued by the police, and police permission must be asked for every change of residence, which is then entered in the document. Without this passport, a Soviet worker cannot be hired; and in coal mines, armament factories, banks, and savings banks, the management is even obliged to take it away from him for the duration of his employment. It is significant that on March 23, 1956, just one month before the repeal of the prohibition against change of employment, the Moscow City Soviet passed a special decree to enforce strict observance of the passport regulations, and that further similar decrees were promulgated in April and August of 1958. Thus the worker who has left his job, especially if he did so against the wishes of the plant management, may meet with a refusal when he presents his passport to the police for permission to move elsewhere.

Even if he finds work in the locality where he lives, he runs the risk of not being able to keep it for long, thanks to the system of organized recruitment known as *orgnabor*. A special government body is charged with procuring a given number of workers every year for enterprises with a manpower problem. This body can order a plant to release some of its workers for reassignment, and the plant thus tapped must surrender the number of workers requested. It stands to reason that it will select those who have least seniority or are otherwise considered undesirable. The men recruited in this way must usually sign a contract for two or three years and are often transferred over great distances to fill unskilled labor jobs. The number of such labor conscripts has grown considerably in recent years, most of them being sent to the remote eastern and northern regions where, until fairly recently, the corrective-labor camps were the principal suppliers of labor.

Thus, the constraints on the mobility of labor are being diffused rather than significantly relaxed. During the 1930's and 1940's, Soviet labor policy aimed at concentrating the apparatus of coercion as much as possible. In the 1950's, however, the tendency has been to disperse the means of compulsion, exposing the wage earner to a variety of pressures that can be applied with greater flexibility.

Labor Discipline

A similar trend can be observed in the modifications of disciplinary labor regulations. Gliksman's research shows that after the enactment of the unpublished 1951 decree, only those guilty of prolonged or repeated absences from work were brought to court. The decree of 1956 went even further in the direction of moderation in that action even in such cases was left to the discretion of the plant managers, who are authorized to impose such disciplinary measures as temporary reduction or suspension of seniority bonuses and dismissal from work with notation in the labor book that the employee has been "dismissed for absence without a valid reason." The workers, as we shall see later, can still be taken to court; but instead of being automatic, this measure is now restricted to particularly serious infractions and has become procedurally more complicated.

At the same time, the authority of factory managers, as well as of supervisors at various levels of responsibility, has been significantly increased in many other respects. The Soviet leadership quite clearly attaches a good deal of importance to this decentralization of disciplinary authority, and the process can be expected to be carried still further in the future, particularly if the system proves efficient in practice. The following extract from an article by G. Podorov, "The Strengthening of Labor Discipline, an Important Factor of the Growth of Productivity," which appeared in *Sotsialisticheski Trud* in 1957, may be indicative of the future trend:

> The consolidation of the principle of unified command, the extension of the rights not only of plant managers, but also of superintendents, foremen, and group chiefs, is of immense importance for the strengthening of labor discipline, since it enables them better to stimulate the workers and to deal with those who violate discipline. If a certain member of a group has infringed labor discipline, if he has been absent without valid reason, if he has come late or has not carried out his task, the group chief, according to the procedure in force, cannot punish him, just as he cannot reward a good worker. Real life demands that such rights should be given to leaders at lower levels also. This will increase their authority and have a good influence on . . . labor discipline.

It would be well to bear in mind, however, that respect for the managers and supervisors as competent technicians and organizers of production could easily be undermined if, in the eyes of the workers, they should become watchdogs primarily preoccupied with discipline. In view of the extraordinary rigor with which labor discipline is enforced in the Soviet Union, this could indeed become a real danger, and it is unlikely that either the government or the managers are oblivious to it. The managerial and supervisory personnel are thus likely to be circumspect in asserting their disciplinary authority, and this may well have entered into the policy-makers' calculations. Viewed in this light, the recent reforms assume yet another aspect: In newly articulating the system of labor constraints, the Soviet leadership may be trying not only to put an end to the clumsiness and red tape that habitually result from excessive concentration of authority, but also to develop a system of discipline enforcement that would be flexible and resilient and would avoid violent shocks to labor morale and productivity.

The Shock Absorbers

To ease the managers' task of enforcing discipline, so-called comrades' courts have been set up in enterprises employing 100 persons or more. Regulations concerning the organization of these "courts," their jurisdiction and rules of procedure, were adopted—though not published—in 1951, very probably in conjunction with the abolition of regular court jurisdiction in the field of labor discipline. In most enterprises, however, they were not actually made public until after the promulgation of the decree of April 25, 1956.

Comrades' courts have an old tradition in the Soviet Union. First established in units of the Red Army after the Bolshevik Revolution, they were transplanted by a decree of November 14, 1919, to industrial enterprises in order to punish noncompliance with labor laws, wage agreements, factory rules, and the like. The "workers' disciplinary courts," as they were then known, were attached to trade-union bodies and were composed of three members representing the factory administration, the trade union, and the general workers' meeting respectively. The punishments they were authorized to impose included public reprimand, suspension from trade-union elections for a period not exceeding six months, demotion and reduced pay for a maximum of one month, and subjection to "socially useful hard labor" with corresponding pay; and particularly obstructive workers could be dismissed and sent to concentration camps (*kontsentratsionnye lageri*). A decree published in April, 1921, just after the inauguration of the NEP (New Economic Policy), specified that workers could be summoned before these courts either by the trade union or by the management. It also enumerated a number of offenses that were made actionable before the courts and extended the range of punishments. With the launching of the Five-

Year Plans, a series of new provisions was promulgated that systematized the institution.

For some twenty years, the comrades' courts were an important instrument in the perpetual Soviet campaign to "strengthen discipline." Judging from the description of a session held in 1937, given by Harold J. Berman in *Justice in Russia*, the procedure gave the accused little chance to defend himself. At the end of a trade-union meeting, the president read the charge against a worker who, without having received any previous notice, had to improvise his own defense; all those present, even if they knew nothing about the case under examination, had the right to intervene in the discussion, and after half an hour, a conclusion was reached, which the accused was compelled to accept. A few years later, probably as a result of the 1940 decrees, which fixed regular court penalties for infringement of labor discipline, the comrades' courts fell into temporary disuse.

As constituted at present, the comrades' courts are composed of five to seven members in small plants, and eleven to fifteen in larger establishments. The members are "elected" in a single-list election by secret ballot, and they, in turn, by a show of hands, "choose" the president of the court, who at every session is assisted by two members of the "court" panel, selected by himself. This collegium is called upon to punish the following offenses: absence without valid reason, late arrival at work, early departure, arriving in a state of intoxication, noncompliance with orders of superiors, unsatisfactory performance and interruption of work due to a worker's negligence, careless attitude toward plant property, neglect of safety regulations, and other infringements of labor discipline. The punishments it can impose include public reprimand, public disgrace, recommendation to the plant manager to demote or dismiss the culprit or to submit the case to investigating or judicial bodies for possible prosecution. Regulations now being prepared would also empower the comrades' courts to impose fines up to 100 rubles and make recommendations to managers that offenders be switched to lower-paid work for periods not exceeding three months.

Only the plant manager, however, can bring a case before a comrades' court, and this is a most important point. He can, by his own authority, punish all the infractions mentioned above by disciplinary sanctions; he resorts to the comrades' courts merely in cases where he finds it more convenient not to act on his own authority. Moreover, if the decision adopted by the court displeases him, he can send the case back for reexamination. The managers have probably had little need so far to resort to such action, as the comrades' courts are, according to *Trud*, the official Soviet trade-union daily, "mainly composed of members of the factory administration." Since the packing of the comrades' courts with administrative personnel has been alluded to, and recently even criticized, elsewhere in the Soviet official press, it is not unlikely that some changes in this respect may take place in the near future. But even if the "judges" should be chosen mainly from among the workers, there is little doubt that the comrades' courts would still have to help the management enforce discipline. The institution would simply be better adapted to its function as shock absorber.

The advantages, for a manager, of being able to act through a comrades' court rather than act himself to punish workers under his command are obvious. Responsibility for decisions injurious to the workers' dignity is thus shifted from his shoulders to the trade union. Moreover, recalcitrant workers tend to be even more intimidated by the spectacular procedure of the comrades' courts than by the penalties themselves. It is, in fact, stipulated that hearings should take place in the factory itself, at a time when the personnel can "be present and take an active part in the discussion of the cases investigated," and that "the decision should be announced to all those present at the hearing and should be made known to all the personnel." Recently it has even been proposed that the sentence should be made known to the neighbors of the condemned worker.

Intimidation and a continued lack of procedural safeguards thus seem to characterize the comrades' courts now as they did in the 1930's. Perhaps the most eloquent indication of the Soviet workers' confidence in this "socialist" institution is the comment of a court president in a large chemical concern, cited by I. I. Yankin in an article on the comrades' courts published in *Sovetskoe Gosudarstvo i pravo*: "From our experience of the work in a comrades' court, we know that many transgressors would prefer to be absent while the comrades' courts judge their case."

The Role of Trade Unions

The renewal of certain rights which had once been granted to the factory committees but had later fallen into disuse, points to the same tendency to use trade-union bodies as shock absorbers between management and labor. Thus in 1958, the regulation requiring the approval of the factory committee before any worker could be dismissed was reintroduced. These committees are so subservient to management, however, that it is hard to see how they could protect workers from arbitrary firing, especially since the committees have more than once proved their impotence in this respect. On the other hand, in view of this additional opportunity to place the responsibility for objectionable practices at the door of the trade unions, the usefulness of the regulation to the regime becomes apparent.

Another example of this type of exploitation of trade unions is the reintroduction of certain old provisions concerning the fixing and revision of output norms. During the Stalin era, management had gradually assumed full control in these matters and made its decisions on a completely unilateral basis. In 1956, the government issued new regulations, which specified that management could change output norms only in agreement with the factory committee and also outlined the procedure for settling conflicts between management and the committees in such cases. It is characteristic, however, that a decree of the Central Trade Union Council quickly asserted that in exercising this new prerogative, the factory committees should regard themselves as the managers' auxiliaries and should make every effort to increase output. Under these circumstances, the intent of the new regulations seems to be little more than to make the factory committees responsible for dealing with workers irritated by the manipulation of norms.

Nevertheless, trade union co-responsibility for fixing norms does have its dangers. As they cannot hide behind a wall of bureaucratic indifference, the unions, especially those on the lower levels, sometimes find it difficult to resist pressures put on them by aggrieved workers. Dissatisfaction provoked by revisions of the norms occasionally contaminates the union organizations themselves. Here, for example, is what *Sotsialisticheski trud,* a monthly journal of the State Commission on Labor and Wages, had to say on the subject:

> Some trade-union committees have declared themselves in an unprincipled manner against the revision of output norms that no longer correspond to changed technical and organizational conditions. A wrong attitude of this kind was taken, for example, by the factory committee of the Leningrad electric-clock factory and later by the Leningrad Regional Committee of the Machine Builders' Union.

On another occasion, the same paper complained again: "Some plant directors claim that no preparation for a revision of output norms are being made because the factory committees do not agree to revisions planned by the management." Under somewhat similar circumstances, it was reported later, the Central Committee of the Machine Builders' Union had to step in and discipline the factory committee of the Luben Machine Factory Kommunard, which obstinately refused to give its consent to a revision of output norms. Even where the trade unions do not actually adopt the workers' attitude, the union officials are obliged to step rather warily. Thus the author of a recent article on labor discipline deplored the lack of diligence of the comrades' courts and explained ironically that "some trade-union and Party officials" seemed unable to find time "to deal with this necessary but embarrassing and stormy business."

The comrades' court is only one of the new organs recently introduced in the Soviet factory in order to increase efficiency of production. In 1955, the Scientific and Technical Societies, composed of engineers and technicians, were integrated into the trade unions and transformed into a "mass organization." Their membership rose from about 200,000–300,000 in 1955, to 600,000 in 1957, 800,000 in 1958, and 1 million in 1959. By 1957, 17,000 units of the Scientific and Technical Societies were established inside the Soviet plants, and at the beginning of 1959, their number had risen to 24,000. A national congress of these societies met in October, 1959.

Simultaneously, another "mass organization," grouping together the "rationalizers" and inventors, was founded under the trade unions' guidance. The purpose of this association—which also has set up units within the plants and already boasts a membership of 2 million—is to improve the training of its members, help them out in their projects, and protect their copyrights. The association held its final national congress in September, 1959.

While both these organizations are intended to protect the privileges of their members, recruited mostly from the industrial bureaucracy, they also play an auxiliary part in the organization of production. Thus, in 1958, "permanent production conferences" were inaugurated in plants employing not less than 100 persons. These conferences are partly elected by the employees and partly appointed by management and the plant organizations of the Party, the Komsomol, and the Scientific and Technical Societies. Within the limits of the initiative allowed the plants, they are expected to take part in working out plans and investment schemes, examine the organization of labor and production, submit suggestions bearing on these matters to the management, and so forth.

At the same time, the functions of the factory committee, i.e., the trade-union organ that to some extent patronizes all these bodies, have been redefined. Some of its prerogatives have been transferred to one or the other of the new organizations. Thus, for example, most of the factory committees' functions in the fields of organization of labor and industrial relations, such as control of wage scales and output norms, drives for improvement in the quality of production and reduction of prime costs, checking the application of inventions, etc., have been assigned to the permanent production conference. In some respects, indeed, the powers of this body are greater than were those of the factory committee:

[The production conference] examines plans for industrial, residential, and cultural buildings, as well as the projected measures for the actual utilization of investment funds; it puts forward suggestions for perfecting the utilization of investment funds; it puts forward suggestions for perfecting the administration within the plant and for improving the working of its apparatus.*

On the other hand, the factory committees have been granted some new rights they did not enjoy before. Thus they are now to take part, apparently in an advisory capacity, in the working out of production programs, and to give their opinion of candidates for a large number of executive jobs. Even though they have no voice in the appointment of top management officials who are not designated by the plant manager, this new role considerably increases the trade-union committees' influence in plant management.

All these measures tending to give the trade unions a larger share in the organization of production are indicative of an attempt to counterbalance the economic bureaucracy and keep its aspirations for independence in check. It is significant that the decree establishing the permanent production conference provides for direct communication between this body and the plant manager's superior authorities. "The sovnarkhozes, ministries, and other high economic bodies are expected to assist the production conferences in every possible way in their work and in carrying out the decisions adopted by them," reads the revelant provision of the decree.

The government thus tries to make use of friction between the workers and the executives in order to uncover shortcomings in plant management. Much stress is laid on the fact that "the worker knows what hinders improvement in the productivity of labor" and, to stimulate him to expose the faults of his bosses, he is insistently told that "he personally suffers from the consequences of the various kinds of disorganization in production."† This trend, which recalls the operation of Mussolini's state corporations, is not new in the Soviet Union. As early as 1947, when collective agreements (designed in the U.S.S.R. not to protect

* _Trud,_ July 18, 1958.

† I. Mishin, "Increase in the Trade Unions' Role in the Factory," _Partiinaia zhizn,_ No. 24 (1959).

the interests of the wage or salary earners, but to guarantee "the fulfillment or overfulfillment of the state production plan for the given establishment") were reintroduced, the Soviet authorities endeavored to use workers and trade unions as sources for obtaining facts and data the managers were wont to hide from them. "The conclusion of collective agreements and the trade-union bodies' systematic endeavors to bring them into effect," wrote M. Kaganovich, a trade-union officer,* "will help to expose the intolerable antistate practice by which various factories set themselves targets that fall short of their capacity."

On the other hand, the government makes sure that the trade unions and associated organizations do not undermine the management's authority over its employees, and they are called to order whenever they overreach their competence. Thus *Partiinaia zhizn*, contradicting somewhat the decree that had established the permanent production conference, wrote:

> It is necessary to examine some errors in the work of the production conferences. Sometimes they exceed their powers. There have been cases where the production conference has applied directly to the sovnarkhoz, over the heads of the management, for raw materials, equipment, etc. needed by the factory. This is wrong. A production conference operates within the limits of its factory, plant, or complex.†

Nor is it permissible, according to *Trud* (July 18, 1958), that a production conference question regulations and orders from above: "After studying the problems, the production conference adopts resolutions in strict conformity with the legislation in force and with the plans approved for the plant or site and for the workshops."

The Channelization of Discontent

The Soviet effort to use trade-union organizations as brakes on the power of the industrial bureaucracy is, however, only a

* *Profesionalye soyuzi*, No. 2 (1947).
† I. Mishin, *op. cit.*

secondary aspect of the extension of union responsibilities in the managerial field. The main purpose of the policy is to keep in check the centrifugal tendencies of labor and direct them into channels profitable to the government.

For several years now, the workers in Soviet industry have demanded that the barracks regime should be abolished, that the relations between management and employees should be based on agreement, and that workers should no longer be forced, in the name of planning and discipline, to accept without discussion orders not in their power to carry out. As early as 1955, *Sovetskoe trudovoe pravo,* the official handbook of labor law, laboriously attempted to refute this agitation on ideological grounds. Nevertheless, the demands continued to be voiced and became particularly insistent after the Twentieth Congress and the emergence of workers' councils in Poland and Hungary; indeed, in many places they were even openly discussed at factory meetings. It is within this context that the measures discussed here must be considered. While they serve to increase productivity, the trade unions' new responsibilities are meant to make the worker feel that he is no longer a tool carrying out decisions in which he has no say.

But while the trade unions are assigned greater responsibilities, steps are being taken to increase the obligations of each of their members. The first attempt to transform all union members into stooges of the management was made at the Eleventh Trade Union Congress in 1954, when the article of the statutes imposing on each union member the duty to "observe strictly state and labor discipline" was amended to read that union members would henceforth be obliged to "fight against every manifestation of indiscipline in production." In March, 1959, a new amendment was voted by the Twelfth Congress, which declared that it is the duty of each member to "carry out the social orders of the trade-union organs." What "social orders" means was not explained, but there is little doubt that this grotesque expression was used to camouflage the full implications of a provision that authorizes the union bodies to give the workers whatever orders the Party may deem necessary. Nor are the broader motives of the amendment hard to interpret. In the past, unions have been invited to take part in the organization of production, and in every instance, they were simply used to transmit to the workers such orders as the managers preferred not to impose directly for fear of antagonizing the workers. The extension of the unions' responsibility in production, insofar as it affects the position of the worker, thus tends to amplify their function as shock absorbers between management and labor.

At the same time, with the trade unions' increasing share of authority in plant management, their concern for the social welfare of the workers seems to be vanishing altogether. At the Twelfth Congress, in March, 1959, the workers' interests were discussed even less than at previous congresses. At the Tenth Trade Union Congress, in 1949, there had at least been some serious criticism of the housing and food deficiencies, and at the Eleventh, in 1954, of the chaos in wages. But the Twelfth Congress dealt almost exclusively with the fulfillment of the current Seven Year Plan. The immediate reason for this is clearly discernible in the following passage of the message addressed to the Congress by the Party Central Committee:

> At present, the most fundamental, the most essential task of Soviet trade unions lies in mobilizing the efforts of the great working masses in view of the struggle for the carrying out of the historic decisions of the Twenty-first Congress of the Party, for the timely fulfillment of the Seven Year Plan and the targets fixed for 1959, the first year of this plan.*

The Twelfth Congress followed up the Party's instructions by inserting into the statutes a new definition of the purposes of Soviet trade unionism:

> The central task of the trade unions is the mobilization of the masses in view of the struggle for a further powerful expansion in all branches of the national economy, for the further strengthening of the economic and defensive power of the Soviet state, for the fulfillment and overfulfillment of the economic plans, for technical progress, for an uninter-

* *Trud*, March 24, 1959.

rupted increase in the productivity of labor, for stricter economy and parsimony in all sectors of the national economy,
for the maximum exploitation of all resources and possibilities with the aim of a rapid increase in industrial and
agricultural production and an uninterrupted rise in the material and cultural standards of the workers' well-being.*

The order in which the union tasks are enumerated speaks for
itself; it is quite clear that the Party is in no mood to heed the
criticisms that Soviet workers have been directing in recent years
at the attitude of the unions, particularly the fact that they
neither represent nor defend the workers' interests.

As far as the practical effect of union participation in management is concerned, published information, particularly on the
subject of the permanent production conferences, indicates that
the experiment is a failure. It appears notably that the factory
committees show little inclination to take part in the study and
elaboration of production plans; that the production conferences
meet rarely and some not at all; that they tend to become the
business of engineers and technicians, since the workers ignore
them; that in those cases where they take their work seriously,
they frequently exceed the scope of their authority and have to
be called to order; that the managers and the economic administration still generally disregard proposals put forward by the
unions. By the same token, it is very unlikely that the new efforts
to transform the workers into tools of the management will prove
successful. The institutional devices used to bring about this aim
are too transparent to achieve now what the Soviet state over the
past several decades has variously attempted and always failed
to accomplish.

Though it is true that the power of the unions has recently
been increased in some respects, nothing has been done to enable
them to fulfill the primary function of genuine trade unions: the
protection of workers' rights. Yet, this is a task that, as even the
Soviet authorities know, cannot remain altogether neglected. It
is quite apparent, however, that in the U.S.S.R. the unions are not

* *Ibid.*, April 2, 1959.

expected to perform it; instead, the protection of workers' rights is being increasingly entrusted to the judiciary. Accordingly, steps have been taken to improve the examination of workers' complaints in the courts, and the role of the judiciary in settling individual labor conflicts has been considerably enlarged.

Judges and attorneys are thus called upon to fill the gap left open by the unions in controlling the observance of labor laws by plant managers and other bodies of the economic administration. Unfortunately, the judicial process is in its very nature clumsy and slow, and virtually all industrial countries have therefore established special procedures to ensure flexible and speedy enforcement of workers' rights. The Soviet decision to relegate the settlement of industrial conflicts to the regular court system neglects social reality.

To sum up, the status of the worker in Soviet society remains largely unchanged. The exercise of repressive discipline, which has always been a barrier to a rational regulation of industrial relations in the U.S.S.R., is still the predominant factor in labor policy. On balance, the recent labor reforms are an improvement to the extent that they moderate the pressures weighing on the shoulders of the worker; but they clearly do not go far enough. Now as before, he performs manual work under conditions that only constraint can impose on him, and for a wage arbitrarily fixed by the employer—the state. The reforms favoring social mobility may perhaps permit his son to raise himself to a higher position, but their effect on the class structure is inevitably very restricted, since the worker remains unable to assert his interests and truly improve his lot.

The Peasant, the Party, and the System

——ARCADIUS KAHAN

THE PREOCCUPATION OF top Soviet policy-makers with problems of agriculture in recent years has been one of numerous interesting facets of the post-Stalin era. The significance of this concern in terms of further Soviet development makes it important to scrutinize closely what attitudes and policies have been adopted by the new leadership, in what sense they show continuity with past policies, and to what degree they depart from the past.

Such an examination requires an understanding of the initial basic relationship between the Soviet state and the peasantry. In spite of the fact that Russia had always been a predominantly agrarian country, few of the early Bolshevik leaders understood the "mystery" that was the Russian peasant. Among them, Lenin came closest to grasping the problem, but was very often blinded by doctrines he believed to be true and self-evident and that he passed on to his followers. Primarily concerned with the strategy of seizing and maintaining power, Lenin viewed the peasants in terms of a potential political force that he wanted either to control or at least to neutralize. Although he recognized the peasants' deep-seated conservatism, it was apparently beyond his comprehension that they might constitute an unrelenting or permanent adversary.

In line with this attitude, he invented (or used) an explanation of peasant social behavior that was typically Russian—one, in fact, that could well have been originated by Dostoevski. According to this theory, the peasant was possessed of a split personality. On the one hand, he harbored a "diabolic" soul, characterized by attachment to private property, resistance to trends of social change, and hope for personal advancement through command over an increasing volume of resources. But there was also an "angelic" side to the peasant soul, one that would accept social transformation; this side was associated with the small proprietor who could not protect himself from exploitation in the market by profit-seeking capitalists. In Lenin's view, the latter side of the peasant's nature made it possible and, indeed, imperative for the industrial proletariat to seek the peasants' cooperation before and during the "bourgeois-democratic" revolution. One of Lenin's contributions to Marxist literature concerned the means of achieving such an alliance; noting the social stratification within the peasantry, he pointed out how a skillful policy, making use of differences of interest at various levels, could prevent the peasants as a whole from taking concerted action during the transformation of the bourgeois-democratic into the proletarian revolution.

This strategy was not, of course, aimed at a permanent alliance with a section of the peasantry, but was simply part of Lenin's blueprint for power, designed to neutralize the resistance he expected would develop, though in what form or to what degree he would not calculate. As early as 1905, he had written:

> Class antagonism between the rural proletariat and the peasant bourgeoisie is inevitable, and we reveal it in advance, explain it and prepare for the struggle. . . . At first we [will] support to the end, by all means including confiscation, the peasantry generally against the landlords, and then (or rather, not "then" but at the same time) we [will] support the proletariat against the peasantry in general. To try now to calculate the combination of forces among the peasantry on "the morrow" of the (democratic) revolution is sheer utopia.

Leninism in Practice

Thus fortified with a political strategy and rules for tactical maneuvering, Lenin did not stop to aanlyze the socioeconomic role of the peasant as a producer in the market, involving such problems as commodity prices, incomes, profits, investment opportunities, taxation, and so on. Indeed, in his various writings, he never exhibited a genuine interest in devising solutions for major economic problems, concentrating instead on the political expression of those problems. Thus he launched the revolution and stepped over the threshold of power without any clear notion of what ought to be the long-run objectives of his agrarian policy. The language of his speech accompanying the Decree on Land, issued immediately after the November 7 coup, aptly reveal his state of mind in this respect:

> Russia is great, and local conditions vary. We believe that the peasants will be able to solve the problem [of agrarian adjustment] correctly better than we could ourselves. Whether in our spirit, or in the spirit of the program of the Socialist Revolutionaries is not the point. The point is that the peasants should be firmly assured that there are no more landlords in the countryside, that they must themselves arrange their own lives.

After embarking on the tragic (in terms of consequences) experiment of war Communism, Lenin proceeded with his divide-and-rule tactics among the peasants, again in an effort to neutralize their political reaction. Specifically, he tried to foment an intravillage struggle between the poor and the rich peasants, with the medium stratum as spectators. Unmindful of the economic consequences of such conflict, he created his *Kombiedy* (Committees of the Poor Peasants), which acted as agents of government policy in each village in the suppression of the richer landholders. This tactic contributed to the general chaos created by war Communism, characterized on the economic side by food requisitioning, galloping inflation, and the return to a virtual barter economy. Under these conditions, the peasants obstinately refused to produce any agricultural surplus, leading to a catastrophic decrease in output.

Agriculture in the 1920's

In 1921, the outbreak of peasant rebellions, along with the Kronstadt uprising, signaled the imminent political dangers of the situation confronting the regime. Unable to admit that the Kronstadt uprising represented his moral defeat by workers and sailors—the alleged pillars of his authority—Lenin, in his speech to the Tenth CPSU Congress in March, 1921, hastily admitted defeat at the hands of the peasants and sounded the horn for retreat. He acknowledged this failure in plain words: "The peasants are not content with our attitude toward them, and they will not tolerate it any longer." The first battle between the Soviet state and the peasants thus ended with a victory for the peasants, and the era of the NEP began.

The NEP's comparatively liberal policies toward the agricultural sector and internal trade demonstrated the possibilities of some sort of a symbiosis between a largely nationalized industry and a relatively free peasant agriculture, as had been visualized and advocated by the Populists in the nineteenth century. Simple agricultural cooperation (later used as a steppingstone to collectivization) and an essentially free market for agricultural products proved beneficial to the task of reconstruction and recovery, the major goal of the NEP period. For the peasants themselves, the first years of NEP represented in a sense a golden era in their history, with incomes on the rise and investment outlays in agriculture increasing.

Yet new troubles were not long in arising. "Scissors crises"— a widening discrepancy between industrial and agricultural prices, or between peasant purchasing power and available consumer goods—in combination with faulty government price and procurement policies, led to a curtailment of the peasants' incentive to produce and thus to a decrease in the agricultural output available for the market. A major dilemma arose over conflicting demands on the short agricultural supply for home consumption of the peasants on the one hand, and urban consumption and exports on the other. Concomitantly, the regime faced the problem of deriving sources for and minimizing costs of rapid industrialization without access to foreign investment markets.

This situation led to the regime's attempts, in 1928, to shift the burden of industrialization onto the peasants by decreasing their home consumption and by procuring grain at prices below the market rate. Stalin himself best described the effect of these measures, in a speech of July, 1928:

> The way matters stand with the peasantry in this respect is as follows: it not only pays the state the usual taxes, direct and indirect; it also *overpays*—in the relatively high prices for manufactured goods . . . in the first place, and it is more or unless *underpaid* in the prices for agricultural produce . . . in the second place. This is an additional tax levied on the peasantry for the sake of promoting industry, which caters to the whole country, the peasantry included. It is something in the nature of a "tribute," of a supertax, which we are compelled to levy for the time being in order to preserve and accelerate our present rate of industrial development . . . to raise further the well-being of the village and then to abolish altogether this additional tax, these "scissors" between town and country.*

It is worth noting that Stalin's avowed intention of eventually abolishing the supertax was never acted upon in his lifetime; it remained a pious wish for the record, fulfilled only recently and only partially by the successor regime.

The Onset of Collectivization

The squeeze put on the peasants naturally met with resistance. The government forced a showdown by launching the brutal campaign against the kulaks and then initiating the collectivization of agriculture. Thus in the process of trying to find a short-run remedy for economic ills, the regime created a new institutional set-up for agriculture—one that, from an administrative point of view, solved both of its major problems by curtailing the peasants' home consumption and procuring the required surplus at terms dictated by and favorable to the state.

Collectivization did have other important effects and purposes: The political scientist, for example, is apt to see as its main aim the tightening of control over the peasantry; the sociologist

* J. V. Stalin, *Works* (Moscow: Foreign Languages Publishing House, 1954), IX, 167.

analyzes it as the preparatory stage for increased social mobility and occupational shifts from agriculture to industry; while a student of legal institutions is most interested in it as a form of landholding. But the economist's viewpoint on collectivization comes closest to its primary purpose—the acquisition of a larger part of agricultural output at a low monopsonist price, thereby decreasing the costs borne by the state in the industrialization process. In the implementation of the program, the chief criterion of success became the effectiveness of techniques for siphoning off the volume of output desired by the state.

The policy-makers also hoped that a change in the attitude of the peasants toward their labor, to result from the Marxian mechanics of a changing relationship between the base and the superstructure, would accompany the reorganization—in short, that the "diabolical" side of the peasant nature would disintegrate. This doctrinal supposition was combined with a strong conviction that higher efficiency in farming could be achieved more rapidly through forced collectivization than through the gradual process of eliminating marginal producers. That the institutional revamping of the farm unit would create both an optimum size, with economies of scale, and attitudes favorable to the interest of society as a whole was a prevailing belief among many planners. Where they were mistaken is that such processes do not take place automatically, and that the impact of a particular organizational form on agricultural output itself is only incidental. In short, to collect taxes in kind efficiently and to compel or induce peasants to work harder to increase production are two entirely different tasks.

With regard to the latter, the brutal methods used to enforce the collective form of agriculture in fact produced just the opposite effect than that desired. Being motivated in part by political considerations, the regime frequently disregarded the economic rationale altogether. In the preliminary campaign to liquidate the kulaks, for example, it set up ostensibly economic criteria of property and income for the purpose of classifying peasant households, yet these criteria were kept vague enough to allow discrimination on political grounds when deemed expedient or necessary. Unable to muster sufficient support in the rural milieu, the Party simply sent thousands of its trusted urban followers to the villages to act as its agents in carrying out its policy. These agents operated through the political departments of the Machine Tractor Stations; as vigilant political overseers, they were charged with the function of crushing not only actual but potential resistance—in effect, a *carte blanche* for the enormous brutalities that ensued. The peasants' reaction to these tactics, was to destroy, in Samsonian fashion, the most readily destructible production assets—the livestock—during the years 1930–32. The longer-range effect of regime policies was a drastic decline in agricultural output—in fact, the precollectivization level was not reached again until about 1955.

Throughout the 1930's and 1940's, the Stalin regime continued in a silent wrangle with the peasantry, mainly over their relative share in total agricultural output. The fact that the peasants resorted to passive forms of resistance, defying the spirit of the law rather than the law itself, has been erroneously interpreted in some quarters as an indication that the regime made solid inroads toward their "conversion." Yet the peasants never gave up their tacit efforts to enlarge their private garden plots at the expense of collective farmland (leading twice—in 1939 and again in 1946—to government decrees to reduce the size of peasant landholdings). The same tenacious resistance was apparent in the "battle for the cow"—the peasant's stubborn effort to hold onto his farm animals, in many cases a single cow, despite an enormous burden of taxation placed upon privately owned livestock.

Stalinist policy persisted in its orientation, inherited from the 1920's, toward concern with distributing agricultural ouput rather than with devising means to increase production. As earlier, it was the size of the procurement and the efficiency of the collection apparatus that occupied most of the attention of the planners and the government bureaucracy, rather than the size of output or measures to increase it. In fact, the dictatorship kept investment in agriculture to a minimum, while at the same time imposing a standard of living on both the peasants and the urban workers below the precollectivization level.

Several factors (aside from the existence of a coercive apparatus) contributed to the regime's ability to pursue its course of economic expansion without promoting any growth of agriculture. The transfer of labor from agriculture to industry, while decreasing the food requirements of the countryside, also facilitated the maintenance of urban consumption at a level to which the transplanted former peasants were accustomed. Drawing millions of women into the labor force, thus converting them from consumers into producers, in a real sense resulted in an increase of the national product without any appreciable increase in food consumption. The gradual rise in the educational level and in labor productivity also played an important role in sustaining industrial growth without a corresponding growth in agriculture. Finally, the planners were greatly "aided" by the very slow rate of population growth during the 1930's and then the grave loss of life during World War II, easing the pressures of population against the available food supply.

That such a situation could not continue indefinitely was clear, however, even to the most naïve observers of the Soviet scene. The state of stagnation in agriculture toward the last years of Stalin's rule caused it to come "into conflict with the productive forces of the society," to borrow a familiar phrase from the Marxist lexicon: from being an asset in the process of economic growth, it turned into a definite liability. In strictly economic terms, it was unable to meet either the increasing demand for agricultural raw materials for industry or the demand for food on the part of a population once more on the increase and able to make its demands more vocal. The need for a change in agricultural policies—not to mention other spheres of Soviet life— was only too obvious. Yet Stalin at this point in his life was unwilling or constitutionally unable to cope with problems requiring a deviation from the established pattern. It fell to his successors to meet these problems and to introduce changes that, although affecting all aspects of the national life, have had a particularly pronounced effect upon Soviet agriculture.

The Social Bases of Post-Stalin Policy

There is need for caution in defining the areas and scope of post-Stalin changes. Observers generally agree that there has been no basic shift in the priority scale of the Soviet economic planners, nor any far-reaching democratization of the political decision-making process. Where then has the change occurred? Answering this question requires a deviation from the major topic here and a brief discussion of the existing relationships between the Party and the rest of society in the Soviet Union.

Traditionally, the Party has required from the Soviet citizen (a) acknowledgment of the supremacy of Party judgment over individual judgment; (b) identification of Party policies with such advantages as derive from the system; (c) dissociation of negative features of the society from Party policies, and their attribution instead to imperfect execution by individuals or to outside factors; (d) acceptance of the basic doctrinal assumptions on which Soviet society and the political system are based; (e) readiness to execute Party orders regardless of the effect upon individual welfare. Popular acquiescence in these requirements—doubly insured by the existence of the secret police—was taken for granted during the Stalin period, yet there is no doubt that resistance to them was on the increase. The basic change in the post-Stalin leadership's approach has been an awareness that submission on the part of the populace could not be assumed matter-of-factly and that something had to be done in order to create favorable attitudes toward the Party. Two of the Party's requirements seem to have come under particular question from a fairly large and influential stratum of the citizenry—namely, acceptance of the excessive and arbitrary terrorism of the political system and obedience to Party orders, regardless of personal welfare. Only in the light of this changed popular attitude can one properly interpret the post-Stalin demotion of the secret police, Khrushchev's famous speech to the Twentieth CPSU Congress (shifting the blame for oppression from the Party as such to Stalin personally), and the regime's various moves to appeal to the citizens' self-interest.

The changes in popular attitude were probably the inevitable result of the changes that had occurred in Soviet society. The Soviet industrialization period was marked by a buildup not only of physical capital, but of human capital, possessing particular qualities. Of utmost importance in this process was the acceleration of upward mobility, encouraging traits of leadership. During this period, there were two major channels of upward mobility. One—the rise through Party ranks—emphasized loyalty, acceptance of discipline, and organizational ability as the tests of performance, qualities essential in a totalitarian system of administration and control. The other—the rise through professional (mainly technological) ranks—required education and special technical competence in the fields related to the urgent problems of the economy. Both channels have provided Soviet society with a steady stream of trained leadership, but one that, with the passage of time, has changed in quality and in the demands it makes.

The generation born and raised under the Soviet regime has taken for granted the existing channels of social mobility and has utilized them to the best of its abilities. While some of its forebears may have viewed the state or Party in an aureate glow, as their liberator from capitalist slavery, the newer generation tends much more to expect a relationship of give and take, *do ut des*, with the regime, such as the relationship that exists between a seller and buyer of services. Any excessive "monopsonistic" tendencies on the part of the buyer are bound to be resented. It seems apparent that this fundamental change in attitude toward the Party and state was sensed by Khrushchev and his associates —something the old Stalinist guard was unable or unwilling to accept. The policies that in recent years have led to such trends as higher income for the farmers, increased social services for the workers, decreases in wage differentials and the like, by no means imply that Khrushchev feels greater concern for the welfare of Soviet subjects than did, say, a Molotov or a Kaganovich, but only that he is less inhibited in recognizing that the real Soviet "man in the street" is far removed from the former model of what a Soviet man ought to be.

The new course has made the Communist Party more competitively oriented with respect to other channels of upward mobility, forcing it to focus attention on ways either of attracting new leadership to itself or of controlling the alternative channels more effectively, yet without resort to former coercive methods. Toward the end of safeguarding its supremacy—without endangering the efficient operation of the economic system—the Party has placed increasing emphasis on controls located closer to the local scene. The creation of the sovnarkhozes (regional Councils of the National Economy), organized under a system of effective political checks, as well as the strengthening of the command position of area Party secretaries, has reflected this tendency.

The trend of Khrushchev's policies has given rise to two basic questions: How far is the present Party leadership willing (or able) to go in meeting the people's demands? Is there a possibility of retreat to formerly held positions? The total evidence of regime attitudes seems to suggest that it will yield only to the extent necessary to maintain the stability of the system and a sense of personal security among the citizenry. It will stop short of any real political concessions, and it will not change the basic priorities established for economic development. Political freedom and consumers' choice in the broadest sense are still incompatible with the Soviet system. On the other hand, though a retreat to Stalinist positions would probably be feasible under conditions of dictatorship, it is very unlikely that the regime would resort to such a course except in a dire situation of international or domestic unrest.

Against this background, let us turn to the changes of attitude on the part of the present policy-makers toward agriculture and the peasants.

Incentives and Organizational Reforms

Without question, the most important policy shift has been the regime's emphasis on the need for a substantial increase in agricultural output and its professed willingness to direct new resources toward the achievement of this goal. For the first time since collectivization was instituted, Soviet policy-makers have taken stock of their agricultural resources, openly admitted their failures, and initiated a series of measures to rescue agriculture from the dead end in which Stalin had left it.

As a preliminary step, the policy-makers showed a long overdue realization of the importance of the human element in the success or failure of any economic program or policy. Recogni-

tion of this factor—virtually ignored since the early industrialization period—led, among other early moves of the regime, to the
granting of major price increases for agricultural products (since
raised further, though now under consideration for downward
revision as we shall see). By raising incomes of the collective
farms, the Soviet government provided the means both for a
higher volume of capital investment and for a rise in individual
peasant incomes, obviously designed as an incentive to raise
productivity.

The regime's next step was to provide a proving ground for
a "new look" in agriculture that would capture the imagination
of the country as a whole: The result was the campaign for the
development of the so-called new lands, glamorized as a pioneer-
ing effort on virgin soil. There were, of course, practical considerations involved in this project: It was hoped that the plowing
up of over 30 million hectares to create a new grain region in
Kazakhstan and Siberia would augment the total food and feed
supply while mitigating the fluctuations in output caused by the
periodic droughts in the principal existing grain regions. These
potential gains apparently outweighed considerations of the complex technical problems and risks involved in bringing vast semi-
arid areas under cultivation. What the long-range outcome of this
program will be is as yet difficult to tell.

Both in the new-lands project and in agriculture generally,
one of the most interesting facets of post-Stalin policy has been
the regime's attitude with regard to the optimal size of farm
units and to the relative advantages of state-farm as against
collective-farm organization.

Soviet agricultural experts and planners have taken various
positions at various times with respect to the optimal size of
farms. The notion that economies of scale could be achieved
almost indefinitely by increasing the size of farms was very
popular at the beginning of collectivization, but was later discarded in the face of mounting deficits and inefficiencies on the
gigantic state farms that had been created. Nonetheless, the idea
again took hold after World War II, leading to an amalgamation
of the collective farms in 1950, which reduced their number by

two thirds and increased the size of individual units correspondingly.

The post-Stalin period has seen a definite trend toward the further amalgamation of the collectives and, since 1957, toward the conversion of collective farms into state farms. These moves have been accompanied by much debate and a series of inquiries into the most efficient size of farms in specific regions and into the relative costs of output in the collective and state-owned units. In the new-lands project, the planners have put heavy preferential stress on the formation of state farms of huge acreage, on the basis that they would be easier to administer and would show greater labor productivity, particularly in view of the need for the large-scale use of machinery on the flatlands. The recent conversion of collectives into state farms in other areas is explained by the regime as a move to help out poorer farms, which were unable to effect improvements on their own, despite the increased prices decreed for agricultural products. In such cases it is probable that the farmers indeed preferred the guaranteed money wage of state-farm workers (while retaining their own livestock and a part of their garden plot) to eking out a meager income from inferior farms.

With regard to the amalgamation of collectives, a main argument put forward in its favor has been the possibility of a more efficient utilization of skilled managers and agricultural experts, who prior to 1950 were spread sparsely over many farms. It has also been predicted that amalgamation would result in decreased administrative expenditures, though there is little indication to date that such economies have been achieved.

Income and Investment Policies

The continued emphasis on amalgamation has been accompanied by a new focusing of attention on the deficient quality and low productivity of the agricultural labor force. As noted, it has been recognized that the relative scarcity of capital in conjunction with the relative abundance of agricultural labor (causing the more ambitious or semiskilled workers to be attracted to better-paid industrial work) have been major factors in preventing the rise of productivity. Accordingly, in the process of amalgamation, attempts have been made to keep the more skilled farmers and tractor drivers on the farms by increasing their incomes and other incentives. At the same time, the regime has applied pressure and devised special inducements to supply agriculture with skilled manpower from the urban areas. Moreover, there has been a rapid increase in the quantity and quality of machinery made available to agriculture, paralleled by the transfer of existing machinery from the Machine Tractor Stations to the collective farms themselves.

The rise in the prices for agricultural commodities paid by the state to the farms has resulted in a rapid increase in the farms' money receipts. A part of this increment has been paid out to the collective-farm members, and attempts are now being made to recompense them more frequently, in the form of advance payments on a quarterly or monthly basis, with some guarantee of a minimum income. One of the results of this incentive policy has been an increase in the number of days the farmers have worked on the collective land. Incentives—including price differentials—have also been used to supplement administrative measures in the regime's efforts to introduce changes in the output mix.

Out of the greater money income of the collectives, the farm administrations are ordered to reserve a share for investment, the proportion of which has been raised in recent years—though there are signs the government has had to apply pressure on this score to counter the peasants' desire for larger labor payments. The demand for increased investment funds was attributed to the transfer of farm machinery to the collectives' charge, necessitating expenditures for repair, maintenance, and new equipment, as well as to the needs for funds for a massive program of farm-building construction. The present Seven Year Plan envisages a further broadening in the scope of such investments.

In addition to their direct investment in physical plant and equipment, the collective farms have been charged since 1955 with the responsibility for investment in what is termed social overhead and services—the expenditures necessary for building and maintaining rural roads, providing small power plants, constructing schools and other cultural facilities, setting up bakeries, etc. The regime was probably correct in assuming that these forms of expenditure would meet with the approval of the rural population, however grudging. While the peasants are anxious for a larger share of farm income, these investment demands must seem preferable to the previous indirect discriminatory taxation of agricultural producers based on vague promises of services, which generally were not forthcoming.

It is difficult to measure the precise economic effect of any of the various policies outlined above—indeed, any effort to do so would be the subject of an entire paper in itself. It seems clear, however, that the collective impact of these policies has been responsible in large part for the significant increases in agricultural production and labor productivity in recent years.

Social Aims of the Agricultural Course

Turning from the economic and technical aspects of recent policy to the broader issue of the present leadership's sociopolitical attitudes toward the peasants, it is possible to distinguish three trends of importance: The first is the Party's tighter control over the execution of its agricultural program; the second, already touched upon, is the move toward a further socialization of agriculture; the third is the attempt to raise the social status of the peasantry, conditioned upon the success of the first two objectives.

One of the major weaknesses of the Party throughout its history has been its comparatively small membership in the rural areas. At the farm level, the collective chairman and possibly a few lesser administrators have been the only Party members—and it is difficult to tell whether their Party membership led to their farm positions or vice versa. This situation was caused by the old regime's preference for controlling agriculture through a hierarchical line of command from above. An elaborate system of Party as well as government supervision was established, operating through various channels and institutions. The cumbersome functioning of this control apparatus was resented both because of its alien nature—i.e., its imposition of orders from without—

and because its bureaucratic actions were often detrimental to the interests of efficiency on a particular farm.

By contrast, the present tightening of Party control has had the effect of moving the center of authority closer to the farms. The new collective amalgamations, the influx of agricultural specialists and former MTS personnel (often Party members) into the farm organizations, along with a drive for new Party recruits in rural areas, have made it possible to organize regular Party cells on most collective and state farms. The consequent opportunity to exercise control from within, and to present the Party to the mass of peasants as a local rather than an alien force, has undoubtedly increased the Party's influence over the behavior of the farm population. The existence of local Party cells may well lead to the increased autonomy of the collectives with respect to minor internal decisions, but it will also insure that major decisions are carried out in accordance with Party recommendations.

An interesting indication of the Party's emphasis on control at the local level—and with this condition met, its positive preference for preserving an atomized society—was provided by a recent debate during the December, 1959, Plenum of the Party's Central Committeee. The subject of the debate was the desirability of establishing an intercollective organization to help implement investment and construction projects involving more than one farm, particularly to represent the farms in dealings with construction agencies and other industrial branches. Although many of the speakers recommended an all-Union organization of the collectives for these purposes, the final resolution —which must be presumed to have reflected the high authorities' wishes—called for organizing the farms at the county or district level. Inevitably, one is reminded of the difficulties the Soviet government had in controlling the *Kolkhoz-Tsentr* of the late 1920's, a similar organization of the collectives, which became a forum for the expression of "nonconformist" ideas against regime policies. It would seem that the Party policy-makers of 1959 are mindful of this experience and entirely unwilling to take the chance that history might repeat itself.

The March Toward Socialization

With regard to the second trend specified above, the fact that policies aimed at the further socialization of agriculture—meaning in effect a further "proletarianization" of the peasantry—were being tried out could be surmised from the following tendencies: (a) the decline of payments in kind and the increased use of money payments for the collective farmers' labor; (b) the decrease in the size of the private garden plots left to the peasantry, and in certain places their elimination; (c) the further conversion of the number of collectives into state farms. Some of the economic problems involved in these policies were discussed earlier, but their noneconomic aspects are just as interesting. The trend of regime thinking is reflected in two frequently repeated slogans. The first declares that the differences between the collective and state forms of ownership are diminishing. By implication, the basis for this claim is that collective farmers are being transformed into money-wage earners and that a part of the collective's profits is being appropriated directly to tasks of a social nature, i.e., beyond the interests of a single farm.

The second slogan proclaims the disappearance of differences between town and country; the implication here is that there will be a further equalization of industrial and agricultural income, along with an increase of social services and cultural facilities (still largely restricted to urban areas) in the countryside. There is no doubt that certain policies of the regime have been directed up to now toward narrowing the differential between urban and farm income, but the gap is still very substantial. The effort represents only the dimmest hint of a start toward Khrushchev's long-professed dreams of establishing "agro-cities," his descriptions of which have raised up the vision of a modernized countryside peopled by educated, skilled, and prosperous agricultural workers participating as equals in a smoothly functioning utopia.

It is absolutely clear—even to the most optimistic Soviet planner—that many years will have to elapse and a very large volume of investment will have to be committed before Khrushchev's

version of Fourier's "phalansteries" becomes reality. The question
to be asked, then, is why Soviet politicians are talking in terms
which imply that this town-country equalization is just around
the corner. One explanation is that they really believe in equalization as an ultimate goal of social policy, and that they want
to enlist the peasants' aid by presenting them with a dream
world, the achievement of which will depend on hard work, the
sacrifice of certain tangible assets for the present, and, above all,
faith in the guidance of the Party and the state. Another explanation—which may supplement rather than exclude the first—is
that the regime is attempting to condition the peasants to "proletarianization" and to make its consequences more acceptable to
them by visions of future rewards.

Yet at the same time—in virtual contradiction of the talk that
has gone on—there have been signs of late that the start toward
town-and-country equalization may be slowed down. The most
crucial indication in this respect has been the paving of the way
for a cut in the commodity prices paid to agricultural producers,
thus reversing the trend of previous policy. Ironically, the "demand" for such a cut has been put forward by agricultural
planners and executives who claim to be expressing the wishes
and speaking in the name of the peasants. It is clear, of course,
that the regime has instigated such talk, with an eye to immediate needs or gains and in neglect of whatever long-run plans
may exist. To understand such an inconsistent and contradictory
measure—as well as the tactics by which it was initiated—one
must take into account the deep-rooted paternalistic attitude of
the Soviet leaders toward the peasantry, their conviction that
superior knowledge is a monopoly of the Party and that the
peasant is deficient in outlook and judgment. Changes such as
the price cut must be introduced from above, but the peasants
must be cajoled along by subterfuge, by the sham impression
that their opinions and "endorsement" have been taken into
consideration. This paternalism, which Khrushchev apparently
believes should be constantly exhibited (Stalin did not think it
necessary), is in a sense the substitute for the individual freedom
denied to the peasants and, indeed, the whole population.

Peasant Viewpoints

In considering the peasants' attitude toward regime policies for further socialization, one is forced to cross over the boundary from facts to educated guesses. It is probably correct to assume that the idea of a return to private ownership has much less psychological appeal for the new generation on the collective farms than for its predecessor. For many of the new generation, farm work has become simply a matter of employment opportunities and income needs, rather than a preference for what used to be a "way of life." The peasants' garden plots and private cows undoubtedly still have symbolic meaning for them as the last bastion of proprietorship, but their deep attachment is also rooted in hard economic fact, since the plot is a dependable source of income in contrast to the uncertain and inadequate supply of money or income in kind from the collective farms. As long as the peasants' share in the product of their labor continues to constitute a residual, they will preserve their suspicious attitude toward the benefits bestowed upon them by the state. In other words, a change in their attitude will require substantial acts on the part of the regime to provide them with what they consider a fair return for their toil.

Another element in the peasants' attitude toward the state is their deep-rooted resentment over the long-professed supremacy of industrial workers in Soviet society. The innate superiority of the industrial working class over other classes of the population is a cornerstone of Bolshevik ideology—witness the basic concept of the "dictatorship of the proletariat." Until recently, the distinction between the industrial worker and the peasant was often emphasized in the regime's dealings with the peasants, and in fact provided the Soviet leaders with a self-made justification for many of their policies.

A consistent policy committed to raising both the income and the social status of the agricultural population might, with time, mollify much of the existing resentment of the peasants. The rise in the status of a particular group depends much more upon government policy in the Soviet Union than it does in other countries, so the choice in this respect is really up to the regime—

and there are signs that a change of approach is under consideration. Whereas in the past a peasant desiring higher social status
had to join the urban working force and work his way up
through the ranks of industry (or, of course, rise through the
Party), there are now a number of indications that greater social
prestige may be accorded to the upper layers of the agricultural
labor force, eliminating the intermediate step of urbanization.

This article has only scratched the surface in its attempt to
review the new features of Soviet agricultural policy and to
compare them with former attitudes and policies. A few basic
observations should perhaps be summarized. The underlying
assumption here has been that post-Stalin policies make sense
primarily in terms of the evolutionary social changes going on
in Soviet society, changes to which the Soviet state and Party,
as well as the peasants themselves, are seeking to adjust. In this
process, the relationship between the state and the agricultural
sector of the population has increasingly exhibited elements of
rationality, although both sides are showing caution with respect
to firm policy commitments or behavior.

If, however, the regime persists in its present course, the
likelihood certainly exists that some of its policies will have a
socially desirable effect upon the way of life of the peasantry.
It is even possible that this course will tend to transform peasant
attitudes toward the regime over a long period. To say this is not
to imply by any means that the peasants could become a zealous
and enthusiastic "proletariat" of the countryside. However much
the regime might improve the peasants' economic lot, it will
continue to deny them other rights. It would be degrading to
the Russian tradition of *Zemlia i Volia* (Land and Freedom) to
accept the view that the desire for material well-being could
permanently displace the desire for personal freedom—though
how, when, or whether the urge for greater freedom will be able
to assert itself in Soviet society are questions for a distant future.

Soviet Nationality Policy in Perspective

——ALEX INKELES

IN THE CURRENT ATMOSPHERE of "peaceful competition between systems," increasing emphasis is placed on the economic factor of production and consumption levels in comparisons of Soviet and non-Soviet achievement. In the process, some observers have all but lost sight of the fundamental political, social, and cultural characteristics that continue to differentiate the two systems. Among relevant issues, one of importance is the status of the national and racial minorities in the Soviet Union. At a time when the Western democracies are granting full independent statehood to one after another of the formerly subject peoples of Africa and Asia, it seems particularly appropriate to inquire into the position of the Soviet minorities. Unfortunately, this subject has received less attention than it deserves, perhaps because many have uncritically accepted Moscow's claim that any issues of nationality and race have long since been successfully resolved. If this were true, Soviet policy would still merit close examination. The fact is, however, that despite some substantial attainments, the Soviet regime has far from solved the problem of minority status either to the satisfaction of the groups themselves or to the particular credit of the Soviet system.

In order to assess Soviet nationality policy intelligently, it is necessary to know certain distinctive historical and demographic facts about the minorities.

Population Patterns

While the Great Russians are the single largest group in the Soviet Union, they hold only a precariously slim margin of

numerical superiority over the combined population of the national minorities. Indeed, as a result of the rapid expansion of
the Czarist Empire, the Russians were formerly in a minority,
comprising only 45 per cent of the population in the 1897 census.
The loss of certain territories during the Revolution and the Civil
War somewhat redressed the balance, and in the 1926 census,
the Great Russians emerged as 52.9 per cent of the total. With
the apparent aim of widening this slight margin, the basis of
classification was changed in the 1939 census: People were no
longer asked what they regarded as their "ethnic origin"
(*narodnost*), but rather what they thought of as their "nationality," the Russian term for which (*natsionalnost*) is closer in meaning to culture or citizenship than to race. With the aid of this
device, the regime was able to report a Russian majority of 58
per cent in 1939.

The 1959 census—preliminary results of which have just been
published—reveal a new downward trend, undoubtedly due to
the incorporation of the Baltic states, a section of Poland, and
part of Bessarabia (Moldavia) since 1939. Today, somewhat
under 55 per cent of the Soviet people think of themselves as
Russian by nationality.

The minorities generally live in homogeneous and compact
groups on the outer edge of the central land mass that is the
territory of the Great Russians. This basic demographic structure
persists despite a great increase in the dispersion of peoples—
especially of Russians—into other nationality areas during World
War II and its aftermath. The fifteen national republics strung
around the outer borders of the Soviet Union contain the
overwhelming bulk, 80 per cent or more, of the country's national
minorities. In the northwest, the three Baltic republics include
close to 4.5 million Latvians, Lithuanians, and Estonians. On
the western frontier there are some 8 million Belorussians and
36 million Ukrainians who, when added to the Russians, give
the Soviet Union its overwhelmingly Slavic majority. On the
same frontier, 2.2 million Moldavians live mainly in the republic
of the same name, and almost 1.5 million Poles, who for obvious
reasons have no identifying territorial unit. Further to the south
and east, along the Black Sea and in the Caucasus, there are

numerous nationalities distributed in a complex pattern of settlement. These include the Georgians, Armenians, and Azerbaijanis,
each in their own republic and each more than 2.5 million strong
—as well as several million Tatars. In Central Asia, the four
republics of the Turkmens, Uzbeks, Tadzhiks, and Kirghiz, along
with the people of adjoining Kazakhstan, contribute some 15
million Turkic people of Moslem faith. Other Moslems, living in
areas further in from the border, include several million Volga
Tatars and almost a million of the closely related Bashkirs. A
neighboring area contains close to 1.5 million Chuvash, a Christian and often Russianized remnant of the old Bolgar Empire on
the Volga. The Volga was mainly the site of a large settlement
of German-speaking colonists, now largely dispersed but still
numbering 1.5 million. To complete the census of nationalities
numbering more than a million, we must cite the Mordvinians,
who occupy an autonomous republic in Central Russia, and the
2.2. million Jews. The Jews are the only large group not com-
pactly settled in a territory historically associated with their
nationality.

Some 85 per cent of all the Great Russians live in the vast,
sprawling Russian Soviet Federated Socialist Republic. The rest
are spread throughout the surrounding ring of nationality areas,
usually living in enclaves in the cities within a countryside that
is solidly non-Russian. In this limited sense, minority status is
at least as typical of the Russian as any other Soviet nationality.
Collectively, Russian groups constitute a median proportion of
13.5 per cent of the population in the fourteen republics other
than the R.S.F.S.R. In certain areas, however, the influx of
Russians has been far greater. In Kazakhstan, for example, the
Russians are now the most numerous group (43 per cent) of the
population; together with other Slavic residents, the Ukrainians
and Belorussians, they constitute a majority of that republic.
Thus, the Kazakhs have become a minority in the area presumably set aside for them as a national home, and by a process
over which they have had little to say and less control.

Most of the important minorities represent separate and distinct nationalities, with their own language and literature, and
in many cases an earlier history of independent existence as a

nation-state. Their sense of separate identity is intensified by the fact that ethnicity is generally linked with religious identification, without the crosscutting of religion and race found in some lands. Thus, to be Russian is to be Orthodox, to be Polish, Catholic; Armenians are in the Armenian National Church and Georgians in the Georgian Church; and the Asiatic peoples, especially the Turkic, are overwhelmingly Moslem. It seems fairly clear that the last thing these people wish is the loss of identity as separate nationalities through absorption into the larger homogeneous culture of the Russian nation. Indeed, although there are often important historical ties that bind them to the center in Moscow, the nationalities seldom share much in common with other peoples of the Soviet Union beyond their minority status. How, then, did these diverse peoples all come together in common Soviet citizenship? The answer is not to be found, as in some other ethnically heterogeneous nations, in voluntary emigration or incorporation into Russia. It must be sought in the history of Russian state policy going back many centuries.

Czarist Expansionism

Following their subjugation by the Khans, the Russian people lived for centuries under the rule of the Tatar hordes, compressed into a modest area in central Russia and cut off from other major Slavic groups such as the Poles and Ukrainians, who were variously under domination by peoples from the West, Scandinavia, and the Baltic. The starting point of Russian colonialism may be taken as 1552, when Ivan the Terrible took Kazan, and thus liquidated the Tatar Khanate. The expansion of the previously small Muscovite state thus began with the incorporation of large numbers of Turkic peoples, especially from along the Volga and its tributaries. About a century later, a comparable major movement to the west was completed, when the left-bank regions of the Dnieper were established as a protectorate, bringing Cossack and Ukrainian peoples under Russian hegemony. Peter the Great added the peoples along the coast of the Baltic Sea. In her turn, Catherine the Great made further acquisitions in the west, including parts of Poland, and drove all the way to the Black Sea in the south. The Caucasus was added later, and most of the rest of Turkestan was acquired by Alexander II, to complete the movement by the end of his reign in 1881.

This extraordinary territorial expansion was estimated to have proceeded at the rate of 50 square miles a day over a period of 400 years—from the end of the fifteenth to the end of the nineteenth centuries. As pointed out earlier, it brought the Russians to the status of being a minority in the land they ruled. To speak of Russia as having a minority problem in the usual sense is therefore misleading. Russia was a huge colonial empire; but in distinction to the other empires of Europe, her colonial possessions were contiguous to the homeland. Thus she *incorporated* her possessions, her dependencies, and satellites, within one continuous border, with the captive nations strung around the outer limits of the solid Great Russian core. It is impossible to understand the nationality problem in the Soviet Union without always keeping in mind that the Soviet regime inherited this "prison of nations" from the Czars when it took power, and it had to operate within the framework thus set by history.

The Leninist Formula

In this situation, the Soviet regime has adopted an essentially dualistic attitude toward Czarist expansionism: On the one hand, it has generally treated the conquest and incorporation of the minorities as a "historically progressive" policy; on the other hand, it has encouraged the myth that Czarist treatment of the captive peoples was uniformly harsh, oppressive, and reactionary, and that it was designed to destroy the character and individuality of the many groups that had come under the empire's sway. Actually, Czarist policy toward the subject minorities varied considerably at different times, depending on the political philosophy of the different rulers. It also varied with respect to different areas and groups. Most modern impressions of this policy tend to concentrate on the period of intensive suppression started after the accession of Alexander III in 1881, and lasting until the revolution in 1905, after which a considerable liberalization again ensued. The depredations of Alexander's reign, especially the marked efforts at Russification and the virtual driving underground of local cultural movements, left a lasting mark not only on world opinion, but on the national groups as well, and this fact was soon to be of great importance to the as yet unborn Soviet government.

Considering how obvious a source of grievance against the Czarist regime here lay ready for exploitation, it is striking that the Bolsheviks were so slow to realize its potentialities as an instrument for shaking the old order. But their whole philosophy inclined them to gloss over the nationality problem. It was a basic belief of Marxists that the path of history would lead toward ever-larger, more homogeneous, centralized, industrial, political units, which in time would yield to a world-wide "proletarian" society. The slogan "the proletariat has no fatherland" expressed the belief that nationalism, patriotism, regionalism, and similar attachments were part and parcel of the social pattern of bourgeois capitalism, which would somehow be outlived and sloughed off once socialism and then Communism came to the world. Lenin himself gave virtually no attention to the nationality problem until 1913, when he was forced to turn to it both because of the growing popularity of the Bauer-Renner program and because of his own growing awareness that the success of his plans must reckon with the fact of national loyalties and aspirations.

The Bauer-Renner program, conceived to meet the multinational situation facing the political parties in the Austro-Hungarian Empire, proposed an unusual degree of autonomy for minorities in the conduct of their own affairs. Had it been put into effect, it would have permitted a great multiplication of small and more or less exclusive national, religious, and ethnic units. Lenin naturally viewed this program as a challenge to the principle of centralization he had steadfastly espoused. He was, however, equally opposed to the alternative idea of federalism, again on grounds that it weakened the chances for the development of a truly international proletarian power. Forced to take a stand, he went to what he thought was the absolute heart of the matter by basing his policy squarely *and exclusively* on the right of each nationality to so-called self-determination. He was unwilling to consider any compromises that might weaken the power of a central Communist government. Any people or nation—theoretically, at least—had the right to secede from the larger society, but if it chose to remain, it had to accept the general system in its entirety, without demanding special status or privilege and without asking for a federal union:

> The right to self-determination is an exception to our general thesis, which is centralism. This exception is absolutely necessary in the face of the Black Hundred type of Great Russian nationalism. . . . But a broad interpretation may not be made of an exception. There is *nothing*, absolutely nothing here, and there must be nothing here, but the *right* to secede.

Lenin felt that this acknowledgment of the abstract "right" to secede was necessary as a political maneuver. But at the same time—in a contradiction that no amount of esoteric language could hide—he held that any attempt at *actual* secession would be retrograde, antiproletarian, bourgeois counterrevolution. He assumed, in short, that no one could want to *exercise* the right of secession should there be a proletarian revolution.

He proved completely wrong, although in this he had the company of most of the other political groups in Russia, all of whom inadequately assessed both the effect of Czarist policy in hardening national feeling against *any* central Russian government, and the effect of the rapid social and cultural changes that were increasing national consciousness in many of the minority areas. In any event, the Bolshevik regime found, to its great embarrassment, that in most of the national areas of the former empire the local political leaders took their right of secession quite seriously. Even where complete separation was not their prime objective, the local leaders viewed themselves as equals with the leaders in Moscow, entitled on that basis to negotiate the nature of their nationality's participation in the new state.

The Bolsheviks did not hesitate to use the force of arms to meet this upsurge of independence, sending their Red Army to regain control over most of the provinces of the former empire. Finland was allowed to slip away without any particular struggle, and Poland and the Baltic States were abandoned after unsuccessful military compaigns. But under the command of such well-known Communist figures as Frunze and Kuibyshev in Central Asia, Kirov and Ordzhonikidze in the North Caucasus, Kaganovich in Belorussia, and Mikoyan in Azerbaijan, almost all the other territories were recaptured by Soviet troops and turned over to the control of the local Communist Parties, reliable subordinates of the central Party apparatus in Moscow. The army that entered Georgia on February 16, 1921, and by February 25 once again placed the Communist flag over the capital, Tiflis, fought the last major round in the effort to reintegrate the rebellious national areas.

The need for force to win back control of these areas brought home to the Soviet leaders the crucial nature of the nationality problem, and it is largely to this realization that we owe the particular forms the so-called nationality policy of the Soviet Union has assumed. Rather than attempting to relate the explicit history of the policy, the writer will turn directly to a consideration of its over-all features, giving the historical context as seems necessary. Perhaps the best approach is to pose four questions that would be important in evaluating the policy of any large-scale colonial power.

Self-Determination: A Paper Right

1) The first question in such an assessment would be: To what extent does the country's nationality policy provide for gradual transition to separate statehood for the major national minorities whose culture, history, and sociopolitical and economic maturity make them reasonable candidates for such status?

The attainment of a condition of self-government and national independence has come to be accepted as a fundamental goal and an inalienable right of people all over the world. Since World War II, we have witnessed a tremendous sociopolitical movement as virtually all the major colonial dependencies of the former British Empire, and to a lesser but striking degree of the French Empire, have achieved national independence. Any nation that tries to maintain control over a colonial area—or even to slow down the pace toward independence—invites serious criticism and often serious trouble; the crisis in Algeria is only the most striking and recent evidence of the explosive nature of this issue. It seems not at all inappropriate, therefore, to address the above question to the Soviet Union, particularly since it takes so much pride in pointing to the provision in its constitution that grants each of the constituent republics the ultimate right "freely" to secede from the Union. What, if anything, is done to implement this right in practice?

It may seem superfluous to observe, in the first place, that the Soviet regime in no way acts to encourage the secession of the minorities. In fact, one might well argue that no central government could be expected to take an active part in urging its constituent parts to achieve independence. The point is made here because there are those who apply a double standard on this score, criticizing other colonial powers for their lack of encouragement to independence movements while turning a blind eye to Soviet practice.

It is of course one thing for a central government to encourage some part of a larger union to detach itself, and quite another to ask simply that minority peoples have the right to advocate and work peacefully for their eventual independence. Since the right of secession is constitutionally guaranteed in the Soviet Union, the right to pursue that goal would logically seem to follow. Yet even to advocate, let alone to work toward, the political independence of any area in the Soviet Union is unthinkable for the Soviet citizen. Such action is identified, both by law outside the Constitution and by long practice of the secret police, as a counterrevolutionary crime against the state, warranting severe punishment. Almost every major purge trial has involved charges that the accused conspired to separate some national area from the Union. At various stages of Soviet history, hundreds and thousands of officials, teachers, writers, and other members of the intellectual classes of different national republics have been purged from the Party and state apparatus, and/or sent into forced-labor camps on charges of harboring "bourgeois nationalist leanings," the official term for identifying with the interests of one's national group and resisting abject subordination to the interests of the Moscow center.

In short, what the Constitution says about the national question bears virtually no relation to Soviet practice. Any lingering doubts on this score should have been destroyed by the action of the Soviet regime during World War II, when it simply erased from the map and from the face of the earth four autonomous socialist republics—the Volga German, the Crimean Tatar, the Kalmyk, and the Chechen-Ingush. Although there was an announcement in the case of the Volga Germans that this action was taken in the interest of national security, and a belated statement that the Chechen and Crimean Tatars had collaborated with the Germans, not even this much explanation was given with regard to the Kalmyks.

Not only were the republics liquidated as political entities, but their millions of people were dispersed to distant regions of the Soviet Union. There were wide repercussions and revulsion against this act; among others, Tito of Yugoslavia went so far as to accuse the Soviet Union of genocide. Certainly the indiscriminate mass dispersion of a whole population because of acts of individuals, no matter how numerous, violated basic standards of humanity and made a mockery of Stalin's assertion that "the national question and the problem of collaboration among nations have been settled better [in the U.S.S.R.] than in any other multinational state." It was not until after Stalin's death that some members of these nationalities were rehabilitated and partially restored to their former status.

Cultural Survivals

2) The second broad question may be phrased: To what degree are the minorities permitted and facilitated in the free expression of their cultural heritage? First and foremost, this involves the right to use one's native tongue in all types of public and private communication and in the education of youth. Cultural expression also includes the preservation and further development of folk and tribal ways, including art forms, ceremonial and religious customs, the national costume, etc. In addition, some hold that free cultural expression should include the right to have economic and political forms of organization distinctive to a particular culture.

That the Soviet approach toward the cultural self-expression of the minorities has been unique is beyond doubt; whether it has been as liberal as is claimed is quite another question. The doctrinal explanation of Soviet policy rests in the distinction that is made between the content and the form of culture, expressed in the well-worn formula "national in form, socialist in content." In theory, this phrase means that the values and ideas of the socialist society should be uniform in every culture, though the means by which they are expressed may be—indeed, should be—of a traditional and indigenous nature. The vagueness of this formula, however, has left wide leeway in its application, and like most Soviet slogans it has become quite meaningless in practice.

Obviously it is important to know *which* institutions and distinctive cultural forms are allowed to persist, and how crucial to the integrity of the original culture are those that have been suppressed because they fall in the realm where "socialist" uniformity is required. In the Soviet totalitarian system, the model for society as developed in Moscow is so rigid and all-pervasive that very little has in fact been left that could qualify as being "national" without conflicting with what must be "socialist."

The outstanding survival has been the native languages. With one exception—Yiddish—the Soviet regime has made no attempt to eradicate local tongues; they are used in the educational system, in communications media, and in indigenous literature. Generally distinctive literary forms associated with the languages in such spheres as poetry, epic writing, and drama have also been permitted. Another class of survivals that has suffered comparatively little interference is folk arts, including folk handicrafts and native art forms. Nor has there been much effort made to alter distinctive modes of native dress (except in the case of the Moslem veil for women, against which a rather successful campaign has been waged). These policies, it might be pointed out, parallel the practice adopted by most colonial powers.

If the Soviet attitude with respect to these several fundamentals of cultural expression has been generally permissive—and certainly represents a vast reform over the depredatory Russification efforts of Alexander III—there is nevertheless much on the record to indicate that tolerance extends only as far as it suits the interests of the central authorities. Even in the matter of language, Moscow's actions have in some cases profoundly affected an indigenous culture. Much is made of the fact that the Soviets provided alphabets for several dozen languages that previously could not be written down, paving the way for newspapers and other literature in these tongues. Less is known of the fact that the Soviet regime used its power, against the overwhelming opposition of the local population, to force the abandonment of the religiously sanctioned Arabic script used by the millions of Soviet Moslems. Not once but twice they did this, first introducing the Latin alphabet, and then, in 1939, substituting the Cyrillic. Even the Czars never dreamed of attempting such a victory for Russian culture among their subject Moslems.

Folk literature and art, too, have been subjected to interference and suppression whenever Moscow chose to see in their various forms any manifestations of "bourgeois nationalism." Frequently, the regime has seized on old or new folk writings, dramas, operas, etc., condemning them for deviation from the official line, forbidding their production, and taking reprisals against their authors. The writing or presentation of native history in particular has suffered from intervention by the authorities, who insist that the Czarist subjugation of the nationality areas be treated as "historically progressive." Among many such acts of repression, one of the more glaring examples was the dissolution of the entire cultural apparatus of the Soviet Jews—including their native theater, newspapers, publishing houses, and writers' association—during the postwar wave of officially inspired anti-Semitism.

All of the minority religions have, of course, been the object of repressive measures. The fact that these moves have, from a doctrinal point of view, been part of the Communist campaign against religious belief per se (including the Russian Orthodox faith) has made little difference to peoples whose religion and nationality are closely identified. For them, the attack on religion has been simply another example of the effort of an alien regime to encroach on indigenous cultural patterns and to shackle national development.

In short, the Soviet attitude toward "national forms" in the cultural sphere has been one of tolerance when—but only when—tolerance has not interfered with the ideological or practical needs of the regime.

System and Sacrifice

Outside of the specific areas of cultural expression mentioned above, few of the traditional ways of the minorities have been allowed to survive. In the political, economic, and generally the social spheres, the uniform institutions of Soviet society prevail in the form of the supreme ruling party, the bureaucratic administrative apparatus, the planned and centrally controlled industrial economy, the collectivized peasant agriculture, and the ubiquitous instruments of ideological indoctrination and control. Thus Soviet nationality policy has allowed no recognition of the fact that economic, political, and social forms of organization may be distinctive and indeed crucial elements in a particular national culture.

The imposition of the Soviet system involved a social and cultural revolution throughout Soviet-held territory. Among the more settled European or Europeanized populations, whose culture was already somewhat geared to the patterns of industrial society, the process of Sovietization was highly disruptive, but no more so than for the majority of the Great Russians—and perhaps even less so in the case, say, of Armenian traders than of the Russian peasants. But among the peoples of the more isolated, underdeveloped areas—mainly in Asia—the depredations caused by Sovietization and the enforced departure from traditional ways were of enormous magnitude.

An outstanding example is the case of the Kazakh people. Before collectivization, the Kazakhs were either nomads who relied extensively on the use of horses on the great Central Asian steppe, or recently settled cattle and sheep herders. Their whole way of life was regulated by and within the tribal structure, especially the clan system. The attempt blindly to impose the pattern of collectivization on these people in the early 1930's met with intensive resistance, leading to an open struggle with the regime. The loss of life was staggering. While some of the Kazakhs escaped with their herds over the border into Chinese Sinkiang, the huge decimation of the population during this period was mainly due to deaths in the fighting or through starvation. Census figures for 1926 and 1939 show that in the interim the Kazakh population dropped from 3.967 to 3.098 million, an absolute decline of 869,000, or 22 per cent. Calculating in what would have been an expectable rate of population growth under normal circumstances (on the basis of 15 per cent for the Soviet population as a whole), the survivors in Kazhakstan were 1.5 million fewer by 1939 than they should have been, a staggering deficit considering the over-all size of the population. Moreover, in the course of the bitter struggle, the greater part of the livestock on which the local economy had rested was lost, through retaliative slaughter on the part of the desperate natives, neglect of the herds while the men were off fighting, or in minor part migration. Taking the stocks in 1928 as a base, only 25 to 50 per cent of the cattle, 13 per cent of the sheep, and 12 per cent of the horses remained by 1934.

Although the stark statistics above are from official sources, the Soviet regime has never put forward any explanation of this chapter of its history. Unfortunately, the statistics are little known to the world and are seldom weighed in the balance when glib estimates are made in praise of "enlightened" Soviet nationality policy. This case represents a relentless fulfillment of Stalin's instruction to the Communist Party in 1923, when he urged that Turkestan—which included Kazakhstan—be transformed into a model republic because of its revolutionary significance for Soviet Russia's eastern policy. He declared: "We have to fulfill this task whatever the price, without sparing efforts and without shrinking from sacrifices. . . ." Stalin, certainly, can never be accused of having shrunk from sacrifices in Kazakhstan.

Equal Opportunity

3) Turning to the third question under consideration, to what extent is Soviet nationality policy nondiscriminatory—that is, to what extent does it offer members of the minority nationalities equal access to such benefits as the society provides for average

citizens? Are opportunities for education, work, pay, social mobility, freedom of movement, and choice of residence the same for all, or does the dominant group enjoy a favored status?

On the whole, the record of the Soviet Union in these respects is good. The data supporting this evaluation are based on republics as a whole, not on pure ethnic or national groups, so that the presence of large Russian and Ukrainian minorities in some of the national republics—and conversely of non-Russian minorities in the R.S.F.S.R.—may distort the picture of Soviet accomplishment to some degree. Still, on the basis of a large number of indices, it seems clear that members of all nationalities (including the Great Russian) have received broadly equal treatment with respect to personal economic and social—if not political —opportunities. Allowance must be made, of course, for the fact that many of the minorities live in predominantly rural or backward regions whose development has expectably lagged behind that of more urban or industrial areas; however, the *relative* position of these groups has improved greatly since the pre-revolutionary era.

Important among the indices considered here is the striking spread of literacy among all groups of the Soviet population. In the intercensus period from 1926 to 1939, the over-all literacy rate in the Soviet Union rose from 51 to 81 per cent. In certain national republics, the low base at the start made the rise much more dramatic. For example, in the Central Asian Tadzhik Republic, the rate of literacy increased from 4 to 72 per cent, and in the Azerbaijan Republic from 25 to 73 per cent. The preliminary release on the 1959 census does not provide data on literacy by nationality, but since the All-Union rate is now reported to be 98.5 per cent, it must be assumed that the nationality areas have continued to advance in this respect. While the Soviet definition of literacy is based on a very rudimentary level of learning, and while in some areas, the improvement can be attributed to the influx of Russian and other literates, the record of accomplishment is nevertheless substantial.

Data on improvements in education follow a similar pattern. In the area of the five Central Asian republics (including Kazakhstan), there were only 136,000 pupils in elementary and secondary schools in 1914–15, representing less than 0.5 per cent of the 9.6 million pupils in all Russia. By 1955–56, the parallel enrollment was 3.59 million, an increase of more than twenty-five times. This number constituted about 13 per cent of the total student enrollment in the same grades, which is about the weight of the population of the Central Asiatic republics in the Soviet population as a whole. Similar progress has been made in higher education: Whereas before the Revolution there were virtually no higher school establishments in these areas, by 1955, local institutions had an enrollment of 155,000 students, or about 9 per cent of the total higher school population in the U.S.S.R.

There are many other ways in which the Soviet regime has accorded equal treatment to the minorities. Available data show that facilities such as libraries, medical clinics, movie and dramatic theaters, sports stadiums, clubs, newspapers and journals, radio and television stations, etc. have been provided in the nationality areas at close to the same per-capita rate as in the Great Russian area.

The sum indication of such statistical evidence is that minority members (again, with the striking exception of Soviet Jews) do not suffer from any discrimination insofar as educational training, economic opportunity, and social benefits are concerned. This impression is supported by the testimony of Soviet refugees. In the Harvard Project on the Soviet Social System, in which this writer participated, questionnaires were submitted to several hundred Ukrainians and to smaller groups of other nationalities —along with Russians—all of whom had escaped from the Soviet Union. The replies showed that people whose occupations had been on a comparable level had, regardless of their nationality, been in very similar circumstances with respect to income, opportunities for education, job satisfaction, and the general rate of social mobility. Such similarity in living conditions produced similarity in values, attitudes, and opinions, again cutting across national lines. In other words, class status rather than national identification determined what people found praiseworthy in the Soviet system and what they condemned. The Russian peasant described and criticized his life very much as did the Ukrainian, Georgian, Tatar, or Kazakh peasant; similarly, professional people of different nationality evaluated their life situations in like terms and shared the same criticisms of the system. Such differences as did emerge between nationalities were largely a reflection of the varying class composition—in particular, the proportion of peasants—from group to group.

Unequal Inopportunity

There was, however, one distinctive complaint voiced by those in the minority nationalities, and this on an issue of profound importance. The reader may have noted that all of the above examples of nondiscrimination have been confined to the economic and social spheres. In the political realm—in the structure of rule—a very different picture emerges. The crucial protest voiced in common by refugees from the minorities was that their people did not share equally in the direction of society and were not free to shape their culture along lines in keeping with native or indigenous traditions. Many saw themselves as still essentially vassals of a foreign power, as ruled by the alien Russian. The basis of these feelings is not just a matter of the sharp restrictions that, as we have seen, the regime places on the development of local nationalism. Just as important is the fact that the institutions of governance, both at the center and within the republics, have not included a proportionate representation of the minorities. The Communist Party has been predominantly a Russian party, with only a weak representation of the nationalities, while in the republics themselves the influence and indeed control of Russians and other outsiders sent in from Moscow has been painfully evident.

The composition of the supreme council of the Party has reflected this imbalance during most of its history. Up to the time of its reorganization in 1952, the Politburo had a total of twenty-eight members, of whom sixteen were Russians and eight others Russified Jews or Georgians. The people of thirteen national republics, containing some 80 million of the population, never had representation on that body, including the third largest nationality, the Belorussians, and some 16 to 20 million Moslems. The 30 to 40 million Ukrainians were not represented after 1938, when the purges claimed the leading figures of Ukrainian nationality. The membership of the Presidium, which replaced the Politburo in 1952, has been somewhat more proportionate, but not markedly so. Of the thirty-three people who have served on the Presidium, only eight—including Stalin before his death—have been non-Russians. The others are Beria (also Georgian), Kaganovich (Jewish), Mikoyan (Armenian), Korotchenko and Kirichenko (Ukrainians), Kuusinen (Finnish), and Mukhitdinov (Uzbek). A number of minority members, however, have been appointed as candidate (alternative) members of the Presidium.

The fact that Stalin himself was a Georgian by birth counts for little, since like many of these leaders he thoroughly identified himself with the Russians, a trait reflected in his extraordinary toast at the end of World War II: "I should like to propose a toast to the health of our Soviet people, and above all of our Russian people. I drink in particular to the health of the Russian people because it is the most outstanding of all the nations of the Soviet Union."

The weakness of national representation has been evident not only at the top of the power hierarchy, but in the rank and file of the Party. In proportion to population, the Communist Party is strongest in the predominantly Great Russian areas, weakest in the nationality regions. In Moscow and Leningrad, for example, the ratio of local to total Party membership is more than twice that of local to total population; in republics like Tadjikistan, the reverse applies. In fact, however, the disproportion is much greater, since within the nationality areas, the Party is not only small, but includes a substantial number of non-natives, preponderantly Russians. The exact ratios are hard to estimate, since the Party generally stopped publishing data according to nationality by 1938. It is known, however, that as late as 1935, Tadzhiks and Turkmens—for example—constituted 75 per cent of the population in the republics bearing their names, but only about 50 per cent of the Party organizations.

Within the lower and middle ranks of the national Parties, both the rank and file and their officials are predominantly of native stock and speak the native languages (the same is even truer of the governmental apparatus). But in the large urban centers, at the seats of power, the Russian image looms large. Access to positions of power is comparatively limited to the native, except insofar as he has become Russified—and in this case he is considered a non-national who may be transferred to work anywhere within the Soviet Union.

The fact that the Party chief in the national areas has often been someone sent in from the outside has been perhaps the most important affront to national pride and symbol of the alien nature of the Party. The best example in this respect is the Ukraine, where the First Secretary of the Communist Party has almost always been a non-Ukrainian, even though sometimes vaguely connected with the Ukrainian area or nationality. Kaganovich, who held the post in 1925–28, was a Russified Jew born in Belorussia. Kossior, who followed, was a Pole. The rest were Russians, and many never even learned to speak Ukrainian with fluency, despite the fact that it was the national tongue of some 40 million subjects. The only exception in the line of rule was Khrushchev's chosen successor in the post—his Ukrainian assistant Kirichenko (who later rose to the Presidium but is now in disgrace).

Economic Development Policy

To pose the fourth and last question: Has there been any economic exploitation of minority regions, by depletion of the land or other natural resources, by the carrying off of wealth produced in the area without sufficient compensation, or by the development of the region's economy in so special or limited a way as to subordinate it unduly to the productive needs and interests of the dominant majority?

In the Soviet case, the answer to these questions is clear-cut: The regime's economic policy as a whole does not discriminate against the minority areas and their economic development in favor of the Great Russians. Soviet industrialization was, of course, based on forced savings, which the government extracted for investment at the cost of popular consumption. But the minorities were not asked to bear a disproportionate share of the resulting hardships of a depressed living standard. The burden fell on all; in fact, it might be argued that the Great Russian majority initially made the greater sacrifice in order to permit the development of the capital-hungry, economically backward areas.

One economist has estimated, for example, that while the all-Union living standard fell markedly during the 1930's, in the four republics of Central Asia (not counting Kazakhstan) it may actually have improved to a slight degree. At that time, the local economy was undergoing rapid change, as indicated by the fact that industrial output, which had been negligible, multiplied six to nine fold between 1928 and 1937. Such an increase could only have been accomplished by the substantial investment of capital drawn from other parts of the country and by the application of new technology. Such help was even more important to the agriculture of the region.

In the initial stage of European colonial development, substantial capital was invested in the colonies, but often only in order to create a one-crop economy that in the long run was economically disadvantageous to the local people. There was an element of this approach in the Soviet regime's insistence on the expansion of cotton acreage in Central Asia, usually at the expense of existing wheat crops. But the area was not treated simply as a vast cotton plantation for the rest of the Soviet Union. On the contrary, existing resources of other kinds were widely developed. A hydroelectric power industry was developed, the output of which increased 8.5 times in the period 1928–37. Earlier, virtually all cotton had been shipped to Russia to be made into textiles, which in turn had to be shipped back, but in the 1930's, a substantial textile industry was established in Tashkent. Leather shoemaking was established to utilize the hides from the region's extensive herds. These efforts make it evident that capital was retained in the area and not syphoned off for accumulation at the center. The data already cited on the growth of education and other cultural and social facilities similarly indicate that a goodly share of the returns accrued from exploitation of the region's natural wealth was reinvested in raising standards in the region.

Although the central Asian case may be one of the more outstanding examples, it reflects the general pattern of Soviet policy in the economic development of backward areas. The allocation of investment during the process of economic expansion has not in any significant degree been guided by considerations of nationality, but rather by those of economic efficiency or the defense needs of the country. And the benefits—as well as the burdens—which have resulted from economic development have been more or less equally shared by all peoples of the Soviet Union.

A Summary View

The main features of Soviet nationality policy sketched above have been consistently manifested since at least the early 1930's. Although the program as a whole is often identified as "Stalinist" nationality policy, only minor modifications have taken place in the post-Stalin era. In line with the general relaxation of terror in the U.S.S.R., the most repressive policies vis-à-vis certain nationalities have been abandoned and some of the iniquities of Stalin's reign (e.g., the dispersion of the Chechen-Ingush, Kalmyks, and so on) have been rectified. In addition, Khrushchev has shown more awareness of the requirements of good "public relations" by such gestures as personal visits to the nationality areas, the appointment of a Ukrainian to the top post in the Ukraine, and the nomination of representatives of the Central Asian peoples to the higher councils of the ruling Communist Party.

In all other respects, however, the present leadership has followed the pattern of the past. On the credit side of the record, this has generally meant equality of social and economic opportunity for the individual of minority status. On the whole it has also meant equal treatment of national groups with regard to the exploitation of resources and economic development on the one hand, and to the elaboration of certain cultural institutions on the other.

Against these features, other factors must be weighed. First, if equality of treatment has been the general rule in the above respects, the exceptions and departures have been numerous enough and in some cases so glaring as to demonstrate that the application of nationality policy remains a matter of arbitrary and expedient decision on the part of the regime. More important, however, are the moral and political issues that underly the question of minority rights. The basic fact—and no amount of achievement can obscure it—is that Soviet nationality policy has constituted a forceful imposition of social, political, and economic forms by a powerful center upon a host of colonial subjects. If these people had little part in choosing their path of national development, they have as little freedom today to alter it.

Communism and Anti-Semitism

—ERICH GOLDHAGEN

Judaism kills the love for the Soviet Motherland.
        —*Sovetskaia Moldavia*, July 23, 1959.

*They do not like collective work, group discipline . . .
They are individualists. . . . Jews are interested in everything, they want to probe into everything, they discuss
everything, and end up by having profoundly different
opinions.*

> —Khrushchev, in an interview with Serge
> Goussard, correspondent of *Le Figaro*
> (Paris), April 9, 1958.

THE EXISTENCE OF anti-Semitism in the U.S.S.R., its employment
as a tool by the Communist leadership, and—indeed—its absorption into the *Weltanschauung* of the "new class" should no longer
come as a surprise to anyone familiar with the realities of Soviet
life. Yet few are aware that the Soviet leaders, in embracing anti-
Semitism, have been acting in a spirit not entirely alien to the
socialist tradition in Western Europe as well as in Russia. Indeed, the precursors of Leninism and Stalinism—the revolutionary terrorists, the so-called Populists, who dominated the
revolutionary scene in Russia in the second half of the nineteenth
century, were not averse to employing anti-Semitism in the pursuit of their aims.

"Lubricant on the Wheel of Revolution"

When socialism as a current of political thought made its
appearance in Western Europe, it tended to look upon the Jews

with unfriendly eyes, regarding them as the embodiment of those qualities of social life that socialists denounced as evil and that they were sworn to undo. Barred from the ownership of land and excluded from the guilds, the Jews had long ago been driven to devote themselves primarily to the pursuit of commerce; and throughout Western Europe the name Jew came to be almost synonymous with that of trader. The belief was thus born that the pursuit of money was a national vocation of the Jews, enjoined by their religion and practiced with unrivaled skill and zeal. It seemed that the spirit of commerce had found its purest embodiment and its consummate practitioners in the Jews.*

The Jews thus incurred the contempt and hatred that socialists harbored against the world of finance. The comprehensive condemnation of commerce and finance as useless and parasitic occupations, as unproductive activities whereby those who shun honest labor could derive undeserved riches from the toil of others, was bound to embrace the Jews. This attitude was reinforced by the sinister tales that popular lore came to weave around the name of Rothschild, whose enormous wealth was believed to be a source of evil power—swaying monarchs, making and unmaking governments, and determining the destinies of nations. The vagaries of history, its irrationalities, the injustices and sufferings which it inflicted were traced not to the impersonal forces of economic and social processes but to villains of flesh and blood to whom one could assign guilt and upon whom one could discharge that hatred in which suffering and discontent often seek relief.

It was this outlook that Marx in part echoed in his famous essay *Zur Judenfrage:*

* It is interesting to note, in this connection, that all utopian reformers viewed money as a pernicious force serving no purpose save that of breeding injustice and perverting authentic human values, and foresaw its disappearance in the desired society of the future. The citizens of Thomas More's *Utopia,* for instance, "hold gold and silver up to scorn in every way. . . . They hang gold rings from the ears of criminals, place gold rings on their fingers, gold collars around their necks, and gold crowns on their heads." And Karl Marx, in his *Nationale Ökonomie und Philosophie,* had the following to say about the evil influence of money: "It turns loyalty into disloyalty, love into hate, virtue into vice, vice into virtue, slave into master, master into slave, stupidity into intelligence, intelligence into stupidity."

What is the object of the Jew's worship in this world?
Usury. What is his worldly god? Money. . . .

Money is the zealous one God of Israel, beside which no
other God may stand. Money degrades all the gods of mankind and turns them into commodities. Money is the universal and self-constituted value set upon all things. It has
therefore robbed the whole world, of both nature and man,
of its original value. Money is the essence of man's life and
work, which have become alienated from him. This alien
monster rules him and he worships it.*

In Russia, too, disdain towards the Jews prevailed among many
of the early revolutionaries. The abysmal conditions of the Jews
—constrained in their movement, compelled to live only in
assigned regions known as the Jewish Pale, and reduced (save
for a tiny minority) to a state of poverty verging on starvation—
evoked little sympathy in the breasts of some of the radical intellectuals of the 1870's and 1880's, however virulent their hatred
of the Czarist autocracy. To be sure, the Jews were wretched and
poor, but their wretchedness and poverty was not graced by
those lofty virtues the fertile imagination of the revolutionaries
ascribed to the Russian peasantry. Unlike the peasants, who
earned their meager subsistence by toil and who were regarded
by the intellectuals as noble beings endowed with the qualities
of selflessness and instinctive communalism, the Jews were a

---

* This is not to say that Marx was anti-Semitic in the accepted sense of the
term. Indeed, the main theme and purport of his essay was to expose the
hollowness of the civic equality granted by the bourgeois order. As for
Marx's linking of Jews and capitalism, the most original and freshest explanation of it, in this author's opinion, was offered by the East German
scholar L. Kofler, in his *Zur Geschichte der Buergerlichen Gesellschaft* (*On
the History of the Bourgeois Society*), pp. 478–96—a unique exception to
the otherwise dreary gibberish that passes off as "social science" in the
Communist bloc. According to Kofler, capitalism found its purest manifestation in the Jewish ethos, because unlike Gentile capitalists who, being
linked to the native proletariat by ties of common nationhood, have endeavored to disguise and temper their avarice and exploitative ambitions,
the Jews knew no such restraint. Strangers to the society in which they have
lived, they pursued their vocation with uninhibited ruthlessness and without an embellishing guise. They thus mirrored capitalism in its stark naked-
ness.

work-shirking lot, engaging in the "parasitic" and "exploitative" occupations. Even poverty, their only reward, could not redeem them.

But some revolutionaries did not content themselves with passive disdain; they acclaimed and encouraged active violence against the Jews.

In the spring and summer of 1881, a wave of violence swept through the southern part of the Pale. Over one hundred Jewish communities were visited by orgies of destruction, claiming, apart from enormous material damage, scores of dead and hundreds of wounded. This outbreak of unprovoked brute force visited upon a defenseless community moved the Executive Committee of the Narodnaya Volya (People's Will)—the largest revolutionary-terroristic organization at that time—to issue a proclamation in Ukrainian on August 30, 1881, blessing the riots and exhorting the peasants to further violence against "the parasitic Jews" and the "Czar of the Jews." "The people of the Ukraine," the proclamation stated, "suffer more than anyone else from the Jews. . . . You have already begun to rise against the Jews . . . you have done well."

This proclamation cannot be explained, of course, by the anti-Semitic spirit of the radical intelligentsia. No doubt its authors were imbued with anti-Semitic prejudices; yet it would be naïve to assume, for instance, that they were in earnest in affixing the label Czar of the Jews on Alexander III: His disdain for the Jews and his oppressive and discriminatory policies against them were certainly known to the leaders of the Narodnaya Volya. Thus there is little doubt that the proclamation was first and foremost a *calculated device*. Underlying it, apart from the Bakuninist conviction that the "passion for destruction is a constructive passion," lay Machiavellian calculation, the wish and the hope that the violence against the Jews would be extended to the autocracy. By linking the Jews with the Czar, the leaders of the Narodnaya Volya sought to telescope the pogroms into the social revolution, to fan its fire into a conflagration engulfing the authorities. They were consciously lying, but to their minds this was a "noble lie," graced by the lofty purpose it served. The blood of the Jews might have been wholly innocent, but it was nonetheless the "lubricant on the wheels of Revolution."

Among the radical émigrés in Geneva, one by the name of Zhukovsky defended the pogroms in the following terms:

Sixty percent of the Jewish population are engaged in commerce. This is the background against which the peasant hunts down the Jew. . . . To be sure, from a humanitarian standpoint, it is a piece of barbarism when peasants fall like savages upon a frightened Jew and beat him until he bleeds. However, take this event in the context of social dynamics. Why does he beat? Because [beating] is his political ballot. He has no other way of venting his wrath against his exploitation by the government. It is indeed a pity that the peasant beats the Jew—the most innocent of his exploiters. But he beats, and this is the beginning of his struggle for liberation. When . . . his fists will have grown strong and hard he will strike those who are above the Jews.*

But even those radicals who did not view the pogroms with approval could not bring themselves to call for an end to the bloodshed. Anti-Semitism was endemic to the Russian peasantry. It was its daily psychic bread, designed to still the grievances and frustrations born of hunger—hunger for land and hunger for food. The Russian intelligentsia, which had for two decades tried with only limited success to strike roots in the Russian peasantry, to secure its confidence, and to persuade it to follow the intellectuals as the champions of its aspirations, feared that by showing concern for the Jews they would unwittingly alienate the peasants. To come out in defense of the Jews would have branded them as "Jewish stooges." Was it worth endangering, for the sake of a small national minority, the cause of socialism? These were the arguments with which some radicals who had dissociated themselves from violence justified their refusal to come out publicly against the pogroms. The radical philosopher P. L. Lavrov, who was to describe anti-Semitism as the "most tragic epidemic of

* F. Kurski, *Historishe Shriftn* (Yiddish, Vilna/Paris), III (1939), 561.

our era," declined to print a pamphlet against the pogroms submitted to him by the Social Democratic leader Akselrod, stating:

> I must confess that I regard this question as a very complicated one, indeed an exceedingly difficult one for a party that seeks to come closer to the people. Theoretically, on paper, the question can be easily answered. But in view of the prevailing popular passions and the need of the Russian socialists to have the people on their side whenever possible, the question is quite different.*

The New Spirit

The succeeding generation of Russian revolutionaries did not share the view—prevalent among many Populist leaders—that anti-Semitic outrages have a redemptive quality. Manifestations of anti-Semitism were not tolerated in the Marxist-Socialist movement, which dominated the Russian revolutionary scene during the next two decades. In his pamphlet *Our Differences* (1884), which set forth the program of the Social Democrats and the reasons for their opposition to the Narodnaya Volya, Plekhanov, the "father of Russian Marxism," condemned the proclamation of 1881 as "a base flattery of the national prejudices of the Russian people." Similarly, Lenin, after the notorious Kishinev pogrom in 1903, recalled with shame the "infamous proclamation" and called on all socialists to defend the Jews against the mob as a matter of honor.

Indeed, by the turn of the century, both Russian and West European socialists tended to view anti-Semitism in a new light. Hitherto, socialists had regarded it as a misguided protest against existing social conditions by petty bourgeois and proletarians—"the socialism of fools" in the words of August Bebel. They had hoped that sooner or later those ensnared by it would recognize that not only capitalist Jews were the cause of their misery, but Gentile and Jewish capitalists alike, and that this recognition would bring them into the fold of socialism. But when it seemed that instead of being a vestibule of socialism, anti-Semitism had become a useful tool in the hands of the ruling class, the socialist

* *Iz Arkhiva P. G. Akselroda* (Russian, Berlin), II (1924), 30.

attitude changed. Anti-Semitism came to be treated unequiv-
ocally as a hostile ideology. During the two decades before 1917,
there were few recorded overt expressions of anti-Jewish bias
in the Russian socialist movement. In fact, there is no doubt
that by and large the leaders of the Russian socialist parties did
not harbor anti-Semitic sentiments. Such sentiments were certainly absent from Lenin, who was a genuine "internationalist,"
singularly free from national intolerance, and determinedly
hostile to any manifestations of xenophobia or "Great Russian
chauvinism" on the part of his comrades-in-arms.

Nevertheless, the Russian Social Democrats still shunned
prominent association with specifically Jewish causes. To be sure,
the central organs of their press denounced anti-Semitism in
forceful terms; but they did not carry these denunciations in
popular leaflets and pamphlets. For a socialist agitator, working
among the grass roots of the working class, it was still unwise to
appear in the role of an advocate of the Jews.

After the October Revolution, the Bolsheviks adopted an uncompromising attitude against anti-Semitism. As the White
armies converged to extinguish the infant regime with the battle-
cry "Beat the Jews and Save Russia," the denunciation of anti-
Semitism as counterrevolutionary became not only a duty enjoined by faith, but a course dictated by the imperatives of the
struggle in which the Bolsheviks were engaged. The weapon had
to be wrested from the hands of those seeking to restore the
ancien regime. Anti-Semitism was outlawed and suppressed; and
the Red Army was hailed by the Jews as a protector and liberator from the White troops, which were bringing upon them
nothing but death and destruction. Anti-Semitism could not
figure in any indictment drawn up against the Soviet dictatorship during the 1920's. But with the advent of the 1930's, a new
picture began to unfold.

Stalinist Nationalism

The revival of Great Russian nationalism under Stalin's dispensation in the early 1930's created a climate less congenial to the
Jews than that which had prevailed throughout the preceding
decade. With the building of "socialism in one country" proceed-

ing apace, Bolshevik Russia began to shed many of the features that revolutionary enthusiasm and devotion had bestowed upon her. A new spirit pervaded the Party, disillusioned by the dearth of revolutionary outbreaks in West Europe to which it had looked forward in the days of Lenin and Trotsky, and deeply immersed in its own "revolution from above." Under these circumstances, the Russian nationalist tradition, renounced and abused by the sweeping wave of revolutionary triumph, gradually reasserted its claims, casting the revolutionary *élan* into a more traditional mold. Within these confining walls the cosmopolitan radiance of the revolution grew dimmer and dimmer. The old revolutionary leadership, reared in the tradition of Marxist internationalism, was replaced by a new generation of bureaucrats imbued with that peculiar mixture of Marxist militancy and Russian chauvinism that henceforth was to mark the ethos of Soviet society.

A chilly wind began to envelop the Jews, especially the Jewish intelligentsia, which had been everywhere in the modern world the bearer of cosmopolitanism. In this new climate the dictatorship was less disposed to resist the envious and subdued demands that the high proportion of the Jews in administrative positions and universities be reduced and that the vacancies thus created be filled by native sons. Indeed, the dictatorship viewed such restrictive measures as salutary: They would earn the regime fresh popularity at home, and at the same time blunt the edge of anti-Communist propaganda throughout the world (emanating from the extreme right) that Mother Russia had fallen under the domination of the Judeo-Communist conspiracy. Accordingly, the Soviet government proceeded to reduce sharply the number of Jews in the leading bodies of the Party and government, to introduce a *numerus clausus* into some institutions of higher learning, and virtually to exclude Jews from the diplomatic service.* To be a Jew again became a source of discomfort and a handicap.

* Hitler revealed in the course of one of his celebrated table talks that "Stalin made no secret before Ribbentrop that he was waiting only for the moment of maturation of a sufficiently large indigenous intelligentsia to make short shrift (*Schluss zu machen*) of Jews as a leadership stratum that he still needs today." *Hitlers Tischgespraeche* (Bonn, 1951), p. 119.

These measures did not spring from anti-Semitic sentiment in the strict traditional sense of the term, but were motivated by coldly calculated *raison d'état*. They were sometimes accompanied by regrets (privately voiced) about the necessity of sacrificing principles to this greater consideration. *Lex revolutiae suprema est*, Plekhanov had proclaimed in faulty Latin at the Second Congress of the Russian Social Democratic Party (1903), scarcely aware of the horrifying deeds with which that tenet was pregnant. Would a movement that could massacre proletarians in the name of the dictatorship of the proletariat, practice terror in order to achieve social harmony, glory in autocracy in order to establish universal self-government—would such a movement shrink from the appeasement of anti-Semitism if it thought such appeasement would further the "lofty" cause of Communism? The head of the Central Committee's department on national minorities met the complaints of a Yiddish writer, Katcherginski, concerning the discrimination against Jews practiced by Soviet authorities in Lithuania, with the explanation that "the Jews of Lithuania may have to be sacrificed to the general cause." The rich and indiscriminate armory of means wherewith Bolshevism professed to pursue Utopia acquired a fresh instrument, time-honored and of proved efficacy; and the anti-Semitic spirits, which had been outlawed by Bolshevism and driven to lead a repressed existence in the subterranean dwellings of Soviet society, were now emboldened to emerge and engage in their practice in the guise of a Communist *raison d'état*.*

* Trotsky diagnosed the first stealthy manifestations of official anti-Semitism in Soviet Russia as symptoms of the bureaucratic degeneration afflicting Soviet society. According to him, the Stalinist bureaucracy, having usurped the dictatorship of the proletariat and betrayed the spirit of the Marxist-Leninist legacy, was seeking to use the Jews as a scapegoat for its misrule and betrayal (Leon Trotsky, "Thermidor and Anti-Semitism," *The New International* [New York], May, 1941, pp. 91–94). The article bears the date February 22, 1937. This diagnosis, however, was less applicable for the 1930's than to the period after World War II. Thus in 1956, during the ferment in the Polish Communist Party that brought Gomulka to power, the Stalinist elements, known as the Natolin faction, proposed that the popular hatred besieging the Communist rulers be placated by offering the Jewish Party members as sacrificial lambs. They advocated, in the words of a contemporary revisionist account, that the governmental and Party apparatus be reconstructed by applying "the criterion of pure Aryan

From Intolerance to Repression

In 1948, Soviet policy toward the Jews acquired a fresh and disturbing dimension. If, hitherto, anti-Semitism had been a tool wielded with dispassion and calculated moderation without deeply engaging the spirit of the Communist leaders, and affecting only those Jews aspiring to careers in certain fields, now it was fed by passion and conviction, and was directed against the entire Jewish community. It was not only anti-Semitism *de logique*, to paraphrase Camus' famous phrase; it was at once logical and passionate.

The affection and enthusiasm displayed by the Jews of Russia for the newly created state of Israel to whose birth the Soviet Union itself had made a modest contribution, provoked Stalin's suspicion that the Jews were an untrustworthy element whose ties with their numerous brethren abroad made them potential traitors. He proceeded to treat them accordingly. He decided not only to render them harmless by encouraging their removal from jobs as security risks, but also to extinguish their ethnic consciousness. With characteristic totalitarian swiftness, all Jewish cultural institutions were abolished and several hundred Yiddish writers were arrested: The more prominent among them were executed after a secret trial (in 1952), while others expired in the penal camps of the Arctic wasteland. The entry "Jews" in the Soviet Encyclopedia published during that period described the Jews as if they were an extinct tribe. Before World War II, an elaborate network of cultural institutions had served the Jews of Russia: schools attended by over 100,000 children, a Yiddish press, a large and prolific Yiddish literary community, and a theatre rated among the best in the Soviet Union. By the autumn of 1948, almost nothing remained in existence. By a stroke of the dictator's pen, all organized Jewish endeavor came to an abrupt end. Only a score or so of defunct synagogues survived. These and the withered label of Birobidzhan still incongruously attached to that region on the Amur, which had never acquired a

blood" (Ryszard Turski, in *Po Prostu* [Warsaw], October 28, 1956). See also Czeslaw Milosz, "Anti-Semitism in Poland," *Problems of Communism*, May–June, 1957.

Jewish character and in which the Jews formed a hopeless minority, were the only visible signs of a community of 2.5 million.

From 1948 until the death of Stalin, Soviet Jews lived under a reign of terror amid rumors of their imminent mass deportation.

Rehabilitation with a Difference

The death of Stalin and the acquittal of the doctors involved in the "doctors' plot," as well as *Pravda's* (April 6, 1953) admission that the affair of the doctors was a "fabrication" intended to "inflame nationalist hostilities among the Soviet peoples," removed the nightmare that had hovered over the Jewish community. The terror relented. But the fundamentals of Stalin's policies towards the Jews were retained. As in many other spheres of Communist endeavor, the Stalinist aims were preserved, only the methods were changed. The carrot gained ascendancy over the stick, the peaceful incentive over terror, the indirect approach over the direct brutal assault.

Stalin's heirs, in the process of their cautious detachment from the most severe features of Stalin's legacy, set out to right the wrongs inflicted on some nationalities. It will be recalled that seven other ethnic groups had fallen victim to Stalin's suspicion and vindictiveness: the Ingushes, the Chechens, the Volga Germans, the Crimea Tatars, the Kalmyks, the Karachai, and the Balkars. All of them were uprooted at various times during World War II and banished in their entirety, including members of the Party and the Komsomol, to remote places. While the expulsion of the Volga Germans was justified by the authorities as a security measure—and it was perhaps a more rational measure than the removal of the Japanese-American from the Pacific coast during World War II—the deportation of the other national groups was undertaken on the principle of collective guilt. The sins of the few were visited upon the entire community. The preamble to the official decree published in *Izvestia*, June 26, 1946, announcing, two years after the expulsion, the dissolution of the Chechen-Ingush and the Crimean Tatar autonomous republics, stated that collective punishment had been meted out for the failure of the peoples to combat those in their midst who were collaborating with the German enemy. It was this tribal notion of justice that Khrushchev included in his indictment of Stalin at the Twentieth Party Congress:

> Not only a Marxist-Leninist but also no man of common sense can grasp how it is possible to make whole nations responsible for inimical activity, including women, children, old people, Communists and Komsomols, to use mass repression against them, and to expose them to misery and suffering for the hostile acts of individual persons or groups of persons.

The repressed nationalities have since been restored to their public identity and some have even been permitted to return to their native lands. They ceased to be Orwellian "un-peoples." Their names reappeared on maps and in reference works. Even the Volga Germans have been provided with schools and newspapers.

This wholesale rehabilitation has not embraced the Jews. To be sure, the Jews had not been deported—although Soviet Jews are convinced that only Stalin's death saved them from that fate. But condemned to the status of an un-people, they had been marked out for cultural extinction and their institutions had been destroyed. However, it would seem that in Khrushchev's view, this particular action of Stalin did not fall into the category of "monstrous acts" and "rude violations of the basic Leninist principles of the nationality policy of the Soviet state"; it was a deed of prudent statesmanship. In the course of an interview with a Canadian Communist delegation, Khrushchev, in one of the unguarded moments of candor to which he is so often given, showed himself to share Stalin's view of the Jews as inherent security risks. "Khrushchev," relates the Canadian Communist Salsberg (*The New Leader*, September 14, 1959), "agreed with Stalin that the Crimea, which had been depopulated at the war's end, should not be turned into a Jewish colonization center, because in case of war it would be turned into a base for attacking the U.S.S.R. . . ."

Surely a people harboring such a ready propensity to treason could not be allowed to possess cultural institutions fostering and perpetuating that tendency.

Assimilation through Attrition

Stalin's heirs are determined not to revoke the edict against the cultural life of the Jews. The pleadings of a British Communist group that Yiddish schools and the theatre be restored, were met by Suslov with a categorical refusal befitting that grim guardian of orthodoxy: "No, these things will not be reinstituted."

This obduracy has been maintained by the Soviet leaders in spite of its unfavorable impression on Western opinion, which has displayed anxiety over the lot of the Jews, and in spite of the injuries inflicted on Communist Parties with a substantial proportion of Jewish members. Three Communist delegations have taken up the Jewish question with the highest Soviet leaders: a Canadian delegation in August, 1956; a British delegation in October of the same year; and a deputation of French Jewish Communists who journeyed to Moscow with the blessing of Thorez early in 1958 for the express purpose of dissuading the Soviet leaders from their present policy toward the Jewish minority. All returned empty-handed.

Disillusioned and embittered, Jewish Communists in Canada, the United States, and Britain have deserted their Parties in large numbers. For many years, they had nourished a vision of Soviet Russia that bore little resemblance to reality. Their imagination had seen a land in which a multinational brotherhood, informed by love, was laboring toward the realization of Utopia under the guidance of dedicated leaders, all of them paragons of Leninist virtue, stern, determined, ruthless against enemies but full of solicitude for the oppressed everywhere. In the aftermath of Stalin's death, the veil of illusion dissolved. J. B. Salsberg, leader of the Canadian CP and a member of the delegation to the U.S.S.R., after an interview of two hours, found the First Secretary of the Communist Party and presumed custodian of Marxism-Leninism to be a man possessed of "a backward prejudice against the Jewish group as a people . . . a prejudice which sharply contradicts the Marxist mode of thought." His "statements smack of Great Russian chauvinism. . . . His approach to the problem of Jewish nationality is an unforgivable violation of socialist democracy."* Soon afterwards, Salsberg resigned from the Party and was followed in this action by a large number of Jews and non-Jews. The Canadian Party lost some of its ablest leaders and dedicated members. In Montreal, where the Communists had once been strong enough to elect a member of Parliament, the Party organization virtually ceased to exist.

In explanation of the absence of Jewish cultural institutions, Soviet spokesmen usually advance the theory of "integration." According to this theory, the Jews have become so integrated into the body of the Russian people that they have lost all will or capacity for ethnic self-expression. Eager to submerge in the Russian majority, they have abandoned Yiddish for Russian. The breath of life has departed from Jewish culture; it has died from inanition. This consummation, marking an advance on the road of history, deserves the applause of all progressive persons, including Jews. Only reactionaries could lament it. To revive Jewish institutions would, therefore, be tantamount to reviving a corpse in defiance of the will of History. According to Salsberg, "Khrushchev repeated the view . . . that the majority of Soviet Jews have become integrated into the country's general life. He emphasized that such integration is historically progressive, whereas the maintenance of a separate group existence is reactionary."

It is true, of course, that the majority of Jews have come to use Russian in their daily lives—to a large extent as a result of the assimilationist policies that have been enforced on them. Still, according to the last census, 20.8 per cent of Soviet Jews have declared Yiddish to be their most intimate medium of com-

* That Khrushchev harbors anti-Semitic feelings of a rather vulgar nature has been evidenced by many of his utterances made in private. One such adverse pronouncement on the Jews, made in the course of an interview with a French correspondent of *Le Figaro*, April 9, 1958, described the Jews as averse to collective work and group discipline and stung even the most hardened Jewish Communists in the West, whose loyalty survived the *crise de conscience* produced by revelations after Stalin's death. "It is incomprehensible how such a statement could come from the leader of the Soviet state," exclaimed the *Morgn Fraihait* (New York), April 13, 1958. It would be a mistake, however, to infer that the personal feelings of the dictator govern Soviet policy towards the Jews. The operative logic of the Soviet system is sufficient to account for it, although the dictator's sentiments lend a particular acerbity to some of its features.

munication. To be sure, the percentage is lower than of any other ethnic group claiming its national language as the "mother tongue." Yet two factors must be borne in mind: (1) That it must have taken a certain amount of courage for Jews to claim Yiddish as their tongue in the face of official hostility, and that the actual figure may therefore be considerably larger; and (2) that 20.8 per cent still embraces 472,000 people—in absolute figures . . . a far larger number than that of two dozen or so other Soviet nationalities (such as the Buriats, Avars, Ossetians, and so on), whose languages are not only tolerated, but actively encouraged by the Soviet authorities. Such, indeed, are the canons of the Soviet nationality policy, that 472,000 Jews are served by a meager sheet, whose circulation of 1,000 is largely confined to Birobidzhan, while, say, the 12,000 Chukchi inhabiting the northern region of the R.S.F.S.R. are served by a comparable organ of 800 copies.

The picture becomes fuller when we add that about eighty Yiddish writers, survivors of the decimation of the Yiddish literary intelligentsia, are denied a public forum in their own tongue for their creative talents. A chosen few may have their words translated into Russian, if their theme is not of a specific Jewish content. The others must find contentment in manuscripts languishing in the obscurity of desk drawers. According to a report by the highly literate French Jewish Communist Chaim Sloves in *Yiddishe Kultur* (New York, February, 1959),

> The Soviet Jewish writers are more creative today than perhaps ever before. "Not a day passes that I don't write," everyone tells you. And everyone has his own work ready for the press—volumes of poetry, novels, stories, dramas. It is not merely literary impetus or prolific creativity: It is, in the highest sense, sacred dedication.

Immediately after the Revolution, Hebrew was declared a counterrevolutionary language. Since 1948, Yiddish literature has been treated as a force inimical to the purposes of the Soviet government. A unique application, indeed, of the official formula "socialist in content—national in form"!*

---

* In late 1961, the Soviet authorities finally relented and permitted the publication in Moscow of a Yiddish bimonthly called *Sovyetishe Heymland.*

Pursuing the goal of total assimilation of the Jews, the regime has for the past three years embarked on a campaign against the last fragments of communal life in Russia—the synagogues and the religious life associated with them. The purpose of this campaign, conducted through the familiar medium of the feuilleton in the press and the occasional radio broadcast, and practically reinforced by the closing of synagogues in outlying regions, is to deter the Jews from congregating in compact groups. The process of atomization is to be brought to its ultimate conclusion. By insulating the Jews from their co-religionists and co-nationals in the rest of the world and by isolating them from each other, the regime hopes to extirpate the consciousness of kind and thus remove what it thinks is a source of disaffection from within the Soviet Union. For Judaism, Soviet propagandists insist, is not only "opium for the people," but also a creed implanting in its adherents allegiance to foreign powers and infidelity to the Soviet Union. In a recent broadcast (December 9, 1959) emanating from Kirovograd in the Ukraine (a town, incidentally, with a notorious record of pogroms in pre-Revolutionary Russia, including the one which the Narodnaya Volya welcomed with such glee), the speaker inveighed in language of unusual virulence against the local synagogue and its officials. The broadcast was saturated with sheer medievalism:

> The Jewish faith has been strongly intermixed with Jewish bourgeois nationalism and Zionism, already possessing a strong reactionary essence. . . . Sermons by Rabbi Ayzik Spektor hardly differ from the woeful theory of the uniqueness of the Aryan race and its destiny to rule over the peoples of the entire world. . . .
>
> Among the numerous Jewish feasts, a special place belongs to Saturday, which should be inspiringly observed by every Orthodox Jew, for according to the teaching of the Talmud this is the day of absolute inactivity. And so, on a Saturday,

---

The one issue that has appeared thus far (November, 1961) makes it clear that the journal is designed to serve the needs of Soviet propaganda rather than that of the Soviet Jews. The stories and poems (most of them written in the spirit of "socialist realism" *par excellence*) deal with subjects such as Soviet patriotism, the glories of collective farming, the "anticolonialist struggle," and the like.—*Ed.*

when the divine service ends, the faithful disperse, and . . .
the table is laid, vodka, wine, and snacks appear, and toasts
to the health of "God's servants" are raised. The drinking
feast (sic) is led by the rabbi's wife, Roza Spektor.

Jewish ministers and circumcisers execute the rite of
circumcision, which has a strikingly nationalistic character.
Its specific significance lies in the fact that it gives proof of
belonging to the "chosen" people—the Jews. At the same time
it imbues Jews with repugnance and hatred of those who do
not possess this special sign. . . .

Judaic sermons are sermons of bourgeois Zionists. Such
sermons are tools of the nationalistic, Israeli, cosmopolitan
American bourgeoisie. With their tentacles, the Jewish
bourgeois nationalists, with the help of Judaism, try to reach
into our Soviet garden. But they will never succeed.*

The treatment of the Jews by the Soviet dictatorship is without a full parallel among its policies toward the other national
minorities. A unique people, the Jews have drawn upon themselves singular treatment. As Stalinism departed from the ideals
of internationalism and cosmopolitanism that had inspired the
Bolshevik Revolution, it cynically resorted to anti-Semitism as a
tool of its designs, harkening back to the methods used by the
Narodnaya Volya. The xenophobia born of its totalitarian
isolation—a xenophobia incongruously linked to its international aspirations and professions—exposed the Jews to grave
suspicion. They were members of a world-wide fraternity,
the greater part of which lived in the camp of "imperialism,"
and the creation of the state of Israel intensified that suspicion.
Alone among all the national minorities, the Jews have been
condemned to total assimilation. The Jews are indeed a "chosen
people" in Russia—chosen for cultural extinction.

* Throughout 1959, a high percentage of the feuilletons appearing in
the Soviet press were devoted to the pillorying and denunciation of individuals bearing unmistakable Jewish names, and of synagogues: e.g., 20–25
per cent of the pieces in *Vechernaia Moskva;* 20 per cent in *Sovetskaia
kultura;* 10 per cent in *Komsomolskaia pravda;* 33 per cent in *Sovetskaia
Latvia.* For representative samples, see *Prikarpatska pravda,* September 24,
1958; *Vechernaia Moskva,* March 13, 1959; and *Sovetskaia Moldavia,* November 12, 1959. See also *The New Leader,* September 14, 1959.

THE LITERARY SCENE

Introduction

It is no accident (as Marxists would put it) that the literary scene in the Soviet Union is often referred to officially as the "literary front." For no other area of Soviet culture has been visited by so many onslaughts and so much destruction—artistic as well as human—as has Soviet literature. In no other area has the Party bureaucracy interfered so rudely—censoring, suppressing, or rewriting published works, demanding adherence to spurious aesthetic principles ("socialist realism," "partyness"), villifying those who did not conform, driving some into exile (e.g., Zamiatin), some to suicide (Yesenin, Mayakovski), some into silence (e.g., Zoshchenko and—until shortly before his death—Pasternak), and some into concentration camps, where they perished without trace (Pilnyak, Babel, Tarasov-Radionov, Ivan Kataev, to mention but a few).

Yet it is a curious, and in a sense profoundly encouraging fact that despite all these ravages the creative spirit of Soviet literature has not been crushed. Somehow, side by side with the plays celebrating romances between rosy-cheeked milkmaids and sturdy Stakhanovites, doggerel about Stalin, and novels full of stock characters, both negative (sinister foreign agents) and positive (upstanding Party secretaries)—somehow, amidst this sorry and sterile output, a few writers continue to write good works, some of which managed to get past the censors' eyes, and some of which were left "in the drawer" in the hope that they may yet one day be allowed to emerge into the open.

If proof of the viability of Soviet literature is needed, it is to be found in the astonishing outburst of creative writing soon after Stalin's death. The most oppressive Party controls having been lifted, Soviet literary journals in late 1953 and 1954 began to publish essays demanding "sincerity" and "truthfulness" in literature, as well as poems, plays, and fiction bristling with real emotions, believable characters, and realistic plots. Toward the end of 1954, the Party reacted to this flood of unorthodox writing by reimposing stricter controls, but in 1956, and particularly in 1957, following Khrushchev's speech on Stalin and the October events in Poland and Hungary, there was a new rash of bold and rebellious writings—so much so that by the end of the year, Khrushchev felt compelled personally to threaten the writers with dire consequences unless they mended their ways and followed more faithfully the dicta of socialist realism.

With the exception of Victor Erlich's article, which offers a historical sketch of literary criticism in the U.S.S.R., the articles in this section are concerned with the second "thaw" in Soviet literature—the one that began in 1956, and that continues to this day, Khrushchev's grim warning of 1957 notwithstanding. Two of the articles (one by Harry Willets and one by George Gibian) analyze specific works that have appeared during the past few years; the one by Max Hayward, on the other hand, traces the vicissitudes of the Party's literary policy from 1956 onward. The section ends with a set of anonymous poems, which, even under the current quasi-liberal regime, could not possibly be published, as well as an essay by their (equally anonymous) translator, who comments on the poems against the searching, restless, and unsurrendering mood of today's Soviet intelligentsia.

Soviet Literary Criticism: Past and Present

——VICTOR ERLICH

OVER A FORTY-YEAR PERIOD, Soviet literary criticism—like other fields of Soviet culture—has been forced along a tortuous course of development, twisted in one direction and then another by successive changes in the Communist cultural line. The attempts of the Party dialecticians to rationalize these shifts have done more to obscure than to clarify the real issue involved. Cutting through the smokescreen of official rhetoric, it seems clear that what has been at stake throughout all the twists and turns in Soviet literary theory is nothing less than the survival of literary criticism as an autonomous activity. For at the heart of all significant critical controversy has been the problem of the relative status of literary vis-à-vis ideological values, of the critic's right to discuss and evaluate literature in its own terms rather than in those of social utility or of political orthodoxy.

The degree of candor and explicitness with which this question could be debated has varied from period to period. During the first decade of the Soviet era, when some measure of intellectual freedom still prevailed, bona fide discussion of critical principles was not impossible. The tug of war between the literary and the crudely "social" emphasis could still assert itself in a free-swinging debate, in which the contenders were now the "formalists" versus the "sociologists," now the "Right-Wing" Marxist-Leninists versus the "Left-Wing" Marxist-Leninists.

By 1930, however, genuine methodological controversy had virtually ceased. Literary theorizing became increasingly a matter of intellectual shadowboxing, of timid exegesis on insipid or ambiguous official pronouncements. The struggle between politi-

343

cal expediency and residual literary values was driven underground but not resolved. Thereafter, it found expression not in
an open clash between well-defined critical positions, but in
embarrassing contradictions within official doctrine, in unwitting
confusion or deliberate double talk.

Basic Precepts and Early Protests

The doctrine that, since 1917, has held sway in Russian criticism has combined Marx's economic determinism with Lenin's
relentless political instrumentalism. Marxist-Leninism has tended
all too often to reduce the work of literature to its alleged
"sociological equivalent," and to supplant a total critical judgment with a political verdict—an "unmasking" of the writer's
"class ideology." In effect, such doctrinaire excesses have been a
far cry from the Marx-Engels "philosophy of art" the Soviet
literary theorists have invoked with such reverence. Actually,
philosophy of art is much too grand a term for a number of
casual observations scattered across the writings of the founders
of historical materialism. They had neither the time nor the urge
to evolve a full-dress theory of artistic creation. But they were
undoubtedly interested in literature, and in responding to it they
showed sound, if somewhat conventional, judgment.

While emphasizing the social relevance of art, Marx and Engels
refused to measure it by narrowly ideological yardsticks. They
discouraged preaching and overexplicit messages in imaginative
literature and urged strongly that vivid, credible, individualized
characters would serve the socialist playwright better than
abstract rhetorics and mere noble sentiments. "Vividness," "con-
creteness," "accurate portrayal of life in all its complexity and
many-sidedness"—all these criteria came to be part and parcel of
the Soviet political canon. The Party hacks have paid them mere
lip service, but more sensitive Marxists have cited them time and
again to bolster the fight against the cruder excesses of political-
ized literature and art.

The Formalists

The most vigorous plea for the autonomy of literary values
came not from the Right-Wing Marxists, but from a heterodox

school of criticism—the "formalists"—and constituted the only serious challenge ever made to the hegemony of Marxism-Leninism in Russian literary studies.

The term "formalism" has been bandied about so recklessly in latter-day Soviet propaganda that one is likely to forget its initial meaning. What can be legitimately referred to as Russian formalism is a school in Russian literary scholarship which originated in the years 1915–16; its champions were a number of philologists and students of literature, including B. Eikhenbaum, R. Jakobson, V. Shklovsky, and Y. Tynyanov. The formalists viewed literature as a distinct field of human endeavor, as a verbal art rather than a reflection of society or a battleground of ideas. In attempting to delimit literary studies from contiguous fields, such as psychology, sociology, or cultural history, the formalist theoreticians were quick to focus on "distinguishing features" of literature. "The subject of literary scholarship," said Ramon Jakobson in *Noveishaia russkaia poeziia* (*Modern Russian Poetry*), an early study published in Prague in 1921, "is not literature in its totality, but literariness, i.e., that which makes of a given work a work of literature." To the formalists, "literariness" means primarily artistic devices peculiar to imaginative writing, techniques whereby the creative writer reshapes his subject matter—reality— and manipulates his medium—language.

On the basis of these precepts, the adherents of formalism subjected the "golden age" of Russian literature to a drastic reexamination. Gogol's famous story "The Overcoat," hailed by the nineteenth-century Russian critics as a deeply moving plea for the "little man," became under the critical eye of B. Eikhenbaum primarily an intricate piece of grotesque stylization. The moral crisis of the young Tolstoi was reinterpreted in aesthetic terms as a struggle for a new style, as a recoil from romantic conventions grown stale. In dealing with contemporary literary production in the new Soviet era, the formalist critics showed the same single-minded concern with craftsmanship. They praised the linguistic experiments of the "futurist" poets, the aesthetic and psychological sophistication of the nonconformist novelists. In visual arts, they encouraged such trends as cubism and constructivism.

Youthful exuberance as well as the initial shrill tenor of Soviet critical controversy impelled the formalists to overstate their case. In their early studies, Shklovsky and Jakobson played down the links between literature and society and denied the relevance of any considerations other than aesthetic ones. In so doing, they provided easy targets for their Marxist-Leninist opponents, who were becoming increasingly concerned over the growing influence of the formalist school not only in literary criticism, but also in academic scholarship.

Attacks and Counterattacks

By the mid-1920's, a full-dress offensive against formalism was under way: It was spearheaded by no lesser figures than Trotsky and Bukharin.

Trotsky's attitude towards formalism was sharply critical, but not altogether hostile. The brilliant Communist chieftain had a field day punching holes in V. Shklovsky's witty but extravagant raid on sociological criticism. At the same time, Trotsky admitted grudgingly that "a certain part of the research done by the formalists" (concerning problems of style and rhythm) was useful. Treated as an auxiliary device, he argued, formalism was a legitimate, indeed a rewarding, critical method; raised to the status of a full-fledged theory of literature, it became inadequate, in fact dangerous. In *Literature and Revolution*, he emphatically upheld the monopoly of dialectical materialism as the only legitimate world view and philosophy of history: "Marxism alone can answer the crucial question of why and how a given tendency in art has originated in the given period of history." But he admitted that if in the realm of causal explanation the dialectician had no equals, this in itself did not make him capable of sound aesthetic judgment; Marxism could not yield any criteria for evaluating artistic phenomena.

In short, while the cruder practitioners of Marxist criticism saw in literature merely a medium for "registering social phenomena," Trotsky was aware that artistic creation was "a deflection, a transformation of reality, in accordance with the *peculiar laws of art*." (Italics added.) "A work of art," he added, "should in the first place be judged by its own law, the law of art." Since Marxists qua Marxists were unable to identify these laws, they should not completely disregard whatever assistance they could get from the ideologically alien formalist writings.

A similar position was taken by Bukharin. He, too, saw some merit in the formalist explorations of poetic art, even while going beyond Trotsky in minimizing the actual scope of formalist analyses. If one is to believe Bukharin, all that the formalists were trying to do was to compile a "catalog" of individual poetic devices. This "analytical job," declared Bukharin, "is wholly acceptable as long as you treat it as spadework preliminary to future critical synthesis," but it is no substitute for such a synthesis.

Trotsky and Bukharin were very broadminded indeed by comparison with some other Party stalwarts. P. S. Kogan, a prolific literary historian who prided himself on never having had "time for the study of literary form," had no use whatever for formalist "spadework." He saw in the formalists' concern with literary craft a symptom of distasteful "aesthetic gourmandise."

Equally vehement was the reaction of A. V. Lunacharsky, the first Soviet Commissar of Education, an influential critic and publicist. He spoke grimly of "formalist escapism," and diagnosed the enemy as "the last refuge of the unreconstructed intelligentsia looking furtively toward bourgeois Europe." Proclaiming emotional intensity and spontaneity as ultimate tests of greatness in art, Lunacharsky termed the formalist preoccupation with artifice a sign of intellectual and moral poverty.

While Kogan and Lunacharsky were thus labeling formalism an alien limb in the Soviet body politic, an attempt was under way at the opposite pole of the Marxist spectrum to incorporate formalist procedures into the scheme of Marxian criticism. A. Tseitlin spoke out boldly against the tendency to reduce literary scholarship to a mere subdivision of social history. "There is no point," he wrote, "in discussing the sociological implications of literary facts, as long as the facts themselves are not established" —hence the importance and timeliness of the formalist contribution. By focusing on the close analysis of the text, on systematic description of literary facts, formalism was breaking ground for the truly scientific study of Russian literature.

Tseitlin's was clearly a minority view. Few Soviet Marxist critics were prepared to go along with his sensible caveat that in order to explain a phenomenon, one ought first to find out what it was. In fact, to the more rigid exponents of Marxism-Leninism, the latter question seemed irrelevant, if not illicit. For those who saw the critic's task as one of tracing the literary work back to its "class roots," the problem of the nature of literary creation was bound to be submerged by concern with "underly-- ing social forces." As the critic V. Pertsov put it:

> I cannot visualize a Marxist raising the question: "How is this work of literature constructed?" without this question being immediately superseded by another question: "Why is this work of literature constructed this way and not another?"

The "sociological" analysis of literature gave way in short order to crude label-mongering and to partisan vituperation. A programmatic statement of the doctrinaire Marxists, published in their organ *Na Postu* (On Guard) in 1923, charged that the poetry of Anna Akhmatova, one of modern Russia's foremost lyricists, "organized the reader's psyche toward the clerical-feudal-bourgeois restoration"; that Turgenev was a "slanderer of nihilists"; that Andrei Bely (a brilliant Symbolist writer who sought frantically to come to terms with post-Revolutionary Russia) was "not only an anti-Soviet element, but an antisocial one as well."

To the spokesmen of the "On Guard" group, such as Vardin, Averbakh, and Lelevich, art was a potent weapon in the class struggle. A 1925 resolution of the group stated in part: "Imaginative literature is one of the last areas in which an implacable class war is taking place between the proletariat and the bourgeoisie for hegemony over intermediate groups." A statement in *Proletariat i literatura* defined art as an "instrument of emotional infection, a means of organizing the reader's psyche in conformity with the interests of the given class." The logical consequence of such views was a demand that all voices but those of "proletarian" (i.e., orthodox) writers be silenced. If, as Lelevich maintained, a writer always fulfills the unwritten "social command" —that of infecting his audience with the attitudes of his class— the "petty-bourgeois" interlopers could not be tolerated; they were liable to poison the trusting Soviet reader with socially alien emotions.

The thick-headed orthodoxy of the "On Guard" group found its most articulate opponent in A. Voronsky, the editor of the influential literary magazine *Krasnaia nov* (Red Virgin Soil). To Voronsky, art was not primarily a matter of mobilizing and manipulating group emotions. It was a form of cognition, a largely intuitive mode of apprehending reality. As a Marxist, Voronsky had to concede that the way in which the artist perceives the world, the degree to which he is likely to achieve insight into things as they really are, is strongly affected by his social background. But a great writer manages time and again to rise above the limitations of his milieu; often he cannot help seeing and embodying in his work certain truths that run counter to his conscious bias and to the interests of his class. Indeed, said Voronsky, this ability to transcend one's environment is the earmark of truly great art. Going a step further, he asserted that a non-Party writer of talent and integrity could be not only aesthetically, but also ideologically, more valuable than a mediocre "proletarian," since the former could provide more accurate insight into the social situation and thus a safer guide to political action.

The form-conscious Western critic would find much to argue with in Voronsky's literary theorizing and critical practice, with their strong psychoideological bent. Moreover, his broad-mindedness had its limitations; while he tolerated, indeed encouraged, certain independent writers who sympathized with the October Revolution, he showed little patience with such militant nonconformism as that of the brilliant writer E. Zamyatin. Nevertheless, viewed against the background of his era, Voronsky inspires respect because of his steadfast refusal to surrender literary criteria, to disregard the uniqueness of artistic creation.

Whatever the rigors of his ideological position, it did not quite succeed in dampening his genuine delight in creativity or dulling his impatience with orthodox mediocrity. No wonder Voronsky's was one of the first heads to roll when the doctrinaires and the zealots whom he had fought so valiantly gained the upper hand in Soviet letters.

From RAPP's Frying Pan into the Fire

Toward the end of the 1920's, the methodological debate was rudely interrupted. Formalism, declared to be "false because it was reactionary and reactionary because it was false," was driven from the scene. Marxist-Leninism criticism was whipped into uniformity. Voronsky's philosophy of art stood convicted of such deadly sins as "Bergsonian idealism." Soviet criticism was inexorably moving toward the single aesthetic canon of "socialist realism."

The period of 1929–32 saw the beginning of the end of Soviet criticism as a relatively independent cultural force. Under the aegis of L. Averbakh's ultraorthodox faction, the so-called RAPP (Russian Association of Proletarian Writers), critics and writers alike were enlisted in the service of the Five Year Plan. RAPP's overriding control was made possible through initial regime and Party support; so dismal were the results of its "literary shock-brigade" tactics, however, that it was disbanded in 1932, to the accompaniment of much vituperation about "sectarianism" and "ideological sabotage."

At the time, many friends of Russian literature heaved a sigh of relief. But their belief that the end of RAPP signified a respite from political interference proved purely illusory. Recent research strongly supports the thesis that the *real* crime of RAPP, as far as the Party leadership was concerned, was not excessive narrow-mindedness and utilitarianism, but excessive intransigence, or, if one will, literary vigilantism. Apparently what was at issue was not so much the degree of political interference with literature as the mode of control. From this standpoint, the shift from the RAPP hegemony to a single, all-embracing Union of Soviet Writers, responsible to and supervised by the Party Central

Committee, meant the substitution of direct Party controls for the rule of a zealous, yet increasingly erratic, coterie.

For a while, the new "line"—which, adopted in 1932 and proclaimed with much fanfare at the First All-Union Congress of Soviet Writers came to be known as socialist realism—seemed to be a victory for sense and sensibility. Some of the statements made at the Congress sounded very promising indeed. In his judicious report on "Poetry, Poetics, and Problems of Poetry in the U.S.S.R.," Bukharin gently but firmly rebuked the shrillness and slogan-mongering of some Bolshevik versifiers. Poetic "paraphrases of newspaper articles," he argued, were no longer enough. What was needed was a richer, more sophisticated fare, which would do justice to the "growing complexity, the heightened tone, the changed dimensions of our social life."

Was the new aesthetic doctrine of "socialist realism" thus a vindication of literary values? Scarcely. It is true that the strident call for better craftsmanship encouraged some manifestations of artistic integrity in creative writing and of sensitivity in criticism. But such efforts were ill fated. When, for example, Sholokhov in *And Quiet Flows the Don* portrayed the ethical dilemmas of an "uncommitted" Cossack, Gregori Melekhov, with a degree of candor and complexity, he was castigated by a number of official critics for failing to make Gregori ultimately "see the light" of Communist infallibility. Shortly afterwards, the Soviet reviewers were waxing rhapsodic over Aleksei Tolstoi's slick and dishonest Civil War novel, *Bread*. That this thinly disguised piece of Stalinist falsification could have been hailed as a triumph of "socialist realism" calls into question the validity and the true meaning of the crucial term of official Soviet aesthetics.

Clearly, "socialist realism" is "realism" of a unique sort. According to an authoritative statement by Zhdanov in 1934, Soviet literature cannot be content with merely "reflecting" or "truthfully portraying" reality; it must be *instrumental in the ideological remolding of the toiling people in the spirit of socialism.* The duality of Zhdanov's criteria of "truthful portrayal" and "ideological remolding" reflects a basic internal contradiction in Soviet literary theory. As soon as "ideological remolding of the toiling people" is translated as "Party-mindedness," the precarious character of the definition becomes obvious. It is difficult enough to conceive how conscious promotion of any set of political objectives could be reconciled with a "vivid and many-sided portrayal of life." Such a reconciliation becomes an utter impossibility when the objectives that are to be promoted are those of a totalitarian regime that has a vested interest in, and a physical capacity for, suppressing information about "whole vast tracts of Soviet reality" (Gleb Struve, *Soviet Russian Literature 1917–1950*, p. 371).

To put it differently, the internal contradiction within the official aesthetic doctrine could be construed as a tension within the concept of socialist realism, between the adjective "socialist" and the noun "realism." The latter calls for the portrayal of "life as it really is"; the former points toward "life as it ought to be," or as it supposedly is, according to the extravagant claims of Party propaganda.

Latter-Day Dialectics

Recent Soviet criticism has sought to bridge the gap between realism and idealization by means of manipulating the notion of the "typical" for all it is worth. This emphasis has its ultimate source in Engels' often-quoted definition of realism as the "accurate portrayal of typical characters under typical circumstances." Georgi Malenkov, in a speech of October, 1952, before the Nineteenth CPSU Congress, summarized the prevailing official attitude toward "typicality" as follows:

> In Marxist-Leninist understanding, the typical by no means signifies some sort of statistical average. Typicalness corresponds to the essence of the given social-historical phenomenon; it is not simply the most widespread, frequently occurring, and ordinary phenomenon.

As if the import of these remarks were not sufficiently clear, Malenkov added disingenuously: "The typical is the basic sphere of the manifestation of party-minded *[partiinost]* in realistic art. The problem of typicalness is always a political problem."

This was a significant admission. In effect, what has been

played up as "typical" by the Soviet critic often depends not on the actual social relevance of the phenomenon under discussion, but on its status in the official view of reality. Whenever necessary, dialectics, or more exactly, "double-think," has been called upon to explain away the rule as nontypical and to claim typicalness, i.e., a higher order of reality, for the exception.

One of the by-products of the post-Stalin cultural "thaw" has been a somewhat more flexible interpretation of the typical in literature. A representative statement, appearing in the Party's theoretical organ, *Kommunist*, in December, 1955, belabored the tendency on the part of some Soviet writers to "varnish our reality," glossing over actual difficulties and shortcomings, and warned sternly against excessive schematism. In a seemingly direct slap at Malenkov's earlier position, the article sharply criticized the "current formulas that . . . construe the typical as the chief expression of Party-mindedness in literature, indeed insist that the problem of the typical is always a political problem." Lenin's authority was invoked to bolster a plea for a more differentiated literary characterization, while Engels was quoted in support of the sensible thesis that the "objective meaning" of a literary work can be a far cry from the author's conscious bias.

Did this mean that the principle of "Party-mindedness"—and the concomitant tendency to explain away embarrassing realities —had been abandoned? The answer, unhappily, is no: After all its vigorous disclaimers, *Kommunist* (December, 1955) went right on to restate Malenkov's distinction between the statistically representative and the typical, albeit in a slightly modified form. "In realistic art," it declared, "the infrequent becomes typical whenever it reflects the seeds [sic] of the new," whenever it represents a lawful rather than a fortuitous development. Since at each given moment it is up to the Party dialecticians to decide what is lawful and what is fortuitous, the Party's right to define and impose its own view of "reality" remains basically unchallenged.

The Phases of Post-Stalin Policy

The same pattern of fundamental orthodoxy tempered by occasional ventures toward open-mindedness has characterized literary criticism, along with other fields of Soviet culture, throughout the post-Stalin era. In seesawing motion through various periods, pressures to accelerate the "thaw" of culture—to give wider berth to creative expression and to liberalize the crippling dictates of socialist realism—have been countered by retrenchment pressures from the Party and its cultural henchmen, reaffirming the basic principle of political control over the arts.

In the initial phase of the "thaw" (1953–54), a number of Soviet writers and critics raised their voices to issue a plea that sincerity be recognized as a *sine qua non* of good literature. Notably among these was V. Pomerantsev, who persuasively argued that "the degree of sincerity, i.e., the spontaneity, of a work . . . must be the main yardstick" of its worth, rather than its political "correctness." Such sentiments, however, were not long voiced with impunity. Pomerantsev's position was soon labeled a threat to the still-binding principle of Party-mindedness and was the specific target of a number of denunciatory speeches at the Second Congress of Soviet Writers in December, 1954. During the year 1955, there were few authoritative articles bearing on literary policy or theory that did not deal harshly with the hapless champions of sincerity, who stood convicted of "philistinism, apoliticality, and subjectivism."

Then came the Twentieth CPSU Congress (February, 1956), and in its wake a period of ideological relaxation. "Sincerity" and nonconformism were given a new lease on life. A mood of revulsion against bureaucratic controls and stale official rhetorics became increasingly apparent on the literary scene, even finding its way into the critical pronouncements of some of the prominent writers who have been semiofficial spokesmen of the regime. In a significant article published in *Novy mir*, for example, Konstantin Simonov spoke ruefully of the part he had played in the Zhdanovite literary purge and counseled a broadening of the rigid criteria of socialist realism, which, he added, "has been compromised by the Halleluiaism of recent years." In urging that the label "socialist realism" ought to apply to any literary work so long as it was imbued with a "socialist" spirit, Simonov conceded in effect the precariousness of the Soviet critical canon as an aesthetic yardstick.

Some of the less prominent critics were still more explicit. In decrying the "disastrous consequences of the personality cult in literary criticism," S. Shtut in *Novy mir* paid tribute to the artistic integrity and courage of Boris Pasternak and boldly took issue with the doctrinaire view that advocating "untrammeled freedom of creative personality" represented a regression to bourgeois individualism. Several drama critics—A. Nazarev and V. Granin in *Voprosy filosofii*, and A. Kron in *Literaturnaia Moskva*—struck out against obtrusive interference with the Soviet theatre. Kron, for example, blamed the "stagnation" in Soviet drama on three factors—the "ignoring of the objective laws of artistic creation [shades of Leo Trotsky!], the hypertrophy of editing, and the creation of a bureaucratic hierarchy in art."

Such outspoken criticism was under constant counterattack from the doctrinaires, but it was tolerated through most of the year 1956. Once again, however, the trend toward freer and franker self-expression was to shift. The complex forces set in motion by the Twentieth Congress—climaxing in the profoundly disturbing events in Hungary and Poland in the fall of 1956—had severe repercussions on the Soviet scene. In the cultural sphere, the pendulum swung back to a full-scale reassertion of Party primacy and ideological discipline. Today, "Party spirit" (*partiinost*) and "principle-mindedness" (*principialnost*) have once again become the chief themes of Soviet criticism. In wordy harangues, the Party stalwarts have charged that dissident elements grossly exaggerated the damage done to literature by the "cult of personality," that they overemphasized the dangers of "varnishing" Soviet realities while complacently ignoring the opposite pitfall of "denigrating our achievements."

The monopoly of socialist realism as the only permissible artistic method has been grimly reasserted and Simonov's argument for a more flexible yardstick demeaned. To make socialist realism largely a matter of socialist *Weltanschauung*, argued B. Solovev in *Literaturnaia gazeta*, is to declare it theoretically compatible with a variety of artistic styles, including "formalism" and "naturalism," which is clearly out of the question.

"Ideological confusion" among Soviet writers and critics

apparently was adjudged a serious enough matter to warrant direct interference by the Party leadership. In his speeches on literature and art, delivered in May and July, 1957, Khrushchev laid down the line in no uncertain terms. He inveighed against the tendency of "some intelligentsia" to pin the label of "varnisher" (*lakirovshchik*) on those loyal writers who aimed at glorifying the virtues of Soviet society rather than at gloating maliciously over its shortcomings. More importantly, he referred ominously to the misguided champions of creative freedom who, under the guise of a campaign against the cult of personality, sought to challenge the basic tenet of *partiinost*. The principle of Party guidance over literature was thus authoritatively reaffirmed, even while bureaucratic abuses and excessive apologetics came in for a measure of criticism.

A Summary View

While the tightening of ideological screws that followed the relatively "free" 1956–57 period is discouraging, the fluctuations in Party cultural policy in the post-Stalin era require that we take a longer view in summarizing the situation of literary criticism and of Soviet culture in general. If we compare the post-Stalin period as a whole with the era of Stalinism, we must certainly recognize an over-all change in the intellectual climate, to the extent that some controversy and flexibility have become possible *within* the bounds of basic orthodoxy.

The example of two specific categories of literary criticism may serve to illustrate this change, indicating both the scope and the limitations of the thaw as it has affected Soviet critical practice. The first concerns the treatment accorded foreign authors, and particularly Western literature. Whereas the hysterical xenophobia of the Zhdanov era resulted in the virtual isolation of the Soviet intelligentsia from foreign literary output (except that of loyal Party-liners), the post-Stalin regime has adopted a somewhat saner attitude: A number of foreign works have now been judged "permissible" reading, and a special journal *Inostrannaia literatura* (Foreign Literature), has been founded to publish and evaluate acceptable output. Judging by its issues, the choice of works to be translated and discussed is still determined far more often by the author's position vis-à-vis the Soviet Union than by his literary talents; nevertheless, the recognition that any non-Communist literature at all can have merit represents a significant modification of past policy.

To cite a single example, William Faulkner—a "decadent" reactionary by Stalinist definition—now occasionally appears in print, and it even seems possible to credit him with some "progressive" attitudes. In a rather simple-minded but sympathetic article that appeared in *Inostrannaia literatura* in December, 1955 (but is still representative), E. Romanova praises this "outstanding prose writer of contemporary America" for his "faith in the strength of the human soul" and his genuine opposition to war.

Similarly, there has been a significant softening in some aspects of the official attitude toward the pre-Revolutionary cultural heritage. The outstanding example of this has been the recent Dostoevski revival. In the Zhdavonite era, Dostoevski was *persona non grata* in the Soviet cultural world. Critics either ignored him completely or bitterly attacked him as an obscurantist—a view that found its crassest expression in a 1948 pamphlet by V. Ermilov and in the vociferous articles of D. Zaslavsky. His works were not reprinted, and some of his major novels, such as *The Possessed* and *The Brothers Karamazov*, became virtually inaccessible.

In the past two years, however, Dostoevski has been readmitted to the ranks of the favored, in a revival pegged to the seventy-fifth anniversary of his death. *Pravda* has discovered him as "a great Russian writer," and the state publishing house, Goslitizdat, has embarked upon a new edition of his works (several volumes of the edition, including two "ideological" novels, *Crime and Punishment* and *The Raw Youth*, have already appeared). A number of articles in the Soviet press seem to indicate a concerted effort to make Dostoevski palatable to, and safe for, the Soviet reader. It is now urged that, in spite of his ideological weaknesses, Dostoevski was a great literary artist, a "writer of immense talent." It is further maintained that fundamentally Dostoevski's heart was on the right side: He felt deeply for the downtrodden, he had no use for capitalist civilization, he mercilessly exposed the pitfalls of bourgeois individualism and the degrading impact of money. Unfortunately, this line of reasoning continues, Dostoevski failed to understand that the nature of the evils he decried was social rather than moral or metaphysical; his attempts at a positive ideology were futile and even harmful, and his portrayal of the nineteenth-century Russian revolutionary movement in *The Possessed* slanderous. According to the critics it is therefore no accident that this, dubbed Dostoevski's most reactionary novel, is also artistically his weakest.

However strained this analysis, the present-day Soviet attitude toward Dostoevski is a distinct improvement over the censure of Stalinist days. Under the new "dispensation," Dostoevski's masterpieces are at least being made available to the Russian reading public. Moreover, the new emphasis on Dostoevski's greatness as a *writer* helps to focus attention on the importance of literary versus political criteria. Yet the principal grounds on which Dostoevski is being readmitted to the Soviet literary pantheon are ideological rather than aesthetic. In undertaking to make him ideologically acceptable, the Party-line critics have demonstrated their stock techniques of dealing with an "embarrassing" master— among them, partial distortion of the writer's message (exemplified by gross overemphasis of the anticapitalist character of Dostoevski's critique of individualism); fatherly chiding (e.g., condescending remarks concerning Dostoevski's "confusion"); and outright doctrinaire inanity (*Pravda* notwithstanding, *The Possessed* is far from a "weak" novel). It is noteworthy, too, that virtually all of the recent articles on Dostoevski make precisely the same points in their analyses, down to the "insight" that *The Possessed* was an artistic failure. In short, the rediscovery of Dostoevski has all the earmarks of a carefully blueprinted Party line, albeit a somewhat more "liberal" one.*

---

* Following the publication of this article, a few works appeared that indicated a slight change in the official attitude toward formalism, too. Thus, A. Skaftymov's *Essays on Russian Literature,* published in late 1958, featured formal analysis and contained references to formalists and other "idealistic" critics such as N. Strakhov, K. Leontiev, and Vyacheslav Ivanov,

To sum up what has been said, with all of the manifest limitations of the thaw in Soviet literary criticism, the controversies that have been aired in the course of a vacillating Party policy are proof that at least some critics in the Soviet Union have survived the long Stalinist winter of intellectual stagnation, that they still care deeply about literature and are able to discuss it intelligently whenever given a chance. Will this chance be offered, without further crippling restrictions and caveats? Will Soviet critics be allowed to think for themselves? As long as the totalitarian tutelage over literature remains as obtrusive as it is today, the prospects for the development of genuinely free criticism seem poor.

---

who hitherto had been either ignored or abused. As far as current literary criticism is concerned, however, it still pays obeisance to the doctrine of socialist realism, which remains the official guideline of Soviet aesthetics.

The "Literary Opposition"

——HARRY WILLETS

In June, 1957, Khrushchev, after a long struggle, succeeded in expelling from the Soviet inner leadership a group of rivals whom some foreign commentators have chosen to call "Stalinists." Even while the struggle was reaching its climax, he found time to attack a very different "opposition": all those writers who had ignored or interpreted in their own way the Party's demands on literature. He took advantage of his victory over the anti-Party group to silence the "literary opposition," whose members had been the most enthusiastic supporters of de-Stalinization.

Many a Soviet reader must have learned with a twinge of grim amusement that the anti-Party group had encouraged revisionism and ideological indiscipline. Did Kaganovich, then, who had done as much as any man alive to create the Soviet industrial system, accept Dudintsev's devastating strictures in *Not By Bread Alone?* Had Nikolai Zhdanov's parable about town and country, peasant and bureaucrat, drawn a *mea culpa* from agriculture's former overlord, Malenkov? The meaning of the charge was of course quite different. It no doubt contained an element of truth. We can easily imagine, for instance, that Molotov, when he was in charge of cultural affairs in autumn, 1958, "took no practical measures" against ideological disarray, but was content to wag his head self-righteously at Khrushchev and suggest that only a radical modification of the latter's policies could restore order.

Moreover, the very existence of divisions within the Presidium —and the Soviet intelligentsia never doubted their seriousness—

encouraged indiscipline. Some writers may have hoped that the expositions of the Party line on the arts, which began to appear in the middle of 1956, were a tactical concession to the "reactionaries" rather than an expression of Khrushchev's own views. Others, more realistic, must have calculated that Khrushchev, while the struggle lasted, would do nothing that his opponents could represent as an admission of error or a proof of inconsistency. Khrushchev was determined that nobody should draw the wrong conclusions from his victory, that the revisionists should take no comfort from the defeat of the "dogmatists." And so he coolly blamed his rivals for the previous disarray.

The emergence of a new, courageous, realistic, and humanitarian trend in Soviet literature was one of the most heartening results of the Twentieth CPSU Congress. It has now been suppressed, and, with one or two notable exceptions, the leading figures of the literary establishment have joined in condemning it. Khrushchev's own prescription for writers and artists have appeared in the form of an article, "For a Closer Tie Between Literature and Art and the Life of the People" (*Kommunist*, No. 12, 1957) that was widely reprinted in the press, and which was conflated from three of his speeches. It would seem that this is a suitable moment to try and decide what the dissident writers wanted to do, and why they angered the Party.

The term "literary opposition" is used above. It originated in Western accounts of the writers' meetings of March and May, 1957, at which Dudintsev and a group of contributors to the periodical anthology *Literaturnaia Moskva* (*Literary Moscow*) resisted the demands of their senior colleagues, who were clearly backed by the authority of the Party, that they humble themselves and recant, and chose instead the "heroism of silence." Some commentators see political significance in their action, and in fact use "literary opposition" in the sense of "political opposition on the part of writers." It is important to decide whether there is any justification for this equation.

In its most literal sense the term "literary opposition" is a true and useful description of the silent heroes, along with others who shared some of their ideas. They opposed in the first place the false values of Stalinist literature and the stultifying controls set up to enforce them. The yearning for creative freedom had, of course, shown itself long before the Twentieth CPSU Congress. Yet the Congress seemed to offer the long-awaited assurance that the Party would look tolerantly on bolder writers, provided that their general loyalty to the purposes of the regime was not in doubt. Moreover, the laureate hacks who for so many years had ruled over Soviet literature were discredited and their authority impaired by Khrushchev's revelations about the master whom they had so slavishly extolled. Many young writers, and even some who had borne the burden without a murmur under Stalin, felt free to refuse the strain of circumspection and the tedium of forced complacency. They were united in one thing: their determination to write spontaneously and honestly. Beyond this, there was no real unity of mood and aspirations. Writers very different in outlook and intentions were later forced together into a defensive alliance. We must not be misled into regarding them as a homogeneous school.

True, all of them reflected thoughts and feelings aroused in the Soviet intelligentsia by the Twentieth Congress. But reactions to this event, and especially to Khrushchev's secret speech, varied widely. Some intellectuals felt only disgust and despair, sharpened sometimes by a sense of personal guilt. In others, revulsion against the past brought about a rebirth of primitive socialist enthusiasm. While some were confirmed in their dislike of the Party and all its works, other identified themselves with what they believed to be the purposes of the dominant group at the Twentieth Congress.

The Party, however, was less concerned with intentions than with effects, and the literary opposition at large, in spite of differences between its members, expressed and encouraged undesirable political attitudes among the intelligentsia. In particular, it stimulated a critical re-examination of the Soviet past and present, proceeding not from political and economic formulas, but from direct social observation.

The Party itself has raised the question, What is wrong with Soviet society? and had answered, Nothing that the cult of the individual does not explain, or that the elimination of the cult cannot cure. It is remarkable how little attention the literary opposition paid to the concept of the cult. Recent literary work unmistakably expresses the awareness of the more politically conscious that these pat code words conceal the true nature of the disease and are of little help in treating it. The writers chose to ignore the history of the disease, and to offer instead a realistic description of certain symptoms, with a few hints as to where a cure should be sought.

They noted especially a hardening of the arteries, a failure of civic consciousness and social courage, a cowardly or complacent avoidance of awkward problems. This theme is treated symbolically in Semion Kirsanov's "Seven Days of the Week"— a bizarre poem about the poet's efforts to produce a new heart to save a dying friend, published in *Novy mir* (No. 9, 1956). The need for a change of heart, for a spiritual reawakening, is a frequently recurring motif. In several works we meet ordinary, decent people who have come to terms with Soviet society by suppressing the promptings of conscience and common sense: Dudintsev's military judge (in *Not by Bread Alone*), who comfortably assumes that the inventor Lopatkin would never have been sent to trial if his work were of any use; Nikolai Zhdanov's bureaucrat (in "Journey Home"), who feels a brief uneasiness about the plight of the peasantry while on a belated visit to his native village but relapses into complacency upon his departure, Alexander Yashin's kolkhoz officials (in "Levers"), who solemnly enact the empty bureaucratic ritual they know to be meaningless;* and many others.

Sometimes callousness and indifference are frankly shown to be the results of official terrorism, as in the case of Yuri Nagibin's escapist (in "Khazar Decoration"), who had been "frightened once and for all" and had ever since averted his eyes from the present. The return from prison camps of many thousands of innocent victims of the purges stirred the conscience of the Soviet intelligentsia, and sharpened their awareness that only a rebirth of social courage could guarantee that such crimes would never

* Both these stories appeared in *Literaturnaia Moskva*, No. 2 (1957).

happen again. Margarita Aliger, one of the editors of *Literatur-naia Moskva*, in her poem "The Most Important Thing," bitterly accuses "Soviet man" of moral cowardice. He had tempered steel, hewn stone, planted gardens in the steppes, built houses, spanned broad rivers with straight bridges, written countless books, fought the Fascists and built the Communist world, "but suddenly he sounded a false note, lied without cause, self-consciously tried to extricate himself, and slandered his friends. The flicker of fright in his eye showed that he would hide in stormy weather." She herself does not deny the indictment. Her poem "The Real Truth" (*Novy mir*, Nos. 2 and 4, 1957), is an anguished admission of guilt:

> The enemies cunningly concealed themselves behind dictatorial orders and pompous phraseology. . . . We said: There must be something in all that; we raised our hands and voted for their calumny. We should have known. . . . But, oh bitter shame, I did not try to defend him. I thought: Perhaps I did not really understand him? Perhaps I failed to notice something.

Common to most members of the literary opposition is the realization that an oppressive society corrupts its citizens. With it goes the knowledge that those who win and hold high places in such a society are especially liable to deformations of character; and conversely, that it is frighteningly easy for the unscrupulous to manipulate the system in their own interests. The Party had mentioned "bureaucratic distortions" as an evil consequence of the personality cult. The writers offered an anatomy of bureaucracy that suggested that the fault was in the system itself, and that it could not be corrected by the mere act of pious self-dissociation from Stalin's excesses.

The most important contribution was certainly Dudintsev's novel. Most of the officials and scientific administrators who throng its pages live to "occupy a comfortable chair" and to enjoy the material benefits of success. Dudintsev depicts with fascinated horror their materialism, snobbery, servility to authority, arbitrary use of power, habits of intrigue, and above all their

detachment from the ideals to which, in theory, they are dedicated. His most memorable creation is Drozdov, whose name
became for the Soviet intelligentsia a symbol of all that is most
detestable in an overpowerful, overprivileged bureaucracy. He
has something of the old fictional commissar about him—his
proletarian origin, his roughness, his defiantly simple outlook.
But virtue has deserted him. Instead of single-minded concentration on the achievement of an ideal, he is capable only of
narrow-minded devotion to routine. He is obsessed to the point
of mania with his belief in the system, that "planners' fallacy"
that thrives in closed societies. But his beliefs have long ago
fused with his personal ambitions and taken on their coloration.
He has only contempt for original ideas and creative individuals.
To the inventor Lopatkin he says:

> You are a truly tragic figure. You personify an age that has
> vanished, never to return. . . . We can do without your
> invention, even if it is an important one. And we shall lose
> nothing because strict planning and calculation ensure
> steady progress. . . . If your invention is one of genius, our
> collective will nonetheless solve the same problem when it
> becomes necessary. We are builder ants and necessary. You
> are a solitary genius, and not needed, with your giant idea
> on feeble legs.

The bureaucrats in *Not by Bread Alone* have their own ideology—a set of convenient rationalizations to justify claims to
authority and prosperity. Drozdov defends his rejection of fine
ideas about the higher nature of things with the statement: "I
belong to the producers of material values. I am strengthening
the basis of society." His wife objects to his vulgarization of
the Marxist concept of the basis. "Well," says Drozdov, "I am
producing the things that will enable people to enter into social
relations. Once the things are there, anybody can enter into
social relations—there'll be no difficulty about that." The *nouveau-
riche* snobbery of the Soviet bourgeoisie is strong in him. When
his wife asks why only bigwigs are invited to their parties, he
says that "ordinary people would identify us with the things

that surround us [their luxurious home] and would envy us."
He is adept in the use of political clichés (the "basis," the "collective," "interests of state," etc.) to serve his own purpose, but
his political consciousness goes no further than awareness of
what will please his superiors and awe his subordinates.

Dudintsev shows that narrow authoritarian routineers of the
Drozdov type are not even efficient, that they retard rather than
accelerate material progress. But it is their lack of scruple, their
readiness to slander and destroy anyone who challenges them,
that particularly horrifies him. The story of the plot against
Lopatkin and his condemnation reveal the terrible helplessness
of the private citizen against a monopolistic bureaucracy more
powerfully than anything else in Soviet literature.

Other writers joined in the indictment of the bureaucrats.
Kaverin, for instance—whom few would regard as a member of
the literary opposition—in a curious story about Soviet attempts
to produce penicillin (*Literaturnaia Moskva*, No. 2, 1957), further develops Dudintsev's proposition that an oppressive,
intrigue-ridden bureaucracy hinders technical progress. His positive characters speak of their bureaucratic enemies with a violence that is foreign to Dudintsev. "I listen, and feel with horror
that I want to kill this man, with his politeness . . . and his
profound, barbarian indifference to everything that does not
affect his brilliant career." This of a deputy minister. Of another
successful and unscrupulous careerist:

He is a thief. He stole all this—his money, luxurious apartment, carpets, furniture, and connections. Why does he have
all these things? What has he ever done? There are hundreds
like him—no, thousands. They stick together. They fear and
hate each other, but all the same how they stick together,
how they cover up for each other!

Two other contributors to *Literaturnaia Moskva* dealt with
the bureaucrat more gently. Nagibin, in "Light in the Window,"
and Zhdanov, in "Journey Home," showed the bureaucrat as alien
to the people and unresponsive to their needs; but he is himself
a victim of the system and unable to change his ways. Both are

slight stories, hardly more than anecdotes, but richly symbolic.

In the first, a small official, the guardian of exorbitant bureaucratic privileges and the helpless executor of senseless orders, prevents the staff and patients of a sanatorium from using a room that, year in and year out, is kept ready for a great official who never arrives. In Zhdanov's story the symbolism is starker. The bureaucrat Varygin leaves his office routine, his discontented wife and overfed children, to attend his mother's funeral in the backward kolkhoz village of his birth. He had not seen his mother for a long time and feels uneasily that he had neglected her. How had she managed? Not too badly, the village watchman tells him. "Sometimes she even ate white bread and indulged in factory tea. Why, last year they brought us sugar ever so many times, and she got some."

In conversation with local people he learns something of the miseries and frustrations of collective life. One woman tells him how petty officials had compelled the peasants to get the wheat in, although it was urgently necessary to harvest the flax, and the wheat could have waited. The peasants, through no fault of their own, missed the flax harvest, and while their record for grain production was among the best of the local farms, they got no bread for themselves because their over-all performance was unsatisfactory. "Did they do right by us?" the woman asks. Varygin can only mumble garbled political clichés: "It is a political question. We must always put the state above everything else. Everything depends on the level of consciousness of the masses." The poor woman is pathetically pleased. "You've put it well! There's not enough consciousness in the masses."

Oppressed by the bareness of his mother's hut and the evidences of misery and dissatisfaction all around him, Varygin carries away the picture of a sad, forgotten and neglected world. In his imagination he sees the rough wooden crosses against the sky, the house that had been warm and comfortable in his childhood, the old samovar in the corner. His mother sits behind the wooden table and asks him with hope and expectation: "Did they do right by us or not?" But when his car leaves the stark country road for the smooth highway to the railroad station, he gradually begins to return to his habitual even mood, and thinks with pleasure that tomorrow he will go into his warm, well-appointed office and take his seat in the armchair at his desk.

In Kirsanov's poem we find a more savage attack on the bureaucrats. They are not mere routineers, cliché-mongers, evaders of awkward questions, but vicious self-seekers. When the hero of this fantasy (narrated in the first person) puts his "new hearts" on display, the bureaucrats force their way to the head of the inspection line: "Who is entitled to new hearts? Not those who are too tired. Not those who have never reached the upper ranks. Not those who cannot be called persons." The "smaller fry" are pushed aside and "somebody's favorites" placed in the line—"the double-dealers, the turncoats, the slanderers, the traitors, all had permits for new hearts. . . ." Yet in the end, the bureaucrats declare: "These hearts are not needed. . . . We need useful hearts, like iron locks"—hearts that will do whatever they are told. (See excerpt at the end of this article—*Ed.*)

The above discussion offers no more than a glance at a few of the works that most clearly reveal why the literary "opposition" excited the admiration of the critical intelligentsia and the anger of the Party. These references are enough to show the truth of one of the gravest charges of the official criticism leveled against the opposition writers. They did indeed dwell almost exclusively on the dark side of Soviet reality. But, in the view of many thousands of Soviet intellectuals, the dark side needed attention: The masters of Stalinist chiaroscura had for years past toned it down almost to invisibility.

Many intellectuals also felt that the dominant group at the Twentieth Congress had recognized the need for a regeneration of Soviet society. Clearly the essential preliminary was honesty about the past and the present. Yet the Party, in spite of Khrushchev's secret speech, was slow to particularize in a public statement about those crimes ("infringements of socialist legality") and abuses ("bureaucratic distortions") that, on its own admission, had characterized the period of the personality cult. The writers insisted that the task should not be shirked. A. Kron summarized their attitude in his brilliant essay, "A Writer's Remarks" (*Literaturnaia Moskva*, No. 2, 1957):

It is usual to say that the personality cult did our society incalculable harm. Incalculable, immeasurable, unbounded, unprecedented, unlimited—these words, used in large quantities, have an unpleasant flavor of irrationality, and it is no accident that they were very much in fashion a few years back. . . . No, however great the harm done by the personality cult, it is calculable and must be calculated. At the same time, we must soberly estimate our strength and our possibilities, and we shall see that they more than suffice to overcome thoroughly and decisively the consequences of the cult. . . .

Certainly it should not be assumed that there was any subversive intention in the action of the literary opposition. After all, the Party itself had called for frank, unvarnished accounts of "Soviet reality" and fearless satire of bureaucratic abuses. Indeed, the first authoritative reviews of Dudintsev's book praised it as a work in the true Bolshevik literary tradition. It was only when the deeper implications of the new, bold literature —implications the writers themselves did not always realize— became clear from the reactions of critical intellectuals, and particularly of turbulent university students, that Dudintsev, for instance, could be accused of "blackening all that the Soviet people has created."

There were certain inescapable conclusions that any free-thinking Soviet intellectual was bound to draw from writings such as those described above. One was that if the literary opposition gave a true picture of Soviet reality—and there were even complaints that it had not been frank enough (that Dudintsev's half-happy ending, for instance, was an optimistic falsification)—then there was a need for a radical reform of Soviet institutions to prevent the recurrence of such abuses. Another, that although the chief culprit was dead, many others were alive and entrenched in positions of power, enjoying authority and prosperity, which they had won by crimes against the people. Should they not be exposed and called to account?

In many ways Dudintsev and some of his fellows reminded their admirers of the opposition literature of Czarist times. It was almost as though they had deliberately revived some of the strongest traditional themes of Russian literature. Here, once again, were the two Russias: official Russia and the Russia of the people—the one oppressive, corrupt, inhuman; the other exploited, innocent and helpless. Here, too, was the traditional hatred of the intelligentsia for the Philistine, the *meshchane*—identified now with the luxury-loving, complacent, pompous bureaucratic class. For there is no denying that the work of the literary opposition is full of hatred and contempt for the false ideals and political emptiness of bureaucrats as a social species, not just of particular bad bureaucrats.

The critical intelligentsia drew positive as well as negative conclusions from the new literature. Dudintsev, again, supplied the text for the lessons the literary opposition as a whole seemed to teach. The most important such lesson is that the health of a society depends not on unconditional loyalty to some collective (which, says one of Dudintsev's characters, often means in practice a monopoly), not on unquestioning acceptance of political clichés, such as "the interests of the state" ("always inquire whose interests are really at stake," wrote Dudintsev), but on the courage and initiative of ordinary citizens. It seemed to readers of *Not by Bread Alone* enormously significant that the Party as such plays no role in the story, for good or ill. In the conventional Soviet novel on the same theme, the Party would certainly have intervened like a *deus ex machina* to vindicate the hero and punish his persecutors. The only Party official in Dudintsev's book is one who clownishly abases himself before Drozdov.

It may very well be that Dudintsev's silence about the Party was tactful, not malicious. But his heroes, Lopatkin and Galitsky, the vehicles of a pure and primitive Communist faith, are pitted against enemies who are in the Party for careerist reasons, who have influence with important Party organs, yet who have no sincere political creed, who at best believe in what Lopatkin calls "petty-bourgeois Communism." The inference is clear: that grace resides in individuals, not in organizations.

Some elements of the critical intelligentsia, particularly student groups at Moscow and other universities, saw in the work of the literary opposition support for certain demands they began to voice widely in the autumn of 1956—demands for the freer exercise of public opinion; for the right to criticize, within the bounds of loyalty, the Soviet past and present; and for the establishment of genuine popular controls to expose and check abuses in high places. Not one of the opposition writers formulated any sort of political program. Many of them undoubtedly believed that they were expressing the spirit of the Twentieth Congress and that the Party itself would take action in the sense their writings seemed to demand. There is no mistaking the notes of socialist faith, and indeed of Soviet patriotism, in the work of Dudintsev and Margarita Aliger, for instance. Their later obstinacy in refusing to "recant" in the face of Party pressure was due to hurt resentment against those who misrepresented their intentions and called in doubt their loyalty to the Soviet system. They could not believe that the Party would not recognize in them its truest and best supporters.

But the Party could not afford to let writers serve its purposes in their own way, let alone suggest what those purposes should be. Undisciplined literature, however loyal its intentions, could only encourage indiscipline in the population and lead to "demagogic" utterances of the sort the Party considered a challenge to its own authority.

And so the writers found themselves forced, unwillingly, into "opposition" not merely to their professional superiors, but to the Party leadership. At the very least they were guilty, in the official view, of washing the Soviet Union's dirty linen before gloating foreign eyes; of usurping the Party's prerogatives in diagnosing and prescribing for the ills of Soviet society; of encouraging demagogy and homebred revisionism. Khrushchev, at a gathering of Party leaders, writers, and artists on May 19, 1957, drew a sinister comparison between the literary opposition and those Hungarian writers who had played such an important part in events leading up to the October uprising. Dudintsev and some of his colleagues, to their dismay we can be sure, certainly contributed to the disaffection among university students, both in the autumn of 1956, and later in the spring of 1957. And their example had spread to far corners of the Soviet Union. In both Kazakhstan and the Baltic States, literary oppositions sprang up.

The opposition writers had set out to elaborate in their own way the lessons of the Twentieth Congress. Khrushchev has now, at long last, given his own views as to how literature can best assist his policies. His positive prescriptions go no further than loyalty to Party policies, identification of the Party with the people, and an optimistic and inspiring, but businesslike treatment of reality. It seems probable that he has no wish to bind the arts as tightly as Stalin did. Stalin's personal taste, as well as ideological controls, was to blame for the degradation of Soviet art in the 1930's. If the novel was an inflated slogan, paintings banal posters, and music a tedious succession of sanctimonious marches and plodding hymns, it was in part because Stalin, a provincial, Victorian philistine, fancied himself as an infallible connoisseur. Khrushchev is less interested in the arts and probably less bigoted.

Nonetheless, his intervention will almost certainly have other damaging effects on Soviet literature, besides circumscribing its choice of themes and treatment. He has strengthened the hand of Stalin's literary yes-men, confirmed most of them in their posts as literary overseers, and even spared a word of sympathy for their sufferings during the campaign against the Stalin cult. He has also subordinated the troublesome Moscow writers' organization to a new Union of Writers of the R.S.F.S.R., dominated by dreary and reliable provincial hacks who now will enjoy (in theory) the same prestige and (in fact) the same rates of pay and opportunities for publication as their nationally famous colleagues.

"All kinds of lies were sold as hearts," says Kirsanov. So far his words may be prophetic for the future of Soviet literature. But we may doubt the applicability of the line that follows: "And the people swallowed them with great delight."

"WE NEED USEFUL HEARTS . . ."

. . . . They come
      as a large commission
with some important mission.

I recognize
          the Double-Faced One—
he will never say a superfluous word.
The Indifferent One strides along
so sedately and confidently,
and next to him, moderately sedate,
is his personal assistant.
It is stupid to resist!
They shove their fingers
          into the artery.
They come up and feel it
like fabric for trousers.
A short Statement is already drawn up.
—Unsuitable.
          Correct.
                    It is a fact.
For public consumption
          such hearts are not needed.
And in general, novelties
are not required
                    on our market.
We need useful hearts,
like iron locks,
uncomplicated,
          convenient,
capable of executing any order:
To blacken? To blacken!
To value? To value!
To annihilate? To annihilate!
To feed? To feed!
To roar? To roar!
To keep silent? To keep silent!
To destroy? To destroy!
To love? To love!
And no cardiograms whatever,
and in the future, for good order—
A penalty of two hundred grams
will be imposed for "seekings!"

The statement is signed
          and that's that!
The workers get the order—go home!
Because of this statement
          we are helpless.
What now? Go off to our respective streets?
And across the street
          my friend
is lying with his pulse not beating.
This is how—
          with a stab of a knife
they catch you from behind . . .
But perhaps we shall revive him again?
But shall we have time, during one day?
. . . . There is one more day in the week,
but the work
          is enormous!
Our shop is on the verge of tears.
This is what happened on Friday.
I leave, and on my heels
leave the women laboratory workers,
holding their hearts, as though in them
were gaping wounds.

—From "The Seven Days of the Week,"
By S. Kirsanov, *Novy mir*, September, 1956.

The Struggle Goes On

———MAX HAYWARD

IN FEBRUARY, 1959, the French journal *Esprit* published an anonymous essay by a young Soviet writer on the topic of socialist realism, a brilliant and original effort to explain the stagnation of Soviet literature. Early in his discussion the writer observes:

> Art does not fear dictatorship nor severity, nor repressions, nor even conservatism and clichés. If needs be, art is narrowly religious, stupidly *étatiste*, without individuality, and yet it is great. We are enthusiastic about the style of ancient Egypt, Russian iconography, folklore. Art is fluid enough to fit the Procrustean bed imposed by history. There is only one thing that it cannot tolerate: eclecticism.*

The author points out that in a "theological" society, where everything is subordinated to the achievement of a supreme Purpose, it is incongruous to employ modes of expression adequate only to lack of faith, skepticism, and self-deprecating irony. A "religious aesthetic" cannot be based on nineteenth-century models. Yet this is precisely what is demanded of Soviet writers. Ever since Gorki commanded them to "learn from the classics," they have been trying to glorify the "positive hero" and his devoted, single-minded struggle for Communism in the style of Balzac, Tolstoi, De Maupassant, and Chekhov. There is, then, a patent contradiction between form and content. Positive heroes

---

* The essay has now been published in book form: Abram Tertz, *On Socialist Realism*, Introduction by Czeslaw Milosz (New York: Pantheon Books, 1961).—*Ed.*

and militant optimism cannot be convincingly portrayed in language associated with the "superfluous man" and deeply pessimistic uncertainty about the purpose of life. Thus, says the author:

> If many writers are going through a crisis at the moment
> .... it is because they have to seek a compromise and unite
> what cannot be united: the positive hero who logically lends
> himself to schematized, allegorical treatment—with psychological character-study; an elevated, declamatory style—with
> description of prosaic, everyday life; a sublime ideal—with
> verisimilitude to reality. This results in a monstrous salad.
> The characters [of Soviet fiction] torment themselves almost
> à la Dostoevski, grow sad almost à la Chekhov, arrange their
> family life almost à la Tolstoi and yet at the same time vie
> with each other in shouting platitudes from the Soviet press:
> "Long live peace in the whole world," "Down with the warmongers." This is neither classicism nor realism. It is semiclassical demiart of a none too socialist demirealism.

In the author's view, the only Soviet writer who has ever given original artistic expression to the Soviet epoch was Mayakovski. He hated analysis and psychologism. He never described everyday life (*byt*) or nature. He did not try to imitate the Russian classics, but devised a hyperbolic, Homeric style of his own. Since his day, Soviet writers have been condemned to a ludicrous eclectic epigonism, including, if they are poets, even elements of Mayakovski. This eclecticism was imposed in the 1930's and was in line with other extraordinary miscegenated forms (e.g., the combination of one-man rule with a "democratic" constitution) invented by Stalin.

The greatest source of contradiction and tension in Soviet intellectual life since the famous Twentieth Congress of 1956 is that these ideological hybrids have not been allowed to lapse with the partial eclipse of their maker.

Free Content Versus Free Form

Students of Communism have tended to ascribe all the ills of Soviet literature and art to the principle of *partiinost* (i.e., conformity to Party guidance), with special emphasis on the restrictions that this places on *what* they writer says. As the author of the *Esprit* article suggests, however, perhaps an even greater handicap for the Soviet writer is the fact that Party doctrine prevents him from freely elaborating an original style. Freedom to express certain ideas is less important in art than freedom in the choice of form. It is only this latter freedom that is essential to art.

It is odd that the more imaginative post-Stalin leadership has not realized that by granting this freedom, it might win much more effective support from the writers as propagandists for the Cause (at least from those of them who still have not lost faith in it), and at the same time deflect them from their interest in the extension of more general freedoms. Since the events of 1956, this has been understood by the Party leadership in Poland and even in Hungary and Czechoslovakia, where considerable discretion is allowed the writers in their choice of style. Thus, while it retains control in the realm of political ideas, the Party gives the writer relative freedom to be an *artist*, and by removing a major frustration, reduces his potentialities as a rebel. This particular lesson of the Polish-Hungarian revolts has not been learned by the Soviet Central Committee. Instead of allowing writers to be artists, it forces them to be second-rate publicists—second-rate, because to be a first-rate publicist one needs a political and intellectual freedom much wider than the license of form required by an artist. The policy of the Central Committee, therefore, has compelled Soviet writers to seek an improvement in their position by striving for a measure of liberty that, if granted, would undermine the political and ideological foundations of the regime.

The "controversial" novels, plays, and articles of the last few years (Ehrenburg's *Thaw*, Zorin's *Guests*, Pomerantsev's "Sincerity in Literature," Dudintsev's *Not by Bread Alone*, etc.) were the first truly publicist works to appear in the Soviet Union for decades. They also demonstrated that the realist style is effective only when it is employed to express the mood and outlook of those Russian writers of the last century who created it. In other words, they broke down the specious distinction between "socialist realism" and "critical realism." *The Thaw* reintroduced the theme of the Superfluous Man into Russian literature. Instead of faith in the future, we find uncertainty in the present. Reality becomes complex and hence rather sad, instead of simple and joyous. Doubt, hesitation, and introspection ("What is the meaning of life?" asks a character in one of Vera Panova's novels) belie the optimism of the still-obligatory happy ending. In all this post-Stalin literature, however conformist the author tries to be, the "shining heights of Communism" are gradually being overcast by a haze.

Since the counterattack against revisionism in 1956, the Party's policy in literature has been to suppress overt challenges to its authority while encouraging the writers to give a more balanced and truthful picture of life. They have been asked to write on contemporary themes with greater plausibility and artistic skill. Since perfection is always unconvincing, positive heroes may be endowed with human weakness, and the difficulties and hardships of the transitional stage between socialism and Communism may be frankly exposed. These concessions to greater realism have, if anything, made the writers' educational task more difficult. Virtue is tedious and Soviet readers are not exceptional in being far more interested in vice.

A Grounded Literature

The official speeches at the Third Congress of Soviet Writers, which was finally held in May, 1959, after two unexplained postponements, showed little evidence of concern at the obvious inadequacy of this modification of literary formula.* In its formal address to the Congress, the Central Committee told the writers that their "high calling" is "to show truthfully and vividly the beauty of the people's labor exploits . . . to be passionate propagandists of the Seven Year Plan, and to imbue the hearts of Soviet people with courage and energy." They are to do this by "giving every support to realist art which is opposed to formalist, idea-less art."

* The Congress convened on May 18th and closed on May 23rd. This article is based on its most important speeches, published in *Literaturnaia gazeta*, May 18-27.

The monumentally tedious speech delivered by Andrei Surkov, outgoing head of the Writers' Union, spelled out these two incongruous demands at inordinate length. But there are passages that suggest that he was aware of the contradiction between them no less than the author of the *Esprit* article. Speaking of the poverty of language in many recent Soviet works he observed that "content that has not found the right form cannot influence the minds and hearts of the readers." He virtually admitted the incompatibility of realism and the portrayal of romantic, inspiring heroes when he said:

> We have many truthful and talented books about the life of the people, but what one of our great writers said ten years ago about our literature not being sufficiently *winged* is as valid now as it was then. Indeed, we seem to have difficulty in poeticizing the people of the present day.

Earth and air, it seems, mix no better in Soviet literature than they did in medieval alchemy. Surkov went even further when he said: "We often forget that the portrayal of what is new in life demands innovation (*novatorstvo*) in form."

What would be simpler, then, than to encourage writers to go ahead and experiment? The answer is that it cannot be done because freedom to experiment might lead to formalism and "pseudo innovation." Surkov's argument at this point is quoted in full because nothing could better illustrate the crabbed, infantile perversity of pseudo-dialectical logic:

> In the 1920's and the beginning of the 1930's, there was often heated discussion among writers about the novelty of Soviet literature in general, and innovation was understood as the search for a new form, for new linguistic possibilities of expressing the new material of revolutionary reality. Admittedly, there was much that was false and pseudo-revolutionary in the debates of those days. Formalist quirks were often passed off as innovation. . . . The struggle against these false interpretations of the idea of innovation was successfully concluded about a quarter of a century ago, because the rich literary practice of the Soviet epoch mercilessly

destroyed all the inventions of the pseudo theoreticians. Formalism now manifested itself only in certain cases of recidivism. But now it has come about that serious discussion of innovation in our literature has ceased altogether. Our literature is not subjected to a profound analysis from the point of view of the compatibility of the form of literary expression with the new material of reality.*

The older writers at the Congress will have remembered sadly that in many cases the pseudo theoreticians were destroyed together with their inventions. They will also have wondered how it is possible to seek for new forms without courting the charge of formalism. Everybody will have thought back to the period just after Stalin's death when the Party launched an appeal for "boldness" and when those who responded were soon being charged with "pseudo boldness."

A Plea for Growing Room

It was one of the older writers, Vsevolod Ivanov, who gently pointed out the absurdity of asking people to experiment without allowing them to do so. In what was almost the only noteworthy speech from the floor, he made a plea that the younger writers be given their head in this respect:

Young writers must be allowed and helped to experiment, to find their own style, their own manner of writing. . . . It would occur to nobody to dispute the fact that progress in science is unthinkable without experiment. Yet attempts to experiment in literature are not met with approval and the experimenter risks being classed as a formalist. In my opinion this is nonsense. There is not and cannot be any danger of formalism in our literature, because formalism was a short and bygone stage in the lives of certain literary critics and it by no means embraced the whole of Soviet literature.

* Surkov's reference to recidivism is a fascinating example of how the language of criminology has become commonplace in Soviet literary debate. It is quite natural to talk of an "amnesty" for erring intellectuals.

The last sentence makes an important and obvious point that has probably never been publicly made before, namely that the very use of the term "formalism" (as in the Central Committee's message to the Congress) is an unwarranted extension of its original meaning. In the 1920's, it was the term chosen by a small but very influential group of literary critics to describe their method of analyzing the linguistic and structural aspects of works of literature. Its pejorative application to writers was a misappropriation of the term.

Apart from Khrushchev's address, the only other notable contribution to the Congress came in the shape of an article by Konstantin Paustovsky, one of the more outspoken and rebellious of the older writers.* He discussed with notable frankness some of the factors that "impede the free development of literature." The first is the lack of tolerance toward various, as he put it, "isms." He spoke of them with unprecedented indulgence:

> All these isms are the children of extravagant Paris and America. Beyond the outer ring of the Paris fortifications, they lose their glamour, the soil that feeds them, and they look far-fetched and unnatural. But even these extravagances (surrealism, decaphonism, dadaism, and other isms) are essentially a completely normal expression of youthful impetuosity. There is no reason whatsover to sound the tocsin and shout with panic, for the recklessness of youth is useful—it prevents the older generation from going to seed and regarding itself as infallible and "untouchable."

His second point was even more radical. Flying in the face of antirevisionist orthodoxy, he disputed the standard charge that writers who fail to make a judicious balance between "negative" and "positive" have lost contact with the people. In a cautious phrase that could well refer to Pasternak as well as Dudintsev,

---

* Paustovsky has used the comparative immunity of old age once before to plead for a more common-sense approach to literary questions, particularly as they affect the right of the younger generation to break new ground. In 1957, he made a sensational speech at a public discussion on Dudintsev. It was never printed in the Soviet press, but a transcript appeared in a French newspaper.

he asked whether those writers accused of "isolation from the people" are really the ones guilty of it.* His answer, in so many words, was that the writers who are alien to the people are rather those who try to combine realism with phony optimism (*bodryachestvo*), who lace their work with high-minded sentiment, insert saving clauses, and devise happy endings. "Perhaps," he wrote, "we shout so much and so loudly about truth in literature just because there is a lack of it. . . . The people see everything and understand everything and they will never excuse falsity and deceit in a writer, however talented he may be." Comparing the saving clauses and the happy endings to the bows a clown makes to the spectators before he leaves the ring, he commented:

> It is well that Tolstoi was able to write *Anna Karenina* before the appearance of this tradition. He did not have to "bow" to anybody, not even to the publisher, and he allowed Anna to disrupt her family and die for purely personal and, therefore, impermissible, reasons. It is not acceptable to write about defects, however harmful they may be for the life of our society, without first making an exculpatory "bow" by mentioning our achievements. . . . Another useless and burdensome tradition is the reluctance to write about suffering, the fear of any suggestion of sadness, as though our lives should take place under a sugary sky to the cheerful laughter of "militant" men and women. . . .

This article by Paustovsky amounted to a manifesto, audaciously close in spirit and tone to the demands for freedom (at least freedom from the absurd formulas bequeathed by Stalin and Zhdanov) that caused such a furor when they were first enunciated in 1953–54 and again, with even greater insistence, in 1956. The fact that these demands could be reiterated at the

---

* The Pasternak affair was scarcely mentioned at the Congress. Only Surkov saw fit to refer to his "treacherous activities." But one of the other speakers took up the subject. The only other reference is by Galina Nikolaeva in an article published in *Literaturnaia gazeta* on May 18, the opening day of the Congress. In a strikingly different tonality to Surkov's remark, she speaks *en passant* of Pasternak's "mistake."

Congress by a writer who previously had compromised himself as their ardent champion shows very clearly that, surface appearances to the contrary, the movement toward the emancipation of literature (and hence of intellectual activity in general) was still strong and undefeated. Talk in the West about the end of the "thaw" has been grossly exaggerated. The current flows even more strongly than before, but under a thin covering of ice. In a curious, negative way, the Writers' Congress indeed bore witness to the victory of the opposition. The lack of controversy, the calculated absence (or at least failure to participate) of all those writers who could have injected a spark of life into the proceedings, turned the Congress into a rather pathetic parade of old-timers.* It was all reminiscent of a demonstration by some dwindling political group whose members turn out to keep the flag flying, but whose arguments and slogans are so irrelevant that nobody bothers to contradict them any more.

Culture and Corn

It was only the appearance of Khrushchev that enlivened the Congress and perhaps saved it from being a fiasco. His speech was an impressive example of his impromptu oratory in the intimate and rather bantering style that he adopts in his discourses to the peasants and other producers of material goods. There are even agricultural similes: The fostering of young literary talent, for instance, is elaborately compared with the cultivation of corn.

It would be useless to look for any new thinking on ideological or cultural questions in Khrushchev's address. What he said was so conventional as to be irrelevant to the problems that vex the writers. Gone was the angry exhortative note that marked his three "literary" speeches of 1957, when he personally intervened to rap the knuckles of the revisionist recalcitrants. Indeed he now evinced something close to boredom with literary questions, and

* Mikhail Sholokhov, who arrived back in Moscow from his foreign tour two days before the opening session, did not speak, even though he attended. At the previous Congress in 1954 he had spoken scathingly of the "Olympian calm" of the proceedings and all but disrupted them by a series of scurrilous personal attacks on various conformist colleagues. It would be interesting to know what he thought of this Congress.

there was a note of mock humility in his constant assurance to the audience that he is not really competent to judge literary matters. He informed them apologetically that he did not really have much time left over from matters of state to do much reading, and even then he often needed to prick himself with a pin to keep awake. One can only imagine the discomfiture of certain people in the hall when he went on to mention one book he had read recently without the aid of a pin, namely *Not by Bread Alone:* "Anastas Ivanovich Mikoyan, who read this work before me, said to me, 'Read it—from some of the things he says it looks as though he has been eavesdropping on you!" The embarrassment of those who led the campaign against Dudintsev can have been matched only by the relief of the majority on hearing that their works were no longer being passed upon by an omniscient and malignant judge.

Khrushchev's main concern was evidently not that the writers should be ideologically pure, but that they should keep the peace and not trouble the government with their interminable squabbles. He also made it quite clear that they were no longer regarded as being so important as they believed themselves to be: "Life is incomparably richer, more full-blooded and deeper, than any work of art." Their mistakes, therefore, scarcely warrant all the fuss made about them. The following passage in his speech could very well have significant implications, since it suggests a certain abdication by the Party of its exclusive prerogatives in the control of literature in favor of the corporate judgment of the writers themselves:

You will ask: What guarantee is there against mistakes? Yes, it is difficult to give guarantees, because a writer, if he is a real Soviet writer, makes mistakes not consciously, not intentionally, but for a whole number of reasons, such as inadequate knowledge of life and incorrect premises, etc. In order to prevent this, one must remember that writers live in society, reflect the life of society, that their work must be guided by the criticism of society, and that they must take account of this criticism. . . . Again you may say: "Criticize us, control us; if a work is incorrect, do not print

it." But you know that it is not easy to decide right away
what to print and what not to print. The easiest thing would
be to print nothing, then there would be no mistakes. . . .
But it would be stupidity. Therefore, Comrades, do not
burden the government with the solution of such questions,
decide them for yourselves in a comradely fashion.

This grant of relative autonomy to the writers was accompanied by guarantees that there would be no return to the "intolerable phenomena" associated with the cult of personality, and
also by a plea for tolerance and tact in dealing with colleagues,
however seriously they may have erred. Wayward intellectuals,
like hardened criminals, are not incorrigible if they are given
every chance to reform. Apologizing for the "crudity" of his
analogy, Khrushchev told his audience how he himself had
recently reformed a thief with a little kindness. In calling for
comradely love and reconciliation, however, Khrushchev made it
quite plain that forgiveness depends on penitence and a contrite
admission of defeat. One must "not strike a man when he's
down"; but neither must one forget the immortal words of Maxim
Gorky: "If the enemy does not surrender, he must be destroyed."
Nor must the writers be allowed to forget that their role is primarily to assist the Party in the education of man. At the end of
his speech, through a remarkable unconscious blunder, he refor-
mulated this sacred task of the Soviet writers in words rather
familiar to Western ears:

> I saw some Americans three days ago. Among them was an
> old man, a judge. At the end of our talk he said . . . "I fear
> that when I get back and tell my friends about my impres-
> sions, some of them will say, 'The Russians have washed the
> old judge's brain.'" That's literally what he said. Not a bad
> expression. So there you are, Comrades, you should wash
> people's brains with your works.

Despite the ominous reservations in Khrushchev's speech, it
gave some hope that the life of the writers would now be easier,
that it would encourage editors to take greater risks in publishing
ambiguous works, and give a weapon to the opposition against

the hacks. If this comes to pass, the latter will feel much less sure of their ground in exposing "mistakes," and they will have to fight out their battles within the writers' organization instead of appealing to the Central Committee for arbitration. The composition of the new Secretariat of the Writers' Union, elected immediately after the Congress, showed that the conservatives will now have to contend with formidable opposition from liberals, who wish to free literature from the trammels of the past. It included Tvardovski and Panfyorov, the editors of *Novy mir* and *Oktiabr* respectively, both of whom were temporarily relieved of their posts by Surkov a few years earlier for pursuing an overly independent line in their editorial policies. Surkov himself was dismissed as First Secretary of the Union and replaced by K. A. Fedin, who takes a rather cautious but tolerant view of the new mood among the writers. In his speech at the Congress he in fact came out on the side of freedom to experiment in form: "We value and respect innovators in science, industry, and agriculture. The question is, may a writer rest content with the working methods of the nineteenth century?" It seems highly likely that under this new leadership there may at last appear in the Soviet Union some literary works of lasting and distinctive artistic quality. We may see the emergence of a new style, which will give adequate expression to the age. It is idle to speculate what new forms might arise, but the author of the *Esprit* article offers one intriguing suggestion:

> It put my hope in a phantasmagorical art, with hypothesis instead of a Purpose, an art in which the grotesque will replace realist description of everyday life. This is what would best correspond to the spirit of our epoch. Let the *outré* images of Hoffmann, Dostoevski, Goya, Chagall, and Mayakovski . . . teach us how to be truthful with the aid of absurd fantasy.

Postscript

The events of the past two years lend some substance to the note of optimism with which this article concluded. Yet the path of progress has not been smooth, and the dangers of a return to the type of controls imposed in the 1957–58 period are still present.

The change in the climate the followed the Third Writers' Congress may be illustrated by two examples: In December, 1958, the Union of Writers of the R.S.F.S.R., a recently created body dominated by reactionaries (its president is L. Sobolev, who made quite a career out of baiting revisionists in the difficult months after Hungary), held its constituent congress. Several of the speakers made vicious attacks on Pasternak, and one of them added a new charge, namely that of "corrupting youth." It appears that two young poets, Pankratov and Kharabarov, students of the Moscow Literary Institute, had fallen under the spell of Pasternak, made "secret" visits to his *dacha*, written verse in imitation of him, hung his portrait in the Institute hostel, and circulated a manuscript copy of *Doctor Zhivago* among their fellow students. For these heinous offenses they "underwent their deserved punishment"—expulsion from the Komsomol.

In August, 1960, the Central Asian newspaper *Kazakhstanskaia pravda* announced that the two well-known young Moscow poets Pankratov and Kharabarov had arrived in Kazakhstan on a travel warrant issued by the Central Committee of the Komsomol and had honored the editorial board of the paper with a visit. The announcement was accompanied by two specimens of their work. Kharabarov's poem is entitled "On an Untrodden Path" and is a moving appeal for the right to go one's way. Evidently there has been very powerful intervention on their behalf since December, 1958, and it seems highly likely that their total rehabilitation was made possible by the changes at the Third Congress of Writers in May, 1959.

The second example is an interview given by Ehrenburg in August to a correspondent of *Literature and Life*. He said there what he had said in a rather more disguised way in an article on Chekhov published just before the Writers' Congress. Among other things, he makes an unprecedented appeal for "solidarity" among writers:

In the very difficult times of the eighties, Chekhov spoke of the solidarity of the writers of that generation. Is it not time to give serious thought to the question of solidarity among writers in our Soviet epoch? Savage attacks on young writers, cliquishness, and novels in which authors settle accounts with their fellow writers [i.e., Kochetov's infamous Brothers Vershov] would be incompatible with such solidarity....*

In addition, a considerable amount of interesting work has appeared in the literary journals in the past two years, no doubt as a result of the improved atmosphere since the Writers' Congress. What is striking about it is its unorthodoxy, in formal rather than political terms, by the traditional standards of socialist realism. There has been no reversal to the openly "critical" realism of 1956, but there is a new prose style of almost Chekhovian objectivity, and the once-obligatory distortion of Soviet reality, with the presentation of shortcomings in human nature as transitory "survivals of capitalism" untypical of Soviet society, is much less common than it was. *Three, Seven, Ace*, by the gifted young writer V. Tendryakov is a case in point. It would have been unthinkable a few years ago to suggest, however obliquely, that it would be possible for a whole collective of honest Soviet working men to be corrupted by one evil man. Even more striking is the ending, which leaves the reader in doubt as to whether justice—even socialist justice—will be done or not. Evtushenko's short poem "The Nihilist" also flies in the face of officially accepted ideas by suggesting that a person who harbors "dangerous thoughts" is not necessarily a bad citizen.

Since the end of 1960, however, there have been ominous signs of a comeback on the part of the neo-Stalinists. In July of that year, Kochetov, writing in the popular illustrated weekly *Ogonyok*, described *Novy mir* as "that paltry little journal that spreads its nihilistic poison among our intelligentsia," and his friend in Leningrad, V. Arkhipov, writing in the neo-Stalinist *Neva*, attacked Ilya Ehrenburg for undermining the principle of

---

* This is not the only example of Ehrenburg's recent writings that places him clearly in the camp of the "progressives." In various articles and reviews, as well as in his memoirs—published serially in *Novy mir*—Ehrenburg has made a determined attempt to remove the Stalinist blights from the Soviet literary scene.

partiinost and denounced the *Literary Gazette* for publishing an article by the American writer Norman Cousins, calling it "cosmopolitan balderdash." At the end of 1960, though probably not as a result of this attack, Smirnov was dismissed as editor of the *Literary Gazette* and replaced by his deputy, Kosolapov. Worst of all, at the beginning of 1961, Kochetov was appointed editor of one of the leading literary monthlies, *Oktiabr*, succeeding Feod Panfyorov, who died in 1960.*

It is not certain that the re-emergence of Kochetov, which could scarcely have happened without strong official support, is a sign of some impending regression in Soviet literature. The most likely explanation is that the Party wishes to restore the balance between the two camps that now, for the first time since the 1920's, openly exist among the Soviet writers. There is even a clear identification of certain journals with both sides: The monthlies *Novy mir* and *Yunost* and the biweekly *Literary Gazette* are on the whole "progressive," while *Neva* (and hence, presumably *Oktiabr*) and the biweekly *Literatura i zhizn* are "reactionary." This is, perhaps the way the Party likes things. The "progressives," who are now overwhelmingly strong in numbers, are, it is no doubt considered, best kept in check by having the threat of total reaction always hanging over them. This is a better and more intelligent way of imposing restraint on them than by gross administrative interference. Whether the Party will continue to tolerate this unprecedented "two-camp" situation or whether it will find itself compelled—much of course depends on the international situation—to arbitrate decisively in favor of one side or the other, remains to be seen. For the moment, at any rate, there is a free struggle between them.

---

* Just before his death, Panfyorov completed a novel that was attacked for its near-pornographical elements. The author of these lines, who was Panfyorov's host during his month's visit to England in 1958, is introduced at one point, under the thinly disguised name of "Mister Wood," in the role of an unsuccessful pimp.

Recent Soviet Literature

——GEORGE GIBIAN

THE LITERARY FARE recently available to the Soviet public has
been more varied than at any time since the tightening of controls
over literature early in Stalin's reign. In some ways, it is true, the
liberalization of the years 1954–56 has been arrested or reversed.
Works containing serious attacks on the established order—such
as those, for example, printed late in 1956 in *Literary Moscow*,
Vol. II—are no longer being published. On the other hand, certain favorable consequences of the thaw of the mid-1950's were
slow in working themselves out and are only now reflected in
what is being printed.

The main improvements, from the point of view of the Soviet
reader, have been: (a) a more plentiful supply of translations
from contemporary foreign literatures; (b) more editions of
Russian classics; (c) the reprinting of works by Soviet authors
who, to all intents and purposes, have been rehabilitated after
years of suppression (Olesha, Babel, Zoshchenko); (d) more
"entertainment" literature and undidactic works, particularly
short stories of adventure; (e) efforts at innovations in technique,
especially in drama; (f) the rise of young authors—most valuable
from the point of view of art—who write feelingly of the purely
personal lives of ordinary individuals.

While the main stress of current publishing remains on Soviet
works, it is important to remember that in Soviet Russia, even
more than in other countries, what is published is not identical
with what is read. Foreign and Russian classics and contemporary foreign writing primarily seem to capture the interest of

390

many Soviet readers. One would probably be justified in claiming that a correlation exists between the level of education and literary sophistication of a Soviet reader and the degree of interest he takes in foreign writing—far greater than his interest in new Soviet books. It may be that workers on farms and in factories (about whose reading tastes outsiders admittedly know least) constitute the element that takes current Soviet literature most seriously. At the other end of the spectrum, some members of the metropolitan university and intellectual elite privately profess to be utterly bored by contemporary Soviet writing. The literary intellectuals are preoccupied with whatever they can find of the exciting, different, to them eternally *avant-garde*, Western writing.

Recently, the writer attended a meeting in Leningrad at which the editors of *Voprosy literatury* (*Problems of Literature*) announced the results of a questionnaire they had submitted to their readers. One of the responses reported was the readers' desire for more discussion of modern foreign literature. The work of Remarque was frequently cited in answers to the questionnaire. (Later in the same evening, one of the official speakers reported in another connection that the readers had urged franker treatment of love and eroticism in Soviet literature. Remarque is famous in Russia for writing about sex, a possible explanation why his work was frequently mentioned.) Laxness, the Icelandic Nobel and Stalin Prize holder, is also popular in Soviet Russia. The Russian readers, it became clear through the reports read at the conference, have been asking for critical analyses of foreign works and for articles about the "artistic side" and the "technical experience" of foreign authors.

The extraordinary interest of Soviet citizens in Western books is evident to anyone who has had any conversations about literature inside the Soviet Union. The subject comes up in every discussion. Hearing the report at the *Voprosy literatury* meeting served only to confirm—statistically and officially—the validity of the writer's own experiences.

During two brief visits to Russia, in 1956 and 1960, I asked everyone with whom I spoke what Soviet readers were reading— or, as I sometimes phrased it: "What is there that is really worthwhile in current Soviet literature—what would you advise me not to miss in the mass that is being published?" I asked this of students, officers I met on trains, representatives of the Writers' Union, artists living on the thin margin between official tolerance and rejection. The differences in the answers were largely predictable. The officials of the Writers' Union took a very rosy view, finding many writers of promise, while a poet who opposed controls held that there were few works worth reading. The official spokesmen would include praise for the Stalinist Kochetov (author of the antirevisionist *Yershov Brothers*); the dissidents would only jeer when Kochetov's name was brought up. An official tried to dissuade me from reading Panfyorov's latest book ("It is not necessary to read that," he said), though others recommended it.

Allowing for inevitable differences, however, there was, in some respects, a surprising degree of agreement in November, 1960, during my last visit. Certain names recurred on the list of recommended authors. These were, first of all, established writers of the top rank, like Sholokhov and Simonov, who had published new novels. In second place were a number of authors, ranging from middle-aged to very young, some of whom had sprung to the center of literary attention suddenly, who were unknown a year earlier but were now being watched by everyone interested in literature. The appearance of these new names on the literary scene is the most hopeful aspect of Soviet literature today.

The writers most frequently mentioned were: Sergey Antonov, Yuri Bondarev, Georgi Baklanov, Sergey Voronin, Yuri Kazakov, Yuri Nagibin, Viktor Nekrasov, Anatoly Kuznetsov, Eduard Shim, Vera Ketlinskaia, Vladimir Soloukhin, V. Tendriakov, and Yulian Semyonov.

Two Outstanding Novels

One of the most important novels of recent years is Konstantin Simonov's *The Living and the Dead*, published toward the end of 1960. Like all Simonov's works, *The Living and the Dead* is slick, competent, and very readable. To some extent it is reminiscent of *The Days and the Nights*, Simonov's famous novel on

Stalingrad written during World War II. The present novel, though a more reflective work, also deals with the war. It relates the adventures of an officer named Sintsov stationed in Grodno (then Poland), who happens to be vacationing in the Crimea at the time of the German attack. Sintsov attempts to return to Grodno with his wife, Masha. Traveling as far west as he can, he discovers how quickly the Germans have advanced, how inaccurate the official Soviet communiqués are. His odyssey in search of his unit is a modern equivalent of Fabrice's confused wanderings in Stendhal's *Charterhouse of Parma:* trucks, disabled tanks, wounded soldiers, Russians and Germans mix kaleidoscopically in a situation in which nobody knows where the front lines are or who is infiltrating whom. Unable to find his own unit, Sintsov joins another outfit, fights in it bravely, and is seriously wounded. A friend, expecting him either to die or fall into enemy hands, takes his papers away from him and leaves him behind unconscious.

Sintsov regains consciousness and fights his way back to the Russian lines. His worst experiences—and the book's main theme —only begin at this point. Since he has no documents, he is suspected, challenged, questioned. He manages to slip into Moscow and thereby adds to his troubles: He is considered a potential deserter, possibly even a German agent. The question of trust in human beings becomes one pole of the novel: "What is more valuable, papers or people," the hero asks. The other pole, related to trust, is truth. Simonov's characters watch Messerschmitts outmaneuver and shoot down Russian fighters and bombers; they think of former assurances that in Spain and Mongolia their planes proved superior to foreign models. Recurrently they ask themselves the question: Why were they not told the truth about the strength of the enemy? Whose fault is it that the Soviet armies were unprepared? Why were the Germans able to penetrate deeply into Russia?

Serpilin is another character in the novel who embodies Simonov's challenge. He is a former instructor at the War School who had specialized in the study of foreign armies. Accused in the 1930's of overestimating the strength of the German armed forces, Serpilin had been arrested, personally interrogated by

Yezhov twice, and imprisoned. During the war, he fights in the field as commander of the unit in which Sintsov serves.

The distrust toward a brave fighter who cannot explain how he lost his papers, the lies to the population about the real state of affairs, the evidence of officialdom's "not looking the truth in the eye" and failing to prepare adequately for the war—all merge into one complex through which Simonov expresses doubts about the prewar leadership and implicitly accuses it.

The appeal of Simonov's book is broad. Sheer narrative interest is high; the novelist is a master of creating suspense. There are escapes, break-throughs, tales of daring resistance and super-human endurance. To satisfy some readers, Simonov includes a few scenes of conventional Soviet piety, such as a prison scene in which Serpilin, himself the innocent victim of Yezhov's purge, beats a fellow prisoner—a Trotskyist—to a pulp for saying the revolution is dead and the Party corrupt. But the main impor-tance of the book lies in the implications of the questions it raises.

The only recent book that may have surpassed *The Living and the Dead* in popularity in the Soviet Union is Mikhail Sholokhov's concluding volume of *Virgin Soil Upturned* (1959), published in the West under the title *Harvest on the Don* (1961).

The first part of Sholokhov's work, dealing with the brutal years of war Communism, was published more than a quarter century ago, in 1932; the concluding volume completes the action with the victory and establishment of the Communist order. The White conspiracy in the Don region is crushed, its leaders appre-hended. The Bolshevik hero, Davidov, has shaken off the seduc-tive slut Lushka Nagulnova and become engaged to a virginal girl. He dies, but he dies as a Soviet martyr, a triumphant hero. In the village of Gremyachy Log, Soviet power and collective farming are firmly enthroned.

This robust novel is very uneven. Dull scenes describing Party meetings and agricultural problems overlie the exciting story of the conspiracy. Yet Sholokhov's genius occasionally does reappear in its full power. He still has an ear alert to the strong speech of Cossack peasants, a heart attuned to their primitive, earthy passions, and a mind obsessed by the horrible, fascinating enormities of all the beating, killing, conspiring, and raping his blood-soaked homeland has endured.

The best parts of the book, which are as good as anything in *And Quiet Flows the Don* (his first volume) are those reminiscences and interpolated tales in which Sholokhov deals with events of the past, particularly the Civil War—tales of violence and torment, human suffering and exaltation. Occasional diversion is provided by comic passages suggestive of William Faulkner's scenes of rustic humor.

The siren, Lushka Nagulnova, eventually marries a mining engineer and climbs into the new Soviet technocratic bourgeoisie. She has lost her fire, her body, her lust, trading them in for respectability and self-satisfied fatness. It is evident that Sholokhov shares the feelings of his character Razmiotnov, who says: "I felt a touch of regret for the old Lushka, young, smart with her tongue, and beautiful. Now you might almost say I'd seen her in a dream a long, long time ago, once upon a time, so to speak, but never lived with her in the same village. Well, that's our life, boys, that's the way things go."

Sholokhov, too, seems to yearn for the bad, wild days, which were also the heroic days. For all the horror, the bloodshed, for all the resistance to Communism and collectivization—due, as Sholokhov sees it, to human greed and blindness—the old days were the time when human experience was vivid. The mining engineer on the city's paved streets in modern industrialized Russia may gain Sholokhov's formal endorsement (he ends his book with a look forward to the horizons of the future), but not his emotional allegiance. That belongs to the preindustrial days, of which he gives us a glimpse here and there through the flashbacks and reminiscences in his *Virgin Soil Upturned*.

Millions of Soviet readers have read Sholokhov's novel, first in magazine form, then as a book. Sholokhov was awarded a Lenin Prize for it.

The Short Story Today

One difference between the current crop of Soviet short stories and those of both the Stalinist period and the years 1954–57 is that now adventure stories are more prominent. This is true not only, as one would expect, of the shorter, less pretentious stories of a popular magazine like *Ogonyok*, but also of the monthlies—*Novy mir*, *Neva*, *Oktiabr*, and others. In almost every issue one finds stories aimed at attracting the reader's interest primarily through thrilling action. Many are set in exotic locations.

This category of fiction can be considered an effort to give relief from the eternal didacticism of Soviet life. The stories have color; they supply some amusement for its own sake. None that the writer has read is a masterpiece, but many are competently done. A number of them are fairly slick and craftsmanlike war stories. Just like their colleagues in the West, Soviet writers are now going through a "second wave" of war fiction. V. Korablinov's "The Secret Shelter of the Forests" (*Neva*, January–February, 1960), for instance, is an adventure story of guerrilla warfare against the Germans. Leonid Pervomaysky's "Coffee, Budapest Style" (*Ogonyok*, No. 27, 1960) portrays a Hungarian Communist who, having fought with Bela Kun and fled to the U.S.S.R., returns to Budapest as a Soviet soldier after the city's capture by the Soviet army. The main interest of the story lies in the soldier's search for his mother, whom he has not seen for over twenty years. He is sent from one address to another until he finally finds her, and in a simple ending she brews coffee for him from beans he had sent her years before from abroad. The author leans heavily on the sentimental possibilities of the returning-son-seeking-his-mother theme. He does not, however, take advantage of the wartime situation to preach patriotism or Communist ideology.

A more interesting story is I. Efremov's "Afaneor, the Daughter of Akharkhellen" (*Neva*, January, 1960), which has the Central Sahara as its setting. Tiressuen, a young man of the Tuareg tribe, is offered employment as a guide by a French expedition. The French party is portrayed as a combination of sincere, scholarly archaeologists looking for the ruins of an ancient city, and disguised military officers secretly looking for sites for nuclear tests that will contaminate vast regions of the Sahara.

Tiressuen's tribe believes that many years previously a man they call El-Issey-Ef (to wit, the Russian traveler Eliseef) had

come to their land, and unlike other white men, had demonstrated genuine respect and interest in the Tuaregs. At the urging
of Afaneor, a woman of the tribe, Tiressuen consents to lead the
French expedition on condition that he be promised a trip to
the Soviet Union as his reward. Afaneor wants Tiressuen to take
a look at the homeland of El-Issey-Ef, which in her opinion must
be superior to other white men's homelands.

Tiressuen is the noble hero throughout the story. When the
expedition's truck breaks down, he saves everyone by walking
alone through the desert on a five-day search for help. Such
sections of the story are a gripping, even if hackneyed, tale of
desert adventure, danger, and salvation in the nick of time.
Toward the end, however, political motifs and Russian nationalist
self-congratulation gain the upper hand, along with anticolonial-
ism, tributes to the Arabs, and attacks on French atomic tests in
the Sahara. For example, the author interweaves praise for the
noble desert savage with the theme of the superiority of Russians
(pre-1917 as well as Soviet) over other white men: "The soul
of the Russian sees more deeply into nature and has richer
feelings than the soul of other Europeans. That is why El-Issey-Ef
understood the desert nomads so well, and they understood him."
In the end, Tiressuen does visit Leningrad, enjoys a sympathetic
reception by the Russians, and returns enlightened about French
"designs" in the Sahara. The story ends with Tiressuen and
Afaneor watching with hostility the advance of a column of
French armored vehicles.

Thus Efremov weaves into his tale every possible thread of
interest. He flatters his Russian audience and pushes every stock
response button, but he does it so skillfully that even while one
is aware of the author's designs and the fallacies of his implications, one reads with absorption.

A story without any official propagandistic bias is I. Metter's
"Murat" (*Novy mir*, June, 1960). It follows a police dog's life
from the moment of his purchase by the Leningrad criminal-
investigation police to his retirement from active service because
of bullet injuries to his nervous system. Murat, the dog, is a great
hero, a skilled tracker and brave fighter. The story describes a
number of missions on which Murat was sent with his policeman-

guide. In Rin-Tin-Tin fashion, Murat caught criminals, found stolen goods, and attacked evil-doers.

The author employs two other time-tested devices to catch human interest: a detailed, almost documentary account of the training of police dogs and police methods; and a sentimental ending, in which the dog, unfit for further service and about to be destroyed, is saved after much supplication by his guide and permitted to live out his days as a "pensioner" in the police kennels.

The increase of adventure stories in recent years may have contributed to a certain decrease in the popularity of two other categories of fiction—"production" stories (dealing with problems of factory management or labor) and collective-farm stories, both of which were prominent under Stalin, and again from 1954 to 1958. The adventure stories to some extent are escape literature. By turning to a war fought twenty years ago, to the Sahara, or to crime detection, the authors offer something exciting and different from the readers' day-to-day lives. At the same time, the writers forestall possible criticism for "turning their backs on topical issues" by stressing the documentary value of their works. Many of the stories begin or end with a link to journalistic reporting. In the conclusion to "Murat," for instance, the author states that he wrote the story after seeing in the Leningrad Police Museum a stuffed police dog that had taken part in 4,000 operations and had helped to apprehend 2,858 criminals. "Coffee, Budapest Style" contains a paragraph claiming that all the events described had actually taken place. "Afaneor" is topical and praiseworthy from the Party's point of view because it under-scores the Soviet propaganda line on colonialism and nuclear testing.

Questions and Negations

A few stories have appeared recently that continue the so-called "negative trend" of the years 1954–57 by dealing with deli-cate topics or by subtly challenging the stereotypes of the officially accepted versions of Soviet life. For example, Sergey Antonov in "First Voyage" (*Yunost*, October, 1960), describes a

newspaperman's trip to a remote lumber district in Siberia and
his gradual discovery that Kolya Khromov, ostensibly a hero of
labor who had been honored for such feats as driving his truck
100,000 kilometers without any repair, is in reality a nihilist, a
cynic, and a criminal.

In the first interview, Kolya reels off to the journalist the
Soviet honorific clichés about himself: "My character was formed
in the period of the postwar Five Year Plans, when our nation
achieved great triumphs of labor and the bright stars of the
sputniks directed themselves toward remote skies." Kolya even
offers to lend the journalist an old clipping describing his accomplishments, so as to save him the trouble of having to write his
own story. But Antonov's narrator hears hints of foul play. He
discovers that Kolya has been dumping gasoline in the woods
in order to simulate mileage, and cheating on production records.

The newspaperman turns amateur detective. He talks to
Kolya's girl friend. A fantastic story of fraud and collusion is
revealed in which the main villain is the *tekhnoruk* Akim, Kolya's
superior, who has corrupted the young man. Yet more interesting
than the bare facts of the "economic crimes" uncovered are
Kolya's cynical pronouncements about human nature, which run
counter to all Soviet ideology. This man, outwardly a Soviet
hero, despises fellow beings, work, love. In a diatribe, which
begins with his view of his girl friend, he says:

Here in the woods it is boring for girls to spend their eve-
nings alone, so they look for someone to pet with. . . . Today
she likes candy, tomorrow she will like a pickled cucumber.
. . . Men are no better, of course. On the whole, man is a
slimy creature. Everybody thinks only of himself and does
not care a hoot for anyone else. That is the way it has been
and the way it is going to be. They talk about building Communism, but they try to grab the most they can, as quickly
as they can, all they need, at the cost of the Communism of
the future. . . . I respect a goat more than a man. In comparison with a goat, man has only one advantage, and that
is that he has more intelligence. And as far as intelligence
goes, I am not sure if it is an advantage or a disadvantage.

It is not important to have a lot of intelligence. The main thing is to use it. Intelligent people invented atomic energy, but they did not have enough sense to send powdered sugar to the lumberworkers. That is intelligence for you. Look into man's soul: all greed, cowardice, lies. Intelligence gives way before greed, cowardice, and lies.

On the whole, this story of lumberworkers—whose way of life is normally glorified in the U.S.S.R.—seems to convey the message that surface appearances are not always the reality, that what seems real may be pretense.

Two stories by Sergey Voronin do not challenge Party dogma, but raise embarrassing questions. In "At the Birthplace" (*Neva*, September, 1959), Voronin describes the dilemma of Ivan Kasimov, a veteran who returns to his native village years after the war to find that Vasily, a fellow villager who, as a prisoner of war, had joined the Germans and guarded Russian prisoners, was living at home again, with the story of his wartime treason unknown to anybody. Ivan speaks with Vasily, who admits his guilt and pleads with Ivan not to denounce him. Vasily makes a moving case for himself: "I wanted so badly to live," he affirms. Ivan feels a great revulsion, yet to some extent also pity. After much hesitation, he leaves the village without having informed on Vasily.

Sympathy for a traitor, indulgence for a collaborator—such are the emotions about which the author compels his readers to meditate. In Russia, the subject of the story was certain to stir old, deep memories, and the inevitable result was controversy. *Literaturnaia gazeta* published an attack on Voronin which in effect made it appear that he and not his character had been the turncoat.

In another story, "The Blue Danube" (*Neva*, November, 1959), Voronin depicts the successive stages of a quarrel between two former friends, Ivan and Nikolay. As he presents it, the increasing bitter enmity between the two was guided and made inevitable by some force greater than either of them. One of them hits the other and breaks his jaw; he is sent to prison. When the prisoner is released, the other man, feeling threatened, stabs his former friend with a butcher knife and, in turn, is sentenced to five years in jail.

Voronin's objectivity of narration and his failure to assign any blame for the brutal acts of these country ruffians are striking. He sees every deed from the point of view of the character who committed it; in that perspective, the act seems innocent or inevitable. Thus Ivan "was quiet and slow to anger." But Nikolay "had drunk his vodka, pulled his shirt out of his trousers, and this made Ivan lose his patience." Seen from the other side, however: "Nikolay did not like to fight. But it seemed to him very insulting that Ivan did not give him his money back, that he spilled vodka on him, that he hit him in the chest."

In this story, as in the earlier one, Voronin shows sympathy for the weak and fallen. He concludes his story by reporting the reaction of the wife of one of the men, who "shrugged her shoulders, not understanding where this hostility between them had come from and why it was necessary to man." Voronin himself seems to share this attitude of puzzled wonderment; certainly he does not convey the official Soviet attitude of condemning the wrongdoer and using the example to make optimistic proposals for the elimination of crime.

The New Wave in Soviet Fiction

For several years after the war, Vera Panova stood out as the one Soviet author of talent who wrote about the emotional life of her characters without feeling obliged to involve them in topical industrial, agricultural, or political concerns. She has now been joined by various other writers, for the most part young men who, unlike their Stalinist predecessors, show no interest in writing for the sake of illustrating current public issues or the Party line, and who, unlike the "dissidents" of the mid-fifties, are equally uninterested in any "negative" movement based on a reversal of Party desiderata. These writers (men like Sergey Antonov, Eduard Shim, Yuri Nagibin, Yuri Kazakov) simply turn their backs on public affairs. Their sole concern is to present —as delicately as possible and for the story's sake alone—the small events of daily life. They often write about people who are victims of fate. As is to be expected, love preoccupies them, and unrequited, unhappy love is more frequent in their stories than happy and married love. Much in their works reminds us of the traditions of Turgenev, Chekhov, and Bunin.

A recent sketch by Eduard Shim, "Night Journey" (*Pravda*, March 5, 1961), exemplifies this type of story. It is a brief account of a trip by truck. The chief passenger is a girl going to see her fiancé. Previously married, she had been deserted by her husband, a scoundrel, and left with a son, but has not dared to tell her present fiancé about the child. On this night journey she is traveling to her fiancé's house in order to tell him the truth. The sketch solves nothing. We do not even know the outcome of the conversation between the lovers. Shim merely suggests a delicate human situation—a girl's fear of being rejected because of having a child, her need to tell her young man about it, the involvement of other people in her predicament.

The best writers in this genre are Kazakov and Nagibin. Yuri Kazakov, a young man, writes stories perhaps still more melancholy and subtle than Nagibin's and Antonov's. They are imbued with a sense of life's ironies. He writes of lovers who have parted because the girl fell in love with someone else; or lovers of whom one is married, who meet casually yet fall deeply in love, spend only one night together, and then must part— questioning whether "this was really love," whether it brought more pain or more happiness.

In his story "At the Railroad Stop," Kazakov describes a simple girl, very much in love, saying good-by to her boy, the local weight-lifting champion, who is about to take a train from their collective farm to a town where he will receive expert coaching. The boy, impatient to leave both the village and the girl, thinks only of his future athletic career, of his eventual successes in Moscow. The story builds to a cruel climax, when the boy, from an already moving train, shouts to the girl: "No, I shall never come back here, no!"

Kazakov's story "The Renegade" (*Oktiabr*, July, 1959) is typical of his lyrical stories at their best. Egor is a "young man who is already a drunkard." He lives in a riverside hut, working as a ferryman and keeper of four lights on his stretch of the river.

He once had a wife, who, however, drank too much vodka one night, tried to dance on the thin ice, broke through, and drowned before Egor's eyes. Now Alenka, a girl from a nearby village, comes to see him on three-day visits. Thus Egor lives the life of a semi-derelict, a drunkard who spends his time sleeping, drinking, daydreaming about his service in the navy, and from time to time putting up hunters, to whom he sings and tells boastful stories in exchange for their vodka.

Egor, then, is disreputable; he is far from a Soviet hero. Yet the author does not moralize or condemn. On the contrary, Kazakov describes the solitary, broken-down Egor with sympathy, and, when he is singing, even with admiration. The story concludes with an account of a ritualistic, heroic "duet" by Egor and Alenka. They choose a proper place outdoors and sing old, soul-stirring Russian songs. Both feel, at such moments, as if their hearts might burst: "It is sweet, it is torture." The two characters, in other respects insignificant, seem to Kazakov to deserve attention and, in their passion for music, to achieve a certain simple nobility.

Yuri Nagibin is more widely known in Russia than Kazakov. His first story was published in 1939, when he was nineteen; selections from his latest collection, *Clean Ponds*, were printed in *Znamia* (January, 1961). His stories are usually less poetic, more factual than Kazakov's, but they, too, focus on psychological analysis. Nagibin is aware of the ironies arising out of the failures of communication between men. His stories are usually bittersweet. His view of human nature is far more complex and less optimistic than the official Soviet view. Thus he is interested in the confusion of a girl who reaches puberty ("Before the Holiday," *Rasskazy 1959 g.*); in the inability of a game warden to say what he wants to say to a visiting novelist, and the latter's error in taking the warden for a drunken country fool ("Conversation," *Oktiabr*, January, 1960); and generally in human frustration as well as in men's small joys and triumphs.

Like Kazakov, Nagibin focuses his art on everyday incidents and ephemeral impressions. This, together with his utter disinterest in public issues, makes his work stand out in sharp contrast to the bulk of officially approved Soviet literature.

Among the most talented writers of fiction are Viktor Nekrasov —the author of *The Second Night* (*Novy mir*, May, 1960) and the stirring tale *Kira Georgievna* (*Novy mir*, June, 1961)—and V. Tendriakov, whose latest work is *The Trial* (*Novy mir*, April, 1961). The brightest stars in the realm of Russian poetry are Andrei Voznesensky and Evgeny Evtushenko.

Innovation At All Cost

In other areas of literary expression, there are also signs of change and innovation. In the Russian theater, for example, the great popular successes of the day are plays whose only claim to attention is that they are different from the run-of-the-mill repertory. Unfortunately, the mere fact of novelty is not a guarantee of quality. The greatest hit of the past two seasons is Arbuzov's *Irkutsk Story*. When I visited Russia in November, 1960, it was impossible to find tickets to any Moscow production; I finally did obtain one in Leningrad. The play centers around a flighty girl who, after flirting with many men, marries the one really serious man who is in love with her. She settles down; they have twins. Then her husband drowns while trying to save a child. One of the girl's former suitors returns; he claims he has now matured to the point where he can truly love her. She postpones her decision—and the play ends.

To the Russians, this play is exciting. It deals with love; it presents situations of decision-making in love and marriage. It moves the audience to frequent tears—especially in the scenes when the husband awaits the children's birth, and later when he drowns. Moreover, the play is novel in technique. In a departure from the stilted forms of socialist realism, it uses a chorus. In the production I saw, men dressed in grayish uniforms (rather like elevator operators) stood on a pyramidlike structure and solemnly commented on the events taking place.

The audience wept and applauded. The play is indeed "new and different" by Soviet standards, but it seemed to me no better than the average soap opera on American radio or TV. It was a tissue of sentimental clichés. In addition to being naïve *Kitsch*, Arbuzov's play is pretentious and takes itself very seriously.

Another interesting facet of literature is the remarkable number of memoirs and autobiographies now being published in Russia. Ilya Ehrenburg's *People, Years, Life* has been appearing in installments in *Novy mir*. It describes his Bohemian days in Paris forty-five years ago, his acquaintance with Picasso, Rivera, and other artists. Konstantin Paustovsky has been publishing his memoirs in a five-volume cycle, *A Tale About a Life*. The last part, *A Jump South*, deals with the exciting post-revolutionary days in the Abkhazian state in Sukhumi. Kaverin has published sketches about his childhood, his early loves, his father.

The reasons for the popularity of such memoir literature are not difficult to find. Since the thaw, writers are a little freer in referring to past events and experiences. Thus Paustovsky now mentions his meetings with Isaac Babel, while Ehrenburg makes favorable comments on French civil liberties and Bohemian life in Paris. To the reading public, such memoirs are exciting for reasons similar to those that make Mediterranean and North Sea cruises on the *Pobeda* and *Gruziia* popular among Soviet tourists: they are windows opening on different forms of life.

By the same token, however, Soviet readers still do not even know of the existence of many important foreign authors, and they still chafe at their inability to obtain translations (not to mention originals) of works by some authors of whom they do know. Reading (and life) in Russia still seems to them uniform, gray, in comparison with what they suspect exists in the West— hence their drive to see or read or discuss anything foreign, un-Soviet.

Literary criticism in Russia continues to languish. Reviews and learned studies still usually bog down in the marshes of such topics as the "positive hero" and the "representation of contemporary reality." It is difficult to exaggerate the dullness of much current book reviewing. The situation improves when there is a controversy over some work, as there was over V. Tendryakov's novel, *After the Running Day*. Then, at least, certain issues come into the open, differences of opinion are heard. It is perhaps a good sign that I. Vinogradov's long article in the January, 1961, issue of *Voprosy literatury*, which seems to aspire at summing up and concluding the Tendryakov controversy, takes a rather liberal position. A similarly tolerant attitude is implicit in a recent article in *Literaturnaia gazeta* (March 2, 1961) by K. Bukovsky, "Story or Sketch," which looks with favor on Sergey Antonov's provocative "First Voyage."

To sum up, much in Soviet literature remains what it was: stereotyped, tendentious writing on public, contemporary themes. The departure of Smirnov from his influential post as editor of *Literaturnaia gazeta* and the appointment of Kochetov as the chief editor of *Oktiabr* are recent evidences of the power of men standing for an "antirevisionist," strict Party line in culture.

Nevertheless, there is now in existence a whole corpus of a "new literature" that presumes a new kind of reader and addresses itself to a different aspect of the human personality. One could even say that it is aimed at the larger, more complete human being. It does not assume that its audience is composed of "economic men" or political-social Party enthusiasts. Rather it demands a response based on the presence, in the reader, of emotional subtlety and of sensitivity to the nuances of human relationships.

In 1927, in his short novel *Envy*, Yuri Olesha created Ivan Babichev and Nikolai Kavalerov, two characters who feared that human emotions were doomed in Soviet Russia and that only machinelike human beings would survive. The two men organized a "conspiracy of feelings" in protest against the threatened de-emotionalization of life. The literature of the late Stalinist years seemed to confirm many of the fears of these "conspirators." However, the "new writing" of the last few years offers reassurance insofar as the survival of feelings is concerned. It not only assumes the existence of a lasting interest in man's private, emotional life, but tacitly gives this interest primacy over other areas of human concern.

In a programmatic editorial statement in *Oktiabr* (February, 1961), its new editor, Kochetov, sarcastically attacked those who thought "the road to Communism" had anything to do with Ilya Ehrenburg's views on Chekhov and Stendhal, formalism in painting, and "that world they call the world of feelings." Party-line ridicule cannot, however, change the evidence that the "world of feelings" has appeal for many Soviet readers, that they find in the new literature something fresh and creative, something that adds a lost dimension to life and evokes in their consciousness a response long dormant but never dead.

СВОЕВРЕМЕННЫЕ РАЗМЫШЛЕНИЯ

В то утро в мавзолее был похоронен Сталин,
А вечер был обычен — прозрачен и хрустален.
Шагал я тихо, мирно,
Наедине с Москвой
И вот что думал, верно,
Как парень с головой:
Эпоха зрелищ кончена,
Пришла эпоха хлеба.
Перекур объявлен
У штурмовавших небо.
Перемотать портянки
Присел на час народ,
В своих ботинках спящий
Нивесть который год.

Нет, я не думал этого,
А думал я другое:
Что вот он был и нет его,
Гиганта и героя.
На брошенный, оставленный
Москва
            похожа
                    дом.
Как будем жить без Сталина?

Я посмотрел кругом:
Москва была не грустная, Москва была пустая.
Нельзя грузить без устали. Все до смерти устали.
Все спали, только дворники
Неистово мели,
Как будто рвали корни и
Скребли из-под земли,
Как будто выдирали из перезябшей почвы
Его приказов окрик, его декретов почерк:
Следы трехдневной смерти

Poems from the Underground

CONTEMPORARY REFLECTIONS

On that morning, in the mausoleum, Stalin was buried,
And the evening was ordinary—crystal clear and limpid.
I walked quietly, tranquilly,
Alone with Moscow
And here is what I thought, verily,
Like a clever fellow:
The epoch of spectacles has ended,
The epoch of bread has arrived.
A smoking-break has been declared
For those who have been storming the heavens.
The people, asleep in its shoes
For God knows how long
Has sat down for an hour
To rewind its footcloths.

No, I didn't think that,
I thought something else:
That here he was, and now he is not,
The giant and the hero.
Moscow is like
      a forsaken
         deserted
            house.
How will we live without Stalin?

I looked around:
Moscow did not lament, Moscow was vacant.
You cannot grieve unceasingly. All are tired to death.
Everyone was sleeping, only the janitors
Were furiously sweeping.
As if they were tearing at roots and
Raking from beneath the earth,
As if they were ripping from the frozen soil
The shriek of his orders, the handwriting of his decrees:
The traces of a three-day death

И старые следы —
Тридцатилетней власти,
Величья и беды.
Я шел всё дальше, дальше,
И предо мной предстали
Его дворцы, заводы —
Всё, что воздвигнул Сталин:
Высотных зданий башни,
Квадраты площадей...

Социализм был выстроен.
Посели в нем людей.

* * *

Надо, чтобы дети или звери,
Чтоб солдаты или, скажем, бабы,
К вам питали полное доверье
Или полюбили вас, хотя бы.

Обмануть детей не очень просто.
Баба тоже не пойдет за подлым,
Лошадь сбросит на скаку прохвоста,
А солдат поймет, где ложь, где подвиг.

Ну, а вас, разумных и ученых?
О, высокомудрые мужчины —
Вас водили за нос, как девчонок,
Как детей, вас за руку влачили.

Нечего ходить с улыбкой гордой
Многократно купленным за орден.
Что там толковать про смысл и разум,
Многократно проданный за фразу.

Я бывал в различных обстоятельствах,
Но видна бессмертная душа
Лишь в освобожденной от предательства
В слабенькой улыбке малыша.

And old traces—
Of a thirty-year reign,
Of grandeur and calamity.
I walked on and on
And before me rose
His palaces, factories—
Everything that Stalin built:
The towers of his skyscrapers,
The quadrangles of his squares. . . .

Socialism was constructed.
They settled people in it.

* * *

It is necessary that children or animals,
That soldiers or, say, women,
Should put their whole trust in you
Or love you, even.

To deceive children is not very simple.
Nor will a woman take up with a rascal,
A horse will throw a scoundrel from the saddle,
And a soldier will understand what is a lie, and what is valor.

But, you, you men of reason and scholars?
Oh, you Solons—
You were led by the nose, like silly girls,
Like children, you were dragged by the hand.

You have no reason to walk with a proud smile
You who were repeatedly bought for a medal.
What have you to say about wisdom and reason,
You have repeatedly sold yourself for a phrase.

I have been in various circumstances,
But the immortal soul can be seen
Only
          in the smile of a child
Weak, and free from treachery.

Лакирую действительность —
Исправляю стихи.
Перечесть удивительно:
И смирны и тихи,
И не только покорны
Всем законам страны —
Соответствуют норме!
Расписанью верны!

Чтобы с черного хода
Их пустили в печать,
Мне
     за правдой
          охоту
Поручили начать.
Чтоб дорога прямая
Привела их к рублю,
Я им руки ломаю.
Я им ноги рублю.
Выдаю с головою,
Лакирую и лгу.

Всё же кое-что скрою,
Кой-кого сберегу.
Самых сильных и бравых
Никому не отдам.

Я еще без поправок
Эту книгу издам!

*   *   *

Мы все ходили под богом,
У бога под самым боком.
Стоя на мавзолее,
Был он сильнее и злее,
Мудрее того, другого,
По имени Иегова,

I varnish reality—
I emend verses.
To reread them is astonishing:
They are compliant and tranquil,
And not only obedient
To all the laws of the land—
I meet my norm!
They correspond to the plan!

To get them into print
Through a back door
I have been commissioned
To begin
    to hunt
       down truth.
But for a direct road
To lead them to the ruble
I break their hands.
I hack off their legs.
I betray them utterly,
I varnish and I lie.

Nevertheless, some I shall hide,
Someone I shall keep safe.
The strongest and the bravest
I shall give up to no one.

I shall publish this book yet
Without corrections!

*   *   *

We all walked under god,
By god, at his very side.
Standing on the mausoleum,
He was more powerful and wrathful,
Wiser than that other,
Whose name is Jehovah,

Которого он низринул,
Извел, пережег на уголь,
А после из мрака вынул
И дал ему стол и угол.

Мы все ходили под богом,
У бога под самым боком...

Однажды я шел Арбатом.
Бог ехал в пяти машинах.
От страха почти горбата
В своих пальтишках мышиных
С ним рядом дрожала охрана.

И было поздно и рано.
Серело. Вставало утро.
Бог глянул жестоко и мудро,
Всепроницающим взглядом,
Всепонимающим оком...

Мы все ходили под богом
И даже стояли с ним рядом.

*   *   *

Я строю на песке, а тот песок
Еще недавно мне скалой казался.
Он был скалой, для всех скалой остался,
А для меня распался и потек.

Я мог бы руку долу опустить,
Я мог бы отдых пальцам дать корявым.
Я мог бы возмутиться и спросить,
За что меня и по какому праву?..

Но верен я строительной программе...
Прижат к стене, вися на волоске,
Я строю, на плывущем под ногами,
На уходящем из-под ног песке.

Whom he cast down,
Tormented, burned on hot coals,
Then pulled out from the blackness
And gave a corner and a stool.

We all were under god,
By god, at his very side. . . .

Once I was walking along the Arbat.
God was driving in five automobiles.
From fear almost hunched
In their mouse-colored coats
His guard trembled beside him.

And it was early and it was late.
It was turning gray. The dawn was rising.
God looked out cruelly and wisely,
With an all-piercing glance,
With an all-knowing eye. . . .

We all were under god
And even stood beside him.

*   *   *

I am building on sand, and that sand
Only recently seemed to me to be a rock.
It was a rock, and has remained a rock for everybody,
But for me it fell apart and began to flow away.

I might have thrown up my hands,
I might have given rest to my gnarled fingers.
I might have grown indignant and asked,
Why me, and by what right? . . .

But I am faithful to the construction program. . . .
Backed up against a wall, hanging by a hair,
I am building on sand which is flowing under my feet,
Slipping out from under my feet.

ЧЕЛОВЕК

Царь природы, венец творенья
Встал за сахаром для варенья.

За всеведеньем или бессмертьем
Он бы в очередь в эту не влез,
Но к вареньям куда безмерней
И значительней интерес.

Метафизикам не чета я
И морали ему не читаю:

Человек должен сытно кушать
И чаи с вареньем пивать,
А потом про бессмертие слушать
И всезнаньем мозги забивать.

*   *   *

Я судил людей и знаю точно,
Что судить людей совсем несложно —
Только погодя бывает тошно,
Если вспомнишь как-нибудь оплошно.

Кто они, мои четыре пуда
Мяса,
        чтоб судить чужое мясо?
Больше никого судить не буду.
Хорошо быть не вождем, а массой.

Хорошо быть педагогом школьным
Иль сидельцем в книжном магазине
Иль судьей...
                Каким судьей? Футбольным!

MAN

The sovereign of nature, the crown of creation
Queued up for sugar for his jam.

For omniscience or immortality
He would not have gotten into that line,
But how much greater and more significant
His interest in jam.

I am no metaphysician
And am not reading him a moral.

A man must eat his fill
And drink his tea with jam,
And afterward listen to stories of immortality
And stuff his head with omniscience.

*   *   *

I have judged people and know exactly,
That to judge people is quite simple—
Only later one is sick,
If he remembers somehow inadvertently.

What is my hundredthweight
Of flesh
   to judge another's flesh?
I shall never judge anyone again.
It is good to be not a leader, but one of the masses.

Good to be a school master
Or a salesman in a book store
Or a judge. . . .
   What kind of judge? A soccer referee!

Быть на матчах пристальным разиней.

Если сны приснятся этим судьям,
Так они во сне кричать не станут.
Ну, а мы? Мы закричим,
                         мы будем
Вспоминать былое неустанно.

Опыт мой особенный и скверный —
Как забыть его себя заставить?

Этот стих ошибочный, неверный.
Я неправ.
Пускай меня поправят.

ПРОПАГАНДА

Сегодня я ничему не верю —
Глазам — не верю.
Ушам — не верю.
Пощупаю — тогда, пожалуй, поверю.
Если наощупь — всё без обмана.

Мне вспоминаются хмурые немцы,
Печальные пленные сорок пятого года,
Стоявшие — руки по швам — на допросе.
Я спрашиваю — они отвечают:

— Вы верите Гитлеру? — Нет, не верю.
— Вы верите Герингу? — Нет, не верю.
— Вы верите Геббельсу? — О, пропаганда!
— А мне вы верите? — Минута молчания. —
— Господин комиссар, я вам не верю.
Всё пропаганда. Весь мир — пропаганда.

To be a rapt gawk at the matches.

If such judges dream,
They will not cry out in their sleep.
And us? We will scream,
                              we will
Remember the past unremittingly.

My experience is a special and vile one—
How can I force myself to forget it?

This poem is mistaken, untrue.
I am wrong.
Let them correct me.

PROPAGANDA

Today I don't believe anything—
My eyes—I don't believe.
My ears—I don't believe.
I'll feel it—then, perhaps, I'll believe.
When it can be touched—everything is without deception.

I recall the frowning Germans,
The sad prisoners of 1945,
Standing—hands at sides—at the interrogation.
I ask—they answer:

—Do you believe Hitler?—No, I don't believe.
—You believe Göring?—No, I don't believe.
—You believe Goebbels?—Oh, propaganda!
—And do you believe me?—A moment of silence.
—Mister Commissar, I don't believe you.
Everything is propaganda. The whole world is propaganda.

Четыре слога слова пропаганда
Гудят в ушах моих еще сегодня:
«Всё пропаганда. Весь мир — пропаганда».

Если бы я превратился в ребенка,
Снова учился в начальной школе,
И мне бы сказали такое:
Волга впадает в Каспийское море! —
Я бы, конечно, поверил. Но прежде
Нашел бы эту самую Волгу,
Спустился бы вниз по течению к морю,
Умылся его водой мутноватой
И только тогда бы, пожалуй, поверил.

Лошади едят овес и сено!
Ложь! Зимой тридцать третьего года
Я жил на тощей, как жердь, Украине.
Лошади ели сначала солому,
Потом — худые соломенные крыши,
Потом их гнали в Харьков на свалку.
Я лично видел своими глазами
Суровых, серьезных, почти что важных
Гнедых, караковых и буланых,
Молча, неспешно бродивших по свалке.
Они ходили, потом стояли,
А после падали и долго лежали.
Умирали лошади не сразу.

Лошади едят овес и сено!
Нет. Неверно. Ложь. Пропаганда.
Всё — пропаганда. Весь мир — пропаганда.

A word of four syllables—propaganda—
Sounds in my ears to this day:
"Everything is propaganda. The whole world is propaganda."

If I were to turn into a child,
Studying again in an elementary school,
And it was said to me:
The Volga falls into the Caspian Sea!
I would, of course, believe it. But first
I'd find that Volga,
Follow its current down to the sea,
Wash myself in its turbid waters
And only then, perhaps, would I believe.

Horses eat oats and hay!
A lie! During the winter of 1933
I lived in the emaciated Ukraine.
At first the horses ate straw,
Then—the sparse straw from roofs,
Then they were driven to Kharkov to a dump.
I saw with my own eyes horses
Severe, serious, almost pompous
Bay ones and dun ones and dark-brown colored horses
Silently, unhurriedly wandering around the dump.
They walked, then stood
And fell and lay a long time.
They did not die quickly, the horses.

Horses eat oats and hay!
No. Not true. A lie. Propaganda.
Everything is propaganda. The whole world is propaganda.

The Conscience of a Generation—
A Commentary

——A. ZR

THE POEMS THAT APPEAR here in translation were given to me in Warsaw last summer by a Polish friend I had known in Moscow. The manuscript, as it was given to him, was unsigned, and the person who gave it to him would tell him no more than that the poems were written by someone who is not young, and who is a known poet in the Soviet Union. We sat by an open window in my friend's tiny apartment and read the poems on that warm Sunday afternoon; and, drawing on our experiences of the previous year in Moscow, we discussed them in the light of what we had learned about Russian intellectuals.

We agreed that the poems provided not only a powerful example of Soviet "underground" literature, but a key to the mentality, conscience, and experiences of the intellectual generation represented by the poet. So many of the thoughts expressed in them in ideal form, in verse, were thoughts familiar to us from conversations with Russian friends and acquaintances. Many of them are not new, even in Soviet literature. During the short-lived literary movement of social protest in 1956–57, the outside world listened with strained attention to the distant voices of people who, for the first time since the beginning of Stalin's long rule, spoke in honest accents. We heard Russian writers cry out with outrage and pain as they cast aside their habitual facti-tious social optimism and laid bare the anatomy of a rotten society festering with bureaucratic corruption, callousness, and arbitrariness. They exposed a nation disfigured by ubiquitous dishonesty and social cowardice; and some even acknowledged, with revulsion, their own complicity in the death or exile of innocent comrades.

All of this is contained in these poems. If anyone has any question about the grounds of the guilt expressed in "I have judged people. . . . ," they were quite clearly stated in early 1957 in a poem by Margarita Aliger, "The Real Truth." She admits having voted to condemn writer friends who had fallen victim to Stalin's purges, describes her shame for not having spoken out in their defense, and offers in her own defense that she had been misled and deceived by the "pompous phraseology" of the charges against them. No doubt, in Stalin's time the fearful consequences of daring to defend his victims encouraged people to be stupid and actually to convince themselves of things that were patently unreasonable, but which it was healthier to believe. Perhaps our anonymous poet could claim with equal right to have "judged people" in blindness and stupidity, and not in cowardice; but he says nothing of this. His agony is unextenuated, though it is graced by pathetic defiance in the poem's last lines: "This poem is mistaken, untrue./I am wrong./Let them correct me."

But there are also new themes in these poems. Even during the height of the thaw in 1956–57, Soviet editors had not softened to the point of permitting writers the full expression of their views, nor did the writers sense that the time had arrived to express themselves freely. Among the very authors of the startlingly critical works of those years were some who saved the unpublishable residue of their criticisms for just such manuscripts as the one we have before us. From these poems we can discern the full range of their partially revealed discontents.

We have never before heard a Soviet writer speak, for example, on the subject of propaganda, that indigestible staple of the Soviet citizen's daily intellectual diet; nor have we ever had, as in "I varnish reality," a writer's confession of the unpleasant work he does in the Soviet Union. The last poem is interesting on another count, for it gives us a glimpse of that highly developed underworld of Soviet literature that one suspects must exist as an outlet for writers whose public pursuit of their craft is degraded by dishonesty. The honest ones do indeed write—"for the desk drawer," as they say—whatever has personal or artistic meaning for them. And it is a further measure of the powerful longing of both Soviet readers and writers for truthfulness that to speak of a writer as "honest" (*chestnyi*)—not in the sense that he scrupulously avoids sentimentality or any of the other failures of the imagination that betray artistic truth, but in the unadorned sense that he does not write lies or propaganda—is to give him the highest praise possible in the Soviet Union.

There are two main avenues whereby Soviet writers of "desk-drawer" manuscripts may reach an audience. One is the private literary evening, an institution that seems to have vanished from the American scene, but that continues to flourish in the Soviet Union. Apart from this, underground manuscripts are circulated in typewritten copies, and judging by the complete files that some writers have of their colleagues' unpublishable works, there must be a good number of self-sacrificing authors who are willing to take the trouble of making extra copies to pass on to friends, or else a well-developed system of clandestine reproduction and loan. The typing of forbidden manuscripts has, incidentally, been turned to profit by some enterprising, if not so self-sacrificing, spirits. In 1958, typewritten copies of *Doctor Zhivago* were selling in Moscow for 1,000 rubles, and smuggled copies of the printed American (Russian-language) edition, I am told, went for 2,000 rubles.

It is hard to say how widespread and typical the writing of these manuscripts is. My guess is that apart from the arrant hacks who are content to write according to the official formulas purely for money, very many Soviet authors are troubled by areas of creative unfulfillment that demands satisfaction. Not everything they write is of a direct political character. Young writers, in particular, are often more interested in experimenting with literary forms that are too *outré* for the tastes of Soviet editors than they are in politics. Then, too, I have seen manuscripts that have no political ax to grind but still would be considered heretical, either because they describe Soviet life in too tragic, satirical, or simply too objective a fashion, or because the artistic temperament they reveal is too defiantly individualistic. An interesting sidelight is that considerably less prose than poetry is written for nonpublication, so to speak. The reason is that prose works are normally longer and require a greater investment of time. Obviously, it takes unique dedication and character to write for a doubtful posterity, especially when this has to be done at a financial sacrifice.

The poems in our manuscript are undated. They show evidence, however, of having been written under the immediate impact of the two most important events of the last decade of Soviet history—Stalin's death and Khrushchev's secret speech at the Twentieth Party Congress—which would date them between 1953 and 1957. They span a period of deepening disillusionment in the author as he comes more and more to grasp the significance of Stalin's rule. The poems "Contemporary Reflections" and "We All Walked Under God," which are among the first in order of appearance in the manuscript, were unquestionably written before the Twentieth Congress, and the awakened critical thought reflected in them is not yet as devastating as it is in the later poems in the manuscript. The poet's initial reaction to the shock of Stalin's death seems to be one of bewildered ambivalence—a balancing of the material achievements of the dictator's rule against its calamities. But in the end the negation is complete, and one is aware only of the unrelieved burden of terrible pain and knowledge. The last remaining rock of intellectual support that, despite everything, the poet thought Stalin had bequeathed to him—"socialism was constructed"—has crumbled into the shifting sand of total disbelief.

What will perhaps surprise and shock the non-Soviet reader is the genuine sense of loss the poet experienced at Stalin's death. The attitude expressed in the earlier poems combines at least equal parts of horror and admiration, even veneration. The official line since 1956 has right along been that Stalin possessed as many virtues as he did vices, and this is the line one would expect to find in "legal" literature about him. Condemnation mixed with admiration is characteristic, for example, of A. T. Tvardovsky's reflections on Stalin in *Za daliu dal*. Yet here it is also, in poetry written not for the eyes of the Soviet censor, but for the poet himself and his friends. I, for one, was struck by the reference to Stalin as a "god"—ironic, it is true, but not so destructively ironic as to turn the appellation into a bitter joke and remove all foundation from it.

It is worth dwelling for a moment on the attitude of the Russians toward Stalin. One recent autumn evening in Leningrad, he was described to me as a "vampire"—an image more in keeping with the one we have of him in the West. I had met a young man in a restaurant, where he had overheard a waitress telling me about the terrifying sacrifices the Russians had made during the last war, of how miserable life had been just afterward and how much better it was now, of her faith in the future and her hope that we Americans would leave her people in peace. Her tears were sincere. (It is a rare Russian who can talk about the last war without a display of genuine feeling that evokes pity and terror in the listener.) Having overheard the waitress' outburst, the young man came up to me as I was leaving the restaurant and introduced himself. He apologized for what he had mistaken as a propaganda harangue by the waitress—actually I was sympathetic and not in the least offended—and then invited me for a stroll. We walked for hours through the *Marsovoye Pole* (Mars Field), where an eternal light burns for the heroes of the revolution whose names are inscribed in stone on the low walls surrounding the memorial area in the middle of the field, along the Nevsky Prospekt, and through back streets deserted in the cool late-autumn evening. (I was to take many a walk like that one, sometimes in freezing winter weather, to hear the story of some Russian acquaintance who preferred to talk on the street, where one could be certain of not being overheard. And such is the Russian's talent for talking, and his irrepressible desire to express his pent-up thoughts to someone he knows will listen sympathetically and will not betray him, that I always returned home on these occasions with a pain in the small of my back from having walked too long.)

My young acquaintance turned out to be a scientist and amateur writer. He told me of everything that troubled him and seemed in a rush to get it all said in this one night. Normally, he said, he was taciturn and guarded in talking with other Russians, except a very few close friends. What poured out of him was astonishing. Though born into a family of mixed faith and himself an atheist until early manhood, he told me that he was now a religious man, and that if he were ever to go to the West, he would embrace Catholicism, because its strong discipline and ritual appealed to him. He could not understand how his countrymen could bear the realities of Soviet life without strong religious faith. His own faith was his sole consolation, and it gave him the strength to work and to be patient. He was one of the few religious Russians I met—and also one of the few who fitted the picture of the intensely spiritual Russian made familiar by Dostoevski.

I was impressed by the passion, excitement, and intelligence of his talk, by the dark handsomeness of his features, and by his wonderful eyes, now bright with wit, humor, and friendliness, now still with inwardness. When we reached the Neva, in front of the Admiralty, by the two blackened bronze lions that stand on pedestals above the stepped stone embankment leading down to the river, he asked if I would like him to recite parts of a story he had written about the events of the days following Stalin's death. He had once put it on paper, but then, having destroyed the manuscript for fear that it might fall into the wrong hands, had committed it to memory. The story was about the crushing to death of large numbers of young people in the stampede that took place in Moscow the first day that Stalin's body lay in state for public view. (The little girl, Katya, in Abram Tertz's story *The Trial Begins*, was also a victim of this stampede.) Countless thousands of people had crowded into the streets to have a last look at Stalin and confirm with their own eyes the awesome fact of his death. The approaches to the Red Square were jammed beyond belief. Suddenly, something happened; the crowd began to move uncontrollably, panic seized it, and many—mainly young people—were crushed underfoot, against the walls of buildings or in passageways. I remember the words with which my friend's story ended: "And even in death, this vampire in the uniform of a generalissimo demanded sacrificial vctims."

To this young Russian, Stalin represented pure evil and was

as hateful as the system of government he created. But my friend's attitude was by no means shared by all Russians, many of whom still speak of Stalin with a curious lack of bitterness and with a willingness to admit a positive side to his rule that seems unthinkable and morally blind to an outsider. This attitude undoubtedly stems from a retrospective evaluation of Stalin's social and economic programs, and I want for a moment to consider what the Russians thought of him while he was alive; otherwise, it will be impossible to understand how the adult, intelligent author of "Contemporary Reflections" could have written soon after Stalin's death: "How will we live without Stalin?" and could even have called him a "god."

In the first place—and this is a purely psychological datum—if most Russians did not actually regard Stalin as a kind of divinity during his lifetime, they at least regarded him as a figure of superhuman proportions, one that the imagination could assimilate only by mythic hyperbole. Abram Tertz, in *The Trial Begins*, also needs to call Stalin "The Master" and "a god" in order to convey something of his psychological impact on the people he ruled. Everything about Stalin was calculated to contribute to this mystique—his Eastern origins, his remote inaccessibility, the strength, absolutism, and swift arbitrariness of his rule—not to speak of the prodigious propaganda effort, embracing every printed and spoken word in every sphere of culture, that was made to portray Stalin as an omniscient and omnipotent being. If it did not actually induce belief, this effort certainly staggered the imagination by its all-pervasiveness and myth-making quality. It is a striking testimonial to the grip of this mystique that even to many mature intellectuals, our poet among them, the 1956 denunciation of the personality cult and the revelation of the horrendous crimes of the Stalin era came as a deep traumatic shock. It is less surprising that this was true of the young. An artist, who was a first-year university student at the time of these events, told me how the attack upon the benevolent god they actually had believed Stalin to be produced in himself and his friends a mood of insupportable despair: Their faith had been shattered, and henceforth they could believe in nothing.

There were other powerful considerations that blinded Russian intellectuals, especially of the generation of the author of these poems, to the evils of Stalin's rule. The Russian intelligentsia traditionally—and this applies with special force to the Soviet Russian intelligentsia—has been haunted and driven by the desire to shake off their country's economic backwardness. Thus whatever doubts and questions some of Stalin's acts inspired in them were stilled by the fact that others brought grand accomplishments: "And before me rose his palaces, factories—/Everything that Stalin built:/the towers of his skyscrapers,/The quadrangles of his squares. . . ." For those Russian intellectuals who identified the objectives of the Revolution with economic progress and a rich modern life—there were a majority in the 1930's, and are still a majority today—there was no question that Stalin was pushing Russia toward these ultimate goals. And according to the gigantic, concerted propaganda chorus, he was doing it singlehandedly.

Every success that was scored, from the astonishingly rapid transformation of Russia into a powerful industrial nation, to the victory over Germany, was Stalin's personal success. Vsevolod Kochetov is not a writer who can be trusted to present anything but the official point of view; nevertheless, in his novel *The Yershov Brothers*, there is a character who describes his uncritical attitude toward the Stalin cult in the days when it was being promoted in a way that, I believe, accurately reflects the popular mood of the time: "We saw the successes of the country, saw how it was growing and getting strong. We saw great works. We participated in those works, we participated in the war in which German fascism was buried. And, for us, these were the main things."

The effectiveness of the propaganda glorifying Stalin was thus, in large part, based on the solid achievements people saw around them; the nation was ripe for mass hypnosis. This helps to explain why in the last war Russian soldiers—and not just the simpleminded ones—went into battle with the cry "For the Fatherland! For Stalin!" on their lips.

During the dreadful purges of the 1930's and the renewed terror of the postwar period, even the most convinced believers

in Stalin must have undergone a crisis of faith. It requires no
great stretch of the imagination to picture men like our poet in
the dilemma of a Job—bewildered and outraged by a sense of
injustice, yet anxious, through an act of faith, to find some reason in what was taking place around him. Apart from everything
else, they had personal motives for wanting to do so: There was
so much for them to lose by saying "no" to Stalin's Russia. They
were old enough to have made sacrifices in the cause of the
Revolution during its early years and to have played a part in
the establishment of Stalin's power; many were personally impli-
cated in events that were distasteful to them and troubled their
consciences ("I have judged people. . . ."), and, finally, they
had behind them a lifelong commitment to the Marxist ideology.
A man's integrity and self-esteem, indeed his whole previous
person, were at stake in rejecting Stalin and his works.

The type of mentality I am trying to describe, with its tendency
to assert faith through an act of will and to interpret disturbing
contradictions in their most hopeful light, is well represented in
The Trial Begins. The grandmother in the story, Ekaterina
Petrovna, is an old Bolshevik, older than our poet, but like him
an intellectual. We gather from what she tells her grandson,
Seryozha, that she was once imprisoned by the Czarist authorities for revolutionary activities. Seryozha has begun to notice
contradictions between Soviet ideology and Soviet reality, and
he frequently embarrasses his elders by speaking out about
things that trouble him. Seryozha says of the kind of Soviet
fiction that varnishes reality: "I know those books, I've read
them. They're nothing but model window dressing—all lies."
Ekaterina Petrovna has just been defending a novel about a
collective farm on the ground that, though badly written, it
depicts a model farm as an example for other farms to follow.
The point is that Ekaterina Petrovna is capable of recognizing
the aesthetic weaknesses and falseness of the book, but has made
a choice of priorities that—temporarily, she would say—places the
immediate aims of social and economic progress above all other
values. For many Russian intellectuals, we can well imagine, this
involved a willful amputation of a vital part of their consciousness. Ekaterina Petrovna says something like this to Seryozha:

"You think I'm old and haven't got eyes in my head. Well, I dare say I see more things wrong than you do. But don't you understand, Seryozha, you must have faith, you simply must believe. . . . The whole of our life is devoted to this. It's—our aim. . . ."

We can be sure that our anonymous poet once reconciled himself to reality by very much the same sort of rationalization. Today, however, all the flames of faith are burned out in him. Still, one hope desperately refuses to be extinguished—one hope, he says, keeps him working and prevents him from succumbing altogether to disillusionment and bitterness. For me, the most significant poem in the group is the one beginning with: "I am building on sand." Here, the hope that characteristically sustains not only its author but most critically thinking Russian intellectuals in their middle years or older is expressed in the line: "But I am faithful to the construction program. . . ."

Let me illustrate the meaning of this last line. One evening I was standing on the crest of the Lenin Hills with a philosophy teacher in his late thirties, who was in from the provinces to do advanced work at Moscow University. We had walked from the university along the spacious tree-lined promenade that leads to the top of a tall bluff overlooking the Moscow River. There, with the river flowing far below, we could see the whole of Moscow laid out before us, illuminated and sparkling in the night. Along the way we had been arguing, playing our tiny roles in the great contemporary dialogue between East and West. Russians were incomparably freer now than before, my companion said; life, in general, was much better, and he was confident it would continue to improve still more. How could he be sure? I asked; what guarantees did he have, and didn't he realize that without free political institutions, a free press, and civil liberties, all the gains made since Stalin's death might be wiped out by the Party if it decided this was necessary? What was to prevent a repetition of the bloody purges of the 1930's if the Party felt its power threatened or if it spawned some new maniac like Stalin? My friend did not seem to regard these as real possibilities; nevertheless, unknowingly, I had touched him in a sensitive spot. His own father, he told me, had been arrested during the

Yezhovshchina and had spent many years in exile, but despite that had never lost "faith." Nor had he himself and other Russians lost faith, he added; and then, to support this last contention, he pointed with a triumphant gesture toward the new residential construction sites on Lenin Prospekt, and beyond to the gigantic and burgeoning new southwest quarter of Moscow, with its miles of gargantuan apartment houses, each seven stories high and several city blocks long. This was his faith and his guarantee of the future.

If there still are Russian intellectuals today who find it possible to look back on Stalin as a modern Peter the Great, a ruler of monstrous iniquities but one to whom they are grateful for forcing Russia along the road to modernity, and if these intellectuals can and do find things in their society that are worthy of assent, it is because they, like our poet, are absorbed—mesmerized, I should say—by a compelling vision of their country's economic future.

Nevertheless, I met many intellectuals in their thirties and older whose political disaffection was fierce—unmodulated by any such vision. They were consumed by bitterness, and while they believed that with time material standards of life would improve, perhaps even radically, they were more concerned about the future of political and intellectual freedom, and not hopeful about it. The younger intellectuals, especially, seem to live exclusively in a world of present needs: They want, right *now*, to be free and modern in their style of life and dress as well as in their art and literature, and they are impatient with talk about the necessity of present sacrifices for the sake of future goals. But the majority of adult intellectuals, including those who are opposed in principle to the regime, give their primary allegiance to the "construction program" and are willing to restrain their criticisms of the regime because they believe that it shares this allegiance.

I think that despite all we have learned in recent years about the importance of economic development for the intellectuals in the underdeveloped countries and how it tends—to our dismay—to overshadow issues of political, individual, and intellectual freedom, it is still difficult for us to appreciate the problem vividly enough, in all its ramifications. What disturbs Russian intellectuals is not only that they and their countrymen still suffer material hardship, though this is of course most important; it is also the special tone which their country's relative economic backwardness gives to other aspects of Soviet social life.

My first insight into this problem came from a person who was not an intellectual. Shortly after my arrival in Moscow, I was lucky enough to run into one of those talkative Russian taxi drivers I had read about. He seized the occasion of having a foreign fare to get what was bothering him off his chest, and he did so simply and vehemently, but with an intelligence and incisiveness that simple people seem to acquire under hard living conditions. "We work, and we work, and we work—and for what? For nothing!" he said. "For forty-two years they have been promising us a better life, and we have nothing to show for it. People are still starving in the villages—I've been there and I know— while *they* [he said with special vehemence] live like kings, in palaces." (This is a peculiarly working-class view of the government and Party leaders. To discontented workers they are "bandits," out only for their own personal gain. The oppositionist intelligentsia will attribute any number of vices to the leaders, but they seldom regard them as animated solely by venal motives.) He complained that workers' children rarely get higher education and that nearly all the students at universities and institutes were sons and daughters of "Party workers, intellectuals, writers and television people."

I told him I had heard that Jews were disliked in the Soviet Union and asked if this was true. Yes, he replied, Russians hate the Jews because Jews don't want to work with their hands, because they are all educated and shrewd, and if one gets a good job somewhere, he drags all his Jewish friends in. He thought for a moment and then added: "But, you know, the reason we hate Jews is because life is so hard. And we don't hate just Jews, we hate one another. If life were better for all of us, we wouldn't care that they had good jobs."

I thought that this was a rather sophisticated explanation, at least of popular anti-Semitism in the Soviet Union. (I remembered that anti-Semitism had been most virulent in the United States during the Great Depression.) During the months that followed, I noticed many things—the rudeness of salesgirls, waitresses, and bus conductors; the easily aroused irritability of people generally and the frequent altercations between them in stores, restaurants, and on the street; an old *dvornik* deliberately sweeping street dust onto two young girls who had had the temerity to expect that he would stop his work long enough to let them pass by. As these observations accumulated, they grew into a conviction about a certain quality of Soviet life, and I found myself recalling the taxi driver's words: "We hate one another."

"Hate" is perhaps too strong a word for the tension in Soviet life that explodes often enough to make the foreigner take notice. I asked some of my Russian friends, who had the economic development complex I have been describing, how they accounted for this tension, and they would come up with several answers: the constant waiting in lines that Soviet shoppers have to put up with; the frequent shortages of consumer goods, which compel them to waste time going from store to store in search of what they are after; low pay and the tightness of the average Soviet citizen's budget; and, most of all, the housing shortage.

I already had some idea of the housing problem before I went to the Soviet Union; American newspapers described it as "appalling." But to understand how unspeakably bad conditions actually are, one has to see them with one's own eyes and measure them in terms of their social consequences—a total lack of privacy, separated families, an astronomical divorce rate and a low birth rate, widespread drunkenness, and national irascibility. The typical setup is the communal apartment consisting of four or more separate rooms with a common kitchen and common bathroom, each of the rooms usually occupied by one family, sometimes with odd relatives thrown in. The Russian housewife starts the day waiting her turn to use the kitchen stove so that she can prepare breakfast, which she will carry back to the family's single room. Her husband starts his day waiting for the bathroom to be free. It is not exactly the kind of morning to put either in a friendly frame of mind for the rest of the day. But life at home in the evening is enough to drive one to drink.

I have had the situation described to me vividly: The Russian *pater familias* gets home from work and sits down to relax after dinner; the children are playing at his feet and making a racket; his mother-in-law is sitting in the corner complaining about her rheumatism; his neighbor on the left, separated from him by a thin wall, is abusing his wife, while the neighbor on the right has his radio receiver turned up full blast, blaring forth the Soviet national anthem for all the world to hear. So, the hell with it, says *pater familias* and goes out for a couple of drinks. Small wonder that there is such a staggering amount of drunkenness in Soviet cities!

I knew of divorces that took place because husbands could not stand living in the same room with their in-laws, or because couples lived apart too long—often in the same city—unable to find a place to live together. One man whose wife left him over mother-in-law trouble wound up still living in the same room with his former mother-in-law, because neither of them could find another place to stay.

These are some of the social costs of economic backwardness. They are less easy to assess than the actual material privations, but they are equally important in shaping the political state of mind of the Russian intelligentsia. There are still other hidden costs. For many of my educated Russian friends, who knew that they were every bit as articulate and sophisticated as Western intellectuals, it was humiliating to know that they could be invidiously distinguished from the latter by a suit of clothing. They experienced their country's poverty as a personal and national degradation, and so long as they saw hope of economic progress, they were willing to be incredibly patient in regard to other things.

Before going to the Soviet Union, I had expected to find the Soviet working class pacified by recent improvements in living standards, and the intelligentsia, on the contrary, the focal point of disaffection, because of the continued pinch of restrictions on intellectual freedom. The situation turned out to be the reverse. In general, it was my most sophisticated friends who were willing to stand behind the government, because they saw it as the only hope of moving forward economically, and who

were ready to tolerate—and sometimes even justify—practices
directly affecting themselves, such as censorship of literature, the
prohibition of internal political criticism, and curbs on cultural
exchange with the outside world. They felt that the Soviet Union
could not yet afford democratic freedoms, that at the present time
such freedoms would only invite disorders, and probably revolution, by the working class, which they thought was unhappy
enough—with proper provocation—to raise the cry, *doloi kom-
munizm* (down with Communism) and plunge the country back
into chaos.* In the meantime, they themselves had agreed not to
rock the boat, not to focus, by word or deed, the disaffections
of the working class, so as to buy the time necessary for their
country to develop a richer material life. The formula was:
"We've had enough of idle talk and criticism. You have to have
been born and to have grown up here to know what a peculiar
Russian curse it is. We're so given to self-deprecation and admiration of the West. What we need is *work* and *efficiency!* When
we have that, we'll become rich, and then we won't have to be
afraid of comparison with the West, our borders will be opened,
and freedom will come."

"Work," indeed, is the one subject on which even the most
unorthodox Russian intellectuals agree with their government,
the one subject about which they can speak sincerely and still
give a foreigner the impression that he is listening to a lead
article from *Pravda*. One evening I attended a reception held at
a well-known Moscow institute for the entering freshman class.

---

* Even people whose first commitment was to intellectual and political
freedom, and not to economic development, did not welcome the prospect
of a new working-class revolution. "The workers don't only hate 'them,'
they also hate intellectuals. They think we're all living in ease, while they're
living in poverty," said one intellectual friend who would have liked nothing
better than to see the regime blasted from the face of the earth. Actually,
only a small percentage of intellectuals live well—have their own apartments, for example—but workers generalize their envy and hatred toward
all intellectuals. It is significant that the taxi driver I mentioned earlier
believed that the universities and institutes were attended exclusively by the
children of either Party workers or "intellectuals, writers, and television
people." One sees frequent evidences of the smoldering antagonism the
working class feels toward the intelligentsia. "Educated one," "intelligent,"
"bespectacled one," and even "student" are terms of abuse on the lips of
workers.

The director of the institute, a very sophisticated man with a reputation for liberalism and independence, delivered an address, but all he managed to say to his young protégés dealt with work, and his were words with which they had been assailed since first learning to read and to understand the spoken word. He began by speaking of the institute's scholarly traditions, of the great scholars who had worked there and the contributions they had made to the enlightenment and material well-being of the nation; he concluded by emphasizing the duty of the students to work conscientiously so that they, too, might make the contributions the nation required of them. It was the same old call to labor that has hounded Soviet citizens since the days of the Revolution; yet, as I listened to this man, I had the deep impression that his words were sincere, his enthusiasm genuine, and his belief in the saving power of work a first article of faith.

For disillusioned people, people with no other hope, work is often a last refuge, as it was for Chekhov's Uncle Vanya. Many Russians, when asked what they can do to change things in their country, will tell you that the only thing left for them is to work as hard and honestly as they can in their own occupations and hope that change will come about through more and more people doing the same thing. Yet, for Russians today, "work" does not as a rule have the pathetic significance that it did for Uncle Vanya. They do not work, as he did, to forget—because there was nothing else a man of conscience could do in a tired old empire strangling in sloth and social injustice. They work rather because they are drawn by a goal and a hope—the goal of forging not their country's might and destiny, but simply its economic well-being, and the hope that this will bring ultimate freedom.

This brings me to another crucial aspect of the problem of economic development as it appears to Russian intellectuals. Khrushchev's celebrated remark, "We are getting richer, and when a person has more to eat, he gets more democratic," reflects a widely held belief. It is a belief that, in different terms, is implicit in the poem "Man." Russian intellectuals see freedom and material abundance as two sides of the same coin, and if many of them are willing to remain passive in the face of the oppressive features of their society today, it is because they are convinced that these features are fated to disappear with the arrival of an abundant tomorrow. The usual argument is that freedom will be unattainable as long as living standards are so low that they engender discontent to the point of threatening the position of the Party and making it unwilling to relax controls. In line with this, Russians argue that restrictions on intercourse with the West exist because official circles fear the effect that the knowledge of Western material conditions and political life might have upon the Russian people. Rising living standards, they believe, will lift these barriers to the freedoms they are now denied. I often asked friends who argued this way how they could be sure the Party would surrender its power monopoly, but beyond a vague confidence that it would somehow have to do so, I never got any satisfactory answers. It was my impression that they did not think too deeply about the question—that it is a bridge they will cross when they come to it. Meanwhile, they are absorbed in the problem of getting to a point where the bridge will at least be in sight.

In conclusion, I should like to return to one last poem and to consider a question it raises. The poem is "Propaganda," and the question is: To what extent are the sentiments expressed in it typical of the attitude of Soviet citizens and, by extension, how successful has the official indoctrination program been in anesthetizing them to their political condition? To anyone who goes to the Soviet Union with even the smallest expectation of finding it a never-never land of thoroughly indoctrinated political robots, the experience of getting to know Russian intellectuals—and not only intellectuals, but intelligent, thinking Russians in whatever walk of life—will come as a big surprise. He will be astonished by their open-mindedness and lack of dogmatism, by the way they have managed to keep their heads clear despite the concentrated effort of the most insidious, highly saturating propaganda machine yet devised by any government. He will be overwhelmed by their eagerness to know about life in the West, touched by their humility about their ignorance of the outside world, and impressed by their sophisticated understanding of their own life. Of course, he will meet many Russians who exhibit all the qualities of mindlessness and stereotyped thinking that Soviet indoctrination is designed to inculcate. But he will be struck much more by the numbers of people who want to be free and know they are not, and who show an ironic disregard both for official dogma and for their leaders.

That is, of course, *if* he has an opportunity to know them genuinely and honestly. For this, two elementary rules have to be remembered: First, a Russian can never be expected to speak candidly with a foreigner in the presence of other Russians, unless they are his trusted friends; second, no Russian speaking in an official capacity can be expected to risk his job or his freedom by revealing his private self. Often the same person who, in the presence of others, beleaguers you with hostile questions about unemployment in the United States, starving workers, and discrimination against the Negroes, will in private ask about these things simply and unprovocatively, because he wants to know the facts—sometimes, even, in a way that clearly conveys his own disbelief of the official propaganda.

Bearing this in mind, it is particularly important to avoid judging the attitudes of Russian intellectuals in general by what they may say as Soviet official representatives in group discussions with visiting foreign cultural delegations. For one thing, these representatives are often likely to be members of the despised Stalin generation—careerists, sycophants, intellectual mediocrities who rose to the top while those who were really talented and independent-minded were swept away in the purges. Yet even among these, the rule is cynicism and ambition rather than stupidity, and what they say cannot be taken as expressing what they actually believe.

It is a wicked fact, but nevertheless a fact, that whatever genuine intellectual life there is in the Soviet Union goes on beneath the surface, and that Russians, when they feel they have to, can lie (not only to foreigners, unfortunately, but also to one another) with an adroitness that comes from living so long under conditions of political and intellectual repression. After all, lying—in one way or another—not only is the daily work of Soviet writers, as our poet confesses; it is the business of every Soviet citizen who writes or speaks publicly, just as it is a necessary precaution of everyday life in a society where one can never be sure of one's neighbor.

But when one succeeds in penetrating this protective screen,

one soon discovers the plain and simple fact that the enormous
official indoctrination effort has made surprisingly little inroads
on the private attitudes and thinking of Russian intellectuals,
and for that matter of intelligent Soviet citizens in general.
Indeed, it is perhaps the least successful of all Soviet government
enterprises. Chances are today that by the time a young Russian
is of university age, he will already have arrived at a fundamental understanding of his political condition. A friend
described the three ages of the New Soviet Man to me in this
way. Up to the age of eighteen, give or take a couple of years,
he is apt to be an enthusiastic supporter of the regime, an active
Pioneer or *komsomolets* thoroughly imbued with the ideals and
ideology of Marxism-Leninism. Between eighteen and twenty-
five, the process of independent thought sets in, and with it
comes the high tide of disillusionment. (It is, significantly,
among persons of this age group that what little organized
opposition there is to the regime usually develops.) Finally, by
the age of twenty-five, most Russians have already become convinced that they are powerless to change things, or they are too
afraid of the chaos that might result from trying to change them,
and too concerned with keeping their families in food and
clothing to do anything but settle back into the "wait-and-see"
attitude that is typical of thinking people in the Soviet Union.

Obviously, there are Russians who never outgrow their childhood naïveté and who go on believing to the end the official
picture of the world. But the only educated adults I encountered
who seemed to fit in this category either were persons with
whom I had official contacts—and who may or may not have
really believed what they said—or else individuals of deficient
intelligence. Among uneducated Russians, one often encounters
a species of cynicism that might be characterized as a belief in
universal evil: Life is bad in the Soviet Union, but it is no better
anywhere else. Perhaps they would subscribe to a literal interpretation of our poet's words: "Everything is propaganda. The
whole world is propaganda." But, for other Russians, these lines
have a more limited meaning. They know that *their* world is
propaganda, but they suspect that there is a different world
beyond.

MISCELLANEA

Introduction

The following articles could not be fitted into any other section of this book, yet each one of them is of crucial importance
in understanding the realities of contemporary Russia. The first
deals with the attempts to establish some kind of rule of law in
a country where the judiciary has been merely a tool of the
Party's political and economic policies. The second article is
concerned with the writing of history in the U.S.S.R. As Alexander Dallin points out, Soviet historiography is still essentially
a method of adjusting the past to the political requirements of
the present; inasmuch as the current policy calls for a renunciation of some segments of the Stalinist past, however, Soviet
historiography under Khrushchev has lifted the veil on events
and personages whose existence had long been misrepresented
or denied altogether. Finally, in "The Soviet Theater," we get
not only a fascinating picture of what has happened to Soviet
theatrical art within the past four decades, but of the profound
transformation of Soviet culture in general; for Mr. Rühle provides a revealing account of the chasm between the intoxicating
hopes and achievements of the early, revolutionary period, and
the cultural bankruptcy of the succeeding eras, including the
present one.

Socialist Legality: The Road Uphill

——LEON LIPSON

OF ALL THE BANNERS that were waved in the rhetorical winds of
the Twentieth Congress of the CPSU, the banner of "socialist
legality" was one of the largest and bravest. The Party, it was
stated, had brought to light some crude, though only occasional,
violations of socialist legality committed in the preceding twenty
years by Beria "and his band," and tolerated under the spell of
the cult of personality. Good Communists had suffered. It was
now the task of legal science, guided by the Party, to strengthen
and even to perfect the legal system so that such abuses could
not recur.

This banner was not new; it had only been refurbished. Soviet
legal scholars for a generation had used the phrase "socialist
legality" as the successor to the "revolutionary legality" of the
early 1920's, and an official periodical entitled *Socialist Legality*
had been regularly published long before Stalin's death. The
prevailing public interpretation of the concept among Soviet
lawyers has stressed the elements of stability of the laws and the
protection of socialist property.

Around the time of the promulgation of the Constitution of
1936—and therefore near the climactic phase of the Great Purges
—Stalin said in a report to the Extraordinary Session of the
Eighth All-Union Congress of Soviets, "We need stability of
laws now more than ever." A little army of legal writers, led by
Andrei Y. Vyshinsky, gave this slogan a jurisdictional interpretation, reading it to mean respect for the constitutional and statutory distribution of functions among the Supreme Soviet, its

Presidium, and the courts. Even in this sense, of course, legality was freely violated: The Supreme Soviet was not convoked with anything like the frequency required by the Constitution, and its legislative functions were regularly usurped by the Presidium; the Constitution was several times amended illegally; the Supreme Court occasionally "re-enacted" new laws in the guise of explanatory directives handed down to lower courts; and the secret police often bypassed even the very loose restraints placed on them by law.

In the latter part of the Stalin period, the protection of socialist property moved into the foreground as the chief theoretical task of socialist legality. Most Soviet theorists would have had scant sympathy with the comment of Justice Oliver Wendell Holmes that "for my part, I think it less evil that some criminals should escape than that the government should play an ignoble part." What mattered to them was rather that the citizen should walk a straight and narrow path when dealing with the government. In their eyes, it was precisely this requirement that made socialist legality specifically socialist.

Even in the Stalin era, a few voices were heard to object that there was more to socialist legality than the integrity of governmental tables of organization and function, or the sanctity of socialist property. For these few, the legal order ought also to protect the citizen against arbitrary or cruel persecution by the state. The criminal law, they said, was deficient in procedural guarantees on such points as the right to counsel, control by the courts over police activity, and the pretrial investigators' independence of the public prosecutors. Theirs, however, were voices crying in the wilderness—indeed, in more than just a figurative sense, for some of them were banished for a time to the remote Russian wastes.

The thaw that followed Stalin's death attained its warmest temperature in the legal field, as in several others, in late 1956 and early 1957. Reform of many phases of criminal procedure and of the substantive law of crimes was publicly debated. One of the salient features of the debate was the propensity toward fond recollection of the period prior to the supremacy of Stalin, especially the early 1920's. Mikoyan, at the Twentieth Congress, praised Soviet legal science of the early days, and juridical scholars combed the works of Lenin for quotations to support their particular recommendations and opinions—including their own righteous scorn of "quotationism." When no apt quotation could be found, nor even one capable of being ingeniously warped into pertinence, it was thought sufficient to observe that something like the law or regulation or legal institution being defended or advocated had existed during Lenin's lifetime, the implication being that no sparrow could have fallen without his remarking it. Many of the proposals for legal reform made in the mid-1950's had little to do with the good old days and might have been vetoed by Lenin; but that is beside the point. Their authors' purpose in invoking, however tenuously, the letter of the older law was, probably, to evoke the memory of the noble, mythical past when the Revolution was young, the Party was virtuous, life was simple, and laws were just.

Even at its peak, the agitation for legal reform was restricted within well-defined limits. There was and is no public question of curbing the Party or making the Party subordinate to the law. To a Soviet lawyer in good standing, this would be a false issue because (he would say) the law has no other function than to facilitate the execution of policy, and policy is made by the Party. Specific measures to achieve greater legality are, in fact, often advocated on the ostensible ground that they would guard the Party's policy against distortion. For example, it is urged that statutes must be strictly construed and applied because the legislator is supreme; and the legislator is supreme because he enacts the measures decided upon by the Party. Thus, contemporary Soviet lawyers have transcended the conflict that appeared to convulse an older generation of scholars, the conflict between socialist legality and revolutionary expediency.

The limits imposed upon legal reform, however, still leave some room for maneuver. Legality and expediency flow into each other. What should be done, for instance, about laws that are obsolete but still on the books? Should the trouble be taken to repeal them, should they be enforced according to the letter, or should the prosecutor—or the court—simply be allowed to ignore them at his discretion? This problem, encountered in all modern societies, can be approached in various ways, depending on the relative values assigned to the various institutional processes involved. Vyshinsky said, "If a law has lagged behind life, it must either be amended or, as Comrade Stalin puts it, be laid aside." The more liberal of the Soviet legal reformers of today would insist that the law must be applied until it is formally repealed or amended, which in turn entails recommendations for longer and more frequent sessions of the Supreme Soviet or recommendations to legitimize the *de facto* law-making of its Presidium.

To cite another example, the conviction of innocent men is attacked, and the virtues of what an American lawyer would call "procedural due process" are stressed, not so much on the ground of humanitarian reasons or principles of justice, as for the reason that if an innocent man is convicted and the real culprit goes free, the state is endangered.

An appraisal of the extent and significance of the agitation for legal reform is complicated by several factors that, in combination, are peculiar to Soviet society. First, it is hard to distinguish from outside the U.S.S.R., and perhaps even from inside, between reforms of major importance and mere technical improvements that are exaggerated for political effect. Second, suspicion naturally arises that the topics most freely agitated are those of least concern to the Party; yet it would hardly be safe to conclude, on this basis, that the Party line remains wholly untouched by the agitation. Third, the lack of publicity given to Soviet statutes, edicts, decrees, and court proceedings—many of which have not been published at all—makes it difficult, in the intervals between fits of self-criticism, to assess the practical effect of the laws on the books.

Finally, the role of the law as an organizing principle of society is much less important in the Soviet Union than in many other countries, though how much less is difficult to say. For years, while the state grew ever stronger, it was supposed that law itself was about to wither away with the state. The bar has never attracted a high percentage of talented youth, though some highly capable people may be found in various branches of the Soviet legal profession. Lawyers as mediators between the government and the people, as experts in the complex, interwoven structure of a pluralistic society, as custodians of parliamentary and other political traditions, have been almost "technologically unemployed" in the Soviet Union. These qualifications must be borne in mind in assessing the importance of the reforms sketched in the following paragraphs.

Some Areas of Change

The recent debate on socialist legality centered on the preparation of new codes of substantive criminal law and of criminal procedure. The old codes of the Soviet republics, patched and seamed by many amending statutes, decrees, and interpretations, were out of date; the new all-Union codes called for by the 1936 Constitution never came into being. In February, 1957, it was ordained that only fundamental principles should be enacted for the U.S.S.R. as a whole, and that detailed new codes should be drawn up separately for each republic. Some of the draftsmen favored a slight modification in the structure of the new codes, hoping merely to tidy up the old material; others wanted something new under the sun. Soviet experts in criminal law told foreign acquaintances that they were ranging over the experience of all countries regardless of social system and were prepared to borrow whatever seemed best, regardless of source.

Despite this eclectic ambition, the institutional organization of the Soviet legal process was not radically altered, either by the basic legislation enacted by the Supreme Soviet of the U.S.S.R. in December, 1958, or by the measures enacted before and since. For instance, the summary military-trial procedure previously enforced for certain political crimes—the so-called "Lex Kirov"— was abolished in 1956 for all offenses except espionage;* the

---

* Sergei Kirov, a prominent Communist Party worker and member of the Politburo, was assassinated in late 1934. The circumstances, as finally acknowledged by Khrushchev in his Special Report to the Twentieth Congress of the CPSU, suggested a "frame-up" from above. On the pretext of the assassination, directives were issued on Stalin's initiative, requiring that defendants accused of terrorism be notified of charges only 24 hours before

Special Boards of the Ministry of Internal Affairs (the famous *troikas*) had already been abolished in 1953 by a well-publicized, though still unpublished, edict.* The new laws specify that "criminal punishment shall be applied only by the sentence of a court" and that "justice in criminal cases shall be meted out only by a court. No one may be acknowledged guilty of crime and subjected to criminal punishment save by sentence of a court."

These principles seem to be regarded as excluding the practical possibility of a return of the Special Boards. Military courts remain and indeed will try—in addition to ordinary military cases—all cases on espionage; they may cover also all civil and criminal cases in places where, because of exceptional circumstances, the regular boards are not sitting. A number of other special courts have been abolished. Nevertheless, the possibility of the imposition of penal sentences through extrajudicial procedures lacking reasonable safeguards is still very much alive, as will be seen from the description given later of the new law against "social parasites."

The procuracy, conservatively reformed in 1955, retains its treble functions of conducting criminal prosecutions in court, overseeing the legality of criminal and civil decisions through the right of protest to higher tribunals, and supervising to a certain extent the legality of executive action. There was some sentiment in favor of decentralizing the procuracy as far down

---

trial, providing for trial without the participation of the defendant, forbidding appeals and petitions for clemency, and ordering execution of the death penalty immediately upon sentencing. These provisions, which were carried into the criminal codes of the various republics, were repealed in the spring of 1956. *Vedomosti*, No. 9 (1956), item 193. (The sinister circumstances surrounding Kirov's death were further aired by Khrushchev in his speech to the Twenty-second Congress on October 27, 1961.—*Ed.*)

* The Special Boards, established in 1934, appear to have been modeled roughly after the pre-Revolutionary system of "open police supervision." They were empowered to sentence "socially dangerous" persons to a maximum of five years of exile or "corrective labor." The procedure was secret, outside the court system, with no right of appeal. The unpublished 1953 edict, which purportedly abolished the Special Boards, was mentioned in an editorial in *Sovetskoe gosudarstvo i pravo* (*Soviet State and Law*), No. 1 (1956), p. 3. News of the abolition had reached the West as early as 1954; see Johnson, Book Review, *Journal of the Society of Public Teachers of Law* (new series), II (1954), 244, 245.

as the level of the individual republic, in a fashion partially analogous to the abolition of the Union Ministry of Justice. The proposed change would have made the procurator of a republic responsible to the republic instead of to the all-Union Soviet, although his local subordinates would still report to him rather than to their local soviets; the procurator of the U.S.S.R. would watch over the conformity of the regulations of the republican governments to Union and republican laws, and to decrees of the Union government.

In the field of procedure, the question had arisen whether criminal pretrial investigators should remain functionally subordinate to the procuracy, be restored to their former subordination to the courts,* or be empowered to operate independently. The ostensible impartiality of the investigators was said to have suffered because of their dependence upon conviction-seeking prosecutors. An allied question concerned the desirability of continuing the system of double investigation, under which the police made one investigation—before or after arrest, or both—and the investigators made another for the procurator's file and the court. This dual system was retained for an (unspecified) assortment of crimes. Certain state crimes, indeed, appear to have three sets of investigators, the third coming from the organs of state security; some minor crimes may be investigated by police only. The investigator has been afforded what may or may not prove to be a substantial working authority over the police. Some Soviet authorities with responsibilities in the training of prosecutors have contended informally that the supervision of the police by the investigator, or, in default of that, the independent investigation by an investigator not connected with the police, was not a tool in aid of conviction but rather an instrument of fairness and justice.

In the period of debates in 1956–57, some support was found

---

* Shortly after the Revolution, the preliminary investigation of criminal cases was in the hands of people's investigators, who were under the jurisdiction of the "people's courts." See *"Polozhenie o narodnom sude"* ("Decree on the People's Court"), Art. 30 (October 21, 1926), reprinted in *Sovetskaia prokuratura v vazhneishikh dokumentakh (Principal Documents on Soviet Procuracy)* (1956), p. 150.

for a suggestion that trials of major crimes be conducted before an enlarged tribunal. Besides a judge, the proposed tribunal would have comprised half a dozen people's assessors, instead of the customary two; it was suggested also that the expanded group of assessors should determine the guilt or innocence of the accused, leaving it to the judge to fix the sentence in the event of a guilty verdict. This innovation, which will be recognized as similar in concept to the foreign (or pre-Revolutionary Russian) jury, was not adopted. The judge's term of office has been extended from three to five years; the term within which a people's assessor remains subject to call has been reduced from three years to two.

Not much public attention was paid to the categories or types of crime. By legislation prior to the adoption of the Fundamentals, a few acts were added to the category of separate, criminally punishable offenses, such as hooliganism, which had posed an awkward problem until it was given special status as an offense punishable by a suitably light sentence. The Presidium of the Supreme Soviet had also decreed that repeated failure to deliver goods to other economic regions, to other republics, or to the Union government, was a criminal offense. Other acts, including absenteeism, train hopping, and, in some circumstances, abortion, had been removed from the category of crimes and were already being dealt with by other measures than criminal prosecution.

Occasionally such changes have been entirely *de facto*. We are told, for instance, that the state is no longer enforcing the notorious provision that subjected the relatives and dependents of deserting servicemen to criminal punishment (five years in exile) even if they had not assisted or even known of the desertion; however, the statute still remains on the books, though it may have "lagged behind life." It is quaintly consistent with this informality that the *de facto* suspension of the statute was disclosed by the Deputy Procurator General of the U.S.S.R. in an interview in which he inadvertently admitted, by implication, that when the provision had been in effect, it had been misapplied to the relatives of subversive but nondeserting servicemen.

Other acts regarded as state crimes have been redefined. The

definition of treason, according to D. S. Poliansky (Chairman
of the Commission on Draft Legislation of the Soviet of the
Union), places a new emphasis on the necessary element of
intent; it still includes, however, flight from the U.S.S.R. or the
refusal to return to the U.S.S.R. from abroad. Terrorism, which
Poliansky conceded had often been broadly interpreted in the
past because it had not been defined with sufficient precision,
is now specified as "the killing of a state or public official or
representative of authority, committed in connection with his
state or public activity, with the aim of undermining or weakening Soviet power"—or "grievous bodily harm inflicted with the
same purposes" upon a victim of the same status. Concealment
of crimes and failure to report crimes are, as before, punishable
only where the criminal law specifically says so, but a specific
provision establishing punishment for failure to report is included
in the new law on state crimes.

Until the republican codes are enacted, it will not be possible
to enumerate all of the acts that have lost their criminal character as a result of the new reforms. The criminal responsibility
of juveniles has been lightened somewhat; persons who commit
crimes between the ages of fourteen and sixteen are criminally
responsible only for specified major crimes, and persons who,
before reaching the age of eighteen, have committed crimes
"representing no great social danger" may at the discretion of
the courts be treated by compulsory measures "of an educational
character" without formal criminal punishment.

The Aims of Criminal Justice

The handling of Soviet citizens who have been convicted of
crime evinces several interwoven threads in Soviet legal and
social thought. Soviet attitudes toward sentencing and punishment have been said by scholars to illustrate the "parental theory" of Soviet law; but this suggestive distinction becomes
ambiguously attractive when one considers that there are parents
. . . and parents. To say that Soviet criminals are considered
wayward youths who must be re-educated to take their place
in Soviet society, and that the process of trial and sentence is

intended to instruct the populace, does help to call attention to that component of Soviet criminological theory that lays stress on the goal of rehabilitation, and to the moralizing conscious-ness-of-community that has long been observed in Russian his-tory and society. Other notions bearing on the purpose of punishment—the notions of revenge, prevention, and deterrence—also play their role in Soviet doctrine. If we bear in mind the popular bit of Soviet folklore to the effect that the population of the Soviet Union is divided into three groups—prisoners, ex-pris-oners, and future prisoners—the situation is worth studying in some detail.

Stimulated by Marxist sociology and Italian penology, early Soviet writers sought to dehydrate the concept of crime by squeezing out its moral element. Traces of the attempt can be found in the legal codes, which (though the wording was not consistent throughout) often used the terms "socially dangerous act" instead of crime, and "measures of social defense" instead of punishment. The typically prescribed measure of social defense was corrective labor, with or without deprivation of freedom. Nonpolitical crimes were attributed at first to the fragmentary survival of bourgeois economic relations of production, and later, when crime refused to disappear after the achievement of socialism was proclaimed, to survivals of capitalist ways of thought in the minds of the criminals. The range of permissible sentencing represented, as it does elsewhere in varying degrees, a compromise between the desire to allow the court to individual-ize the punishment and the "menu" theory, which assumes that a prospective lawbreaker has the right to know the exact price attached to the crime he is about to commit. A special feature was the power given to the regular courts to convict, and sen-tence to exile, even a defendant who had not committed a "socially dangerous act" if, by reason of his previous activity or present associations, he was considered in his own person a social danger. (This provision, though still in the Soviet criminal code, was in effect judicially repealed in 1946.)* Places of pun-

* The repealer took the form of a directive of the Plenum of the U.S.S.R. Supreme Court of July 12, 1946, which stated that the code provision authorizing the conviction of socially dangerous elements in the absence of

ishment included prisons, corrective-labor camps, and corrective-labor colonies; in addition, some lesser offenses were punishable by compulsory labor at the offender's usual place of work, without deprivation of freedom. Corrective labor in the camps and colonies was supposedly regulated by a fairly elaborate code in the interests of rehabilitation through work.

Almost every aspect of this system came under fire in the past few years. Some of the criticisms may be translated into specific provisions in the new codes; relatively more of them may only contribute to a lingering uneasiness, to a feeling that crime may be intractable even to Marxist-Leninist analysis. Some effort may be made to differentiate more sharply between the treatment of minors and casual criminals and that of professional, adult, and recidivist criminals. Corrective-labor camps, at which (it is now conceded) economic targets took precedence over the aims of rehabilitation, are said to be superseded by, or merged into, colonies governed by a looser regime. The use of prisons may be restricted to what might be called "maximum security" cases. Exile or banishment for socially dangerous elements not guilty of specific criminal acts may be deleted from the new codes, and the "objective imputation of guilt" rejected. Rudimentary efforts are being made to study the causes of crime, and unless they are balked by theoretical or political obstacles, these studies should in time affect sentencing practices. It is a promising sign that one Soviet writer—Sadnovnikov, a local prosecutor reporting from the grass roots on the prevalent and troublesome offense of hooliganism—scoffed at the official habit of trying to attribute crime to vestiges of capitalist consciousness; he states flatly that "the basic reason for hooliganism is drunkenness." Perhaps it is not too much to expect that such a man, or others like him, may begin to inquire into the basic reasons for drunkenness.

There is a curious unreality in Soviet writing on the subject of capital punishment. In line with the contemporary emphasis on the humaneness of Soviet laws, the legal analysts hold that the

---

forbidden acts had been superseded by subsequent legislation incompatible with it. See notes to Article 7 of the Criminal Code of the R.S.F.S.R. This repealer, of course, did not affect the activity of the Special Boards of the Ministry of Internal Affairs.

Soviet Union has been consistently opposed in principle to capital punishment, though the number of officially inflicted deaths both for crimes punishable by death as well as for other offenses has been large. This professed humaneness is now being bleakly expressed in the solemn posthumous rehabilitation of some of the prisoners who died in corrective-labor camps while serving sentences now acknowledged to have been unjust.

Under the new Fundamentals of Criminal Law, punishment "not only is a penalty for the crime committed, but also is aimed at the correction and reformation of those convicted, . . . [instilling] an honorable attitude toward work, exact obedience to the laws, respect for the rules of socialist community life, and also [is aimed at] the deterrence of those convicted, as well as of others, from new crimes." Perhaps the draftsmen of the new legislation considered deterrence more important than rehabilitation for a number of offenses, for the death penalty is to be retained for treason, espionage, diversion (defined in the Law on State Crimes as a sort of major sabotage), terrorism, banditry, and intentional homicide in "aggravating circumstances"; it will also be applied in special cases to other "heinous crimes." From the text it is not clear what will be covered in the catch-all provision at the end of the list. A deputy from Adygei Autonomous Oblast, addressing the Supreme Soviet while the new laws were under consideration, complained of the action of appellate courts in reversing convictions for intentional homicide on the ground that the victim had survived; his protest was based on the fact that the defendant had after all "done all he could to carry out his intent to kill." The catch-all provision, when spelled out by detailed republican laws, may make it possible in such cases to apply the death penalty without distorting the definition of homicide as the speaker wished to do. Many of the maximum sentences were somewhat shortened; on the other hand, the criteria for parole, especially for major criminals and recidivists, were stiffened, and an attempt was made to stop the practice of speeding eligibility for parole by the overliberal crediting of "labor days" for time served in confinement.*

* On May 5, 1961, the Presidium of the Supreme Soviet of the U.S.S.R. issued a decree extending the death penalty (still "pending its complete

The Doctrine of Analogy

Though the list of crimes was not much altered by reform measures, the character of the list was in some measure hardened, to the protection of defendants, by the abolition, no less certain for being implicit, of the doctrine of Analogy. That doctrine, which had been embodied in Article 16 of the Criminal Code of the R.S.F.S.R. and in corresponding articles of the codes of other republics, permitted the courts, in cases of "socially dangerous" acts not specifically covered by law, to apply the punishment that the law prescribed for the most closely similar offense. Several judicial limitations developed that, had they ever been followed consistently, would have blunted most of the sting of the article: It was held, for example, that Analogy could not be applied where the act *was* expressly covered by some other law, and also that Analogy could not be used as a means of increasing the severity of a sentence. Nevertheless, the article came to stand for arbitrary brutality in the Soviet penal system, and the necessity of its abolition figured prominently in the public discussions of legal reform. After a lively dispute, the abolitionists won out.* The official explanation is that the cultural level of the Soviet citizenry has now risen so high that "socially dangerous" acts either will not be committed or can be anticipated sufficiently to enable the legislature to outlaw them in advance by specific statute.

The technical importance of the abolition of Analogy will be slight, however, since the same purpose can be achieved, if necessary, by other means—for instance, by enactment of retro-

---

abolition") to cover, among others, "the case of especially dangerous habitual offenders and persons convicted of serious crimes who, in places of deprivation of freedom, terrorize prisoners who have taken the path of reform...." (See this author's "The Criminal Reconsidered," *Problems of Communism,* July–August, 1961.)—*Ed.*

* Fundamentals of Criminal Law, Art. 3: "No one shall be subject to criminal liability and punishment save one is guilty of the commission of a crime, that is, a socially dangerous act committed intentionally or negligently and *specified by criminal law*. . . ." (Italics added.) The Russian term used for "law" here is equivalent to *lex*, not *ius;* some would even translate it as "statute," thus strengthening the implication that conviction by analogy is forbidden.

active legislation fixing a criminal penalty for an act that was legal when committed, or by broad interpretation of existing legislation, to say nothing of the possibilities of prosecution outside the regular system of the courts. All these expedients have been repudiated by the legal reformers, but they are supported by Soviet precedent and may be resorted to again should the abolition of Analogy prove awkward for the regime. Even more likely is the insertion in the new codes of a catch-all category of crimes, defined with sufficient breadth and vagueness to permit an astute prosecutor and court to fill almost any gap not covered by the new, exhaustive list of specified crimes. Still, to say that the abolition of Analogy will have mainly a symbolic effect is not to say categorically that it will make no difference in the administration of Soviet justice: At least for a time, the courts can be expected to refrain from resorting to substitute devices.

Due Process?

Before the enactment of the Fundamentals, the Soviet legal and general press entertained a three-way debate on the desirability of stating expressly the principle of the presumption of innocence. The debate appears to a foreign observer to have been remarkable all round for its dubious logic and its naïve attitude, both toward burdens of proof and toward the dynamics of courtroom procedure. Some held that the presumption could not exist in Soviet law, because the mere fact that a man was accused in court by a public prosecutor on the basis of a preliminary investigation showed that some responsible officials believed him guilty. Others contended that the right to counsel implied that the defendant was presumed innocent until proved guilty, for if he was presumed guilty from the beginning, there would be no point in granting him the right to be defended. The proponents of the latter view, in turn, were divided among themselves on the question whether or not the inferred presumption should be spelled out.

As finally enacted, the Fundamentals of Criminal Justice set forth a formula bearing all the stigmata of a compromise that makes none of the compromisers happy: "The court, procurator, investigator, and person conducting the [police, etc.] inquiry do not have the right to shift the burden of proof onto the accused."

This formula may be combined with the principle, stated elsewhere in the Fundamentals, that "conviction cannot be founded on presuppositions and shall be pronounced only in the event that the guilt of the accused has been proved in the course of the judicial hearing. Even so, it fails to illuminate the problem of the quantum of proof necessary to translate an "inner conviction" into an outer conviction, and gives no clear guidance to local officials.

The contrasting inferences still possible may be seen in two of the official remarks accompanying the "discussion" of the drafts in the Supreme Soviet. A. F. Gorkin of the U.S.S.R. Supreme Court, speaking as a Deputy from the Kirghiz S.S.R., referred to "the principle, flowing from the sense and spirit of our legislation, according to which the proof of an accusation rests at the charge of the accuser and the accused is not obliged to prove his innocence." Yet Deputy B. S. Sharkov, of the Lithuanian Republic, inveighing against "certain scholars who still have not emerged from their ivory towers" (*Izvestia*, December 3, 1958), scolded those who had "attempted to introduce into our theory and practice the outworn dogmas of bourgeois law in the nature of a presumption of innocence." He ridiculed a suggested formula to the effect that the accused should be considered innocent until his guilt was established by the lawfully pronounced sentence of a court, and went on:

Enactment of such a formula into our law would entail irreconcilable contradictions. Take a case like this: A murderer, a bandit, is caught at the scene of the crime with the goods on him. The investigator and procurator make a careful investigation in full conformity with the law and establish the guilt of the bandit, though even without that his guilt was evident to everyone. On the basis of the law and the indisputable evidence collected, the investigator and the procurator not only have a right, but are obliged in duty, to hale the murderer to criminal liability and take

him into custody. At the same time, according to the formula
being proposed, if it were enacted into law, the investigator
and the procurator would be obliged to consider that bandit
innocent. More than that—inasmuch as it is stressed that the
accused shall be considered innocent up to the time the
sentence enters into lawful force, the result is that even
the court, when it has considered the case and is issuing its
sentence of conviction, is obliged to consider the accused
innocent. The absurdity of such a state of affairs from the
viewpoint of common sense is beyond dispute. The only
thing that passes understanding is, why is this not clear to
the said theoreticians?

One of the most problematic of the procedural rights of a
criminal defendant, in Soviet circumstances, was the right to
counsel. Before the new Fundamentals, the right to counsel
was, generally speaking, confined to the period of actual trial
proceedings. Counsel was not permitted, as of right, during the
stage of investigation by the pretrial investigator; nor was it the
defendant's right, though it is said to have been the common
practice, to have counsel present during review of his case by
an appellate tribunal. The absence of counsel during the pretrial
investigation, while not in itself unusual, did particular harm
under Soviet conditions, because the investigator's findings, upon
approval by the public prosecutor, became the basis of the activity of the court during the trial; this meant that the initial report
of facts, placed before the court, had not been previously tested
by cross-examination or countered by professionally martialed
evidence on the defendant's behalf.

The Fundamentals of Criminal Procedure broadened the right
to counsel at both ends of the trial process. The accused is now
to be permitted counsel from the time the accusation is communicated to him, though not necessarily as of the beginning of the
preliminary investigation, and defense counsel now has the
express right to take part in a hearing on appeal after conviction.

In the past, counsel's role during the trial proper was restricted
by several factors, among which formal statutory restraints were
not necessarily the most important. Time was when defense

counsel even vied with the public prosecutor in abusing the defendant, especially in political cases; there are grounds for belief that this was no mere forensic tactic, designed to prepare the way for a plea for clemency, but rather a recognition of the "educational" importance of the trial and the delicacy of counsel's own position. The new law directs counsel "to use all means and methods of defense laid down in the law in the interest of eluci- dating the circumstances that exonerate the accused or mitigate his responsibility, and to render the necessary legal assistance to the accused."

Even the small changes in the role of defense counsel appear to have met with some opposition, which D. Rasulov (Chairman of the Commission on Draft Legislation of the Soviet of Nation- alities) endeavored to allay in his presentation to the Supreme Soviet (*Izvestia*, December 26, 1958):

> The drafting committees proceed from the idea that defense counsel is obliged to use all means envisaged by the law in the defense of the accused and to furnish the accused the necessary legal assistance. Together with this it must be emphasized that from the viewpoint of Soviet law and the principles of socialist morality, defense counsel may not conduct himself so as by any method whatever to hedge his defendant about with protection against condign justice. Soviet defense counsel must serve the greater humane cause of the defense of socialist society, law, truth, and justice. That is the way to define his course of conduct in the defense of the accused—that is where the task of defense counsel lies, and not in the defense of illegal chicanery on the part of the accused, which would inevitably grow into defense of a criminal and thus of crime.

As for quantum of proof, the Soviet criminal system, like others on the European continent, is roughly accusatorial or inquisitorial rather than adversary. That is, the court, instead of sitting passively in judgment on the evidence furnished by opposing parties, and regulating its decision in doubtful cases with the help of such Anglo-Saxon legal concepts as the "risk of nonpersuasion" or the "necessary quantum of proof," is supposed to penetrate to the "objective truth" of the case, continuing the proceedings as long as necessary to establish the facts and taking appropriate initiative to uncover relevant evidence. To what extent it actually does this, except in exemplary cases occasionally publicized for the edification of the profession, is a matter of some doubt. At all events, it now seems to be largely agreed that conviction is improper in the absence of "objective truth," and that the old formulas of maximal, relative, or approximate truth facilitated improper convictions.* This latter could well be a restrospective exaggeration of the influence of theory on practice.

The warmest period of the thaw produced, in particular, a number of attacks upon the emphasis that Soviet legal doctrine used to place on the confession of the accused. The critics recalled that confessions have occasionally proven false and that some—whether true or false—were extorted by improper means. As late as 1950, an official had written: "With what a feeling of moral satisfaction an investigator compiles an indictment when he has the confession of the accused. . . . The accused has confessed—that is a great achievement, especially in a case where there is no direct evidence of his guilt." Now, however, it is felt that this went too far, or at least that the official's choice of words was unhappy. Confessions probably will not be ruled altogether inadmissible in evidence under the new codes, but they will very likely cease to be regarded as the Queen of Proof—an ancient notion that, in Vyshinsky's day, was practically official dogma. Soviet law still seems far away from developing a distinction between confessions that may be admitted in evidence because

* Soviet theorists busied themselves for years with questions of judicial epistemology, but they have not always distinguished the problems of quality of evidence, the hazards of fact-finding, and the burden of proof, on the one hand, from the general question of the nature of cognition, on the other. Some of them have also been accused by others of slanting their scholarly assertions in order to make convictions easier (or harder). Several warring theories are reviewed in Starchenko, "The Problem of Objective Truth in the Theory of Criminal Procedure," *Voprosy filosofii*, No. 2 (1956), pp. 105–17.

they are voluntary, and confessions that are inadmissible because coerced.

When Is a Court Not a Court?

The changes in Soviet criminal law and procedure will be celebrated by Moscow as new strides in the history of mankind. It will not matter if some of the reforms appear only to bring the Soviet system up to the level of the eighteenth century, for any given principle or institution that would, by definition, be reactionary under bourgeois conditions is, also by definition, revolutionary and progressive when adopted in the Soviet Union. Thus, one Soviet legalist, rediscovering in 1957 the principle of *nullum crimen, nulla poena sine lege*, reported that it "was inscribed on the flag of the bourgeoisie as it came to power and was vitiated soon thereafter, like all the other principles of bourgeois democracy." He added that it now "can find its consistent and genuine realization only in socialist society."*

The paper reforms, when completed, are unlikely to take account of all the criticisms voiced in the relatively outspoken era of 1956–7, and even then they will be of dubious effectiveness until tested in practice. Soviet writers occasionally concede this. Some of them have shown themselves to be aware of the vast gulf between the *Soll* and the *Ist* in criminal law: between the "issuance of lawful norms" and the "unlawful and incorrect application of the norms," between the pious morality behind the Corrective Labor Code and the grim truth of the camps, between the principle of judicial independence and the facts of judicial practice

---

* Shliapochnikov, "On the Stability of Soviet Criminal Law," *Sovetskoe gosudarstvo i pravo*, No. 12 (1957), p. 19. Cf. Chkhikvadze, *ibid.*, No. 11 (1957), pp. 130, 139: "Coercion applied by the Soviet state differs in principle from coercion applied by bourgeois states. The Soviet state applies coercion for the defense of the conquests of the socialist revolution, for the annihilation of exploitation of man by man, for the construction of a classless Communist society; therefore it bears a progressive, revolutionary character. Coercion applied by bourgeois states, on the other hand, is directed toward the subjugation and exploitation of the toilers, the defense of the power of the exploiters; it is directed against the historical development of mankind; therefore it bears a reactionary, antipopular character." Circular reasoning has—by definition—no gaps.

in some cases, between the ideal of the impartial pretrial investigator and his actual zeal for conviction. They are aware that a
statute means little until (as Shliapochnikov put it with typical
aplomb) it is interpreted "in the dialectical unity of its sociopolitical content and form."

These qualifications need not, however, prevent us from recognizing what may be a genuine and widespread sentiment for the
improvement of Soviet criminal law and procedure in the direction of genuine legality. The mere fact that there is so much
smoke does not prove that there is no fire. If the new substantive
provisions are buttressed by improved institutions and procedures—more independence for the pretrial investigator, wider judicial review of executive and administrative acts, a more impartial procuracy, a better-trained corps of judges and people's
assessors, fuller and more regular publication of court cases,
statutes, and decrees—much may be achieved, at least in the area
of nonpolitical cases.

What reformers have not touched and will not touch is the
political basis that necessarily prevents "socialist legality," Soviet-
style, from meeting the standards of legality upheld—though
imperfectly—in other countries. There will be no sure legal
guarantees that the *troikas* and purges will not recur, that the
cult of (some other) personality will not again become the religion of the state, and that terror will not lay waste another generation of Soviet citizens; indeed, there can be none as long as the
Party, and the elements of Soviet society striving for supremacy
through or against the Party, remain unwilling to grant effective
autonomy to the legal system, keeping it above the political struggle as a safeguard of general order and liberty.

The reasons for this unwillingness are almost as complex as
Soviet society itself, but that it exists seems clear. Its most conspicuous recent illustration is provided by the new law against
social parasites already enacted by statute in several of the smaller
republics in 1957 and 1958, though not yet passed in the R.S.F.S.R.
or the Ukrainian Republic. The most remarkable feature of this
law is not that it fixes deportation to remote areas for the term
of two to five years at compulsory labor as the penalty for "malicious evasion of socially useful work" or living "on unearned in-

come" (but, incidentally, not for ordinary vagrancy, which is specifically excluded from the law's application). Such severity is not unusual in the light of Soviet and earlier Russian history, though it is hardly to be reconciled with the current professions of humaneness and parental solicitude. Nor is it particularly astonishing that, in fact, the law has been applied to such malefactors as a collective farmer accused of neglecting work for the collective in favor of working his own plot and an artisan who bought, repaired, and sold musical instruments on his own.

The really striking feature of the law is the procedure by which it is enforced. Judgment is pronounced, without court trial, by a public assembly of the defendant's neighbors; the necessary vote is a simple majority of those present, provided they represent a quorum of the neighborhood. The judgment is then reviewed by the executive committee of the appropriate local soviet, but not by any judicial body, and becomes final and executory upon approval by the executive committee.

This procedure, halfway between that of a Nazi people's court and the medieval Russian folkmoot (*Veche*), shows little consistency with the claims and purported aspirations of the Soviet legal reformers. It has encountered some, but not much, public opposition. On its face it seems to be an effort to place a powerful weapon of discipline in the hands of local party leaders, who of course dominate the executive committees of the local soviets and probably are also able to wield the initiative in the public assemblies of the neighborhoods. At the same time, from the Party's point of view, it would seem to contain, among other things, a threat of haphazard and inconsistent administration, the danger of "localism" in a special form, which may have to be countered by providing for secondary review in Party or perhaps administrative channels. However, that would hardly cure the other vices of the law.

Nothing was said in the new legislation to indicate that it must lead to the repeal of the antiparasite laws. Moreover, the care with which some of the references to the new laws stress the "criminal" character of the proceedings over which the regular courts are to have exclusive jurisdiction, may hint at a plan to preserve or even extend the antiparasite statutes on the ground that the offenses at which they aim and the penalties that they authorize are not "criminal."

One clue to the future of the antiparasite tribunals may be found in a broader setting. Mr. Khrushchev, in one of the neo-Periclean passages of his address to the Twenty-first Congress of the CPSU(January, 1959), showed himself to be (ex officio) a leading legal philosopher as well as a theoretician of Marxism-Leninism. The First Secretary told the Congress:

> Social [nongovernmental] organizations must acquire juris-diction more and more over problems of the security of public order and the rules of socialist communal life. At the present time there are no instances of court liability in the Soviet Union for political crimes. This is doubtless a great achievement. It bespeaks the unprecedented unity of the political convictions of our entire people, of its solidarity around the Communist Party and Soviet rule.

> But there are still not a few instances of violations of public order, and a decisive struggle must be waged against them. Cannot Soviet society cope with the violators of socialist legal order? Of course it can. Our organizations have no fewer possibilities, equipment, and power for this than the organs of the police, the court, and the procuracy!

> The point is that functions of security of public order and safety should be fulfilled by organizations as well as by such state institutions as the police and the courts. . . .

The theme of the larger role envisaged for extragovernmental machinery in sustaining the Soviet legal order was echoed—with a difference—by A. N. Shelepin, then Chairman of the Committee on State Security. He congratulated the Party on the full restora-tion of "revolutionary legality," in a possibly inadvertent revival of the phrase, and assured the Congress that "the shameful business of violations of legality will never be repeated any more. The Party and its Central Committee will not allow it."

Shelepin, like Khrushchev, spoke of prophylactic measures to be undertaken, especially by nongovernmental organizations, supplementing or substituting for the regular legal machinery. He stressed the supervision of "work therapy" by social organizations:

> I think we ought to consider affording rights to social organizations—Komsomols, trade unions, collective plants and factories, and kolkhozes—to take under their wing misguided people who have committed insignificant crimes, so as to give them the opportunity of reforming themselves in the collective instead of serving a punishment imposed by a court.

It may be wondered whether part of the impetus for this suggestion came from considerations of the needs of Soviet manpower. Shelepin may have reflected that corrective-labor colonies were not as efficient users of convict labor as labor unions and collective farms could be, and he may have had his eye focused not so much on rehabilitation through work as on work through rehabilitation.

The comments made by Mr. Khrushchev and others portend the possibility of a substantial incursion of unofficial tribunals—whether folkmoots or kangaroo courts or comrades' courts—into the jurisdiction of the regular criminal courts. This development would appear to be regarded as a part of the progressive transfer of various supervisory functions from governmental to nongovernmental hands. As Khrushchev said in his speech at the Twenty-first Congress:

> Socialist society is creating such voluntary organs . . . as the people's police, comrades' courts, and similar bodies. They will operate afresh, fulfill public functions afresh. Voluntary detachments of the people's police must take on themselves the securing of public order in their settlements. . . . The time has come to pay great attention to the comrades' courts, which must in the main endeavor to avert various kinds of violations. They must take up not only questions of an industrial-productive character but also of a moral and daily-living character, instances of incorrect conduct of members of the collective, which permit deviations from the norms of

public order. . . . The main thing is this prophylactic, educational work.

It seems likely that a generation of Soviet legal and governmental officials will be kept busy attaching some meaning to Mr. Khrushchev's extensive but cryptic remarks. One thing seems fairly certain: If the gradual transition from what he calls socialism to what he calls communism is to be accompanied by this progressive "degovernmentalization" of legal functions, the Party must prepare itself to take over the active supervision of nominally unofficial institutions to an even greater degree than has been the case up to now.

Vitally involved in this issue of "degovernmentalization" is the theoretical question of the relative roles of coercion and suasion in the advancing socialist order. M. A. Suslov, the leading theoretician (after Khrushchev) in the Presidium, touched on this point of theory in his speech to the Twenty-first Congress:

With the development of Soviet society, the methods of activity of state organs are also changing; the organization and persuasion of the masses acquires greater and greater significance. Coercion was never the main method in the activity of the socialist state; now, the sphere of coercion is becoming still narrower, and is pointed [sic] only against agents sent by the imperialistic states, and also against thieves and swindlers, plunderers of public property, idlers, malicious hooligans, murderers, and other antisocial elements.

Rather ironically, the "persuasive" sphere is far less clearly defined in Suslov's statement than is the "coercive"—the area in which the state's official constraints remain applicable. On the question of how coercion may be made to give way to persuasion—whether the agent be governmental or extragovernmental—the Soviet leaders seem unwilling, or unable, to proceed beyond obscure generalities. Of interest in this respect is the plaintive though guarded request voiced by one of the most distinguished specialists in Soviet criminal law, Professor S. A. Golunsky, in the course of a recent address that on the whole was remarkable for the care with which he avoided specific approbation of the new efforts (*Izvestia*, December 27, 1958).

We must have a fresh resolution of the problem of the relationship between persuasion and coercion as a method of the state's guidance of society, about which there is a direct mention in the remarks of Comrade Khrushchev [in his November presentation of the Seven Year Plan]. . . . The task of our science of law is to find criteria that would enable us to determine rightly in each particular instance whether it is expedient in that case to establish norms of law presupposing the possibility of coercion or to apply a complex of other measures of an organizational and educational character. So far, our science of law has not gone beyond general statements about the union of persuasion and coercion in Soviet law.

No one observing this confused scene from outside can now guess with any confidence whether the development of new criteria for liability, the substitution of new types of sanction, and the alteration of institutional arrangements will follow parallel lines or will proceed at the same speed. To judge from the official criminology, there still is agreement on the idea that criminal tendencies are to be referred to as "remnants of capitalism in the consciousness of people" or "birthmarks of the past, inherited from capitalism." "The vitality of these remnants of the past," said Suslov at the Twenty-first Congress, "is explained by the lag of consciousness behind the facts of social existence and by the penetration into our midst of alien views and bourgeois ideology from the capitalist world." Unless statements of this type can be dismissed by Soviet legal scholars as mere Soviet equivalents for the statement that Evil comes from Satan, the search for the causes of crime will make little progress, and the universally difficult problem of the proper relationship between suasion and coercion will elude their grasp. Perhaps the gravest danger to Soviet legality is that coercive measures will be placed at the disposal of nongovernmental, irregular courts, lacking even the procedural safeguards of the new laws, and empowered to enforce the tenets of "suasion" by means of an organized and irremediable system of injustice.

These forebodings are creatures of the middle distance, not of the here and now. To the mass of Soviet citizens concerned with the law from below, the legal system after the changes of late 1958 will probably appear a little more rational, a little less harshly punitive, a little smoother in its operation. But it is unlikely that they will consider it in any significant sense "their" legal system, since it remains one imposed from above, one dependent for its elements of stability and decency on the fateful caprice of an elite ultimately responsible to no one but itself. To the thoughtful Soviet citizen it must be cold comfort to think that his protection against future excesses depends on the assurance that, in Shelepin's phrase, "the Party and the Central Committee will not allow it."

In no country does the history of legal procedure, of substantive criminal law, of constitutional safeguards, justify an attitude of complacency. The handling of petty offenses, in particular, requires in all contemporary societies a difficult consideration of penological, administrative, sociological, economic, and other factors. An observer of the struggles on the legal scene in the Soviet Union must look with sympathy on the efforts of Soviet legal reformers to deal with some of the same problems, aggravated as they are by the special circumstances of the Soviet political system, and must hope that the concept of "socialist legality" will become something less of a contradiction in terms than it appears to be today.

Recent Soviet Historiography

——ALEXANDER DALLIN

No OTHER REGIME has tried so hard and so brazenly to rewrite the past to suit its political needs as has that of the Soviet Union. Step by step, history has been reduced to an ancillary instrument of propaganda. There is only one official, mandatory version, and with each change of tactics, inconvenient historical figures and events (and at times historians, too) are relegated to the Orwellian memory hole. The reversals in historical interpretation that followed Stalin's death, however, have been somewhat more complex and far-reaching than their predecessors. By 1953, Soviet historiography—like most other fields of endeavor—had reached the nadir of sterility and rigidity. Personally and professionally insecure, subject to the wiles of charlatans, many a scholar yearned for a breathing spell and a reassertion of truth.*

Two trends converged to produce the present turn in Soviet historical writing. One has been the general climate of greater security and relaxation—characteristic of the more flexible

---

* Despite political dictation, some excellent work has been done, whose scientific worth has been assessed elsewhere at length. See, *e.g.*, Horst Jablonowski in *Historische Zeitschrift*, Nos. 1–2 (1955); Günther Stökl and Georg von Rauch in *Jahrbücher für Geschichte Osteuropas*, No. 1 (1955). The standard Soviet compendium was A. L. Sidorov, *Osnovnye problemy i nekotorye itogi razvitiia istoricheskoi nauki* (*The Basic Problems and Some Results of the Development of Historical Science*) (Moscow, 1955). On the political background, see Klaus Mehnert, *Stalin vs. Marx* (New York: The Macmillan Company, 1951); Bertram D. Wolfe, "Operation Rewrite," *Problems of Communism*, No. 3–4 (1953); and Cyril E. Black, ed.: *Rewriting Russian History* (New York: Frederick A. Praeger; 1956).

approach of the new rulers. In this spirit of "more breadth, more elasticity, more daring," the historian finally won an opportunity to voice, with seeming impunity, certain judgments that heretofore had been but mental reservations.

In addition, however, the new leadership has been as eager as the old to rewrite the past to bolster its own status, to find new heroes and new scapegoats. Even while attacking the Stalinist practice of labeling foes as enemies of the people, Khrushchev calls Beria an enemy of Party and state; and while the adulation of Stalin is dismissed as a despicable cult of the individual, Lenin is made the object of a similar cult. A by-product of this officially inspired search for a new legitimacy happens to be increased opportunities for somewhat less distorted writing of history.

The Thaw

This "new era" was not born overnight. While laudatory references to Stalin declined rapidly after his death, most writings continued to present the recent past in Stalinist terms. Continued intolerance and intransigence were mixed inconsistently with revisions of particularly abhorrent interpretations.

Sometime in the winter of 1954–55, a decision seems to have been adopted to end the years of enforced academic isolationism and resume some contacts with the outside world. The Soviet Union agreed to participate in the International Conference of Historical Science in Rome in September, 1955, and to join the UNESCO project on the history of science and culture. By mid-1955, the politically opportune position was that "history can nowhere lead an isolated existence." As in the 1920's, limited collaboration was possible even with non-Communists.*

At the same time, an increasing sense of personal independence and security among historians was discernible when they were told in *Voprosy istorii* not to idealize the recent past "as a smooth, linear road, as an utter victory parade," or when, in an instance of courageous integrity, one historian accused another of writing

---

* *Voprosy istorii*, No. 8 (1955) and No. 5 (1956). In early 1955, work ceased on a collective volume in the old "militant" vein, parts of which were to have been violently critical of American scholarship.

"as if all were clear, as if there were no room for discussion, and as if all that remained to be done was to repeat once again quotations that everybody knows only too well." Indeed, one could increasingly sense camouflaged attempts to push beyond the old framework and raise questions that had been taboo for years.

After this careful prelude, the "new era" in the field of history was ushered in several months before February, 1956, when the Twentieth Congress of the Communist Party staged a political "turn." In October, 1955, a conference of historians, held to discuss a new volume of Russian historical writing, bared "serious doubts and disagreements" on a number of basic problems. The official spokesman summarized "the general defects in our historical science" frankly as "an attempt to isolate Russian historical science from that of Western Europe, an immodest insistence on its superiority, a nihilist attitude toward pre-Marxian science, its reduction to a mere accumulation of factual knowledge, an effort to idealize past representatives of Russian social thought. . . ." Four months later, when the Party Congress was told that Soviet historical writing was the most backward of the social sciences, the new revisionism was given the highest stamp of approval.

The de-Stalinization campaign launched at that Congress gave the historians a new task. As usual, specific changes had to be reinforced by broader "theoretical" formulations—this time centering in the attack on the role of the individual in history. Under Stalin, it had been imperative somehow to uphold the inevitability and omnipotence of historical laws and at the same time to inflate the part of the Leader's genius. A by-product of Stalin's posthumous demotion was a shift of emphasis toward the "role of the masses" in history. Dozens of politically timely but substantively empty pamphlets and articles sought to provide a foundation for this new course. The loyal historians even discovered that Pushkin and Herzen had recognized the "role of the masses" as a prime mover of history.

These were the Soviet historian's habitual tributes to authority. More basic were the consequences of the invitation to review the entire Soviet past, as proffered by the ban on the official *Short Course of the History of the CPSU* and the so-called *Brief*

Biography of Stalin. In closed session, Khrushchev lashed out against these works, while Mikoyan made the first public criticism of the Course—which until then had been considered sacrosanct as Stalin's own "unequaled model of a scientific, Bolshevik statement of history."

Initially, the leadership made known its views on only a few isolated events in Party history. Yet there was a need, sensed by both politicians and historians, to do a more systematic job of rewriting. Who, after all, was still an enemy and who was not? When and how did Stalin become a villain? What had been suppressed and falsified in his days? The immediate impact of the new "line" was confusion and flux. It was the historical journal *Voprosy istorii* (*Problems of History*), that made itself a medium for revisions and a vehicle for "rehabilitations"—the by-word of the new era.

Rehabilitations: Not All Is Forgiven

The process of rehabilitating individuals previously purged or tacitly dropped from grace combines the present leadership's denigration of Stalin with a realization that it is politically profitable to correct such injustices—albeit posthumously. It began soon after Stalin's death with the unheralded reappearance of some surviving victims. Wholesale rehabilitations, however, came to public attention only after Mikoyan's speech of February, 1956.

The butt of his attack was a book by A. B. Likholat published in 1954, which attributed to two old Bolsheviks, Vladimir Antonov-Ovseyenko and Stanislav Kosior—both purged by Stalin—responsibility for anti-Bolshevik activity in the Ukraine during the Civil War. The volume had been officially acclaimed as a model of writing on Soviet problems and reviewed as a "great, valuable work." It was tragicomically reminiscent of Stalinist practice, therefore, when in the wake of Mikoyan's strictures *Voprosy istorii* "re-reviewed" the book. Now it was called "a model of how not to write history," and the author was exposed for willful distortions and suppressions of facts.

The same review in passing gave favorable mention to two

other prominent victims of Stalin—Mykola Skrypnik and Andrei Bubnov. This was typical of the oblique fashion in which Bolsheviks, dead or alive, were being restored to grace. Articles deplored the omission in various studies of such "vanished" Party stalwarts as Chubar, Postyshev, and Rudzutak—men whom Khrushchev had in effect exonerated in his secret speech of February 25. Next came a group of Red Army commanders who had vanished during the Great Purges: Historians were encouraged "to show the merits of outstanding commanders and political workers—commissars of the Red Army" like Marshals Blücher, Gamarnik, Tukhachevsky, and Egorov.*

For several months, uncertainty prevailed. The explicit restorations remained highly selective. Trotskyites as well as Bukharinites are still excluded; Radek and Tomsky, Zinoviev and Kamenev have remained outside the pale. None of the prominent victims of the public show trials of the 1930's has been rehabilitated under the recent "unrewriting" of history. Equally important, no non-Bolsheviks have been exonerated: The entire process has remained restricted within the Party fold.

Meanwhile pre-Bolshevik revolutionaries and non-Bolshevik Marxists such as G. V. Plekhanov were again placed in a somewhat more rational—though still "partisan"—light. Intra-Party disputes of the 1917–27 era emerged in a slightly more factual version, and future students may at least be able to consult standard (but also thoroughly Bolshevik) histories of the Party by Bubnov, Popov, and Yaroslavsky, which had been proscribed under Stalin. Indeed, they will be encouraged to go back to original sources and stenographic records of past Communist gatherings, which (for good political reasons) have become "bibliographical rarities." An important change was the admission that anti-Leninist Bolsheviks, both before and after 1917,

---

* *Ibid.*, Nos. 2 and 3 (1956). The revisions soon extended to the satellite states as well. In February, 1956, Warsaw announced the rehabilitation of the Polish Communist prewar leadership, whom the Comintern, in 1938, had branded as permeated with traitors and police agents. The "new line" also brought the exoneration of Laszlo Rajk in Hungary and Traicho Kostov in Bulgaria. After some awkward double talk, the Hungarian Communists in February, 1956, also rehabilitated Bela Kun, leader of their 1919 revolt, who had been purged in Moscow in 1937.

were sincere opponents and not merely "cliques of exposed spies and wreckers" or "agents of hostile classes."[*] Their arguments—still emphatically rejected and denounced—could now be discussed on their merits rather than in the official caricature of recent years. In substance, then, Party history returned to pre-1934 orthodoxy, rejecting many of Stalin's subsequent deeds but endorsing the Bolshevik "general line" against Rightist and Leftist opposition.

Pokrovsky Redivivus?

The towering figure—and victim—of Soviet historiography was Mikhail N. Pokrovsky. Once the unchallenged Bolshevik master historian, he was in the 1930's subjected to a posthumous attack that highlighted the Party's interference in the field of history. A series of decrees (over Stalin's, Kirov's, and Zhdanov's names) demanded, among other things, greater "appreciation of the national past" and greater stress on leading personalities in history. Pokrovsky had rejected these as "bourgeois" and "idealist" theses—a view intolerable under full-blown Stalinism, and the leading Soviet historians were rounded up to denounce him as a "hireling of fascism."

In spite of his extreme economic determinism and "sociological schematism," Pokrovsky's latently anti-Stalinist record made him a candidate for resurrection. The rewriting did not come easily. Only in the spring of 1955 did the switch become apparent: The new Soviet encyclopedia carried an article on Pokrovsky that, while not favorable, was at least factually correct. (Indicative of the coordination of such politically sensitive decisions, the first casual reference to Pokrovsky appeared in *Voprosy istorii* during the same month—May, 1955—as did Volume XXXIII of the encyclopedia.) Since then references to him have multiplied: He could again be discussed as an extremist who had erred but had done valuable work.

[*] *Ibid.*, No. 2 (1956), p. 202; No. 3, p. 9. Memoirs of "old Bolsheviks" were republished in stupendous quantities—primarily for their political value as reminders of a Leninist lineage and a pre-Stalinist prototype, *faute de mieux*, of "collective leadership." Stenographic records of certain earlier Party Congresses have been reissued in recent years.

A somewhat more modest reappraisal was accorded to Russian "bourgeois" historians. Though still violently scored on ideological ground, they could (as in the 1920's) be cited and discussed. Thus Soloviov, Kliuchevsky, and Rostovtsev became again part of the national heritage. E. Kosminski, a veteran medievalist, again referred favorably to non-Communist Russian scholars like Maxim Kovalevsky, Sir Paul Vinogradoff, and Dmitri Petrushevsky. As the head of the Soviet Academy's Institute of History declared: "While critically examining the heritage of prerevolutionary historiography, Soviet historians by no means jettison the findings of its concrete investigations, just as they do not discard the valuable factual results of investigations of contemporary foreign authors who adhere to a different methodology."

It was convenient to reduce the gap between Soviet and Western historians to one of methodology. This enabled Soviet scholars to extend their toleration to some Western historians as well. A new volume on Russian historiography, published in 1955, soon came in for attack as excessively derogatory toward non-Soviet scholarship. Negative references to De Tocqueville, Herder, Dahlmann, Lefebvre were called too crude or mechanistic: not all non-Soviet and pre-Marxian history, it turned out, was *ipso facto* unscientific.

The pendulum began to swing to the other extreme. Historians were castigated for "ignoring the influence of progressive Western European thought on the development of historiography in Russia." One could again discuss Hegel's or Montesquieu's influence on their Russian contemporaries, and travelers reported that "Western influences"—taboo for years—became favorite dissertation topics in Moscow and Leningrad.

From Ivan to Shamil: Turning Back the Clock

Along with Stalin, his favorite historical protagonists came in for denigration. The prime exhibit for this reversal is Ivan the Terrible. As late as 1955, Robert Wipper, the old historian who had raised Ivan to a peculiar respectability of political craft and statesmanship, was praised for his "correct evaluation of Ivan's personality." But a year later, just prior to Khrushchev's attack on the "Stalin myth," Ivan the Terrible was proclaimed to have been just another unworthy object of the cult of the individual. Marshal Suvorov, much extolled as a military genius, came in for severe strictures for suppressing the "progressive" Pugachev uprising and fighting against the French Revolution.

Even more basic was the termination of the ludicrous "Russia First" spirit, the insistence on Great Russian predominance and priorities in inventions. Lifting the ban on "foreign influences" was a relatively simple matter, and a systematic debunking of earlier falsifications (such as the claim of the invention of the airplane by Mozhaisky in 1882) proceeded apace. The reassessment of the Czarist past was more difficult to handle. Now one could again attack the "idealization" of Russia's role in the Crimean War and in nineteenth-century Far Eastern politics. Yet the key issue was that of Czarist annexations.

Pokrovsky's downfall ushered in the politically convenient theory that Russian conquest of neighboring nationalities had been culturally and economically a progressive development and hence a "lesser evil" than permitting them to stagnate or fall under British rule. One of the purposes of this thesis was to bolster the sense of "fraternity" between Russians and non-Russians within the empire. The same drive for multinational cohesion—now minus the overtones of Russian chauvinism—still obtains. Hence there has been considerable reluctance to jettison the theory of the lesser evil in its entirety. Yet, as one historian commented publicly, for a while all national movements in Central Asia had been considered progressive; then "certain comrades" came to regard them all as reactionary. They could not be both. What was to be done? The authorities apparently preferred to sidestep the issue. If after Stalin's death "the thesis about the progressive nature of the annexation of non-Russian peoples was no longer controversial," in 1956 it was still being maintained —a bit apologetically—that the conquests had their "progressive side."

A natural candidate for rehabilitation was Shamil, the North Caucasian independence fighter of the mid-nineteenth century. Considered a popular hero in the early Soviet era, he fell prey to the efforts of the Zhdanovites to deny the positive nature of anti-Russian resistance movements. After World War II, Shamil was subjected to a viciously hostile "review," which was forced upon an exceptionally reticent professional audience. Only in mid-1955 did Moscow publish a piece that, in effect, assailed his condemnation. While not daring to defend him, the author denied that Shamil had been a mere tool of the Turks or the British. Now the whole "distortion" was conveniently blamed on Mir Dzhafer Bagirov, former boss of Azerbaijan, who was executed in 1956 as an associate of Beria. The new version was that, while the annexations by Russia were "progressive," Shamil's opposition to them cannot be considered "reactionary." Here is a piece of dialectical double talk typical of the transitional stage in post-Stalinist historiography.

Flexibility and Ferment

Whatever the alterations, the regime's view that history is a weapon to be wielded by the political power has undergone no change. As before, historical anniversaries serve as the occasion for the fulfillment of state plans *in academe*. As before, an individual can become an "un-person." In the new chapters of "Operation Palimpsest" (to use Bertram Wolfe's term), the Great Soviet Encyclopedia suggested in 1954 that subscribers "carefully cut out" the pages referring to the purged police chief Lavrenti Beria, substituting an item on the Bering Strait; again in 1956, the encyclopedia urged the excision ("using scissors or razor blade") of a page containing an article on Kao Kang, a Chinese Communist leader, who, accused of conspiracy, allegedly committed suicide in 1954.

Political considerations dictate the diversion of emphasis— and funds—for the study of underdeveloped areas in the United States. Anti-Americanism in historical studies can be turned on and off at will. A more "truthful" study of Bolshevik history is requested in order to help "develop the contemporary tactics of foreign Communist and labor parties," to overcome "sectarianism" in them or promote "proletarian internationalism"—under Moscow's guidance.

The past is but a means to an end. As a Party historian remarked in *Voprosy istorii* (No. 2 [1956], p. 211), he objected to a re-evaluation of Shamil not on the basis of fact, but because "it would not further the strengthening of friendship among the nationalities" of the U.S.S.R. Just as it recognizes no art for art's sake, so the Soviet state denies knowledge for the sake of knowledge or history for the sake of historical truth. This is reflected in the frank, continued concern for conformity on the "historical front" and in the official demand for new history texts, which would serve "not only historical but also practical interests."*

Thus one may scarcely expect the regime itself to pioneer for dispassionate history. It is the historians who must speak out for higher professional standards, and—while many of the best men have died or vanished—some of them have done precisely that: So much so, that they have already been rebuked for excessive zeal, political naïveté or opportunism.

A recent critique of Soviet dissertations found one historian trenchantly condemning them as superficial, offering stereotypes in place of evidence, and idealizing the official favorites. The demand for "facts instead of theories" has become a leitmotiv of the craft. In 1954, S. Yakubovskaia, one of the leading women historians, began to urge young scholars to be more careful in their assertions, to read more original documents, and in general to use historical data more conscientiously.

How successful the new endeavors will be remains to be seen. Yet *Kommunist*'s (No. 5, 1956) official endorsement of freer use of archival sources marks the victorious culmination of an effort begun in 1954 to make more materials—until then, largely in the custody of the MVD—available to scholarship.

Recent reports from the Soviet Union speak of widespread

---

* The same concern with practical consequences has produced a symptomatic ambiguity within the Soviet leadership regarding history in general. While the effort documented above seeks to use history to prove the present rulers right, there is a countertrend toward "present-mindedness," and an inclination to let bygones be bygones (partly to exonerate themselves). This makes for a willingness—particularly in some bureaucratic and managerial quarters—to move away from the intense preoccupation with the past that characterized the Stalin era.

intellectual ferment and questioning of axioms. Students have been jolted out of their ideologically secure existence; the old Stalinist routine of cynicism and clichés no longer satisfies. University youths, including apprentice historians, are reportedly groping, politically at sea, and often inclined to sympathize with what Soviet editorials have chastised as "rotten elements," taking advantage of the anti-Stalin campaign to "slander the Party's policy and its Leninist foundations." The situation was climaxed by the decision to suspend examinations in Party history for the spring of 1956. Never before has there been such reluctant "ambiguity tolerance"—something the totalitarian organism inherently abhors and seeks to combat.

Yet there are distinct germs of hope in the present quest for more elbow room and more truth—demands that Soviet historians (like other professionals) voice with increasing vigor. One wing of the intelligentsia promptly took advantage of the new thaw to publicize sentiments suppressed for years. Their refrain was expressed by one who appealed to "distinguish between honest error and malicious fabrication, between mistaken views and outright untruths" (*Voprosy istorii*, No. 2, 1956, p. 194). Underneath the display of conformity and subservient mimicry, alongside mediocrities and charlatans, there remains a finer self.

The iron logic of "de-control"—even within the Soviet framework—imposed a ticklish dilemma on the leadership. The political lords permitted the intellectual to whet his appetite. Henceforth, *l'appétit vient en mangeant*. Will they be willing to permit more questioning, further inquiry and research? And can they stop the present trend without attempting to revert to the rigidity of their predecessor?

In the long run, the present situation is untenable: It contains the seeds of its own destruction (to use the Bolshevik phrase), for it is beset by the inherent contradiction between political insistence on monolithic conformity and the emboldened demands of the professionals for academic and artistic freedom.

The new turn in Soviet historiography may well have unleashed dynamics unwelcome to its sires. Until they come to fruition, the Soviet historian must continue to navigate between cynical abandon to political dictation and courageous emancipation into scientific scholarship—scientific not in label but in method and spirit.

The Crisis

This is where matters stood when the original article was written in mid-1956. The crisis was indeed not far off. Just as the thaw in historiography began prior to the Twentieth Party Congress, which sanctioned the new course, so the first rumblings of a return to Bolshevik orthodoxy were audible months before the Kremlin decided to reverse its course—in the wake of the Hungarian and Polish crises—and flail the cardinal sins of revisionism and bourgeois objectivism.

It is symptomatic of the ferment and disarray that in 1955–56 an organ like *Problems of History*, so thoroughly controlled and so subservient to the regime, could pioneer in de-Stalinization. In prior years the journal had, in effect, the status of legislator in historical matters. Its chief editor, Anna Pankratova, was one of the few female members of the Central Committee. A prolific author, she had a remarkable record of shifting with the changing Kremlin winds. A fervent follower of Pokrovsky until his demise, she later wrote the lead article denouncing him. In 1939, she went so far as to insist that the Pokrovsky school was "the basis for the wrecking by the Trotskyite-Bukharinite hirelings of fascism, wreckers, and spies." She hailed Stalin on his seventieth birthday as the creator of Soviet "historical science" who had "extended the limits of Soviet history by 1,500 to 2,000 years." Now and until her death, she professed to stand in the vanguard of the new course, pontificating about a more "truthful," "scientific" anti-Stalinist approach.

The associate editor, E. N. Burdzhalov, who had written a variety of popular booklets and lectured at the Party's Higher School, had endeared himself to the *apparat*. Since mid-1953, he was apparently the guiding spirit of the journal. His tone at recent conferences was self-assured, if not dictatorial, and it was over his signature that in May, 1956, there appeared an article in *Voprosy istorii* going beyond Khrushchev's attack in identifying Stalin with an anti-Leninist position in the spring of 1917, making in effect an "opportunist" of him. Burdzhalov was rapidly made the target of the counterthrust by the Party's orthodox. Indeed, his piece on the Bolsheviks in 1917 permitted the implication that the Party had not been exactly infallible. Now the Party chastised *Voprosy istorii* in *Kommunist* (No. 10, 1956, p. 24) for having published—under the pressure of "rotten" or at least "hasty" elements—during the months of relative flux, some articles that slurred over or ignored "the full significance of the Party's struggle against Trotskyites, right opportunists, and deviationists," and others that "glossed over the differences of principle between Mensheviks and Bolsheviks." Before long, the journal and several of its contributors were reprimanded for having exaggerated the populist roots of Bolshevism, overstressing Western influences, and going too far in wishing to publish non-Communist materials.

In the lax atmosphere of mid-1956, Burdzhalov was able to reply to E. Bugaev's attacks on him, published in *Partiinaia zhizn* (Nos. 14 and 23). But soon the Party secured the help of a Moscow university professor, V. Smirnov, who assailed Burdzhalov in the pages of *Pravda* (November 20, 1956); and before the end of the year, the Presidium of the Academy of Sciences called for public confessions of guilt by the editors of the historical journal.

It is well to remember that Burdzhalov was but one target in the broad attack that followed the paroxysm of October–November, 1956, in the Soviet orbit. The Party leadership was determined to curtail the experiment in controlled liberalization, which had threatened to get out of hand. On March 9, 1957, the Central Committee of the Communist Party adopted a resolution, "On the Journal *Problems of History*," which was not published then, but was later allowed to appear in print (just as Krushchev's remarks on "partyness" [*partiinost*] in arts and letters were to be published half a year later). The highest authority was thus invoked to condemn the journal's heresies in theory and practice—errors that had allegedly carried it away from the Leninist principles of "partyness"—the watchword of the post-1956 era. Reiterating the various charges leveled against *Problems of History* in the Party press during the preceding eight

months, the Central Committee firmly took its stand on the side
of political orthodoxy in scholarship.

While the resolution remained secret, *Kommunist* (going to
press on March 15, 1957) carried a stern editorial demanding
strict "partyness" in history and calling for an "uncompromising
struggle against bourgeois objectivism and revisionism. . . ." As if
stunned, *Problems of History* failed to appear for the next two
months—and when the next issue came out in mid-June, it became
apparent that a purge had taken place. While the ailing Pankratova (who now admitted "serious errors") and three editorial
assistants remained, seven editors—including Burdzhalov—were
ousted. Oddly enough, for more than a year *Problems of History*
appeared without an editor in chief. Burdzhalov has not been
heard from since. The new editors, led by N. I. Matyushkin,
faithfully adopted the "new orthodoxy," joining in the various
changes and innuendos earlier raised against the old staff. The
days of flux were over. Ideological and organizational discipline
was reimposed. Since then a spirit of rigid obeisance has prevailed anew.

What Has Improved . . .

All in all, by comparison with the late Stalin era, some
improvement remains unmistakable. This is most obvious with
regard to the quantity and variety of publications. New journals
have made their appearance. Excellent series of documentary
publications have been issued, especially on the 1905 and 1917
Revolutions and on Soviet diplomatic history.* While many of
these are no more than compilations and often have politically
significant omissions, they are in general conscientiously presented and contain valuable data. Some subjects previously
neglected as too ticklish or taboo can now be handled more

* See the useful survey by S. V. Utechin, "The Year 1917: New Publications," *Soviet Survey*, November–December, 1957. The volumes include
the wartime correspondence of the Big Three; the records of the August,
1939, military-staff negotiations in Moscow; Russian relations with China
and India; and the first three of five volumes on Soviet foreign policy. Works
of several historians are being republished, and several series of diplomatic
documents and encyclopedias have been launched.

sensibly—World War II, Soviet foreign policy, and the Party's top organs.

Access to primary sources has improved, and recent studies use original materials to a far greater extent than was possible before 1953. The long struggle to gain access to governmental archives was at least partially won by the scholars: A decree of February 7, 1956, gives them permission to use such archives. Contacts with the outside world have multiplied, and while it would be an error to speak of a meaningful exchange of ideas, it is true that Soviet historians now take much greater cognizance of foreign writings and opinions even in the field of Russian history.

In a move away from Russia-centered education, the Soviet secondary-school curriculum has, since 1957, included the "recent history of foreign countries." Training of historians—whatever its many inadequacies and distortions—is rigorous and strives for high standards. The rather unceremonious appeal to authority has been amply assailed. Modest, "business-like" criticism is no longer shunned; and journal reviews condemn other historians for "primitiveness," "scientific inadequacy," "schematism," "declarativism" in lieu of research, and—a terminological jewel— "quotationism" (*tsitatnichestvo*). While very much remains to be desired, the old extremes of mandatory misinterpretation remain abandoned.

. . . And What Has Not

The major trend since 1957 has been the increased politicalization of the social sciences. History has again been made a docile tool in the Party's omniscient conduct of the secular struggle, and Moscow is proud to say so. Indeed, any suggestion that there might be a conflict between Party dictate and the demands of historical truth is rebuffed with studied indignation. How to explain the successful creative development of historical science in the Soviet Union? *Problems of History* editorially explains: "Above all by the fact that the entire work of our scholars is always guided by the Communist Party." The necessity of "party-ness" remains, for "Communist partyness and bourgeois objectivism express entirely different class purposes and methodologies, different approaches to the evaluation of social phenomena. In the last analysis, this is due to the opposite interests of capital and labor. . . ."*

With the victory of the proponents of "applied history," the secretary of the Academy of Sciences' historical division told the Soviet historians that they "must direct all their energy and creative capabilities to the solution of problems posed by life and directly connected with the great process of building a Communist society." Their work must be "subordinated" to the needs of "Communist education, ideological struggle, and the study of contemporary world processes in the epoch of transition from capitalism to Communism."†

Another token of the increased "partyness" are the frequent contributions to *Voprosy istorii* and *Novaia i noveishaia istoriia* (*Modern and Contemporary History*) by such Communist stalwarts as Walter Ulbricht, Harry Pollitt, Ferenc Munich, and Roger Garaudy. Their articles underscore the tighter linkage of the historical craft with the Party's organs.

One of the consequences of the 1957 purge was a restructuring and tightening of jurisdictional lines. The leading position has been held by the Department of Historical Branches of the U.S.S.R. Academy of Sciences, whose task it has been to draft research plans for Soviet historians. Indeed, Soviet historians, much as the rest of the "national economy," are governed by a Seven Year plan. More recently, particular stress has been placed on direct links with the AON—the Academy of Social Sciences of the Communist Party's Central Committee in Moscow. One conference sponsored by it analyzed "bourgeois" writings on the

* *Voprosy istorii*, No. 4 (1958), pp. 4, 8. See also *ibid.*, No. 10 (1957), p. 11. The need for vigilance must also have domestic roots, since, we are told, "It is essential to rebut the efforts of certain historians and participants of past events who seek to revise and gloss over the errors of 'Leftists' and 'Rightists' and national deviationists in the Ukraine. . . ." (*Ibid.*, No. 2 (1959), p. 177.)

† *Ibid.*, No. 6 (1959), p. 157. Soviet pedagogues have frankly posited as purposes of history training "to develop [among Soviet youth] hatred for the enemies of the toilers, to strengthen devotion to Party and people, readiness to give all its forces to the struggle for the victory of Communism." (*Ibid.*, No. 7 (1959), p. 48. See also *Pravda*, September 16, 1959.)

history of the U.S.S.R. as well as research on Soviet Russia carried on abroad. Another, in the first half of 1959, reviewed the quality of *Problems of History*. While finding much to criticize, it determined that the journal had become far more "goal-oriented" and was serving the cause of struggle against bourgeois objectivism and revisionism. It is symptomatic that the first commentator at this conference was K. V. Gusev, Secretary of the Communist Party organization at the AON, and that the new Editor in Chief of *Voprosy istorii*, S. F. Naida, publicly acknowledged the need for "more systematic and closer cooperation" with the AON.

Totems and Taboos

In May, 1959, a special conference in Tashkent reopened the old argument over the character of Czarist aggrandizement. While avoiding the blanket statements that had characterized Stalin's last years, it found that the absorption of backward areas by Russia had had a "progressive significance" in that it put the more primitive peoples "in contact with the advanced Russian culture." Now it is proper to speak of the "civilizing role of Russia."

Recent publications on the Revolution of 1917 methodically underplay the significance of the February Revolution, play up the part of the Bolsheviks, and weave fanciful stories about the coup's impact on the revolutionary activities of non-Russian toilers. Historical publications abound in political blasts against writers abroad critical of the U.S.S.R. It is hardly necessary to stress that Soviet historiography continues to operate within a narrowly circumscribed universe whose official boundaries have been set and within which the margin of debate may concern only matters of relative emphasis or detail. The taboos remain: The true story of collectivization, of intra-Party "deviations," of Katyn, of assassinations and kidnappings abroad, of the secret terms of the Nazi-Soviet Pact of 1939, of the background of the Korean war—all these and many more problems are still concealed, ignored, or denied.

The phase of "rehabilitations" is over, and the demands of

accuracy and completeness (let alone the requirements of morality) remain completely ignored. Republication of memoirs—say, on the Revolution—gives evidence of curious distortions and suppressions that mirror the latest "line." For, while a given line may change, there is always *a* line. And the gaping memory holes remain. Indeed, it is a neat feat of academic brinkmanship to write an entire volume (as a Soviet historian did) on Anglo-Soviet relations in the mid-1920's without mentioning Comintern President Zinoviev himself or the famous "Zinoviev letter" a single time—simply because this would have meant identifying the purged Zinoviev with the Soviet cause.*

At times, one suspects, the Soviet writer is not fully aware of the implications of his statements. *Kommunist* (No. 4, 1957, p. 21) editorially attacked Burdzhalov for treating facts in a manner contrary to the requirements of Marxist science. Apparently the choice of data must be guided by conformity with requisite conclusions. On another occasion, replying to the charge (made abroad) that political considerations take precedence over scholarly standards for Soviet historians, *Problems of History* (No. 5, 1958, pp. 121–22) indignantly proclaimed: "It is foreign to Communists to contrast politics, 'partyness,' and science, [which are] indissolubly linked with one another," thus by implication admitting the charge of heeding political imperatives. The Secretary of the Academy's Historical Branches, Eugene Zhukov, frankly declared that "individualism in the scholarly work of historians is a menacing phenomenon" and demanded more "collective" writing. Zhukov is no less outspoken in regard to restrictive publication policies: "One must carefully approach the problem of selecting manuscripts destined for

* F. D. Volkov, *Anglo-sovetskie otnosheniia 1924–1929 gg.* (*British-Soviet Relations in 1924–1929*) (Moscow, 1958). Even more blatantly mendacious is the recent volume on foreign policy in 1945–49. It contains nothing on the Stalin-Tito split, on Soviet demands on Turkey, or on the Soviet-Iranian crisis. It describes the Nazis in their attack on the U.S.S.R. as a tool of American imperialists and landlords, and Point Four as a form of American aggression. *Mezhdunarodnye otnosheniia i vneshniaia politika SSSR 1945–1949* (*International Relations and the Foreign Policy of the U.S.S.R., 1945–1949*) (Moscow, 1958). On the rewriting of Soviet military history, see also Raymond L. Garthoff, *Soviet Strategy in the Nuclear Age* (New York: Frederick A. Praeger, 1958), Chapter II.

appearance, publishing only those books that are most necessary for the people and most topical in subject matter."*

There is no doubt that some Soviet historians continue to wage a muted battle on the homefront.† It is no less obvious that the reimposition of controls has been generally successful. Specific instances of historical falsification, a good many crudities of analysis, and a certain "primitivism" have been abandoned, but the Bolshevik straightjacket of monistic determinism and infallibility is still with us. Stalins come and go, but the totalitarian spirit prevails.

---

* *Voprosy istorii*, No. 6 (1959), p. 158. In a "fundamental" article on the relation of history to the present, Zhukov also stated that "Marx, Engels and Lenin always subordinated their scholarly work, in history as in other social disciplines, to the actual tasks of the present." Since "history is a political science," historians must stop devoting "unjustifiably" much effort to academic subjects without relevance to the present. (*Kommunist*, No. 11 (1959), pp. 42–46.)

Since then, the changes in composition of editorial boards and policy directives have continued, but without introducing anything fundamentally novel in quality, toleration, or outlook. For a more recent policy statement, see "Sovetskaia istoricheskaia nauka na novom etape razvitiia," *Voprosy istorii*, No. 8 (1960), pp. 3–18.

† Soviet scholars have apparently been successful in beating off the extremist endeavors of Trofim Lysenko (whose return to grace is itself an index of the increased politization in the arts and sciences) to see to it that "payment for work of scholars would henceforth depend on the practical value of their scientific studies and recommendations," as he put it at the Twenty-first Party Congress. In a sense, Lysenko merely elaborated on the complaint of *Kommunist* (No. 17, 1958, p. 18) that topics of many dissertations are picked without regard for the fact that "they are needed neither for the promotion of science nor for the people."

The Soviet Theater

————JÜRGEN RÜHLE

PART I: RISE AND DECLINE

HISTORIANS OF THE Soviet theater of the 1920's advance two opposing theses: One school says that the brilliant artistry of the theater in that early period of the Soviet Union was but an afterglow of the Silver Age that preceded the Revolution, that the Bolsheviks simply had not yet had time to liquidate the Russian theater; the other school holds that the Soviet theater of the 1920's was a product of the Bolshevik cultural revolution, a testimony to the fertility that revolutionary ideas bring to the arts.

The first thesis predominates among Western historians of the theater; it seems to have been formulated under the influence of Russian émigrés to whom the triumph of Bolshevism meant the destruction of the Russian way of life and, hence, of Russian art as well. It is interesting to note that a similar view, although with a different evaluation, was held by the Stalinists—i.e., the adherents of Stalin's and Zhdanov's cultural policies—who likewise saw in the early, and to their minds formalistic and decadent, phase of Soviet art nothing but a vestige of reactionary bourgeois ideology and therefore liquidated it.

The second thesis was maintained by the Bolshevik leadership during the early, pre-Stalinist phase of the Soviet era. At that time, the Bolshevik Party laid claim to the achievements of Russian revolutionary art, which was attracting attention all over the world, as a triumph of its own ideas. After Stalin's death, this thesis was reinstated and the artists of the 1920's were rehabilitated. The partial revival of the revolutionary theater was one of the elements of de-Stalinization (1953–54), an aspect of the so-called Leninist renaissance.

Pre-Revolutionary Origins

The roots of the revolutionary theater reach deep into Russian and also West European tradition. The leading figures of the theatrical world were mature and publicly acclaimed personalities who had developed their fundamental conceptions of art by the time the Revolution broke out. To illustrate this point, let us consider the foremost revolutionaries of the theater: Stanislavski, Meyerhold, Tairov, and Vakhtangov.

When Stanislavski stepped onto the stage of the Russian theater, the need for "naturalness" was the cry of the day. The commercial and industrial circles, who by then were setting the fashion in the arts, demanded the replacement of the decorative court theater by a "theater of truth." Konstantin Stanislavski (real name, Alekseev, 1863–1938) was himself the product of this newly self-assertive bourgeoisie. The son of a Moscow manufacturer, he dedicated his entire fortune to the theater as the years went by. The Moscow Art Theater was financed initially by the directors of the Philharmonic Society, an institution established by rich Moscow merchants, and later by the big industrialist Morozov alone.

Stanislavski's early ideas, comprising the first, naturalistic phase of his prerevolutionary work (beginning with the founding of the Moscow Art Theater in 1898), must be understood against this social background. They were born of the optimistic belief in progress prevalent during the last quarter of the nineteenth century and of the materialistic philosophy of the then triumphant natural sciences. "I was born at the meeting point of two eras," Stanislavski begins his autobiography. "Thus I witnessed the progress from the tallow candle to the spotlight, from the stagecoach to the airplane, from the sailboat to the submarine, from the mail courier to telegraphy, from the flint-lock musket to the Big Bertha, from serfdom to Bolshevism." As one of the generation that had accomplished all these marvels, Stanislavski wondered why "a patriarch as venerable as our theater . . . should to this day remain in an almost primordial state." He saw his life's mission in raising dramatic art to a state of perfection commensurate with the demands of the scientific age.

This indeed was a time when new ideas began to assert themselves in theaters throughout Europe—Germany and France in particular. Stanislavski's program corresponded largely to the trends in French and German naturalism:

> We protested against the former art of acting, against the histrionic routine, against the false pathos, against the declaiming, against the dramatic exaggeration, against the foolish conventions in staging and stage scenery, against the star system that destroys the teamwork—in effect against the whole manner of the performances as well as against the worthless repertoire of the theater at that time.

This is not to say, of course, that the Art Theater was merely an echo of theatrical movements in Western Europe. The Russian love of and gift for the theater, fed from deep inner springs, brought performances to a perfection approaching the miraculous.

Symbolism and the "System"

When it is said that Stanislavski established naturalism in the Russian theater, it must not be forgotten that he introduced symbolism and surrealism to the Russian stage as well. The production in 1907 of Hamsun's *The Play of Life* marks the opening of the second, symbolist, phase of his development.

The events of the year 1905 (Russia's defeat in the war with Japan, the first Russian Revolution, and the subsequent period of militant reaction) ushered in the era of wars, revolutions, and dictatorships for Russia, sweeping away the bourgeoisie's complacent belief in progress. In the European theater a new literary movement with which naturalistic techniques could no longer cope, made its appearance. The repertoire of the Art Theater was henceforth dominated not by Tolstoi, Chekhov, and Gorki, but by Hamsun, Maeterlinck, Dostoevski, Andreev, the Hauptmann of the middle period, and the later Ibsen.

Stanislavski responded to the signs of the times with extraordinary consistency and courage. He enlisted the cooperation of *avant-garde* artists (Gordon Craig, Benoit), and the surrealistic and visionary stage settings he designed himself. In collaboration with Tolstoi's disciple, Sulerzhitski (who injected many elements of Tolstoiism into Stanislavski's ethical views) and with Meyerhold, who had severed his ties with the Art Theater some years before because of his aversion to naturalism, Stanislavski founded several experimental studios.

At this time Stanislavski also came under the influence of Indian mysticism, then in vogue in Russia, with important effect on his methodology of acting. His new basic idea—the stimulation of intuition by physical exercise—was evidently borrowed from the teachings of the Indian yogis. The merging into one's environment, which Stanislavski demanded of the actor, thus acquired a new and ultimate significance: Acting, he now believed, was not an imitation of reality but a penetration into the sphere of the subconscious, which is possible only in an authentic environment, in a concrete situation. "If the body does not begin to live, the soul cannot believe either."

To describe the Stanislavski System (as it eventually emerged), one can simply say that it rests on two conceptual pillars: "bodily freedom" and the "supreme task." The first principle, bodily freedom, consists in urging the actor not to *feel* on the stage as though he were the character to be portrayed, but to *act* that way. The term "bodily freedom" is in fact not quite precise, for it refers to human action as a whole, including the psychic expression, the will, and the utterance of words, in addition to physical action as such. Stanislavski formulated his guiding principles in order to stress simple realistic behavior, to show the contrast between his method and convulsive attempts to engender emotion out of the blue (which leads to "ham acting"), and to distinguish it from a routine mastering of certain standardized forms of human expression. The actor was to relive his role each time by going through its actions. For the mature (postnaturalistic) Stanislavski, bodily freedom meant not only an imitation of nature but a means of bringing intuition and the subconscious into play.

The supreme task, which is distilled from the movement and the spoken words of the play as well as from the roles, is the creative basic formula for the production. The purpose of postulating a supreme task is first to eliminate the rambling—and consequently ineffective—type of staging, and secondly to concentrate the attention of the director and the actors on the text proper, rather than on moods or what might be termed "stage tricks." The connection between the elements of bodily freedom and the supreme task is formed by the "trunkline of action." This concept links the individual actions, eliminating those that are unsuited to the supreme task, digressive, or superfluous.

The Stanislavski System is neither an outmoded stylistic form, nor a stale species of nineteenth-century naturalism, as many critics say, nor a dramatic panacea, as its apologists maintain. The System is the point of departure, the basis of all dramatic art, just as the study of nature is the foundation of all painting. Most great actors—consciously or unconsciously—lean on the methodology that Stanislavski for the first time formulated in scientific categories. Means of representation such as stylizing, the grotesque, exotic effects, lighting effects, etc., were used repeatedly by Stanislavski himself. If he did not take them into account in his System, it is because his development was broken off by the October Revolution, when he fell into tragic isolation. Moreover, he himself always regarded his System as not yet completed.

Other Innovators

Although Meyerhold, Tairov, and Vakhtangov, too, passed through the *purely* naturalistic school, they developed their individual styles in sharp opposition to naturalism. In so doing they went beyond Stanislavski, who never completely outgrew his naturalistic origins.

Vsevolod Meyerhold (1874–1939), who was the son of a provincial vodka manufacturer, was the best student at the Art Theater's school of acting. He played the male lead in the memorable première of Chekhov's *Sea Gull*. Stanislavski, highly demanding though he was, entrusted Meyerhold with tasks of stage directing, notwithstanding his youthful years. After several years, Meyerhold parted company with his teachers, Stanislavski and Nemirovich-Danchenko, and went to St. Petersburg, where the famous actress Komisarzhevskaia had opened an *avant-garde* theater. In opposition to the naturalism of the Art Theater, Meyerhold developed the principles of the "symbolical" stage. His goal was the decorative, pictorial composition of the stage; he grouped his actors like living bas-reliefs or frescoes. When Stanislavski began to have doubts about his own work, he called back his most gifted pupil, but their joint studio failed for financial reasons. In the years before World War I, Meyerhold— although denounced as a revolutionary—conquered the Imperial theaters in St. Petersburg, reshaping them with his stunning stagings of drama and opera.

Alexander Tairov (whose real name was Kornfeld, 1885–1950), after becoming disillusioned with naturalism, accepted a call from Marzhanov, a rich theater enthusiast in Moscow, to direct the Free Theater, which aimed to promote all the various forms of the theatrical arts under the banner of "synthetic theater." Given the task of producing a pantomime, Tairov was thrust upon the path which he was thenceforth to follow faithfully, even after Marzhanov's undertaking ended in bankruptcy. In 1914, after the war had already broken out, Tairov opened his own experimental stage, the Moscow Chamber Theater.

Tairov defined the aims of his theater negatively, distinguishing it from Stanislavski's naturalistic theater and from the symbolical theater of Meyerhold. To his mind both these schools did violence to the stage and most of all to its essence, the art of acting, which he conceived as the human body's art of expression. In Tairov's opinion, the naturalistic system turned the actor into a psychopath burrowing about in his own soul, while the symbolical stage debased him to a mere speck of color or an element of construction on the stage. Tairov strove for a theater of pure acting, liberated from all psychological, literary, pictorial or mechanical aspirations. It is in this sense that the slogan, "the unfettered theater," is to be understood. Derived from the title of Tairov's book, it has come to stand for Tairov's entire work in the field of drama. The actor should be allowed to unfold freely on the stage, unfettered by any influence alien to his art, bound alone by his physical structure. What Tairov aspired to, then, was *l'art pour l'art*, the art of acting for its own sake. In practice, this meant that his stage methods approached the modern expressionistic dance: His actors moved rhythmically, striding, tripping, skipping on a stage set with monumental cubes, squares, cones, sloping platforms, and flights of steps.

Yevgeny Vakhtangov (1883–1922), like Meyerhold a product of the Moscow Art Theater and one of Stanislavski's favorite pupils, awoke to artistic originality in the period of transition between the revolutions of 1905 and 1917. This was the time when Gorki and Stanislavski, both brimming over with new ideas, discussed plans for a "stage of improvisation." Under the influence of the impromptu folk plays he had seen in Naples, Gorki suggested a revival of the *commedia dell'arte*. He visualized it as follows: A playwright sketches a scenario indicating the plot, the cast, and the locale of a play. In the course of discussions and rehearsals with the actors, who create their own image of their roles, the "sketched model of characters" is rounded out with detailed, true-to-life traits. As the characters evolve, their inherent contradictions will also evolve, and thus the dramatic conflicts will be created. The dramatist writes the final script during the group's rehearsals. Stanislavski, who was interested in Gorki's idea, set up a studio to try out the procedure in practice; he made Sulerzhitski director of the studio and Vakhtangov his assistant.

Not much came of the experiments, however. For one thing, Gorki's concepts were at variance with the concepts of the Art Theater. Gorki was by temperament always immersed in revolutionary politics—despite his differences with Lenin—whereas Stanislavski and Sulerzhitski, in keeping with Tolstoi's teachings, put their faith in an artistic and humanitarian regeneration. Improvisation, to be sure, would have been a suitable tool for the mere propagandizing of ideas; it was not suited, however, for any penetrating articulation of ideas. Furthermore, the propagandizing of ideas—and here is the second reason for the failure of the experiments—was not yet in demand at that time. After the Revolution, of course, the improvisation technique proved very fruithful.

In any case, under the influence of Gorki's experiments, Vakhtangov broke with the artistic policy of the Moscow Art Theater. After Sulerzhitski's premature death in 1916, Vakhtangov took over the First Studio of the Art Theater and soon stamped it with the imprint of his own personality.

It is clear, then, that the great Russian stage directors were well matured in their ideas even before the Revolution. Yet it is just as evident that all of them—with the exception of Stanislavski—derived from that upheaval creative impulses without which their rise to world fame would have been inconceivable.

The "October in the Theater"

In the early postrevolutionary years, the Soviet theater was dominated by the imposing mass spectacles held, in the manner of mystery plays, on the holidays of the so-called Red Calendar— the anniversary of the October Revolution, for example, or May Day—or in celebration of Bolshevik Party congresses. Arranged by men such as Meyerhold, Yevreinov, Kershentsev—chiefly at Petrograd and Moscow—these presentations dealt with the historic events of the Revolution and enlisted thousands, even tens of thousands of people as participants. This political use of the theater did not remain confined to the large cities. Sent out from the centers, agitation troupes traveled all over the country putting on dramatic performances. During the Civil War, 3,000 theatrical organizations were counted in the Soviet Union, but this figure does not even begin to reflect the importance of theatrical activity at that time. Almost every factory, every village Party organization, every unit of the Red Army played theater in one way or another. In a country whose inhabitants were predominantly illiterate, the stage play—whether performed in a factory shop, in a shed, on the village green, or elsewhere in the open air—was the most effective tool for agitation and propaganda. There were the Red Reviews by the Blue Blouses (or Agitprop

Brigades). There was the Living Newspaper, a sequel of scenes depicting and explaining the latest political events. There were the "agitcourts," which, with the participation of the audience, tried and condemned the White Guardist generals, the members of the Triple Entente, the hoarders, as well as "illiteracy," "famine," and "typhoid epidemics."

It is only through this upsurge of folk-theater playing, with its mass spectacles, its amateur performances, its agitation and propaganda rallies, that the Soviet theater of the 1920's—the "October in the Theater"—can be really understood.* That which sprang up with such elemental force at the mass gatherings later found its way in a refined form to the theaters of Moscow, Petrograd (Leningrad), and Kiev. Many of the characteristics that made the early Soviet theater world famous can be traced to the conditions confronted in staging productions in the streets and in the country. There was, for one thing, the sovereign authority of the director—for he had been the man in charge of the mass spectacles and the agitation rallies, who, like the leader of an army, had to decide on the action and to direct huge numbers of participants. A corollary characteristic was the priority of staging and improvisation over the word of the playwright, which was considered a mere starting point, raw material for the real task, and in any case was drowned out in the general hubbub. Nor was there any use for psychology or individual creation of character by the actors; the need was for forms of expression that could be heard and seen over great distances and that could be mastered by the performers, most of them amateurs without previous training—in other words, mass movements, choruses, heroic and satirical formulas and symbols. The borderline between performers and spectators became blurred; they were all participants in a political action. And the borderline between the various forms of art also vanished, since not only acting but

* The term "October in the Theater" was originally adopted by Meyerhold and his colleagues to identify the movement for a revolutionary theater; more broadly it connotes all of the theatrical trends of the period. See: J. Gregor and R. Fülöp-Miller, *Das russische Theater*; A. Holitscher, *Das Theater im revolutionären Russland, Kunst und Volk* (Berlin: Bühnenverlag, 1924); P. Kershentsev, *Das schöpferische Theater* (Hamburg: Hoym Nachfolger, 1922).

also pantomime, recitation, dancing, music, painting, acrobatics, and buffoonery came into play, depending upon the talent available in the group.

Above all, however, the theater of the masses and the theater of the young Soviet stage groups responded to one and the same decisive impulse: the political mandate. Just as the theater of antiquity sprang from religious worship, so the theater of the Soviet Union sprang from political life, from gatherings, meetings, and demonstrations. Only those theater directors whose aspirations were in keeping with the spirit of the times were thus able to maintain their position.

A Burst of Freedom—And Its Limits

The post of Chief of the Theater Section in the People's Commissariat of Education was given to Meyerhold. Meyerhold's joining the Party was not an act of opportunism; throughout his life and up to his tragic death as a victim of the Great Purge he was never a conformist, but a man of honest convictions. As Russia's most consistent theatrical innovator, who again and again had run into barriers both material and intellectual, he discovered undreamed-of creative possibilities in the Revolution. Suddenly, the entire rigid structure of theatrical conventions and limitations was swept away; the sovereign master of a powerful modern stage apparatus, obeying his own inspirations, he now found himself face to face with an unsophisticated public, which was grateful for every cultural experience offered. The theater of the post-Revolutionary period offered him a free and vast field for his experiments; here he could introduce and try out in the course of a few years all the innovations that were achieved by the *avant-garde* in other countries only after decades of struggle with vested theater interests and a conventionally minded public. To Meyerhold, the Revolution became a mighty wave of liberation—small wonder, then, that he was also in full sympathy with the social emancipation of the workers and peasants and linked his endeavors with theirs. He had no grasp of Bolshevik ideology; and in his theater, he never presented the specifically Bolshevik variant of the Revolution but only revolution *per se*—the revolt of the masses.

Under the impact of the social revolution, Meyerhold's principle of the symbolical stage underwent a change. Meyerhold based his work principally on four components of presentation: biomechanics, folkplay, buffoonery, and constructivism in the stage *décor*. The biomechanics method was designed to achieve the most rational and laconic movements on the stage and the transformation of spiritual and mental experiences into physical expressions. By this means, the emotions were to be converted into formulas, the experiences of the individual were to be socialized and standardized in a way considered desirable by a theater aspiring to collective experiences and mass actions. The buffoonery of the farces at country fairs was revived because it was far more intimately interwoven with Russian folk life than the theatrical arts proper, imported as they were from the West and addressing themselves mainly to the propertied classes. The court jester, who was at liberty to tell the truth even to the Czar himself, was look upon as something of a forerunner of the Revolution. Constructivism, finally, which did away with the picture-frame stage with its curtains and wings, and instead installed on the stage movable ceilings, turntables, platforms that could be raised or lowered, lifts, escalators, and cranes, was designed to "reshape the stage in the image of our technical world."

There was a different relation between the pure aestheticism of Tairov's Chamber Theater and the Bolshevik Revolution. Not only was Tairov in his personal attitude and convictions anything but a Bolshevik; his artistic credo compelled him to reject any tendencies bent on using the theater as a forum for agitation and mobilization of the masses. In this respect, his views differed markedly from those of Meyerhold and his followers. Tairov envisioned the regeneration not of the cultist, but of the aesthetic theater, not a theatricalization of life as proclaimed by the director Yevreinov, but a "theatricalization of the theater." Nevertheless, it was certainly not an accident that Tairov's stagings contained elements of the revolutionary theater.

It must be remembered that Tairov, like Meyerhold, Yevreinov, and most of the other proponents of the October in the

Theater, was the product of that *avant-garde* reform movement that had taken hold of the cultural life of Russia before World War I. This movement was a reaction to the failure of the Revolution of 1905, or, one might say, its sublimation. After their political hopes had been destroyed, the intelligentsia turned their yearning for emancipation into aesthetic channels. The decidedly nonpolitical and anti-ideological character of the cultural reforms may be explained as an act of repression in the psychological sense. When, in the year 1917, the heavy weight of oppression was lifted from political life in Russia, the artistic revolution merged at once with the current of the political revolution. The expressionists, futurists, and symbolists of literature and of the theater became the first protagonists of revolutionary art; their innovations, developed long before and independently of the Revolution, proved fully adequate to the turbulent spirit of the times. Many artistic devices that Tairov had tried out on his experimental stage, such as the synthetic method of representation and the stereometrical stage settings, were adopted by the revolutionary theater without hesitation.

At the same time, the year 1917 meant a decisive change for Tairov personally. For one thing, his Chamber Theater—as well as the Moscow Art Theater—was relieved of its perennial financial woes and enabled to operate on a far larger scale. This by itself might not have been of much help if the post-Revolutionary period had not at the same time offered a fertile climate for Tairov's aspirations. The public, receptive to innovations of any kind, responded with enthusiasm to the most elaborate flights of fancy and hailed them as revolutionary feats, so that Tairov could give free rein to his imagination. His stage work was transplanted from its earlier esoteric exclusiveness into the mainstream of public life. This contact with reality had an invigorating and stimulating effect upon Tairov and freed his productions of their former, somewhat decadent and extravagant, quality.

"Theatrical Theater"

It goes without saying that Vakhtangov, too, with his attachment to improvisation, immediately came under the spell of the

Revolution. He noted in his diary: "We must dramatize the rebellious spirit of the people. . . . It would be well if someone wrote a play without any individual roles. In all acts, the masses are the only players. . . ." He had turned from Stanislavski's extreme individual psychology to the equally extreme mass movement of Meyerhold. Eventually, however, when already marked by death, he found a personal style of his own. The great presentations that constitute his claim to lasting fame were produced in the agony of the last two years of his life, the years 1921 and 1922, which are among the most terrible in Russian history. In the midst of misery, horror, and despair, tortured by cancer and feverish with pneumonia, Vakhtangov unfolded the radiant gaiety of his "theatrical theater." The overwhelming success of his achievement, which was not only enthusiastically received by the public but also approved by his famous colleagues—Stanislavski, Nemirovich-Danchenko, Tairov, and Meyerhold—may clearly be attributed to the circumstance that at a crucial hour he embodied the hopes of the people in theatrical visions. This young director, who had welcomed the Revolution without reservation, now felt that the time had come to put an end to it. In his artistic creations he anticipated the end of the terror, for which the whole nation was longing. The triumphal acclaim accorded his *Turandot,* while he already lay on his deathbed, coincided with the advent of the NEP, which brought the Russian people a brief spell of political and economic freedom. Vakhtangov's presentations seemed a promise of the better life that was to come when the fruits of the Revolution would be harvested.

In this final phase, Vakhtangov's methods of improvisation underwent a change. Improvisation was limited to the rehearsals, where each member of the cast had an opportunity to display his imagination, repartee, and wit. From the wealth of suggestions and ideas presented, the director then crystallized the definitive form of the production. No longer were there any improvisations during the actual performance; what mattered now was the sense of improvisation that had been achieved. In contrast to Gorki and Meyerhold, who believed that the essence of improvisation was the creation of the play by the actors themselves—the actors being considered as representatives of the masses who, as the Communists put it, "take their fate into their own hands"—Vakhtangov's basic point in the use of improvisation was not the collective production of pronouncements on cultural policies but the free, relaxed, and serene play, symbolic of a free, relaxed, and serene life. This difference expressed itself both in the selection of subject matter (literary instead of political) and in stage methods (theatrical theater instead of mass scenes.). Vakhtangov's aversion to all ideology anticipated a similar general trend in the Soviet theater in the years to come.

Stanislavski remained completely aloof from the October Revolution. The radical reorganization of society was a blow to his creative work, from which he never recovered. At first he had attempted to satisfy the mood of the times by staging a symbolistic performance of Byron's mystery play *Cain;* but because of its religious trappings (in a period of violent campaigning against the Church) it was misunderstood and failed. Stanislavski vented his annoyance by including in the repertoire of his musical studio a work most decidedly out of tune with the spirit of the times—Lecocq's old operetta *La fille de Madame Angot,* lampooning the French Revolution. It required the intervention of several high-ranking Party leaders, including Lenin and Lunacharski, to save Russia's most famous theater from being liquidated. The Moscow Art Theater was preserved—as a precious museum piece, so to speak. In 1926, Stanislavski produced Bulgakov's *Days of the Turbines,* which created a tumultuous scandal because White Guardist officers appeared in it as tragic heroes and the Czarist anthem was sung on the stage.* For the tenth anniversary celebration of the October Revolution in 1927, when the Art Theater could no longer avoid taking notice of the new

* Mikhail Bulgakov (1891–1940), one of the best Soviet dramatists, star playwright of the exacting Moscow Theater, wrote to Stalin in the 1930's, when all his plays were banned, that the government ought to let him emigrate or shoot him, because under the circumstances his life no longer had any meaning. Stalin then ordered that *The Days of the Turbines* be put in the repertoire again (slightly retouched) and its author be given a position as a dramatist with the Art Theater. He himself informed Bulgakov of the decision by telephone. (See J. Jelagin, *The Taming of the Arts.*)

era, Stanislavski finally staged a Soviet revolutionary play, Ivanov's *Armored Train 14-69*. But even this production—today interpreted by Soviet historiography as Stanislavski's declaration of allegiance to the Revolution—was sternly denounced at the time by the critics, because Stanislavski's staging had stripped the play of all its poster-style political characteristics. After these repeated failures, the aging Stanislavski retired completely into the shell of his private studio.

Stanislavski was clearly one of the Russian artists whose aspirations were in conflict with the Revolution. We may well ask what prevented this indefatigable experimenter, twice the leader of a revolution in the Russian theater, from joining the October-in-the-Theater movement. Quite clearly, it was his dislike for the political theater, which was incompatible with his conceptions of the humanitarian mission of art. "Tendentiousness and art are incompatible," he wrote in 1925. "The one precludes the other. If one approaches art merely with tendentious, propagandistic, or other nonartistic aims, it will wilt like a flower in one's hand."

The Stalinist Invasion of Art

Why did the revolutionary period of the Soviet theater, which had flowered so richly and colorfully, come to an end so soon? It is very enlightening to read today what an unbiased observer, the Austrian critic René Fülöp-Miller, wrote in the late 1920's, after a visit to the Soviet Union (*Süddeutsche Monatshefte*, Munich, No. 4, 1929):

> At a gala performance given during the last big anniversary celebration for numerous guests at the Bolshoi Theater in Moscow, the stage, decked out in red, was again, as so often before, occupied by the Bengal-lighted, gigantic "Globe Delivered," an indispensable stage prop of the early, solemn period of Soviet art. The globe was surrounded by persons whose heavy chains of papier-mâché were intended to symbolize the slavery under the former world order. A poet of the Leftist Literary Front declaimed revolutionary hymns; presently the stage began to glow with a red light, the slaves threw off their cardboard chains, the "globe" split open and

disgorged from its belly masses of people who immediately
intoned the stereotyped triumphant hymn of the Revolution. But, how false this scene now seemed to the viewer!
What once, in its naïve symbolism, had been the artistic expression of a faith flushed with victory, now no longer corresponded to the real mood of the people. The lofty impulse
that had created this form for the theater had long since been
extinguished by the thousand worries and troubles of everyday life; thus nothing remained of the earlier elation but the
hollow stage tricks.

More clearly than any theoretical discussion, Fülöp-Miller's
account explains why the revolutionary theater was doomed. It
had outlived its time; the revolutionary illusion became a lie.
Russia stood at the crossroads: She either had to revert to despotism or advance toward democracy. From the revolutionary
theater the road led either back to a theatrical byzantinism or
forward to a free theater in a free society. The early development
toward a free, unprejudiced, truthful and human theater had
been staked out by Vakhtangov before his untimely death, and
reached its climax when Meyerhold, the initiator of the October
in the Theater, renounced his previous stage work and publicly
proclaimed himself a disciple of Vakhtangov's. This development
was supported by liberal Party leaders like Lunacharski and
Bukharin, who aimed at a democratization of the Soviet society.
The Party bureaucracy under Stalin, on the other hand, was
bound to see a danger in the theater, both in its revolutionary
and in its postrevolutionary attitudes.

In the early 1930's, an increasing number of plays and productions were banned from the theaters. The censorship was no
longer directed exclusively against non-Communist artists like
Bulgakov, but also against the Communists who deviated from
the general Stalinist line. The following are the two most important cases:

In 1929–30, Meyerhold (in cooperation with the composer
Shostakovich and the artists' co-operative *Kukryniksy*) produced
Mayakovski's satires *The Bedbug* and *The Bath*. In these plays,
Mayakovski had given free reign to his increasing hatred of the

Party bureaucracy. By means of grotesqueries, parodies, and utopias (the plays are laid in the second millennium), he censured the Bolshevik bigwigs and the "new class" in the manner of Djilas. *The Bath* ends with the provocative statement that the functionaries are unnecessary for Communism. The Party critics were indignant; the satires were removed from the repertoire and remained banned until after Stalin's death. The hounding and defamation to which Mayakovski had been subjected undoubtedly contributed to his suicide in 1930.

In 1936, Tairov's Chamber Theater staged the opera *The Knights*, by Borodin. It was produced with a new libretto in which its author, the Agitprop poet Demyan Bedny, poured forth scorn and ridicule on the old Russian knights and heroes. In doing so, he had overlooked the fact that the Party line had in the meantime changed from the revolutionary contempt of the entire Russian past to a new chauvinism. (Stalin, for example, permitted a new production of the opera *A Life for the Czar*, with only its title changed to *Ivan Sussanin*.) Molotov left the premiere of *The Knights* under protest. According to Yelagin, he is supposed to have said: "A dirty shame! The old knights were great men!" The opera was removed from the boards and Bedny expelled from the Writers' Union.

Purges and Gleichschaltung

Censorship now reached into questions of form; the reproach of "formalism" became a fearful anathema. All *avant-garde* and revolutionary elements, and particularly the *Proletkult* (abbreviation of "proletarian culture"—leftist tendency in early Soviet cultural policy) were condemned for substituting "abstract sociological concepts for the concrete and typical artistic form." The Stalin regime desired a theater as conventional and generally understandable as possible for the easy popularization of its propaganda themes; it was just as uninterested in an artistic mastery of the period as it was in a theater serving pure enjoyment. It wanted a political theater of illusion that would hide the bitter reality. It feared revolution in both content and form.

A number of the best-known playhouses were closed, among

them the Moscow Korsch Theater, the Second Moscow Art Theater (a Stanislavski establishment), Okhlopkov's Realistic Theater, the *Proletkult* Playhouse managed by Diki, all experimental and *avant-garde* studios, and, above all, the bulwark of the October in the Theater, the Meyerhold Theater. The Stalinist terror struck mercilessly at the elite of the Soviet dramatic artists. One need only remember the liquidation of Vsevolod Meyerhold and his wife, the well-known actress Sinaida Reich; of the re-creator of the Ukrainian theater, Les Kurbas; the dramatists Isaac Bakel, Vladimir Kirshon, Sergei Tretyakov, and Mikola Kulish; as well as the entire top stratum of Soviet critics. The condemnations took place on political pretexts: Meyerhold, for example, was arrested after a speech against socialist realism, but at the trial he was accused of being a German spy. According to reliable reports from various sources, he succumbed to torture under interrogation.*

Postwar Debilitation

The survivors of the Great Purge of the 1930's, the *Yezhovshchina,* were subjected after World War II to a new wave of persecution—the *Zhdanovshchina.* At the initiative of Andrei Zhdanov, the Central Committee of the Communist Party took a number of decisions regarding literature (August 14, 1946), the theater (August 26, 1946), motion pictures (September 4, 1946), and music (February 10, 1948). Within the framework of these steps, disciplinary action was taken against the following, among others: the writers Anna Akhmatova and Mikhail Zoshchenko; the theatrical directors Alexander Tairov and Nikolai Akimov, who were discharged from their position as heads of the Moscow Chamber Theater and of the Leningrad Comedy, respectively; the motion picture directors Pudovkin and Eisenstein (a Meyerhold pupil); and the composers Shostakovich, Prokofiev, and Khachaturian. The decree of August 26, 1946, "Concern-

* Regarding the death of Meyerhold, there are reports of an NKVD agent who was captured during World War II (see W. Solsky, "Der Grosse Meyerhold," *Der Monat* [West Berlin], No. 21 [1950]), and of Polish intellectuals who after the rehabilitation of Meyerhold were able to examine the interrogation files.

ing the Repertoire of the Playhouses and Measures for Its Improvement," criticized the Soviet theaters because they played Western dramas and the kind of Soviet plays that took a critical view of Soviet life and the Soviet people. The Central Committee made it compulsory for all theaters "each year to put on at least two or three new plays of high ideological and artistic quality dealing with modern Soviet themes." This order led to a flood of trash on the Soviet stage.

On January 28, 1948, an attack on the "antipatriotic group of dramatic critics" appeared in *Pravda*. Several leading Moscow critics, all without exception of Jewish extraction, were thereupon discharged and arrested. This action against the "cosmopolitan critics" and "agents of bourgeois decadence" was the starting signal of Stalin's anti-Semitic campaign, in the course of which all Jewish theaters in the Soviet Union were closed, including the Yiddish Chamber Theater, which had played a part in the October in the Theater. The famous actor Mikhoels, after whom the theater was named, died in 1948, under suspicious circumstances. Shortly after his death, he was accused of cosmopolitanism and espionage for "Zionism."

By a strange irony, Stanislavski's declining days were brightened by the glow of Stalin's favor. While Stanislavski offered his private studio as a last asylum from persecution to his great disciple and antagonist, Meyerhold, the revolution of the theater was being crushed in his name—through no fault of his.

What was it, actually, that induced the regime to appropriate the Stanislavski System? It was probably the circumstance that Stanislavski's method, designed to teach the actor solid craftsmanship, seemed to make possible stage work without any creative artistic spark. By emphasizing certain rational and didactic elements in the system—its naturalistic dross, as it were—and suppressing the irrational and mystical elements of the symbolistic period, the System could be integrated to some extent with dialectical materialism; after all, both stemmed from the same root, the nineteenth-century optimistic faith in progress. The fact that the System's usefulness was limited to the Russian classics and modern plays—a consequence of Stanislavski's isolation after the October Revolution—was flattering to Great Russian chauvinism; the conventionality and plausibility of the acting appealed to the philistine tastes of the functionaries. Still, in order that the System might be adopted without trouble, it was necessary to withhold, and in part suppress, the master's authentic writings. The version of the System declared to be authentic in 1950 and now practiced in the Soviet Union was worked out by a few Stalinist pupils of Stanislavski's only after the death of the entire old guard of the Moscow Art Theater.

The Stalin Era: A Summary

The Soviet revolutionary theater was not an original achievement of the Bolsheviks. The Silver Age preceding the Revolution, with its abundance of talent and ideas, with its high artistic level and a social life permeated with love of the arts, was the indispensable basis for the flowering of the theater in the 1920's. It should be remembered that long before the triumph of the Revolution, Russian intellectual life had assumed a revolutionary character, in the field of politics as well as in the arts, and that it stood in opposition to the Czarist regime.

It is also true, however, that the Russian theater of the 1920's was shaped by the spirit of the Revolution—and specifically by Bolshevism, insofar as it was the most radical expression of revolutionary ideas. In the years of the revolutionary upheavals, Bolshevism seemed to answer the basic demands and desires of the Russian people: Measures such as the conclusion of a peace treaty, the distribution of land in 1917, industrialization, social reforms, expansion of public education, and cultural reforms, were welcomed by large sectors of workers, peasants, and the intelligentsia. Many artists who had held leftist or *avant-gardist* leanings under the Czarist regime approved the abolition of academic conventions and found their creative impulses fired by the ethos of the revolution. When cultural institutions were taken oven by the state, they also found material security and encouragement.

Yet the alliance between leftist art and leftist politics that was forged in the fire of the Revolution never amounted to real identification. Even Communists like Meyerhold and Mayakovski al-

ways had definite opinions of their own and clashed with the
Party again and again. On the other hand, the Party leadership
recognized from the very beginning the problems inherent in
revolutionary art; it classified the artists only as "fellow travelers."
Thus even the early years of the Soviet theater proved that complete accord between art and politics is impossible.

If the Soviet regime in its initial stages nevertheless tolerated
and promoted art, it did so for two reasons: because the intellectual leaders of the Revolution, like Lenin, Trotsky, Lunacharski, Bukharin, Radek, were cultured and educated men for
whom any forcible encroachment upon the creative processes
of art was unthinkable; and because the Party looked upon the
cultural chaos as a natural transitional stage. Even though the
1925 resolution of the Central Committee, which determined the
cultural policy for the succeeding years, did emphasize the class
character of art and denied the possibility of a neutral and nonpolitical art, it acknowledged at the same time that the forms of
art are "infinitely varied," that the proletariat, i.e., the Party, had
not as yet found the time to draw up a universally binding canon
of aesthetics, and that therefore the Party could not identify itself
with any artistic group, however pro-Communist that group
might profess to be. The initial tolerance of the Bolsheviks in
matters of culture was thus an outgrowth of the utopian character
of their policies in general. They were firmly convinced that
sooner or later the classless Communist society would become a
reality. Then there would be only one culture, Communist culture. All other artistic movements, deprived of their basis in
society, would wither away and die. And one day, so they hoped,
the revolutionary eruption of creative powers would bring forth
the ideal art, true to the Party line.

Early Soviet art, and hence the heyday of the Soviet theater,
can then be characterized as an *art of revolutionary illusions,*
from the point of view of the artists as well as from the point
of view of the Party. The break was inevitable when the Bolshevik ideals materialized into Stalinist reality.

PART II: RAVAGES AND SURVIVALS

Nothing summarizes the decline of the Soviet theater under Stalin better than the memorable speech given by Vsevolod Meyerhold in 1939—just a few days before his arrest—at the First Congress of Soviet Theatrical Directors in Moscow:

> How would you describe the present trend in the Soviet theater? Here I have to be frank: If what has happened in the Soviet theater recently is antiformalism, if what is happening today on the stages of the best Moscow theaters is an achievement of the Soviet drama, I prefer to be considered a formalist. I, for one, find the work in our theaters at present pitiful and terrifying. I don't know whether it is antiformalism, or realism, or naturalism, or some other ism, but I do know that it is uninspired and bad.
>
> This pitiful and sterile something that aspires to the title of socialist realism has nothing in common with art. Yet the theater is art, and without art there can be no theater. Go to the Moscow theaters and look at the colorless, boring productions, which are all alike and which differ only in their degree of worthlessness. No longer can one identify the creative signature of the Maly Theater, of the Vakhtangov Theater, of the Kamerni Theater, or of the Moscow Art Theater. In the very places where only recently creative life was seething, where men of art searched, made mistakes, experimented, and found new ways to create productions, some of which were bad and others magnificent, now there is nothing but a depressing, well-meaning, shockingly mediocre, and devastating lack of talent.
>
> Was this your aim? If so, you have committed a horrible deed. You have washed the child down the drain along with the dirty water. In your effort to eradicate formalism, you have destroyed art.[*]

[*] J. Jelagin, *Taming of the Arts* (New York: E. P. Dutton & Company, 1951), pp. 172–73.

The speech cost Meyerhold his freedom and his life.

It was not until some thirteen years later that the Communist Party itself recognized the sad plight of the Soviet theater. In April, 1952, *Pravda* announced in an editorial entitled "Fight Against the Backwardness of the Drama" that the level of the Soviet dramatic arts had sunk to an unprecedented low. "Of the great number of plays written by Soviet playwrights, only a few are suitable for performance. The gross discrepancy between the quantity and the quality of today's dramas indicates that many playwrights are working in the wrong direction." The Soviet writers, so *Pravda* asserted, appeared to be afraid of the truth.

Thus a year before Stalin's death, the signal sounded for the beginning of the cultural thaw in the Soviet Union. That the new trend made itself felt in the field of dramatic literature first was by no means an accident. While Party interference had not completely debased the Soviet performing arts, playwriting in the 1930's had sunk below the lowest artistic standard. This development was clearly the result of official cultural policy as it had emerged over the previous decade.

Early Cultural Policy

The Soviet regime had from its very beginning imposed narrower constraints on literary production than on the performing arts. This attitude found its ultimate expression in a resolution of the Central Committee on June 18, 1925, "On the Policy of the Party in the Field of Belles-Lettres," which stated that while the proletariat, that is the Party, could not yet prescribe artistic form, it could determine the content of art.

In its earliest days Soviet censorship was thus purely political: It suppressed hostile or alien opinions wherever they cropped up—in the theater as well as in the press and at public gatherings; it controlled verbal expression, but it did not feel itself competent to pass on aesthetic forms, such as Stanislavski's physical action, Meyerhold's biomechanics, or Tairov's emotional gesture.

While the art of acting thus remained more or less free, plays had to take positive stands on Bolshevik policy. This insistence on political labeling had important consequences: first, the theater's radical break with Russian tradition (Tolstoi, Chekhov); second, the emigration of all leading prerevolutionary dramatists, with Gorki and Andreev at the head; and third, the provincialism of early Soviet playwriting, which, in contrast to the stagecraft of the "revolutionary theater," hardly penetrated beyond the confines of the Soviet Union.

The revolutionary theater had, as is not surprising under these circumstances, an antipathy toward fiction. Meyerhold, Tairov, and Eisenstein used not dramas but librettos as the basis of their scenic fantasies. Even the best plays that were produced in this period—such as Mayakovski's *Mysterium Buffo,* a "heroic-epic-satiric representation of our era," Ehrenburg's *Trust D. E.,* a fantastic and grotesque assault on capitalism, and Tretyakov's revolutionary play *Roar, China*—are today of historical interest only.

In 1923, when the revolutionary ardor began to wane, People's Commissar Lunacharski—a man of cultivated taste—proclaimed the slogan "Back to Ostrovski!"* He meant by this a return to the realistic, psychologically plausible social criticism of the comedy of manners popular with the Russian classicists at the end of the nineteenth century. Political as well as artistic reasons were responsible for this development. With the introduction of the NEP, capitalistic elements had again arisen in Soviet society, and while the regime approved of their existence, it nevertheless did its best to combat them ideologically. Moreover, in the Soviet administrative machinery itself, a new class emerged—a bureaucracy that in its outlook and mores was far removed from the dedication and puritanism of the men who had made the Revolution. The purpose of the new sociocritical plays, then, was to protect the purity of the revolutionary idea. In this period some highly talented playwrights, such as Bulgakov, Afinogenov, Kataev, Erdman, Faiko, and Shkvarkin, came to maturity; however,

---

* Alexander Nikolaevich Ostrovski (1823–86) was a leading Russian playwright of the second half of the nineteenth century. Russian merchant life of the period, with its isolation, smugness, and double-dealing, was the favorite subject of his dramas. Turning out some forty plays in prose as well as eight in blank verse, Ostrovski created the first great corpus of Russian national drama. He remains to this day the most popular Russian dramatic writer of the Soviet stage.—*Ed.*

it was again Mayakovski who, with his satires *The Bedbug* and *The Bath,* dominated the Soviet stage.

But the more it became evident that the degenerative symptoms appearing in Soviet society were characteristic of the Communist system itself rather than being vestiges of capitalism, the more embarrassing did the comedy of manners become. To be sure, the Soviet dramatists tried—through ideological window-dressing, *deus ex machina,* the happy ending—to explain away the evils as "growing pains," but the public only felt confirmed in its rejection of Communism and drew its own politically unorthodox conclusions. The sociocritical period of Soviet drama, which had inspired great hopes, passed away as swiftly as the NEP; nearly all the dramatists of this persuasion fared badly under Stalinism.

The Theater of the 1930's

In the late 1920's and early 1930's, the Party gave its approval to two new dramatic forms. One was the "construction play" promoted by the writers' organization RAPP,* which aimed to popularize the First Five Year Plan in industry and agriculture. The best-known example of the construction play was Pogodin's *Aristocrats,* a macabre comedy dealing with forced labor in the construction of the Baltic–White Sea Canal. But this type of play, too, was soon banned by the Party because of its genuinely realistic features. The other new type of drama officially promoted in those years was the so-called "classical revolutionary play," the best-known examples of which were Trenyov's *Lyubov Yarovaia,* Vishnevski's *First Cavalry Army* and *Optimistic Tragedy,* and Vsevolod Ivanov's *Armored Train 14-69.* Despite their Bolshevik ideology, these plays were characterized by relative verisimilitude and candor in the depiction of the Civil War; they described tragic human destinies with gripping pathos and revolutionary

---

* Abbreviation of Russian Association of Proletarian Authors, an artists' organization of the Left, succeeding *Proletkult,* which regimented literature during the First Five Year Plan. Accused of excessive zeal and sectarianism, RAPP was dissolved by a decree of the Party Central Committee of April 23, 1932, and replaced by the Union of Soviet Writers. Leopold Auerbach, the leader of RAPP, was liquidated in the Great Purge.

romanticism. In contrast to the sociocritical drama, this group of plays, which met with Stalin's approval, was declared sacrosanct. Yet the stark truth and dynamic quality of the plays apparently made them so explosive in their effect on stage that, while they received much praise, they were not often performed.

A special place in Soviet drama of this period was occupied by the historical plays of Alexei Tolstoi (not to be confused with the nineteenth-century novelist Leo Tolstoi) and the late works of Maxim Gorki. In his plays about Peter the Great and Ivan the Terrible, Count Tolstoi, who had become Stalin's "court poet," skillfully construed historical parallels to the rule of Lenin and Stalin. Although he intended these parallels to be flattering and even discussed them with Stalin, he had to rewrite them in the end. Gorki's last plays, *Yegor Bulychov and Others* and *Dostigayev and Others*, and the second version of *Vassa Shelesnova*, are among the best things he wrote. They deal, however, with prerevolutionary subjects, and they created no school in Soviet drama. The only work of Gorki's that deals with Soviet conditions is *Somov and Others*. Written immediately after Gorki's return to the Soviet Union (1928), and under the impact of the Shakhty trial,* it is far weaker artistically than his other late works. Strangely enough, it was precisely this play that was suppressed by Stalinism. Though Gorki in *Somov* assailed the "enemies of the state," he rejected the "agent theory" of the sham trials.

In the 1930's, Soviet drama ceased to exist as art. With very few exceptions (for example, *The Shadow*, by Yevgeni Schvarts, a phantasy with hidden meaning, and some plays dealing with the war period), the plays of the Stalin era were nothing more

---

* The Shakhty Trial of 1928 concerned an allegedly counter-Revolutionary group of engineers in the town of Shakhty, in the North Caucasus. The engineers were accused of collaborating with the former owners of the Shakhty mines, then living abroad, in a plan to wreck the mines by systematic sabotage. The case against them and the succeeding trial were manufactured by Stalin, without any evidence supporting the allegations and despite the protests of his Politburo colleagues. After having "confessed" to a variety of crimes, five of the engineers were sentenced to death and forty-nine others to terms of imprisonment. The trial opened a period of persecution of the intelligentsia in the Soviet Union and as the first of the notorious "show trials," it initiated Stalin's devastatingly effective method of annihilating political opponents.—*Ed.*

than instruments of totalitarian propaganda. Stalin did not dub his writers "engineers of the human soul" in vain. It became the task of the drama to blacken the West (*The Voice of America,* by Lavrenyov; *The Russian Question,* by Simonov), to cultivate Russian tradition (*Field Marshal Kutusov,* by Solovyev; *The Family,* a Leninst play by Popov), to educate youth in Communist ideology (*Tamerlane and His Band,* by Gaidar; *The Red Scarf,* by Mikhalkov), to stimulate production (*Moscow Character,* by Sofronov; *The Green Signal,* by Surov), and in general to glorify Soviet life (*Forest of Elders,* by Korneichuk; *Dawn over Moscow,* by Sutov). Most of the plays, in fact, fulfilled all tasks at one and the same time.

"Drama Without Conflict"

In the years immediately following World War II, a theoretical justification was advanced in support of the vapid *agitprop* pieces that continued to appear on the Soviet stages. This was the theory of the "drama without conflict" formulated by Nikolai Virta, Boris Lavrenev, and a few other writers. They maintained that the basic principle of the traditional drama, the conflict between positive and negative forces, no longer applied to the Soviet drama, inasmuch as in Soviet society all social antagonisms had been resolved and life had become happy and harmonious. Only one conflict was left, the conflict between the good and the better. No serious disagreements were conceivable among Soviet citizens, they said, only misunderstandings. For this reason they proposed striking the word "conflict" from the playwright's vocabulary.

The concept of the absence of conflict from Soviet life had not, of course, emerged spontaneously in the minds of such writers as Virta and Lavrenev (who had shown no hesitancy to deal with conflicts in plays written not long before). It was, rather, the logical product of the cultural policy of Zhdanov, who in speeches and resolutions had condemned any truthful or critical presentation of Soviet reality as "slander against Soviet life and the Soviet people." The 1946 resolution of the Central Committee, "On the Repertoire of the Theaters," had singled out for condemnation all those plays in which the Soviet people were allegedly caricatured as "philistines in taste and mores."

In practice the tendency to eliminate conflict was carried to the extreme. As the dramatist Nikolai Pogodin said, one saw on the stages "only good, very good, and exceedingly good persons." For instance, the play *Sons of Moscow,* by N. Roshkov, derived its entire plot from an argument between two Stakhanovite workers about the technological details involved in further rationalization of high-speed forging. Another play dealt with the quarrels of two progressive lovers who were unable to agree on the best method of hilling potatoes. The Russian man in the street dubbed such rose-colored presentation of Soviet reality *lakirovka* (vanishing). Nobody had the courage any longer to treat Soviet people or Soviet conditions critically. Some playwrights—among them the dramatist Surov, winner of several Stalin prizes—chose to return to the Theater of Satire the advance payments they had received for projected works of comedy rather than to fulfill their contractual obligations.

This was the situation when the startling *Pravda* editorial appeared on April 7, 1952. It was directed at the state of Soviet drama as well as at the proponents of the "drama without conflict":

The main cause of the poverty of our dramatic production and the weakness of many plays lies in the fact that the playwrights fail to base their works on the deep conflicts of life, avoiding them instead. To judge by these plays, everything in the U.S.S.R. is good and ideal, there are no conflicts. Some playwrights seem to believe that they are actually forbidden to criticize the things that are bad and negative in Soviet life. And some critics demand that works of art should present only ideal types; however, if a writer or dramatist reveals the negative things that are found in life, they try to tear him to pieces with their criticism. Such an attitude is wrong. . . . Not everything is ideal in the Soviet land; there are negative types among us; there is quite a bit of wickedness in our life and quite a few insincere people. We need not be afraid to point out our shortcomings and our difficulties. The short-comings must be cured.

While *Pravda's* attack was aimed, characteristically, at Soviet playwrights rather than at the policy of the Communist Party (which alone was to blame for the sad state of Soviet drama), it nevertheless signaled the end of the worst and most absurd excesses of the *Zhdanovshchina*. The new policy was given official sanction by Malenkov, who in his speech at the Nineteenth Congress of the CPSU (October, 1952) called upon Soviet artists to strike out against "everything that is negative, rotten, and outmoded, and burn to ashes everything that blocks our forward march." Their task was still "to instill in men and women . . . the character, capacities, and habits that are untainted by the sores of capitalism," but at least they were not to close their eyes to "the vices, shortcomings, and manifestations of depravity still existing in (Soviet) society."

Critical Realism of the New Type

Malenkov's statement was the go-ahead signal for the appearance of sociocritical plays about life in the Soviet Union. The new trend emerged haltingly at first, but gained momentum after the death of Stalin in March, 1953.

Sergei Mikhalkov's comedy *Crabs* followed quite faithfully the model recommended by Malenkov, i.e., Gogol's *Inspector General*. The play, produced in 1953, was a sensation in that it put only "negative characters" on the boards. The plot centered around an intelligent young man who hoodwinks a high-ranking plant manager (a Party member) and his conceited wife into believing that he intends to marry their daughter. On the wedding day he absconds, taking the plant's funds with him. A whole swarm of corrupt and dull-witted Soviet bureaucrats, functionaries, and police are led by the nose and exposed to ridicule.

The theaters that staged the play proceeded at first with great caution; depending on the boldness of their managers, they used one of three different versions for its ending. The Party, however, reacted positively, even suggesting that the play was not aggressive enough: "Regrettably, the author failed to rise to truly

satirical criticism. . . ." The Soviet writers did not wait to be told
a second time.

In 1954, half a dozen theaters staged a new play by Leonid
Zorin, entitled *Guests*. Whereas Mikhalkov's *Crabs* was actually
only a gay adaptation of a classical subject, *Guests* aimed its
barbs straight at the heart of Soviet class society. The central
figure of the play is one Pyotr Kirpichov, the son of an old Bolshevik revolutionary, but himself a corrupt, arrogant, and unscrupulous functionary in the Soviet Ministry of Justice.

Toward the end of the action, Kirpichov's father takes him to
task. "The land grew stronger," says the old man, "and the people
became richer. Then, unnoticed and quite gradually, there appeared on the scene, beside the indefatigable, hard-working
toilers, people such as you: gluttonous, conceited, soulless bureaucrats who lost touch with the people." The Party press had criticized Mikhalkov's comedy for failing to explain how it was
possible for such persons to develop and why they were not exposed and curbed long ago. Zorin provided an answer in old
Kirpichov's words to his son: "I worked side by side with the
great toilers of our land. I worked and did not know the taste of
power; but you took a liking to power from childhood, and power
has poisoned you." His favorite daughter, Barbara, agrees laconically: "There is a short word—power!" In Zorin's play, two
hostile groups confront each other throughout: on the one side,
Pyotr Kirpichov and the functionaries of the state apparatus; on
the other side, the intellectuals and the men and women of the
people.

That the Party's policy of de-Stalinization also found its propagandists among playwrights, ready to translate the new line into
stereotyped "heros" and "villains," is exemplified by Alexander
Korneichuk's *Wings*, staged in 1954. In it, the blame for the
terror, purges, and ubiquitous fear that had so long dominated
Soviet life is placed on the "Beria gang," and the new leaders are
portrayed in redeemingly rosy colors. Nevertheless, the fact that
the horrors of the recent past *were*, for the first time, frankly
discussed on the stage (in one scene the Party secretary's wife,
Anna, accuses her husband of basely forsaking and betraying her
at a time when she was being unjustly persecuted) brought

Soviet drama closer to reality than was the case during the Stalinist era.

It soon became apparent, however, that criticism had gone further than the cultural policy-makers in the Kremlin had intended. Many of the writers had not been content to criticize the weaknesses and shortcomings of the bureaucratic apparatus; they had gone as far as to question Communist society as such. In 1954, the Party leadership therefore felt compelled to halt the liberalization of the theater.

At an extraordinary session of the Collegium of the Ministry of Culture of the U.S.S.R., Zorin's play was subjected to scathing criticism. In language reminiscent of Zhdanov's pronouncements ("putrid logic," "harmful rubbish"), the author was accused of deliberately misrepresenting Soviet reality: of portraying "rascals and villains" as typical representatives of the whole Soviet apparatus," of maintaining that "filthy types" such as Pyotr Kirpichov are the natural fruits of Soviet society rather than aberrations. The resolution mentioned by name and reprimanded all the persons and agencies that had approved or at least failed to suppress the play—Zorin's fellow writers Konstantin Simonov and Boris Lavrenev, the critics on the staffs of various newspapers and periodicals, the censors in the Ministry of Culture, and the theaters that had presented the play. The other plays of the sociocritical group were also suppressed. Only Korneichuk's *Wings* escaped the vengeful censure of the Party, obviously because the play's criticism was specifically aimed at the already liquidated Beria faction.

For similar reasons, *mutatis mutandis,* the Party on the very eve of the Twentieth Congress viciously attacked Nikolai Pogodin's play *Three Went to the Virgin Lands,* which had lambasted Khrushchev's pet project, the settlement of the newly opened land in Siberia. Produced in November, 1955, the play debunked the officially propagated picture of enthusiastic virgin-land pioneers. Letavin, the leading character of the play, decides to heed the government's call because "here at home he is fed up with everything" and a girl has jilted him; Rakitkin, a hooligan, joins because he wants to elude the police; the girl Ira, because she cannot adjust to life and feels lonesome. Not much more heroic are the motives of the other pioneers; a seamstress speculates on the possibility of marrying an "interesting person" en route; a stenographer had an unhappy marriage and "escaped that nightmare by going to the virgin lands"; a pupil of the tenth grade was expelled from school; and a village teacher went "to the virgin lands with dreams of supernatural heroism. . . . She thought life was something like a color film." The new life these people encounter in virgin Siberia turns out to be dreary, barbaric, raw, and crushing—quite unlike that of the enthusiastic and glowing legends disseminated by Party propaganda. "There are no virgin lands here at all; there is nothing but snow and more snow, wolves and blizzards." And when in the midst of the frozen steppes the pioneers meet a deportee, Pogodin again conjures up the fearful trauma that Soviet society has for decades been trying to banish from its consciousness: the horror of forced labor.

Between Scylla and Charybdis

The 1953–56 period, then, was one of experimentation and vacillation, of advance and retreat. No sooner were the Party guards lowered than new plays critical of Soviet society reappeared on Russian stages; this brought about further restraints, which in turn produced the very sterility and *lakirovka* the Party wished to eliminate from the Soviet theater as well as from the arts in general. But since Zhdanovite terror was no longer applied in the arts, every period of comparative calm was bound again to engender "unhealthy" tendencies—to wit, Pogodin's *Three Went to The Virgin Lands*. Clearly, a more consistent and effective policy was urgently required; and an attempt to produce one was made on the eve of the Twentieth Congress of the CPSU, in an editorial that appeared in the Party's theoretical organ, *Kommunist*.

The Party now tried to steer a middle course. In an article in *Kommunist* (No. 18, 1955), it rejected, on the one hand, the worst excess of the *Zhdanovshchina*:

One of the fundamental conditions for the development of highly ideological and truly artistic literature and art founded on lofty ideals is the implacable struggle against uniformity and leveling in the creative processes. . . . The task of the Soviet writers and artists consists in appropriating all the wealth of artistic mastery mankind has accumulated, and to augment that wealth by new creative inventions. Socialist realism sets no limits in this respect. It presupposes diversity in the styles and forms of artistic creation, and also diversity in the methods of typification.

On the other hand, it attacked the critical realism that had sprung up during the liberalization phase:

Another great danger inherent in the demand for over-emphasis is that it leads to a hypertrophied presentation of the negative aspects of our society—a kind of presentation that distorts and oversimplifies reality. As is well known, this erroneous tendency became particularly manifest in a number of articles in the magazine *Novi mir* and in stage plays such as *Guests,* by L. Zorin, and *Pompeyev's Downfall,* by N. Virta. The Soviet public and press have firmly rejected these works.

The reasoning that induced the Soviet leaders to chart this course seems clear. They now realized that Stalin's and Zhdanov's narrow-minded cultural policy had destroyed the Soviet art that had flowered in the 1920's. Immeasurable damage had thereby been inflicted on cultural life in the Soviet Union and on the international prestige of Communism. Now, they reasoned, if the petty harassments and the continual interference with the creative processes of the artists are stopped, it should be possible to resurrect the great art of the early Soviet era. Let the writers and artists indulge their experimenting and their formalistic excesses—so long as they create works that bring honor and glory to the Communist regime.

With the laconic remark that they had been the victims of a "violation of socialist legality," the great artists of the revolutionary period like Meyerhold, Babel, Pilnyak, Tretyakov, Kirshon, and Vesyoli, were rehabilitated. The Institute of the History of the Arts at the Academy of Sciences of the U.S.S.R., in co-operation with the All-Russian Theater Association, appointed a commission to act as custodian and administrator of the heritage left by Vsevolod Meyerhold. The Theater of Satire in Moscow included in its repertoire Mayakovski's satires *The Bedbug* and *The Bath,* both of which had been banned for more than two decades. At the Mayakovski Theater, Okhlopkov revived Pogodin's *Aristocrats,* which he had first staged twenty years earlier. Okhlopkov not only revived the original staging to the last detail, but even employed the same leading actor. Gorki's *Somov and Others,* Alexei Faiko's *The Man with the Portfolio,* and other plays long missing from the repertoire of Soviet theaters reappeared on the stage.

This marked the beginning of a change in the appearance of the Soviet theatrical scene. For the first time in many years, productions in the tradition of the "revolutionary theater" again made their appearance—productions which bore the individual stamp of the directors and stimulated creative discussions. Among these were: the already mentioned stagings of Mayakovski's comedies *The Bedbug, The Bath,* and *Mystery-Bouffe* by a group of directors at the Theater of Satire under Plutshek; Okhlopkov's *Hamlet;* Saltykov-Shchedrin's plays produced by Nikolai Akimov; the "epical" presentation of Vsevolod Vishnevski's *An Optimistic Tragedy* under the young director Tovstogonov. In addition, Okhlopkov staged *The Sonnet of Petrarch,* by Pogodin, a period play on love, and perhaps the most noteworthy dramatic work of the second phase of the thaw.

All these performances were sensational hits with the audiences and were played regularly before capacity crowds. The reaction of the critics was divided—which in itself signified progress when compared with the conformity of the Stalin period.

Voices from the Past

The rehabilitation of the "revolutionary theater" encroached, of course, upon the monopoly of the Stanislavski System. The artists, for so long straitjacketed in the name of Stanislavski, began to abandon the System. At a plenary session of the Council of the Soviet Theater Organization (VTO) in 1956, Nikolai Okhlopkov, the most distinguished survivor of the "revolutionary theater," whose theatrical methods were inspired by Meyerhold, asked how it had come to pass that so many Soviet theaters were dominated by pedestrianism, petty realism, and monotony. Why were the performances so devoid of the genuine creative spark, of inspiration, of passion? Was it that the directors had become incompetent? He placed the blame for the wretched condition of the Soviet theater on the domination of the Stanislavski System "as interpreted in their own manner by his disciples Toporkov and Kedrov."* Okhlopkov's speech caused a great stir in the Soviet theater world.

In the periodical *Teatr*, the Vakhtangov disciples Ruben, Simonov, and B. Zakhava took issue with Stanislavski's inclination to draw a sharp distinction between the "art of experience," rooted in his psychological naturalism, and the "art of representation" and called for a revival of Vakhtangov's theatrical principles, which—in their opinion—contained a synthesis of both these theatrical forms.†

An even more biting comment in *Teatr* (No. 12, 1956) came from the stage director Bebutov, who wrote:

It is time for us to wake up to the plain truth that it is not the actor for the System, but the System for the actor. It is time to realize that the Stanislavski System is by no means the only key to the dramatic creations of all periods; rather it is just a method that was born and grew out of the dra-

* W. Toporkov and N. Kedrov were the aged Stanislavski's assistant directors in the experimental production of Molière's *Tartuffe*, which, despite 553 rehearsals, was never performed. Toporkov wrote the book *Stanislavski at a Rehearsal*. Kedrov succeeded Nemirovich-Danchenko as head of the Moscow Art Theater.

† R. Simonov, "*O teatrakh 'perezhivaniia' i 'predstavleniia.'*" (On the Theaters of 'Experience' and of 'Representation'"), *Teatr*, No. 8 (1956); B. Zakhava, "*Za sintes teatra 'predstavleniia' i 'perezhivaniia'*" (For a Synthesis of the Theater of 'Representation' and of 'Experience'"), *Teatr*, No. 1 (1957). By "art of experience," Stanislavski meant the embodiment of a concept of acting that comes from within—by "art of representation," he meant the embodiment of a concept of acting by external artistic means, such as rhetoric, gestures, movement, etc. The revolutionary theater preferred the "art of representation" because it did not put the audience in a trance, but stimulated its thought and actions. Stanislavski considered this method unnatural, false, and artificial.

matic arts as they were at the end of the nineteenth and the beginning of the twentieth centuries. We can hardly expect to achieve positive results by applying this method without modification to the presentation of the classical heritage, for example the works of the Renaissance. And lastly, it is time to stop denouncing as contemptible formalists all those actors and stage directors who go their own way, and by their experiences and their searching enrich the art of the Soviet theater, embracing, as it does, numerous national minorities.

The debate on the state of the Soviet theater received a new vigorous impulse when the *Berliner Ensemble*, the theatrical group created after World War II in East Berlin by Bertold Brecht, played in Moscow and Leningrad in the summer of 1957. Brecht (1898–1956), a German playwright, poet, and novelist, had developed a theatrical theory known as the "epic theater." The theory was an attempt on his part to turn away from the "theater of illusion" (represented in his view by the entire Western theater tradition from Aristotle on), and to evoke in the audience an attitude of detached observation and evaluation. To achieve this "alienation" Brecht often resorted in his plays to interruptions—comments, asides, lectures, songs—all calculated to break off the audience's identification with the performance and to substitute critical awareness. With the same purpose in mind, Brecht trained his actors to emphasize the distance between themselves and their roles; this of course in direct opposition to Stanislavski's ideal of identification.

Bertold Brecht was also a fervent Marxist and widely known as a Communist sympathizer. Because of his involvement in the Marxist movement, the Communists appropriated his name, gave him a theater in East Berlin after World War II, awarded him a Stalin Peace Prize, and made him the showpiece of the Communist theater in their propaganda in the West. Yet, attracted as he was by the humanist elements of Marxist theory, Brecht's views were always unorthodox from the Communist point of view, and he often found himself at odds with the Party. All this, of course, Communist propaganda never mentioned. Nothing was ever said of the fact that Brecht had written all his plays before he went to live in the Soviet zone of Germany, most of them while an emigré in the West; that during his lifetime his plays were never performed in any Eastern bloc country, nor indeed to this day in the Soviet Union; or that in East Germany several of his plays were banned, withdrawn from the repertoire, or rewritten.

Nevertheless, the performance of the *Berliner Ensemble* created much excitement in the Soviet Union, and while the official notices were generally respectful, if somewhat restrained in tone, a few critics seemed to be inching toward admitting Brecht into the pantheon of socialist realism. A characteristic comment by A. Anikst (*Teatr*, No. 8, 1957) ran as follows:

> In my view, Brecht's theater is convincing testimony to the wealth and variety of the art of socialist realism. . . . The *Berliner Ensemble* defends its own peculiar artistic principles. Precisely because its art is so markedly individualistic, it has enriched our comprehension of the broad potentialities of socialist realism.

As in 1954, however, all these tentative advances toward a larger measure of freedom in the Soviet theater again came to an end. The theater could not for long escape the consequences of the campaign against revisionism unleashed by the Kremlin in 1957, and presently new efforts were made to rescue the hegemony of the Stanislavski System, which to the Party seems to constitute a guarantee of ideological hegemony in the theater. In its drive for a general acceptance of the System, the Party employed the same tactics as it had used before in its defense of socialist realism; the concept was broadened and "dogmatic distortions" disavowed.

Thus an essay by V. Prokofief and G. Dristi in *Teatr* in preparation for the All-Union Congress of Creative Theater Workers, Dramatists, and Theater Critics, held in October, 1958, at Moscow, stated:

> The endeavors to exploit creatively what is best in other schools should hardly arouse any objections. It is incomprehensible, however, that the trend toward the traditions of

Meyerhold and Vakhtangov should now be proclaimed as an innovation, while the trend toward the Stanislavski System—which is in use at the Meyerhold and Vakhtangov Theaters as well as at all other good theaters—should be considered by certain critics of the System as routine and traditional. It might be mentioned, incidentally, that Vakhtangov's and Stanislavski's views on art were doubtless more often in agreement than in disagreement. It is therefore hardly justifiable to separate the Vakhtangov tradition from the main current of realism on the stage, i.e., Stanislavski's school. The contradictions which do exist between the two schools—contradictions that are not absolute but relative—cannot alter the fact that Vakhtangov was the disciple nearest to Stanislavski and to the end of his life considered him the ultimate authority on art. Similarly, there are points of contact between the experiments of Stanislavski and the experiments of Meyerhold, who acknowledged with appreciation Stanislavski's new method in the mid-1930's and then joined with him in artistic cooperation.

Having in this way *a priori* incorporated everything "artistically valuable" of Vakhtangov and Meyerhold into the Stanislavski System, the essay then went on to the conclusion: "The theory of a hybrid of various movements in art is as little worthy of serious consideration as a return to Meyerhold's biomechanics or to the theater of the 1920's, which has been suggested by some authors."

At the Congress itself, the then Minister of Culture, Mikhailov, spoke in the same vein, although much more vaguely.[*] The door to a creative renaissance of the "golden era" of the Soviet theater was thus closed once again—this time, it would seem, for good.

Conclusion

1) It has proved impossible to restore the "revolutionary theater." The art of that era derived its persuasive power and the

[*] N. Mikhailov, "O sostoianii i zadachakh sovetskovo teatralnovo iskusstva na sovremennom etape," *Teatr*, No. 12, 1958.

vigor of its expression from the ardor of the still unbroken revolutionary illusions. It sincerely depicted the torments and the contradictions of the times, justifying them by the fervor of its faith in the advent of a better world order. Stalin and Zhdanov destroyed this art along with the international prestige it had gained, not out of malice or sheer philistinism. They sensed— more by instinct than by reasoning—that the revolutionary testimony was bound to turn against Communism itself as soon as its heroic ideals degenerated and became the reality of Soviet society. Then, too, all that had made the revolutionary art of the 1920's unacceptable to the Stalinists—its respect for truth, its denunciation of evil, its passionate will to change the world— alienated it from the post-Stalin era as well. The thaw has shown that any artistic utterance professing the truth undermines the foundations of the Party dictatorship.

Furthermore, it is not possible to grant the artists creative freedom as far as the *form* of their work is concerned and at the same time dictate its *content*. As descendants of Hegel and Marx, the Soviet theoreticians ought to know that form and content cannot be separated: Their unity is a condition of art. The campaign carried on by the Stalinists against "formalism" was never concerned with problems of form only. The true artist, spurred by the "urge to speak," will always create new concepts and new content when he expands the limits set to his art by form. The liberty to experiment will therefore always entail great danger to the regime.

2) The "revolutionary theater" is a historically closed era. Even if the Party permitted a free development of Soviet theater life, the 1920's would not return. The revisionist artists sided with the "revolutionary theater" only in order to break the dogmatic bonds of Stalinism. Moreover, as the discussions and productions during the thaw showed, they flocked instead to Vakhtangov's playhouse, thus joining in a development that the artists of the Soviet theater, with Meyerhold at the head, had tried to encourage back at the end of the 1920's. The fact that the trend toward the "theatrical theater" is now dominant in the whole Western world points to the conclusion that this dramatic conception represents the legitimate form of theatrical expression in contem-

porary democratic society. Not even in the rebellion against the
Party can the devices of the old "revolutionary theater" be successfully employed, since it is the emancipation of the human
being and not—as in 1917—of a revolutionary idea that is involved.
All the works of the period of the thaw, both in the Soviet Union
and in the "people's democracies," were critical rather than emotional; they dealt with the individual and not with the masses.

3) The dilemma of the Soviet theater stems from the fundamental contradiction between humanitarianism and power inherent in a totalitarian society. The regime can, to be sure, banish
truth and humanitarianism from art and replace them with hollow
propaganda slogans; but at the very moment it does so, art
crumbles in its hands. Its power of persuasion, the very quality
that led the Bolsheviks to "occupy" art, has been annihilated by
socialist realism. The regime can punish or even kill the creative
artists who honor the truth; the result, however, will not be
subjection of mind and spirit, but a devastating dearth of initiative and talent. It is clear that such a system must lead to crises.
Neither will the artists, however relentlessly pressured, ever
reconcile themselves to the violation of their aspirations, nor will
a society be able to endure for any length of time without a
cultural life, without the arts and sciences. It was this difficulty
that brought forth the thaw, and the crisis will not be overcome
until the Party relinquishes its ideological monopoly in the arts.

WHITHER RUSSIA?

Introduction

To say that the Soviet Union is changing is one thing. To analyze—as the authors of all the preceding articles have done— the nature of the changes is a formidable task, of course, but not an insurmountable one. But should we not examine the changes *in toto* and thereby try to arrive at an explanation not only of how and why the Soviet Union is changing, but of its future development? Here is a path on which many have trodden, yet only few have done so with any degree of success. For Winston Churchill's famous remark that "Russia is a riddle wrapped in an enigma" is perhaps nowhere more applicable than in the area of prognosis and prediction. In the 1920's, for instance, there was a great deal of talk about "liberalization" resulting from the quasi-capitalist New Economic Policy. The policies of forced collectivization and rapid industrialization put an end to *those* speculations. In the late 1930's, in the wake of the decimation of the revolutionary elite, it was confidently predicted that Soviet society would not withstand this shock and would eventually crumble. The victory over Nazi Germany proved that this, too, was false. Another wave of expectations was aroused at the end of World War II, when it seemed as if the hard-pressed Soviet population would finally be given a breathing spell after the dreadful rigors of the preceding two decades. But then came the "Zdhanovshchina"—that violent and seemingly irrational attack on all forms of nonconformity and "kowtowing to the

531

West"—with its shrill insistence on "eternal vigilance," and again the hopes of the "optimists" were dashed. Examples of this type could be cited in profusion.

This, of course, is not to suggest either that no changes have occurred in the Soviet Union, or that attempts at predicting the future of Russia are doomed to failure. As this book has made abundantly clear—and as the commentary "An Empire in Convulsion" emphasizes—Stalin's death *has* marked a profound break with a whole era; accordingly, it has also made it imperative for those who follow Soviet events not only to understand the present, but to project their analyses into the future. Above all, in assessing the trends of Soviet policies, both domestic and foreign, it has become necessary to distinguish between the elements of continuity and those of change, to understand which aspects of the Soviet system are here to stay and which elements may be expected to evolve—and if so, in what direction.

Of the half dozen or so articles in this section, the one that takes the most general and historic view is that of Raymond Aron. Committed neither to the economic determinism of Isaac Deutscher, who foresees gradual democratization as a result of the growth of industrialization in the U.S.S.R., nor to the school of thought that maintains that no basic changes in the totalitarian structure of the Soviet Union can occur, Mr. Aron takes a calm look at what has actually transpired since Stalin's death and delineates the areas of possible change on the basis of empirical evidence and common sense.

The article by Professor Sidney Hook, written shortly after the launching of the "de-Stalinization" campaign in the Soviet Union and the October revolutions in Hungary and Poland, speculates on the possibility of internal liberalization in the Soviet bloc as a result of the revolution in Marxist thought, particularly in Eastern Europe. An addendum, written this year, is appended. The other articles are even more provocative: The symposium "Toward a 'Communist Welfare State'?" examines the relation between economic rationalism and political liberty, while the last two articles consider the recent attempts to steer Soviet society toward "full Communism." The readers—and time—are left to judge the validity of the predictions offered.

An Empire in Convulsion—
A Commentary

IN THE LAST few weeks, the world has been subjected to an avalanche of staggering events whose outcome is not yet in sight.* What had initially borne the earmarks of an accelerated but orderly retreat from rigid Stalinism soon degenerated into a nightmarish bloodbath, still rampant as these lines are written. After making concessions to "national Communism" in Poland, Moscow is now reported to be subjecting the Polish government to various forms of pressure, all designed to forestall extensive administrative and economic reforms. Soon after the official promise to withdraw its troops from the satellites, the Soviet dictatorship brands the thousands of men, women, and children fighting and dying in Hungary as "fascists," "landlords," and "counterrevolutionaries," brazenly defending its bloody intervention as the "correct position of proletarian internationalism."

Will the brutal suppression of the Hungarian Revolution and strong-arm tactics in Poland spell the end of the "thaw" that has been spreading through the length and breadth of the Soviet empire? Or will there be a return to a process of controlled relaxation once the Soviet Union is convinced that it is not threatened with immediate annihilation and that naked force is no substitute for rational economic and political policies? These are some of the questions that are anxiously raised at this time. But before some tentative answers are advanced, a brief sketch of the forces that underlie the current crisis would seem to be in order.

* This commentary was written in the first weeks of November, 1956.—*Ed.*

Until the eruption of violence at the end of October, the Stalinist system at home and abroad showed every sign of a gradual and inexorable disintegration. Seen in retrospect, this disintegration was due to a number of causes, all of them important, though asserting themselves at different times and with differing effects. The first cause lay in the fact that the social and economic factors that did much to determine Stalinist policies have been playing an ever-diminishing role. Chief among these factors was the over-all backwardness of Russian society and its atomization following the upheavals of 1914–18. This is not to say, as some commentators do, that these factors made totalitarianism inevitable, but to the extent that they did exist, they surely helped to shape the specific form of Stalinist totalitarianism. To industrialize the country in the direction and with the speed desired by the dictatorship, forced collectivization had to be employed. Wholesale collectivization, in turn, was intimately connected with coercion, bloodshed, ruthlessness, a centralized economy—all hallmarks of the Stalinist system. Once Russia emerged as a powerful and in many respects modern industrial state, some of its original social and economic compulsions were bound to become less and less operative.

As Soviet society has changed, so has the Soviet dictatorship. And what was useful and rational—from the Kremlin's point of view—became less useful, less rational—indeed, at times, even dangerous. The Stalin reign was marked by a number of features that in the hands of an arbitrary dictator eventually became liabilities rather than assets. The Stalin cult, which at first played a rational role in legitimizing the rule of the Leader, was gradually getting out of hand. Suspicion and terror, which at first helped to consolidate the Stalinist power apparatus, finally threatened to become a socially disruptive and uncontrollable force. Massive coercion, which facilitated the process of collectivization and the creation of Soviet military might, became, as time went on, an impediment to the growth of the Soviet economy. To eradicate these irrational elements, which comprised what may be called the "senescence of Stalinism," became in many respects an imperative from which the new Soviet leadership could only shrink at its own peril.

The reasons for the post-Stalin changes would thus seem to be a mixture of objective and subjective factors, of irresistible forces as well as conscious engineering, of expediential adaptation to reality as well as deliberate attempts to steer it along new channels. They cannot be explained entirely either as tactical shifts or as policies deliberately staged by this or that faction within the Soviet hierarchy in their internecine struggle for power. Both elements undoubtedly play their roles in the present situation, but though the stress on incentives to peasants, in lieu of continuous repression, may be regarded as a change in tactics, the same surely cannot apply to the dismantling of concentration camps in the U.S.S.R. And while Malenkov may very well have represented the interests of certain groups in Soviet society, and his downfall the rise of a different group, the fact remains that it was his successor, Khrushchev, at first considered an arch-Stalinist, who gave the anti-Stalin campaign its greatest impetus. Khrushchev's reversal may be pure opportunism, but it has important roots that go beyond the machinations of the individuals in question.

The disintegration of Stalinism, described above, has until now been controlled—and even, as pointed out, desired and initiated—by the Soviet leadership. Internally, this situation still holds true. There has been a significant degree of continuity of post-Stalin measures in the U.S.S.R. in almost all areas of public life. Even the Khrushchev assault on Stalin may be regarded essentially as an intensification of a process that took three years to mature. Stalinism, after all, had become not only a symbol, not only a "cult," but a method of government, a mode of behavior, a system of thought and action that had penetrated into every institutional facet of Soviet society. "The cult of the individual fettered the search of the inquiring mind and set limits on scientific research," says *Partiinaia zhizn*, No. 9, of May, 1956. "The cult of the individual did grave harm to the country's defensive capacity," declares *Krasnaia zvezda* of July 19, 1956. "As a result of the cult of the individual, negative phenomena have become rooted in the work of Party and Soviet bodies and in the methods of leadership," according to *Kommunist*, No. 10, August,

1956. There is no reason to doubt the underlying truth of these
statements—or understatements. . . . And there is good reason to
believe that the Soviet leaders had come to the conclusion that
many of these problems must be tackled—and tackled head-on,
through the customary method of *shturmovshchina*, or all-out
assault.

It is externally, however, that the breakdown of Stalinism has
become so conspicuous these past few months—and so dramatic.
The use of force in Hungary can only be understood against the
background of the manifest failure of Stalinist policy in Eastern
Europe and in relation to the numerous concessions that the
Soviets have been compelled to make to their erstwhile under-
lings. Furthermore, Moscow's decision to drown the Hungarian
Revolution in blood, taken after a period of hesitation and
attempted conciliation, must not obscure the fact that in the long
run Stalinism would prove viable only at an enormous price, one
that the Soviet leaders may well not be willing to pay.

The Soviet concessions to Poland, and the declaration of October 30, 1956, promising to discuss with the governments of the
"people's republics" the question of the withdrawal of Soviet
advisers and troops, underlined Moscow's readiness to come to
terms with the liberalization movement sweeping through Eastern Europe—provided it did not go too far. Clearly, the Hungarian Revolution, responsive to its own elemental forces and not
to the limits prescribed in Moscow, did go "too far," and consequently Soviet Russia resorted to wholesale terror in order to
suppress it and prevent its entire East European empire from
falling apart. But does this mean a full-scale return to Stalinist
methods vis-à-vis the satellites, and the complete end of controlled liberalization? As grim and tragic as the situation may
look at this moment, it would seem as if the answer to this question should be in the negative. For one thing, Stalinism has *never*
meant brute force alone, but force enveloped in a myth of
"popular support," the "elimination of elements hostile to the
masses," etc. Soviet seizure of Hungary—or for that matter any
other satellite—did not occur overnight, but progressed piece-

meal, through the use of what Rakosi had dubbed "salami tactics," i.e., the gradual liquidation of all existing or potential enemy forces, under all sorts of hypocritical pretexts, and to the tune of innumerable promises and ideological rationalizations. The promises have now been exploded, the pretexts shown up for what they were, the ideological rationalizations pulverized by the simple fact that force, and only brute force, was used to gain what threats, cajolery, and lies could not achieve. The Soviets realize that a return to a Stalinist position could be accomplished only through the use of the essence, but not the trappings, of Stalinist politics; and it was on the trappings that their appeal had depended so much in the past. Now it is obvious, however, that never again will the captive peoples in Eastern Europe accept Soviet promises and prevarications. And it is doubtful whether the Soviet leaders would consider it either desirable or practical to keep down by brute force alone what might well develop into a continuous movement of passive resistance.

In addition, whatever the innate Soviet contempt for either the views of Communist parties abroad, or for world opinion at large, the fact remains that they can ill afford to disregard them altogether. In particular, they cannot, in the long run, afford to antagonize the very powers in Asia whom they so blatantly have been trying to woo. Their present action in Hungary may have been obscured—at least as far as some parts of the world are concerned—by Anglo-French action in the Middle East. But a *continuous* reign of terror cannot be hidden—or rationalized—forever. Already the Communist world has been rocked by mass defections (e.g., in Italy), angry protests from leaders (in Austria), and genuine soul-searching among intellectual elements (in France). And while Asian opinion, by and large, has thus far been only mildly disturbed by the Soviet massacre in Hungary, it is safe to assume that repercussions in that part of the world will sooner or later make themselves felt as well.

All things considered, therefore, it is possible to assume that Moscow will eventually have to come to terms with reality—and make the best of it. For the outstanding feature of the present situation is that it represents a natural result of the erosion of a system that began with the death of the man who had brought it into being. The same forces that have generated the disintegration of the Stalinist system at home are also at work in the Stalinist empire *in toto*. And as in the case of internal de-Stalinization, the Soviet leaders—whoever they will be—will probably have to reconcile themselves to existing trends—in this case, the growing independence of their former vassals. The process of reconciliation has, for the time being, suffered a setback, and it is more than likely that in the immediate future there will be a resurgence of the type of approach and mentality that the world had grown accustomed to under the reign of the omnipotent Stalin. The duration and precise nature of this approach will depend to a significant extent on the kind of reception it receives from the powers that have thus far successfully resisted Communist expansion in Europe and Asia. Should the Soviet leaders see that the flare-up of militancy is—as in the case of Stalinist aggression—leading them into a blind alley, the earlier pressures for gradual relaxation will be bound to reassert themselves with even greater vigor than hitherto. It will be at that time that we may see the further disintegration of the Stalinist monolith and the emergence of a new genre of Communism—in its ultimate sense perhaps no less abhorrent to the goals and ideals of a democratic society, but certainly different from the type the world has known until now.

A. B.

Soviet Society in Transition

—RAYMOND ARON

THE FUTURE DEVELOPMENT of Soviet society is manifestly one of
the most crucial issues under investigation by social scientists
today. Studies in this field are necessarily speculative, not only
for the obvious reason that they deal with future unknowns, but
because there has been so little opportunity for outsiders to
familiarize themselves with the Soviet-Russian reality. Social
scientists face a further difficulty in that there are several possible
—and somewhat incompatible—approaches, or bases, for an interpretation of Soviet society.

Studies to date have proceeded along three principal avenues
of approach, investigating Soviet society, first, as an industrial
civilization; second, as a totalitarian system (dealt with as a
unique phenomenon without historical precedent); third, as the
successor to Czarist Russia (with stress laid on aspects of cultural
continuity between past and present). Any of these conceptual
approaches can lead to confusion in attempts to predict the Soviet
future. In the first instance, little is known as yet about the laws
of economic development in a system of the Soviet type. Analyses
stressing the totalitarian aspect often suffer for lack of a clear
definition of totalitarianism itself (e.g., does it date back to Lenin
or just to Stalin?). As for the continuity approach, stress on the
constant factors in Russian culture as a key to the future can too
easily lead to underestimation or disregard of the impact of economic and political changes.

Taking all these approaches into account, we may then ask the
following questions: To what extent, if any, will the development
of industrial civilization bring about an evolution of the Soviet

totalitarian regime and of the social forms inherited from the past? What direction will this evolution take? Some observers, in attempting to answer these questions, have put forward theses based on one or another of the above schemes of interpretation in virtual disregard of the issues raised by the others.

Two such theses are worth mention as categorical and contradictory extremes of opinion; both, in this writer's view, are invalid. One asserts that the stupendous development of productive forces in the Soviet Union will pave the way to democracy; the other, that the totalitarian regime is invulnerable to economic forces.

Extremist Theories

The first of these has been expounded in particularly crude terms by Isaac Deutscher. His formulation lends itself to numerous objections, raised so often already that they can be dealt with briefly here. The explanation that terrorism and ideological orthodoxy are determined solely by the needs of primary accumulation or of the Five Year Plans runs up against the incontrovertible fact that the Great Purge of 1936–38 took place after the first Plan had already been carried out and the collectivization of agriculture completed. The terror that accompanied collectivization may, at a stretch, be attributed to economic "necessities," but this explanation cannot apply to the Great Purge, during which millions of real and imagined opponents, faithful Bolsheviks and even Stalinists were thrown into prison.

The tremendous development of Soviet productive forces, on which neo-Marxists always dwell as a portent of the better life to come, is of course no fiction. By and large, however, it applies only to heavy industry. The lot of the Soviet citizenry has not greatly improved, since the living standard is determined not by per-capita production but by the value of goods intended for consumption by individuals. Considering additionally the lag in agricultural output, it is unlikely that the Soviet planners can greatly increase the purchasing power of the population in the foreseeable future.

In any thesis on the Soviet future, the meaning of the word

"democracy" is crucial. If by democracy is meant the organized competition of parties—as it seems to in Deutscher's formulation —then there is no obvious connection between democracy and economic progress. But it is absurd to insist on rigid and unalterable concepts of democracy in its Western form (characterized by multiparty systems, legislative representation, intellectual liberties, and the like) as opposed to totalitarianism (characterized by the single party, ideological terrorism, and police controls). Neither Western democracy nor Stalinist totalitarianism can be considered as fixed entities, as "historic atoms" that cannot be transmuted. Thus, if it is illogical to assert that totalitarianism will develop into full-fledged democracy with the development of productive forces, it is just as illogical to exclude dogmatically a softening up of totalitarianism.

This is the weakness of the second theory, opposite to Isaac Deutscher's, which asserts that totalitarianism is invulnerable to outside forces. It is usually posited as part of a political and almost metaphysical interpretation of totalitarianism, conceived of as a disease liable to infect any modern society—even though, so far, only Russia and Germany have experienced it in its "pure" form. Its proponents argue that although totalitarianism is favored by certain economic and social circumstances, it is essentially something political and ideological. It is supposed to be the outcome of an obsessive drive of a group of people bent on shaping society according to their own ideology. The power of a single party, ideological orthodoxy, police terror, the creation of a world of superimposed conventional meanings, with no reference to the real world and yet forced on the masses as something truer than reality—all these features, we are told, are linked together and constitute the characteristics of a global, or self-contained, phenomenon—a phenomenon that has emerged and will eventually disappear, but which it would be idle to expect to return to normality by gradual stages.

In this definition of totalitarianism, three of the above features are essential: ideological orthodoxy, police terror, and worldwide victory—or else apocalyptic collapse. These three elements are said to be closely linked. The will to set up an arbitrary and often absurd ideology as "The Truth" necessitates the recourse to police inquisition, which is used for hunting not only enemies but also heretics. The truth of the ideology can triumph only when it is no longer rejected by anybody. So long as there is opposition anywhere, Communism will not be entirely true, because its truth will still clash with reality, and its complete truth depends on its universal application. Thus Communism is in a constant state of war with unbelievers both inside and outside its borders. The greater the progress, the more it is impelled to struggle, for nothing has been achieved so long as something still remains to be done. This line of analysis affords an explanation for the Great Purge having descended upon Soviet society after the completion of rural collectivization; the latter is viewed not as an economic and rational measure, however ruthless, but as the expression of a policy *alien* to economic rationalism, and it is intelligible only in terms of an ideological and emotional logic.

This kind of interpretation, which Hannah Arendt has developed with great skills, seems to me to be dangerous. It amounts to creating a certain ideal type, a kind of essence of totalitarianism—and to assuming, thereupon, that the regime, both in the present and in the future, must conform to this type or this essence. If the Soviets behaved as "perfect" totalitarians, as Hannah Arendt understands the word, then it is quite true that we could expect no normalization or evolution of the Soviet regime. The real question is, however, whether the regime has even been completely totalitarian, whether the "essence" has not simply been created by theorists like Miss Arendt on the strength of certain historically observed and historically explicable phenomena. The Soviet regime *became* totalitarian by degrees, under the influence of certain circumstances. Why, then, could it not cease to be totalitarian, or become less totalitarian, under the influence of other circumstances?

The Impact of Economic Development

Once the extremes of the neo-Marxist and the totalitarian theory have been rejected, it must be decided what either of them can contribute to a logical assessment of the Soviet future. What transformations, social and economic, are brought about by the development of productive forces? What is the likely effect of these transformations on the political regime? To what extent is totalitarianism (or certain totalitarian elements) inseparable from the regime, regardless of economic progress?

There are at least three important social and economic consequences of the development of productive forces. The first is a rise in the general level of culture and the creation and development of an intelligentsia whose broad base—in addition to traditional cultural and professional elements—is the swelling ranks of technical and managerial specialists who man the economy. It is as true for the Soviet Union as for the West that industry today requires a higher proportion of technicians and specialized cadres than it did in the past, and Soviet statistics show a steady increase in the proportion of intelligentsia to the whole working population.

Even outside this intelligentsia with its higher-level specialization, the priority given to production and to productivity is bound to encourage the spread of specialized training and of technical education. More than half the Soviet labor force is at present employed in industry or its auxiliary services, and more than half the population is urban. This urban population can read and write, and it is no longer as cowed—or as malleable—as it was in the early years of Stalin's reign.

The second consequence of industrial development, closely related to the first, is an increase in the economic wants and demands of the population. In the Soviet Union, the development of productive forces has not been accompanied by a corresponding rise in the standard of living of the masses. The concentration of capital investments in heavy industry, the failures in agriculture, and the housing shortage have meant that the average citizen is worse housed, worse fed and less well-dressed than the average citizen of the West, even in some of the less prosperous countries. In recent years, however, there has been some improvements in material conditions, and various pressures have led the regime to pay some limited deference to consumer needs. The indications are that this limited satisfaction of certain wants has whetted the population's appetite for more goods. In particular, the intelligentsia has shown increasing eagerness to acquire commodities typical of the way of life of the Western bourgeois (durable consumer goods, automobiles, refrigerators, and so on).

The third consequence of developing productive forces is a trend toward a more rational economy. Over the last thirty years, the Soviet economy has become not only more powerful but technologically far more complex. To what extent and how long the crude planning methods of the first Five Year Plans can continue to be applied is a highly complicated and controversial issue. Yet the general direction of evolution seems fairly clear to this writer. As shortages become less severe, the consumers' choice will tend to be of growing importance to the market. Technological complexity will strengthen the managerial class at the expense of the ideologists and the militants, at any rate on the enterprise level, if not on the state level. The decentralization of industrial administration, in reinforcing the managerial elements, should reduce the part played by fear and coercion in the Soviet management of an industrial society.

Stabilizing Forces in Soviet Society

While the rate at which any of these social and economic trends will develop is hard to foresee, certain political implications seem clear. Briefly, it is the writer's view that none of these trends—toward a higher cultural level, toward increasing popular demands, or toward a more rational economy—constitutes a threat to the basic organization of the Soviet state or society.

Apart from its peculiarly totalitarian features, Soviet society is essentially bureaucratic and hierarchical, just as was pre-Revolutionary Russian society. The reliance of an industrial society on a state bureaucracy with vested interests—under a system that prevents the formation of organized opinion or pressure through professional groups, genuine trade unions, or political parties—obviously creates a certain tendency toward stability. A further stabilizing factor is class mobility; since the intelligentsia is expanding with each generation, it can absorb the ablest children of the masses without the regime's having to resort to purge or to demotion of the children of the already privileged.

As noted above, there is bound to be some tension between the economic desires of the masses and the intelligentsia, on the one hand, and the exigencies of regime policy on the other (requiring the continued priority of heavy industry). There is probably also a latent conflict between the desire for rationality and security on the part of the managerial and technocratic elements, and the desire for power and prestige on the part of the Party men. But such conflicts do not imply any explosions or fundamental changes in the society.

In short, there is nothing to indicate that economic progress will force the ruling class, composed of Party men and higher-level bureaucrats, to authorize the creation of rival forces—in the form of either parties or workers' trade unions. And there is nothing to indicate that such a challenge can come from below; neither the masses nor the intelligentsia have the means of over-riding the ban on organized pressure groups. The leadership seems quite capable of maintaining the principle of the single hierarchy, of the single party, and of the legal *status quo* of the ruling bureaucracy. If any basic change is to take place, it will have to occur *within* the ruling elite—i.e., inside the Communist Party.

Evolution and the Regime

What can be said, then, of the effects of progressing industrialization on the Communist regime itself, and specifically on those aspects of the regime that have come to be identified as "totalitarian"? The question may be discussed under several heads: (1) Will the internal structure of the Party undergo basic changes as a result of the spontaneous evolution of the economy and the society? (2) Will ideology continue, in the long run, to play the same role as it has in the past? (3) Is the movement still inspired by the same boundless ambition, by the same violence, or may it be expected eventually to rest content with what it is —that is, something less than universal?

The most crucial change in the Party structure of recent years —the substitution of collective leadership for one-man dictatorship—is attributable to a historical event, to the death of an individual, rather than to the evolution of either the society or the regime. Nevertheless, the change was, in a way, logical. For the very nature of Stalin's power—or his abuse of it—dictated against the rise of a single successor. None of the members of the Presidium could without anxiety face the prospect of a repetition of the process whereby Stalin, little by little, had liquidated virtually all of the men who had once been his allies in the Party leadership.

Some observers have held that Khrushchev's increasing domination of the ruling clique has already put an end to collective leadership. But Khrushchev has had to lean heavily on the support of allies to push through his policies, and in this sense group rule certainly continues. Acting as a group of leaders, the Presidium has appeared to be less indifferent to public demands, less able or less determined to carry out programs regardless of cost, than was Stalin with his unlimited personal power.

Whether further fundamental changes will take place in the structure and balance of power within the Party is a matter of conjecture at this stage. However, it is worth noting that Khrushchev effected his purge of the so-called "anti-Party" leaders in June, 1957, through appeal to the Central Committee, over the objections of a majority of the Presidium. Before that time, the Presidium appeared to be just as independent of the Central Committee as Stalin had been. Since the authority of the proletariat originally passed from the Party to the Politburo (i.e., Stalin) *through* the Central Committee, it is interesting to speculate on whether the reverse could take place. So far, there is no sign that any such basic shift in power is in the offing; if it were to occur, however, it would be directly attributable to the struggle for power rather than to broader forces of evolution.*

---

* "Soviet Society in Transition" was written in 1957, and is based on a report presented at the St. Antony's (Oxford) Conference on Soviet Communism, organized jointly by the College and the Congress for Cultural Freedom, held in June of that year. Since then, of course, the term "collective leadership" has largely fallen into disuse in the U.S.S.R., and Khru-

The changeover from personal to collective leadership has been accompanied by the mitigation or abandonment of certain aspects of totalitarian rule. Perhaps the epitome of totalitarianism, certainly the feature most frequently mentioned, is the instrument of the purge, characterized by that combination of arbitrary police action, ideological terrorism, and pure fantasy defined by the inquisitor-theologians as more real than reality itself. The confession trials were the symbolic expression of this aspect of totalitarianism.

The collective leadership has renounced such excesses, and in doing so has revealed that it was never taken in by the mad logic of Stalinist ideological terrorism. At the same time, it may reasonably be pointed out that Khrushchev has not hesitated, on occasion, to employ it himself, as for instance when he has called Beria an "imperialist agent" or the Hungarian Revolution a "counterrevolution." This leads us to perhaps the most crucial issue under consideration in this paper: the future role of ideology in the evolving Soviet society.

A Trend Toward Skepticism?

Communist ideology is based on a few simple ideas—e.g., the Party *is* the proletariat; the seizure of power by the Party is the *sine qua non* for the establishment of socialism. In places where

---

shchev's victory over his rivals has become an accomplished fact. He had used the Central Committee to reverse the hostile majority in the Presidium, having first assured himself of a loyal following in the Central Committee through appointments made by the Party Secretariat—of which, of course, he is the supreme master.

Yet another fact seems equally certain: Khrushchev does not exercise control over the Party by terror, as did Stalin. Could he follow in the latter's footsteps? While this question must of necessity be left open, the possibility of an evolution in the direction of full-blown Stalinism seems rather improbable, as it would run counter to the feelings and wishes of the very Party members who had brought Khrushchev to power.

To what extent the current situation is a result of Khrushchev's character and mode of governance, and to what extent it flows from the diffused will of the Party also is a moot point. In any event, even if the leadership of the Soviet Union has assumed a personal character, the fact remains that the person in charge has not become a tyrant, nor have his rivals suffered the fate suffered by Stalin's numerous rivals and adversaries.—R. A.

the Party has not taken over power, capitalism reigns and the masses are exploited. The inevitable culmination will be the extension throughout the world of regimes similar to the Soviet regime.

As is frequently pointed out, this orthodoxy has little connection with either Marx *or* reality. A society that has developed a great industrial complex side by side with a relentlessly low standard of living resembles what Marx called capitalism—a welfare state, albeit "capitalist," in which the additional resources accruing from technical progress are used for the benefit of the masses, does not. The dialecticians have been obliged to place an arbitrary interpretation on facts, often at variance with the most obvious reality. The element of fantasy in the great trials is merely the supreme expression of this logic.

It is the writer's belief that Soviet society, with the improvement in its standard of living, its culture, and its technology, not only is becoming economically more rational, but must in the long run lose its ideological fervor. As it makes further progress and becomes more stable, as its technical level draws closer to that of industrialized Western societies, so both its militants and the people at large are bound to incline to some degree of skepticism. They will come to admit certain incontestable facts, such as the plurality of methods of industrialization, the raising of the standard of living in the West, etc. As soon as Polish writers and educators were able to talk freely, they proceeded to admit these facts and to escape from the absurd logic of Communist ideology.

Orthodoxy Versus Rationality

Does this mean that the dialecticians and Soviet leaders will cease to profess their belief in the universal mission, in the coming, through socialism, of a classless society? Certainly they have shown no such tendency thus far, leading to still another question: Is it possible for Soviet society, under its present organization and ideological restrictions, to go very far in the direction of *either* economic rationalism *or* the return to common sense? In both respects, regime attitudes are the source of basic contradictions in a society in conflict with evolutionary trends.

In the matter of ideology, the Soviet leadership is faced with a profound dilemma: It is hard to maintain a faith, but it is harder still to do without one. The leadership could, without too much difficulty, abandon the absurd excesses of Stalinist orthodoxy. The nightmare of the Stalin era was not confined to the system of trials and confessions; Stalin, by setting himself up as the supreme arbiter in matters of biology and linguistics, extended it to these realms. He also decreed what, in literature, painting, or music, conformed or failed to conform to socialist doctrine. But this kind of madness was not inherent in the system. It was simple for his successors to restore to biologists the right to accept the laws of genetics or to grant novelists or composers a greater measure of freedom in their work.

The leaders cannot, however, permit freedom of discussion to extend to the dogma itself, since its premises, as we have seen, are patently absurd and at variance with the facts. They do not want to return to Stalinist excesses, but they cannot permit any challenge of the dogma that legitimizes their rule and provides the justification for the perpetuation of Communism. The compromise is an uneasy one. The leaders are constantly threatening to deprive the intellectuals of some of the freedoms they have been granted, while the intellectuals, on their side, are continuously straining to transcend the limits that have been set for them.

In Poland and Hungary, where the desire for intellectual freedom was reinforced by the desire for national freedom, the conflict was resolved by explosion. In Hungary, order has been restored—but it is a foreign order, a police and military order. In Poland, a large measure of intellectual freedom still exists, but the dogma *as such* has vanished. The regime still pursues a socialist path of development, but the people are aware that it is simply one of many systems, that it offers no mystical guarantee for the welfare of the masses.

In the Soviet Union, on the other hand, the dogma is still intact; even though it is no longer as comprehensive or imperative as in the past, it continues to permeate the society. Certainly the leaders, judging by their pronouncements, still believe in the perpetuation of Communism. They have not ceased to see themselves as engaged in a relentless struggle with the capitalist camp. Their outlook on the world is a long-term one, dominated by an oversimplified conception of good and evil.

This leads us to the second major contradiction in Soviet society—the obstacles that stand in the way of economic rationalization. From the inception of the Five Year Plans, the objectives and methods of Soviet economic planning have been keyed to the concept of world struggle and to a desperate effort to catch up and surpass the level of industrialization in the capitalist countries. The system has the characteristics of what, in the West, would be a war economy: A rigid system of priorities has been established to ensure that the goals of heavy industry are achieved at all costs, the rest, if necessary, being sacrificed. When these goals have not been reached quickly enough, additional labor has been brought in from the countryside, and out-of-date industrial equipment has remained in operation.

Gradually however, transferable labor reserves have dwindled, with the result that increases have to come, in ever greater measure, from increased productivity. The problems of depreciation, renewal of equipment, and economic planning are becoming more and more acute. Light industry and agriculture can no longer be sacrificed indiscriminately. The situation obviously demands an increasingly rational economy; but what kind of rationality is there in a planning system that concentrates not on satisfying demands but on the expansion of heavy industry, that refuses to grant enterprises more than a bare minimum of independence, that continues to allocate the country's resources on the basis of decisions taken at the top, and that still aims at authoritarian administration in so large a sector of the system? The 1957 reform of industrial administration, while transferring various executive functions to newly created regional authorities, does not basically change these governing principles of the Soviet economic system.

As long as the Soviet leaders adhere to Stalinist principles, insist on the priority of heavy industry, and maintain dispro-

portionate ratios between investment and consumption and heavy
industry and agriculture and light industry, the Soviet economy
will continue to bear the marks of an authoritarian, police regime.
The return to a normal peacetime economy depends, in the final
analysis, on the modification of the objectives fixed by the leaders
—in short, on their outlook.

All of the foregoing suggests two conclusions. It is not true to
say that the Soviet regime is becoming increasingly totalitarian
as the society comes to need totalitarianism less and less. Many
of the worst aberrations of the regime appear to have stemmed
from the abnormality of Stalin himself; and they have disappeared with him. But neither is it true to maintain that the main
features of the economic system and of the political regime are
attributable to Stalin exclusively; they are rooted as firmly in the
views and methods of the men who helped build the U.S.S.R.
and who now rule it.

These conclusions, however, still do not answer the basic issues
of the future; namely, *could* the regime change fundamentally
without crumbling? And what freedoms is it capable of tolerat-
ing?

The Prospects for a Freer Society

When making a simplified analysis, a distinction can be drawn
between three different kinds of freedom: first, what Montesquieu called security; second, the freedom the Hungarian intellectuals claimed, namely, the right to tell the truth about
everything; and finally, Rousseau's freedom—participation in
sovereignty—represented in the twentieth century by free elections and the multiparty system.

Individual security is, as a rule, most favored by a parliamentary type of government. But many nondemocratic regimes
give a fairly broad measure of security to those who do not
engage in politics. The Czarist regime, during its final period,
interfered little with the life and liberty of citizens who minded
their own business. In the Soviet Union, the insecurity of the
Stalin era appears to have been greatly lessened by Stalin's suc-

cessors. But as long as the Soviet regime continues to apply political sanctions in order to make the economy work, as long as it demands unquestioning respect for the dogma, the Soviet citizen will not be able to enjoy a true or stable measure of security.

To what extent could intellectuals and ordinary Soviet citizens be allowed to enjoy the second kind of freedom—to tell the truth about reality, to exchange ideas, to visit the capitalist West? In the writer's opinion, the regime could, without endangering its own safety, grant musicians, painters, and writers more freedoms than it does at present. But the word "could" here has a double application; the question is whether the leaders of the regime and the Party could bring themselves to grant such freedoms. Again, as long as they believe in their dogma, they will not allow it to be discussed, and truth will be harnessed. Yet even if they themselves become skeptical, would they admit it publicly? For the future, this is a matter of speculation; for the present, they certainly would not dare to do so. For even though there may be a tendency in Russia to evolve into a semi-ideological technocracy, the dogma is still a vital factor in less-advanced Communist countries and is crucial in justifying the unity of the socialist camp. To hope that the dogma will fade out in the near future would be overoptimistic.

In the long run, however, this writer holds to his view that increasing ideological skepticism is inevitable among both the leaders and the masses. Already the problems of Soviet planning are completely out of touch with the official economic textbooks, which are simplified versions of *Das Kapital.* Though tribute may still be paid to Marx, the day may come when an industrial society, concerned more with efficiency than with orthodoxy, will cease to follow the Lenin-Stalin ideology. Revolutionary fervor—though revived by the successes of Communism in Asia and the Middle East—is nevertheless bound, in the end, to die down, and probably to die out.

Will the Soviet citizen eventually obtain Rousseau's freedom—participation in sovereignty—through either the development of factions within the Party, or perhaps even the emergence of a multiparty system? The prospect of any move toward full-fledged political freedom of the Western type is so far beyond the scope of present or even predictable evolutionary trends that speculation would be foolish. Only time and the forces already at work in Soviet society will provide the clues to Russia's political future.

The Import of Ideological Diversity

——SIDNEY HOOK

RECENT EVENTS in the Soviet orbit, dating from Stalin's death in March 1953, have posed the problem of what may be termed "liberation by evolution," that is, the gradual transformation, within the ideological tradition of Marxism-Leninism, of the totalitarian system of Communism into a libertarian culture in which the strategic political and cultural freedoms of an open society are legally recognized and *in fact* realized.

Obviously it is impossible to predict if or when such a transformation actually will occur. This depends upon many factors outside the scope of the present discussion. The purpose of this essay is simply to raise the question of whether such a transformation is *possible*, and if it is, to determine which elements in the traditional Marxist ideology and which in current Communist theory and practice would lend themselves to such a development.

Of course, the ideology of Marxism and Leninism cannot so simply be assimilated to the ideal of human freedom. Yet anyone acquainted with the history of ideas knows that the same generic terms and doctrines have encompassed the widest variations in personality, belief, and practice. Communism as a secular religion has often been compared with Christianity, and identified by Toynbee—mistakenly, in this author's view—with one of its sects. But how vast and full of incompatible elements is the spectrum of beliefs called "Christian." The development of Christianity is largely the history of radical changes, both in doctrine and in practice, by those who claimed to be doing no more than returning to the pure essence of the doctrine.

What is true of religious movements is also true of other fields of human experience. Whether we consider the actual content of the slogans "the return to Christ" or "the return to Kant" or "the return to Rome or Jerusalem"—we will find that these returns always mark an original departure in doctrine and movement, sometimes in opposition to the actual intentions of the innovators.

What is for present purposes more to the point, is that even Lenin's slogan "Back to Marx," which he borrowed from Rosa Luxemburg, marked a tremendous revision in what until then had been understood as Marxism. Lenin's extremely voluntaristic *What Is to Be Done?*, although too simply characterized by some critics as spawned under Bakuninistic and Blanquist influences, was certainly not the Marxism of Kautsky and Plekhanov. What Lenin did to Marx in the name of Marxism, Stalin in lesser measure did to Lenin in the name of Leninism. This raises the question of the extent to which it will be possible in the current atmosphere of ambiguous devaluation of Stalin to initiate in other Communist countries even more far-reaching departures in Communist theory and practice by "returning to Marx."

Roads and Inroads

Communist theory and practice hang together more closely than in other ideologies, but it is possible to exaggerate their monolithic unity. Although adherence to a set of doctrines is, and always has been, *de rigueur* for all Communist parties affiliated with the Kremlin, some variations were permitted in the road to power—especially if they proved successful and were not taken in defiance of the Kremlin's orders. Stalin explicitly condemned the American Communist theory of exceptionalism—which simply asserted the banal proposition that each Communist Party must take note of the distinctive peculiarities of national political history and geography—primarily in order to replace one faction by a more compliant one. Yet when the opportunity presented itself after the war, he heartily approved of the manner in which the Czech, Yugoslav, and Chinese Communists seized power, even though in one case (China) it involved making the peasantry, not the proletariat, the basis of the Communist movement, and in no case did it involve the use of soviets, in whose name the Communist Party had seized power in the Russian October Revolution.

When we turn from the consideration of "different roads to power" to "different roads to socialism," we find the variations in the practices of Communist states just as great, but enormously more significant. Different roads to power are comparable to different roads leading to a city. The city is the same, irrespective of the way we reach it. But different roads to socialism, about which the classics of Marxism really say little, may be compared to different ways of building a city. The different ways of building a city result in substantially different cities, because the means used are not like the scaffolding torn away when the building is constructed, but are like the bricks and mortar, the steel and glass, which become intrinsic elements of the finished construction. The architectural metaphor serves admirably to drive home the logic of the means-end relation. If it is true that not pious words but means determine ends, then the adoption of different means of constructing socialism involves the very real likelihood of different kinds of socialism, unwelcome as this may be to the leaders of the Communist movement.

Today, under the name of Communism and Marxism, we find considerable differences in the theory and practice of "socialist society" in four different regions—the Soviet Union, China, Yugoslavia, and Poland. Some of these differences reflect, so to speak, the historical and geographical landscape and the accidents attendant upon origin. The differences may turn out to be even more momentous because to the extent that theory is a guide to action—and it is often only a rationalization of action—differences in doctrine can lead to the intensification of differences in social, economic, and cultural behavior. Thus, when Mao Tse-tung says that socialism is a garden in which many different theories can be permitted to grow, he has said something of which Khrushchev cannot approve without the danger of letting the "thaw" get out of hand. Even though, as seems likely, Mao Tse-tung will destroy as a "poisonous weed" any doctrine he does not like, his words may meanwhile inspire programs of liberalization in other countries—programs hesitant and tentative, to be sure, but still possible bases for further development. Even more significant, when Gomulka proclaims (in his speech to the Eighth Plenum in October, 1956) that "the best definition of the social contents inherent in the idea of socialism is contained in the definition that socialism is a social system that abolishes the exploitation and oppression of man by man," and that "what is immutable in socialism can be reduced to the abolition of the exploitation of man by man," these pronouncements constitute a more radical revision of traditional Marxism-Leninism-Stalinism than do Titoism and Maoism. For it follows at once that socialism, by this definition, is absent in the Soviet Union and the "people's democracies"—since it is not difficult to show that their populations, as they very well know, are exploited and oppressed economically, culturally, and politically. It follows that even a Jeffersonian community of small landowners who till their own soil, or one of individual craftsmen who own their instruments of production, who do not employ others and hence cannot exploit their labor, would have to be called socialistic!

The very conception of "different roads to socialism" gives rise naturally to the notion of "national Communism," so much feared by the Kremlin and, therefore, even by Tito and Gomulka. For "national Communism" is just as much a departure from the classic views of international Communism as "national socialism" is from the socialism of the *Communist Manifesto*. And in a genuine sense, the first expression of national Communism is to be found not in Titoism but in Stalinism, under which the concluding line of the *Communist Manifesto* was in practice made to read: "Workers of the World Unite—to Defend the Soviet Union."

Property and Power

The question here raised is whether, in terms of the official ideology and in the light of incontestable realities, the totalitarian integument of Communist doctrine can be shattered by uncovering, developing, and reinterpreting the rich legacy of ambiguities in the intellectual and social movement of Marxism. The existence of these ambiguities is revealed in the accounts given by former

ideological functionaries of Communist parties, such as Wolf-
gang Leonhard, of the process by which their difficulties developed into cancerous doubts, and Stalin was gradually rejected in
the name of Lenin, and Lenin finally rejected in the name of
Marx. I am not raising the question of whether any profound
institutional changes can take place by way of doctrine alone, for
this seems very improbable. Economic and international political factors are usually more weighty. I am asking only whether
in the struggle for freedom any aspect of the Marxist tradition
can be refashioned and sharpened into a serviceable weapon in
the cause of liberation—a liberation not only from foreign but
from domestic despots.

Let us look at some key Marxist concepts in this light.

There are two conceptions of property in Marx and the Marxist
tradition, one of which provides the basis not only for the critique
of capitalism, but even more powerfully for a critique of what
passes for "socialist economy."

The first conception of property is substantial and legalistic.
It defines property in terms of legal relations where the law is
construed as a decree certifying title of ownership. The development of modern economy in the West has limited the usefulness
of this concept by separating title from actual economic power.
The second conception of property in Marx is functional and
sociological. It is bound up with the Marxist ethical critique of
capitalism. According to this conception, property is a form of
power—the power not so much to use or abuse instruments,
goods, and services (since this is always limited) as the power to
exclude others from using them. Wherever property in land and
instruments of production gives power to exclude individuals
from the land and from access to instruments of production, they
give a very real power over the personal lives of these individuals.

Where legal title to property has been abolished, the continued *de facto* power to deny others access to goods and services,
and especially access to the means of livelihood, in effect gives
those who wield this power most of the traditional rights of
ownership under classical capitalism. This cut rights to the heart
of the fiction that collectivized or nationalized industry, since it
is no *one* man's individual property, *eo ipso* automatically spells

the end of exploitation. Under any system of socialization, where the institutional framework makes it possible for workers to be systematically denied access to the means of production, i.e., to their means of livelihood, it is a mockery to speak of the workers' ownership of the productive plant.

The same applies when it is said that the property in question is *state* property. For this merely pushes the question farther back. To whom does the state belong or who controls the state? If a group is excluded from effective political participation, what sense does it make to say that the state belongs to that group?

In the Soviet Union and in most of the satellite countries, the juridical change in proprietorship transferred title from capitalists and landlords to the collectivity. But the collectivity is a legal fiction whose actual content, according to sound Marxist principles, depends upon how it is actually organized, how it functions, and the different roles played by different groups in the actual processes of production. Almost from the very beginning, the Communist rulers had absolute power to deny any peasant or worker access to farm or factory, to decide what should be saved and spent—and how—and to determine the conditions and rewards of work as well as everything else connected with the use of the industrial plant, natural resources, etc.; this power was in no way susceptible to control by those whom its decisions so fatefully affected. In effect, then—and again according to legitimate Marxist categories—the instruments of production belonged to the Communist Party hierarchy, giving it all the traditional privileges of ownership except the right to buy and sell and the right of testamentary disposition. Under such a setup, workers can be and have been exploited more intensively, i.e., more surplus value has been sweated out of them, than under other forms of legal ownership since the early days of the industrial revolution.

Despite the semantic outrage of referring to the Soviet Union or any other Communist economy as a "workers' state" and to the productive plant as "state property," the facts were really not in dispute. When Lenin brutally proclaimed to the Eleventh Congress of the Russian Communist Party, in 1922, "We are the state," he might as well have stated, "We are the owners of the economy." Insofar as Marxism is a critique of the economies of exploitation, it can be used more legitimately and with greater devastation in present-day Communist countries than in most of the present-day democratic capitalistic countries of the West.

It is obvious when we look at the economies that are called socialist in countries like the U.S.S.R., China, Yugoslavia, Czechoslovakia, and Poland, that considerable differences in practice exist. When we examine Marxist theory, we can detect even greater potential differences in meaning—a democratic or totalitarian variant. Because Marxism is primarily a critique of capitalism, it provides no specific directives but only general guides as to how to build socialism. These guides are more social, political, and moral than economic in nature, because Marx assumed that the processes of accumulation would have progressed to a point where there would be no problem of having to construct capital goods industries. The ambiguities in Marxism are aggravated by the Bolshevik success in refuting (or revising) Marx in their attempt to lay the foundation of socialist economy by political means in industrially backward areas—something presumably ruled out by historical materialism. The most fervent "Marxists" today are those who have actually refuted Marx while excoriating the revisionists of Marx.

There is no historical necessity in the way in which socialism is to be built, otherwise we could not speak of different paths to socialism. No matter what the objective economic conditions, other factors enter into the situation. Among them an important—though not necessarily decisive—factor may be the way in which traditional Marxist principles are interpreted and developed. The direction in which "socialist" economy and society will develop may depend, for example, in some countries upon how the principle of "workers' control," stressed in pre-Revolutionary terms by both syndicalists and Marxists alike, is understood.

Workers' Control

There has always been an ambiguity about the nature and function of "workers' control" in socialist theory. The utopian theory of Marxism, according to which some day the state will disappear, made the organs of workers' control on the level of the factory the administrative unit of a society that would function without coercion by the voluntary cooperation of a historically new species of man. For purposes of revolutionary struggle, "workers' control" was stressed as a means of heightening the pitch of a revolutionary situation. All tendencies within the socialist movement declared themselves for workers' control, but few seemed clear about what it meant. All agreed, however, that workers' control was something exercised for the workers by a political group monopolizing power or, on the other hand, that it was something exercised by the workers themselves, following whatever leadership they chose.

In the early days of Bolshevism, on the eve of taking power and shortly thereafter, the Communists stressed in the most emphatic way the desirability of workers' control in every factory. Before long, however, the control of the Communist Party asserted itself so forcibly that the phrase "workers' control" became a transparent piece of terminological hypocrisy. Lenin himself led the fight against the "workers' opposition"—a group in the Communist Party that took the earlier agitational and propaganda slogans seriously—as an anarcho-syndicalist deviation.

The Yugoslav Communists who speak today of "workers' control" imply that Stalin revised Lenin's position on this question, while they are following the Leninist pattern. This is a misleading oversimplification. It results from confusing decentralization of industry and planning, which permits greater autonomy to the individual plant, and which the Yugoslavs have carried out, with independent workers' control in the decentralized plants, a control that the Yugoslavs only promise. And if they follow Lenin, they will never deliver on their promises. For even in the most liberal period of Soviet economic life, Lenin insisted that in the interests of rapid construction of large-scale industry "it is absolutely essential that all authority in the factories should be in the hands of the management."

It need not be pointed out that management in the so-called capitalist countries has much less power over workers than management in socialist societies, while trade unions in the former enjoy far more control in actual practice than do workers' councils in theory. Lenin recognized the limited role of the trade unions in correcting "the excesses and blunders resulting from the bureaucratic distortions of the state apparatus," and this stand was of tremendous importance in that it provided a justification of the right of the workers to strike in the so-called "workers' state"—to strike in all state enterprises. That this right was hedged in by all sorts of restrictions and qualifications, that it was more honored in the breach than in the observance, does not detract from its significance and its use as a rallying cry in the present and future. It was this truncated right that was lost under Stalin and in all Stalinist regimes. It was a grievous loss, for the abolition of the right to strike means in effect the existence of a system of forced labor with all its multiform kinds of exploitation and aggression.

In Yugoslavia today, a very limited kind of workers' control through workers' councils operates in conjunction with a largely decentralized industry planned to meet the market needs of local regions. This system came into existence more because of economic necessity than because of political virtue. And however limited the control, Soviet critical reaction has not been the less severe. What is interesting is the theoretical justification of these institutional deviations from the Soviet pattern expressed by Kardelj and other Yugoslav Communists in grandiose ideological terms.

Edward Kardelj, the leading Yugoslav theoretician, in his speech of December 7, 1956, before the Yugoslav People's Assembly, frankly accepts the theory of exceptionalism, but he claims Yugoslavia to be exceptional in being most faithful to the conceptions of Marx and Lenin. The development of socialist industry, he asserts, must take place concomitantly with a progressive democratization of all social relations. "Human beings should not in a socialist system become the slaves of a state machine in the name of any higher interests whatsoever." To achieve independence from the state machine, the social and economic position of the worker must be secured by strengthening the democratic control of the workers in the factories and in their communities.

Only in this way can the state wither away in Marxist fashion instead of becoming an all-devouring Frankenstein monster.

For Kardelj, the key issue is to avoid the bureaucratization of socialism. This is inevitable, according to him, unless there is "active, direct, and increasing participation of the producers in the direction of state and industry." Those who, like the Soviet Russian apologists, interpret this as undermining the dictatorship of the proletariat are indifferent, he says, to the fact that "the dictatorship that they characterize as 'proletarian' can be anything else in the world except proletarian, precisely because it is not filled with a democratic content."

The motivation of this theoretical departure from Stalinism, the extent to which it is actually embodied in Yugoslavian practice, and the political uses to which it is put are irrelevant issues in this discussion. Tito, for example, although professing to blame the Hungarian Stalinists for refusing to follow the lead of the Hungarian workers, inconsistently supports the Soviet suppression of their councils. Considerations of *Staatsraeson* obviously determine the official reactions. But once launched upon the world, ideas, although not independent, may develop a life and an influence of their own. It is the direction of the Yugoslav heresy that is important—not only its nationalism, its claim that all Communist states are equal in dignity in a common cause, but its emphasis upon a conception of workers' democracy, which, once material conditions are favorable to it, may turn out to be an ideological hydrogen bomb.

The most significant thing about the ideological position of the Yugoslav regime is that, if it is taken seriously, it spells the end of the political monopoly of the Communist Party. A "workers' control" that is in turn controlled by a Party faction with the secret police behind it collapses of itself—it dies of boredom and disinterest, like the Russian soviets and local trade unions. Some semblance of power, no matter how fearfully guarded by the Party watchdogs, must be given to the workers. This power in time either grows from what it feeds upon or becomes atrophied. It is the natural form through which, where it exists, opposition can be "legitimately" channeled.

That Kardelj, for all his lack of clarity, his inconsistencies and backtracking, is on the right road, from the point of view of intensifying the struggle between the democratic and totalitarian potentials of socialism, is evidenced in part by the character of the embittered reply made to him by a Soviet writer by the name of Rumiantsev in the chief theoretical organ of the CPSU, *Kommunist* (No. 18, 1957). As Rumiantsev recognizes, Kardelj in effect is charging that the Soviet Union is a new form of class state in which, although the legal title of ownership has been transformed to the workers and peasants, these are in fact being exploited by the state apparatus, its functionaries and pensioners, and that consequently the class struggle is still being waged in the alleged socialist society, not between nonexistent capitalists and landlords, on the one hand, and the toiling masses, on the other hand, but between the latter and the new class of Communist officials, managers, and their retainers. Rumiantsev attempts to toss this off with a laugh as a *reductio ad absurdum* too ridiculous to require refutation—and then attempts one anyhow. If the workers by definition own the instruments of production, he asks, how can they be said to exploit themselves? He is oblivious to the possibility that there may be something wrong with his definition, and that to resort to it in the face of the glaring facts of political and economic inequality is merely to fall back on a question-begging definition.

Gomulka's discussion of the function of the workers' councils is something else. He sees their development as one of the three main elements in the "Polish road to socialism." In his speech before the Ninth Plenum of the Party Central Committee (May, 1957), Gomulka outlines seven chief tasks of the workers' councils, which, if taken literally, would make them masters of the factories and, therefore, of all of industry. He warns against regarding the councils "as organs of political power," but at the same time is fearful lest the political leadership of the Communist Party fractions be displaced. He wants workers' councils to be autonomous and at the same time seeks (in vain, it seems to this observer) to limit their functions to purely industrial issues. Because of the nature of the Polish economy, he is undoubtedly sensible in cautioning the workers' councils against a too nearsighted and too decentralized view of the needs of production. But if they are actually given the right to make mistakes in these matters, they are being given very real powers indeed. And he is quite forthright in acknowledging the right of the workers to strike, although he does not regard this as the best way of rectifying grievances.

Gomulka's ambiguous feelings about increasing the power of the workers' councils stem from his fear that they may work free of the influence of the Communist Party, whose leading position he regards as essential to the building of socialism. As if aware that all those who define the "Polish road to socialism," if given their head, may carry Poland out of the Kremlin's orbit, as if to reassure the uneasy Russians, he delivers even stronger attacks against those he calls revisionists, and who really are democratic socialists of the Western type, than he does against the Stalinist dogmatists and conservatives. Gomulka taxes the revisionists with believing that socialism can be built without any class struggles. The accuracy of this characterization can be regarded as very questionable. The difficulty is to know what kind of class struggle can be waged after the capitalists and great landholders disappear. Struggles still go on, but if they are class struggles, they are of the kind that Kardelj describes—between the toilers, the workers, and peasants, on the one hand, and the state and Party officialdom, on the other. More accurate is Gomulka's charge against the revisionists that they are opposed to the dictatorship of the Communist Party. That is true. But it is also true of Marx.

The Dictatorship of the Proletariat

It is perfectly clear by now that "the dictatorship of the proletariat" as interpreted by Lenin and Stalin is substantially the dictatorship of the Communist Party over the proletariat and all other social groups. That this represented a radical departure from the meaning Marx gave to the rarely used phrase in his writings can scarcely be doubted. Marx and Engels pointed to the Paris Commune as illustrating what they meant by "the dictatorship of the proletariat." The Commune was one in which several different political groups or parties participated, and in which the followers of Marx were a tiny minority. In the Communist Manifesto, Marx had said that Communists "do not constitute themselves a special party over and above other working-class parties."

The "dictatorship of the proletariat" in the corpus of Marx's writings is not primarily a political concept but a social one. The opposite of the phrase is the "dictatorship of the bourgeoisie." Since, according to Marxist theory, a "dictatorship of the bourgeoisie" is compatible with many political forms, ranging from monarchy, Bonapartism, and other expressions of dictatorship through an entire spectrum of parliamentary democracies, it is clear that the economic and social content of the dictatorship of the proletariat, in theory at least, is compatible with the existence of one or more political parties and with political structures ranging from dictatorship to democracy.

Socialism declares itself opposed to all forms of exploitation and oppression, to any kind of class society in which coercion, open or veiled, is present. Marxism recognizes, however, that every dictatorship, even when it is considered progressive with respect to expanding the forces of production, is a form of oppression. If one takes Marx literally, the elimination of all coercion from human relations, the complete withering away of the state, is a utopian ideal—but pragmatically it can be interpreted as an ideal of diminishing coercion and exploitation of human society.

If one reads Marx in the light of modern sociology, one understands that classes will continue to exist, class struggles will continue to be fought, even though the role of classes will differ when different social relationships are introduced. A strike under socialism is a struggle, even though some terminological purist may balk at calling it an expression of class struggle. In either case, or in either interpretation, there is an immanent dynamic toward greater democracy in the Marxist ideal, toward a permanent revolution against whatever series of evils the social process generates.

Marxism is a philosophically primitive system, but it never identified the social system of the future with the end or process of history itself in the way in which Hegel identified the Absolute Idea or the Way of God with the Prussian state. Because Communism is a disease of idealism, if only it does not harden into the fanaticism that makes a fetish of the instrument—the instrument of the Communist Party—it may prove to be susceptible to the virus of political liberalism.

Historically, in Russia the Bolsheviks took power with the Left Social Revolutionists as a cover. They permitted other socialist parties to exist for a time in a tortured way. On paper, but only on paper, bourgeois parties could exist. On occasion, in order to bring home the distinction between the dictatorship as a social and economic instrument and dictatorship as a political weapon, Lenin maintained that it is "quite conceivable that the dictatorship of the proletariat may suppress the bourgeoisie at every step without disenfranchising the bourgeoisie; . . . while it is essential to suppress the bourgeoisie as an [economic] class, it is not essential to deprive them of their suffrage and equality."

What this meant with respect to bourgeois parties, and later all other parties, is that if they agreed not to oppose the program of the Communist Party in any way whatsoever after the latter seized power, they would be permitted to exist, although it is not clear what the point of their political existence would be. With respect to other working-class or socialist parties, Bolshevik fanaticism led to the same result. For the Bolsheviks believed that any serious disagreement with the Communist Party by *definition* had counterrevolutionary objective consequences.

The Communist regimes in the Soviet Union, Yugoslavia, and some of the satellites are unabashed one-party dictatorships. In China, Poland, Czechoslovakia, and East Germany, the Communist Party rules with the device of spurious coalition parties. The existence of these parties is in part the price the Communists pay for their hypocritical pretenses to democracy, but under a favorable conjunction of circumstances, especially in the satellite countries, where aspirations to national independence are strong, conditions may compel them to pay an ever-higher price in granting political rights to other parties.

Many of the moves away from total or extreme collectivization and the more conspicuous forms of Party terrorism in Communist countries are motivated today by considerations of political strategy. They may be reversed overnight. Nonetheless, they are all points of ideological and institutional infection in the Communist body politic. If these heretical germs get into the Marxist blood stream, they may produce fevers in the short run and languors in the long run, resulting in profound organic changes in the system.

Recent events behind the Iron Curtain have shown that socialist humanism, despite its exaggerated claims to novelty, has a greater continuity with traditional forms of Western humanism than both its official spokesmen and its hostile Western critics imagined. The new Soviet man, the new Communist man with new criteria of the true, the good, and the beautiful, of whom Stalin boasted and whom the West feared, is a myth. Despite the principle of *partiinost*, or partisanship in dialectical materialism, Communist intellectuals, whether scientists or historians, know the difference between truth and lies, facts and fiction.

Things can never be the same again after the fumbling attempt of Stalin's accomplices to de-Stalinize, after the Polish declaration of independence, after the heroic spectacle of the Hungarian nation in arms against the Soviet occupation. Even without war or foreign intervention, even without violent revolution, the intellectual elite of all Communist countries will produce in each generation, and in every social group or class, critical spirits nurtured on the ideals of freedom expressed in the classics of Marxism as well as in those of the humanist tradition, well aware of the discrepancies between Soviet promise and performance, and of the Communists' betrayal of almost all the liberating ideals that inspired the socialist movement. Their presence, whether articulate or eloquently silent, will constitute a permanent opposition to cultural and political tyranny.

Given the history of the twentieth century, once a "thaw" sets in in any aspect of culture in a totalitarian society, it has a tendency to extend not only into neighboring cultural fields, but to take political form as well. The chagrin and rage of the Soviet Communist leaders at the Hungarian and Polish intellectuals is due to their realization that the heretical cultural ideas of these men will, in the long run, prove politically infectious. The logic of the situation is such that every concession made to artists, writers, or scientists carries with it consequences that call for further concessions, which when denied put into question the sincerity and genuineness of the first concession. History often shows that changes are more rapid when things begin to get a bit better. Despair paralyzes the will to action, especially risky action; hope inspires it. We can be sure that the slight taste of the freedoms given to the peoples of the satellite countries, after having been deprived of them for almost a decade, will generate an enormous appetite for more—and perhaps this hunger will spread to the Soviet Union itself.

POSTSCRIPT

Although the prospects of liberation today are bleaker than they were when I originally wrote the article reprinted here, I am still convinced that, short of sudden changes in the leadership of the Soviet Union, revisionist ideas of Marxism will be the instruments by which the dictatorial character of the Communist regimes in satellite countries will be eased. The more the roads that are opened to cultural coexistence, the more difficult it will be to preserve Bolshevik-Leninist orthodoxy in any cultural field. Today, revisionism has been checked by the Communist regime in Poland through the application of economic sanctions—by the arguments of economic force, and not by the force of arguments. But unless we conceive of the development of an intellectual class without ideas, the intellectuals will sooner or later have to come to grips with the mythology of orthodox Communist doctrine. So long as they take it at its literal face value, in the manner in which the politically orthodox, stone-faced, ivory-headed political commissars believe it, they will quite properly have contempt for it.

The price of their intellectual contempt will be increasing isolation from political opinion-making and educational agencies. They may even be starved out. A whole generation of intellectuals may be destroyed by systematic denial of access to the "instruments of publication."

Whether in this generation or in another generation, since the political rulers of these countries will not abandon their mythology or surrender their power, those who wish to resist them effectively will rediscover the revisionist way. They may even do so by charging those in the seats of orthodoxy with revisionism until no one knows what the meaning of revisionism is and thus, in the ensuing struggle, permit a little common sense and a breath of intellectual sunlight and freedom to waft in. Adam Schaff, the defender of the purity of Bolshevik-Leninist theory against the Polish revisionists, is attempting to marry formal Polish logic to the Communist dialectic. From the standpoint of Leninist orthodoxy, this is in some respects as grave a revisionism as the position of those whom Schaff accuses of revisionism.

I am not saying that this necessarily will occur. Nor am I saying that the Communist countries will necessarily become liberalized as their standard of material life improves. Intellectual and cultural terror against nonconformists is compatible with material comforts for the slavish in spirit. Only those who have not liberated themselves from the dogmas of orthodox Marxism can feel certain that economics always determines politics and freedom. What I am saying is that if there is a change toward liberalization in the totalitarian enclaves of the world, it will very likely be initiated by, and take the form of, a reinterpretation of the official dogmas, the triumph of heresy. What the total complex of causal factors will be, if the change occurs, is hard to predict now. But its integral factors will be the advance of technology, the flowing of a new nationalism, and the revival of the ideal of freedom.

Toward a "Communist Welfare State"?

Social Welfare in the U.S.S.R.

——ALEC NOVE

IN THE EYES OF SOME CRITICS, the Soviet state is exclusively an organ of oppression. The motivations of its leaders, they believe, are to be found solely in the pursuit of world revolution, of national aggrandizement, of personal power—or of all these simultaneously. The attitude of the Soviet leaders toward their own people is often represented as being mainly inspired by the objective of keeping the mass of Soviet citizens on the lowest possible living standard consistent with the necessity of providing minimum work incentives.

Hence such critics are inclined to view all Soviet measures that seem to increase public welfare as "concessions" wrung from a reluctant regime by irresistible force of circumstances or popular pressure. It is but a short step from this view to the conclusion that such measures are, in themselves, proof of the regime's weakness or instability. If more was done to improve welfare in the first years after Stalin's death, these critics might argue, it was only because the struggle for power among Stalin's successors was undecided, and because the police apparatus had lost much of its capacity to intimidate. Inversely, now that Khrushchev has become unquestioned boss, they should logically expect a return to the old ways.

This article is an inquiry into the validity of such interpretations of the "welfare" aspect of Soviet rule. But it is necessary first of all to define the area of discussion. To take a negative approach, the author does not propose to discuss such matters

as wage rates and consumer-goods production. It is an acknowledged fact that real wages in the Soviet Union have been rising
slowly but steadily, that peasant incomes and retail-trade turnover have gone up, and that the present Soviet leadership has
declared its intention to continue this process through the period
of the Seven Year Plan (1958–65). It is also true that the upward
trend in these areas is highly relevant to welfare in the general
sense and should be duly noted. This article, however, will focus
attention on activities of a more direct "public-welfare" nature,
i.e., on the various social services (health, education, etc.), on
housing, and on other state measures that affect the everyday life
of Soviet citizens.

A Look at the Record

Before inquiring into the question of motivation, it is also
necessary to set forth a few facts illustrating what actually *has*
been done, or is being done, by the Soviet Union in the area of
welfare. Such a survey of the record may best begin with an
examination of the budget allocations for social and cultural
expenditures during the 1950–59 period presented in the following
table. Keeping the general trend toward increased outlays in
mind, the individual welfare categories listed are reviewed below,
with particular attention given to changes or retention of policy.

U.S.S.R. Social-Cultural Budgets: 1950–59
(*in billions of rubles*)

	1950	1953	1957	1959
Total Health	21.4	24.2	38.3	44.0
(of which)				
Hospitals and clinics, urban	10.3	12.3	18.6	....
Hospitals and clinics, rural	2.6	3.1	4.6	....
Total Education	56.9	61.1	80.7	94.3
(of which)				
General schooling[a]	30.4	32.2	37.6	....
Higher and technical	18.3	19.3	24.2	....
Science and research[b]	5.4	6.2	13.6	23.1[c]

Total Social Security	22.0	22.8	52.8	88.2
Total Social Insurance	12.7	16.2	23.5	....
Total Maternity Assistance	1.2	4.5	5.2	5.5
Total Social-Cultural Budgets	116.7	128.8	200.5	232.0

Source: *Raskhody na sotsialno-kulturnye meropriiatia po gosudarstvennom biudzhetu SSSR* (*Expenditures for Social-Cultural Measures in the State Budget of the U.S.S.R.* (Moscow, 1958); also Finance Minister Zverev's speech, reported in *Pravda*, December 23, 1958.

Notes: [a] includes kindergarten and adult education. [b] As most all-Union expenditures for science and research are kept secret, no complete breakdown of this item is given in the budget, but nuclear research is doubtless a major element. The item as a whole has practically no relevance for "welfare" in any sense. [c] Part of the big increase in 1959 is accounted for by a change in definition hinted at in Zverev's budget speech.

Health. There is no evidence that Soviet policy in this field has undergone any basic change in recent years. Vigorous efforts to expand medical and health services were already a feature of Stalin's reign, and the progress that was achieved is clearly indicated by the fact that the Soviet Union, as the following figures attest, has, since 1951, boasted a larger number of doctors per thousand inhabitants than most Western countries:

Country	Per thousand
U.S.S.R. (1951)	13.9
U.S.S.R. (1957)	16.9
United States (1954)	12.7
United Kingdom (1951)	8.8
West Germany (1955)	13.5

Source: *Dostizheniia sovetskoi vlasti za 40 let* (*The Achievements of the Soviet Government in Forty Years*) (Moscow, 1957), p. 348.

Thus, while the 1957 and 1959 budget figures show relatively sharp increases in health expenditures, it is clear that these do not represent an innovation in Soviet policy, but rather a continuation of past trends.

It is true that the equipment of many Soviet hospitals is antiquated, that drugs are often scarce, and that the general level of health facilities is not up to the best Western standards. Nevertheless, a great deal has certainly been done to spread hygiene, combat epidemics, and reduce infant mortality. The services of state doctors and hospitals are free, although most medicines have to be bought by the patient.

Education. Here again, recent Soviet policy has not basically altered Stalin's approach aimed at a large-scale expansion of the educational system, but there have been important changes in emphasis and direction. Thus, the decision of the Twentieth CPSU Congress (February, 1956) to extend full-time secondary education to all has since been modified in favor of part-time education after the age of fifteen, and Khrushchev's reform of higher education also seems likely to result in a reduction of the number of *full-time* university students. It is not, of course, within the scope of this article to discuss the detailed causes and consequences of Khrushchev's reforms of Soviet education. Regardless of the effect they may have on academic standards, however, it can be stated that these reforms are unlikely to result in any modification of the upward trend in Soviet educational expenditures (except for a possible large saving in student stipends).

One notable reason for this assumption is the evident rise in the school building program, partly as a result of an overdue effort to remedy the overcrowding, which at present necessitates two-shift, and sometimes even three-shift, schedules, and partly to set up the new-type boarding schools in which Khrushchev plans to train the "new Soviet man." It is only fair to add that, in contrast to the continuing shortage of physical facilities, the situation of Soviet schools with regard to the teacher-pupil ratio compares very favorably with that in many other countries, including the United States, as evidenced by the following figures:

Country	Pupils (in thousands)	Teachers (in thousands)	Pupils per Teacher
U.S.S.R. (1956–57)	30,127	1,811	16.6
United States (1955)	30,531	1,135	26.9
United Kingdom (1956)	7,981	309	25.8

Sources: For the U.S.S.R., *Dostizheniia.* . . . p. 274; for the U.S. and U.K., *United Nations Statistical Yearbook*, 1958.

Mention should also be made of the Khrushchev leadership's action in 1956 to abolish all fees in schools and universities, which reversed one of Stalin's counterreforms. It will be recalled that free education had been a feature of the Soviet regime from the beginning and was explicitly guaranteed by the 1936 Stalin Constitution. Despite the constitutional guarantee, however, educational charges were imposed in the top three grades of secondary schools and in universities by a simple decree of the Council of Ministers in 1940. Although the action did not have such a serious effect on university students, since the large majority were receiving stipends from which the fees simply were deducted, its impact on children of poor families enrolled in secondary schools, where stipends were not granted, was much more severe. Without doubt the restoration of free education was a highly popular act.

Social insurance, social security, and pensions. Sick-pay benefits in the Soviet Union have long been on a relatively generous scale, and there have been no significant changes in rates of payment in recent years, although over-all expenditures for this purpose have increased as a result of the increased labor force and higher average wages. As part of the campaign launched in the 1930's to reduce the high rate of labor turnover, full rates of sick pay were made conditional upon a minimum period of work in the same enterprise or office, except in cases where workers had transferred under official orders. These rules remain in force, although with some modifications in favor of the worker.

A trade-union member who falls ill is paid the following proportions of his actual earnings (non-members receive one-half these rates, subject to the minimums referred to below):

Years of Service	Percentage of Earnings
Less than 3	50
3 to 5	60
5 to 8	70
8 to 12	80
More than 12	90

Present regulations provide for minimum monthly payments of 300 rubles in urban areas and 270 rubles in rural areas, and a maximum payment of 100 rubles per day.* Those who are injured at work or suffer from occupational diseases are entitled to sickness benefits at the rate of 100 per cent of their earnings, regardless of length of service. If a worker leaves his job of his own volition, he is not entitled to sickness pay for ordinary illness during the first six-month period, but this limitation does not apply (since February, 1957) to cases of accident or occupational disease. Of course, the social-insurance rates described here apply only to disability for a limited period of time, permanent disablement being dealt with under pension regulations.

The maternity-benefit rate itself also has not been changed in recent years, but in 1956, the period of paid maternity leave was lengthened to 112 days. This was, in effect, a return to the regulation in force prior to 1938, when the period of maternity leave was reduced from 112 to 70 days.

The biggest recent improvements in this general area have been in the field of old-age and permanent-disability pensions. Their effect, according to Finance Minister Zverev (*Finansy SSSR*, No. 10, 1957, p. 17), was to raise the average rate of all pensions by 81 per cent, but certain groups of workers who had fared relatively worse under the pre-1956 pension regulations secured much bigger gains than this, for the following reasons: The previous regulations nominally entitled a worker qualifying for an old-age pension by length of service to receive payments

---

* To give the reader some idea of the purchasing power of the ruble, here are the official Soviet prices (in rubles) of a few representative commodities (per kilogram in the case of food, unless otherwise stated): chicken, 16.5; beef (stewing), 12; pork, 19.5; average fish, 11; butter, 28; milk, 2.2 per liter; eggs (10), 7.5; rye bread, 1.24; potatoes, 1; cabbage, 1.5-2; coffee, 40; wool-mixture blanket, 100+; cotton print dress, 200; wool dress, 475; man's overcoat, 720; man's all-wool suit, 2,000; shoes (adequate), 200; bicycle, 450-600; motorcycle, 4,200; radio, 400; washing machine, 2,250; family divan, 1,300; toilet soap, (bar) 2.2; lipstick, 4.5-6. Source: Lynn Turgeon, "Levels of Living, Wages and Prices in the Soviet and United States Economies," *Comparisons of the United States and Soviet Economies* (Joint Economic Committee of the U.S. Congress; Washington, D.C.: U.S. Government Printing Office, 1959), pp. 335–36.—Ed.

at the rate of two-thirds of his final wage. This looked extremely generous until one noticed the proviso, often omitted from propaganda statements, that the two thirds was to be calculated on the basis of a *maximum* "reckonable" wage of 300 rubles per month, meaning an effective maximum pension of 200 rubles per month. This figure, when originally fixed some twenty-five years earlier, was quite legitimate, but wages and prices subsequently multiplied without any upward revision of the allowable maximum. The result was considerable hardship for ordinary workers, while on the other hand exceptional treatment was granted to certain categories including not only the professional and official classes, but also workers in some priority occupations. For example, coal miners, steel workers, and those engaged in electricity generation were allotted a much higher reckonable maximum. Similar discriminatory rules applied to pension benefits for surviving dependents and victims of industrial accidents and the like.

The reform of 1956, while reducing certain very high pensions, established an all-round minimum old-age pension of 300 rubles per month for those qualified by length of service, an advance of great importance. In addition, it put into effect a new scale of payments benefiting lower-paid workers, so that those earning up to 350 rubles per month now receive pensions amounting to 100 per cent of earnings, with progressively smaller percentages for those with higher earnings, and with a maximum over-all ceiling of 1,200 rubles per month. An average worker earning, say, 750 rubles per month qualifies for a pension of 487 rubles under the new rules, as against probably only 200 under the old. One offsetting feature of the reform is that working pensioners are no longer permitted to receive full pensions in addition to their wages.* (This provision, together with the better pension rates, has very probably encouraged many old people to retire.) On balance, however, the net gain to Soviet pensioners can readily be measured by the increase in pension expenditures shown in the following table (in billions of rubles):

* The normal payment to working pensioners is now only 150 rubles per month.

	1950	1956	1957 (preliminary)	1958 (estimated)
Total pensions (of which)	30.1	36.5	59.9	66.0
Nonworking pensioners	8.7	12.6	27.6	34.2
Working pensioners	4.7	5.1	5.3	5.8
Ex-military and families	15.6	17.5	23.5	23.4

Source: A. Zverev, in *Planovoe khoziaistvo*, No. 12 (1957), p. 24.

The improvement in old-age pension benefits was accompanied by substantial increases in pensions for those suffering permanent disability of varying degrees and for dependents, the increases reportedly amounting to 50–65 per cent. Further sizable increases in minimum pension rates also have been promised under the Seven Year Plan, along with a raising of minimum wages. No doubt exists regarding the general popularity of these measures.

There has also been a good deal of talk about extending social-insurance and pension rights to collective farmers. Some farms are reported to have adopted a system of paying fixed amounts of money and produce to their sick and aged members, which represents a step forward from the normal collective-farm practice of extending relief to such members out of a small fund set aside for this purpose. Fixed payments are still the exception, since the vast majority of collective farms do not yet have sufficient revenues for this purpose, but it is a fact that the number of such exceptions is steadily growing, and the extensive publicity given to them in the Soviet press indicates that the new system is officially regarded as a desirable development. It must be noted that, at present, all such payments are made out of the resources of each farm, and that the state has no responsibility, financial or otherwise. However, as the regime's policy toward the peasants is, in principle, to reward regular collective work with regular pay and to bring the status of the peasant gradually closer to that of the industrial worker, it seems to follow that the state eventually will have to accept some responsibility for at least ensuring that the collective farms are financially capable of providing social-insurance benefits. This is all the more necessary because the collective farms have now absorbed the workers of the disbanded Machine Tractor Stations, who were promised the continuation of the benefits they formerly enjoyed as state-employed workers. It is too soon, however, to say how the problem will be tackled.

Other Welfare Benefits

Holidays. Turning to other kinds of social-welfare benefits for state-employed persons, there appears to have been no appreciable change in the rules governing paid holidays, which already were on a fairly generous scale under Stalin. These regulations compare favorably with those of West European countries, especially for workers in arduous or unhealthy occupations. For example, miners, steelworkers, and bus drivers are allowed up to four weeks of paid vacation per year. Over-all statistics showing the distribution of the total working force according to numbers of paid (working-day) holidays per year are as follows:

Days of vacation	Percentage of Total Workers
12	43
15	12
18	11
21	3
24	19
Over 24	12
	100

Source: *Vestnik statistiki*, No. 10 (1958), Statistical Supplement.

A less desirable feature of the Soviet holiday system is the practice of spreading vacations over the whole year, so that many are on vacation when the weather is unfavorable. There is also a grave shortage of holiday accommodations. The much-publicized, low-cost trade-union rest homes can accommodate only a small fraction of the workers.

Working Time. There has been significant improvement with respect to working hours, although here again the reform effected by the present leadership so far represents, in large part, a return to the more liberal regulations that prevailed prior to Stalin's oppressive labor legislation of 1938–40. A 1940 decree lengthened the standard workday from seven to eight hours, increasing total hours for the six-day work week to forty-eight. This remained unchanged until 1956, when the Khrushchev leadership, implementing its promise at the Twentieth Party Congress to reduce working hours, took an initial step to cut down Saturday work to six hours, leaving most of the afternoon free and thus creating the beginnings of a Soviet "weekend."

During 1957–58, further reductions of working hours were made effective in certain industries, notably mining and metallurgy. These were followed by still greater promises at the Twenty-first Party Congress in January, 1959, when the leadership explicitly pledged a standard forty-hour week (and a thirty-five-hour week in unhealthy occupations) by 1962, with still further reductions to follow. There was even talk of achieving "the shortest working week in the world" by 1967. The promises have been so definite and attended by such great publicity that it will be hard indeed for the leadership to go back on its word, except in the event of dire emergency. Reduced hours are in fact already being put into effect in several key industries. A statement jointly issued by the CPSU Central Committee, the Council of Ministers, and the central trade-union organization, and published in the Soviet press on September 20, 1959, announced a detailed time schedule for the gradual extension of the seven-hour day to "all workers and employees in the national economy." (With six-hour Saturdays, this will reduce the standard working week to forty-one hours.) The process began on October 1, 1959, and is to be completed in the fourth quarter of 1960.

Some Western critics, pointing to the fact that planned productivity increases more than compensate for the reduction of working hours, conclude from this that the reform is in some way not genuine, since there will have to be greater intensity of effort in the shortened work period.* Such a view hardly seems justifiable. It is obvious, in the first place, that a shorter working week requires greater work intensity and higher productivity. This is so not only in Russia, but also in the United States or any other country. If output per hour remained the same while hours were reduced by 15 per cent, then—other things being equal—total output would go down by 15 per cent and everyone would be correspondingly poorer, a situation no one could possibly want. Nor is it that the Soviet Union intends to increase productivity solely, or even mainly, by imposing heavier physical burdens on labor. This is quite evident from the great attention being paid to the mechanization of labor-intensive processes, especially in auxiliary occupations (loading, moving of materials, etc.).

The charge that weekly wages are being cut as part of the reduction in working hours is equally untenable. The fact that a major reform of the Soviet wage system has coincided with the reduction of the working week makes it difficult to determine the precise effect of either change, but average wages appear to continue to rise slowly. Thus, the cut in the working week is as genuine as these things can be in an imperfect world. Those who assert the contrary are guilty of using against the Soviet Union the very same—quite unfounded—arguments by which Soviet propagandists seek to explain away the reduction of the working week in the United States.

Other Employment Reforms. Brief mention should also be made of recent steps extending the special privileges of juvenile workers. Since May, 1956, workers between the ages of sixteen and eighteen have enjoyed a shortened, six-hour working day with extra piecework pay to compensate for any loss in earnings. In addition, they are allowed a full month's vacation each year and special facilities for study. These privileges have, indeed, caused many managers to try to avoid employing juveniles—a tendency that has aroused official criticism and contributed to the difficulties experienced by high-school graduates looking for

---

* This was argued, for instance by Dr. E. Kux, writing in the *Neue Zürcher Zeitung* (December 16, 1958), in tones suggesting that the reform was practically a fraud.

employment.* The compulsory drafting of young people into labor-reserve schools, introduced in October, 1940, had already been terminated by a decree of March 18, 1955, and has been replaced by voluntary recruitment.

For another thing, the worker's right to change his occupation, while not explicitly recognized, has been strengthened by the abolition, in 1957, of criminal penalties for leaving one's job without permission. These penalties, as well as others for worker absenteeism and unpunctuality, had been instituted by decree in 1940. Although the decree gradually became a dead letter under Stalin's successors and was no longer mentioned in Soviet legal textbooks from 1954 on, it apparently survived on the statute books until 1957.

In still another reversal of Stalinist policy, the 1936 decree, which required the rural population to work six days per year on roads—without compensation—was repealed by the present leadership in November, 1958. Instead, responsibility for building and repairing local roads has been placed on the "collective farms, state farms, industrial, transport, building and other enterprises and organizations." Of course, the job still has to be done, but presumably the individual is now entitled to be paid for doing it.

Wage Questions. Although wages as such are outside the province of this discussion, it may be useful to refer briefly to changes in this field insofar as they are indicative of political attitudes. The practice of the Stalin period was to maximize wage differentials, which indeed reached record dimensions; on the contrary, the trend in recent years has been in the opposite direction. In 1956, a minimum-wage law was adopted, fixing a floor of 300–350 rubles per month in urban areas and 270 rubles in the country. The measure particularly benefited the appallingly underpaid groups of auxiliary personnel (janitors, cleaners, messengers, etc.) and the lowest grades of shop assistants, railroad workers, and others. This process of raising the level of the lowest-paid workers is to continue. The decree on the Seven Year Plan provides for increasing the minimum wage to 400–450 rubles

* A decree to combat this was issued by the Party Central Committee and the government on September 12, 1957.

monthly between 1959 and 1962, and to 500–600 rubles between 1963 and 1965, as well as for a consequential (but smaller) upward revision of the pay of middle-grade workers. Since the average increase in all money wages is to be only 26 per cent, it is evident that the spread between top and bottom will be sharply reduced.

This policy is reflected in other aspects of wage reform now in progress. Apart from introducing smaller differentials in basic rates, the reforms tend to eliminate the more exaggerated forms of progressive piecework bonuses, thus cutting down disparities in actual earnings. The gap between the pay of skilled and unskilled workers on collective farms is also being reduced significantly.* There have apparently been cuts in very high salaries, such as those of government ministers and university professors. (Though no statement to this effect seems to have appeared in print, the cuts are apparently a matter of general knowledge in the Soviet Union and have been confirmed to the writer several times.) The relative position of the lowest paid has also been improved as a result of a decree of March 23, 1957, reducing direct taxation on incomes below 450 rubles per month. All this certainly does not indicate that the Soviets are embracing hithertocondemned "petty-bourgeois egalitarianism," but it does show that the *excessive* inequalities of the Stalin era are being corrected.

Housing. Something must also be said about housing, since the fact that rents in the Soviet Union are far too low to bear any relation to housing costs justifies treating it as a social service rather than as a species of commercial transaction. At 1.32 rubles per square meter per month (somewhat higher for new apartments in some cities), rents are generally insufficient even to cover bare maintenance, which may explain why this factor is so often neglected.† At the same time, the miseries caused by the

* Some farms are adopting a pay ratio of 1:3 for unskilled as against skilled labor, instead of the previously "recommended" 1:5. See *Voprosy ekonomiki*, No. 2 (1959), p. 114.

† In Moscow, for example, the average revenue from tenants for rent and "other items" is 1.75 rubles per square meter, while running costs, inclusive of capital repairs, average 4.31 rubles per square meter. See *Novy mir*, No. 10 (1959), p. 211.

housing shortage and consequent overcrowding are too well known to require comment here. Khrushchev has declared that his aim is eventually to provide a separate apartment for every Soviet family instead of the single room that is the usual situation today. It is evident from the housing provisions of the Seven Year Plan, however, that the separate apartments will be very small by Western standards. The plan calls for the construction of 15 million apartment units with a total floor space (including corridors, bathroom, and kitchen) of 650–60 million square meters—or, at most, 44 square meters (430 square feet) per apartment. An American working-class family would be shocked at having so little space. Still, no one can doubt that Soviet citizens will be much happier if and when each family can have its own front door and no longer have to share the kitchen with several neighbors.

There is no question about the sharp acceleration of housing construction under the post-Stalin leadership. This is fully evident from the following figures, showing housing space (excluding private rural housing) completed in four different years from 1950 to 1958, and the Seven Year Plan goals:

Year	Total	State	Urban Private
	(in million sq. meters of total space)		
1950	24.2	17.8	6.4
1953	30.8	23.2	7.6
1957	52.0	38.5	13.5[a]
1958	70.1	45.6	24.5[a]
1959 (plan)	80.0	—	—
1960 (plan)	101.0	—	—
1959–65 plan, total	650–60.0	—	—
1959–65, annual average	93.0	—	—

Source: *Vestnik Statistiki,* No. 5 (1959), p. 94. [a] These figures include private housebuilding by state-employed persons engaged in agriculture and forestry.

Despite the sharply increased effort since Stalin's death, it is clear that there is still a very long way to go before tolerable housing conditions will be achieved, since a large part of new construction is necessary merely to keep pace with urban population growth. It has been pointed out by S. Wolk in the *Bulletin* of the Munich Institute for the Study of the U.S.S.R. that the Soviet per-capita rate of housebuilding, even allowing generously for rural construction, remains below that of the German Federal Republic. Nonetheless, the facts reveal considerable progress in the U.S.S.R. The ambitious plans for rebuilding villages in connection with Khrushchev's contemplated revival of the *agrogorod* necessarily call for a still greater expansion of housing construction in rural areas, although the financial burden involved is to be shouldered by the collective farms.

Services. Finally, brief mention must be made of improvements in badly needed consumer services—restaurants, cafés, shops, repair facilities, and the like. This is a very backward sector of Soviet life. To cite just one example, an article in *Pravda* (March 14, 1959) estimated the total capacity of shoe-repair establishments in the R.S.F.S.R. at 15 million pairs annually, although 100 million pairs of new shoes are sold each year and may be presumed to require repair at least once annually. A recent decree embodied plans for increasing the turnover of service and repair shops of all kinds to 10.3 billion rubles in 1961, as against 6.2 million rubles in 1958. There have also been measures to increase the number of shops and restaurants.

Motivations of Recent Policy

This, then, is the actual Soviet record in social welfare. It suggests, first of all, that even under Stalin's rule much attention was paid to the expansion and improvement of health services and education, and fairly generous rules were adopted in regard to such things as sickness benefits and paid vacations. In the late 1930's, however, some backward steps were taken that affected hours of labor, maternity leave, and the worker's right to change his occupation, and it was only after Stalin's death that moves got underway to restore the conditions which had prevailed until the mid-1930's. In the last few years, the record shows, much more has been or is being done to improve old-age pensions and disability pay, to reduce working hours, to build more housing, and to provide more consumer services, even though the Soviet citizen certainly still has—and probably will continue to have—much to complain about.

Only the willfully blind will refuse to take all this seriously. But more than *what* has been done, the vital question is *why* has it been done, and what significance, if any, these developments have from the standpoint of assessing the nature of the Soviet system. No single, definitive answer is possible of course, but here, for what they may be worth, are a few thoughts on the subject.

While it is arguable that the Soviet rulers do as little as possible for the citizen in order to devote the largest possible share of national resources to heavy industry and weapons, such a formulation begs the question. One could reverse it and say that they devote as much as possible to improving the citizen's lot, subject to the necessary investment in heavy industry and weapons—which would sound better from the Soviet point of view, but means equally little. Is the glass half-full or half-empty? In any case, neither formulation explains why more is being done for the Soviet citizen today than in the past.

One relevant factor may simply be that the U.S.S.R. is now powerful enough economically to permit the greater diversion of resources to satisfy the needs of its citizens without curtailing ambitious plans for the expansion of heavy industry. To carry out the First Five Year Plan (1928–32), Stalin found it necessary to reduce living standards drastically, but it would be foolish to take this for what lawyers term "evidence of system." It is obviously no part of Communist ideology to make people poorer; on the contrary, Communism lays great stress on abundance. The abundance of Communism may well be—in the author's opinion it definitely is—a meaningless, even nonsensical concept, but it surely was the intention of all Soviet leaders, including Stalin himself, to raise living standards at some future date, once the painful sacrifices of "primitive accumulation" were no longer necessary. The Soviet citizen was, and still is, denied adequate housing, but it would be a mistake to conclude that the leadership believes in bad housing in the same sense that it believes in the undesirability of private peasant enterprise. Soviet leaders have been willing to sacrifice an entire generation, to neglect urgent needs for years, but it would be patently foolish to represent them as favoring poverty and hardship as such. They surely would concede, and even advocate, improvements in popular welfare if doing so would not interfere with the pursuit of their basic aims.

Before leaving the subject of ideology, two other points are worth making. One is the enormous attention Communists always pay to education: However they may twist its content to suit their purposes, they have invariably lavished resources on its development, whether under Stalin or under his successors. It is true that this effort is due, in part, to the urgent need of developing technical skills, but this is far from the whole explanation. Indeed, the promise made at the Twentieth Congress to extend full-time secondary education to all went far beyond practical necessities, and its implementation even tended to aggravate social tensions, which was one reason for Khrushchev's subsequent counter-reforms.

The second point is the great importance, from the standpoint of Communist ideology, of appearing to be doing something to improve the lot of the working masses. Even when nothing or little is actually being done, the Party leaders must of necessity claim to be acting in that direction. Too great a contrast between words and deeds, however, can lead to general cynicism, as in fact it did under Stalin. Khrushchev is now engaged in an evident effort to revive the fervor of the Party and to replace passive bureaucratism with initiative. It is reasonable to suppose, therefore, that with this aim in view he wants to show that the Party is genuinely doing something to carry out its promises to the people.

One example of this ideological influence is the regime's insistence, for political reasons, on cheap bread and low rents even when these are economically irrational and administratively inconvenient. Thus, Khrushchev recently reasserted the *political impossibility* of raising bread prices despite the fact that, at these prices, it pays to feed bread, rather than regular cattle feed, to private livestock. In short, cheap bread is essential to the Party's outward picture of itself.*

The Role of Incentives

Other factors, too, have a bearing on the regime's attitude in regard to welfare. For a number of reasons too complex to be analyzed here, the functioning of the Soviet economy is coming to depend more on incentives and less on compulsion. Prisoners can be kept working even when forced to live in overcrowded barracks on a minimum diet, but unless there is some emergency to spur them, free men work better when they can expect to live better by greater effort. To achieve the leadership's ambitious plans, better work, more efficient organization, more initiative at the grass roots are all objective necessities. To some extent, of course, this was also true under Stalin and was acted upon, as evidenced by the lavish rewards given to Stakhanovites. But few analysts question that there has been a shift toward much *greater* reliance on incentives in recent years, paralleled by a scaling down of the number and powers of the police. To give but one of many examples of how this works in practice, the author, during a tour of the Soviet Union, was shown a new apartment block in Kiev, which he was told was being erected by the building industry for its own workers, because, now that they could change employment without incurring criminal penalties, they would not remain in the industry "unless we replaced the barracks and hostels with decent housing."

Of course, people's attitudes and expectations are relevant to the efficacy of incentives as well as to political stability. The more the Soviet Union boasts of its great technical progress, of its sputniks and moon rockets, of its equality with, or superiority over, the United States in weapons, the more impatient its citizens become with their backward living conditions, and the less

---

* This picture has been obscured in the West by denunciations of an allegedly huge Soviet turnover tax on bread. Although it is true that the tax was for years the major constituent of the price of bread, the reason for this was that the tax was calculated on the basis of a ridiculously low procurement price for grain. The real economic incidence of the tax was not on consumers, but on the producers—the peasants.

reasonable it seems to them that nothing drastic is done to improve them. Confronted by such a popular state of mind, an intelligent leadership is likely to see the wisdom of taking some action.

The increasing range of contacts between Soviet citizens and foreigners plays a dual role in this process. Many more Soviet citizens are now learning at first or second hand how the other side lives, and this affects their own expectations. Then, too, with the increasing flow of foreign visitors to Russia, it must certainly appear politically advantageous to the leadership to impress them with higher standards of living. This is much more than a matter of impressing unsophisticated tourists from the West, who can, if necessary, be fobbed off with Potemkin villages. Much more important are the thousands of students and others from underdeveloped countries, as well as from the Soviet Union's own allies, who actually spend some time living among the Russians and cannot help learning the truth. Khrushchev is well aware that the relative living standards will play an important role in the world impact of the two opposed systems.

Some Points of Logic

For all its simplicity, one should not overlook still another point: Khrushchev wants to be popular. He may genuinely care to reduce poverty, or he may be acting on the basis of cold political calculation—it does not matter which. He may even aspire to go down in history as the man who brought prosperity to the Soviet people—on the foundations laid by his grim predecessor. There are some Western observers who seem to shy away from even considering such motives possible, as if to do so would label them as pro-Soviet. This is clearly an illogical attitude. What is primarily objectionable about the Soviet system is its totalitarian character, its lack of intellectual and political freedom; and this character is not directly affected by the shortening of working hours or the provision of a separate apartment for every family.

It is indeed true that certain features of the Soviet economy are inconsistent with the proper satisfaction of consumer demand.

It may also be true that the ultimate logic of a better-educated and materially more satisfied citizenry is incompatible with the totalitarian one-party state. Let us hope that it will prove so. But that is no reason for closing one's eyes to the realities: Much is being done on the Soviet "welfare" front, and there is no sign that Khrushchev's consolidation of his political power will cause any change in this respect, especially since the policies being followed must, in his judgment, appear rational, right, and necessary.

Commentaries

Why the Changes?

——SOLOMON M. SCHWARZ

IN HIS ARTICLE "Social Welfare in the U.S.S.R.," Mr. Nove sets out to perform two tasks, the first of which is to present "the actual Soviet record in social welfare." In the opinion of this writer, he accomplishes this task with commendable clarity and painstaking attention to detail, producing what is unquestionably a highly impressive picture. Indeed, its impressiveness may come as a shock to those people—and there are many of them—who think that the Soviet system is, *by the very nature of its aims,* socially and economically oppressive. Those who are given to this sort of reasoning have never grasped the fact that the socially and economically oppressive measures with which the history of the Soviet regime abounds have not been expressions of a policy deliberately inimical to the working masses, but rather the inevitable by-products of the general dictatorial policy of the Communist Party.

The second problem to which Mr. Nove addresses himself is even more important. He puts it squarely: "More than *what* has been done, the vital question is *why* has it been done, and what significance, if any, these developments have from the standpoint of assessing the nature of the Soviet system."

Mr. Nove is skeptical about the possibility of answering this "vital question." "No single, definitive answer is possible, of course," he writes, "but here, for what they may be worth, are a few thoughts on the subject." The "thoughts" he presents are not without interest, but they do not go far enough. And if no *single* answer to the question can be given—that is, if "these developments" cannot be explained by one cause only—it becomes all the more necessary to find their *main* cause.

In his introductory remarks, Mr. Nove takes issue with some anonymous critics who, it would appear, have put forward rather peculiar answers to the question. As Mr. Nove formulates it, "such critics are inclined to view all Soviet measures that seem to increase public welfare as 'concessions' wrung from a reluctant regime by irresistible force of circumstances or popular pressure." The accent is—perhaps with a tinge of irony—on "concessions."

The fact is, however, that once the polemics and the "concessions" are put aside, the arguments of "irresistible force of circumstances" and "popular pressure" assume considerable weight. In fact, this may be said of the argument of "irresistible force of circumstances" by itself, since "popular pressure," as will be shown, is often (not always!) only a part, a concomitant, or, if you will, a derivative of the "irresistible force of circumstances."

What is this force that, especially in the last decade, has so deeply influenced the development of the Soviet Union and—to remain within the frame of Mr. Nove's topic—has made the improvement of public welfare so necessary and, indeed, so unavoidable? The answer may be reduced to a simple formula: *The U.S.S.R. has become a modern industrial state, but the great majority of its working population lived until recently, and to a lesser degree continues to live today, under conditions characteristic of economically backward countries.* It is this simple yet fundamental fact—perhaps *the greatest internal contradiction of Soviet life*—that in the past few years has, with "irresistible force," influenced the entire course of development in the U.S.S.R. And it is this contradiction that has engendered not only economic and social but, to some degree, even political adjustments to the conditions and requirements of a modern industrial society.

Again confining our analysis to Mr. Nove's topic, it is important to point out that a modern industrial state can function properly only if it possesses a working class that enjoys a relatively high standard of living, tolerable working conditions, and access to educational opportunities. Ineluctably, a modern working class will also demand more and more freedom. These are not merely social imperatives finding their expression in social tensions and pressures: They are also economic imperatives—that is, necessary preconditions for the required rise in the quality and productivity of labor. It is these economic imperatives that, as will be shown, have played the most important role in recent developments.

A few examples will illustrate this point. They are taken not from the field of social welfare *stricto sensu*—i.e., not from the field of "fringe benefits," in popular American terminology—but from the general area of labor relations, where the causalities of the development appear more clearly.

Throughout the 1930's, that is, during the first decade of intensive Soviet industrialization, Russian workers were subjected to extraordinary strains, which became even more exacerbated during World War II. To further industrial development under general conditions of misery and deprivation, the Soviet government provided relatively better conditions for a small number of highly skilled workers, thus in effect creating a privileged class at the expense of the vast majority of the population. The policy of extreme wage differentiation, which would have been unthinkable in any advanced industrial country, was for many years hailed as a true expression of socialism in action—in contrast, of course, to the "capitalist wage policy," supposedly based on the "leveling" principle. In the last decade, however, this wage policy became more and more of a handicap to further industrial development, making impossible a rational organization of labor. Its continuation caused a creeping demoralization, an increasing tendency to resort to ruses and stratagems of all sorts—in short, a situation harmful to labor and management alike. In 1956, this unique "socialist" wage policy was finally buried, and the Soviet authorities set about reorganizing the wage system, cutting down the extraordinarily high earnings of some privileged workers and raising the wages of the underprivileged ones.

The extreme wage inequality of the 1930's and 1940's was but one aspect of Stalin's antisocial labor policy. Another aspect was the repudiation—as detestable "trade unionism"—of the traditional concept of trade unions as defenders of the workers' interests against management, and the degradation of these

bodies to the status of mere instruments of the state, used solely
to exact greater productive effort from the workers. Yet even the
most fanatical supporters of this policy finally had to recognize
that modern industrialism demanded profound changes not
merely in the position and function of the trade unions, but in the
economic system at large. In recent years changes have actually
been introduced in various phases of industrial planning and
administration—unsystematically, haltingly, and even in a somewhat contradictory manner, but on an ever-increasing scale. Revision of the trade unions' role has been part of this development.
To be sure, the Communist leadership would not think of permitting the unions to reassume their traditional functions. What
it has done is to turn them into organs of social welfare and to let
them participate to some extent in the administration of plants
as a kind of counterbalance to the danger of bureaucratization.
It is worth noting that the initiative in these reforms came from
the Communist Party, that the role of the trade-union leadership
has been merely that of an obedient agent and executor of the
Party's orders, and that the trade-union masses have yet to be
drawn into these practices. The very manner in which the reforms
have been carried out, then, offers convincing evidence that they
have been determined more by economic imperatives than by
social pressure.

One more example. Under Stalin, Soviet labor relations came
to be based not on a free labor contract but on compulsion. The
development in the direction of greater compulsion was climaxed
by a decree of the Supreme Soviet of the U.S.S.R., dated June 26,
1940, which deprived employees of the right to terminate their
employment of their own volition, invested managers with virtually unrestricted power to hire and fire at will, and made not
only unauthorized departure, but even lateness in reporting for
work (by as little as twenty minutes!), subject to criminal punishment. In the postwar years, however, the Soviet leadership came
to realize the impossibility—and, from a practical standpoint, the
undesirability—of keeping the entire working population in a
straitjacket, and it gradually relaxed its labor practices—characteristically, without issuing any open instructions to this effect.
It was not until three years after Stalin's death, in April, 1956,

that the basic provisions of the 1940 decree were finally re-
scinded. To quote Mr. Nove, "the functioning of the Soviet economy is coming to depend more on incentives and less on
compulsion." This, indeed, is the essence of *any* modern industrialism, to which the Soviet system can no longer claim exception.

The need to adjust Soviet realities to the imperatives of modern
industrialism is thus the *main* cause of the recent development
of social welfare in the U.S.S.R. Yet one more factor should also
be mentioned, namely, *the change of generations,* the importance
of which must not be underrated. Those who were children at
the beginning of World War II are now in their early and middle
thirties. Those who were in their teens are now in their late
thirties. Together with their juniors, they comprise the most
active segment of the working population, the great majority in
the newly developed eastern areas. With the exception of the
1948–53 period, which embraced the so-called *Zhdanovshchina,*
the hysterical "vigilance" campaign of 1952, and the ominous
"doctors' plot" in January, 1953, the Soviet youth and young adult
population of today have grown up in a relatively relaxed political atmosphere. The horrors of the prewar decade are relatively unfamiliar to them. In their feelings, in their thoughts, in
their attitudes, they differ considerably from their elders—those
who were psychologically mutilated during the long years of un-
mitigated terror. The urgent needs and demands of these young
people—voiced or still in the process of germination—create those
social pressures which, in addition to the economic imperatives
described above, are exercising such a profound influence on the
evolving Soviet system.

Facts and Polemics

——BERTRAM D. WOLFE

Mr. Nove has done a useful job in bringing together in one place so many facts on social welfare in the Soviet Union, and in showing, on the whole, a trend toward more education, better health conservation, some improvement in housing, less draconic labor laws than in Stalin's last years, and a lessening of extreme differentiation in wages in favor of the most poorly paid. I think that in some cases he has taken official statement for fact and promise for performance, but on the whole his picture is undoubtedly correct, and no useful corrections could be offered in so brief a space as a commentary affords. This comment, therefore, is limited to two general points: (1) The historical framework in which these changes should be viewed; and (2) the polemical use Mr. Nove has tried to make of his material.

1) The historical framework. Most writing on the Soviet era suffers from a lack of consideration of the earlier history of Russia; the history of the postwar upsurge of other war-ruined countries such as Germany and Japan; and the history of industrialization in general.

Thus our whole perspective on the rate of recovery and industrial expansion in post-World War II Russia is altered if we stop to consider the faster rate of recovery and expansion of, let us say, Germany and Japan during the same period.

Or again, in examining the Soviet Union's rate of industrial growth, we get a fresh perspective if we examine the history of the sudden march of other countries into industrialism. Thus in the period 1860–1900, Russian industrial productivity increased more than seven times, German almost five times, French two and one half times, English a little over two. When we attempt to evaluate Soviet industrial growth at various periods, we must regard it in the context of these comparative figures.

It is no less interesting to examine the standard of living during the industrial upsurge in Czarist Russia. There were two distinct periods so far as labor was concerned. In the decade of the 1890's, the upsurge of industry was accompanied, and in fact partly achieved, by a decline in the standard of living. But in the next decade, the still more stormy advance was accompanied by a *rise* in the standard of living. May this not be characteristic of the earlier and later phases of industrialism under any socio-political system?

The same applies to such "welfare" features as health. When Mr. Nove retreats from the comparative figure on doctors (of little meaning, incidentally, unless we define the degree of training) to the sounder "nevertheless, a great deal has certainly been done to spread hygiene, combat epidemics, and reduce infant mortality," is it not incumbent on us to remember that medical progress is fatefully easier and cheaper than industrial progress, and that this generalization on hygiene, epidemics, and infant mortality applies even to the most underdeveloped countries.*

Again, does not advancing industrialism—under any "system" —require more literate, better-trained workers? In the Khrushchev era, for the first time in the history of the Soviet Union, there is a shortage of the rural "reserve" population that hitherto has made up any deficiency of capital investment per worker and productivity per worker. Does this not make mandatory more capital investment per head? And more "investment" in the training of "human capital"? Do not these questions on the historical framework of industrialization take precedence over an examination of the special role of totalitarianism in shaping industrialization?

When Mr. Nove comes to the proportions of the national product devoted to consumer goods on the one hand and "power" goods (means of production plus military might) on the other, his question ("Is the glass of water half-full or half-empty?") is

---

* This is the source of the "population explosion" in underdeveloped countries.

anything but helpful. For if we compare a society that devotes three quarters of its GNP to consumption and one quarter to expansion of production with a society that reverses these fractions, then the question of whether the glass is one-quarter full or three-quarters full is far from meaningless to those who drink.

2) *Totalitarianism and the motives of the rulers.* Mr. Nove says that the "purpose" of the article is to inquire into the validity of some interpretations of the interrelations between the sector devoted to "welfare" and the sector devoted to the expansion of power. But some of the "interpretations" he chooses seem to border on the fatuous.

Thus his first target (sentence one) is those "who see the Soviet state exclusively as an organ of oppression." But is it not ABC that we are dealing with the greatest managerial and ownership state in all history? If there are any serious students of Soviet affairs who do not know that, do we need all of Mr. Nove's statistical ammunition on "welfare" when we can dispose of it by the simple reminder that a state that seeks to own and run everything must be primarily an organ of the administration of the economy itself?

In sum, I find the factual material Mr. Nove has assembled highly useful. His interpretation of the facts he has assembled is weakened by the failure to put them into the perspective of the history of modern industrialization, and of the features common to industrializing societies whatever their political form— republic, monarchy, limited despotism, and totalist despotism.

As for the polemical framework, it is scarcely worthy of the material he has been at pains to assemble. The analysis of the nature of totalitarianism is an even more difficult subject, and one on which far less progress has been made than on the analysis of industrialization—or, for that matter, on the problems of how much of the Soviet product is devoted to the expansion of "power," and how much to "welfare." Indeed, it is even difficult to decide such a simple question as the degree to which such a "welfare" feature as health is also a "power" problem, for does not any modern state need healthy soldiers, schooled workingmen, and at least some measure of mass acceptance of things as they are?

The Logic of Economics

——BERTRAND DE JOUVENEL

AT THE OUTSET I must emphasize that since I do not have the slightest qualification as a "Sovietologist," I can appraise the facts, figures, and interpretations presented by Mr. Nove, an eminent expert in that field, only on the basis of general knowledge and simple logic.

I should like, first of all, to state a point I consider to be of fundamental importance in discussing the topic of Soviet welfare policy. It is a basic characteristic of democratic capitalist economies that they are governed by the free and widely diversified choices of individual citizens, to which entrepreneurs must necessarily adjust. In general, as consumers, the citizens much prefer consumption to saving, and as voters they voice their preference for spending their own money on the goods and services they themselves desire rather than having it taken in taxes and spent for them by the government on health, education, and other social services. By contrast, the main feature of the Soviet economy is the concentration of all choice in such matters in the hands of the state.

This is not meant to imply that there is any reason to question the intent of the Soviet state to cater to the needs of the people as *it* interprets them, and to the extent that *it* deems possible. But at the same time there is no doubt whatever that the preferences of the individual citizen in the U.S.S.R. have been ruthlessly disregarded. It is regrettable from this viewpoint that Mr. Nove's article addresses itself almost exclusively to the sphere of social-welfare benefits proper, rather than to the over-all situation of the

Soviet citizen as a consumer. Welfare benefits obviously cannot serve as a reliable index of over-all welfare for the simple reason that the more authoritarian the government, the more extensive one can usually expect these benefits to be. Speculatively speaking, I would readily assume that, in the Soviet case, they have expanded a good deal more than private consumption as we know it. At the same time, I would guess that there has also been rapid, though not commensurate, progress in private consumption.

The reasoning that leads me to these suppositions is roughly outlined below:

1) Upon acceding to power, Stalin found the Russian economy in a bad way. While industrial production had been increasing quite rapidly up till 1914,* it was hardly any higher in 1928 than it had been in 1913†, and the output of many individual items was even lower. Stalin then decided to channel maximum resources into the expansion of productive facilities (i.e., investment) and indirect aids to production (e.g., education). Backed by the compulsive power of the state, this policy permitted a far higher rate of investment than would have been possible under the system of voluntary saving as we know it as well as a much higher level of government consumption than voters in a democratic society would grant in taxes.

2) Increasing the shares of investment and government consumption in national production obviously narrows the share of private consumption. But if—as economists universally agree—the allocation of a large share to investment fosters a high rate of increase in over-all output, then it is a simple matter of arithmetic to show that output for consumption, in absolute terms, will also rise rapidly, even though as a proportion of the total product it may continue to decline.

3) However preponderant a place military expenditures may occupy within government consumption, there is still room for

* From 1870 to 1913, Russian industrial production moved up at the yearly rate of 5.3 per cent, or 3.7 per cent per head of population, as pointed out by Warren G. Nutter.

† This lack of overall increase stood in sharp contrast to the considerable gains in output achieved by the "capitalist" economies from 1913 to 1928.

increasing the health and educational services, which the Soviet planners consider not only "good for the people," but also necessary for raising productivity.

4) Given a certain allotment of productive resources to private consumption, the quantitative output of consumer goods will be greatest if the utilization of these resources is geared to the satisfaction of a uniform standard of consumer needs fixed by the government, thus obviating the necessity of adjusting to diverse and changing consumer requirements.

The argument presented above rests essentially upon the well-established notion that a high rate of investment, by raising the rate of economic growth, tends to increase the production of consumer goods as well. We must, however, beware of making economic nonsense out of sound arithmetic. It can be argued, for example, that, living as we do in consumer-oriented economies, we naturally think of investment (however high its rate) as being allocated to asset-building between producer-goods industries and consumer-goods industries in proportions suitable to a short-term increase in consumer-goods output, but that this assumption does not hold true for the U.S.S.R. where the extreme emphasis on building up basic industries undoubtedly caused an investment lag in consumer-goods industries. It could also be maintained, in a more sophisticated argument, that the emphasis on developing producer-goods industries has resulted in a "good mix" of productive factors in that sector at the cost of a "poor mix" in the consumer sector, with attendant lags in over-all factor productivity within the latter. There are still other possible criticisms, too subtle to be dealt with in this space.

Turning now from the abstract to the concrete, three points stand out:

1) The volume of consumer goods turned out by Soviet industry has increased considerably. It is claimed that in 1958 the index for purchases of textile products stood at 183 (1940=100) for workers' families, and at 204 for the families of collective farmers; and that the corresponding index figures for purchases of leather footwear were 201 and 217 respectively. These figures do not strike me as implausible. Indeed, it would be hard to imagine any countervailing factors powerful enough to prevent a build-up

of productive capacity such as has been taking place in the
U.S.S.R. from resulting in a considerably increased output of
industrial consumer goods.

2) The present Soviet leadership admits that Stalin made a
frightful mess of Russian agriculture. From 1931 to 1936, over-all
agricultural output consistently was well below what it had been
in 1928, and it is only since the death of Stalin that a considerable
rise has occurred. The evidence goes to show that it was a lack
not of capital input, but of common sense that caused the great
lag in this vital sector.

3) In a period of enormous population transfers, the Soviet
housing effort was quite inadequate and produced conditions of
overcrowding far worse than any known during the industrial
revolution in Europe. Here, the cause is to be sought in the deliberate and, from the Soviet point of view, economically justifiable
sacrifice of investment in housing in favor of other, more productive, forms of investment. This sacrifice of consumer comfort
probably played an important part in bringing down the capital-
output ratio for the Soviet economy as a whole.

It is clear from experience that augmenting the supply of industrial consumer goods has a less significant effect on the standard
of living than does the provision of more ample food and housing. (As a particularly striking illustration of this point, one
could cite the example of France under the German occupation,
when people were willing to trade quite a remarkable amount of
industrial goods for a leg of lamb or a pound of butter, while
almost no amount of industrial goods was worth as much as a
room of one's own.) Worth noting in this connection is the fact
that while it is theoretically impossible in the Soviet system for
products to remain unsold, this is exactly what appears to have
happened on a large scale recently in the case of consumer
durables. The only explanation is that Soviet consumers, rather
than spend their money for these items, preferred to spend it on
marginal increments of vital goods in short supply. A change of
relative valuations will, of course, occur in the Soviet Union as
the food supply becomes less tight (which already seems to be
the case) and once the housing situation starts improving significantly (which will be a far lengthier process). With the

establishment of such a solid base for improved living standards, the subjective value of industrial consumer goods will inevitably rise.

There is, indeed, no obvious reason why we should *not* expect a rapid rise in Soviet living standards. Insofar as food is concerned, the serious deficiencies of the past were a paradox that would never have occurred had it not been for the ill-conceived policies that sought to exact agricultural deliveries at arbitrarily low prices. These mistakes have now been corrected by considerable increases in the prices paid to farmers, and it should be added that the latter have been able to translate their higher earnings into increased purchases of industrial consumer goods, which have become more abundant as a consequence of the expansion of this industrial factor.*

As for the outlook in regard to housing, it is probable that very rapid progress can be made as soon as adequate priorities are granted, since Soviet housing construction is standardized and therefore extremely economical in cost, compared to building to the individual customer's taste, as is usual in the West. Finally, intangible goods such as health and education services have all along enjoyed a high priority in the Soviet Union, and no change in policy in this respect is to be expected.

It is, of course, very difficult to compare the standard of living in the U.S.S.R. with the standards of Western countries, because the choices made for the people by the Soviet authorities have been so very different from those made freely by the people in democratic societies. Not only has the Soviet government disregarded the time preference of the people and forced them to accept investment to the detriment of consumption, but even those goods and services it has provided have reflected authoritarian choices. This shows up first of all in the fact that the ratio of the share of national income spent on education to the share

---

* It is probable that in the case of the textile industries, expansion of production was delayed, compared to what it could have been under unplanned development, because the amount of equipment allotted to textile manufacturing failed to compensate for the diversion of manpower from this sector of industry.

spent on the production of tangible consumer goods is very much higher in the U.S.S.R. than in Western countries. It is equally apparent in the pricing pattern of goods bought and sold in the market. For instance, such items as newspapers, a medical thermometer, a toothbrush, and such services as the telephone and urban transit are all very cheap in the U.S.S.R. in comparison to what they cost in the United States, while commodities such as a bed, a blanket, a pound of butter, or a suit of clothes are relatively very expensive.

Obviously comparisons like these require no fixed "rate of exchange." It is sufficient to observe that when a 10-cent phone call costs 15 kopeks and a 50-dollar bed and mattress 1552 rubles, the purchasing power equivalent of one dollar in the case of the phone call is 1.5 rubles and in the case of the bed and mattress more than 30 rubles. There are clear indications here that the Soviet economy has been slanted toward the provision of goods and services which the Soviet regime considers "progressive." Its choices in production have patterned Soviet consumer habits, whereas in the West consumer responses have patterned production. It is true that after having so long forced upon the people "what is good for them," the Soviet leaders may now increasingly let the people have what they would like, but even so, they will insist upon forming the people's taste—as a new rash of publications devoted to this purpose indicates.

Nevertheless, a tendency toward greater regard for the tastes of Soviet consumers is apparent, and there is hardly any need for special explanations of this phenomenon, since it fits into the general pattern of recent Soviet developments. The Soviet rulers have always thought of themselves as working for the good of the people even when, as in Stalin's day, their arbitrary judgment as to what was the people's best interest led them ruthlessly to disregard the preferences and feelings, the liberties and even the lives of the citizens. Was this really necessary in a country whose pre-World War I rate of economic growth led all economists of the time to predict that by mid-century Russia would become the dominant industrial and commercial power of Europe? Certainly not. Was it unsuccessful? Again, certainly not. Those who insist on finding it unsuccessful display the dangerous brand of "moralism" that, for fear of compromising ethical judgment by an acknowledgment of success, prefers to translate a moral condemnation of procedure into a judgment of objective failure.

What can we expect, then, from the material betterment of the lives of the Russian people? Surely it would be monstrous not to feel pleased about it. But whether this betterment is likely to promote an eventual change in the political regime is another matter. I can, indeed, find no evidence in the history of the Western world that would indicate that economic wealth inevitably nurtures political freedom, and as far as the recent history of the U.S.S.R. is concerned, I am inclined to believe that it was the death of Stalin, rather than economic development, that caused the current amelioration of Soviet political life. However, let us hope that here the Marxian model will prove valid.

The Consumer and the System

——PETER WILES

THE EDITORS have asked me to comment specifically on the ideas expressed in Mr. Nove's last paragraph. I agree that "certain features of the Soviet economy are inconsistent with the proper satisfaction of consumer demands"—in one sense, indeed, so radically inconsistent that to achieve such satisfaction would require a fundamental change. I mean that central physical planning of the economy is, in the present state of human knowledge, incompatible with the consumers' sovereignty and the rational allocation of scarce resources between competing ends. In the far future, perhaps, the application of so-called "activity-analysis" mathematics, aided by electronic machines into which a vast nationwide network will feed information about the availabilities of production capacity and the current needs of consumers, may make it possible both to plan centrally and to allocate rationally; indeed this now seems, in response to the influx of Western economic techniques, to be the ultimate hope of the Gosplan itself.

But that is for the distant future. At present, there are only two ways of attaining the "proper satisfaction of consumer demand." The first is by means of what I have called elsewhere a "centralized free market." In this system the state, as monopolist of all products, so disposes of the means of production as simply to transmit the push and pull of consumer demand to them. Using a system of rational prices, it transmits consumer preferences as the consumers themselves would have transmitted them. The second alternative would be decentralized free-market socialism as in Yugoslavia (decentralization without a free market would, of course, only make things worse).

Now both these systems cut at the root, not of socialism, but of much else that is dear to the Communists: the habit of command, the ideology of arbitrary physical allocations, contempt for money profit, and so on. The latest changes in the Soviet Union do indeed move in the directions outlined above, but not very far. For instance, if enterprises are given planned directions only of the most general kind and expressed in money rather than physical values, and which leave other details of what they are to produce to decentralized contract-making with the individual enterprises specified in the plan, the consumer continues to have no choice between suppliers such as he has under conditions of proper competition. Undoubtedly the Soviet system is now better than it was, but it could still be vastly improved.

On the other hand, even if we assume some truly radical reconstruction of the Soviet economy on Titoist lines, we must ask whether it would really matter. Minds trained in Western economics are often just as fundamentally Marxist as their Communist opposite numbers. Why should we suppose that decentralization and a free market would lessen political totalitarianism? Have they done so in Yugoslavia? The connection between totalitarianism and central physical planning (as opposed to the mere abolition of private ownership) is subtle and indirect. We can only go so far as to say that the desire to sit in a central office and give physical orders to enterprises is but one of many possible expressions of a totalitarian mentality; it is neither sufficient of itself nor necessary for political totalitarianism. Indeed, in a complex modern economy, those who give such orders must have technical skills of a high order, and the acquisition of these skills tends to dilute the totalitarian mentality. This results in the growth of a huge bureaucracy of undogmatic technicians, and the really dogmatic ideologues find their dynamism swamped in a morass of detail. The latter might well choose to revert to a comparatively free market, or at least to very limited types of planning, simply in order to draw themselves clear of the bureaucrats. The conflicts between Malenkov and Khrushchev, or Chou En-lai and Liu Shao-ch'i, express this same dichotomy. Thus, it has been precisely the ideologues who have stood for less complex—albeit not necessarily more rational—methods of planning.

Moreover, the survival of Yugoslav totalitarianism does not say much for the liberalizing effects of consumer sovereignty.

But there is another sense in which the "proper satisfaction of consumer demand" is inconsistent with "certain features of the Soviet economy." This is the Soviet obsession with investment and with a more rapid rate of growth for heavy industry. Maximum consumer satisfaction at any moment of time would require a relaxation here also. But it is far from clear that the Western policy in this regard is right, and the Soviet wrong, if we are thinking of consumer satisfaction not merely now but in the future. In the long run, if Soviet consumption continues to grow at anything like its present rate, it will exceed the American rate; hence it is not clear why this policy should be altered or that it is, in any permanent sense, a defect of the Soviet system. Moreover, in particular short periods, the policy obviously can be altered, and indeed was altered during the Second Five Year Plan, as it also was in Hungary during the first prime ministership of Nagy, and elsewhere in the bloc.

But more important than this is the question, does prosperity itself, regardless of what kind of economic organization or policy brings it about, threaten Soviet political totalitarianism? An optimistic answer has been given far too often by people who clearly have not thought the matter out. On the one side, the ruled will be grateful to those who have increased their prosperity: As the recent British general elections showed, the important thing is not to have any particular policy, but merely to be the government in office during a period of enrichment. And again, the leaders—of *whatever* political complexion—will be enriched and emboldened and confirmed in their failings, whatever those failings are. On the other side, increasing wealth has to be shared with those outside the party, who gain confidence and search for new outlets for their wealth. "We are a grown-up people," said the young man at an exhibition of *avant-garde* Polish paintings, and a grown-up people will want not only Polish paintings, but also trips abroad, foreign newspapers, etc.—or at least the intelligentsia will. Moreover, prosperity must bring with it a certain general relaxation of the atmosphere. Rich and comfortable people are on the whole more tolerant and find it more difficult to hate. Indeed, Marxism itself associates freedom (in the half-nonsensical Marxist meaning of the word) with prosperity. The ultimate utopia of the doctrine—full Communism—has prosperity and "freedom" as its two main constituents. In their off-moments, in fact, Marxists promise themselves quite liberal bourgeois Western freedoms in the more prosperous future.

On balance, then, it is very difficult to prophesy the effect of prosperity on freedom in the Soviet Union. While the kind of optimism that has been standard is in my opinion superficial, there also does not appear to be any compelling ground for pessimism.

Ideology, Power, and Welfare

——RICHARD LOWENTHAL

IN MY OPINION, Mr. Nove has performed a most useful service in pointing out that the achievement of substantial improvements in the welfare standard (and, by extension of the same argument, also in the general living standard) of Soviet citizens can be explained, and the possibility of further improvements admitted, *without assuming a basic change in the political and ideological motivations of the ruling Communist Party and its leaders.* I am not quite sure whether this was Mr. Nove's main intention; I feel certain that it is the general upshot of his argument, and its great merit.

The people's welfare is not, of course, the principal moving force of the Soviet economy, any more than it is of the capitalist economy. The principal moving force of the Soviet economy has been and remains power, just as the principal moving force of the capitalist economy has been and remains profit. But once we clear our minds of both Communist and capitalist cant, it is obvious that this formulation does not imply the impossibility of welfare improvements under Communist dictatorship, just as it does not imply a "law of absolute and relative impoverishment of the proletariat" under capitalism.

There are two reasons for this. The first is that, given the achievement of a certain degree of capital accumulation and productivity, it becomes possible for both economic systems to satisfy secondary objectives as well. The second is that the nature of the modern industrial process—independent of the economic and political systems—increasingly requires educated workers with a sense of responsibility toward the maintenance of their tools and the quality of their output. For building pyramids in Egypt or railway lines in Arctic Russia, it may be just as effective (and certainly cheaper) to employ masses of underpaid and undernourished laborers as it is to maintain a well-fed and well-trained working class. For operating modern machinery efficiently, however, you need the latter, particularly if the birth-rate and the influx of manpower from the countryside slows down; and that means a guaranteed minimum standard, plus incentives.

The transformation of living and working conditions in post-Stalin Russia, which has included the welfare measures noted by Mr. Nove, thus amounts to a somewhat belated adjustment by the U.S.S.R. to the stage of "industrial maturity" it has already reached. The adjustment has not conflicted with the ideological and power objectives of the regime; in fact, as Mr. Nove points out, Soviet action to improve welfare has satisfied certain low-priority propaganda objectives without hampering in the slightest the high-priority pursuit of producer goods, armaments, and so on. All this parallels corresponding developments at corresponding stages in the history of the older capitalist-industrial countries.

In most of the advanced industrial countries of the West, however, the pursuit of profit is modified not only by the need to keep the labor force efficient and responsible, but also by two other major factors. One is the existence of political democracy, including the role played by independent trade unions and political labor groups. The other is the ideology of consumption. These two modifying factors have no parallel in the Soviet Union; on the contrary, they are incompatible with the power structure and ideology of any Communist Party dictatorship. It follows that the pressure for higher standards of living and consumption is less strong in the Soviet Union and its satellites than in democratic industrial countries, and that the improvement is likely to remain within narrower limits than in democratic countries with comparable productivity.

Mr. Nove points out that there is no need to *assume* the existence of democratic pressures in Russia in order to explain what has happened. There is also no *evidence* for the existence of such pressures, except for the mass strikes in the slave-labor camps during the immediate post-Stalin years, and possibly some pressure among the ruling group for increased personal security. There has been no sign of independence on the part of the Party-controlled "trade unions," and no hint of giving them any bargaining rights in determining the wage level fixed by the plan: As for the peasants, they are not even "organized" (in unions) as a class. To grant such rights to independent pressure groups would, of course, be the beginning of the end of the totalitarian power structure, unless these rights were quickly revoked again—witness Gomulka's Poland after October, 1956.

The ideology of consumption, as widely held in advanced capitalist countries, maintains that the demand of consumers is the ultimate driving force of capitalist economies. This is a misleading picture of reality, partly because capitalist production tends to create its own demand by "synthesizing wants," and partly because a growing sector of effective demand emanates from public funds and is directed to goods that either do not enter private consumption at all, such as armaments, or are not individually paid for, such as public education, roads, and so on. But the ideological stress on consumption, together with the capitalist producers' continuous efforts to create new wants, tends to reinforce democratic demands for an ever-higher minimum standard. Hence the tendency of democratic capitalist societies not only to provide the workers with the minimum required for training and incentives, but to channel at least part of all productivity gains into mass consumption.

Of course, Communist ideology also proclaims that abundant satisfaction of all wants is the ultimate purpose of the economic system; and the recent stress on catching up with American consumption has made this utopian vision appear more concrete and practical. Yet the Stalinist principle of continued priority for heavy industry has not been abandoned either in theory or in practice; nor could an economic system of total planning, in which literally all demand emanates from the state, ever become dependent on "want creation" to the extent that characterizes the

American economy. No doubt the Soviet rulers are genuinely interested in increasing mass consumption, and there is little question that within the limits set by higher priority objectives, and given normal circumstances, they should be able to do so. But the idea that because of their propagandist promises they are "committed" to a consumption race with the United States, whatever its effect on their other objectives—an idea frequently advanced in current discussion on the prospects of "peaceful coexistence," though not of course in Mr. Nove's paper—overlooks the fact that the Soviet system has neither the political mechanism of democratic pressures, nor the economic mechanism of partial dependence on demand, that would give such promises the weight of a "commitment" in democratic capitalist conditions.

Assuming, therefore, that continued economic growth in the U.S.S.R. will make further improvement of welfare and consumption standards possible, the actual rate of such improvements will depend not only on the total rate of growth, but also on the changing allocation of resources between consumption on the one hand, and such competing claims as continued investment, development aid (particularly to the countries within the Soviet bloc), and armaments on the other. This is not the place, nor am I competent, to give an estimate of the likely development in regard to such allocation. But it may be confidently asserted that as long as the totalitarian power structure and its ideological dynamics last, the share of individual consumption in the national product will continue to be far below that in the capitalist democracies—just as it is now, after all the recent improvements.

Against this, a view now fashionable in Western discussions on the future of the Soviet Union contends that the very emergence there of a modern industrial economy based on material incentives and a high level of technical education, and "committed" to rising consumption standards, is bound to erode the ideological dynamism of the regime, as traditional ideological goals come to be replaced in the minds of its rulers and managers by the material standards of efficiency and affluence familiar in the West. The obvious objection to this latest revival of nineteenth-century materialist optimism is that it completely neglects the experience of Nazi Germany. I do not, of course, equate the ideological goals and political methods of Mr. Khrushchev with those of Hitler; if they were the same, we should probably all be dead by now. The relevance of Nazi experience lies not in the particular content and direction of its ideological dynamism, but in the fact that the pursuit of dynamic ideological goals, *whatever their content*, proved compatible with the conditions of a highly developed industrial country under totalitarian rule.

Nazi Germany, it will be remembered, looked back to a long tradition of universal education and technical development. Its economy was based not on terror but on a modern system of material incentives: in contrast to Stalin's labor camps, Hitler's concentration camps, however important politically, were marginal to economic life. By overcoming mass unemployment, the regime achieved a considerable improvement of living standards; it boasted of this fact and "committed" itself to mass production of "people's cars," but whenever a choice had to be made, it subordinated butter to guns. Its highly efficient economic managers took little interest in race theories; but though they were far more independent in their work than their Soviet colleagues are even today, they did not rule the country and determine its policies.

Among the goals pursued by the ruling party of the Soviet Union, the people's welfare and consumption standards do indeed have a place, but a subordinate one. In the official ideology, the "building of Communism" is not defined as a *direct* achievement of material abundance; before this can be attained, further changes have to be carried out in the structure of society—above all, in assimilating the living and working conditions of collective farmers to those of wage laborers on the state farms. From the point of view of the Soviet rulers, the most important development now proceeding in the U.S.S.R. is not the improvement in living standards, proud as they are of this, but rather the new transformation of agriculture—a transformation hardly reported in the West. They are engaged in further amalgamating collective farms into giant units (their number has diminished by one quarter in the eighteen months from December, 1957, to June,

1959); they are forcing up kolkhoz investments in the state-controlled "indivisible fund," whose percentage share of kolkhoz income has doubled since 1953, reaching 24 per cent in 1958; they are preparing to introduce "labor books" for all collective-farm members next year; they are laying the groundwork for the abolition, within two years, of the private plots of state-farm laborers, and for the eventual liquidation of collective farmers' plots—the latter to disappear more slowly as the members of the new giant collectives come to be centrally resettled in "agrotowns"; and they are pressuring the members of the more efficient kolkhozes "voluntarily" to sell their cows to the collectives.

All these measures, which absorb a great deal of the time and energy of the ruling Party, are based on its ideological vision, which is very real to the Party leaders. And while Khrushchev and his associates are trying to avoid Stalin's mistakes and to diminish as far as possible the risk that such revolutionary measures may cause production setbacks, they are nevertheless pursuing their ideological goals in the awareness that the only way of obviating all risk would be to abandon their ideology, which would expose them to an even greater and more vital risk—that the Party to which they owe their position would lose its cohesion, and hence its power.

En Route to Utopia

The Glorious Future: Realities and Chimeras

> SUKARNO: *Indonesian socialism is not a severe socialism. It aims at a good life for all, without exploitation.*
>
> KHRUSHCHEV: *No, no, no. Socialism should mean that every minute is calculated, a life built on calculation.*
>
> SUKARNO: *That is the life of a robot.*
>
> —The New York Times, March 2, 1960.

THE IDEA OF PROGRESS, the belief in the irresistible advance of human society to ever-greater social and moral perfection, which had been, in the words of the distinguished historian J. B. Bury in his *Idea of Progress,* "the animating and controlling idea of Western civilization," is virtually extinct in the West today. Two world wars, the eruption of inhumanity and barbarism—all the more terrifying for their technological refinement and the ever-present danger of universal nuclear destruction—have banished the optimism characteristic of the nineteenth century. Gloom, pessimism, and uncertainty have enveloped Western civilization. The prophecy of Condorcet that "the perfectability of man is in fact unlimited and can never be reversed" could only evoke a smile in a generation that has witnessed Auschwitz and that is condemned to live in the shadow of the hydrogen bomb.

But the vision of utopia, extinct in the West, continues to shine

616

in the Communist East, deriving its splendor from the artificial illumination of the propaganda engines of *Agitprop*. At the Twelfth International Congress of Philosophers held at Venice in 1958, M. B. Mitin, a leading Soviet philosopher, portrayed the future society to which the Soviet Union is allegedly advancing in terms worthy perhaps not so much of Marx as of his more imaginative predecessors—Condorcet, Saint-Simon, and Fourier. The society to come, he solemnly prophesied, would attain such heights of social perfection that the individuals nurtured by it would develop—"as if by magic"—qualities hitherto possessed only by men of genius. The common man would grow to the stature of a Michelangelo, a Liszt, or a Paganini. Just as Communism would abolish the distinction between rich and poor by providing abundance for all, so would it reduce the differences between the mental capacities and achievements of individuals by liberating the potentialities of man from the oppressive shells of human institutions. To the Western philosophers present, it must have seemed as if the ghost of Condorcet had descended upon Venice in the guise of the Soviet philosopher to preach the doctrine of inevitable progress towards utopia. Some might even have reflected that it was odd, though symbolic, that this Soviet Condorcet combined the lofty vocation of philosophical visionary with the mundane pursuit of police agent and propagandist.*

But the theme of utopia is not confined to philosophers alone. In the Soviet Union, economists, writers and a vast army of propagandists have been dwelling on it with increasing frequency, reflecting the guiding and inspiring hand of the Party— the chief dispenser of spiritual nourishment to the Soviet populace.

Addressing a plenary session of the Board of the Writers' Union of the R.S.F.S.R., L. Sobolev, its Chairman and an official guardian of literary orthodoxy, envisaged the future Communist society to be peopled by citizens endowed with intellectual capacities of a degree hitherto confined to a gifted minority. The

---

* Mitin, entrusted by Stalin with the conduct of the campaign against Tito, distinguished himself by such zeal that he earned the Titoist epithet "the best philosopher among the NKVD men and the best NKVD man among philosophers."

art of literary creation, instead of remaining the property of a chosen few, will become the natural attribute of everyone. The citizens of Communism, released from the toil to which humanity has been condemned, would take to the pen; and a new golden age of art and literature would dawn upon the human race. Just as "work will become the primary vital need of man, so the mastery of [literary] craftsmanship will cease to be the achievement of single individuals to become the natural practice of everyone exactly in the same manner in which, under Soviet rule, literacy ceased to be the privilege of the ruling estate and became universal." Soviet society, Sobolev continued, stands in the "forefield" of that golden age, separated from it only by a road of great but surmountable obstacles. In describing the manner in which these obstacles are to be overcome, Sobolev abandoned the mellow and gilded language of the utopian dreamer for the warlike metaphor of the cavalry officer, his former vocation (*Pravda*, May 11, 1960):

> We find ourselves in the forefield of Communism. I adduce this military term consciously, because, in the course of the unfolding advance our society is now effecting, we must still overcome some minefields laid thousands of years ago—the so-called survivals of capitalism in the consciousness of people.

Many would be naturally tempted to dismiss such utterances as ritualistic lip service, as mechanical and meaningless recitals of the Marxist creed. But to do so would be to obscure not only the sincere devotion with which many of the Marxist formulas are held, but also the vital role played by utopia in the Communist order.

The Opiate of the Rulers

The secular eschatology of Marxism is one of the ideological and psychological pillars of Soviet society. Just as the power of the church and indeed the cohesion of the medieval order rested on the belief in the hereafter, so the ideal terrestial future is an essential element of the spiritual foundation of the Communist world. The awe-inspiring firmament of the hereafter was a living psychic reality for medieval man, providing the anchor chain for the power of the church over his mind. Earthly power was firmly rooted in the heavenly domain, investing the authority of the church with a claim to obedience equaled by few temporal rulers. All political power seeks to legitimize itself, to rely not on naked force but on the voluntary consent of its subjects. But the Bolshevik claim to obedience could rest on few tangible benefits offered to the people. It has demanded much in toil, suffering, and anxiety, but it has offered little in return, save the assurance that the privation of the present would yield abundant fruit in the undetermined future. Until recently, utopian dreams were the only gratification the regime could supply in plenty.

It would be impossible to determine the efficacy of utopia as an opium for the people. It is doubtful, for instance, that the peasantry was at all susceptible to it, particularly during the collectivization drive. Terror seems to have been a more potent instrument in securing submission to the will of the Party than the blandishments of the glorious future. But if Marx's eschatology has served only imperfectly as an opium for the people, it has been a powerful self-administered opium for the ruling class. It would be difficult to exaggerate the *élan* derived by Bolsheviks from the utopian vision. It has endowed them with an unwavering singleness of purpose, with a missionary zeal that retains, undaunted, the fullness of its fervor even in adversity, and it has imparted to them an immunity to scruples in the pursuit of power.

For the Bolshevik mind, from the very beginning, endowed the future with the dimensions and qualities of a deity—or rather a moloch. Whenever a Bolshevik would be beset by doubts caused by the contradiction between precept and practice, between the humane goal and the inhuman deed, he would summon up the radiant future, thus rationalizing the present, appeasing his conscience, and enabling himself to resume his vocation undisturbed by qualms. Perhaps the power of rationalization conferred by utopia is best revealed in those Communist victims of the Stalinist terror who, languishing innocently in prisons and concentration camps, nevertheless found comfort and justification for their ordeal in the belief that their lot was but part of the heavy toll humanity must pay in order to enter the gates of the future. The Polish poet Czeslaw Milosz has brilliantly described the arguments of Communist theodicy in *The Captive Mind*. His expressions of disquiet over the mass deportations from the Baltic were met by a Communist friend, more strongly anesthetized by faith than he himself, with reproach:

> If you keep thinking about the Baltics and the camps, do you know what will happen to you? . . . You will use up the rest of your time to live and you will present yourself before Zeus; and the god, pointing his finger (here my friend gestured accusingly), will cry: "Idiot! You ruined your life by worrying about trifles!"

Or:

> The present moment is dark but, seen from a distance, for example from the year 2953, it will appear as short as the Reign of Terror in the French Revolution seems to us today; and the number of victims (200–300 million, more or less) will seem scarcely more important than a few thousand beheaded French aristocrats.

The Bolshevik is one of the purest incarnations of the Faustian Man. He is constantly on the historical road in pursuit of the Goal, overcoming obstacles and warding off enemies. To pause, content with past achievements, would signify that his mission has been completed, his role exhausted, and his claim to total power ended. Totalitarian Communism can dispense neither with enemies nor with utopia.*

Challenge from Within

During the past three years, the theme of the transition to Communism has occupied a prominent place in Party propaganda. Not since the "heroic days" of the Revolution has the

---

* The totalitarian regime must constantly affirm a boundless optimism. For pessimism is the blood-brother of skepticism, and skepticism is the enemy of all absolute creeds. It is, in the words of the *Soviet Encyclopedia*, "one of the forms of the struggle against science and against dialectical materialism."

shape of the future society been the object of such intense pre-occupation. It was the subject of a special session of the departments of social sciences of the U.S.S.R. Academy of Sciences in June, 1958. It was a conspicuous item in Khrushchev's speech to the Twenty-first CPSU Congress. A seminar held in Prague in April, 1960, attended by leading economists of all the Communist countries, made this the single point on its agenda. During 1959 and 1960, Soviet presses turned out about one hundred books and countless magazine and newspaper articles devoted to the image of the ultimate society. Clearly, the final stage of social evolution has become one of the major preoccupations of theoreticians and propagandists alike.

Three interrelated circumstances seem to have combined to produce the current emphasis on Marxist eschatology: the challenge of libertarian Marxist revisionism; the Party's endeavor—in response to the revisionist challenge—to recast its ideology into a mold consistent with the demands of totalitarianism so as to prevent its use as a weapon of heresy; and finally, the greater clarity the hitherto blurred picture of the future has assumed in the minds of the Soviet leaders.

Revisionists in Hungary and Poland and Yugoslavia brought to life some of the tenets of Marxism that for years had slumbered peacefully and innocuously in the official text. Phrases like "workers' control," "the withering away of the state," "the leap from necessity to freedom," which had been invoked on ceremonial occasions with automatic solemnity, now became slogans of revolt raised against the terroristic dictatorship. The Soviet leaders were dismayed to see their ritualistic phrases turned into "armed doctrines," challenging the foundations of their power. They were awakened to the fact that their own ideological armory contained two-edged swords. Indeed, one of the lessons derived by the Soviet leaders from the events in Hungary and Poland in 1956, and from the faint intellectual stirrings in their own domain, was the power inherent in ideas. True—to paraphrase a Latin saying—amidst terror ideas are silent. But the veil of silence conceals a dormant life. When terror relents, or when circumstances prevent its full use, those ideas may spring into insurgent action.

The slogans of revisionism were all the more dangerous to the Communist regime because they appeared not in the alien and vulnerable garb of bourgeois doctrine, but in the legitimate and familiar attire of Marxism, asserting their purity against the alleged official adulterators of the Marxist creed. In the words of a Soviet writer (*Voprosy filosofii*, No. 4, 1960, p. 14): "The problem of the withering away of the . . . socialist state is the main thesis, indeed a veritable *idée fixe* of contemporary revisionism. No sooner does the question of the state arise than they steer it to the issue of the withering away."

The need arose to remove heretical overtones from such doctrines by placing upon them an interpretation compatible with the perpetuation of totalitarianism. New wine had to be poured into the old libertarian bottles of Marxism, a wine that would not intoxicate with the desire for freedom but would instill a quiescent submission to an everlasting totalitarian order.

Reality Versus Promises

One of the contradictions of Communism has always been its demand for absolute obedience and punishment of any sign of resistance to its will on the one hand, and its simultaneous inculcation, through Marxist texts, of the dream of a different social order on the other. A populace exposed to the ubiquitous power of the police and the state, experiencing glaring inequalities in income and status, chained serflike to their jobs, could nevertheless speak aloud about a future state to the fulfillment of which their leaders themselves were pledged, a state in which the police, indeed the very organs of government, would not exist, in which full social equality would reign, and in which every individual would be able to fulfill himself.

Now, with the material conditions for fulfillment of the great promise at last in sight, Soviet citizens, according to *Kommunist*, have begun to raise specific questions about "the nature of the future organs of government in the villages and cities, about other details of Communist life." An agitator in the Saratov area appealed to Moscow for guidance and knowledge of the future society; for, "deluged" by questions he was unable to answer, he was in danger of "forfeiting his authority as an agitator." One Soviet writer expressed his apprehensions lest an "unreasonable person" might entertain the following notion of Communism: "You rise in the morning and you begin to reflect: Where shall I go to work today—to the factory as the chief engineer, or shall I gather and lead the fishing brigade? Or pehaps fly to Moscow to conduct an urgent session of the Academy of Sciences?" *Kommunist,* quoting this flight of imagination, remarked laconically, "Thus it will not be."

Ideas are a force no dictator can ignore with impunity. The eschatological imagination threatens to become a source of indiscipline, a breeder of "dangerous" expectations incompatible with the total claims of the state. Totalitarian order has to be imposed upon the anarchic vision without, however, robbing it of the enthusiasm and purposefulness that it imparted to its bearers. As early as October 13, 1952, Poskrebyshev, Stalin's secretary and the *éminence grise* of the Soviet system, denounced in *Pravda* "those among us who await the coming of Communism as if it were some heavenly paradise. They sit there and ask themselves: 'When will Communism finally be proclaimed? Will we soon be getting things from society according to our needs?' " Eight years later, the theoretical organ of the Party warned that the treatment of the future society must admit neither "oversimplification" nor "harebrained plans" (*prozhektorstvo*), that "to write now about the future is more complicated than ever before. The days of utopia, of arbitrary flights of fancy, have passed, giving way to higher responsibility in analyzing reality and in foresight." And Khrushchev, at the Twenty-first Party Congress, sought to dispel with oracular authority the "vulgar" conception of Communism "as a formless, unorganized, and anarchic mass of people. No, it will be a highly organized and arranged cooperation of workers. In order to direct machines, everybody will have to fulfill his functions as a laborer and his *social duties* at a determined time and in an established order." (Italics added.)

It was in the course of purging Marxist eschatology of its heretical elements that the Party gained a clearer conception of the ultimate goal of its endeavor. What had heretofore been a tacit and only half-conscious conception became a more articulate vision.* Upon inspection, that vision reveals the hallmarks of a dream typical of Party bureaucrats. If utopia mirrors the imaginary fulfillment of desires thwarted by reality, then the utopia of the Party bureaucrats—the *apparatchiki*—reflects lust for unobstructed power: a perfected totalitarianism. As such, it bears a greater affinity to the ideals of Sparta or the Republic of Plato, to Rousseau's ideal state or to Thomas More's *Utopia*, than to the vague vision of Marx, although it is not altogether alien to it. Some strands of the Marxist ideal future are lifted from their original context, severed from the libertarian elements to which they had been organically linked, and woven into a new pattern that Marx would scarcely recognize. But before outlining the utopia of the *apparatchiki*, a brief excursion into political philosophy is in order.

The Quest for Harmony

Plato's Republic is the archetype of a political ideal that has found exponents in almost every period of Western civilization. Its adherents, for all their differences on the details of social organization, have been united by an impatience with the discordant diversity displayed by all human communities, impatience with the fact that at each moment of history the shape and organization of the community is determined not by conscious human planning in accordance with a system of logic and order, but by the vagaries of spontaneous social forces. Their aim has been to create concord and harmony in human affairs by reducing the complexity of society to a comparatively simple formula. All men should be brought into harmonious communion by inculcating in them ideas that would move them to cooperative endeavor, that would make them accept their social status, however lowly, as a natural and unalterable condition, and that would nip the seeds of social envy and resentment before they take root. Thus the perennial problem of the rival claims of freedom and author-

* Vladimir Dedijer records, in his biography of *Tito* (New York: Simon and Schuster, 1953, p. 296), a statement by Malenkov at the founding conference of the Cominform in 1947, that the Soviet Union was about "to adopt a fifteen-year plan of the transition from socialism to communism ... drawing in detail upon the utopian socialists."

ity, of the reconciliation of the private will with communal
demands, would find its final and permanent resolution. Repose
and social solidarity will replace the restlessness and conflict that
have been the inescapable collective human condition.

Plato proposed that an enlightened elite of philosopher-kings
train its subjects to such obedient solidarity by inculcating in
them "noble lies." Rousseau advocated that a "sovereign" be
vested with the power to "fix the articles of a civil religion" that
would beget an attitude making for "social unity" and abolish
those conditions that set man in "contradiction to himself." Saint-
Simon wished to see a "New Christianity," that is, a society in
which the individuals would be held together by bonds of social
consonance. The French "conservative reaction" and the group
that the *Communist Manifesto* denounced as "feudal socialists"
preached abandonment of the "anarchy" of bourgeois society for
a social system framed in the image of the hierarchical order of
the Middle Ages, allegedly blessed by universal concord. The
Right and the Left in the nineteenth century, for all their differences and mutual enmity, were nourished by kindred psychic
sources.

Marx and Engels were heirs to the same tradition. They, too,
sought social harmony. But unlike most others, they did not seek
to achieve it through a reordering of society into a new harmonious hierarchy by an enlightened elite employing force and
suasion. They believed that once private property and the means
of production were abolished, the triumphant revolutionary
majority would naturally merge into a cooperative community of
equals. The division of humanity into classes would then disappear. The state as an instrument of coercion would be replaced
by an apparatus for the "administration of things" or, to use
Lenin's suggestive term, into a "nonpolitical" state. The highest
degree of human freedom would thus produce the most perfect
harmony ever experienced by man since the mythical days of
primitive Communism.

The vision of Marx has proved less realistic than that of the
"utopian socialist" Saint-Simon and the "elitist" Right. It was a
coincidentia oppositorum. Solidarity was to be achieved not by an
elite consciously fostering *Bindung* and *Ganzheit,* the twin ideals

of the conservative Right, but by a voluntary union of autonomous individuals governed by Reason. Harmony was to be bred by anarchy. It was left to the Bolshevik disciples of Marx to "correct" the teachings of their master, thus exposing the kinship between the reactionary Right and the radical Left.

Thus, while Bolshevism retains the economic ideals of Marx, it finds that *Bindung* and *Ganzheit* can be realized only by the means prescribed by the Right. Marx's utopia has been "dialectically" transmuted by the *apparatchiki*. Freedom is denounced as anarchy, self-government of society as anarcho-syndicalism, the autonomy of artistic creation as an antisocial propensity, the demand for privacy against the all-embracing claims of the collectivity as pernicious individualism. And as for the *apparatchiki* themselves, they have become the indispensable guides, wardens, and tutors of society.

The aim of the Party functionaries, then, is to impose upon society what might be termed totalitarian harmony; to remove, in the language of Soviet scholasticism, all contradictions from the body social; to prevent the coagulation of any social groups that threaten to assert themselves against the total embrace of the Party. No spontaneous group-will must exist save that imparted by the ruling elite. "Spontaneity (*stykhiinost*), Comrades," Khrushchev remarked at a Plenum of the Party Central Committee in 1958, "spontaneity is the deadliest enemy of all." As for the divergent forces that spontaneity breeds, they are succinctly and revealingly summarized in the following excerpt from a major theoretical discussion of "Communist transformation" by B. Ukraintsev in *Kommunist* (No. 13, 1960, p. 72). According to its author, the aim of the Party is:

. . . the unity of the working class, not its fragmentation; the strengthening of the alliance between the working class and the peasantry, not discord between these two nonantagonistic classes; the strengthening of the unity of the ranks of the Marxist-Leninist Party, not factionalism and ideological rambling; the unified, planned socialist economy, based on public socialist property, not the anarcho-syndicalist economic fragmentation; the ideological, political, and moral unity of the people, not ideological dispersion; reunion of people of various nationalities . . . not national differences and nationalism; the strengthening of a single socialist governmental power, not provincial separatism. . . .

Or, in the words of Khrushchev: "Just like bees toiling from dawn to dusk, creating a new building and filling it with honey, so our people fulfill their obligations and functions in society."*

The Shape of the Future

Let us pause here to explore some of the specific features of the social beehive into which the Party seeks to transform Soviet society.

The Ruling Elite. The Communist Party, having been the demiurge of Soviet society, will become its perpetual animator. To be sure, some functions of government will devolve upon "public organizations," and the "state would wither away" (whatever that may mean). But the role of the Party will grow; for *Kommunist* asks, "Who but the Party is capable of uniting and coordinating the manifold activities of the ramified system of public organizations? The party is a higher form of public organi-

---

* *Pravda,* November 18, 1959. There is a striking similarity between Khrushchev's vision and Plutarch's description of Spartan life: "To be brief, he (Lycurgus) did accustom his citizens so, that they neither would nor could live alone, but were as men incorporated one with another and were always in company together, as the bees be about their master bee. Still in a continuall love to serve their countrie, to winne honour, and to advance the commonweale." (*Plutarch's Lives,* trans. Sir Thomas North, I, 148.)

Khrushchev, however, would do well to acquaint himself also with the judgment of the English philosopher Thomas Hobbes, who wrote in the *Leviathan,* published in 1651: "It is true that certain living creatures, as Bees and Ants, live sociably with one another (which are therefore by Aristotle numbered amongst politicall creatures); and yet have no other direction, than their particular judgment and appetites; nor speech, whereby one of them can signifie to another, what he thinks expedient for the common benefit; and therefore some man may perhaps desire to know, why Man-kind cannot do the same. To which I answer, First that men are continually in competition for Honour and Dignity, which these creatures are not; and consequently amongst men there arises on that ground, Envy and Hatred, and finally Warre; but amongst these not so."

zation [and public organizations, as is well known, never wither away]. It alone can and does give correct political direction to all organizations. Unlike all other organizations, the Party is not connected with any professional, departmental, and local interests. The Party sees farther than others. It has organizational and political experience."

The Party, however, will rule without coercion. The practitioners of violence will assume the role of philosopher-kings, whose main tasks will be to "conquer human souls," "to convert the truth of Marxism-Leninism into the inner convictions of all without exception," until "every Soviet man" will be guided by it. "What has been confirmed by world history must find confirmation in the psyche of the individual." The totalitarian ethos will become internalized—part and parcel of the psychic household of the individual. Ideological work will be the foremost task of the Party, holding custody of the purity of men's minds, preventing their contamination by alien ideologies, and safeguarding against the emergence of a no less dangerous apolitical mental vacuum. Indeed, Khrushchev, fascinated by the suggestive term "brainwashing" (which he learned from an American), exhorted Soviet writers "to wash the brains of people with your works, not clutter up their minds."

Freedom. Significantly, this word rarely appears in the voluminous discussions on the "transition to Communism." But it is not difficult to divine, from the official texts, the extent and nature of freedom in the projected order. Obedience to the Party will become an "organic necessity" of man, his second nature, as it were. The desire for emancipation from its tutelage will be regarded as a pernicious rebellion against the ideal of collectivism, an expression of baneful individualism leading to "anarchy." But such anarchistic propensities will be as rare as they will be unnatural—a form of psychopathology. In Khrushchev's words:

Will there be criminals in Communist society? I personally, for example, as a Communist, cannot vouch that there will not be any. A crime is a deviation from the generally recognized standards of behavior in society, frequently caused by mental disorder. Can there be any diseases, any mental disorders among some men in a Communist society? Evidently there can be. If that is so, then there can be delinquencies of which people of an abnormal mind are capable.

In other words, a deviation from the totalitarian norm will be treated as a form of insanity.

Equality. By 1930, the cry for equality of the disinherited, upon which the Bolsheviks had ridden to power, was silenced; and those who defiantly continued to demand that the promise of the Revolution be redeemed were denounced as petty-bourgeois deviationists. Utopia had yielded to the inexorable dictates of human nature, for which egalitarianism is a noble but impracticable ideal. To be sure, the Communist dictatorship continued to affirm its commitment to the Marxist principle "from each according to his abilities, to each according to his needs"; but its realization, it was now argued, must await the distant day when the poverty to which Bolshevik Russia was heir should have been conquered by abundance, and when inequality of material rewards would no longer be needed to induce man, cleansed of capitalistic habits, to render his most efficient service to society.

Current Soviet discussion of the transition to Communism again lays stress on egalitarianism as a vital feature of the future society. But the Party's quest for equality is no longer sustained by the passion that originally brought it into being. The yearning of the disinherited for equality, nourished by resentment and envy, has turned into a calculated technique of totalitarian domination.

The distribution of goods and services according to need, already partially realized in such spheres as medical services, nurseries, and boarding schools, will ever widen, until it embraces the full scope of human consumption. Such a mode of distribution will serve to strengthen the collectivist nature of Soviet society against manifestations of individualism, especially against "tendencies to private property," that "most terrible of all the survivals of capitalism" (*Pravda*, May 11, 1960). In terms strongly reminiscent of Plato's argument in favor of "communism," the Party has been encouraging a widening of the scope of the "public satisfaction of 'needs.'" According to *Kommunist* (No. 14, 1960, p. 19):

> There is no doubt that all objects necessary for personal use will remain in personal use under Communism as well. However, the outlook for the future does not correspond to the provision of workers and employees with immovable property—with private dwellings and country houses, with means of transportation [presumably automobiles], i.e., with property that would allow them in certain cases to derive income without toil. . . . It would be inexpedient to encourage . . . private building.

But not only housing is to become "cooperative." All forms of distribution will eventually become collectivized. *Kommunist* goes on to say:

> Even now a substantial and ever-growing part of material and cultural goods are distributed among citizens regardless of the quality and quantity of their work. . . . The widening of the collective forms of satisfying the personal needs of the workers will constitute an important condition for sealing off the channels through which tendencies favoring private property might leak out.

Thus, in the conception of the Party, egalitarian collectivism is a safeguard against individualism and the desire for private property, which might create "islets" of social autonomy eluding the control of the Party. History has known many absolute rulers who sought to fortify their rule by leveling society and reducing it to an undifferentiated mass of impotent and obedient subjects. In the words of Shakespeare's *King Richard II:*

> Go thou and, like an executioner,
> Cut off the heads of too fast growing spray
> That look too lofty in our Commonwealth.
> All must be even in our government.
>
> (*Act III, Scene 4*)

The Family. Communism will be a period of *"consistent monogamy"* (*Kommunist*, No. 7, 1960; italics in original). "Communist morality is in principle opposed to [liaisons born of] dissoluteness and flightiness." While rejecting with contempt the "slanders" heaped upon Communist society in Orwell's *1984* and Aldous Huxley's *Brave New World*—both of which portrayed love under Communism as controlled by the state and procreation practiced by artificial means—Communist theoreticians make it clear that abjuration of the Leftist deviation of free love, which the regime briefly sanctioned during the 1920's, remains in force. Marital infidelity and sexual promiscuity, it would seem, breed a frame of mind that militates against the discipline of totalitarianism. The puritanical code must permeate the whole of society. As *Komsomolskaia pravda* (April 11, 1959) asked, in reporting a case of marital "betrayal": "How many steps are there from this to treason in the broader sense . . . ?"

As for the household functions of the family, they will be gradually replaced by public restaurants and laundries, both of which will increase in volume as well as in quality. Yet the family will definitely retain its "moral and educative" functions. Although the rearing of children will, to a considerable extent, be transferred to the expanding network of boarding schools, the family will continue to share in that task. In the words of *Kommunist*, the "joys of fatherhood and motherhood are indispensable to man and represent an important factor in the education of children." At the same time, the boarding schools will be expected to play an ever-increasing role, inasmuch as they are best equipped to eradicate "egoistic" tendencies—i.e., individualism.

The Discipline of Leisure. In the past few years, the Party has evinced a growing concern with the uses to which Soviet citizens put the leisure gained by technological advances. For it is, indeed, endemic to a totalitarian regime that it insist on integrating *res privata* into *res publica*. In this respect, the similarity between Communism and fascism is striking. "In National Socialism," one Nazi official proclaimed, "there is no such thing as a private individual."

Leisure encourages privacy and the pursuit of "idle pleasures."

It offers many opportunities for social activities beyond the sphere of control of the totalitarian regime. Sensual gratification may become the dominant preoccupation of man, making him impervious to political discipline. In the conception of the Party, all men must be imbued with political consciousness; for, Mao Tse-tung maintained in his Hundred Flower speech, "not to have the correct political view is like having no soul." Accordingly, the levers of the totalitarian regime must embrace individuals at home as well as at work. It is in this context that the recent stream of denunciatory articles against "idlers, sluggards and parasites" can best be understood. To cite from one such article chosen at random from *Pravda* (September 6, 1960):

> We conduct political, cultural, and educative work primarily in enterprises and establishments, i.e., at places of work. But man does not work twenty-four hours a day. He spends the greater part of his time at home where he rests, studies, and amuses himself. Can we be indifferent to the manner in which he conducts his mode of life?

The remedies proposed are: (a) the intensification of vigilantism by "public organizations," such as the "neighborhood courts against parasitism" and citizens' brigades, which, under the discreet guidance of the Party, would ferret out idlers and guard against such frivolities as cardplaying, drunkenness, and eccentricities of dress. (b) The enlargement of facilities for public entertainment and recreation, such as clubs and cafés where citizens would amuse themselves under a watchful public eye. (c) The fostering of a distinctive Communist mode of life providing aesthetic gratification. The ceremonial occasions in the life of an individual (weddings, funerals, birthdays, etc.) should be suffused with the symbols of the collective. In short, the private domain must be transformed into the public domain—controlled, supervised, and dominated by the Communist Party.

Such, in broad outline, is the ideal society envisioned by the Party. Yet this ideal is probably no more than a chimera. For all that we know about man and society seems incompatible with its realization. Even the tools of modern technology have not endowed a dictator with the capacity to mold society as if it were clay in his hands; and the means available to the *apparatchiki* are ludicrously inadequate to the enormity of the task. They hesitate to use the incalculable weapon of terror, which tends to recoil upon its wielder. "Man," said Khrushchev (*Pravda*, July 4, 1960), "must not be driven into paradise by means of the club." And the ideology of Marxism-Leninism, which aims to instill obedience to the Party, is growing less and less relevant and meaningful. Instead of animating Soviet citizens with enthusiasm, it often induces somnolence in them.

The Communists aspire to "leap" from the "necessity" of compromising with *stykhiinost* into the realm of absolute "freedom" from it, to sway the wayward course of social change into a narrow channel fixed by the Party. But it is doubtful that the complex course of history can be made fully to obey the dictates of a political machine. The mark of unpredictability is written on all historical action. Almost every historical deed breeds unintended consequences. "Man makes his own history, but he does not know the history he is making." Will the Party be exempt from this rule, which has hitherto governed human destiny?

But perhaps, in their heart of hearts, the Communist leaders cherish less the ideal goal than the pursuit of it. Tension and struggle are the pith and marrow of their endeavor. They lend meaning and purpose to their existence. The reward of ultimate conquest would be intolerable ennui. The mantle of philosopher-king ruling a populace trained to unswerving obedience would ill fit an *apparatchik* who has imbibed the ethos of perpetual struggle. To the question "What is your idea of happiness?" the typical *apparatchik* would probably reply with Marx, "To fight." *Subconsciously*, he would thus echo the words of Mussolini: "We have created our myth, the myth is a faith, it is a passion, it is not necessary that it shall be a reality. It is a reality by the fact that it is a goal, a hope, a faith that is courage."

The Bolshevik dictatorship may long endure, always pursuing the unattainable goal—the conquest of spontaneity. "The movement is everything, the end is nothing."

Totalitarianism Without Coercion?

——HERBERT RITVO

MILOVAN DJILAS, in *The New Class*, his classic probe of the fallacies of the Communist system, characterized "the question of the state," and its role in society as the most important problem for Communism, in theory and practice. During the first four decades of the Soviet Union's existence, its political leaders all espoused the theoretical axiom of the ultimate "withering away of the state," but none of them was seriously confronted with the problem of implementing it in practice. Today, however, with the declaration that the U.S.S.R. is well advanced economically along the road to full Communism, the issue has become of crucial importance for the Soviet leadership—especially for the man who has successfully reasserted personal dictatorship over the Party-state. The purpose of the present paper is to examine: (a) Khrushchev's approach to this vital issue, both in theoretical pronouncements and in practical policies, which has resulted in a unique readjustment of the Party-state relationship; (b) the effect of his innovations on the present Soviet scene and their portent, real or visionary, for the future of the society; (c) the intimately related problem, again both in theory and practice, of the shifting balance between coercion and persuasion in Soviet life.

Doctrinal Precedents

Khrushchev's theory of state quite naturally uses the doctrinal heritage left by his predecessors as its take-off point. Lenin, in his *State and Revolution*, stressed that "it is clear there can be no question of defining the exact moment of the *future* withering away—the more so as it must be a rather lengthy process." Stalin treated the indeterminate duration of the state as contingent upon two independent but related factors: (a) the continued existence of *internal* enemies, causing an inevitable intensification of the class struggle during the advance toward socialism; (b) the presence of hostile *external* forces, constituting a "capitalist encirclement "of the solitary socialist state. He thereby asserted the indispensability of maintaining the strongest possible state apparatus.

At the Twentieth CPSU Congress in 1956, Khrushchev—already the *primus inter pares* in the "collective leadership"—bitterly condemned the first of these Stalinist notions in his famous secret speech. Subsequent developments, however—particularly the Hungarian uprising in the fall of 1956—led him to some retreat from this stance. The concept of increasing class conflict, which Stalin used to rationalize the total terror of the 1930's, has been partially rehabilitated (along with Stalin himself), in the sense that it is no longer characterized as one of his major errors. Indeed, the conspicuous absence of either criticism or affirmation of this notion in recent theoretical discussions suggests that it is probably viewed as an ideological weapon to be held in reserve —for potential use not so much at home, where socialism is ostensibly an "irreversible reality," as in the peoples' democracies, where the organs of coercion may again be required to suppress open opposition.

With much less ambiguity, the second of Stalin's explanations for the longevity of the state has been retained and adapted to cover the period of building Communism. Although it is admitted that the "capitalist encirclement" of the Stalin era ceased to exist after the creation of a "socialist commonwealth," Khrushchev's case for the continued strengthening of the military might of the state as long as hostile blocs exist is practically indistinguishable from his predecessor's talk of "external enemies."

The rejection—if now only by implication—of Stalin's concept of the "inevitable intensification of the class struggle" is directly connected with the new approach to the coercive functions of the state and their partial transfer to "public" organizations. To understand this relationship, the role of terror as a mechanism of social control under Stalinism should be recalled. Until the day of his death, the dictator used terror primarily in the negative sense—i.e., to guarantee the suppression of opposition, imaginary as well as genuine. It could be argued that the application of terror also facilitated the speedy accumulation of capital needed by a fledgling planned economy aiming at rapid industrialization, by effectively preventing any organized protest against the huge sacrifices imposed on an unwilling population. Yet even the Stalin regime recognized that the resort to mass arrests to fill the slave-labor camps was decisive only for extending rudimentary industrialization to the more remote corners of the Soviet Union and for achieving the initial phase of Marxist "primitive accumulation." Moreover, untold damage was done to the economy as a result of the liquidation of scarce technicians and administrators in the purges. Thus it would be as misleading to consider Soviet industrial accomplishments the direct consequence of terror and forced labor as it would be to attribute Soviet achievements in atomic research to successful espionage or to the forced contributions of captured German scientists.

The announcement of Stalin's death clearly reflected the apprehension of other leaders over the cumulative impact of Stalinist terror; in the joint statement issued by the Central Committee and the Council of Ministers, the collective of his successors warned against "disorder and panic" in words pregnant with their own doubts and fears. Within a month, a limited amnesty had been announced, the reform of the criminal code promised, the "doctors' plot" exposed as a fraud, and the top secret police official, S. D. Ignatiev, removed in disgrace. Precisely why or how these decisions, clearly designed to reduce the degree of terror, were made remains unknown even today, but their broader consequences—foreseen by few at the time—have become increasingly evident. The regime has not renounced the main instrument of terror, the secret police, but has simply re-established the principle (and practice) of Party control over the police apparatus as the guarantee of a new "socialist legality."

At the same time, the promise that the methods of the past were not to be employed in the future—accompanied by the release of thousands from the forced-labor camps and prisons—became the starting point of a process of rationalizing the worst heritage of Stalin's rule, the first step out of the darkness of Stalin's all-embracing terror onto the path of what Adam Ulam has called "enlightened totalitarianism," or, in the words of Leonard Schapiro, the "relatively benevolent despotism" of the post-Stalin dictatorship, today again exercised by one man.

Khrushchev's Innovations

It is of course natural that Khrushchev, as head of the Party-state, should now have emerged as the major interpreter of the Marxist-Leninist theory of state and as the arbiter of the changing ratio of coercion and persuasion in the regime's accelerated approach to Communism. While no real attention was paid to these doctrinal problems before the final resolution of the power struggle in the Presidium, the first sign of the theoretical innovations to come was the inclusion of the following charge in the bill of particulars presented against the "anti-Party" group in July, 1957: "[The anti-Party group] tried to elevate the state above the Party . . . challenged the Party's basic right to take the leading role in the affairs of the Soviets . . . tried to reduce the Party to a position where it would be subordinate to the governmental apparatus. . . ." Having thus defined one of the basic issues of conflict with his opponents—one that compares interestingly with the charges against Beria by Malenkov four years earlier—Khrushchev was ready to venture forth onto the troublesome ideological terrain of clarifying the Party-state relationship of the future. In the fall of 1957, and in early 1958, he issued a series of pronouncements in press interviews and speeches establishing the framework on which current doctrine is based. The dominant refrain in these statements, as well as in comments by the professional theoreticians, was an assurance that there will be no weakening of the role of the state in [the period of] building Communism, more explicitly though less frequently expressed as the notion retained from Stalinism that the state proceeds toward its withering away via its maximum strengthening. In an attempt, evidently, to instill more logic into this dialectical detour of the state on the road to Engels' "museum of antiquities," Khrushchev added a notion of his own, which has become his major contribution to Marxism-Leninism. He resolved the "nonantagonistic" contradiction between the eventual disappearance of the state and its immediate strengthening by the disarmingly simple solution of substituting the ruling Party for the state. In an interview early in 1958 with A. I. Macdonald of the London *Times*, Khrushchev propounded this theme as follows:

> A certain loosening of the administrative ties between *raions*, regions, and republics is now taking place here. At the same time, the ideological ties between regions and republics and the unity of the Soviet peoples are being strengthened. The Communist Party plays an important role [in this process] and this [role] will grow stronger. . . . Changes in the functions of the state are also taking place. The process of change in these functions derives from our conceptions, from the theoretical principles of Marxism-Leninism on the state. When the conditions for the transition to Communism have been created in our country, many administrative organs of the state will gradually die away. . . . The Party has stronger foundations than the state organs. It has arisen and exists not as a result of duties of a legislative nature. Its development was called for by circumstances stemming from the political concepts of people . . . from principles of a moral nature. And mankind will always need moral factors.

From these and other statements, in combination with various practical measures undertaken to elevate Party authority, the concept of the ruling party (*praviashchaia partiia*) emerged in full outline. An important aspect of this concept is the direct link established between the changing Party-state relationship and the allegedly shifting balance of coercion and persuasion in Soviet society. The direction set by Khrushchev in this respect has recently been defined by G. Shitarev in *Politicheskoie samoobrazovaniie* (No. 8, 1960) in the following terms:

If the Communist Party and the socialist state existed and worked together in the past, do [so] in the present, and will [do so] in the future under certain conditions, this does not mean that such will be the case forever. . . . The Communist Party and the socialist state, in their roles and position in society and in their given functions are not identical. The Party takes the leading position in the system of the dictatorship of the proletariat, it directs the internal and foreign policy of the state. . . The Party as an ideological political organization depends completely and fully on persuasion in the direction of the masses, the state on force as well as on persuasion. . . . The Party is the only force in a position to guarantee, through its leadership, the transition from a socialist state to the Communist administration of society. . . . The methods of persuasion . . . are winning more and more ground in the life of Soviet society, and under Communism they will become the sole regulator of relations among people. Together with this, the importance of the Party will grow still more since its leadership of the masses . . . rests upon the propagation of the great ideas of Marxism-Leninism.

The Theory of Participation

The concept of the gradual substitution of persuasion for coercion under the guidance of the supreme party has as its crucial corollary the development of proper attitudes in the population at large and the broadening of popular participation in the regulation of society, to be effected mainly through the expansion of so-called "public" or "social" organizations. In theory such participation is linked to the future expiration of the state; as Khrushchev has put it in a speech to the Thirteenth Komsomol Congress:

Which organizations will be preserved [under Communism]? Public organizations. Whether they are called Komsomol, trade unions, or some other names, they will be public bodies through which society will regulate its relations. . . .

We now have to prepare for this and to teach people to develop habits for these functions.

It is significant that the two types of organizations mentioned—the Komsomol and the trade unions—have long been described as the "transmission belts" or "loyal helpers" of the Party and have been effectively subordinated to its direction and control. What will happen to the Party itself under full Communism is never explicitly spelled out; but insofar as the period of building Communism is concerned, it was frankly stated by Shitarev that the "voluntary" public organizations now emerging on the Soviet scene and any others created in the future will be as closely controlled by the Party as the existing veteran auxiliaries of its rule:

> The Party is now the highest form of political organization . . . in the U.S.S.R. As long as there are [other] organizations . . . on a state level . . in production, trade unions, cooperatives, or by age [ie., the Komsomol], the Party remains the leading force with respect to each one individually and with regard to all altogether; only the Communist Party is capable of coordinating and guiding the work of all state and social organizations in the interest of building Communism. . . .

In propounding the various ideas outlined above, Mr. Khrushchev has, in a sense, killed two birds with one stone: He can point to the beginning, however feeble, of the "withering away of the state" under Communism through the transfer of some state functions to "social organizations"; at the same time his innovations serve the purpose of diminishing the previous duality of Party-state guidance of Soviet society in favor of increasingly monistic rule. Putting it more broadly, the line now pursued by Khrushchev reflects the two constants in terms of which Soviet policy must always be judged: first, the need to meet the demands of an ideology which forecasts a process of continuing change in the social order on the basis of a dialectical development toward Communism; second, the need to maintain the monopoly of power of the leadership (today through the reassertion of the ruling party) in a historically unique form of totalitarian dictatorship, the Soviet one-party state.

It is tempting, given the forty-three-year record of absolute rule by successive Soviet regimes, to dismiss the picture now being painted of the coming Communist future as mere propaganda or as visionary nonsense. Yet whatever the prospects of Khrushchev's version of utopia ever being realized, one cannot ignore the current effects of the stress on substituting persuasion for coercion and of replacing control through the state machine with correction through the community. While the measures that have been initiated in the name of these ideas are transparent in their aim of buttressing the role of the Party, their impact on the society has other important implications which are crucial to an assessment of the present and future Soviet scene.

Something Old, Something New . . .

The measures spoken of here constitute an attempt by the regime to storm the remaining barriers between public and private life in the Soviet Union, in an atmosphere of "revolutionary" fervor designed to recall the enthusiasm of the early days of struggle under Lenin. Under the slogan of "work, study, and live in a Communist manner," the apparatus of the totalitarian Party-state has been mobilizing the population for a vast exercise in "self-control," which seeks to penetrate not only into the factories and the fields, but into the schools, all social and public activity, and indeed into the most intimate spheres of family life. While many of the forms that this mobilization has taken have their roots or prototypes in the Leninist and Stalinist past, the scope of the effort is perhaps unprecedented. As mentioned earlier, primary stress has been laid on the creation of a network of so-called "public organizations" through the initiative of activists at the local level. These organizations cover a broad range of special functions or activities, major and minor.

One of the pressing practical aims of the regime is, of course, to promote cooperation in the accelerated Seven Year Plan. In this connection, a crucial example of public mobilization is the nationwide campaign to enlist workers in the Brigades of Communist Labor, a movement initiated in 1958, and said to have rallied over 5 million workers in more than 40,000 brigades as of June, 1960. Throughout Soviet history—from the *Subbotniks* [voluntary labor days] of the Civil War period through the *Stakhanovite* competitions of the Stalin Five Year Plans, the primary function of "spontaneous movements" among Soviet workers has been to increase labor productivity and efficiency. The new movement follows suit in the priority of the three vows demanded of its members (*Voprosy filosofii*, No. 10, 1959):

1) To increase production, organize well . . . economize, insistently introduce new equipment and technology, use advanced methods at work.
2) To study constantly, strive to master modern knowledge in the fields of science and technology . . . [and] of socialist culture, so as to be of use not only to oneself, but to the entire collective, to society.
3) To cultivate in oneself the best features of the new society, develop yourself in an all-around manner mentally and physically, be exemplary in daily life [and] in your attitude toward public duty, and struggle actively for a new morale.

In commenting on the last of these pledges, a Soviet writer asserted in the same issue of *Voprosy filosofii:*

Communist labor-brigade members and shock workers, for the first time in the history of competition, are imposing on themselves obligations of a moral character. They pledge to combat the vestiges of the past in the consciousness of the people, to strengthen comradely solidarity and collaboration in work and living, and to be the guardians of the norms of socialist society. This is one of the most essential characteristics of the new movement.

Insofar as the members of the brigades now pledge themselves *explicitly* not only to increase production, but to cultivate the new "Soviet morality," the writer's enthusiastic description of the third vow is justified. At the same time, inculcation of "proper" attitudes toward work and society is hardly a new feature of such "spontaneous movements" among workers. Here, for instance, is a random selection from a 1949-issue of *Trud*, strikingly similar to the exhortations that fill its pages. "In every brigade, in every department, in every factory, one must create such conditions that poor work is a personal disgrace for everyone." The difference between the past and the present is one of emphasis, reflecting the social and economic changes that have taken place in the Soviet Union within the past two decades. Whereas in the 1930's and 1940's, the primary goal of the regime was to expand production, almost regardless of cost, the aim now is also to *refine* it—and to do that, mere pressure and exertion are not enough; "reform from without" must slowly give way to "reform from within."

Granting this difference of emphasis, there is a basic similarity between past labor drives and the present movement epitomized in the claim of their "spontaneous" development. It would be premature to state categorically that the personal pledges of the current movement will degenerate into the ritualistic stereotypes and pressures that characterized those of the past. Yet the evidence so far available permits a skeptical view of the predicted emergence of the "new Communist man" striving for that ideal admixture of production and personality development envisioned in regime propaganda. In a recent theoretical discussion in *Oktiabr*, for example, the following complaint was aired:

> Despite the simultaneous solution of the most important Communist tasks in the spheres of labor, education, and way of life, the brigades as a rule show the greatest successes in raising productivity. It frequently happens that some members of the brigades . . . attain high production figures [but] do not always behave in everyday life as they should.

The Vehicles of "Public Order"

Among other "public" organizations now in operation, none are more important than the parapolice and parajudicial institutions, whose function, in Khrushchev's words, is to act "alongside and parallel with such agencies as the militia and courts to perform the functions of safeguarding public order and security." Although the network of these organizations has existed, in one form or another, for some time, the scope of their specific activities and authority is still subject to considerable discussion. Chief among them are the people's militia and the comrades' courts, along with the forms of public activity authorized by the antiparasite laws of 1957–58.

The people's militia (*druzhiny*) are the direct descendants of the *brigadmils* formed in the early 1930's to aid in the collectivization drive. Discredited as a result of their collaboration with the police and the NKVD during the purge period, the *brigadmils* died out almost completely until late 1956, when the idea of using them was revived in connection with the renewed "struggle against antisocial elements." The start of the present countrywide mobilization is credited to the initiative of a "workers' militia group" in Leningrad in November, 1958. Early in 1959, the militia's role was formalized in a joint decree of the Central Committee and the Council of Ministers, "On Participation of Workers in the Maintenance of Public Order." It was subsequently announced that within a month of the decree's issuance, "voluntary" militia units had been formed in most large industrial and agricultural enterprises; according to latest claims (*Kommunist*, No. 10, 1960), there are now 80,000 units with more than 2.5 million members. In Moscow, at least, entire factory units and labor brigades have joined the militia, strongly suggesting that it is intended to develop into a full-fledged mass movement.

Past criticism in the Soviet press, indicating that the regular police was unequal to the task of dealing with petty public disorders, seemingly provided sufficient practical reason for the formation of an ancillary police force. But the regime, as might be expected, chose to stress an ideological explanation for the re-emergence of the people's militia, and in his speech to the Twenty-first Congress, Khrushchev cited it as an example of "the inclusion of the widest strata of the population in the management of the affairs of the country during the transition to Communism."

In the decree governing their activity, the authority of the people's militia was clearly restricted to warning offenders and to listing their names, so that subsequent misdemeanors could be dealt with more severely by the comrades' courts or the regular police. In practice, however, their actions frequently have involved transgressions of the law and frightening invasions of personal privacy. The Soviet press has cited cases of illegal nighttime searches to check on individual moral behavior, beatings administered to young people, and in one case, a citizen's death by assault.

While such negative excesses are criticized by the press and may be considered exceptions in the early phase of a unique experiment in social control, the praise generally accorded to militia activities affirms the basic concept of public intervention in private life. As a report by Radio Vologda on December 16, 1959, pridefully stated, "no antisocial act escapes the attention of squad members." Among the legitimate concerns of the people's militia, a favorite project is the "re-education of drunkards," the typical approach to which is described as follows (*Sovetskaia yustitsia*, No. 3, March, 1960):

> The members of [a militia] unit listed all the inhabitants of the settlement who regularly got drunk and in that state . . . committed antisocial acts. These people were summoned to a meeting . . . and warned of the necessity to mend their ways. In addition, a member of the unit was attached to each one of them for the purposes of daily education work. The members of the unit visited [their assignees] in their homes, found out how they behaved . . . and tried to get them to take part in mass communal activities. In a number of instances, on payday the members of the unit met the lovers of strong liquor at the pay office [and] escorted them home. . . . The number of drunkards in the settlement dropped sharply. . . .

People's Justice

The area of parajudicial activity is a more difficult one to assess, mainly because of the confusion that exists over the division of responsibility between the "public meetings" authorized under the aforementioned "antiparasite" draft laws and the "comrades' courts," more recently stressed as the chief instruments of social correction.

The antiparasite laws, presented for public discussion in 1957–58, have not yet been ratified in the three largest Soviet republics (the R.S.F.S.R., the Ukraine, and Belorussia, containing over 80 per cent of the total population), and since they have been treated with considerable reserve even in Soviet publications, it is possible they may still be subjected to further change. As they now stand, the laws authorize public organizations to hold open trials against "parasitic elements," only loosely defined. The public meetings, at which a minimum of fifty persons must be present, can act, by simple majority vote and even in the absence of an alleged offender, to impose sentences of exile with compulsory labor for two to five years—this despite the provisions in criminal legislation adopted in 1958, which state that "criminal punishment shall be imposed only by judgment of a court." There is no appeal from the decision of these meetings, although sentences must be confirmed by the executive committees of local soviets.

It is hardly necessary to point out the potential dangers of the return to this sort of extrajudicial power, the easy abuse of which was amply demonstrated in Stalin's day by the terroristic "special conferences" of the NKVD-MVD. Ostensibly directed against "useless" members of society, the present laws could be turned against any individual on artificially contrived pretexts, by the action of any of the Party's "transmission belts." Even to those who view other recent developments in Soviet law in an optimistic light, the possibilities of unrestrained "mob rule" inherent in the antiparasite laws are portents of trouble; for those who take a more skeptical view, the extrajudicial show trials constitute simply a new instrument of terror available in the arsenal of the totalitarian state. At the least, all knowledgeable observers join in deeming the laws a threat to the already shaky security of the legal procedure of the U.S.S.R. In short, the laws, though presented as a remedy for behavior injurious to the body politic, seem much more likely to raise the public fever than to cure those social ills juridically still beyond the competence of the regular courts.

The recent revival of the comrades' courts, a more formal institution than the "public meeting," may reflect the regime's response to the apprehension over the antiparasite laws apparent within the Soviet Union itself. On the other hand, the Soviet press has indicated a disposition on the part of participants in the "public meetings" not only to refrain from harsh penalties for serious first offenses but to be excessively considerate (from the regime's viewpoint) of multiple offenders—a fact that could also explain the current signs of official dissatisfaction with this lowest form of "citizens' justice." In any event, since 1959, there has been a determined effort to reestablish and to extend the activities of comrades' courts, which have roots dating back to the first years of the regime. The present scope of their functions and authority, like that of the public meetings, is still defined only in draft regulations, but the indications are that the Party now intends to make the courts a chief instrument in regulating the balance between persuasion and coercion in Soviet society.

The forerunners of the present comrades' courts were concerned almost exclusively with violations of labor discipline; created during the Civil War, they operated from 1919 until 1923, and again from 1928 until 1940, when Stalin's severe labor legislation made them superfluous. By contrast, the revived courts, like other public organizations, have been directed to concern themselves with all aspects of social behavior. Set up wherever a collective exceeds fifty persons—in industrial, agricultural, and educational institutions, apartment blocks, etc.—the comrades' courts, in Khrushchev's words, are "to seek mainly to anticipate all kinds of infringements; they must deal not only with questions of production, but with questions of everyday life and of a moral nature, cases of wrong behavior by members of a collective who have . . . [digressed] from standards of public order. . . ." Under this broad umbrella, the list of offenses falling to the courts' consideration would seem to be limitless; reported cases range from charges involving citizens' failure to bring up children properly, uttering insulting remarks, or spreading falsehoods, to a variety of minor property and housing disputes. In many instances, the comrades' courts handle problems, allocated by the regular courts and police, that are not considered to involve "social danger" and for which penalties are not mandatory under the law. Outside the factory, most of their work involves cases initiated by trade-union and Komsomol committees, local soviets, the people's militia, or street and housing committees.

Although the proposed procedural rules for the comrades' courts constitute a marked improvement over those of the informal "public meetings," they are still a far cry from the judicial standards prevailing in the regular court system. For example, there is no real pretrial hearing or attempts at an investigation, but merely a "check-up on facts," on the assumption that the community, including court members, is already acquainted with the problem at hand; there is also no provision for a defense counsel, and only the court can call witnesses. If a citizen refuses to stand trial, the court can proceed in his absence. As in the case of the "public meetings," decisions are taken by a majority vote, and there is no right of appeal. However, the courts are responsible to the trade unions in enterprises or the executive committees of local soviets, in the sense that the latter may suggest a second trial if there has been an obvious contravention of Soviet law.

Partially offsetting these shortcomings, and in marked contrast to the provisions of the antiparasite laws, the decisions of the comrades' courts are restricted to: (1) expressing public reprimand or censure, imposing a fine up to 100 rubles on offenders, and/or expressing regrets to victims; (2) in cases of labor violations, recommending transfer or demotion of the offenders to less important and lower-paid work, or in extreme cases, their dismissal; (3) ordering compensation for damages up to 500 rubles; (4) referring criminal cases, as well as cases involving housing evictions, to the regular courts. It seems clear that all major crimes—and in fact the more serious of those now classified as minor—will remain within the competence of the regular court system and the police.

In short, the basic function assigned to the comrades' courts is not to administer punishment, but to demonstrate the redemptive powers of the assumption of communal responsibility for citizens who have erred in their ways but who can still be saved for society. Since the educative role of Soviet law has always been an important consideration in theory, the emphasis on community cures for delinquency is not, as pointed out earlier, a new feature in itself. But as a result of the vastly broadened and also loosely defined competence of the comrades' courts, there will be a tremendous increase in the number of people, in no legal sense criminals, who now come within the reach of these parajudicial organizations. As explained "dialectically," this temporary *quantitative* increase, due to the elevation of norms of behavior as the society approaches Communism, will involve the corrective participation of ever greater numbers of citizens, resulting eventually in the *qualitative* transformation of the character both of Soviet law and of the citizens themselves.

Coercion with a Sugar Coating

Together with the increased emphasis on popular self-regulation through public organizations, there has been a notable change of emphasis in the depiction of the roles of the regular police and courts, about which a word must be said. Though the call for public order still uses the time-worn slogans exhorting "vigilance," reminiscent of the coercive excesses of the past, an effort has been made to project to the public a new image of the instruments of coercion—notably the secret police—as organs rather of prevention and persuasion, as friends and helpers of the populace. Thus the KGB, for example, is portrayed as playing a passive yet important role in guiding the new course of social justice, through propaganda stressing its cooperation and assistance to the comrades' courts and the people's militia. Its present work, as *Kommunist* (No. 11, 1960) describes it, is primarily "prophylactic," symbolizing the enlightened dictatorship's efforts gradually to alter the coercion-persuasion ratio in society. As one Soviet expert, P. S. Romashkin, writing in *Sovetskoe gosudarstvo i pravo* (No. 2, 1960), has expressed this aspect of the current line:

> The agencies of coercion are still necessary for guarding the nation from the intrigues of the imperialistic forces and their agents, also for protecting the lawful interests of the citizens, and for carrying on the struggle against antisocial parasitical elements, speculators, hooligans, and other criminals. Still,

one cannot fail to note that the trends in the activities of the agencies of coercion are changing. . . . The sphere of coercion, which had never been the chief method in the activities of the socialist state, is now being narrowed down still further. The activities of such agencies as the police are being more and more closely combined with the activities of the people's militia and are gradually acquiring a more social character. The development of the courts is proceeding . . . along the lines of combining their work with the activities of comrades' courts and the more extensive recruitment of the public into the administration of justice. The punitive measures applied by the courts are acquiring an ever-increasing educational character. . . . Of course, all this does not mean that coercion is already dying out. However . . . direct administrative coercion is being replaced to an ever-greater extent by other forms of economic, political, and moral action.

The Control of Mass Control

The last sentence quoted, and its key word—"replaced"—provide an apt point from which to summarize what is really happening in the Soviet Union today. The transfer of certain functions from the coercive apparatus of the regime to public organizations in no way means a lessening of social controls in Soviet society; on the contrary, it constitutes an effort to penetrate more deeply than ever before into the private and personal spheres of people's lives. The latest experiment in mass control is being conducted without the instrument of active police terror used in the past; but in spite of all the emphasis on persuasion, the aim of this experiment has been defined by the last-quoted writer, in a phrase borrowed from Lenin, as the development of a *"machinery capable of coercing"* in place of one "applying legal norms ensured by the coercive force of the state."

Claims of current progress in this vast experiment have been buttressed with statistics asserting a 20.6-per-cent decrease in the number of crimes in eleven months of the year 1959, over a comparable period in 1958. For the R.S.F.S.R., the largest Soviet republic, the decline of convictions during the first nine months of 1959 over 1958 was broken down as follows: for hooliganism, 10.9 per cent less; for petty theft of public property, 14.2 per cent less; and for thefts of private property, 19.7 per cent less. While these figures presumably were intended to convey the impression of a marked improvement in mass social behavior, logic suggests that they are simply the inevitable statistical consequence of the transfer of functions from the regular courts and police to the public organizations, coupled with the "chase for favorable statistics" that accompanies any major program launched by the leadership.

It is clear, furthermore, that the current offensive is moving forward under the strict control of the ruling Party as the "leading and guiding force in all state and social organizations." Thus the Party leadership, and at the apex Khrushchev himself, has operated through the CPSU proper and the traditional coercive apparatus to set clear limits on the pace and scope of public mobilization. The fact that the Party leadership seems presently secure in its control, however, only underscores the continuing dilemma that confronts it, namely: Too much intervention from above could ruin the desired initiative from below, while too little involves the risk that compromise and leniency might lead the experimental social controls in the direction of anarchy.

Expanding Struggle?

This pressure on the regime to maintain a dynamic equilibrium has been expressed in the theory, supported by some political analysts, that the Soviet Party leadership must conduct a constant "revolution from above" in order to maintain and justify its power. The same idea has been offered by Milovan Djilas when he said: "Communist regimes are a form of latent civil war between the government and the people." In terms of this generalization, the early battles of the present phase of "struggle" seemed to be directed only against a minority element of errant or noncooperative citizens, the "parasitical" flotsam of society. Thence the offensive was expanded into a general mobilization of the public for the fulfillment of official goals. In the course of recent theoretical comment, there have been indications that the regime's "civil war" will in time be extended to still another target—in a battle, necessary sooner or later, against remaining forms of private property. The implications for the future in this respect emerge most clearly in a recent comprehensive essay on the coming society by the noted Soviet economist S. Strumilin:

> Insofar as Communism eliminates the property that divides people, it liquidates that basis from which all property crimes and most other violations arise. The public opinion of commune members will be sufficiently strong to exclude practically all other crimes in time. At the same time, therefore, there will be less and less need, and finally none at all, for penal justice and police, courts and prisons . . . and all other professional agents of justice. Moreover, the entire criminal code will become superfluous. . . . After the liquidation of private property the norms of civil law will also be superfluous. The same fate will befall the various sectors of state institutions and laws one by one.

Clearly discernible in Strumilin's vision of the "brave new world" is the thesis that private property, not only as a form of ownership of the means of production, but also in the form of personal possessions is, under socialism, the root of the "vestiges of the past" that must still be eradicated before the new Soviet man can emerge in his pristine form and the state can wither away. By the logic of this argument, the regime must at some point make an attempt to abolish private personal property, affecting most direly and directly the upper strata of Soviet society—the "haves" in a predominantly "have-not" society.

Supporting this trend of theory, there has been some recent stress in the popular press on the evils of private property. The reaction of those who see themselves threatened by such propaganda is cogently expressed in the letter of a man who identified himself with the words: "My address . . . any house on any street":

> Allow me to ask the editorial staff the following question: Does it know that this bourgeois—or rather many millions of

those bourgeois whom it attacks so vehemently—has fought against autocracy . . . has helped to overcome the chaos and continues to carry on his shoulders all the hardships of development—without receiving any compensation for these titanic achievements? . . . As for myself I can say: I would be, in the opinion of Likhodeyev [author of the article under criticism] a bourgeois, because I have 12,000 rubles in my savings account. I want to own an automobile and a *dacha*. I do not consider this to be shameful. But this did not prevent me from suffering hunger and defending my country and carrying on my shoulders all the Five Year Plans.*

Despite their certain unpopularity in some quarters, the possibility that the incipient steps of an offensive against personal property may not be too far off seems indicated by the recent revelation in the Party's leading theoretical journal (as reported in *Izvestia*), that "in accordance with the proposals of toilers, the construction of individual *dachas* and the development of individual plots is considered to be inexpedient"; ambiguous as this wording may be, it portends some form of new restrictions in a crucial area of property rights. Thus, behind the smoke screen of popular participation, the public organizations may be pushed forward not only toward a new form of dispensation of justice, but toward a new redistribution of property. How extensive the latter is to be will largely determine the harshness of the former.

The Present and the Future

In the largest sense, the regime's "civil war" might be viewed as a struggle against the common citizen, in the demands that he continue to make economic sacrifices and strive to improve his attitudes for the sake of the bright future ahead.

The vision of this future depicts an ideal society in which the new Communist man, guided by the leaders of the ruling Party,

* *Literaturnaia gazeta*, Sept. 3, 1960; the letter is in criticism of an article by L. Likhodeyev, "The Grimace of a Petit Bourgeois," *ibid.*, July 30, 1960.

will enjoy the fruits of abundance produced by an "association of free individuals," for whom useful work has become a necessity of life, for whom the interests of the collective have been recognized as superior to those of the individual, for whom possession of private property has become meaningless. Yet for the outside observer as much as for the Soviet citizen, the utopian aspects of this blueprint for the future are hard to reconcile with the picture of the present as it emerges from the pages of the Soviet press. In particular, the economic drive now being waged under the slogan "Who does not work, does not eat," constitutes a mocking negation of the predicted emergence of a whole society of "new Soviet men." T. Stepanyan, a leading Soviet theoretician has attempted to deal with this issue in Marxist terms:

> Despite the connection and interrelation of the material and moral foundations of Communism, the former develop more quickly than the latter. . . . We will in the near future attain the abundance and surplus of many consumer goods necessary for distribution according to scientifically fixed norms. A much more difficult matter, which will take much more time, will be to form in every member of society the inner urge to work in a Communist manner and to make work the first necessity of life for each.

In sum, while the Soviet leadership claims to have made decisive progress toward producing the material abundance essential to the Marxian vision of society, it has by its own admission only begun to approach the problem of producing the ideal citizens equally necessary to that society—an infinitely more complicated task inherited from the past.

Stated in another way, the problem initially posed by Marx and Engels in the *Communist Manifesto* was how to replace the coercive instruments of the state with a rational social order in which "the free development of each [individual] is the condition for the free development of all." Lenin grappled with this problem for only a brief moment; the barren fruit of his effort was anarchy, poverty, and the Chekist terror of war Communism. Stalin's approach to the problem—justifying maximum coercion and terror as means to the end of the eventual withering away of the coercive apparatus—made a travesty of the original Marxian concept. Today, under Khrushchev, another effort has been launched to actualize this concept, through a mobilization of citizens that stresses the desired "development of each" as the prerequisite for the desired "development of all."

According to Khrushchev, the present program for constructing Communism ultimately will lead not only to the transformation of the individual citizen and of the social order, but to the total substitution of persuasion for coercion in society. Yet these aims of the future are to be pursued through the control mechanisms and methods of the present: The ruling Party will continue to exercise its supreme authority over the populace through a coercive apparatus that has been de-emphasized but remains in ready reserve if needed; moreover, the Party will use its monopoly of control over mass organizations and mass media in a frank attempt to narrow the latitude of free choice still remaining in the personal lives and behavior of Soviet citizens.

Given the present nature of the Party dictatorship, the vision of a future society where persuasion and sweet reason reign supreme must be dismissed as utopian nonsense at best, political cynicism at worst. In no sense, however, is this to write off as meaningless the *relative* shift of emphasis away from coercion and toward persuasion in current Soviet policy. Whether or not the population believes in the promises of the Communist future, it well remembers the purgatory of the Stalinist past. Popular relief over the retreat from Stalinist coercion has been manifest in the greater measure of support accorded to the present regime, and the leadership is not likely to risk dissipating this feeling by a return to past excesses. The dividends accruing to the regime as a result of its greater emphasis on persuasive methods, coupled with its greater attention to consumer needs, have so far considerably outweighed any potential dangers to its power. Short of a serious crisis, then, the gauges on the regime's control machinery may be expected to continue veering toward persuasion rather than coercion. The total pressure on the population will be no less, but to the extent the regime can effectively substitute "social" controls through the new public organization for the traditional controls of the past, it will do so. At the same time, since the apparatus of power will remain at the disposal of the regime, we may expect to see a further development *not* toward a new genre of "totalitarianism without coercion," but toward a totalitarianism in which the latent threat of coercion remains the main source of the effectiveness of persuasion.

CONTRIBUTIONS

The following listing gives the dates on which the articles and essays in this volume originally appeared in *Problems of Communism*.

THE IDEOLOGICAL SETTING

"Ideology and Power: A Symposium," March–April, 1958; "Ideology: The Fourth Stage," November–December, 1959.

KTO KAVO? THE POLITICS OF THE STRUGGLE FOR POWER

"Iconoclasm in Moscow—A Commentary," March–April, 1956; "Anatomy of Tyranny: Khrushchev's Attack on Stalin," July–August, 1956; "The Permanent Revolution Is On Again," September–October, 1957; "What Happened to 'Collective Leadership'?" July–August, 1959; "The Nature of Khrushchev's Power," July–August, 1960; "The Twenty-second Party Congress," November–December, 1961.

THE ECONOMY: PROBLEMS, PROSPECTS

"*Blat* Is Higher Than Stalin," January–February, 1954; "Taxes and the Soviet Citizen," September–October, 1959; "The Soviet Industrial Reorganization," November–December, 1957; "Communism in a Hurry," May–June, 1959; "The Soviet Economy in Transition," January–February, 1961.

THE SOCIETY

"Equality and Inequality Under Khrushchev," March–April, 1960; ". . . But Some Are More Equal Than Others," March–April, 1960; "The Current Status of the Soviet Worker," July–August, 1960; "The Peasant, the Party, and the System," July–August, 1960; "Soviet Nationality Policy in Perspective," May–June, 1960; "Communism and Anti-Semitism," May–June, 1960.

THE LITERARY SCENE

"Soviet Literary Criticism: Past and Present," January–February, 1958; "The 'Literary Opposition'" (originally published under the pseudonym of Tom Scriven), January–February, 1958; "The Struggle Goes On" (original title: "Soviet Literature in the Doldrums"), July–August, 1959; "Recent Soviet Literature," May–June, 1961; "Poems from the Underground" and "The Conscience of a Generation," May–June, 1961.

MISCELLANEA

"Socialist Legality: The Road Uphill" (adapted from two articles: "The New Face of 'Socialist Legality' " and "Socialist Legality: The Mountain Has Labored") July–August, 1958, and March–April, 1959, respectively; "Recent Soviet Historiography" (revised version of original article), November–December, 1956; "The Soviet Theater," Part I, November–December, 1959; Part II, January–February, 1960.

WHITHER RUSSIA?

"An Empire in Convulsion—A Commentary," November–December, 1956; "Soviet Society in Transition," November–December, 1957; "The Import of Ideological Diversity," November–December, 1957; "Toward a 'Communist Welfare State'?" January–February, 1960; "En Route to Utopia," November–December, 1960.

THE CONTRIBUTORS

RAYMOND ARON, the distinguished French political scientist, is a contributor to *Le Figaro* and the author of *The Century of Total War* (1954), *The Opium of the Intellectuals* (1957), and other works.

PAUL BARTON, a Czech sociologist and economist now living in France, has written *L'Institution Concentrationnaire en Russie* (1959) and various other works dealing with Soviet economic and social problems.

JOSEPH S. BERLINER is Associate Professor of Economics at Syracuse University. He is the author of *Factory and Manager in the U.S.S.R.* (1957), *Soviet Economic Aid* (1959), as well as a variety of scholarly articles on the Soviet economy.

SEWERYN BIALER, a former functionary in the Agitprop Department of the Central Committee of the Polish CP and teacher at the Party's Institute of Social Research, is a free-lance political analyst now residing in the United States.

ALEXANDER DALLIN, Professor of International Relations at the Russian Institute of Columbia University, is the author of *German Rule in Russia, 1941–45*, and of the soon-to-be-published *The Soviet Union at the United Nations*.

JANE DEGRAS, a historian specializing in Soviet foreign policy and the activities of the Comintern, is the editor of *Soviet Documents on Foreign Policy, 1917–1951* and *The Communist International, 1919–1943*.

ADDENDA

GREGORY GROSSMAN, one of the most prominent American experts on the Soviet economy, is Associate Professor of Economics at the University of California (Berkeley). He is the author of *Soviet Statistics of Physical Output of Industrial Commodities* (1961) and numerous other studies.

MAX HAYWARD, formerly with the British Embassy in Moscow, is now Fellow of St. Antony's College, Oxford. He is the co-translator (with Manya Harari) of Boris Pasternak's *Dr. Zhivago*, as well as the author of numerous articles on Soviet literature.

LEON M. HERMAN, who has written extensively on various facets of the Soviet economic system, was formerly with the U.S. Department of Commerce and is now with the Library of Congress, Washington, D.C.

SIDNEY HOOK, the eminent American philosopher, is Chairman of the Department of Philosophy at New York University, and author of *Reason, Social Myths and Democracy* (1944), *Marx and the Marxists* (1955), and many other works.

VICTOR ERLICH, an Associate Professor of Slavic Languages and Literature at the University of Washington, is the author of *Russian Formalism* (1955) and other studies on Soviet literature.

MERLE FAINSOD is Professor of Government at Harvard University. He is the author of *How Russia Is Ruled* (1953), *Smolensk Under Soviet Rule* (1958), and other specialized studies.

ROBERT A. FELDMESSER is Assistant Professor of Sociology at Brandeis University and the author of a forthcoming study on social mobility in the U.S.S.R.

GEORGE GIBIAN, Professor of Russian Literature at Cornell University, is the author of *The Interval of Freedom: Soviet Literature During the Thaw, 1954–57* (1960) and of other works dealing with Soviet literature.

ERICH GOLDHAGEN, Assistant Professor of Political Science at Hunter College, is the author of a forthcoming book on Jews in the Soviet Union—*A Political and Cultural History of Soviet Jewry*—and of scholarly articles dealing with Soviet political and social problems.

R. N. CAREW HUNT (1890–1959) served with the British civil service and later taught at St. Antony's College, Oxford. Among his works are *Theory and Practice of Communism* (1950) and *Marxism Past and Present* (1954).

ALEX INKELES is an American social scientist specializing in the study of the Soviet social system. He is Professor of Sociology at Harvard University and the author of *Public Opinion in Soviet Russia* (1950).

BERTRAND DE JOUVENEL, a noted French economist and head of the Bureau de Recherche, Association d'Études pour l'Expansion de l'Economie Française, is the author of *Du Pouvoir* (1945), *De la Souveraineté* (1956), and other studies.

ARCADIUS KAHAN is Assistant Professor of Economics at the University of Chicago, an expert on Soviet agriculture, and the author of several studies of the Soviet economy.

LEOPOLD LABEDZ, a sociologist living in London, is the author of numerous papers on the U.S.S.R. and Eastern Europe and co-editor of *Soviet Survey*.

LEON LIPSON, a well-known American specialist on Soviet law, is Associate Professor of Law at the Yale University Law School.

RICHARD LOWENTHAL, formerly political analyst for the London Observer, now is a professor at the Free University of Berlin. He is the author of *Jenseits des Kapitalismus* (1947, published under the pseudonym Paul Sering) and a frequent contributor to European and American journals.

ALEC NOVE, one of the foremost authorities on the Soviet economy, teaches at the London School of Economics. He is the author of *The Soviet Economy* (1961), the co-author of *Trade with Commu-*

nist Countries (1960), and has written numerous articles and monographs on the Soviet economic system.

HERBERT RITVO, formerly a political analyst for Radio Free Europe, Munich, now is associated with the Center for International Studies, Massachusetts Institute of Technology. He is the author of a forthcoming book on post-Stalin Russia.

JÜRGEN RÜHLE, for six years an art editor and theater critic in East Germany, sought asylum in the West in 1955. He is the author of *Das Gefesselte Theater* (1957) and *Literatur und Revolution* (1960).

SOLOMON M. SCHWARZ, a Russian-born economist and sociologist, now resides in the United States. He is the author of *Labor in the Soviet Union* (1951) and other studies.

SAMUEL L. SHARP is Professor of International Relations at American University, Washington, D.C., and the author of *New Constitutions in the Soviet Sphere* (1950) and *Poland: White Eagle on a Red Field* (1953).

PETER WILES, formerly of New College, Oxford, is now head of the Department of Economics, Brandeis University, Waltham, Mass. He is the author of *Price, Cost and Output* (1956) and other studies on Soviet statistics and economics.

HARRY WILLETS, a frequent contributor to *Soviet Survey* and other journals, is a Research Fellow at St. Antony's College, Oxford.

BERTRAM D. WOLFE is the author of *Three Who Made a Revolution* (1948), *Khrushchev and Stalin's Ghost* (1956), and numerous articles in the field of Soviet studies.

A. ZR is the pseudonym of an American student of Soviet literature.